Fixed Income Analysis
for the
Chartered Financial Analyst® Program

Frank J. Fabozzi, Ph.D., CFA

Sponsored by

 **Association for Investment Management and Research**

Published by Frank J. Fabozzi Associates

Dedication

This book is dedicated to the countless volunteers who have made the CFA Charter the most respected professional designation in the financial world today.

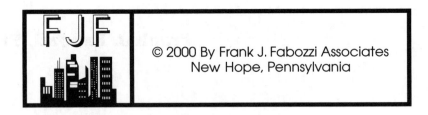

© 2000 By Frank J. Fabozzi Associates
New Hope, Pennsylvania

This publication is designed to provide accurate and authoritative information in regard to the subject matter covered. It is sold with the understanding that the publisher is not engaged in rendering legal, accounting, or other professional services.

ISBN: 1-883249-83-X

Printed in the United States of America

Foreword

These two volumes in fixed income analysis and portfolio management represent an effort by the Association for Investment Management and Research to produce a set of coordinated, comprehensive, and practitioner-oriented textbook readings specifically designed for the three levels of the Chartered Financial Analyst® Program.

In producing these books, AIMR was actively involved in establishing the tables of contents, drawing on inputs from CFA Charterholder volunteer reviewers, fixed income specialist consultants, and AIMR professional staff. Amy F. Lipton, CFA and Richard O. Applebach, CFA were especially helpful. The chapters were designed to include detailed learning outcome statements at the outset, illustrative in-chapter problems with solutions, and extensive end-of-chapter questions and problems with answers, all prepared with CFA candidate distance learners in mind. This treatment of fixed income materials represents a substantial improvement over the previous collections of articles and chapters by various authors. These books provide the evenness of subject matter treatment, consistency of mathematical notation, and continuity of topic coverage so critical to the learning process. Given the expected favorable reception of these fixed income books in the CFA Program, coordinated textbooks in other topic areas are planned for the future.

When considering possible authors or editors of the volumes, one name stood out among the rest: Frank J. Fabozzi, Ph.D., CFA. Because his published work has been used extensively in the CFA Program fixed income curriculum for almost 20 years and because of his widely recognized involvement in fixed income practice, Dr. Fabozzi was an obvious first choice. Given the quality of the completed project, it was an excellent choice and we are grateful he accepted the challenge.

The treatment in these volumes, intended to communicate practical fixed income knowledge, skills, and abilities for the investment generalist, is a hallmark of the CFA Program. Starting from a U.S.-based program of about 2,000 examinees each year in the 1960s and 1970s, the CFA Program has evolved into a pervasive global certification program involving over 70,000 candidates from 136 countries in 2000. Through curriculum improvements such as these two coordinated fixed income textbooks, the CFA Program should continue to appeal to potential new candidates in future years.

Finally, the strong support of Tom Bowman and the AIMR Board of Governors through their authorization of these fixed income volumes should be acknowledged. Without their encouragement and support, this project, intended to materially enhance the CFA Program, could not have been possible.

Robert R. Johnson, Ph.D., CFA
Senior Vice President
Association for Investment
   Management and Research

Donald L. Tuttle, Ph.D., CFA
Vice President
Association for Investment
   Management and Research

June 2000

Preface

Since 1993, I have authored, edited, and published numerous books on fixed income securities and portfolio management for my press, Frank J. Fabozzi Associates. Chapters from some of these books have been included in readings required of CFA Candidates. In mid-1999, the Association for Investment Management and Research approached me with a list of chapters from several books I published and asked if I would be willing to use those chapters as the basis for writing a book for the fixed income part of the Level I and Level II CFA examinations. The book was not to be a mere compilation of these chapters. Rather, it was to be an integrated, comprehensive product written under the direction of AIMR.

In addition to providing me with content direction, AIMR also provided feedback from professional staff and reviewers in the practitioner and academic communities. (These individuals are acknowledged elsewhere.) Every topic and concept was scrutinized with great care. The book that was desired was to be written keeping the following in mind.

First, because some CFA candidates have had limited exposure to fixed income securities, I was asked to make sure that every concept was thoroughly explained when it was first introduced. Second, because CFA candidates come from all over the world, I was asked to avoid idiomatic expressions and jargon that would be unfamiliar to non-North American candidates. Third, I was asked to prepare meaningful end-of-chapter questions designed to test candidates' knowledge of topics covered.

Of all the books I have authored, this book has been the most difficult to write. To the benefit of the reader, the reviewers made me an almost "paranoid" writer. By this I mean that every word and statement was scrutinized to make sure it would be clearly understood by the CFA candidate. In particular, members of the Executive Advisory Board of the Candidate Curriculum Committee guided me through topics that, based on their experience, required special attention. As a result, chapters that typically would take me nine days to write took about 16 days to write for this book.

There is no doubt that this book will generate supplemental publications from vendors who seek to provide products and services for CFA candidates. I expect two types of books to appear. The first is a publication that will simply dilute the contents of this book, claiming that a candidate can review summary points without reading the full book. I think that a CFA candidate who accepts such a claim will be misled. The reason why is that there is no extraneous material in this book. All the topics are critical and were carefully selected. The end of chapter questions and problems were designed to bring out major points. Given the resources and time involved in producing this book, to believe that a vendor could put together a comparable book in a short period of time (without violating copyright laws) — especially if the author is not a specialist in fixed income and is effectively staying one step ahead of the candidate — would be a mistake. On the topic of summaries, I do believe that good summary points are helpful to the candidate in assessing what may need to be reviewed before an examination. For this reason, I have put together an extensive listing of key points at the end of each chapter.

The other type of supplemental book that I believe, and hope, will be produced is one that seeks to expand on some of the concepts in this book and provide additional problem-oriented questions. While I believe that all concepts are clearly explained in this book, there is no doubt that someone with extensive fixed income teaching experience has developed a different approach to explain some of the concepts and this approach will provide additional insights for the candidate. Assuming the author has solid qualifications, I would applaud such an effort.

Frank J. Fabozzi, Ph.D., CFA

Acknowledgments

I would like to acknowledge the assistance of the following individuals.

Dr. Robert R. Johnson, CFA, Senior Vice President of AIMR, reviewed more than a dozen of the books published by Frank J. Fabozzi Associates. Based on his review, he provided me with an extensive list of chapters that contained material that would be useful to CFA candidates for all three levels. Rather than simply put these chapters together into a book, he suggested that I use the material in them to author a book based on explicit content guidelines. His influence on the substance and organization of this book was substantial.

My day-to-day correspondence with AIMR regarding the development of the material and related issues was with Dr. Donald L. Tuttle, CFA, Vice President. It would seem fitting that he would serve as one of my mentors in this project because the book he co-edited, *Managing Investment Portfolios: A Dynamic Process* (first published in 1983), has played an important role in shaping my thoughts on the investment management process; it also has been the cornerstone for portfolio management in the CFA curriculum for almost two decades. The contribution of his books and other publications to the advancement of the CFA body of knowledge, coupled with his leadership role in several key educational projects, recently earned him AIMR's highly prestigious C. Stewart Sheppard Award.

Before any chapters were sent to Don for his review, the first few drafts were sent to Amy F. Lipton, CFA of Lipton Financial Analytics, who was a consultant to AIMR for this project. Amy is currently a member of the Executive Advisory Board of the Candidate Curriculum Committee (CCC). Prior to that she was a member of the Executive Committee of the CCC, the Level I Coordinator for the CCC, and the Chair of the Fixed Income Topic Area of the CCC. Consequently, she was familiar with the topics that should be included in a fixed income analysis book for the CFA Program. Moreover, given her experience in the money management industry (Aetna, First Boston, Greenwich, and Bankers Trust), she was familiar with the material. Amy reviewed and made detailed comments on all aspects of the material. She recommended the deletion or insertion of material, identified topics that required further explanation, and noted material that was too detailed and showed how it should be shortened. Amy not only directed me on content, but she checked every calculation, provided me with spreadsheets of all calculations, and highlighted discrepancies between the solutions in a chapter and those she obtained. On a number of occasions, Amy added material that improved the exposition; she also contributed several end-of-chapter questions. Amy has been accepted into the doctoral program in finance at both Columbia University and Lehigh University, and will begin her studies in Fall of 2000.

After the chapters were approved by Amy and Don, they were then sent to reviewers selected by AIMR. The reviewers provided comments that were the basis for further revisions. I am especially appreciative of the extensive reviews provided by Richard O. Applebach, Jr., CFA and Dr. George H. Troughton, CFA. I am also grateful to the following reviewers: Dr. Philip Fanara, Jr., CFA; Brian S. Heimsoth, CFA; Michael J. Karpik, CFA; Daniel E. Lenhard, CFA; Michael J. Lombardi, CFA; James M. Meeth, CFA; and C. Ronald Sprecher, Ph.D., CFA.

I engaged William McLellan to review all of the chapter drafts. Bill has completed the Level III examination and is now accumulating enough experience to be awarded the CFA designation. Because he took the examinations recently, he reviewed the material as if he were a CFA candidate. He pointed out statements that might be confusing and suggested ways to eliminate ambiguities. Bill checked all the calculations and provided me with his spreadsheet results.

Martin Fridson, CFA and Cecilia Fok provided invaluable insight and direction for the chapter on credit analysis (Chapter 9 of Level II). Dr. Steven V. Mann and Dr. Michael Ferri reviewed several chapters in this book. Dr. Sylvan Feldstein reviewed the sections dealing with municipal bonds in Chapter 3 of Level I and Chapter 9 of Level II. George Kelger reviewed the discussion on agency debentures in Chapter 3 of Level I.

Helen K. Modiri of AIMR provided valuable administrative assistance in coordinating between my office and AIMR.

Megan Orem of Frank J. Fabozzi Associates typeset the entire book and provided editorial assistance on various aspects of this project.

Frank J. Fabozzi, Ph.D., CFA
June 2000

Table of Contents

Web Site Updates

While I made every effort to produce an error-free book, it is highly likely that there will be errors in this book. If you find an error, please send me an email identifying the error. The email should be sent to: info@frankfabozzi.com.

All errors will be posted on my web site: http://www.frankfabozzi.com/cfa/analysis. In addition to any corrections, I may make some comments to clarify the explanation of a topic. Please note that the web site is *not* a vehicle for asking questions about topics or for assistance in explaining topics.

You should check the web site periodically. Alternatively, you can register on line (www.frankfabozzi.com) so that when any change is made to the web site, you will be notified.

Frank J. Fabozzi, Ph.D., CFA

About the Author

Frank J. Fabozzi, Ph.D., CFA, CPA, is editor of the *Journal of Portfolio Management*, an Adjunct Professor of Finance at Yale University's School of Management, and a consultant in the fixed income and derivatives area. From 1986 to 1992, he was a full-time professor of finance at MIT's Sloan School of Management. Dr. Fabozzi, who has earned the Chartered Financial Analyst and Certified Public Accountant designations, has edited and authored numerous books in finance. He has coauthored three books with Franco Modigliani, the 1985 Nobel Prize winner in economic science. In 1993 he started a publishing company, Frank J. Fabozzi Associates, specializing in finance books. Dr. Fabozzi developed *BondVal* software for fixed income valuation jointly with Andrew Kalotay Associates. He is on the board of directors of the Black-Rock complex of funds and the Guardian Life family of funds. He earned a doctorate in economics from the City University of New York in 1972 and in 1994 received an honorary doctorate of Humane Letters from Nova Southeastern University. Dr. Fabozzi is a Fellow of the International Center for Finance at Yale University.

Note on Rounding Differences

It is important to recognize in working through the numerical examples and illustrations in this book that because of rounding differences you may not be able to reproduce some of the results precisely. The two individuals who verified solutions and I used a spreadsheet to compute the solution to all numerical illustrations and examples. For some of the more involved illustrations and examples, there were slight differences in our results.

Moreover, numerical values produced in interim calculations may have been rounded off when produced in a table and as a result when an operation is performed on the values shown in a table, the result may appear to be off.   Just be aware of this. Here is an example of a common situation that you may encounter when attempting to replicate results.

Suppose that a portfolio has four securities and that the market value of these four securities are as shown below:

Security	Market value
1	8,890,100
2	15,215,063
3	18,219,404
4	12,173,200
	54,497,767

Assume further that we want to calculate some weighted average of a characteristic of this portfolio. At Level I, a measure called "duration" will be introduced. For our purposes here, it is not important to know what duration means. All that is of concern to us to demonstrate how rounding differences creep in is that the duration of a portfolio is to be computed. This value is found by computing the weighted average of the duration of the four securities. This involves three steps. First, compute the percentage of each security in the portfolio. Second, multiply the percentage of each security in the portfolio by its duration. Third, sum up the products computed in the second step.

Let's do this with our hypothetical portfolio. We will assume that the duration for each of the securities in the portfolio is as shown below:

Security	Duration
1	9
2	5
3	8
4	2

Using an Excel spreadsheet the following would be computed specifying that the percentage shown in Column (3) below be shown to seven decimal places:

(1)	(2)	(3)	(4)	(5)
Security	Market value	Percent of portfolio	Duration	Percent × duration
1	8,890,100	0.1631278	9	1.46815
2	15,215,063	0.2791869	5	1.395935
3	18,219,404	0.3343147	8	2.674518
4	12,173,200	0.2233706	2	0.446741
Total	54,497,767	1.0000000		5.985343

I simply cut and paste the spreadsheet from Excel to reproduce the table above. The portfolio duration is shown in the last row of Column (5). Rounding this value (5.985343) to two decimal places gives a portfolio duration of 5.99.

There are instances in the book where it was necessary to save space when I cut and paste a large spreadsheet. For example, suppose that in the spreadsheet I specified that Column (3) be shown to only two decimal places rather than seven decimal places. The following table would then be shown:

(1)	(2)	(3)	(4)	(5)
Security	Market value	Percent of portfolio	Duration	Percent × duration
1	8,890,100	0.16	9	1.46815
2	15,215,063	0.28	5	1.395935
3	18,219,404	0.33	8	2.674518
4	12,173,200	0.22	2	0.446741
	54,497,767	1.00		5.985343

Excel would do the computations based on the precise percent of the portfolio and would report the results as shown in Column (5) above. Of course, this is the same value of 5.985343 as before. However, if you calculated for any of the securities the percent of the portfolio in Column (3) multiplied by the duration in Column (4), you do not get the values in Column (5). For example, for Security 1, 0.16 multiplied by 9 gives a value of 1.44, not 1.46815 as shown in the table above.

Suppose instead that the computations were done with a hand-held calculator rather than on a spreadsheet and that the percentage of each security in the portfolio, Column (3), and the product of the percent and duration, Column (5), are computed to two decimal places. The following table would then be computed:

(1)	(2)	(3)	(4)	(5)
Security	Market value	Percent of portfolio	Duration	Percent × duration
1	8,890,100	0.16	9	1.44
2	15,215,063	0.28	5	1.40
3	18,219,404	0.33	8	2.64
4	12,173,200	0.22	2	0.44
Total	54,497,767	1.00		5.92

Note the following. First, the total in Column (3) is really 0.99 (99%) if one adds the value in the columns but is rounded to 1 in the table. Second, the portfolio duration shown in Column (5) is 5.92. This differs from the spreadsheet result earlier of 5.99.

Suppose that you decided to make sure that the total in Column (3) actually totals to 100%. Which security's percent would you round up to do so? If security 3 is rounded up to 34%, then the results would be reported as follows:

(1)	(2)	(3)	(4)	(5)
Security	Market value	Percent of portfolio	Duration	Percent × duration
1	8,890,100	0.16	9	1.44
2	15,215,063	0.28	5	1.40
3	18,219,404	0.34	8	2.72
4	12,173,200	0.22	2	0.44
	54,497,767	1.000		6.00

In this case, the result of the calculation from a hand-held calculator when rounding security 3 to 34% would produce a portfolio duration of 6.

Another reason why the result shown in the book may differ from your calculations is that you may use certain built-in features of spreadsheets that we did not use. For example, you will see in this book how the price of a bond is computed. In some of the illustrations in this book, the price of one or more bonds must be computed as an interim calculation to obtain a solution. If you use a spreadsheet's built-in feature for computing a bond's price (if the feature is available to you), you might observe slightly different results.

Please keep these rounding issues in mind. You are not making computations for sending a rocket to the moon wherein slight differences could cause you to miss your target. Rather, what is important is that you understand the procedure or methodology for computing the values requested.

LEVEL I

Chapter 1

FEATURES OF
FIXED INCOME SECURITIES

LEARNING OUTCOME STATEMENTS

After reading this chapter you should be able to:

- describe the basic features of a bond (maturity, coupon rate, par value, provisions for paying off bonds, currency denomination, and options granted to the issuer or investor)
- identify the wide range of coupon rate structures (zero-coupon bonds, step-up notes, deferred coupon bonds, and floating-rate securities)
- describe the structure of floating-rate securities (that is, the coupon formula and caps and floors) and the different types of floating-rate securities (inverse floaters, dual-indexed floaters, ratchet bonds, stepped spread floaters, and non-interest rate index floaters).
- define accrued interest, full price, and clean price.
- describe what affirmative and negative covenants are.
- describe the provisions for paying off bonds including the distinction between a nonamortizing security and an amortizing security.
- explain the provisions for early retirement of debt including call and refunding provisions, prepayment options, and sinking fund provisions.
- differentiate between a bond being nonrefundable and noncallable.
- explain the difference between a regular redemption price and a special redemption price.
- identify embedded options (call provision, prepayment provision, accelerated sinking fund provision, put option, and conversion option) and explain whether they benefit the issuer or the bondholder.
- explain the importance of options embedded in a bond issue.
- state the typical method used by institutional investors in the bond market used to finance the purchase of a security (margin buying versus repurchase agreement).
- explain a repurchase agreement.
- distinguish between hot collateral (or special collateral) and general collateral.

SECTION I
INTRODUCTION

In its simplest form, a fixed income security is a financial obligation of an entity that promises to pay a specified sum of money at specified future dates. The entity that promises to make the payment is called the **issuer** of the security. Some examples of issuers are central governments such as the U.S. government and the French government, government-related agencies of a central government such as Fannie Mae and Freddie Mac in the United States, a municipal government such as the state of New York in the United States and the city of Rio de Janeiro in Brazil, a corporation such as Coca Cola in the United States and Yorkshire Water in the United Kingdom, and supranational governments such as the World Bank.

Fixed income securities fall into two general categories: debt obligations and preferred stock. In the case of a debt obligation, the issuer is called the **borrower**. The investor who purchases such a fixed income security is said to be the **lender** or **creditor**. The promised payments that the issuer agrees to make at the specified dates consist of two components: interest payments and repayment of the amount borrowed. Fixed income securities that are debt obligations include **bonds**, **mortgage-backed securities**, **asset-backed securities**, and **bank loans**.

In contrast to a fixed income security that represents a debt obligation, **preferred stock** represents an ownership interest in a corporation. Dividend payments are made to the preferred stockholder and represent a distribution of the corporation's profit. Unlike investors who own a corporation's common stock, investors who own the preferred stock can only realize a contractually fixed dividend payment. Moreover, the payments that must be made to preferred stockholders have priority over the payments that a corporation pays to common stockholders. In the case of a liquidation of a corporation, preferred stockholders are given preference over common stockholders. Consequently, preferred stock is a form of equity that has characteristics similar to bonds.

Prior to the 1980s, fixed income securities were simple investment products. Holding aside default by the issuer, the investor knew how long of a time period interest would be received and when the amount borrowed would be repaid. Moreover, most investors purchased these securities with the intent of holding them to their maturity date. Beginning in the 1980s, the fixed income world changed. First, fixed income securities became more complex. There are features in many fixed income securities that make it difficult to determine when the amount borrowed will be repaid and for how long interest will be received. For some securities it is difficult to project the amount of interest that will be received periodically. Second, the hold-to-maturity investor has been replaced by the institutional investor who actively trades fixed income securities.

The major focus of this book is on fixed income securities that are debt obligations. We will frequently use the terms fixed income securities and bonds interchangeably. In addition, we will use the term bonds generically at times to refer collectively to mortgage-backed securities, asset-backed securities, and bank loans.

In this chapter we will look at the various features of fixed income securities and in the next chapter we explain how those features affect the risks associated with investing in fixed income securities. The majority of our illustrations throughout this book use fixed income securities issued in the United States. While the U.S. fixed income market is the largest fixed income market in the world with a diversity of issuers and features, in recent years there has been a significant growth in the fixed income markets of other countries as borrowers have shifted from funding via bank loans to the issuance of fixed income securities. This is a trend that is expected to continue.

SECTION II INDENTURE AND COVENANTS

The promises of the issuer and the rights of the bondholders are set forth in great detail in the bond's **indenture**. Bondholders would have great difficulty in determining from time to time whether the issuer was keeping all the promises made in the indenture. This problem is resolved for the most part by bringing in a trustee as a third party to the contract. The indenture is made out to the trustee as a representative of the interests of the bondholders; that is, a trustee acts in a fiduciary capacity for bondholders.

As part of the indenture there are **affirmative covenants** and **negative covenants**. Affirmative covenants set forth activities that the borrower promises to do. The most common affirmative covenants are (1) to pay interest and principal on a timely basis, (2) to pay all taxes and other claims when due, (3) to maintain all properties used and useful in the borrower's business in good condition and working order, and (4) to submit periodic reports to a trustee stating that the borrower is in compliance with the loan agreement. Negative covenants set forth certain limitations and restrictions on the borrower's activities. The more common restrictive covenants are those that impose limitations on the borrower's ability to incur additional debt unless certain tests are met.

SECTION III MATURITY

The **term to maturity** of a bond is the number of years over which the issuer has promised to meet the conditions of the obligation. The **maturity date** of a bond refers to the date that the debt will cease to exist, at which time the issuer will redeem the bond by paying the amount borrowed. The maturity date of a bond is always identified when describing a bond. For example, a description of a bond might state "due 12/1/2010."

The practice in the bond market is to refer to the "term to maturity" of a bond as simply its "maturity" or "term." As we explain below, there may be provisions in the indenture that allow either the issuer or bondholder to alter a bond's term to maturity.

Some market participants view bonds with a maturity between 1 and 5 years as "short-term." Bonds with a maturity between 5 and 12 years are viewed as "intermediate-term," and "long-term" bonds are those with a maturity of more than 12 years.

There are bonds of every maturity. Typically, the longest maturity is 30 years. However, Walt Disney Co. issued bonds in July 1993 with a maturity date of 7/15/2093, making them 100-year bonds at the time of issuance. In December 1993, the Tennessee Valley Authority issued bonds that mature on 12/15/2043, making them 50-year bonds at the time of issuance.

There are three reasons why the term to maturity of a bond is important:

Reason 1: Term to maturity indicates the time period over which the bondholder can expect to receive interest payments and the number of years before the principal will be paid in full.

Reason 2: The yield offered on a bond depends on the term to maturity. The relationship between the yield on a bond and maturity is called the **yield curve** and will be discussed in Chapter 4.

Reason 3: The price of a bond will fluctuate over its life as interest rates in the market change. The price volatility of a bond is a function of its maturity (among other variables). More specifically, as explained in Chapter 5, all other factors constant, the longer the maturity of a bond, the greater the price volatility resulting from a change in interest rates.

SECTION IV
PAR VALUE

The **par value** of a bond is the amount that the issuer agrees to repay the bondholder by the maturity date. This amount is also referred to as the **principal**, **face value**, **redemption value**, and **maturity value**. Bonds can have any par value.

Because bonds can have a different par value, the practice is to quote the price of a bond as a percentage of its par value. A value of "100" means 100% of par value. So, for example, if a bond has a par value of $1,000 and the issue is selling for $900, this bond would be said to be selling at 90. If a bond with a par value of $5,000 is selling for $5,500, the bond is said to be selling for 110.

When computing the dollar price of a bond in the United States, the bond must first be converted into a price per US$1 of par value. Then the price per $1 of par value is multiplied by the par value to get the dollar price. Here are examples of what the dollar price of a bond is given the price quoted for the bond in the market and the par amount involved in the transaction:

Quoted price	Price per $ par value	Par value	Dollar price
90½	0.9050	$1,000	905.00
102¾	1.0275	$5,000	5,137.50
70⅝	0.7063	$10,000	7,062.50
113¹¹⁄₃₂	1.1334	$100,000	113,343.75

Notice that a bond may trade below or above its par value. When a bond trades below its par value, it said to be **trading at discount**. When a bond trades above its par value, it said to be **trading at a premium**. The reason why a bond sells above or below its par value will be explained in Chapter 2.

PRACTICE QUESTION 1

Given the information in the first and third columns for a U.S. investor, complete the information in the second and fourth columns:

Quoted price	Price per $1 of par value	Par value	Dollar price
103¼		$1,000	
70⅛		$5,000	
87⁵⁄₁₆		$10,000	
117³⁄₃₂		$100,000	

SECTION V
COUPON RATE

The **coupon rate**, also called the **nominal rate**, is the interest rate that the issuer agrees to pay each year. The annual amount of the interest payment made to bondholders during the term of the bond is called the **coupon**. The coupon is determined by multiplying the coupon rate by the par value of the bond. That is,

$$coupon = coupon\ rate \times par\ value$$

For example, a bond with an 8% coupon rate and a par value of $1,000 will pay annual interest of $80 (= $1,000 × 0.08).

When describing a bond of an issuer, the coupon rate is indicated along with the maturity date. For example, the expression "6s of 12/1/2010" means a bond with a 6% coupon rate maturing on 12/1/2010.

In the United States, the usual practice is for the issuer to pay the coupon in two semiannual installments. Mortgage-backed securities and asset-backed securities typically pay interest monthly. For bonds issued in some markets outside the United States, coupon payments are made only once per year.

In addition to indicating the coupon payments that the investor can expect to receive over the term of the bond, the coupon rate also affects the bond's price sensitivity to changes in market interest rates. As illustrated in Chapter 2, all other factors constant, the higher the coupon rate, the less the price will change in response to a change in market interest rates.

A. Zero-Coupon Bonds

Not all bonds make periodic coupon payments. Bonds that are not contracted to make periodic coupon payments are called **zero-coupon bonds**. The holder of a zero-coupon bond realizes interest by buying the bond substantially below its par value (i.e., buying the bond at a discount). Interest is then paid at the maturity date, with the interest being the difference between the par value and the price paid for the bond. So, for example, if an investor purchases a zero-coupon bond for 70, the interest is 30. This is the difference between the par value (100) and the price paid (70). The reason behind the issuance of zero-coupon bonds is explained in Chapter 2.

There is another type of fixed income security that does not pay interest until the maturity date. This type of zero coupon bond has contractual coupon payments but those payments are accrued and distributed along with the maturity value at the maturity date. These instruments are called **accrual bonds**. For example, an issuer may sell a 3-year bond with a par value of $1,000 and agree to pay 6% interest compounded semiannually at the bond's maturity. The accrued interest over this period of time would be $194.05. The issuer would then pay at maturity $1,000 plus the accrued interest of $194.05.[1]

B. Step-Up Notes

There are securities that have a coupon rate that increases over time. These securities are called **step-up notes** because the coupon rate "steps up" over time. For example, a 5-year step-up note might have a coupon rate that is 5% for the first two years and 6% for the last three years. Or, the step-up note could call for a 5% coupon rate for the first two years, 5.5% for the third and fourth years, and 6% for the fifth year. When there is only one change (or step up), as in our first example, the issue is referred to as a **single step-up note**. When there is more than one change, as in our second example, the issue is referred to as a **multiple step-up note**.

An example of an actual multiple step-up note is a 5-year issue of the Student Loan Marketing Association (Sallie Mae) issued in May 1994. The coupon schedule is as follows:

---

[1] The accrued interest is computed by using the formula for the future value of an annuity. Alternatively, it can be computed by simply accruing the coupon interest at the semiannual interest rate (3% in our illustration). In the case of the first semiannual coupon payment, it is compounded for 5 periods (one less than the 6 semiannual periods). The second semiannual coupon payment is compounded for 4 semiannual periods, and so on. That is:

first coupon payment plus accrued interest	=	$30 (1.03)^5$	=	$34.78
second coupon payment plus accrued interest	=	$30 (1.03)^4$	=	$33.77
third coupon payment plus accrued interest	=	$30 (1.03)^3$	=	$32.78
fourth coupon payment plus accrued interest	=	$30 (1.03)^2$	=	$31.83
fifth coupon payment plus accrued interest	=	$30 (1.03)^1$	=	$30.90
sixth coupon payment plus accrued interest	=	$30 (1.03)^0$	=	$30.00
total coupon payments plus accrued interest			=	$194.05

$$6.05\% \quad \text{from} \quad 5/3/94 \quad \text{to} \quad 5/2/95$$
$$6.50\% \quad \text{from} \quad 5/3/95 \quad \text{to} \quad 5/2/96$$
$$7.00\% \quad \text{from} \quad 5/3/96 \quad \text{to} \quad 5/2/97$$
$$7.75\% \quad \text{from} \quad 5/3/97 \quad \text{to} \quad 5/2/98$$
$$8.50\% \quad \text{from} \quad 5/3/98 \quad \text{to} \quad 5/2/99$$

C. Deferred Coupon Bonds

There are issues whose coupon payment is deferred for a specified number of years. That is, there is no coupon payment for the deferred period and then a lump sum payment at some specified date and coupon payments until maturity. The bonds are called **deferred coupon bonds**.

D. Floating-Rate Securities

The coupon rate on a bond need not be fixed over the bond's life. **Floating-rate securities**, sometimes called **variable-rate securities**, have coupon payments that reset periodically according to some reference rate. The typical formula (called the **coupon formula**) for the coupon rate at the dates when the coupon rate is reset is as follows:

coupon rate = reference rate + quoted margin

The **quoted margin** is the additional amount that the issuer agrees to pay above the reference rate. For example, suppose that the reference rate is the 1-month London interbank offered rate (LIBOR). Suppose that the quoted margin is 100 basis points.[2] Then the coupon formula is:

coupon rate = 1-month LIBOR + 100 basis points

So, if 1-month LIBOR on the coupon reset date is 5%, the coupon rate is reset for that period at 6% (5% plus 100 basis points).

The quoted margin need not be a positive value. The quoted margin could be subtracted from the reference rate. For example, the reference rate could be the yield on a 5-year Treasury security and the coupon rate could reset every six months based on the following coupon formula:

coupon rate = 5-year Treasury yield − 90 basis points

So, if the 5-year Treasury yield is 7% on the coupon reset date, the coupon rate is 6.1% (7% minus 90 basis points).

A **deleveraged floater** is a floater that has a coupon formula where the coupon rate is computed as a fraction of the reference rate plus a quoted margin. The general formula for a deleveraged floater is:

coupon rate = $b \times$ (reference rate) + quoted margin

where b is a value between zero and one.

Banker's Trust issued such a floater in April 1992 that matures in March 2003. This issue makes quarterly coupon payments according to the following formula:

$0.40 \times$ (10-year Constant Maturity Treasury rate) + 2.65%

with a minimum interest rate of 6%. For this issue b is 0.40 and the quoted margin is 2.65%.

---

[2] In the fixed income market, market participants refer to changes in interest rates or differences in interest rates in terms of basis points. A **basis point** is defined as 0.0001, or equivalently, 0.01%. Consequently, 100 basis points are equal to 1%. (In our example the coupon formula can be expressed as 1-month LIBOR + 1%.) A change in interest rates from, say, 5.0% to 6.2% means that there is a 1.2% change in rates or 120 basis points.

It is important to understand the mechanics for the payment and the setting of the coupon rate. Suppose that a floater pays interest semiannually and further assume that the coupon reset date is today. Then, the coupon rate is determined via the coupon formula and this is the interest rate that the issuer agrees to pay at the next coupon date six months from now. That is, the coupon rate is determined at the coupon reset date but paid in arrears.

1. Caps and Floors

A floater may have a restriction on the maximum coupon rate that will be paid at any reset date. The maximum coupon rate is called a **cap**. For example, suppose for a floater whose coupon formula is 3-month Treasury bill rate plus 50 basis points, there is a cap of 9%. If the 3-month Treasury bill rate is 9% at a coupon reset date, then the coupon formula would give a coupon rate of 9.5%. However, the cap restricts the coupon rate to 9%. Thus, for our hypothetical floater, once the 3-month Treasury bill rate exceeds 8.5%, the coupon rate is capped at 9%.

Because a cap restricts the coupon rate from increasing, a cap is an unattractive feature for the investor. In contrast, there could be a minimum coupon rate specified for a floater. The minimum coupon rate is called a **floor**. If the coupon formula produces a coupon rate that is below the floor, the floor rate is paid instead. An example of a floor would be the 6% minimum interest rate in the Bankers Trust deleveraged floater. Thus, a floor is an attractive feature for the investor. As we explain in Section X, caps and floors are effectively embedded options.

Some issues have declining floors. For example, for a Citicorp floater issue that was due September 1, 1998, the minimum rate was 7.50% through August 31, 1983, then 7.00% through August 31, 1988, and then 6.50% to maturity.

A floater can have both a cap and floor. This feature is referred to as a **collar**. There are some floaters, referred to as **drop-lock bonds**, which automatically change the floating coupon rate into a fixed coupon rate under certain circumstances.

PRACTICE QUESTION 2

A floating-rate issue has the following coupon formula:

6-month Treasury rate + 50 basis points with a cap of 7%

The coupon rate is set every six months. Suppose that at the reset date the 6-month Treasury rate is as shown below. Compute the coupon rate for the next 6-month period:

	6-month Treasury rate	Coupon rate
First reset date	5.5%	?
Second reset date	5.8%	?
Third reset date	6.3%	?
Fourth reset date	6.8%	?
Fifth reset date	7.3%	?
Sixth reset date	6.1%	?

2. Types of Coupon Formulas

There is a wide range of coupon formulas. These are discussed below. The reasons why issuers have been able to create floating-rate securities with offbeat coupon formulas is due to the use of derivative instruments in offering securities. These offbeat coupon formulas are typically found in "structured notes," a form of medium term note. We will discuss structured notes in Chapter 3.

a. Inverse Floaters

Typically, the coupon formula for a floater is such that the coupon rate increases when the reference rate increases, and decreases when the reference rate decreases. There are issues whose coupon rate moves in the opposite direction from the change in the reference rate. Such issues are called **inverse floaters** or **reverse floaters**. (When first issued, these floaters were also referred to as "yield curve notes.")

In the agency, corporate, and municipal markets inverse floaters are created as structured notes. Inverse floaters in the mortgage-backed securities market are common and are created without the use of derivatives, as will be discussed at Level II.

The coupon formula for an inverse floater is:

$$\text{coupon rate} = K - L \times (\text{reference rate})$$

where K and L are values specified in the prospectus for the issue.

For example, suppose that for a particular inverse floater K is 20% and L is 2. Then the coupon reset formula would be:

$$\text{coupon rate} = 20\% - 2 \times (\text{reference rate})$$

Suppose that the reference rate is the 3-month Treasury bill rate, then the coupon formula would be

$$\text{coupon rate} = 20\% - 2 \times (\text{3-month Treasury bill rate})$$

If at the coupon reset date the 3-month Treasury bill rate is 6%, the coupon rate for the next period is:

$$\text{coupon rate} = 20\% - 2 \times 6\% = 8\%$$

If at the next reset date the 3-month Treasury bill rate declines to 5%, the coupon rate increases to:

$$\text{coupon rate} = 20\% - 2 \times 5\% = 10\%$$

Notice that if the 3-month Treasury bill rate exceeds 10%, then the coupon formula would produce a negative coupon rate. To prevent this, there is also a floor imposed on the coupon rate. There is a cap on the inverse floater. This occurs if the 3-month Treasury bill rate is zero. In that unlikely event, the maximum coupon rate is 20% for our hypothetical inverse floater.

An example of an actual inverse floater is one issued by one of the Federal Home Loan Banks in April 1999. The issue matures in April 2002 and makes payments quarterly based on the following coupon formula:

$$\text{coupon formula} = 18\% - 2.5 \times (\text{3-month LIBOR})$$

Contractually, this inverse floater has a floor of 3% and a cap of 15.5%.

b. Dual-Indexed Floaters

The coupon rate for a **dual-indexed floater** is typically a fixed percentage plus the difference between two reference rates. For example, the Federal Home Loan Bank System issued a floater in July 1993 (the issue matured in July 1996) whose coupon rate (reset quarterly) was as follows:

(10-year Constant Maturity Treasury rate) − (3-month LIBOR) + 160 basis points

c. Range Notes

There are floaters whose coupon rate is equal to the reference rate as long as the reference rate is within a certain range at the reset date. If the reference rate is outside of the range, the coupon rate is zero for that period. This floater is called a **range note** and is another example of a structured note.

For example, a 3-year range note might specify that the reference rate is the 1-year Treasury rate and that the coupon rate resets every year. The coupon rate for the year is the Treasury rate as long as the Treasury rate at the coupon reset date falls within the range as specified below:

	Year 1	Year 2	Year 3
Lower limit of range	4.5%	5.25%	6.00%
Upper limit of range	5.5%	6.75%	7.50%

If the 1-year Treasury rate is outside of the range, the coupon rate is zero. For example, if in Year 1 the 1-year Treasury rate is 5% at the coupon reset date, the coupon rate for the year is 5%. However, if the 1-year Treasury rate is 6%, the coupon rate for the year is zero since the 1-year Treasury rate is greater than the upper limit for Year 1 of 5.5%.

Let's look at an actual range note. In August 1996 Sallie Mae issued one that matures in August 2003. This issue makes coupon payments quarterly. The investor earns 3-month LIBOR plus 155 basis points for every day during the quarter that 3-month LIBOR is between 3% and 9%. Interest will accrue at 0% for each day that 3-month LIBOR is outside this range. As a result, this range note has a floor of 0%.

d. Ratchet Bonds

In 1998 a new adjustable-rate structure was brought to market by the Tennessee Valley Authority. This structure, referred to as a **ratchet bond**, has a coupon rate that adjusts periodically at a fixed margin over a reference rate. However, it can only adjust downward based on a coupon formula. Once the coupon rate is adjusted down, it *cannot* be readjusted up if the reference rate subsequently increases.

e. Stepped Spread Floaters

Some issues provide for a change in the quoted margin at certain intervals over a floater's life. These issues are referred to as **stepped spread floaters** because the quoted margin could either step to a higher or lower level over the security's life. For example, consider Standard Chartered Bank's floater that matures in December 2006. From issuance until December 2001, the coupon formula is 3-month LIBOR plus 40 basis points. From December 2001 until maturity, the quoted margin "steps up" to 90 basis points but the reference rate remains 3-month LIBOR over the life of the security.

f. Reset Margin Determined at Issuer Discretion

There are floaters which require that the issuer reset the coupon rate so that the issue will trade at a predetermined price (typically above par). These issues are called **extendible reset bonds**. The coupon rate at the reset date may be the average of rates suggested by two investment banking firms. The new rate will then reflect: (1) the level of interest rates at the reset date, and (2) the margin required by the market at the reset date. The second element reflects economic conditions in the market.

Notice the difference between an extendible reset bond and a typical floater that resets based on a coupon formula. For a typical floater, the coupon rate resets based on a known margin (i.e., the quoted margin) over some reference rate. For example, suppose that the coupon formula is the 6-month Treasury rate plus 100 basis points. The 100 basis points is the quoted margin and does not change over the life of the floater. In contrast, the coupon rate on an extendible reset issue is reset based on the margin required by the market at the reset date (as determined by the issuer or suggested by several investment banking firms) for the security to trade at par value. For example, suppose that the coupon formula for an extendible reset bond is 6-month Treasury rate plus 100 basis points. At a coupon reset date suppose that investment bankers are contacted about what the price of the issue would be if the margin is 100 basis points. Assume that the investment bankers agreed that the price would be below par and that if the issue is to trade at par, the margin must be 125 basis points. Then at the coupon reset date, the coupon rate will be 6-month Treasury rate plus 125 basis points.

g. Non-Interest Rate Indexes

While the reference rate for most floaters is an interest rate or an interest rate index, a wide variety of reference rates appear in coupon formulas. This is particularly true for structured notes. The coupon for a floater could be indexed to movements in foreign exchange rates, the price of a commodity (e.g., crude oil), the return on an equity index (e.g., the S&P 500), or movements in a bond index. In fact, through financial engineering, issuers have been able to structure floaters with almost any reference rate.

In several countries, there are government bonds whose coupon formula is tied to an inflation index. The U.S. Department of the Treasury in January 1997 began issuing inflation-adjusted securities. These issues are referred to as **Treasury Inflation Protection Securities** (TIPS). The reference rate for the coupon formula is the rate of inflation as measured by the Consumer Price Index for All Urban Consumers (i.e., CPI-U). The first issue was a 10-year Treasury note with a coupon interest rate equal to 3.375% plus the rate of inflation. The mechanics of the payment of the coupon will be explained in Chapter 3 where these securities are discussed.

Corporations and agencies in the United States began to issue **inflation-linked** (or **inflation-indexed**) **bonds** shortly after the Treasury issuance. For example, in February 1997, J.P. Morgan & Company issued a 15-year bond that pays the CPI plus 400 basis points. In the same month, the Federal Home Loan Bank issued a 5-year bond with a coupon rate equal to the CPI plus 315 basis points and a 10-year bond with a coupon rate equal to the CPI plus 337 basis points.

PRACTICE QUESTION 3

Identify the following types of bonds based on their coupon structures:

a. Coupon formula:

coupon rate = 32% − 2 × (5-year Treasury rate)

b. Coupon structure:

Years 1-3	5.1%
Years 4-9	5.7%
Years 10-20	6.2%

c. Coupon formula:

5-year Treasury rate − 3-month Treasury rate + 100 basis points

d. Coupon structure:

Year	If the 1-year Treasury rate is between:	Coupon rate is 1-year Treasury rate plus	If not coupon rate is:
1	3.4% and 4.7%	40 basis points	0%
2	3.8% and 5.1%	40 basis points	0%
3	4.0% and 5.7%	40 basis points	0%
4	4.3% and 6.0%	40 basis points	0%

e. Coupon formula:

3.1% + change in the consumer price index

E. Accrued Interest

Bond issuers do not disburse coupon interest payments every day. Instead, typically in the United States coupon interest is paid every six months. In some countries, interest is paid annually. For mortgage-backed and asset-backed securities, interest is usually paid monthly. The coupon payment is made to the bondholder of record. Thus, if an investor sells a bond between coupon payments and the buyer holds it until the next coupon payment, then the entire coupon interest earned for the period will be paid to the buyer of the bond since the buyer will be the holder of record. The seller of the bond gives up the interest from the time of the last coupon payment to the time until the bond is sold. The amount of interest over this period that will be received by the buyer even though it was earned by the seller is called **accrued interest**. We will see how to calculate accrued interest in Chapter 5.

In the United States and in many countries, the bond buyer must pay the bond seller the accrued interest. The amount that the buyer pays the seller is the agreed upon price for the bond plus accrued interest. This amount is called the **full price**. (Some market participants refer to this as the "dirty price.") The agreed upon bond price without accrued interest is simply referred to as the **price**. (Some refer to it as the "clean price.")

A bond in which the buyer must pay the seller accrued interest is said to be trading *cum-coupon*. If the buyer forgoes the next coupon payment, the bond is said to be trading *ex-coupon*. In the United States, bonds are always traded *cum coupon*. There are bond markets outside the United States where bonds are traded *ex-coupon* for a certain period before the coupon payment date.

There are exceptions to the rule that the bond buyer must pay the bond seller accrued interest. The most important exception is when the issuer has not fulfilled its promise to make the periodic payments. In this case, the issuer is said to be in default. In such instances, the bond is sold without accrued interest and is said to be **traded flat**.

SECTION VI PROVISIONS FOR PAYING OFF BONDS

The issuer of a bond agrees to repay the principal by the stated maturity date. The issuer can agree to repay the entire amount borrowed in one lump sum payment at the maturity date. That is, the issuer is not required to make any principal repayments prior to the maturity date. Such bonds are said to have a **bullet maturity**. The bullet maturity structure has become the most common structure in the United States and Europe for both corporate and government issuers.[3]

There are bond issues which consist of a series of blocks of securities maturing in sequence. The blocks of securities are said to be **serial bonds**. The coupon rate for each block can be different. Bonds issued by municipalities are sometimes issued as serial bonds. For example, a $250 million par issue of The Port Authority of New York and New Jersey, Special Project Bonds, Series 4 issued on May 1, 1996 had the following serial bonds:

Installment	Par Amount	Coupon (%)	Maturity Date
First	$5,400,000	6.25	October 1, 1999
Second	6,800,000	6.50	October 1, 2001
Third	52,200,000	7.00	October 1, 2007
Fourth	48,600,000	6.75	October 1, 2011
Fifth	137,000,000	6.75	October 1, 2019

One type of bond issued by a corporation in which there are serial bonds is an **equipment trust certificate**.

Fixed income securities backed by pools of loans (mortgage-backed securities and asset-backed securities) often have a schedule of partial principal repayments. Such fixed income securities are said to be **amortizing securities**. For many loans, the payments are structured so that when the last loan payment is made, the entire amount owed is fully paid off.

Another example of an amortizing feature is a bond that has a **sinking fund provision**. This provision for repayment of a bond may be designed to liquidate all of an issue by the maturity date, or it may be arranged to repay only a part of the total by the maturity date. We discuss this provision later in this section.

Many issues have a call provision granting the issuer an option to retire all or part of the issue prior to the stated maturity date. Some issues specify that the issuer must retire a predetermined amount of the issue periodically. Various types of call provisions are discussed below.

A. Call and Refunding Provisions

An issuer generally wants the right to retire a bond issue prior to the stated maturity date because it recognizes that at some time in the future the general level of interest rates may fall sufficiently below the issue's coupon rate so that redeeming the issue

---

[3] The reason for this will be explained at Level III.

and replacing it with another issue with a lower coupon rate would be economically beneficial. This right is a disadvantage to the bondholder since proceeds received must be reinvested at a lower interest rate. As a result, an issuer who wants to include this right as part of a bond offering must compensate the bondholder when the issue is sold by offering a higher coupon rate, or equivalently, accepting a lower price than if the right is not included.

The right of the issuer to retire the issue prior to the stated maturity date is referred to as a **call provision**. If an issuer exercises this right, the issuer is said to "call the bond." The price which the issuer must pay to retire the issue is referred to as the **call price**. Typically, there is not one call price but a **call schedule** which sets forth a call price based on when the issuer can exercise the call option.

When a bond is issued, typically the issuer may not call the bond for a number of years. That is, the issue is said to have a **deferred call**. The date at which the bond may first be called is referred to as the **first call date**. The first call date for the Walt Disney 7.55s due 7/15/2093 (the 100-year bonds) is 7/15/2023. For the 50-year Tennessee Valley Authority 6⅞s due 12/15/2043, the first call date is 12/15/2003.

Bonds can be called in whole (the entire issue) or in part (only a portion). When less than the entire issue is called, the certificates to be called are either selected randomly or on a **pro rata basis**. When bonds are selected randomly, a computer program is used to select the serial number of the certificates called. The serial numbers are then published in *The Wall Street Journal* and major metropolitan dailies. Pro rata redemption means that all bondholders of the issue that is partially called will have the same percentage of their holdings redeemed (subject to the restrictions imposed on minimum denominations). Pro rata redemption is rare for publicly issued debt. It is common for debt issues directly or privately placed with borrowers.

A bond issue that permits the issuer to call or refund an issue prior to the stated maturity date is referred to as a **callable bond**. At one time, the callable bond structure was common for corporate bonds issued in the United States. However, since the mid-1990s, there has been significantly less issuance of callable bonds by corporate issuers of high credit quality. Instead, as noted above, the most popular structure is the bullet bond. In contrast, corporate issuers of low credit quality continue to issue callable bonds.[4] In Europe, historically the callable bond structure has not been as popular as in the United States.

1. Call Schedule

Generally, the call schedule is such that the call price at the first call date is a premium over the par value and scaled down to the par value over time. The date at which the issue is first callable at par value is referred to as the **first par call date**.

For example, the Becton Dickinson & Co. 8.70s due 1/15/2025 were issued on 1/10/95. The first call date is 1/15/2005. Thus, at issuance this corporate bond had a 10-year deferred call. The call schedule for this issue is as follows:

---

[4] As explained in Chapter 2, high credit quality issuers are referred to as "investment grade" issuers and low credit quality issuers are referred to as "non-investment grade" issuers. The reason why high credit quality issuers have reduced their issuance of callable bonds while it is still the more popular structure for low credit quality issuers is explained at Level III.

If redeemed during the 12 months beginning January 15:	Call price
2005	103.949
2006	103.554
2007	103.159
2008	102.764
2009	102.369
2010	101.975
2011	101.580
2012	101.185
2013	100.790
2014	100.395
2015 and thereafter	100.000

The $150 million Anheuser Busch Company 8⅝s due 12/1/2016 issued 11/20/1986 also had a 10-year deferred call (the first call date was December 1, 1996) and the following call schedule:

If redeemed during the 12 months beginning December 1:	Call price
1996	104.313
1997	103.881
1998	103.450
1999	103.019
2000	102.588
2001	102.156
2002	101.725
2003	101.294
2004	100.863
2005	100.431
2006 and thereafter	100.000

Not all issues have a call schedule in which the call price starts out as a premium over par. There are issues where the call price at the first call date and subsequent call dates is par value. In such cases, the first call date is the same as the first par call date. For example, Transcontinental Gas Pipe Line Corp. issued on 11/22/96 a 7.25% issue maturing on 12/01/99. The call price is unchanged at 100.

2. Noncallable versus Nonrefundable Bonds

If a bond issue does not have any protection against early call, then it is said to be a **currently callable** issue. But most new bond issues, even if currently callable, usually have some restrictions against certain types of early redemption. The most common restriction is that prohibiting the refunding of the bonds for a certain number of years or for the issue's life. Bonds that are noncallable for the issue's life are more common than bonds which are nonrefundable for life but otherwise callable.

Many investors are confused by the terms **noncallable** and **nonrefundable**. As far back as 1962, Hess and Winn wrote:

> The terms "noncallable" and "nonrefundable" are often used rather loosely as interchangeable entities, although from a technical standpoint they have different meanings.[5]

---

[5] Arleigh P. Hess, Jr. and Willis J. Winn, *The Value of the Call Provision* (Philadelphia, PA: University of Pennsylvania, 1962), p. 24.

Call protection is much more absolute than refunding protection. While there may be certain exceptions to absolute or complete call protection in some cases (such as sinking funds and the redemption of debt under certain mandatory provisions discussed later), it still provides greater assurance against premature and unwanted redemption than does refunding protection. Refunding prohibition merely prevents redemption only from certain sources, namely the proceeds of other debt issues sold at a lower cost of money. The holder is protected only if interest rates decline and the borrower can obtain lower-cost money to pay off the debt.

For example, Anheuser Busch Company issued on 6/23/88 10% coupon bonds due 7/1/2018. The issue was immediately callable. However, the prospectus specified in the call schedule that

> prior to July 1, 1998, the Company may not redeem any of the Debentures pursuant to such option, directly or indirectly, from or in anticipation of the proceeds of the issuance of any indebtedness for money borrowed having an interest cost of less than 10% per annum.

Thus, this Anheuser Busch bond issue could not be redeemed prior to July 2, 1998 if the company raises the funds from a new issue with an interest cost lower than 10%. There is nothing to prevent the company from calling the bonds within the 10-year refunding protected period from debt sold at a higher rate (although the company normally wouldn't do so) or from funds obtained through other means. And that is exactly what Anheuser Busch did. Between December 1993 and June 1994, it called $68.8 million of these relatively high-coupon bonds at 107.5% of par value (the call price) with funds from its general operations. This was permitted because funds from the company's general operations are viewed as a more expensive source of funds than the interest cost of the company. Thus, this issuer was allowed to call this issue prior to July 1, 1998.

Some prospectuses specifically clarify refunding and redemption. For example, the prospectus for one of Cincinnati Gas & Electric Company's bond issues due in 2020 states,[6]

> The Offered Bonds are redeemable (though CG&E does not contemplate doing so) prior to May 1, 1995 through the use of earnings, proceeds from the sale of equity securities and cash accumulations other than those resulting from a refunding operation such as hereinafter described. The Offered Bonds are not redeemable prior to May 1, 1995 as a part of, or in anticipation of, any refunding operation involving the incurring of indebtedness by CG&E having an effective interest cost (calculated to the second place in accordance with generally accepted financial practice) of less than the effective interest cost of the Offered Bonds (similarly calculated) or through the operation of the Maintenance and Replacement Fund.

Refunding means to replace an old bond issue with a new one, often at a lower interest cost. In the Florida Power & Light case the judge said:[7]

---

[6] There are terms in this passage that will be discussed later in this chapter or in later chapters.

[7] Lucas *et al* v. Florida Power & Light Company, Final Judgment, paragraph 77.

The terms "redemption" and "refunding" are not synonymous. A "redemption" is simply a call of bonds. A "refunding" occurs when the issuer sells bonds in order to use the proceeds to redeem an earlier series of bonds. The refunding bond issue being sold is closely linked to the one being redeemed by contractual language and proximity in time so that the proceeds will be available to pay for the redemption. Otherwise, the issuer would be taking an inordinate risk that market conditions would change between the redemption of the earlier issue and the sale of the later issue.

The key point to remember is that investors should not be lulled by a nonrefunding provision. The following two examples illustrate this.[8]

In 1973 Bristol-Myers Company redeemed at 107.538 $25 million of an issue with an original maturity of 1995. Issued in 1970, they traded as high as 111 in 1972 and were about 108-109 when the call was announced. A number of holders, including institutional investors and at least one Wall Street corporate bond dealer, were confused by the call, having mistaken "nonrefundable" for "noncallable." The bonds were nonrefundable for 10 years but were currently callable.

Archer-Daniels-Midland Company (ADM) presents a particularly interesting and important case. In May 1981, the company sold a 16% issue maturing in 2011. The issue was currently callable and had a 10-year prohibition against lower-cost refunding. Subsequent to the issuance of this security, ADM raised money in 1982 and 1983 through a lower-cost borrowings than the 16% coupon issue. It also sold common stock in January 1983 and again on June 1983. On June 1, 1983, the Dow Jones Capital Markets News Wire Service announced that the company would redeem on August 1, at 113.95 plus accrued interest, all of the outstanding 16% issue. The corporate bond market was in an uproar. This call was well within the 10-year refunding protected period. One investment banking firm sued to bar the redemption, claiming that

> investors expected the debentures to continue on the market until 1991 (which) kept the trading value of the debt at about $1,250 per $1,000 face value and misled investors into believing the debentures would continue to be traded... it wouldn't have purchased the debentures if it believed Archer-Daniels would redeem the bonds so soon.[9]

The company said that the proceeds for this redemption came from the sale of the common stock. The plaintiff claimed that ADM was not allowed, by the issue's terms, to call the bonds from lower-cost funds and it pointed to the 1982 and 1983 debt financings. It contended that the money raised from the common stock sales was little more than a subterfuge for circumventing the refunding protection provided in the indenture. The court upheld ADM's right to call the issue with the proceeds from the sales of common shares saying the redemption was within the company's legal rights and in accordance with the indenture. The decision in this case was an important event, as it substantially eroded the effectiveness of standard refunding provisions.

---

[8] These examples are from Chapter 5 in Richard S. Wilson and Frank J. Fabozzi, *Corporate Bonds: Structures & Analysis* (New Hope, PA: Frank J. Fabozzi, 1996).

[9] "Morgan Stanley Sues Over Archer-Daniels' Plan to Redeem Debt," *The Wall Street Journal* (July 11, 1983).

3. Regular versus Special Redemption Prices

The call prices for the various issues cited above are called the **regular redemption prices** or **general redemption prices**. Notice that the regular redemption prices are above par until the first par call date. There are also **special redemption prices** for bonds redeemed through the sinking fund and through other provisions, and the proceeds from the confiscation of property through the right of eminent domain or the forced sale or transfer of assets due to deregulation. The special redemption price is usually par value. Thus, there is an advantage to the issuer of being able to redeem an issue prior to the first par call date at the special redemption price (usually par) rather than at the regular redemption price.

A concern of an investor is that an issuer will use all means possible to maneuver a call so that the special redemption price applies. This is referred to as the **par call problem**. There have been ample examples, and subsequent litigation, where corporations have used the special redemption price and bondholders have challenged the stance of the issuer.

B. Prepayments

For amortizing securities that are backed by loans that have a schedule of principal repayments, individual borrowers typically have the option to pay off all or part of their loan prior to the scheduled date. Any principal repayment prior to the scheduled date is called a **prepayment**. The right of borrowers to prepay is called the **prepayment option**.

Basically, the prepayment option is the same as a call option. However, unlike a call option, there is not a call price that depends on when the borrower pays off the issue. Typically, the price at which a loan is prepaid is par value. Prepayments will be discussed when mortgage-backed and asset-backed securities are discussed at Level II.

C. Sinking Fund Provision

An indenture may require the issuer to retire a specified portion of the issue each year. This is referred to as a **sinking fund requirement**. The alleged purpose of the sinking fund provision is to reduce credit risk (discussed in the next chapter). This kind of provision for repayment of debt may be designed to retire all of a bond issue by the maturity date, or it may be arranged to pay off only a part of the total by the end of the term. If only a part is paid, the remainder is called a **balloon maturity**.

An example of an issue with a sinking fund requirement that pays off the entire principal by the maturity date is the $150 million Ingersoll Rand 7.20s issue due 6/1/2025. This bond, issued on 6/5/1995, has a sinking fund schedule that begins on 6/1/2006. Each year the issuer must retire $7.5 million.

Generally, the issuer may satisfy the sinking fund requirement by either (1) making a cash payment of the par value of the bonds to be retired to the trustee, who then calls the bonds for redemption using a lottery, or (2) delivering to the trustee bonds purchased in the open market that have a total par value equal to the amount that must be retired. If the bonds are retired using the first method, interest payments stop at the redemption date.

Usually, the periodic payments required for sinking fund purposes will be the same for each period. A few indentures might permit variable periodic payments, where payments change according to certain prescribed conditions set forth in the indenture. Many indentures include a provision that grants the issuer the option to retire more than the amount stipulated for sinking fund retirement. This is referred to as an **accelerated sinking fund provision**. For example, the Anheuser Busch 8⅝s due

12/1/2016 whose call schedule was presented earlier, has a sinking fund requirement of $7.5 million per annum beginning on 12/01/1997. The issuer is permitted to retire up to $15 million each year.

Usually the sinking fund call price is the par value if the bonds were originally sold at par. When issued at a price in excess of par, the call price generally starts at the issuance price and scales down to par as the issue approaches maturity.

D. Index Amortizing Notes

There are securities whose principal repayments are made prior to the stated maturity date based on the prevailing value for some reference rate. The principal payments are structured to accelerate when the reference rate is low. These structures are referred to as **indexed amortizing notes**.

SECTION VII CONVERSION PRIVILEGE

A **convertible bond** is an issue that grants the bondholder the right to convert the bond for a specified number of shares of common stock. Such a feature allows the bondholder to take advantage of favorable movements in the price of the issuer's common stock. An **exchangeable bond** allows the bondholder to exchange the issue for a specified number of shares of common stock of a corporation different from the issuer of the bond. These bonds are discussed at Level II where a framework for analyzing them is also provided.

SECTION VIII PUT PROVISION

An issue with a **put provision** included in the indenture grants the bondholder the right to sell the issue back to the issuer at a specified price on designated dates. The specified price is called the **put price**. Typically, a bond is putable at par if it is issued at or close to par value. For a zero-coupon bond, the put price is below par.

The advantage of the put provision to the bondholder is that if after the issuance date market rates rise above the issue's coupon rate, the bondholder can force the issuer to redeem the bond at the put price and then the bondholder can reinvest the proceeds at the prevailing higher rate.

SECTION IX CURRENCY DENOMINATION

The payments that the issuer makes to the bondholder can be in any currency. For bonds issued in the United States, the issuer typically makes both coupon payments and principal repayments in U.S. dollars. However, there is nothing that forces the issuer to make payments in U.S. dollars. The indenture can specify that the issuer may make payments in some other specified currency.

An issue in which payments to bondholders are in U.S. dollars is called a **dollar-denominated issue**. A **nondollar-denominated issue** is one in which payments are not denominated in U.S. dollars. There are some issues whose coupon payments are in one currency and whose principal payment is in another currency. An issue with this characteristic is called a **dual-currency issue**.

SECTION X EMBEDDED OPTIONS

As we have seen, it is common for a bond issue to include a provision in the indenture that gives the issuer and/or the bondholder an option to take some action against the other party. These options are referred to as **embedded options** to distinguish them from bare options (i.e., stand alone options that can be purchased on an exchange or in the over-the-counter market). They are referred to as embedded options because the option is embedded in the issue. In fact, there may be more than one embedded option in an issue.

A. Embedded Options Granted to Issuers

The embedded options that are granted to the issuer that were discussed above include:

- the right to call the issue
- the right of the underlying borrowers in a pool of loans to prepay an amount in excess of the scheduled principal repayment
- the accelerated sinking fund provision
- the cap on a floater

The accelerated sinking fund provision is an embedded option because the issuer can call more than is necessary to meet the sinking fund requirement when interest rates decline below the issue's coupon rate even if there are other restrictions in the issue that prevent the issue from being called.

The cap of a floater can be thought of as an option requiring no action by the issuer to take advantage of a rise in interest rates. Effectively, the bondholder has granted to the issuer the right not to pay more than the cap.

Notice that whether or not the first three options are exercised by the issuer or borrower depends on the level of interest rates prevailing in the market relative to the rate on the issue or the borrowing rate of the underlying loans (in the case of mortgage-backed and asset-backed securities). These options become more valuable when interest rates fall. The cap of a floater also depends on the prevailing level of rates. But here the option becomes more valuable when interest rates rise.

B. Embedded Options Granted to Bondholders

The most common embedded options granted to bondholders are:

- conversion privilege
- the right to put the issue
- floor on a floater

The value of the conversion privilege depends on the movement of the price of the stock that can be acquired if the bondholder exercised the conversion option. The put privilege benefits the bondholder if interest rates in the market rise above the issue's coupon rate. While a cap on a floater benefits the issuer if interest rates rise, a floor benefits the bondholder if interest rates fall.

C. Importance of Understanding Embedded Options

At the outset of this chapter, we stated that fixed income securities have become more complex. The reason for this is that the complexity of embedded options means that it is difficult to project the cash flows of a security. The cash flow for a bond is defined as the interest and the principal.

What this means is that to value a fixed income security with embedded options, it is necessary to:

1. model how the factors that affect whether or not an embedded option will be exercised change over the life of the security, and
2. in the case of options granted to the issuer/borrower, model the behavior of issuers and borrowers to determine the conditions necessary to exercise the embedded option.

For example, consider a callable bond issued by a corporation. Projecting the cash flow requires (1) modeling how interest rates at which the issuer can refund the issue can change over the life of the security and (2) developing a rule for determining the economic conditions necessary for the issuer to benefit from calling the issue. In the case of mortgage-backed or asset-backed securities, again it is necessary to model how interest rates at which the underlying borrowers can refinance the loan can change over the life of the loan. But then a model is necessary to model the default behavior of borrowers and the conditions when borrowers will prepay. Models for valuing bonds with embedded options will be covered at Level II.

It cannot be overemphasized that embedded options not only affect the value of bond but also the performance of a bond. In the next chapter, the risks associated with the presence of an embedded option will be explained. What is critical to understand is that due to the presence of embedded options it is necessary to develop models of interest rate movements and rules for exercising embedded options. This means that any analysis of securities with embedded options exposes an investor to **modeling risk**. This risk will become clearer at Level II when we describe models for valuing bonds with embedded options. We will see all of the assumptions set forth when describing these models. Modeling risk is the risk that the valuation model produces the wrong value because the assumptions are not correct or the assumptions were not realized.

SECTION XI BORROWING FUNDS TO PURCHASE BONDS

At Level II, we will discuss investment strategies in which an investor borrows funds to purchase securities. The expectation of the investor is that the return earned by investing in the securities purchased with the borrowed funds will exceed the borrowing cost. There are several sources of funds available to an investor to borrow funds. When securities are to be purchased with the borrowed funds, the most common practice is to use the securities as collateral for the loan. In such instances, the transaction is referred to as a **collateralized loan**. Two collateralized borrowing arrangements are used by investors — margin buying and repurchase agreements.

A. Margin Buying

In a **margin buying arrangement** the funds borrowed to buy the securities are provided by the broker, and the broker gets the money from a bank. The interest rate that banks charge brokers for these transactions is known as the call money rate (also called the broker loan rate). The broker charges the investor the call money rate plus a service charge. The broker is not free to lend as much as it wishes to the investor to buy securities. The Securities and Exchange Act of 1934 prohibits brokers from lending more than a specified percentage of the market value of the securities. The 1934 act gives the Board of Governors of the Federal Reserve the responsibility to set initial margin requirements, which it does under Regulations T and U. While margin buying is the most common collateralized borrowing arrangement for common stock investors (both retail investors and institutional investors) and retail bond investors (i.e., individual investors), it is not the common borrowing vehicle for institutional bond investors.

B. Repurchase Agreement

The collateralized borrowing arrangement used by institutional investors in the bond market is the repurchase agreement. We will discuss this arrangement in more detail at Level II. However, it is important to understand the basics of the repurchase agreement because it affects how some bonds in the market are valued.

A **repurchase agreement** is the sale of a security with a commitment by the seller to buy the same security back from the purchaser at a specified price at a designated future date. The price at which the seller must subsequently repurchase the security for is called the **repurchase price** and the date that the security must be repurchased is called the **repurchase date**. The implied interest rate is called the **repo rate**. When the term of the loan is one day, it is called an **overnight repo** (or overnight RP); a loan for more than one day is called a **term repo** (or term RP). The transaction is referred to as a repurchase agreement because it calls for the sale of the security and its repurchase at a future date. Both the sale price and the purchase price are specified in the agreement. The difference between the purchase (repurchase) price and the sale price is the dollar interest cost of the loan. The advantage to the investor of using this borrowing arrangement is that the interest rate is less than the cost of bank financing.

For example, suppose that a dealer firm needs to finance $10 million of a Treasury security that it just purchased and plans to hold the security for one day. Suppose also that a customer of the dealer firm, say a municipality, has $10 million in cash from taxes collected that it wants to invest for one day. The dealer firm would agree to deliver ("sell") $10 million of the Treasury security to the municipality for $10 million and simultaneously agree to buy back (i.e., "repurchase") the same Treasury security the next day for $10 million plus interest. The amount of the interest is determined by the repo rate.

There is a good deal of Wall Street jargon describing repo transactions. What is important to remember is that one party is lending money and accepting a security as collateral for the loan; the other party is borrowing money and providing collateral to borrow the money. It is common to use the term **reverse repurchase arrangement** (or reverse repo) when a non-dealer is using a repurchase agreement to borrow funds (i.e., the non-dealer is the seller) and the term repurchase arrangement when a dealer is borrowing funds.

As will be explained at Level II, there is not one repo rate. The rate varies from transaction to transaction depending on a variety of factors. The one important factor that we highlight here is the availability of collateral. The more difficult it is to obtain the collateral, the lower the repo rate. To understand why this is so, remember that the borrower has a security that lenders of cash may want the use of, for whatever reason. (For example, a dealer may be short a security and needs it to cover the position.) Such collateral is referred to as **hot collateral** or **special collateral**. Collateral that does not have this characteristic is referred to as **general collateral**. The party that needs the hot collateral will be willing to lend funds at a lower repo rate in order to obtain the collateral.

We'll see in later chapters the implications of hot collateral on how a bond will trade in the market relative to a bond that is general collateral.

SECTION XII KEY POINTS

❑ *A fixed income security is a financial obligation of an entity (the issuer) who promises to pay a specified sum of money at specified future dates.*

❑ *Fixed income securities fall into two general categories: debt obligations and preferred stock.*

❑ *The promises of the issuer and the rights of the bondholders are set forth in the indenture.*

❑ *The par value (principal, face value, redemption value, or maturity value) is the amount that the issuer agrees to repay the bondholder by the maturity date.*

❑ *Bond prices are quoted as a percentage of par value, with par value equal to 100.*

❑ *The interest rate that the issuer agrees to pay each year is called the coupon rate; the coupon is the annual amount of the interest payment and is found by multiplying the par value by the coupon rate.*

❑ *Zero-coupon bonds do not make periodic coupon payments; the bondholder realizes interest at the maturity date equal to the difference between the maturity value and the price paid for the bond.*

❑ *A floating-rate security is an issue whose coupon rate resets periodically based on some formula; the typical coupon formula is some reference rate plus a quoted margin.*

❑ *A floating-rate security may have a cap which sets the maximum coupon rate that will be paid, or a floor that sets the minimum coupon rate that will be paid.*

❑ *A cap is a disadvantage to the bondholder while a floor is an advantage to the bondholder.*

❑ *The various types of coupon formulas include inverse floaters, range notes, ratchet bonds, and dual indexed.*

❑ *A step-up note is a security whose coupon rate increases over time.*

❑ *Accrued interest is the amount of interest accrued since the last coupon payment and in the United States (as well as in many countries), the bond buyer must pay the bond seller the accrued interest.*

❑ *The full price (or dirty price) of a security is the agreed upon price plus accrued interest; the price (or clean price) is the agreed upon price without accrued interest.*

❑ *An amortizing security is a security for which there is a schedule for the repayment of principal.*

❑ *Many issues have a call provision granting the issuer an option to retire all or part of the issue prior to the stated maturity date.*

❑ *A call provision is an advantage to the issuer and a disadvantage to the bondholder.*

❑ *The call schedule specifies when the issuer can call the issue and the call price at each call date.*

❑ *When a callable bond is issued, typically the issuer may not call the bond for a number of years; that is, there is a deferred call.*

❑ *The call prices in the call schedule are the regular or general redemption prices; there are special redemption prices for debt redeemed through the sinking fund and through other provisions.*

❑ *A currently callable bond is an issue that does not have any protection against early call.*

❑ *Most new bond issues, even if currently callable, usually have some restrictions against refunding.*

❑ *Call protection is much more absolute than refunding protection.*

❑ *For an amortizing security backed by a pool of loans, the underlying borrowers typically have the right to prepay the outstanding principal balance in whole or in part prior to the scheduled principal repayment date; this provision is called a prepayment option.*

❑ *A sinking fund provision requires that the issuer retire a specified portion of an issue each year.*

❑ *An accelerated sinking fund provision allows the issuer to retire more than the amount stipulated to satisfy the periodic sinking fund requirement.*

- *A putable bond is one in which the bondholder has the right to sell the issue back to the issuer at a specified price on designated dates.*

- *A convertible bond is an issue giving the bondholder the right to exchange the bond for a specified number of shares of common stock at a specified price.*

- *The presence of embedded options makes the valuation of fixed income securities complex and requires the modeling of interest rates and issuer/borrower behavior in order to project cash flows.*

- *An investor can borrow funds to purchase a security by using the security itself as collateral.*

- *There are two types of collateralized borrowing arrangements for purchasing securities – margin buying and repurchase agreements.*

- *Typically, institutional investors in the bond market do not finance the purchase of a security by buying on margin; rather, repurchase agreements are used.*

- *A repurchase agreement is the sale of a security with a commitment by the seller to buy the security back from the purchaser at the repurchase price at the repurchase date.*

- *When a non-dealer uses the repo market to borrow funds, it is called a reverse repurchase transaction; when a dealer uses the repo market to borrow funds it is called a repurchase transaction.*

- *The borrowing rate for a repurchase agreement is called the repo rate and while this rate is less than the cost of bank borrowing, it varies from transaction to transaction based on several factors.*

- *Hot collateral or special collateral is collateral that is highly sought after by dealers and can be financed at a lower repo rate than general collateral.*

END OF CHAPTER QUESTIONS

1. Consider the following two bond issues.

   Bond A: 5% 15-year bond
   Bond B: 5% 30-year bond

   Neither bond has an embedded option. Both bonds are trading in the market at the same yield.

   Which bond will fluctuate *more* in price when interest rates change?

2. Given the information in the first and third columns, complete the information in the second and fourth columns:

Quoted price	Price per $1 of par value	Par value	Dollar price
96¼		$1,000	
102⅞		$5,000	
109⁹⁄₁₆		$10,000	
68¹¹⁄₃₂		$100,000	

3. A floating-rate issue has the following coupon formula:

   1-year Treasury rate + 30 basis points with a cap of 7% and a floor of 4.5%

   The coupon rate is reset every year. Suppose that at the reset date the 1-year Treasury rate is as shown below. Compute the coupon rate for the next year:

	1-year Treasury rate	Coupon rate
First reset date	6.1%	?
Second reset date	6.5%	?
Third reset date	6.9%	?
Fourth reset date	6.8%	?
Fifth reset date	5.7%	?
Sixth reset date	5.0%	?
Seventh reset date	4.1%	?
Eighth reset date	3.9%	?
Ninth reset date	3.2%	?
Tenth reset date	4.4%	?

4. What is an accrual bond?

5. A ratchet bond is a bond whose coupon rate can be adjusted down periodically if interest rates decline but cannot then be increased if interest rates subsequently rise. Why is this bond effectively a bond that has multiple call options embedded?

6. An assistant portfolio manager reviewed the prospectus of a bond that will be issued next week on January 1 of 2000. The call schedule for this $200 million, 7.75% coupon 20-year issue specifies the following:

   The Bonds will be redeemable at the option of the Company at any time in whole or in part, upon not fewer than 30 nor more than 60 days' notice, at the following redemption prices (which are expressed in percentages of principal amount) in each case together with accrued interest to the date fixed for redemption:

If redeemed during the 12 months beginning January 1,

2000 through 2005	104.00%
2006 through 2010	103.00%
2011 through 2012	101.00%
from 2013 on	100.00%

provided, however, that prior to January 1, 2006, the Company may not redeem any of the Bonds pursuant to such option, directly or indirectly, from or in anticipation of the proceeds of the issuance of any indebtedness for money borrowed having an interest cost of less than 7.75% per annum.

The prospectus further specifies that

The Company will provide for the retirement by redemption of $10 million of the principal amount of the Bonds each of the years 2010 to and including 2019 at the principal amount thereof, together with accrued interest to the date of redemption. The Company may also provide for the redemption of up to an additional $10 million principal amount... annually,... such optional right being non-cumulative.

The assistant portfolio manager made the following statements to a client after reviewing this bond issue. Comment on each statement.

a. "My major concern is that if rates decline significantly in the next few years, this issue will be called by the Company in order to replace it with a bond issue with a coupon rate less than 7.75%."

b. "One major advantage of this issue is that if the Company redeems it *for any reason* in the first five years, investors are guaranteed receiving a price of 104, a premium over the purchase price at offering which is 100."

c. "A beneficial feature of this issue is that it has a sinking fund provision that reduces the risk that the Company won't have enough funds to pay off the issue at the maturity date."

d. "A further attractive feature of this issue is that the Company can accelerate the payoff of the issue via the sinking fund provision, reducing the risk that funds will not be available at the maturity date."

e. In response to a client question about what will be the interest and principal that the client can depend on if $5 million par value of the issue is purchased, the assistant portfolio manager responded: "I can construct a schedule that shows every six months for the next 20 years the dollar amount of the interest and the principal repayment. It is quite simple to compute — basically it is just multiplying two numbers."

7. What is meant by an embedded option?

8. a. What is an accelerated sinking fund provision?
   b. Why can an accelerated sinking fund provision be viewed as an embedded option granted to an issuer?

9. There are some securities that are backed by a pool of loans. These loans have a schedule of interest and principal payments every month and give each borrower whose loan is included in the pool the right to payoff their respective loan at any time at par value. Suppose that a portfolio manager purchased one of these securities. Can the portfolio manager rely on the schedule of interest and principal payments in determining the cash that will be generated by such securities (assuming no borrowers default)? Why or why not?

10. The importance of knowing the terms of bond issues, especially those relating to redemption, cannot be overstressed. Yet there have appeared numerous instances of investors, professional and others, who acknowledge that they don't read the documentation. For example, in an Augusts 14, 1983 article published in *The New York Times* titled "The Lessons of a Bond Failure," the following statements were attributed to some stockbrokers: "But brokers in the field say they often don't spend much time reading these [official] statements," "I can be honest and say I never look at the prospectus.... Generally, you don't have time to do that," and "There are some clients who really don't know what they buy.... They just say, 'That's a good interest rate.'"

    Why it is important to understand the redemption features of a bond issue?

11. Here is an excerpt from Cincinnati Gas & Electric Company's prospectus for the 10⅛% First Mortgage Bonds due in 2020 states,

    > The Offered Bonds are redeemable (though CG&E does not contemplate doing so) prior to May 1, 1995 through the use of earnings, proceeds from the sale of equity securities and cash accumulations other than those resulting from a refunding operation such as hereinafter described. The Offered Bonds are not redeemable prior to May 1, 1995 as a part of, or in anticipation of, any refunding operation involving the incurring of indebtedness by CG&E having an effective interest cost (calculated to the second place in accordance with generally accepted financial practice) of less than the effective interest cost of the Offered Bonds (similarly calculated) or through the operation of the Maintenance and Replacement Fund.

    What does this excerpt tell the investor about provisions of this issuer to pay off this issue prior to the stated maturity date?

12. a. What is the typical arrangement used by institutional investors in the bond market: bank financing, margin buying, or repurchase agreement?
    b. What is the difference between a term repo and an overnight repo?
    c. Give one reason why the repo rate for a given maturity can vary from transaction to transaction.
    d. How is the term "reverse repo transaction" commonly used in the bond market?

SOLUTIONS TO END OF CHAPTER QUESTIONS

1. All other factors constant, the longer the maturity, the greater the price change when interest rates change. So, Bond B is the answer.

2.

Quoted price	Price per $ par value	Par value	Dollar price
96¼	0.9625	$1,000	962.50
102⅞	1.0288	$5,000	5,143.75
109⁹⁄₁₆	1.0956	$10,000	10,956.25
68¹¹⁄₃₂	0.6834	$100,000	68,343.75

3.

	1-year Treasury rate	Coupon rate
First reset date	6.1%	6.4%
Second reset date	6.5%	6.8%
Third reset date	6.9%	7.0%
Fourth reset date	6.8%	7.0%
Fifth reset date	5.7%	6.0%
Sixth reset date	5.0%	5.3%
Seventh reset date	4.1%	4.5%
Eighth reset date	3.9%	4.5%
Ninth reset date	3.2%	4.5%
Tenth reset date	4.4%	4.7%

4. An accrual bond is a form of zero-coupon bond. The issuer agrees to make the interest payment at the maturity date. The interest payment will include all of the coupon payments plus interest earned on the coupon payments themselves.

5. One of the reasons for the introduction of ratchet bonds by issuers was to save the issuer from the costs of calling the issue and replacing it with another issue at a lower interest rate. Since the coupon rate can never increase, a ratchet bond is effectively a bond where the issuer is permitted to call the bond at no premium and reissued at the new, lower rate each time that the rate has declined at a coupon reset date.

6. a. While it may be true that the Company can call the issue if rates decline, there is a nonrefunding restriction prior to January 1, 2006. The Company may not refund the issue with a source of funds that costs less than 7.75% until after that date.

b. This is only true if the issuer redeems the issue as permitted by the call schedule. In that case the premium is paid. However, there is a sinking fund provision. If the issuer calls in the particular certificates of the issue held by the investor in order to satisfy the sinking fund provision, the issue is called at par value. So, there is no guarantee that the issue will be paid off at a premium at any time if the issue is called to satisfy the sinking fund provision.

c. It is commonly thought that the presence of a sinking fund provision reduces the risk that the issuer will not have sufficient funds to pay off the amount due at the maturity date. But this must be balanced against the fact that a bondholder might have his or her bonds taken away at par value when the issuer calls a part of the issue to satisfy the sinking fund provision. If the issue is trading above par value, the bondholder only receives par value. So, for example, if the issue is trading at 115 and it is called by the Company to satisfy the sinking fund provision, the investor receives par value (100), realizing a loss of 15.

d. As in part c, while it may seem that the right of the issuer to make additional payments beyond the required amount necessary to satisfy the sinking fund provision will reduce the likelihood that the issuer will have sufficient funds to pay off the issue at the maturity date, there is still the potential loss if the issue is called at par. Moreover, the issuer is likely to make additional payments permitted to retire the issue via the sinking fund special call price of 100 when the bond is trading at a premium, because that is when the bond the interest rate in the market is less than the coupon rate on the issue.

e. There is no way that this assistant portfolio managers knows for certain how long the bond issue will be outstanding because it can be called as per the call schedule. Moreover, because of the sinking fund provision, the particular bonds held might be called. (One of the major topics in this book is that because of the uncertainty about the cash flow of a bond due to the right to call an issue, sophisticated analytical techniques and valuation models are needed.)

7. An investor can purchase a stand alone option on an exchange or in the over-the-counter market. When an investor purchases a bond, there are choices or "options" provided for in the indenture that grants either the bondholder or the issuer to do something. These choices are what are commonly referred to as embedded options.

8. a. An accelerated sinking fund provision grants the issuer the right to redeem more than the minimum amount necessary to satisfy the sinking fund requirement.
   b. An accelerated sinking fund provision is an embedded option granted to an issuer because it allows an issuer to retire the issue at par value when interest rates have declined. The issuer can do this even if the issue is nonrefundable at the time or is noncallable.

9. Even if the borrowers whose loans are included in the pool backing the security do not default, they can take advantage to refinance their loan if interest rates in the market decline below the rate on the loans. Consequently, there is no way that the security holder can rely on the schedule of principal and interest payments of the pool of loans.

10. When an investor is contemplating the purchase of a bond, one of the concerns is how long the issue will be outstanding so that the coupon rate on the bond will be received. Moreover, when an investor is contemplating the purchase a bond in the secondary market that is trading above its par value, the concern is that the issue may be paid off prior to the maturity date. The result may be the loss of the premium. So, for example, if an investor believes that a bond is noncallable but the issue has a sinking fund requirement, it is possible that the issue held by an investor can be called at the special redemption price of 100 when the issue is trading at a premium.

11. For this bond the excerpt tells us that the issue may be redeemed prior to May 1, 1995 but they may not be refunded — that is, they cannot be called using a lower

cost of funds than the issue itself. As of this writing, the issue may be redeemed via a refunding. That is, the issue can be called using any source of funds such as a new bond issue with a lower coupon rate than the issue itself.

12. a. Institutional investors typically use a repurchase agreement to finance the purchase of a bond.
   b. A term repo is a repurchase agreement where the borrowing is for more than one day; an overnight repo involves borrowing for only one day.
   c. While there are several reasons (and they are covered at Level II), the reason discussed in the chapter is the availability of the collateral. Hot or special collateral commands a lower repo rate than general collateral.
   d. The term "reverse repo transaction" is commonly used to describe the financing of the purchase of a bond by a non-dealer via a repurchase agreement.

SOLUTIONS TO PRACTICE QUESTIONS

1.

Quoted price	Price per $ par value	Par value	Dollar price
103¼	1.0325	$1,000	1,032.50
70⅛	0.7013	$5,000	3,506.25
87⁵⁄₁₆	0.8731	$10,000	8,731.25
117³⁄₃₂	1.1709	$100,000	117,093.75

2.

	6-month Treasury rate	Coupon rate
First reset date	5.5%	6.0%
Second reset date	5.8%	6.3%
Third reset date	6.3%	6.8%
Fourth reset date	6.8%	7.0%
Fifth reset date	7.3%	7.0%
Sixth reset date	6.1%	6.6%

3. a. Inverse floater
   b. Step-up note (or multiple step-up note)
   c. Dual indexed floater
   d. Range note
   e. Inflation-linked bond

Chapter 2

RISKS ASSOCIATED WITH INVESTING IN BONDS

LEARNING OUTCOME STATEMENTS

After reading this chapter you should be able to:

- explain the various risks associated with investing in bonds (interest rate risk, call and prepayment risk, yield curve risk, reinvestment risk, credit risk, liquidity risk, exchange-rate risk, volatility risk, inflation risk, and event risk).
- explain why there is an inverse relationship between changes in interest rates and bond prices.
- identify the relationship between the coupon rate, yield required by the market, and a bond's price relative to par value (i.e., discount, premium, or par value).
- explain how features of a bond (maturity, coupon, and embedded options) affect its interest rate risk.
- identify the relationship between the price of a callable bond, the price of an option-free bond, and the price of the embedded call option.
- explain how the yield level impacts the interest rate risk of a bond.
- explain the interest rate risk of a floating-rate security and why its price may differ from par value.
- interpret the meaning of the duration of a bond.
- compute the duration of a bond given how its price will change when interest rates are changed.
- use duration to approximate the percentage price change of a bond and compute the new price if interest rates change.
- explain yield curve risk and explain why duration does not account for yield curve risk for a portfolio of bonds.
- explain one measure of yield curve risk called key rate duration.
- identify the factors that affect the reinvestment risk of a security.
- explain the disadvantages of a callable and prepayable security to an investor.
- explain why prepayable amortizing securities expose investors to greater reinvestment risk than nonamortizing securities.
- describe the three types of credit risk: default risk, credit spread risk, and downgrade risk.
- explain what a rating agency does and what is meant by a rating upgrade and a rating downgrade.
- distinguish between investment grade bonds and noninvestment grade bonds.
- explain why liquidity risk is important to investors even if they expect to hold a security to the maturity date.
- compute the market bid-ask spread for a security from the bid-ask spreads provided by dealers.
- describe the exchange rate risk an investor faces when a bond makes payments in a foreign currency.
- explain why inflation risk exists.
- explain why yield volatility affects the price of a bond with an embedded option and how changes in volatility affect the value of a callable bond and a putable bond.
- describe the various forms of event risk (including regulatory risk and political risk).

SECTION I INTRODUCTION

Armed with an understanding of the basic features of bonds, we now turn to the risks associated with investing in bonds. These risks include:

- interest rate risk
- call and prepayment risk
- yield curve risk
- reinvestment risk
- credit risk
- liquidity risk
- exchange-rate risk
- volatility risk
- inflation or purchasing power risk
- event risk

We will see how features of a bond that we described in Chapter 1 — coupon rate, maturity, embedded options, and currency denomination — affect several of these risks.

SECTION II INTEREST RATE RISK

As will be demonstrated in Chapter 5, the price of a typical bond will change in the opposite direction from the change in interest rates or yields.[1] That is, when interest rates rise, a bond's price will fall; when interest rates fall, a bond's price will rise. For example, consider a 6% 20-year bond. If the yield investors require to buy this bond is 6%, the price of this bond would be $100. However, if the required yield increased to 6.5%, the price of this bond would decline to $94.4479. Thus, for a 50 basis point increase in yield, the bond's price declines by 5.55%. If, instead, the yield declines from 6% to 5.5%, the bond's price will rise by 6.02% to $106.0195.

Since the price of a bond fluctuates with market interest rates, the risk that an investor faces is that the price of a bond held in a portfolio will decline if market interest rates rise. This risk is referred to as **interest rate risk** and is the major risk faced by investors in the bond market.

A. Reason for the Inverse Relationship between Changes in Interest Rates and Price

The reason for the inverse relationship between price change and the change in interest rates (or change in market yields) is as follows. Suppose investor X purchases our hypothetical 6% coupon 20-year bond at par value (100). As explained in Chapter 6, the yield for this bond is 6%. Suppose that immediately after the purchase of this bond two things happen. First, market interest rates rise to 6.50% so that if any investor wants to buy a similar 20-year bond, a 6.50% coupon rate would have to be paid by the bond issuer in order to offer a bond at par value. Second, suppose investor X wants to sell the bond. In attempting to sell the bond, investor X would not find an investor who would be willing to pay par value for a bond with a coupon rate of 6%. The reason is that any investor who wanted to purchase this bond could obtain a similar 20-year bond with a coupon rate 50 basis points higher, 6.5%.

What can the investor do? The investor cannot force the issuer to change the coupon rate to 6.5%. Nor can the investor force the issuer to shorten the maturity of the bond to a point where a new investor might be willing to accept a 6% coupon rate. The only thing that the investor can do is adjust the price of the bond so that at the new

---

[1] At this stage, we will use the terms interest rate and yield interchangeably. We'll see in Chapter 6 how to compute a bond's yield.

price a buyer would realize a yield of 6.5%. This means that the price would have to be adjusted down to a price below par value. It turns out, the new price must be 94.4479.[2] While we assumed in our illustration an initial price of par value, the principle holds for any purchase price. Regardless of the price that an investor pays for a bond, an instantaneous increase in market interest rates will result in a decline in a bond's price.

Suppose instead of a rise in market interest rates to 6.5%, interest rates decline to 5.5%. Investors would be more than happy to purchase the 6% coupon 20-year bond for par value. However, investor X realizes that the market is only offering investors the opportunity to buy a similar bond at par value with a coupon rate of 5.5%. Consequently, investor X will increase the price of the bond until it offers a yield of 5.5%. That price turns out to be 106.0195.

Let's summarize the important relationships suggested by our example.

1. A bond will trade at par value when the coupon rate is equal to the yield required by market. That is,

   coupon rate = yield required by market → price = par value

2. A bond will trade below par (sell at a discount) or above par (sell at a premium) if the coupon rate is different from the yield required by the market. Specifically,

   coupon rate < yield required by market → price < par value (discount)

   coupon rate > yield required by market → price >par value (premium)

3. The price of a bond changes in the opposite direction to the change in interest rates. So, for an instantaneous change in interest rates the following relationship holds:

   if interest rates increase → price of a bond decreases
   if interest rates decrease → price of a bond increases

PRACTICE QUESTION 1

The following information is reported in the business section of a newspaper:

Issue	Coupon	Maturity	Yield required by market	Price
A	7⅜%	16 years	6.00%	114.02
B	6¾%	4 years	7.00%	99.14
C	0%	10 years	5.00%	102.10
D	5½%	20 years	5.90%	104.15
E	8½%	18 years	8.50%	100.00
F	4½%	6 years	4.00%	96.50
G	6¼%	25 years	6.25%	103.45

For which of the issues is there an error in the reported price? (No calculations are required.)

---

[2] We'll see how to compute the price of a bond in Chapter 5.

B. Bond Features that Affect Interest Rate Risk

The degree of sensitivity of a bond's price to changes in market interest rates (i.e., a bond's interest rate risk) depends on various features of the issue, such as maturity, coupon rate, and embedded options. While we discuss this in more detail in Chapter 7, we provide a brief discussion below.

1. The Impact of Maturity

All other factors constant, *the longer the bond's maturity, the greater the bond's price sensitivity to changes in interest rates*. For example, we know that for a 6% 20-year bond selling to yield 6%, a rise in the yield required by investors to 6.5% will cause the bond's price to decline from 100 to 94.4479, a 5.55% price decline. For a 6% 5-year bond selling to yield 6%, the price is 100. A rise in the yield required by investors from 6% to 6.5% would decrease the price to 97.8944. The decline in the bond's price is only 2.11%.

2. The Impact of Coupon Rate

A property of a bond is that all other factors constant, *the lower the coupon rate, the greater the bond's price sensitivity to changes in interest rates*. For example, consider a 9% 20-year bond selling to yield 6%. The price of this bond would be 134.6722. If the yield required by investors increases by 50 basis points to 6.5%, the price of this bond would fall by 5.13% to 127.7605. This decline is less than the 5.55% decline for the 6% 20-year bond selling to yield 6%.

An implication is that zero-coupon bonds have greater price sensitivity to interest rate changes than same-maturity bonds bearing a coupon rate and trading at the same yield.

3. The Impact of Embedded Options

In Chapter 1 we discussed the various embedded options that may be included in a bond issue. As we continue our study of fixed income analysis, we will see that the value of a bond with embedded options will change depending on how the value of the embedded options change when interest rates change. For example, we will see that as interest rates decline, the price of a callable bond may not increase as much as an otherwise option-free bond (that is, a bond with no embedded options).

For now, to understand why let's decompose the price of a callable bond into two parts, as shown below:

price of callable bond = price of option-free bond − price of embedded call option

The reason for subtracting the price of the embedded call option from the price of the option-free bond is that the call option is a benefit to the issuer and a disadvantage to the bondholder. This reduces the price of a callable bond relative to an option-free bond.

Now, when interest rates decline, the price of an option-free bond increases. However, the price of the embedded call option increases when interest rates decline because the call option becomes more valuable to the issuer. So, when interest rates decline both components increase, *but* the change in the price of the callable bond depends on the relative price change of the two components. Typically, a decline in interest rates will result in an increase in the price of the callable bond but not by as much as the price change of an otherwise comparable option-free bond.

Similarly, when interest rates rise, the price of a callable bond will not fall by as much as an otherwise option-free bond. The reason is that the price of the embedded call option declines. So, when interest rates rise, the price of the option-free bond declines but this is partially offset by the decrease in the price of the embedded call option.

PRACTICE QUESTION 2

All of the issues below are option-free bonds and the yield required by the market for each bond is the same. Which issue has the greatest interest rate risk and which has the least interest rate risk?

Issue	Coupon rate	Maturity
1	5¼%	15 years
2	6½%	12 years
3	4¾%	20 years
4	8½%	10 years

(No calculations are required.)

C. The Impact of the Yield Level

Because of credit risk (discussed later), different bonds trade at different yields, even if they have the same coupon rate, maturity, and embedded options. How, then, holding other factors constant, does the level of interest rates affect a bond's price sensitivity to changes in interest rates? As it turns out, the higher the level of interest rates that a bond trades, the lower the price sensitivity.

To see this, we can compare a 6% 20-year bond initially selling at a yield of 6%, and a 6% 20-year bond initially selling at a yield of 10%. The former is initially at a price of 100, and the latter 65.68. Now, if the yield on both bonds increases by 100 basis points, the first bond trades down by 10.68 points (10.68%) to a price of 89.32. After the assumed increase in yield, the second bond will trade at a price of 59.88, for a price decline of only 5.80 points (or 8.83%). Thus, we see that the bond that trades at a lower yield is more volatile in both percentage price change and absolute price change, as long as the other bond characteristics are the same. An implication of this is that, for a given change in interest rates, price sensitivity is lower when the level of interest rates in the market is high, and price sensitivity is higher when the level of interest rates is low.

PRACTICE QUESTION 3

For the following four issues that are all option-free bonds, which has the greatest interest rate risk?

Issue	Coupon rate	Maturity	Required yield by the market
4	6½%	12 years	7.00%
5	7¼%	12 years	7.40%
6	6½%	12 years	7.20%
7	7½%	11 years	8.00%

(No calculations are required.)

D. Interest Rate Risk for Floating-Rate Securities

The change in the price of a fixed-rate coupon bond when market interest rates change is due to the fact that the bond's coupon rate differs from the prevailing market interest rate. For a floating-rate security, the coupon rate is reset periodically based on the prevailing value for the reference rate plus the quoted margin. The quoted margin is set for the life of the security. The price of a floating-rate security will fluctuate depending on three factors.

First, the longer the time to the next coupon reset date, the greater the potential price fluctuation.[3] For example, consider a floating-rate security whose coupon resets every six months and the coupon formula is the 6-month Treasury rate plus 20 basis points. Suppose that on the coupon reset date the 6-month Treasury rate is 5.8%. If on the day after the coupon is reset, the 6-month Treasury rate rises to 6.1%, this means that this security is offering a 6-month coupon rate that is less than the prevailing 6-month rate for the remaining six months. The price of the security must decline to reflect this. Suppose instead that the coupon resets every month at the 1-month Treasury rate and that this rate rises immediately after the coupon rate is reset. In this case, while the investor would be realizing a sub-market 1-month coupon rate, it is for only a month. The price decline will be less than for the security that resets every six months.

The second reason why a floating-rate security's price will fluctuate is that the required margin that investors demand in the market changes. For example, consider once again the security whose coupon formula is the 6-month Treasury rate plus 20 basis points. If market conditions change such that investors want a margin of 30 basis points rather than 20 basis points, this security would be offering a coupon rate that is 10 basis points below the market rate. As a result, the security's price will decline.

Finally, a floating-rate security will typically have a cap. Once the coupon rate as specified by the coupon formula rises above the cap rate, the coupon will be set at the cap rate and the security will then offer a below market coupon rate and its price will decline. In fact, once the cap is reached, the security's price will react much the same way to changes in market interest rates as that of a fixed-rate coupon security. This risk for a floating-rate security is called **cap risk**.

PRACTICE QUESTION 4

A floating-rate issue of NotReal.com has the following coupon formula that is reset every six months:

coupon rate = 6-month Treasury rate + 120 basis points with a cap of 8.5%

a. Assume that subsequent to the issuance of this floater, the market wants a higher margin than 120 basis points for purchasing a similar issue to NotReal.com. What will happen to the price of this issue?

b. Assume that the 6-month Treasury rate was 4% when this issue was purchased by an investor but today the 6-month Treasury rate is 7%. What risk has increased since the time the NotReal.com issue was purchased?

E. Measuring Interest Rate Risk

Investors are interested in estimating the price sensitivity of a bond to changes in market interest rates. We will spend a good deal of time looking at how to quantify a bond's interest rate risk in Chapter 7, as well as other chapters. For now, let's see how we can get a rough idea of how to quantify the interest rate risk of a bond.

What we are interested in is a first approximation of how a bond's price will change when interest rates change. We can look at the price change in terms of (1) the

---

[3] As explained in Chapter 1, the coupon reset formula is set at the reset date at the beginning of the period but is not paid until the end of the period.

percentage price change from the initial price or (2) the dollar price change from the initial price.

1. Approximate Percentage Price Change

The most straightforward way to calculate the percentage price change is to average the percentage price change resulting from an increase and a decrease in interest rates of the same number of basis points. For example, suppose that we are trying to estimate the sensitivity of the price of bond ABC that is currently selling for 90 to yield 6%. Now, suppose that interest rates increase by 25 basis points from 6% to 6.25%. The change in yield of 25 basis points is referred to as the "rate shock." How to determine how much the rate shock should be is discussed in Chapter 7. For now, let's simply use 25 basis points. The question is, how much will the price of bond ABC change? To determine what the new price will be if the yield increases to 6.25%, *it is necessary to have a valuation model*. A valuation model provides an estimate of what the value of a bond will be for a given yield level. We will discuss the various models for valuing simple bonds and complex bonds with embedded options in later chapters.

For now, we will assume that the valuation model tells us that the price of bond ABC will be 88 if yields increase from 6% to 6.25%. This means that the price will decline by 2 points or 2.22% of the initial price of 90. If we divide the 2.22% by 25 basis points, the resulting number tells us that the price will decline by 0.0889% per 1 basis point change in yield.

Now suppose that the valuation model tells us that if yields decline from 6% to 5.75%, the price will increase to 92.7. This means that the price increases by 2.7 points or 3.00% of the initial price of 90. Dividing the 3.00% by 25 basis points indicates that the price will change by 0.12% per 1 basis point change in yield.

We can average the two percentage price changes for a 1 basis point change in yield up and down. The average percentage price change is 0.1044% [=(0.0889% + 0.12%)/2]. This means that for a 100 basis point change in yield, the average percentage price change is 10.44% (100 times 0.1044%).

A formula for estimating the *approximate percentage price change for a 100 basis point change in yield is:*

$$\frac{\text{price if yields decline} - \text{price if yields rise}}{2 \times (\text{initial price}) \times (\text{change in yield in decimal})}$$

In our illustration,

price if yields decline by 25 basis points = 92.7
price if yields rise by 25 basis points = 88.0
initial price = 90
change in yield in decimal = 0.0025

Substituting these values into the formula we obtain the approximate percentage price change for a 100 basis point change in yield to be:

$$\frac{92.7 - 88.0}{2 \times (90) \times (0.0025)} = 10.44$$

There is a special name given to this estimate of the percentage price change for a 100 basis point change in yield. It is called **duration**. As can be seen, duration is a measure of the price sensitivity of a bond to a change in yield. So, for example, if the duration of a bond is 10.44, this means that the approximate percentage price change if yields change by 100 basis points is 10.44%. For a 50 basis point change in yields, the approximate percentage price change is 5.22% (10.44% divided by 2). For a 25 basis point change in yield, the approximate percentage price change is 2.61% (10.44% divided by 4).

Notice that the approximate percentage is assumed to be the same for a rise and decline in yield. When we discuss the properties of the price volatility of a bond to changes in yield in Chapter 7, we will see that the percentage price change is not symmetric and we will discuss the implication for using duration as a measure of interest rate risk.

We will discuss the concept of duration in more detail in later chapters. Specifically, we will see the limitations of this measure of price sensitivity. *What is critical to understand here is that the computed duration of a bond is only as good as the valuation model used to get the prices when the yield is shocked up and down. If the valuation model is unreliable, then the duration is a poor measure of the bond's price sensitivity to changes in yield.*

2. Approximating the Dollar Price Change

It is simple to move from duration which measures the approximate percentage price change to the approximate dollar price change of a position in a bond given the market value of the position and its duration. For example, consider again bond ABC with a duration of 10.44. Suppose that the market value of this bond that a manager owns is $5 million. Then for a 100 basis point change in yield, the approximate dollar price change is equal to 10.44% times $5 million, or $522,000. For a 50 basis point change in yield, the approximate dollar price change is $261,000; for a 25 basis point change in yield the approximate dollar price change is $130,500.

The approximate dollar price change for a 100 basis point change in yield is sometimes referred to as the **dollar duration**.

PRACTICE QUESTION 5

a. A portfolio manager wants to estimate the interest rate risk of a bond using duration. The current price of the bond is 106. A valuation model employed by the manager found that if interest rates decline by 25 basis points, the price will increase to 108.5 and if interest rates increase by the same number of basis points, the price will decline to 104. What is the duration of this bond?

b. If the portfolio manager purchased $10 million in market value of this bond, using duration to estimate the percentage price change how much will the value of the bond purchased change if interest rates change by 50 basis points?

SECTION III YIELD CURVE RISK

We know that if interest rates or yields in the market change, the price of an individual bond will change. One of the factors that will affect how sensitive an individual bond's price is to changes in yield is the bond's maturity. A portfolio of bonds is a collection of bond issues typically with different maturities. So, when interest rates change, the price of each bond issue in the portfolio will change and the portfolio's value will change.

As you will see in Chapter 4, there is not one interest rate or yield in the economy. There is a structure of interest rates. One important structure is the relationship between yield and maturity. The graphical depiction of this relationship is called the **yield curve**. As we will see in Chapter 4, when interest rates change, they typically do not change by an equal number of basis points for all maturities.

Exhibit 1: Illustration of Yield Curve Risk
a. Composition of the Portfolio

Bond	Coupon (%)	Maturity (years)	Yield (%)	Par value ($)
A	5.00	2	5.00	5,000,000
B	5.25	5	5.25	10,000,000
C	5.50	20	5.50	20,000,000
D	5.75	30	5.75	30,000,000
Total				65,000,000

b. Parallel Shift in Yield Curve of +25 Basis Points

Bond	Coupon (%)	Maturity (years)	Original Yield (%)	Par value ($)	New yield (%)	New bond price	Value
A	5.00	2	5.00	5,000,000	5.25	99.5312	4,976,558
B	5.25	5	5.25	10,000,000	5.50	98.9200	9,891,999
C	5.50	20	5.50	20,000,000	5.75	97.0514	19,410,274
D	5.75	30	5.75	30,000,000	6.00	96.5406	28,962,166
Total				65,000,000			63,240,997

c. Nonparallel Shift of the Yield Curve

Bond	Coupon (%)	Maturity (years)	Original Yield (%)	Par value ($)	New yield (%)	New bond price	Value
A	5.00	2	5.00	5,000,000	5.10	99.8121	4,990,606
B	5.25	5	5.25	10,000,000	5.45	99.1349	9,913,488
C	5.50	20	5.50	20,000,000	5.75	97.0514	19,410,274
D	5.75	30	5.75	30,000,000	6.20	93.9042	28,171,257
Total				65,000,000			62,485,625

d. Nonparallel Shift of the Yield Curve

Bond	Coupon (%)	Maturity (years)	Original Yield (%)	Par value ($)	New yield (%)	New bond price	Value
A	5.00	2	5.00	5,000,000	5.05	99.9060	4,995,300
B	5.25	5	5.25	10,000,000	5.40	99.3503	9,935,033
C	5.50	20	5.50	20,000,000	5.75	97.0514	19,410,274
D	5.75	30	5.75	30,000,000	6.10	95.2082	28,562,467
Total				65,000,000			62,903,074

For example, suppose that a $65 million portfolio contains the four bonds shown in Exhibit 1. All bonds are trading at par value.

If we want to know how much the value of the portfolio changes if interest rates change, typically it is assumed that all yields change by the same number of basis points. Thus, if we wanted to know how sensitive the portfolio's value is to a change in yields of 25 basis points, we would increase the yield for the four bond issues by 25 basis points in the portfolio and determine what the new price of each bond will be, what the market value of each bond will be, and what the new value will be for the portfolio. For our hypothetical portfolio, the value of each bond issue will change as shown in panel b of Exhibit 1. The portfolio's value has decreased by $1,759,003 from $65 million to $63,240,997.

Suppose that instead of an equal basis point change in the yield for all maturities that the 20-year yield changes by 25 basis points, but the yield for the other maturities changes as follows: (1) 2-year maturity changes by 10 basis points (from 5% to 5.1%), (2) 5-year maturity changes by 20 basis points (from 5.25% to 5.45%), and (3) 30-year maturity changes by 45 basis points (from 5.75% to 6.2%). We will see later in this book that this type of movement (or shift) in the yield curve is referred to as a "steepening of the yield curve." For this type of yield curve shift, the portfolio's value based on these new yield levels is shown in panel c of Exhibit 1. The decline in the portfolio's value is then $2,514,375 (from $65 million to $62,485,625).

Suppose, instead, that if the 20-year yield changes by 25 basis points, the yield for the other three maturities change as follows: (1) 2-year maturity changes by 5 basis points (from 5% to 5.05%), (2) 5-year maturity changes by 15 basis points (from 5.25% to 5.40%), and (3) 30-year maturity changes by 35 basis points (from 5.75% to 6.1%). The new value for the portfolio based on this yield curve shift is shown in panel d of Exhibit 1. The decline in the portfolio's value is $2,096,926 (from $65 million to $62,903,074). The yield curve shift in the second illustration does not steepen as much as in the first case when the yield curve steepens.

The point here is that portfolios have different exposures to how the yield curve shifts. This risk exposure is called **yield curve risk**. The implication is that any measure of interest rate risk that assumes that the interest rates changes by an equal number of basis points for all maturities (referred to as a "parallel yield curve shift") is only an approximation.

This applies to the duration concept that we discussed above. We stated that the duration for an individual bond is the approximate percentage change in price for a 100 basis point change in yield. A duration for a portfolio has the same meaning: it is the approximate percentage change in the portfolio's value for a 100 basis point change in the yield *for all maturities*.

Because of the importance of yield curve risk, a good number of measures have been formulated to try to estimate the exposure of a portfolio to a shift in the yield curve. We defer a discussion of these measures until Chapter 7. However, we can introduce one basic, but the most popular approach, here. In the next chapter we will see that the yield curve is a series of yields, one for each maturity. It is possible to determine the percentage change in the value of a portfolio if only one yield changes while the yield for all other maturities is unchanged. This a form of duration called **rate duration**, where the word "rate" mean an interest rate of a particular maturity. So, for example, suppose a portfolio consists of 40 bonds with different maturities. A "5-year rate duration" of 2 would mean that the portfolio's value will change by approximately 2% for a 100 basis point change in the 5-year yield assuming all other key rates do not change.[4]

Consequently, in theory there is not one rate duration but a rate duration for each maturity. In practice, a rate duration is not computed for all maturities. Instead, the rate duration is computed for several key maturities on the yield curve and this is referred to as **key rate duration**. We'll discuss what maturities practitioners compute a key rate duration for in Chapter 7.

---

[4] At Level II, we will see that an assumption is made in computing the duration for rates between the key rates. Those rates are not held constant.

PRACTICE QUESTION 6

Suppose that an $85 million portfolio consists of the following five issues:

Issue	Maturity	Market value
1	2 years	$20 million
2	5 years	$15 million
3	10 years	$30 million
4	15 years	$5 million
5	28 years	$15 million

a. The portfolio manager computed a duration for the portfolio of 5. Approximately how much will the value of the portfolio decline if interest rates increase by 50 basis points?

b. In your calculation in part a, what is the assumption made in using the duration of 5 to compute the decline in the portfolio's value?

c. Suppose that the portfolio manager computes a 5-year rate duration of 1.5. What does that mean?

SECTION IV
CALL AND
PREPAYMENT
RISK

As explained in Chapter 1, a bond may include a provision that allows the issuer to retire or call all or part of the issue before the maturity date. From the investor's perspective, there are three disadvantages to call provisions:

Disadvantage 1: The cash flow pattern of a callable bond is not known with certainty because it is not known when the bond will be called.

Disadvantage 2: Because the issuer is likely to call the bonds when interest rates have dropped below the bond's coupon rate, the investor is exposed to reinvestment risk, i.e., the investor will have to reinvest the proceeds when the bond is called at interest rates lower than the bond's coupon rate.

Disadvantage 3: The price appreciation potential of a bond will be reduced relative to an otherwise comparable option-free bond. (This property is called **price compression**.)

We explained the third disadvantage in Section II when we discussed how the price of a callable bond may not rise as much as an otherwise comparable option-free bond when interest rates fall.

Because of these three disadvantages faced by the investor, a callable bond is said to expose the investor to **call risk**. The same disadvantages apply to mortgage-backed and asset-backed securities where the borrower can prepay. In this case the risk is referred to as **prepayment risk**.

SECTION V
REINVESTMENT
RISK

Reinvestment risk is the risk that proceeds available for reinvestment must be reinvested at a lower interest rate than the instrument that generated the proceeds. We already saw how reinvestment risk is present when an investor purchases a callable or prepayable bond. When the issuer calls a bond, it is typically done to lower its interest expense because interest rates have declined after the bond is issued. The investor faces the problem of having to reinvest the proceeds received from the issuer when the bond is called in a lower yield environment.

Reinvestment risk also occurs when an investor purchases a bond and relies on the yield of that bond as a measure of return potential. At this point of our development, this is a technical point. We have not explained how to compute the "yield" for a bond. When we do, it will be demonstrated that for the yield computed at the time of purchase to be realized, the investor must be able to reinvest any coupon payments at the computed yield. So, for example, if an investor purchases a 20-year bond with a yield of 6%, to realize the yield of 6% every time a coupon interest payment is made, it is necessary that the payment be reinvested at a 6% rate until the maturity of the bond. So, it is assumed that the first coupon payment can be reinvested for the next 19.5 years at 6%; the second coupon payment it is assumed can be reinvested for the next 19 years at 6%, and so on. The risk that the coupon payments will be reinvested at less than 6% is the reinvestment risk.

When we deal with amortizing securities (i.e., securities that repay principal periodically), reinvestment risk is even greater. Typically, amortizing securities pay interest and principal monthly and permit the borrower to prepay. Now the investor is concerned with reinvestment risk due to prepayments resulting from a decline in interest rates, just as in the case of a callable bond. However, since the payments are monthly, the investor has to make sure that the interest and principal can be reinvested at no less than the computed yield for the security at the time of purchase.

This reinvestment risk for an amortizing security is important to understand. Too often it is said by some market participants that securities that pay both interest and principal monthly are advantageous because the investor has the opportunity to reinvest more frequently and to reinvest a larger amount (because principal is received) relative to a bond that pays only semiannual coupon payments. This is not the case in a declining interest rate environment which will cause borrowers to accelerate their prepayments and force the investor to reinvest at lower interest rates. In fact, amortizing securities that pay monthly expose investors to greater reinvestment risk than standard bonds that pay interest semiannually and retire the entire principal at maturity.

With an understanding of reinvestment risk, we can now appreciate why zero-coupon bonds may be attractive to certain investors. Because there are no coupon payments to reinvest, there is no reinvestment risk. That is, zero-coupon bonds eliminate reinvestment risk. Elimination of reinvestment risk is important to some investors. That's the plus side of the risk equation. The minus side is that as explained in Section II, the lower the coupon rate the greater the interest rate risk for two bonds with the same maturity. Thus, zero-coupon bonds of a given maturity expose investors to the greatest interest rate risk.

Once we cover our basic analytical tools in later chapters, we will see how to quantify the exposure of a bond issue to reinvestment risk.

SECTION VI CREDIT RISK

An investor who lends funds by purchasing a bond issue is exposed to **credit risk**. There are three types of credit risk:

1. default risk
2. credit spread risk
3. downgrade risk

We discuss each type below.

A. Default Risk

Traditionally, credit risk is defined as the risk that the issuer will fail to satisfy the terms of the obligation with respect to the timely payment of interest and repayment of the amount borrowed. This form of credit risk is called **default risk**.

Studies have examined the probability of issuers defaulting. The percentage of a population of bonds that is expected to default is called a **default rate**. If a default does occur, this does not mean the investor loses the entire amount invested. There is a certain percentage of the investment that can be expected to be recovered. This is called the **recovery rate**. Given the default rate and the recovery rate, the estimated expected loss due to a default can be computed. We will explain the findings of studies on default rates and recovery rates in Chapter 3.

B. Credit Spread Risk

Even in the absence of default, an investor is concerned that the market value of a bond will decline and/or the price performance of that bond will be worse than that of other bonds against which the investor is compared. To understand this, recall that the price of a bond changes in the opposite direction to the change in the yield required by the market. Thus, if yields in the economy increase, the price of a bond declines, and vice versa.

As we will see in Chapter 3, the yield on a bond is made up of two components: (1) the yield on a similar default-free bond issue and (2) a premium above the yield on a default-free bond issue necessary to compensate for the risks associated with the bond. The risk premium is referred to as a **spread**. In the United States, Treasury issues are the benchmark yields because they are believed to be default free, they are highly liquid, and Treasury issues are not callable (with the exception of some old issues).[5] The part of the risk premium or spread attributable to default risk is called the **credit spread**.

The price performance of a non-Treasury bond issue and its return that the investor will realize by holding that issue over some time period will depend on how the credit spread changes. If the credit spread increases — investors say that the spread has "widened" — the market price of the bond issue will decline (assuming Treasury rates have not changed). The risk that an issuer's debt obligation will decline due to an increase in the credit spread is called **credit spread risk**.

This risk exists for an individual issue, for issues in a particular industry or economic sector, and for all non-Treasury issues in the economy. For example, in general during economic recessions investors are concerned that issuers will face a decline in cash flows that would be used to service its bond obligations. As a result, the credit spread tends to widen for non-Treasury issuers and the prices of all such issues throughout the economy will decline.

C. Downgrade Risk

While there are portfolio managers who seek to allocate funds among different sectors of the bond market to capitalize on anticipated changes in credit spreads, an analyst investigating the credit quality of an individual issue is concerned with the prospects of the credit spread increasing for that particular issue. But how does the analyst assess whether he or she believes the market will change the credit spread attributed to the issue?

Market participants gauge the default risk of an issue by looking at the credit ratings assigned to issues by rating companies, popularly referred to as **rating agencies**. There are three rating agencies in the United States: Moody's Investors Service, Inc., Standard & Poor's Corporation, and Fitch. (Fitch is the new entity created from the merger of Fitch IBCA and Duff & Phelps Credit Rating Co. in April 2000.)

---

[5] Because of the reduction of issuance by the U.S. Treasury and its buyback of long-term Treasury securities, other benchmarks are being considered by market participants. However, any benchmark other than a U.S. Treasury security will reflect credit risk.

Exhibit 2: Summary of Bond Rating Systems and Symbols

Moody's	S&P	Fitch	Summary Description
Investment Grade — High Credit Worthiness			
Aaa	AAA	AAA	Gilt edge, prime, maximum safety
Aa1	AA+	AA+	
Aa2	AA	AA	High-grade, high-credit quality
Aa3	AA−	AA−	
A1	A+	A+	
A2	A	A	Upper-medium grade
A3	A−	A−	
Baa1	BBB+	BBB+	
Baa2	BBB	BBB	Lower-medium grade
Baa3	BBB−	BBB−	
Speculative — Lower Credit Worthiness			
Ba1	BB+	BB+	
Ba2	BB	BB	Low grade, speculative
Ba3	BB−	BB−	
B1		B+	
B2	B	B	Highly speculative
B3		B−	
Predominantly Speculative, Substantial Risk, or in Default			
	CCC+	CCC+	
Caa	CCC	CCC	Substantial risk, in poor standing
Ca	CC	CC	May be in default, very speculative
C	C	C	Extremely speculative
	CI		Income bonds — no interest being paid
		DDD	
		DD	Default
	D	D	

A **credit rating** is an indicator of the potential default risk associated with a particular bond issue. It represents in a simplistic way the rater's assessment of an issuer's ability to meet the payment of principal and interest in accordance with the terms of the debt contract. Credit rating symbols or characters are uncomplicated representations of more complex ideas. In effect, they are summary opinions. Exhibit 2 provides a summary of the ratings assigned by Moody's, S&P, and Fitch for bonds and the meaning of each rating.

In all systems the term **high grade** means low credit risk, or conversely, high probability of future payments. The highest-grade bonds are designated by Moody's by the symbol Aaa, and by S&P and Fitch by the symbol AAA. The next highest grade is denoted by the symbol Aa (Moody's) or AA (S&P and Fitch); for the third grade both rating companies use A. The next three grades are Baa or BBB, Ba or BB, and B, respectively. There are also C grades. Moody's uses 1, 2, or 3 to provide a narrower credit quality breakdown within each class, and S&P and Fitch use plus and minus signs for the same purpose.

Bonds rated triple A (AAA or Aaa) are said to be **prime grade**; double A (AA or Aa) are of **high quality grade**; single A issues are called **upper medium grade**, and triple B are **medium grade**. Lower-rated bonds are said to have **speculative grade** elements or be **distinctly speculative grade**.

Bond issues that are assigned a rating in the top four categories (that is, AAA, AA, A, and BBB) are referred to as **investment-grade bonds**. Issues that carry a rating below the top four categories are referred to as **non-investment-grade bonds** or

speculative bonds, or more popularly as **high yield bonds** or **junk bonds**. Thus, the bond market can be divided into two sectors: the investment grade and non-investment grade markets as summarized below:

Investment grade bonds	AAA, AA, A, and BBB
Non-investment grade bonds (speculative/high yield)	Below BBB

Once a credit rating is assigned to a debt obligation, a rating agency monitors the credit quality of the issuer and can reassign a different credit rating. An improvement in the credit quality of an issue or issuer is rewarded with a better credit rating, referred to as an **upgrade**; a deterioration in the credit rating of an issue or issuer is penalized by the assignment of an inferior credit rating, referred to as a **downgrade**. An unanticipated downgrading of an issue or issuer increases the credit spread and results in a decline in the price of the issue or the issuer's bonds. This risk is referred to as **downgrade risk** and is closely related to credit spread risk.

As we have explained, the credit rating is a measure of potential default risk. An analyst must be aware of how rating agencies gauge default risk for purposes of assigning ratings in order to understand the other aspects of credit risk. This is because the agencies' assessment of potential default drives downgrade risk, and, in turn, both default potential and credit ratings changes drive credit spread risk.

A popular tools used by managers to gauge the prospects of an issue being downgraded or upgraded is a **rating transition matrix**. This is simply a table constructed by the rating agencies that show the percentage of issues of each rating at the beginning of a time period that were downgraded or upgraded over some period of time. We'll illustrate a rating transition matrix at Level III where we demonstrate how it is used in portfolio strategies.

SECTION VII
LIQUIDITY RISK

When an investor wants to sell a bond prior to the maturity date, he or she is concerned whether the price that can be obtained by dealers is close to the true value of the issue. For example, if recent trades in the market for a particular issue have been between 90 and 90.5 and market conditions have not changed, an investor would expect to sell the bond somewhere in the 90 to 90.5 range.

Liquidity risk is the risk that the investor will have to sell a bond below its true value where the true value is indicated by a recent transaction. The primary measure of liquidity is the size of the spread between the bid price (the price at which a dealer is willing to buy a security) and the ask price (the price at which a dealer is willing to sell a security). The wider the bid-ask spread, the greater the liquidity risk. Exhibit 3 shows typical indicators of market liquidity by market sector as measured by bid-ask spreads where the spread is as a percent of the price. (We will discuss bid-ask spreads in distressed market periods later.)

A liquid market can generally be defined by "small bid-ask spreads which do not materially increase for large transactions."[6] How to define the bid-ask spread in a multiple dealer market is subject to interpretation. For example, consider the bid-ask prices for four dealers. Each quote is for 92 plus the number of 32nds shown:

	Dealer			
	1	2	3	4
Bid price	1	1	2	2
Ask price	4	3	4	5

---

[6] Robert I. Gerber, "A User's Guide to Buy-Side Bond Trading," Chapter 16 in Frank J. Fabozzi (ed.), *Managing Fixed Income Portfolios* (New Hope, PA: Frank J. Fabozzi Associates, 1997), p. 278.

Exhibit 3: Indicators of Market Liquidity

Sector	Bid-ask spreads (% of price)	
	Typical	Distressed
Treasuries		
Bills	0.002	0.005
On-the-run notes and bonds	0.003	0.006
Off-the-run issues and bonds	0.006	0.009
Corporates (intermediates)		
A rated Finance	0.120	0.500
B rated Industrials	0.500	5.000
Mortgage-backed securities		
Fixed-rate generic	0.060	0.250
Municipals		
Long-term issues rated Aa or Aaa	0.250	0.750

Adapted from Exhibit 1 in Robert I. Gerber, "A User's Guide to Buy-Side Bond Trading," Chapter 16 in Frank J. Fabozzi (ed.), *Managing Fixed Income Portfolios* (New Hope, PA: Frank J. Fabozzi Associates, 1997), p. 279.

The bid-ask spread for each dealer (in 32nds) is:

	Dealer			
	1	2	3	4
Bid-ask spread	3	2	2	3

The bid-ask spread as computed above is measured relative to a dealer. The best bid ask spread is $\frac{2}{32}$ for Dealers 2 and 3.

From the perspective of the market overall, the bid-ask spread can be computed by looking at the best bid price (high price at which one of the dealers is willing to buy the security) and the lowest ask price (lowest offer price at which one of the dealers is willing to sell the security). This liquidity measure is called the **market bid-ask spread**. For the four dealers, the highest bid price is $92\frac{2}{32}$ and the lowest ask price is $92\frac{3}{32}$. Thus, the market bid-ask spread is $\frac{1}{32}$.

A. Liquidity Risk and Marking Positions to Market

For investors who plan to hold a bond until maturity and need *not* mark a position to market, liquidity risk is not a major concern. An institutional investor that plans to hold an issue to maturity but is periodically marked-to market is concerned with liquidity risk. By marking a position to market, the security is revalued in the portfolio based on its current market price. For example, mutual funds are required to mark to market at the end of each day the holdings in their portfolio in order to compute the net asset value (NAV). While other institutional investors may not mark to market as frequently as mutual funds, they are marked to market when reports are periodically sent to clients or the board of directors or trustees.

Where are the prices obtained to mark a position to market? Typically, a portfolio manager will solicit indicative bids from several dealers and then use some process to determine the bid price used to mark (i.e., value) the position. The less liquid the issue, the greater the variation there will be in the bid prices obtained by dealers. With an issue that has little liquidity, the price may have to be determined from a pricing service (i.e., a service company that employs models to determine the fair value of a security) rather than from dealer bid prices. Moreover, lack of dealer indicative bids and concern with models used by pricing services may lead the manager occasionally to override a bid (subject to internal approval beyond the control of the manager).

In Chapter 1 we discussed the use of repurchase agreements as a form of borrowing funds to purchase bonds. We will see that the bonds purchased are used as collateral. The bonds purchased are marked to market periodically in order to determine whether or not the collateral provides adequate protection for the lender of the funds. When liquidity in the market dries up, the portfolio manager who has borrowed the funds must rely solely on the bid prices determined by the dealer.

B. Changes in Liquidity Risk

Bid-ask spreads, and therefore liquidity risk, change over time. Changing market liquidity is a concern to portfolio managers who are contemplating investing in new complex bond structures. While there are opportunities for those who invest in a new type of bond structure, there are typically few dealers making a market when the structure is in its infancy stage. If subsequently the new structure becomes popular, more dealers will enter the market and liquidity improves. In contrast, if the new bond structure turns out to be unappealing to investors, the initial buyers face a market with less liquidity because dealers not only exit the market but dealers willing to make a market offer bids that are unattractive because they do not want to hold these bonds in inventory.

Exhibit 3 shows two columns of bid-ask spreads for a variety of securities. The first column indicates the bid-ask spread available to investors under normal conditions. The second column illustrates the bid-ask spreads that might occur in less benign market environments. Situations such as an unexpected change in interest rates might cause a widening of the bid-ask spread, as investors and dealers are reluctant to take new positions until they have had a chance to assess the new information.

Thus, we see that the liquidity risk of an issue changes over time. Here is an actual example of when a manager purchases an issue there may be a number of dealers making a market in the issue but at a later date the number of dealers interested in participating in the market in a meaningful way may decline. In the Spring of 1994 one sector of the mortgage-backed securities market, called the derivative mortgage market, saw the collapse of an important player — a hedge fund — and the exiting from the market of several dealers. As a result, liquidity in the market dried up and bid-ask spreads widened dramatically.

SECTION VIII EXCHANGE RATE OR CURRENCY RISK

A bond whose payments are not in the domestic currency of the portfolio manager has unknown cash flows in the domestic currency. The cash flows in the manager's domestic currency are dependent on the exchange rate at the time the payments are received from the issuer. For example, suppose a portfolio manager's domestic currency is the U.S. dollar and that manager purchases a bond whose payments are in Japanese yen. If the yen depreciates relative to the U.S. dollar at the time a payment is made, then fewer U.S. dollars will be received.

As another example, consider a portfolio manager in the United Kingdom. This manager's domestic currency is the pound. If that manager purchases a U.S. dollar denominated bond, then the manager is concerned that the U.S. dollar will depreciate relative to the British pound when the issuer makes a payment. As a result, fewer British pounds are received.

The risk of receiving less of the domestic currency when investing in a bond issue that makes payments in a currency other than the manager's domestic currency is called **exchange rate risk** or **currency risk**.

SECTION IX
INFLATION OR PURCHASING POWER RISK

Inflation risk or **purchasing power risk** arises because of the variation in the value of cash flows from a security due to inflation, as measured in terms of purchasing power. For example, if an investor purchases a bond with a coupon rate of 5%, but the rate of inflation is 3%, the purchasing power of the investor has not increased by 5%. Instead, the investor's purchasing power has increased by 2%.

For all but inflation protection bonds, an investor is exposed to inflation risk because the interest rate the issuer promises to make is fixed for the life of the issue.

SECTION X
VOLATILITY RISK

In our discussion of the impact of embedded options on the interest rate risk of a bond in Section II, we said that a change in the factors that affect the value of the embedded options will affect how the bond's price will change. Earlier we looked at how a change in the level of interest rates will affect the price of a bond with an embedded option. But there are other factors that will affect the price of an embedded option.

While we discuss these other factors at Level II, we can get an appreciation of one important factor from a general understanding of option pricing. A major factor affecting the value of an option is "expected volatility." In the case of an option on common stock, expected volatility refers to "expected price volatility." The relationship is as follows: the greater the expected price volatility, the greater the value of the option. The same relationship holds for options on bonds. However, instead of expected price volatility, for bonds it is the "expected yield volatility." The greater the expected yield volatility, the greater the value (price) of an option. The interpretation of yield volatility and how it is estimated are explained at Level II.

Now let us tie this into the pricing of a callable bond. We repeat the formula for the components of a callable bond below:

Price of callable bond = Price of option-free bond − Price of embedded call option

If expected yield volatility increases, holding all other factors constant, the price of the embedded call option will increase. As a result, the price of a callable bond will decrease (because it is subtracted from the price of the option-free bond).

To see how a change in expected yield volatility affects the price of a putable bond, we can write the price of a putable bond as follows:

Price of putable bond = Price of option-free bond + Price of embedded put option

A decrease in expected yield volatility reduces the price of the embedded put option and therefore will decrease the price of a putable bond. Since a decrease in expected yield volatility reduces the price of the embedded put option and therefore the price of a putable bond, this means that the volatility risk of a putable bond is that expected yield volatility will decrease.

This risk that the price of a bond with an embedded option will decline when expected yield volatility changes is called **volatility risk**. Below is a summary of the effect of changes in expected yield volatility on the price of callable and putable bonds:

Type of embedded option	Volatility risk due to
Callable bonds	an increase in expected yield volatility
Putable bonds	a decrease in expected yield volatility

SECTION XI
EVENT RISK

Occasionally the ability of an issuer to make interest and principal payments changes dramatically and unexpectedly because of factors including the following:

1. a natural disaster (such as an earthquake or hurricane) or an industrial accident that impairs an issuer's ability to meet its obligations
2. a takeover or corporate restructuring that impairs an issuer's ability to meet its obligations
3. a regulatory change
4. political factors that alters a government's willingness or ability to repay its obligation

A. Natural Catastrophes and Corporate Takeover/ Restructurings

The first type of event risk will result in a downgrading of the issuer by rating agencies and is therefore a form of downgrade risk. However, the downgrading risk is typically confined to the particular issuer.

The second type of event risk also results in a downgrade but this downgrading can impact other issuers. An excellent example occurred in the fall of 1988 with the leverage buyout (LBO) of RJR Nabisco, Inc. The entire industrial sector of the bond market suffered as bond market participants withdrew from the market, new issues were postponed, and secondary market activity came to a standstill as a result of the initial LBO bid announcement. The yield that investors wanted on Nabisco's bonds increased by about 250 basis points. Moreover, because the RJR LBO demonstrated that size was not an obstacle for an LBO, other large industrial firms that market participants previously thought were unlikely candidates for an LBO were fair game. The spillover effect to other industrial companies of the RJR LBO resulted in required yields increasing dramatically.

Analysts assess the event risk of an issue or an industry subjectively. For example, analysts at Morgan Stanley Dean Witter (MSDW) when analyzing a particular issuer or industry express their view of event risk in terms of "high," "neutral," or "low." In mid May 1999, for example, MSDW viewed every sector of the energy industry as having "high" event risk. At the same time, event risk was viewed as "low" for the retail industry. In the aerospace & defense, technology, and diversified industrial sector, event risk was viewed as follows by industry sub-sector: commercial aerospace (low), defense contractors (high), computers (neutral), PC components (neutral), and software (neutral).[7]

B. Regulatory Risk

The third type of risk listed above is **regulatory risk**. This risk comes in a variety of forms. Regulated entities include investment companies, depository institutions, and insurance companies. Pension funds are regulated by ERISA. Regulation of these entities is in terms of the acceptable securities in which they may invest and/or the treatment of the securities for regulatory accounting purposes.

Changes in regulations may require a regulated entity to divest itself from certain types of investments. A flood of the divested securities on the market will adversely impact the price of similar securities. An example occurred in 1989 where one single event sealed the fate of the non-investment grade bond sector of the market for several years. In that year, Congress passed the Financial Institutions Reform, Recovery, and Enforcement Act (FIRREA) requiring as part of a bailout of the saving and loan (S&L) industry that all thrifts divest their holdings of non-investment grade bonds by August 1994. It was estimated that this effectively removed 10% of the new

---

[7] Morgan Stanley Dean Witter, *U.S. Portfolio Strategy*, Fixed Income Research (May 13, 1999).

issuance buying power from the market. By itself, preventing new investments in non-investment grade bonds would not have caused this market sector to collapse; new deals would have been held back until a sufficient numbers of new buyers could be found to replace the S&Ls who were buying these bonds at issuance. However, when Congress further required these institutions to divest all their non-investment grade bonds within five years, 7% of all non-investment grade holdings were effectively dumped onto the market, and liquidity vanished. Within a month of FIRREA's passage, prices in the non-investment grade sector began to decline dramatically. By early 1990, the additional yield required on these bonds increased an average of 400 basis points. Prices fell by about an average of 20% to 25% as new buyers failed to emerge in sufficient numbers to meet this large supply of issues dumped on the market. It is important to understand that it was not the heightened perception of the market that the default risk of non-investment grade bonds had increased that caused this drop in prices, but the passage of FIRREA. Moreover, at the same time, there were proposed federal and state regulations that would either have pension funds and insurance companies divest their holdings of non-investment grade bonds, severely limit the amount they hold, or impose requirements that make holding these securities less attractive.

C. Political Risk

While some forms of event risk that fall under regulatory risk may be viewed as **political risk**, usually political risk refers to the risk that the actions by a government entity (domestic or foreign) results in a default or increase the likelihood of default. For a sovereign government, the country's leaders may simply repudiate its debt. This can be done by the current central government that accumulated the debt or a change in political regime whose debt repayment policy is different from the previous regime. The same is true for a municipality. New political leaders of a municipality may take the position that the obligation to meet its debt obligation is of minor importance relative to the interests of other parties with greater political clout. This is why in assessing the credit risk of a sovereign government and a municipal entity, rating agencies look at not only the capacity to repay debt but the *willingness* to repay debt.

SECTION XII
KEY POINTS

❑ *The price of a bond changes inversely with a change in market interest rates.*

❑ *Interest rate risk refers to the adverse price movement of a bond as a result of a change in market interest rates; for the owner of a bond it is the risk that interest rates will rise.*

❑ *A bond's interest rate risk exposure depends on the features of a bond — maturity, coupon rate, and embedded options.*

❑ *All other factors constant, the longer the bond's maturity, the greater the bond's price sensitivity to changes in interest rates.*

❑ *A property of a bond is that all other factors constant, the lower the coupon rate, the greater the bond's price sensitivity to changes in interest rates.*

❑ *The price of a callable bond is equal to the price of an option-free bond reduced by the price of the embedded call option.*

❑ *When interest rates rise, the price of a callable bond will not fall by as much as an otherwise comparable option-free bond because the price of the embedded call option decreases.*

❏ *The price of a putable bond is equal to the price of an option-free bond plus the price of the embedded put option.*

❏ *All other factors constant, the higher the level of interest rates that a bond trades, the lower the price sensitivity when interest rates change.*

❏ *The price sensitivity of a bond to changes in interest rates can be measured in terms of (1) the percentage price change from the initial price or (2) the dollar price change from the initial price.*

❏ *The most straightforward way to calculate the percentage price change is to average the percentage price change resulting from an increase and a decrease in interest rates of the same number of basis points.*

❏ *Duration is a measure interest rate risk; it measures the price sensitivity of a bond to rates changes.*

❏ *Duration can be interpreted as the approximate percentage price change of a bond for a 100 basis point change in interest rates.*

❏ *The computed duration is only as good as the valuation model used to obtain the prices when interest rates are shocked up and down by the same number of basis points.*

❏ *There can be substantial differences in the duration of complex bonds as computed by market participants because valuation models used to obtain prices can vary.*

❏ *Given the duration of a bond and its market value, the dollar price change can be computed for a given change in interest rates.*

❏ *The yield curve risk for a portfolio occurs because when interest rates increase, they do not change by the same number of basis points; a bond portfolio has different exposures to how the yield curve changes.*

❏ *A portfolio's duration measures the sensitivity of the value of the portfolio to changes in interest rates assuming that the interest rate for all maturities change by the same number of basis points.*

❏ *Any measure of interest rate risk that assumes that the interest rates changes by an equal number of basis points for all maturities (referred to as a "parallel yield curve shift") is only an approximation.*

❏ *One measure of yield curve risk is rate duration which is the approximate percentage price change for a 100 basis point change in the key rate for one maturity, holding all other key rates constant.*

❏ *Call risk and prepayment risk refer to the risk that a security will be paid off before the scheduled principal repayment date.*

❏ *Reinvestment risk is the risk that proceeds available for reinvestment must be reinvested at a lower interest rate than the instrument that generated the proceeds.*

❏ *From an investor's perspective, the disadvantages to call and prepayment provisions are (1) the cash flow pattern is uncertain, (2) reinvestment risk because proceeds received will have to be reinvested at a relatively lower interest rate, and (3) the capital appreciation potential of a bond will be reduced.*

❏ *Reinvestment risk for an amortizing security can be significant because of the right to prepay and the fact that interest and principal are repaid monthly.*

❑ *A zero-coupon bond has no reinvestment risk but has interest rate risk that is greater than a coupon bond of the same maturity.*

❑ *There are three forms of credit risk: default risk, credit spread risk, and downgrade risk.*

❑ *Default risk is the risk that the issuer will fail to satisfy the terms of the obligation with respect to the timely payment of interest and repayment of the amount borrowed.*

❑ *Credit spread risk is the risk that the price of an issuer's bond will decline due to an increase in the credit spread.*

❑ *Downgrade risk is the risk that one or more of the rating agencies will reduce the credit rating of an issuer.*

❑ *There are three rating agencies in the United States: Standard & Poor's Corporation, Moody's Investors Service, Inc., and Fitch.*

❑ *A credit rating is an indicator of the potential default risk associated with a particular bond issue that represents in a simplistic way the rater's assessment of an issuer's ability to meet the payment of principal and interest in accordance with the terms of the debt contract.*

❑ *Liquidity risk is the risk that the investor will have to sell a bond below its true value.*

❑ *The primary measure of liquidity is the size of the spread between the bid price and the ask price quoted by dealers.*

❑ *A market bid-ask spread is the difference between the highest bid price from among dealers and the lowest ask from among dealers.*

❑ *The liquidity risk of an issue changes over time.*

❑ *Exchange rate risk arises when the interest and principal payments of a bond issue are not denominated in the domestic currency of the investor.*

❑ *Exchange rate risk is the risk that the currency in which the interest and principal payments are denominated will decline relative to the domestic currency.*

❑ *Inflation risk or purchasing power risk arises because of the variation in the value of cash flows from a security due to inflation, as measured in terms of purchasing power.*

❑ *Volatility risk is the risk that the price of a bond with an embedded option will decline when expected yield volatility changes.*

❑ *For a callable bond, volatility risk is the risk that expected yield volatility will increase; for a putable bond, volatility risk is the risk that expected yield volatility will decline.*

❑ *Event risk is the risk that the ability of an issuer to make interest and principal payments changes dramatically and unexpectedly because of certain events such as a corporate takeover, a natural catastrophe, regulatory changes, or political changes.*

END OF CHAPTER QUESTIONS

1. For each of the following issues, indicate whether the price of the issue should be par value, above par value, or below par value:

	Issue	Coupon rate	Required yield by the market
a.	A	5¼%	7.25%
b.	B	6⅝%	7.15%
c.	C	0%	6.20%
d.	D	5⅞%	5.00%
e.	E	4½%	4.50%

2. John Smith and Jane Brody are assistant portfolio managers for an account. The senior portfolio manager for the account has asked them to consider the acquisition of one of two option-free bond issues with the following characteristics:

Issue 1 has a lower coupon rate than Issue 2
Issue 1 has a shorter maturity than Issue 2

Both issues have the same credit rating.

Smith and Brody are discussing the interest rate risk of the two issues. Smith argues that Issue 1 has greater interest rate risk than Issue 2 because of its lower coupon rate. Brody counters by arguing that Issue 2 has greater interest rate risk because it has a longer maturity than Issue 1.

a. Which assistant portfolio manager is correct with respect their selection to the issue with the greater interest rate risk?
b. Suppose that you are the senior portfolio manager. How would you suggest that Smith and Brody determine which issue has the greater interest rate risk?

3. A portfolio manager wants to estimate the interest rate risk of a bond using duration. The current price of the bond is 82. A valuation model employed by the manager found that if interest rates decline by 30 basis points, the price will increase to 83.50 and if interest rates increase by 30 basis points, the price will decline to 80.75. What is the duration of this bond?

4. A portfolio manager purchased $8 million in market value of a bond with a duration of 5. For this bond, determine the estimated change in its market value for the change in interest rates shown below:

a. 100 basis points
b. 50 basis points
c. 25 basis points
d. 10 basis points

5. A portfolio manager of a bond fund is considering the acquisition of an extremely complex bond issue. It is complex because it has multiple embedded options. The manager wants to estimate the interest rate risk of the bond issue so that he could determine the impact of its inclusion on the duration of the current portfolio. The dealer that created the bond structure for the issue was contacted about its estimate for the issue's duration. The dealer's analysts estimated the duration to be 7. The portfolio manager solicited his firm's in-house quantitative analyst and asked her to estimate the issue's duration. She estimated the duration to be 10. Explain why

there is such a dramatic difference in the issue's duration as estimated by the dealer's analysts and the firm's in-house analyst?

6. Duration is commonly used as a measure of interest rate risk. However, when estimated for a portfolio, duration does not consider yield curve risk. Why?

7. Explain why a callable bond would be expected to fall by less than an otherwise comparable option-free bond when interest rates rise?

8. a. Short-term investors such as money market mutual funds invest in floating-rate securities of maturities of greater than 1 year. Suppose that the coupon rate is reset everyday. Why is the interest rate risk small for such issues?
   b. Why would it be improper to say that a floating-rate security whose coupon rate resets every day has no interest rate risk?
   c. For floating-rate securities whose coupon rate is reset every day, issuers may include a put provision. The put price is typically par value. Why does this put provision reduce the interest rate risk of a floating-rate security?

9. What measure can a portfolio manager use to assess the interest rate risk of a portfolio to a change in the 5-year yield?

10. For the investor in a callable bond, what are the two forms of reinvestment risk faced?

11. Investors are exposed to credit risk when they purchase a bond. However, even if an issuer does not default on its obligation prior to its maturity date, there is still a concern about how credit risk can adversely impact the performance of a bond. Why?

12. Identify the difference in the major risks associated with the following investment alternatives:

    a. For an investor who plans to hold a security for one year, purchasing a Treasury security that matures in one year versus purchasing a Treasury security that matures in 30 years.
    b. For an investor who plans to hold an investment for 10 years, purchasing a Treasury security that matures in 10 years versus purchasing an AAA corporate security that matures in 10 years.
    c. For an investor who plans to hold an investment for two years, purchasing a zero-coupon Treasury security that matures in one year versus purchasing a zero-coupon Treasury security that matures in two years.
    d. For an investor who plans to hold an investment for five years, purchasing an AA sovereign bond (with dollar denominated cash flow payments) versus purchasing a U.S. corporate bond with a B rating
    e. For an investor who plans to hold an investment for four years, purchasing a less actively traded 10-year AA rated bond versus purchasing a 10-year AA rated bond that is actively traded
    f. For a U.S. investor who plans to hold an investment for six years, purchasing a Treasury security that matures in six year versus purchasing an Italian government security that matures in six years and is denominated in lira.

13. Sam Stevens is the trustee for the Hole Punchers Labor Union (HPLU). He has approached the investment management firm of IM Associates (IMA) to manage

its $200 million bond portfolio. IMA assigned Carol Peters as the portfolio manager for the HPLU account. In their first meeting, Mr. Stevens told Ms. Peters:

> "We are an extremely conservative pension fund. We believe in investing in only investment grade bonds so that there will be minimal risk that the principal invested will be lost. We want at least 40% of the portfolio to be held in bonds that will mature within the next three years. I would like your thoughts on this proposed structure for the portfolio."

How should Ms. Peters respond?

14. a. A treasurer of a municipality with a municipal pension fund has required that its in-house portfolio manager invest all funds in the highest investment grade securities that mature in one month or less. The treasurer believes that this is a safe policy. Comment on this investment policy.

 b. The same treasurer requires that the in-house portfolio municipality's operating fund (i.e., fund needed for day-to-day operations of the municipality) follow the same investment policy. Comment on the appropriateness of this investment policy for managing the municipality's operating fund.

15. An assistant portfolio manager for a portfolio that includes non-dollar denominated government bonds wants to impress the portfolio manager. (The domestic currency for the portfolio is the U.S. dollar.) Noticing that the reporting system describing features of the portfolio does not include a portfolio's duration, the assistant portfolio manager decided to include this measure by computing the duration for each of the non-dollar government bonds and then computing the duration for the portfolio. What is the meaning of the portfolio duration computed by the assistant portfolio manager?

16. In January 1994, General Electric Capital Corporation (GECC) had outstanding $500 million of Reset Notes due March 15, 2018. The reset notes were floating-rate securities. In January 1994, the bonds had an 8% coupon rate for three years that ended March 15, 1994. On January 26, 1994, GECC notified the noteholders that it would redeem the issue on March 15th at par value. This was within the required 30 to 60 day prior notice period. Investors who sought investments with very short-term instruments (e.g., money market investors) bought the notes after GECC's planned redemption announcement. The notes were viewed as short-term because they would be redeemed in six weeks or so. In early February, the Federal Reserve started to boost interest rates and on February 15th, GECC switched gears and canceled the proposed redemption. Instead, it decided to reset the new interest rate based on the indenture at 108% of the three-year Treasury rate in effect on the tenth day preceding the date of the new interest period of March 15th. *The Wall Street Journal* reported that the notes dropped from par to 98 ($1,000 to $980 per note) after the cancellation of the proposed redemption.*

Why did the price decline?

---

* To complete this story, investors were infuriated and they protested to GECC. On March 8th the new interest rate of 5.61% was announced in the financial press. On the very next day GECC announced a tender offer for the notes commencing March 17th. It would buy them back at par plus accrued interest on April 15th. This bailed out many investors who had faith in GECCs original redemption announcement.

17. A British portfolio manager is considering investing in Japanese government bonds denominated in yen. What are the major risks associated with this investment?

18. Why are certain types of event risk a form of downgrade risk?

19. A portfolio manager is considering the purchase of a new type of bond. The bond is extremely complex in terms of its embedded options. Currently, there is only one dealer making a market in this type of bond. In addition, the manager plans to finance the purchase of this bond by using the bond itself as collateral. The bond matures in five years and the manager plans to hold the bond for five years. Because the manager plans to hold the bond to its maturity, he has indicated that he is not concerned with liquidity risk? Explain why you agree or disagree with the manager's view that he is not concerned with liquidity risk?

20. Suppose that the bid and ask prices of five dealers for Issue XYX is 96 plus the number of 32nds shown:

	Dealer				
	1	2	3	4	5
Bid price	14	14	15	15	13
Ask price	18	17	18	20	19

What is the market bid-ask spread for Issue XYX?

SOLUTIONS TO END OF CHAPTER QUESTIONS

1. a. Below par value since the coupon rate is less than the yield required by the market.
   b. Below par value since the coupon rate is less than the yield required by the market.
   c. Below par value since the coupon rate is less than the yield required by the market.
   d. Above par value since the coupon rate is greater than the yield required by the market.
   e. Par value since the coupon rate is equal to the yield required by the market.

	Issue	Coupon rate	Required yield by the market	Price
a.	A	5¼%	7.25%	Below par
b.	B	6⅝%	7.15%	Below par
c.	C	0%	6.20%	Below par
d.	D	5⅞%	5.00%	Above par
e.	E	4½%	4.50%	Par

2. a. While both assistant portfolio managers are correct in that they have identified two features of an issue that will impact interest rate risk, it is the interaction of the two that will affect an issue's interest rate risk. From the information provided in the question, it cannot be determined which has the greater interest rate risk.
   b. You, as the senior portfolio manager, might want to suggest that the two assistant portfolio managers compute the duration of the two issues.

3. The information for computing duration:

   price if yields decline by 30 basis points = 83.50
   price if yields rise by 30 basis points = 80.75
   initial price = 82.00
   change in yield in decimal = 0.0030

   Then,

   $$\text{duration} = \frac{83.50 - 80.75}{2(82.00)(0.0030)} = 5.59$$

4. Since the duration is the approximate percentage price change for a 100 basis point change in interest rates, a bond with a duration of 5 will change by approximately 5% for a 100 basis point change in interest rates. Since the market value of the bond is $8 million, the change in the market value for a 100 basis point change in interest rates is found by multiplying 5% by $8 million. Therefore, the change in market value per 100 basis point change in interest rates is $400,000. To get an estimate of the change in the market value for any other change in interest rates, it is only necessary to scale the change in market value accordingly.

   a. for 100 basis points = $400,000
   b. for 50 basis points = $200,000 (=$400,000/2)
   c. for 25 basis points = $100,000 ($400,000/4)
   d. for 10 basis points = $40,000 ($400,000/10)

5. To calculate duration, the price must be estimated for an increase and decrease (i.e., a rate shock) of the same number of basis points. A valuation model must be employed to obtain the two prices. With an extremely complex bond issue, the val-

uation models by different analysts can produce substantially different prices when rates are shocked. This will result in differences in estimates of duration.

6. For an individual bond, duration is an estimate of the price sensitivity of a bond to changes in interest rates. A portfolio duration can be estimated from the duration of the individual bond holdings in the portfolio. To use the portfolio's duration as an estimate of interest rate risk it is assumed that when interest rates change, the interest rate for all maturities change by the same number of basis points. That is, it does not consider non-parallel changes of the yield curve.

7. The price of a callable bond can be expressed as follows:

price of callable bond = price of option-free bond − price of embedded call option

An increase in interest rates will reduce the price of the option-free bond. However, to partially offset that price decline of the option-free bond, the price of the embedded call option will decrease. This is because as interest rates rise the value of the embedded call option to the issuer is worth less. Since a lower price for the embedded call option is subtracted from the lower price of the option-free bond, the price of the callable bond does not fall as much as that of an option-free bond.

8. a. A floating-rate security's exposure to interest rate risk is affected by the time to the next reset date. The shorter the time, the less likely the issue will offer a below market interest rate until the next reset date. So, a daily reset will not expose the investor of this floater to interest rate risk due to this factor. However, there is interest rate risk which we will see in part b.
   b. The reason there is still interest rate risk with a daily reset floating-rate security is that the margin required by the market may change. And, if there is a cap on the floater, there is cap risk.
   c. The inclusion of a put provision means that if any of the factors that cause interest rate risk for a daily reset floater occur, the investor can force the issuer to repurchase the floater at par by exercising the put option.

9. The approach briefly discussed in this chapter for doing so is *rate duration*. Specifically, the 5-year rate duration indicates the approximate percentage change in the value of the portfolio if the yield on all maturities are unchanged but the yield for the 5-year maturity changes by 100 basis points.

10. The first form of reinvestment risk is due to the necessity to reinvest the proceeds from the called issue in a lower coupon security. The second form of reinvestment risk is the typical risk faced by an investor when purchasing a bond with a coupon rate. It is necessary to reinvest all the coupon payments at the computed yield in order to realize the yield at the time the bond is purchased

11. Credit risk includes default risk, credit spread risk, and downgrade risk. While an investor holds a bond in his or her portfolio, if the issuer does not default there is still (1) the risk that credit spreads in the market will increase (credit spread risk) causing the price of the bond to decline and (2) the risk that the issue will be downgraded by the rating agencies causing the price to decline or not perform as well as other issues (downgrade risk)

12. a. The purchase of a 30-year Treasury exposes the investor to interest rate risk since at the end of one year, the security is a 29-year instrument. Its price at the end of one year depends on what happens to interest rates one year later.

   b. The major difference in risk is with respect to credit risk. Specifically, the AAA issue exposes the investor to credit risk.

   c. There is reinvestment risk for the 1-year zero-coupon Treasury issue because the principal must be reinvested at the end of one year.

   d. The major difference is the quantity of credit risk exposure of both issues. The U.S. corporate bond issue has greater credit risk. (Note that the sovereign issue is dollar denominated so that there is no exchange rate risk.)

   e. The less actively traded issue will have greater liquidity risk.

   f. There are two differences in risk. First, there is the greater credit risk of investing in Italian government bonds relative to U.S. Treasury bonds. Second investing in the Italian government bonds denominated in lira exposes a U.S. investor to exchange rate risk.

13. Probably the first thing that Ms. Peters should ask is what the investment objectives are of HPLU. Addressing directly the two statements Mr. Steven made, consider the first. Mr. Stevens believes that by buying investment grade bonds the portfolio will not be exposed to a loss of principal. However, all bonds — investment grade and non-investment grade — are exposed to the potential loss of principal if interest rates rise (i.e., interest rate risk) if an issue must be sold prior to its maturity date. If a callable bond is purchased, there can be a loss of principal if the call price is less than the purchase price (i.e., call risk). The issue can also be downgraded (i.e., downgrade risk) or the market can require a higher spread (i.e., credit spread risk), both resulting in a decline in the price of an issue. This will result in a loss of principal if the issue must be sold prior to the maturity date.

   The request that the bond portfolio have 40% in issues that mature within three years will reduce the interest rate risk of the portfolio. However, it will expose the HPLU to reinvestment risk (assuming the investment horizon for HPLU is greater than three years) since when the bonds mature there is the risk that the proceeds received may have to be reinvested at a lower interest rate than the coupon rate of the maturing issues.

14. a. It is reasonable to assume that the municipality will not need to redeem proceeds from the pension fund to make current payments to beneficiaries. Instead, the investment objective is to have the fund grow in order to meet future payments that must be made to retiring employees. Investing in just high investment grade securities that mature in one month or less exposes the pension fund to substantial reinvestment risk. So, while the fund reduces its interest rate risk by investing in such securities, it increases exposure to reinvestment risk. In the case of a pension fund, it would be expected that it can absorb some level of interest rate risk but would not want to be exposed to substantial reinvestment risk. So, this investment strategy may not make sense for the municipality's pension fund.

b. The opposite is true for the operating fund. The municipality can be expected to need proceeds on a shorter term basis. It should be less willing to expose the operating fund to interest rate risk but willing to sacrifice investment income (i.e., willing to accept reinvestment risk).

15. It is difficult to interpret the duration of a portfolio consisting of non-dollar denominated government bonds. In addition to the problem of foreign-exchange risk, one must tackle the question of "when interest rates change" what country's interest rates change? For example, suppose that the assistant portfolio manager computed a duration of 4 for the portfolio. This means that if "interest rates" increase by 100 basis points, the portfolio will change by approximately 4%. But which country's interest rates are assumed to change. Basically it assumes that the interest rates of every country whose issue is held in the portfolio changes by the same number of basis points.

16. When the proposed redemption was announced, the securities were treated as short-term investments with a maturity of about six weeks — from the announcement date of January 26th to the redemption date of March 15th. When GECC canceled the proposed redemption issue and set the coupon rate as allowed by the indenture, the price of the issue declined because the new coupon rate was not competitive with market rates for issues with GECC's rating with the same time to the next reset date in three years.

17. A major risk is foreign exchange risk. This is the risk that the Japanese yen will depreciate relative to the British pound when a coupon payment or principal repayment is received. There is still the interest rate risk associated with the Japanese government bond that results from a rise in Japanese interest rates. There is reinvestment risk. There is credit risk, although this risk is minimal.

18. Certain events can impair the ability of an issue or issuer to repay its debt obligations. For example, a corporate takeover that increases the issuer's debt can result in a downgrade. Regulatory changes that reduce revenues or increase expenses of a regulated company or a company serving a market that is adversely impacted by the regulation will be downgraded if it is viewed by the rating agency that the ability to satisfy obligations has been impaired.

19. If this manager's portfolio is marked to market, the manager must be concerned with the bid prices provided to mark the position to market. With only one dealer, there is concern that if this dealer decides to discontinue making a market in this issue, bids must be obtained from a different source. Finally, this manager intends to finance the purchase. The lender of the funds (the dealer financing the purchase) will mark the position to market based on the price it determines and this price will reflect the liquidity risk. Consequently, this manager should be concerned with the liquidity risk even if the manager intends to hold the security to the maturity date.

20. The market bid-ask spread is the difference between the highest bid price and the lowest ask price. Dealers 3 and 4 have the best bid price ($96^{15}/_{32}$). Dealer 2 has the lowest ask price ($96^{17}/_{32}$). The market bid-ask spread is therefore $^2/_{32}$.

SOLUTIONS TO PRACTICE QUESTIONS

1. • The price for Issue A should be a premium since the coupon rate is greater than the yield required by the market. So, there is no error for Issue A.

   • The price for Issue B should be a discount since the coupon rate is less than the yield required by the market. So, there is no error for Issue B.

   • Issue C's coupon rate (0%) is less than the yield required by the market (5%). So, Issue C should be selling at a discount but the reported price is above par value. Hence, the reported price for Issue C is wrong.

   • Issue D's coupon rate (5.5%) is less than the yield required by the market (5.9%). So, Issue D should be selling at a discount but the reported price is above par value. Hence, the reported price for Issue D is wrong.

   • The price for Issue E should be par value since the coupon rate is equal to the yield required by the market. So, there is no error for Issue E.

   • Issue F's coupon rate (4½%) is greater than the yield required by the market (4.0%). So, Issue F should be selling at a premium but the reported price is below par value. Hence, the reported price for Issue F is wrong.

   • The coupon rate for Issue G and the yield required by the market are equal. So, the price should be par value. Since the reported price is above par value, Issue G's reported price is wrong.

2. Interest rate risk is the exposure of an issue to a change in the yield required by the market or to a change in interest rates. For option-free bonds selling at the same yield, maturity and coupon rate determine the interest rate risk of an issue. Since Issue 3 has both the longest maturity and the lowest coupon, it will have the greatest price sensitivity to changes in interest rates. The issue with the least **interest** rate risk is Issue 4 since it has the shortest maturity and the highest **coupon rate.**

3. Issues 5 and 7 have a higher coupon rate and a maturity less than or equal to Issues 4 and 6 and are trading at a higher yield. Thus, Issues 5 and 7 must have less interest rate risk. Issues 4 and 6 have the same maturity and coupon rate. However, Issue 4 is trading at a lower yield relative to issue 6 (7.00% versus 7.20%). Consequently, Issue 4 has the greatest interest rate risk.

4. a. If the market wants a higher margin than 120 basis points for similar issues to NotReal.com after issuance, the price will decline because the quoted margin for the issue (120 basis points) is a below market margin. Even when the coupon rate is reset it will be less than the market required rate for similar issues.

   b. At the time NotReal.com was purchased by an investor, the coupon rate based on the 6-month Treasury rate of 4% was 5.2% (4% plus 120 basis points) considerably below the cap of 8.5%. With the assumed 6-month Treasury rate at 7.0%, the coupon rate is 8.2% (7% plus 120 basis points). Obviously, this is much closer to the cap of 8.5%. While cap risk was present at the time of purchase of this issue, the cap risk was low. With the rise in the 6-month Treasury rate to 7%, cap risk is considerably greater.

5. a. In our illustration,

> price if yields decline by 25 basis points = 108.50
> price if yields rise by 25 basis points = 104.00
> initial price = 106.00
> change in yield in decimal = 0.0025

$$\text{duration} = \frac{108.50 - 104.00}{2(106.00)(0.0025)} = 8.49$$

b. For a 100 basis point change and a duration of 8.49, the price will change by approximately 8.49%. For a 50 basis point change it would change by approximately 4.245%. Since the current market value is $10 million, the market value will change by approximately $10 million times 4.245% or $424,500.

6. a. The portfolio will change by approximately 5% for a 100 basis point change in interest rates and 2.5% for a 50 basis point change. Since the current market value is $85 million, the portfolio's value will change by approximately 2.5% times $85 million, or $2,125,000.

b. The five bonds in the portfolio have different maturities, ranging from 2 years to 28 years. The assumption when using duration is that if interest rates change, the interest rate for all the maturities changes by the same number of basis points.

c. A 5-year rate duration of 1.5 means that if all other key rates are unchanged but the 5-year rate increases by 100 basis points, the value of the portfolio will change by approximately 1.5%.

Chapter 3

OVERVIEW OF BOND SECTORS AND INSTRUMENTS

LEARNING OUTCOME STATEMENTS

After reading this chapter you should be able to:

- identify the major sectors of the bond market.
- indicate the types of securities issued by the U.S. Department of the Treasury
- outline the Treasury auction process
- differentiate between on-the-run and off-the-run Treasury securities.
- outline how stripped Treasury securities are created
- distinguish between Treasury coupon strips and Treasury principal strips
- identify the problems with using Treasury strips as the spot rate for Treasury securities
- explain the different issuers of federal agency securities (federally related institutions and government sponsored enterprises)
- describe the different types of securities issued by federal agencies
- explain what a mortgage-backed security is
- summarize the cash flows for a mortgage-backed security
- state what a prepayment is and what prepayment risk is
- distinguish between a mortgage passthrough security and a collateralized mortgage obligation
- state the motivation for the creation of a collateralized mortgage obligation
- summarize the types of securities issued by municipalities
- distinguish between tax-backed debt obligations and revenue bonds
- describe the different types of tax-backed debt
- indicate what insured bonds and prerefunded bonds are
- summarize the bankruptcy process and bondholder rights
- list the factors considered by rating agencies in assigning a credit rating to a corporate debt instrument
- describe what secured debt, unsecured debt, and credit enhancements for corporate bonds are
- define what a default rate and a default loss rate are
- review the findings about corporate default rates and recovery rates
- describe what a medium-term note is
- identify the differences between a corporate bond and a medium-term note
- describe what a structured note is and the motivation for their issuance by corporations
- describe what commercial paper is
- list the different types of commercial paper
- describe what an asset-backed security is
- summarize the role of a special purpose vehicle in an asset-backed securities transaction
- state the motivation for a corporation to issue an asset-backed security
- identify the different types of international bonds (foreign bonds, Eurobonds, global bonds, and non-U.S. government securities)
- list the different methods used by non-U.S. governments to issue bonds
- explain why rating agencies assign two ratings to the debt of non-U.S. government debt (local currency debt rating and foreign currency debt rating)

SECTION I
INTRODUCTION

Thus far we have mentioned the various sectors of the bond market and the general features of bonds. In this chapter, we will review the major sectors of the bond market and the securities issued. This includes Treasury securities, stripped Treasury securities, federal agency securities, municipal securities, corporate debt instruments, asset-backed securities, and international bonds. Our coverage in this chapter is simply a description of the products found in these sectors. How to analyze them is covered at Level II.

SECTION II
U.S. TREASURY
SECURITIES

Treasury securities are issued by the United States Department of the Treasury and are backed by the full faith and credit of the United States government. Market participants view Treasury securities as having no credit risk.

A. Types of Treasury Securities

There are two types of Treasury securities: discount and coupon securities. Treasury coupon securities come in two forms: fixed-rate and variable-rate securities.

1. Treasury Bills

Discount Treasuries are issued at a discount to par value, have no coupon rate, and mature at par value. The current practice of the Treasury is to issue all securities with a maturity of one year or less as discount securities. These securities are called **Treasury bills**. As discussed below, Treasury bills are issued on a regular basis with initial maturities of 91 days, 182 days, and 364 days. Because of holidays, these days may be either lower or higher by 1 day. They are more popularly referred to as 3-month, 6-month, and 1-year Treasury bills. At irregular intervals the Treasury also issues **cash management bills** with maturities ranging from a few days to about six months. They are occasionally issued a few days or weeks before a large tax payment is due in March, April, June, and September to tide the Treasury over a brief period of cash shortfall.

As discount securities, Treasury bills do not pay coupon interest. Instead, Treasury bills are issued at a discount from their maturity value; the return to the investor is the difference between the maturity value and the purchase price. We will explain how the price and the yield for a Treasury bill are computed in Chapter 6.

2. Treasury Notes and Bonds

All securities with initial maturities of two years or more are issued as coupon securities. Coupon securities are issued at approximately par, have a coupon rate, and mature at par value. Treasury coupon securities issued with original maturities of more than one year and no more than 10 years are called **Treasury notes**. Treasury coupon securities with original maturities greater than 10 years are called **Treasury bonds**. Treasury notes and bonds are referred to as **Treasury coupon securities**. Treasury coupon securities are currently auctioned on a regular basis with initial maturities of 2 years, 5 years, 10 years, and 30 years. On quote sheets, an "n" is used to denote a Treasury note. No notation typically follows an issue to identify it as a bond.

None of the currently issued Treasury coupon securities are callable. The 30-year bonds issued through November 1984 were callable but issues since then all have been noncallable. Outstanding callable Treasury bonds are callable five years prior to their maturity date and identified by two dates: when the bond is first callable and the maturity date. The call price is par value. There are currently only 16 callable Treasury bond issues outstanding.

---

3. Treasury Inflation Protection Securities

On January 29, 1997, the U.S. Department of the Treasury issued for the first time Treasury securities that adjust for inflation. These securities are popularly referred to as **Treasury inflation protection securities** or TIPS. (The Treasury refers to these securities as Treasury inflation indexed securities, TIIS.) The Treasury has issued TIPS that are notes and bonds. TIPS work as follows. The coupon rate on an issue is set at a fixed rate. That rate is determined via the auction process described later in this section. The coupon rate is called the "real rate" since it is the rate that the investor ultimately earns above the inflation rate. The inflation index that the government has decided to use for the inflation adjustment is the non-seasonally adjusted U.S. City Average All Items Consumer Price Index for All Urban Consumers (CPI-U).

The adjustment for inflation is as follows. The principal that the Treasury Department will base both the dollar amount of the coupon payment and the maturity value on is adjusted semiannually. This is called the **inflation-adjusted principal**. For example, suppose that the coupon rate for a TIPS is 3.5% and the annual inflation rate is 3%. Suppose further that an investor purchases on January 1 $100,000 of par value (principal) of this issue. The semiannual inflation rate is 1.5% (3% divided by 2). The inflation-adjusted principal at the end of the first six-month period is found by multiplying the original par value by the semiannual inflation rate. In our example, the inflation-adjusted principal at the end of the first six-month period is $101,500. It is this inflation-adjusted principal that is the basis for computing the coupon interest for the first six-month period. The coupon payment is then 1.75% (one half the real rate of 3.5%) multiplied by the inflation-adjusted principal at the coupon payment date ($101,500). The coupon payment is therefore $1,776.25

Let's look at the next six months. The inflation-adjusted principal at the beginning of the period is $101,500. Suppose that the semiannual inflation rate for the second six-month period is 1%. Then the inflation-adjusted principal at the end of the second six-month period is the inflation-adjusted principal at the beginning of the six-month period ($101,500) increased by the semiannual inflation rate (1%). The adjustment to the principal is $1,015 (1% times $101,500). So, the inflation-adjusted principal at the end of the second six-month period (December 31 in our example) is $102,515 ($101,500 + $1,015). The coupon interest that will be paid to the investor at the second coupon payment date is found by multiplying the inflation-adjusted principal on the coupon payment date ($102,515) by one half the real rate (i.e., one half of 3.5%). That is, the coupon payment will be $1,794.01.

As can be seen, part of the adjustment for inflation comes in the coupon payment since it is based on the inflation-adjusted principal. However, the U.S. government has decided to tax the adjustment each year. This feature reduces the attractiveness of TIPS as investments in accounts of tax-paying entities.

Because of the possibility of disinflation (i.e., price declines), the inflation-adjusted principal at maturity may turn out to be less than the initial par value. However, the Treasury has structured TIPS so that they are redeemed at the greater of the inflation-adjusted principal and the initial par value.

An inflation-adjusted principal must be calculated for a settlement date. The inflation-adjusted principal is defined in terms of an index ratio which is the ratio of the reference CPI for the settlement date to the reference CPI for the issue date. The reference

CPI is calculated with a 3-month lag. For example, the reference CPI for May 1 is the CPI-U reported in February. The U.S. Department of the Treasury publishes and makes available on its website (www.publicdebt.treas.gov) a daily index ratio for an issue.

PRACTICE QUESTION 1

Suppose an investor purchases $10,000 of par value of a Treasury inflation protection security. The real rate (determined at the auction) is 3.8%.

a. Assume that at the end of the first six months the CPI-U is 2.4% (annual rate). Compute the (i) inflation adjustment to principal at the end of the first six months, (ii) the inflation-adjusted principal at the end of the first six months, and (iii) the coupon payment made to the investor at the end of the first six months.

b. Assume that at the end of the second six months the CPI-U is 2.8% (annual rate). Compute the (i) inflation adjustment to principal at the end of the second six months, (ii) the inflation-adjusted principal at the end of the second six months, and (iii) the coupon payment made to the investor at the end of the second six months.

B. The Treasury Auction Process

Treasury securities are all issued on an auction basis. The auction process is a computerized auction system which can be electronically accessed by qualified broker-dealers.

1. Auction Cycles

The U.S. Department of the Treasury makes the determination of the procedure for auctioning new Treasury securities, when to auction them, and what maturities to issue. There have been occasional changes in the auction cycles and the maturity of the issues auctioned. The current auction cycles are as follows. There are weekly 3-month and 6-month bill auctions; "year-bill" auctions are every fourth week. For coupon securities, there are monthly 2-year note and 5-year note auctions and quarterly auctions for the 10-year note and 30-year bond (the "refunding" auction).[1]

On the announcement day, the Treasury announces the amount of each issue to be auctioned, the auction date, and maturities to be issued. Occasionally an outstanding issue is "re-opened" (that is, the amount of an outstanding note is increased) at an auction instead of a new issue auctioned. In recent years, the Department of the Treasury has re-opened the 10-year note several times.

2. Determination of the Results of an Auction

The auction for Treasury securities is conducted on a **competitive bid basis**. There are actually two types of bids that may be submitted by a bidder: noncompetitive bid and competitive bid. A **noncompetitive bid** is submitted by an entity that is willing to purchase the auctioned security at the yield that is determined by the auction process. Typically, individual investors purchase Treasury securities at the auction by submit-

---

[1] Prior to 2000, the Treasury issued 3-year, 4-year, and 7-year notes and 15-year and 20-year bonds. Recently, the Treasury has reduced its issuance of bonds and has repurchased bonds in the open market. This has reduced the amount of Treasury bonds outstanding and this may have important implications for the use of long-term Trearury bonds as a benchmark for interest rates.

ting noncompetitive bids, as do smaller institutional investors. When a noncompetitive bid is submitted, the bidder only specifies the quantity sought. This quantity in a noncompetitive bid may not exceed $1 million for Treasury bills and $5 million for Treasury coupon securities. A **competitive bid** specifies both the quantity sought and the yield at which the bidder is willing to purchase the auctioned security. Competitive bids are typically submitted by broker/dealers, depository institutions, and some of the larger money management firms.

The auction results are determined by first deducting the total noncompetitive tenders and non-public purchases (such as purchases by the Federal Reserve itself) from the total securities being auctioned. The remainder is the amount to be awarded to the competitive bidders. For example, in April 1996 there was an auction for the 2-year Treasury note. The amount auctioned by the Treasury was $19.946 billion. The non-competitive bids totaled $1.169 billion. This meant that there was $18.777 billion to be distributed to competitive bidders. For this auction, there were bids for $47.604 billion.

The bids are then arranged from the lowest yield bid to the highest yield bid. This is equivalent to arranging the bids from the highest price to the lowest price. Starting from the lowest yield bid, all competitive bids are accepted until the amount to be distributed to the competitive bidders is completely allocated. The highest yield accepted by the Treasury is referred to as the **stop yield**, and bidders at that yield are awarded a percentage of their total tender offer. For the 2-year Treasury auction in April 1996, the stop yield was 5.939%. Bidders higher in yield than the stop yield were not distributed any of the new issue. Suppose at the stop yield there were $2 billion in bids but only $1 billion remaining to be allocated after allocating to all bidders who bid higher than the stop yield. Then each bidder who bid the stop yield will receive 50% of the amount that they bid for. So, if an entity bid for $5 million, then that entity will receive only $2.5 million.

All U.S. Treasury auctions are single-price auctions. In a single-price auction, all bidders are awarded securities at the highest yield of accepted competitive tenders (i.e., the stop yield). This type of auction is called a "Dutch auction." Historically, the Treasury auctioned securities through multiple-price auctions. With multiple-price auctions, the Treasury still accepted the lowest-yielding bids up to the yield required to sell the amount offered (less the amount of noncompetitive bids), but accepted bids were awarded at the particular yields bid, rather than at the stop-out yield. In September 1992 the Treasury started conducting single-price auctions for the 2- and 5-year notes. In November 1998 the Treasury adopted the single-price method for all auctions.

C. The Secondary Market

The secondary market for Treasury securities is an over-the-counter market where a group of U.S. government securities dealers offer continuous bid and ask prices on outstanding Treasuries. There is virtual 24-hour trading of Treasury securities. The three primary trading locations are New York, London, and Tokyo. The normal settlement period for Treasury securities is the business day after the transaction day ("next day" settlement).

The most recently auctioned issue is referred to as the **on-the-run issue** or the **current issue**. For example, in May 1999, the on-the-run 30-year Treasury issue was the 5.25s of 2/15/2029. Securities that are replaced by the on-the-run issue are called **off-the-run issues**. For example, prior to the issuance of the 5.25s of 2/15/2029, the on-the-run 30-year Treasury issue was the 5.25s of 11/15/2028 and in May

1999 became an off-the run issue. At a given point in time there may be more than one off-the-run issue with approximately the same remaining maturity as the on-the-run issue. Issues that have been replaced by several on-the-run issues are said to be "well off-the-run issues." For example, in May 1999, the 30-year 6.5% coupon issued in November 1996 and due in May 2026 was a well off-the-run issue.

Treasury securities are traded prior to the time they are issued by the Treasury. This component of the Treasury secondary market is called the **when-issued market**, or **wi market**. When-issued trading for both bills and coupon securities extends from the day the auction is announced until the issue day.

Government dealers trade with the investing public and with other dealer firms. When they trade with each other, it is through intermediaries known as **inter-dealer brokers**. Dealers leave firm bids and offers with interdealer brokers who display the highest bid and lowest offer in a computer network tied to each trading desk and displayed on a monitor. Dealers use interdealer brokers because of the speed and efficiency with which trades can be accomplished. Interdealer brokers keep the names of the dealers involved in trades confidential. The quotes provided on the government dealer screens represent prices in the "inside" or "interdealer" market.

D. Price Quotes

Treasury coupon securities trade on a dollar price basis in price units of $\frac{1}{32}$ of 1% of par value. Par is taken to be $100. For example, a quote of 92-14 refers to a price of 92 and $\frac{14}{32}$. The number after the hyphen represents the number of 32nds. Thus the quoted price is 92.4375% of par value. If par value is $100,000, the quoted price is $92,437.50. On the basis of $100,000 par value, a change in price of 1% equates to $1,000, and $\frac{1}{32}$ equates to $31.25. A plus sign following the number of 32nds means that a 64th is added to the price. For example, 92-14+ refers to a price of 92 and $\frac{29}{64}$ or 92.453125% of par value. Prices can be refined to intervals even finer than 64ths (to 128ths and maybe even 256ths).

Sometimes a quote is shown with a decimal rather than a hyphen. The convention in the Treasury coupon market is the same as that with a hyphen. That is, a quote of 92.14 means 92 and $\frac{14}{32}$. In the illustrations throughout this book, we will *not* use this convention. Consequently, when a decimal is used in a price quote it represents a percentage of par value. So, 92.14 would mean 92.14% of par value.

PRACTICE QUESTION 2

Below are quotes for Treasury coupon securities. Complete the following table for the price per $100 par value and the price for the par value indicated.

Price quote	Price per $100 par	Par value ($)	Price for par value ($)
86-16		10,000	
97-27+		100,000	
106-11		500,000	
111-4+		1,000,000	

SECTION III TREASURY STRIPS

The Treasury does not issue zero-coupon notes or bonds. However, because of the demand for zero-coupon instruments with no credit risk and a maturity greater than one year, the private sector has created such securities.

Exhibit 4: Coupon Stripping: Creating Zero-Coupon Treasury Securities

Security

Par: $100 million Coupon: 10%, semiannual Maturity: 10 years

Cash flows

| Coupon:
$5 million
Receipt in:
6 months | Coupon:
$5 million
Receipt in:
1 year | Coupon:
$5 million
Receipt in:
1.5 years | .... | Coupon:
$5 million
Receipt in:
10 years | Principal:
$100 million
Receipt in:
10 years |

Zero-coupon Treasury securities created

| Maturity value:
$5 million
Maturity:
6 months | Maturity value:
$5 million
Maturity:
1 year | Maturity value:
$5 million
Maturity:
1.5 years | .... | Maturity value:
$5 million
Maturity:
10 years | Maturity value:
$100 million
Maturity:
10 years |

To illustrate the process, suppose $100 million of a Treasury note with a 10-year maturity and a coupon rate of 10% is purchased to create zero-coupon Treasury securities (see Exhibit 1). The cash flows from this Treasury note are 20 semiannual payments of $5 million each ($100 million times 10% divided by 2) and the repayment of principal ("corpus") of $100 million 10 years from now. Receipts are then issued, each with a different single payment claim on the underlying Treasury note. As there are 21 different payments to be made by the Treasury, a receipt representing a single payment claim on each payment is issued, which is effectively a zero-coupon instrument. The amount of the maturity value for a receipt on a particular payment, whether coupon or principal, depends on the amount of the payment to be made by the Treasury on the underlying Treasury note. In our example, 20 coupon receipts each have a maturity value of $5 million, and one receipt, the principal, has a maturity value of $100 million. The maturity dates for the receipts coincide with the corresponding payment dates for the Treasury security that was stripped.

Today, these zero-coupon instruments are issued through the Treasury's Separate Trading of Registered Interest and Principal Securities (STRIPS) program, a program designed to facilitate the stripping of Treasury securities. The zero-coupon Treasury securities created under the STRIPS program are direct obligations of the U.S. government. Moreover, the securities clear through the Federal Reserve's book-entry system. Creation of the STRIPS program in February 1985 ended the origination of other types of zero-coupon instruments that had been issued by dealer firms.

Stripped Treasury securities are simply referred to as **Treasury strips**. On dealer quote sheets and vendor screens they are identified by whether the cash flow is created from the coupon (denoted "ci"), principal from a Treasury bond (denoted "bp"), or principal from a Treasury note (denoted "np"). Strips created from coupon payments are called **coupon strips** and those created from the principal are called **principal strips**. The reason why a distinction is made between coupon strips and the principal strips has to do with the tax treatment by non-U.S. entities as discussed below.

A disadvantage of a taxable entity investing in Treasury strips is that accrued interest is taxed each year even though interest is not paid. Thus, these instruments are negative cash flow instruments until the maturity date. They have negative cash flow since tax payments on interest earned but not received in cash must be made. One reason for distinguishing between strips created from the principal and coupon is that some foreign buyers have a preference for the strips created from the principal (i.e., the principal strips). This preference is due to the tax treatment of the interest in their home country. Some country's tax laws treat the interest as a capital gain if the principal strip is purchased. The capital gain receives a preferential tax treatment (i.e., lower tax rate) compared to ordinary income.

SECTION IV FEDERAL AGENCY SECURITIES

Federal agency securities can be classified by the type of issuer, those issued by **federally related institutions** and those issued by **government sponsored enterprises**.

Federally related institutions (also referred to as government owned agencies) are arms of the federal government and generally do not issue securities directly in the marketplace. The major issuers have been the Tennessee Valley Authority (TVA) and the Government National Mortgage Association (Ginnie Mae). All federally related institutions are exempt from SEC registration. With the exception of securities of the TVA and the Private Export Funding Corporation, the securities are backed by the full faith and credit of the United States government.

Government sponsored enterprises (GSEs) are privately owned, publicly chartered entities. They were created by Congress to reduce the cost of capital for certain borrowing sectors of the economy deemed to be important enough to warrant assistance. The entities in these privileged sectors include farmers, homeowners, and students. Government sponsored enterprises issue securities directly in the marketplace.

Today there are five GSEs that issue securities: Federal Farm Credit System, Federal Home Loan Bank System, Federal National Mortgage Association (Fannie Mae), Federal Home Loan Bank Corporation (Freddie Mac), and Student Loan Marketing Association (Sallie Mae). The Federal Farm Credit Bank System is responsible for the credit market in the agricultural sector of the economy. The Federal Home Loan Bank, Freddie Mac, and Fannie Mae are responsible for providing credit to the housing sectors. Sallie Mae provides funds to support higher education. With the exception of the securities issued by the Federal Farm Credit Financial Assistance Corporation, GSE securities are not backed by the full faith and credit of the U.S. government, as is the case with Treasury and federally related securities. Consequently, investors purchasing GSEs are exposed to credit risk.

A. Agency Debentures

The securities issued by GSEs are one of two types: **debentures** and **mortgage-backed/asset-backed securities**. Debentures do not have any specific collateral backing the bond. The ability to repay bondholders depends on the ability of the issuing GSE to generate sufficient cash flows to satisfy the obligation. Several GSEs are frequent issuers of securities and therefore have developed regular programs for securities that they issue. For example, let's look at the debentures issued by Fannie Mae and Freddie Mac. (The mortgage-backed securities issued by these two GSEs are described later.)

Fannie Mae issues short-term debentures, Benchmark Bills, discount notes, medium-term notes, Benchmark Notes, Benchmark Bonds, Callable Benchmark Notes, and global bonds. We will discuss medium-term notes and global bonds in Section VI and Section VIII, respectively. Short-term debentures have maturities of one year or less and pay interest semiannually. They may be noncallable (bullets) or have a callable feature. **Benchmark Bills** and discount notes are issued at a discount from their maturity value and have maturities of 360 days or less. **Benchmark Notes** are large issues ($2 to $5 billion in initial size) of 5-year to 10-year maturity and are noncallable. Fannie Mae expects to either issue a new Benchmark Note monthly or reopen a current issue according to a published issuance calendar. Benchmark Bonds are large ($2 to $4 billion initial size) 30-year maturity issues which are issued or reopened twice a year. Both Benchmark Notes and Bonds are eligible for stripping. **Callable Benchmark Notes** are issued with the following call structures: 5-year maturity not callable for 2 years (denoted "5nc2 year"), 5-year maturity not callable for 3 years (denoted "5nc3 year"), 10-year maturity not callable for 3 years (denoted "10nc3 year"), and 10-year maturity not callable for 5 years (denoted "10nc5 year"). The minimum size for a new issue is $500 million and for a reopened issue is $100 million. The Benchmark Notes and the Callable Benchmark Notes were funding programs introduced by Fannie Mae in recognition of the importance of improving liquidity for its issues by offering large-size issues. We will discuss the affect of size on liquidity and therefore on yield spread in Chapter 4.

Freddie Mac issues Reference Bills, discount notes, medium-term notes, Reference Notes, Callable Reference Bonds, Reference Notes, and global bonds. **Reference Bills** and discount notes are issued with maturities of one year or less. **Reference Notes** and **Callable Reference Notes** have maturities of 2 to 10 years and are the equivalent to Fannie Mae's Benchmark Notes and Callable Benchmark Notes. Freddie Mac will issue and/or reopen Reference Bills, Reference Notes, and 30-year Reference Bonds according to a published issuance calendar. Initial Reference Note sizes will be $3 to $6 billion, with $2 billion minimum reopenings and initial Reference Bond sizes of $2 billion with $1 billion minimum reopenings. Freddie Mac Reference Notes and Reference Bonds are eligible for stripping.

B. Agency Mortgage-Backed Securities

The two GSEs charged with providing liquidity to the mortgage market — Fannie Mae and Freddie Mac — also issue securities backed by the mortgage loans that they purchase. That is, they use the mortgage loans themselves as collateral for the securities they issue. These securities are called **agency mortgage-backed securities**. Sallie Mae acquires student loans and issues securities backed by the student loans called asset-backed securities. We will discuss asset-backed securities in Section VII.

Since 1969, pools of mortgage loans on residential properties have been used by federal agencies as collateral for the creation of securities, popularly referred to as **mortgage-backed securities**. These securities include mortgage passthrough securities, collateralized mortgage obligations (CMOs), and stripped mortgage-backed securities. The latter two mortgage-backed securities are referred to as derivative mortgage-backed securities because they are created from mortgage passthrough securities.

A description of even the basic features of mortgage-backed securities is not simple. Two chapters are devoted to a description and analysis of these securities at Level II. Here we provide the most basic elements about two of the mortgage-backed securities issued by federal agencies — Fannie Mae and Freddie Mac (GSEs) and Ginnie Mae — mortgage passthrough securities and collateralized mortgage obligations. At Level II we will discuss mortgage-backed securities not issued by federal agencies.

1. Mortgage Loans

A **mortgage loan** is a loan secured by the collateral of some specified real estate property which obliges the borrower to make a predetermined series of payments. The mortgage gives the lender the right, if the borrower defaults, to "foreclose" on the loan and seize the property in order to ensure that the debt is paid off. The interest rate on the mortgage loan is called the **mortgage rate** or **contract rate**.

There are many types of mortgage designs available in the United States. A mortgage design is a specification of the mortgage rate, term of the mortgage, and the manner in which the borrowed funds are repaid. At Level II we will discuss different types of mortgage designs. For now, we will use the most common mortgage design to explain the characteristics of mortgage-backed security: a fixed-rate, level-payment, fully amortized mortgage.

The basic idea behind this mortgage design is that each monthly mortgage payment is the same dollar amount and includes interest and principal repayment. The monthly payments are such that at the end of the loan's term, the loan has been fully amortized (i.e., there is no mortgage balance outstanding).

Each monthly mortgage payment for this mortgage design is due on the first of each month and consists of:

1. interest of $1/12$ of the fixed annual interest rate times the amount of the outstanding mortgage balance at the beginning of the previous month, and
2. a repayment of a portion of the outstanding mortgage balance (principal).

The difference between the monthly mortgage payment and the portion of the payment that represents interest equals the amount that is applied to reduce the outstanding mortgage balance. This amount is referred to as the **amortization**. We shall also refer to it as the **scheduled principal repayment**.

To illustrate this mortgage design, consider a 30-year (360-month), $100,000 mortgage with an 8.125% mortgage rate. The monthly mortgage payment would be $742.50.[2] Exhibit 2 shows for selected months how each monthly mortgage payment is divided between interest and scheduled principal repayment of principal. At the beginning of month 1, the mortgage balance is $100,000, the amount of the original loan. The mortgage payment for month 1 includes interest on the $100,000 borrowed for the month. Since the interest rate is 8.125%, the monthly interest rate is 0.0067708 (0.08125 divided by 12). Interest for month 1 is therefore $677.08 ($100,000 times 0.0067708). The $65.41 difference between the monthly mortgage payment of $742.50 and the interest of $677.08 is the portion of the monthly mortgage payment that represents the scheduled principal repayment (i.e., amortization). This $65.41 in month 1 reduces the mortgage balance.

---

[2] The calculation of the monthly mortgage payment is simply an application of the present value of an annuity. The formula as applied to mortgage payments is as follows:

$$MP = B \left[\frac{r(1+r)^n}{(1+r)^n - 1} \right]$$

where

MP = monthly mortgage payment
B = amount borrowed (i.e., original loan balance)
r = monthly mortgage rate (annual rate divided by 12)
n = number of months of the mortgage loan

In our example,

$B = \$100,000$ $r = 0.0067708 \ (0.08125/12)$ $n = 360$

Then

$$MP = \$100,000 \left[\frac{0.0067708(1.0067708)^{360}}{(1.0067708)^{360} - 1} \right] = \$742.50$$

Exhibit 5: Amortization Schedule for a Level-Payment, Fixed-Rate, Fully Amortized Mortgage (Selected Months)

Mortgage loan: $100,000   Monthly payment: $742.50

Mortgage rate: 8.125%   Term of loan: 30 years (360 months)

(1) Month	(2) Beginning of Month Mortgage Balance	(3) Mortgage Payment	(4) Interest	(5) Scheduled Principal Repayment	(6) End of Month Mortgage Balance
1	$100,000.00	$742.50	$677.08	$65.41	$99,934.59
2	99,934.59	742.50	676.64	65.86	99,868.73
3	99,868.73	742.50	676.19	66.30	99,802.43
4	99,802.43	742.50	675.75	66.75	99,735.68
. . .	. . .	. . .	. . .	. . .	. . .
25	98,301.53	742.50	665.58	76.91	98,224.62
26	98,224.62	742.50	665.06	77.43	98,147.19
27	98,147.19	742.50	664.54	77.96	98,069.23
. . .	. . .	. . .	. . .	. . .	. . .
184	76,446.29	742.50	517.61	224.89	76,221.40
185	76,221.40	742.50	516.08	226.41	75,994.99
186	75,994.99	742.50	514.55	227.95	75,767.04
. . .	. . .	. . .	. . .	. . .	. . .
289	42,200.92	742.50	285.74	456.76	41,744.15
290	41,744.15	742.50	282.64	459.85	41,284.30
291	41,284.30	742.50	279.53	462.97	40,821.33
. . .	. . .	. . .	. . .	. . .	. . .
358	2,197.66	742.50	14.88	727.62	1,470.05
359	1,470.05	742.50	9.95	732.54	737.50
360	737.50	742.50	4.99	737.50	0.00

The mortgage balance at the end of month 1 (beginning of month 2) is then $99,934.59 ($100,000 minus $65.41). The interest for the second monthly mortgage payment is $676.64, the monthly interest rate (0.0066708) times the mortgage balance at the beginning of month 2 ($99,934.59). The difference between the $742.50 monthly mortgage payment and the $676.64 interest is $65.86, representing the amount of the mortgage balance paid off with that monthly mortgage payment. Notice that the mortgage payment in month 360 — the final payment — is sufficient to pay off the remaining mortgage balance.

As Exhibit 2 clearly shows, the portion of the monthly mortgage payment applied to interest declines each month and the portion applied to principal repayment increases. The reason for this is that as the mortgage balance is reduced with each monthly mortgage payment, the interest on the mortgage balance declines. Since the monthly mortgage payment is a fixed dollar amount, an increasingly larger portion of the monthly payment is applied to reduce the mortgage balance outstanding in each subsequent month.

To an investor in a mortgage loan (or a pool of mortgage loans), the monthly mortgage payments as described above are not the investor's cash flow. There are two reasons for this: (1) servicing fees and (2) prepayments.

Every mortgage loan must be serviced. Servicing of a mortgage loan involves collecting monthly payments and forwarding proceeds to owners of the loan; sending payment notices to mortgagors; reminding mortgagors when payments are overdue; maintaining records of principal balances; administering an escrow balance for real estate taxes and insurance purposes; initiating foreclosure proceedings if necessary; and, furnishing tax information to mortgagors when applicable. The servicing fee is a portion of the mortgage rate. If the mortgage rate is 8.125% and the servicing fee is 50 basis points, then the investor receives interest of 7.625%. The interest rate that the investor receives is said to be the **net interest**.

Our illustration of the cash flow for a level-payment, fixed-rate, fully amortized mortgage assumes that the homeowner does not pay off any portion of the mortgage balance prior to the scheduled due date. But homeowners do pay off all or part of their mortgage balance prior to the scheduled date. A payment made in excess of the monthly mortgage payment is called a **prepayment**. The prepayment may be for the entire outstanding balance or a partial pay off of the mortgage balance. When a prepayment is not for the entire amount it is called a **curtailment**. Typically, there is no penalty for prepaying a mortgage loan.

Thus, the cash flows for a mortgage loan are monthly and consist of three components: (1) net interest, (2) scheduled principal repayment, and (3) prepayments. The effect of prepayments is that the amount and timing of the cash flow from a mortgage is not known with certainty. This is the risk that we referred to as **prepayment risk** in Chapter 2.[3]

For example, all that the investor in a $100,000, 8.125% 30-year mortgage knows is that as long as the loan is outstanding and the borrower does not default, interest will be received and the principal will be repaid at the scheduled date each month; then at the end of the 30 years, the investor would have received $100,000 in principal payments. What the investor does not know — the uncertainty — is for how long the loan will be outstanding, and therefore what the timing of the principal payments will be. This is true for all mortgage loans, not just the level-payment, fixed-rate, fully amortized mortgage.

PRACTICE QUESTION 3

Suppose that a mortgage loan for $100,000 is obtained for 30 years. The mortgage is a level-payment, fixed-rate, fully amortized mortgage. The mortgage rate is 7.5% and the monthly mortgage payment is $699.21. Compute an amortization schedule as shown in Exhibit 2 for the first six months.

---

2. Mortgage Passthrough Securities

A **mortgage passthrough security,** or simply passthrough, is a security created when one or more holders of mortgages form a collection (pool) of mortgages and sell shares or participation certificates in the pool. A pool may consist of several thousand or only a few mortgages. When a mortgage is included in a pool of mortgages that is used as collateral for a passthrough, the mortgage is said to be **securitized.**

The cash flow of a passthrough depends on the cash flow of the underlying pool of mortgages. As we just explained, the cash flow consists of monthly mortgage payments representing net interest, the scheduled principal repayment, and any prepayments. Payments are made to security holders each month. Because of prepayments, the amount of the cash flow is uncertain in terms of the timing of the principal repayment.

To illustrate the creation of a passthrough look at Exhibits 3 and 4. Exhibit 3 shows 2,000 mortgage loans and the cash flows from these loans. For the sake of simplicity, we assume that the amount of each loan is $100,000 so that the aggregate value of all ten loans is $200 million.

---

[3] Factors affecting prepayments will be discussed at Level II.

Exhibit 6: Mortgage Loans

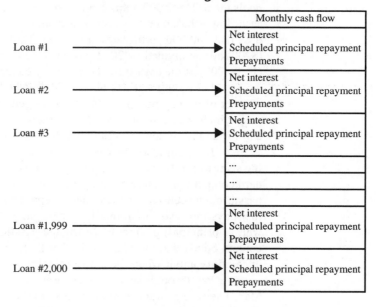

Exhibit 7: Creation of a Passthrough Security

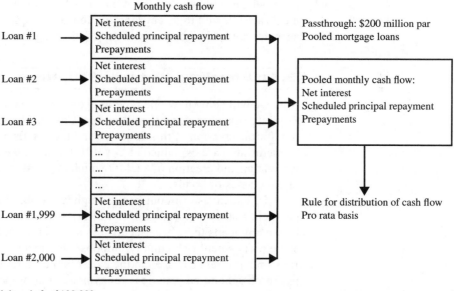

Each loan is for $100,000.
Total loans: $200 million.

An investor who owns any one of the individual mortgage loans shown in Exhibit 3 faces prepayment risk. In the case of an individual loan, it is particularly difficult to predict prepayments. If an individual investor were to purchase all 2,000 loans, however, prepayments might become more predictable based on historical prepayment experience. However, that would call for an investment of $200 million to buy all 2,000 loans.

Suppose, instead, that some entity purchases all 2,000 loans in Exhibit 3 and pools them. The 2,000 loans can be used as collateral for the issuance of a security whose cash flow is based on the cash flow from the 2,000 loans, as depicted in Exhibit 4. Suppose that 200,000 certificates are issued. Thus, each certificate is initially worth $1,000 ($200 million divided by 200,000). Each certificate holder would be entitled to 0.0005% (1/200,000) of the cash flow. The security created is a mortgage passthrough security.

Let's see what has been accomplished by creating the passthrough. The total amount of prepayment risk has not changed. Yet, the investor is now exposed to the prepayment risk spread over 2,000 loans rather than one individual mortgage loan, and for an investment of less than $200 million.

Let's compare the cash flow for a mortgage passthrough security (an amortizing security) to that of a standard coupon bond (a nonamortizing security). For a standard coupon bond there are no principal payments until maturity while for a mortgage passthrough security the principal is repaid over time. Unlike a standard coupon bond that pays interest semiannually, a mortgage passthrough makes monthly interest (as well as principal) payments. Mortgage passthrough securities are similar to standard coupon bonds that are callable in that there is uncertainty about the cash flow due to uncertainty about when the entire principal will be repaid.

Passthrough securities are issued by Ginnie Mae, Fannie Mae, and Freddie Mac. They are guaranteed with respect to the timely payment of interest and principal.[4] The loans that are permitted to be included in the pool of mortgage loans issued by Ginnie Mae, Fannie Mae, and Freddie Mac must meet the underwriting standards that have been established by these entities. Loans that satisfy the underwriting requirements are referred to as **conforming loans**. Mortgage-backed securities not issued by agencies are backed by pools of nonconforming loans.

3. Collateralized Mortgage Obligations

Now we will show how one type of agency mortgage derivative security is created — a **collateralized mortgage obligation** (CMO). A detailed explanation for the motivation for the creation of this structure and the details on how it is created (referred to as "structuring") are explained at Level II. For now, we'll give a brief explanation of the motivation and creation of a CMO which is to redistribute prepayment risk among different classes of bonds.

The investor in our passthrough in Exhibit 4 remains exposed to the total prepayment risk associated with the underlying pool of mortgage loans, regardless of how many loans there are. Securities can be created, however, where investors do not share prepayment risk equally. Suppose that instead of distributing the monthly cash flow on a pro rata basis, as in the case of a passthrough, the distribution of the principal (both scheduled principal repayments and prepayments) is carried out on some prioritized basis. How this is done is illustrated in Exhibit 5.

The exhibit shows the cash flow of our original 2,000 mortgage loans and the passthrough. Also shown are three classes of bonds, commonly referred to as **tranches,** the par value of each tranche, and a set of payment rules indicating how the principal from the passthrough is to be distributed to each tranche. Note that the sum of the par value of the three tranches is equal to $200 million. Although it is not shown

---

[4] Freddie Mac previously issued passthrough securities that guaranteed the timely payment of interest but guaranteed only the eventual repayment of principal (when it is collected or within one year).

in the exhibit, for each of the three tranches there will be certificates representing a proportionate interest in a tranche. For example, suppose that for Tranche A, which has a par value of $80 million, there are 80,000 certificates issued. Each certificate would receive a proportionate share (0.00125%) of payments received by Tranche A.

The rule for the distribution of principal shown in Exhibit 5 is that Tranche A will receive all principal (both scheduled and prepayments) until that tranche receives its entire par value of $80 million. Then, Tranche B receives all principal payments until it receives its par value of $70 million. After Tranche B is completely paid off, Tranche C receives principal payments. The rule for the distribution of the cash flows in Exhibit 5 indicates that each of the three tranches receives interest on the basis of the amount of the par value outstanding.

The mortgage-backed security that has been created is called a CMO. The collateral for a CMO issued by the agencies is a pool of passthrough securities which is placed in a trust. The ultimate source for the CMO's cash flow is the pool of mortgage loans.

Exhibit 8: Creation of a Collateralized Mortgage Obligation

Monthly cash flow

Loan #1 → Net interest / Scheduled principal repayment / Prepayments

Loan #2 → Net interest / Scheduled principal repayment / Prepayments

Loan #3 → Net interest / Scheduled principal repayment / Prepayments

...

...

...

Loan #1,999 → Net interest / Scheduled principal repayment / Prepayments

Loan #2,000 → Net interest / Scheduled principal repayment / Prepayments

Each loan is for $100,000.
Total loans: $200 million.

Passthrough: $200 million par
Pooled mortgage loans

Pooled monthly cash flow:
Net interest
Scheduled principal repayment
Prepayments

Rule for distribution of cash flow
Pro rata basis

Collateralized Mortgage Obligation (three tranches)

Rule for distribution of cash flow to three tranches

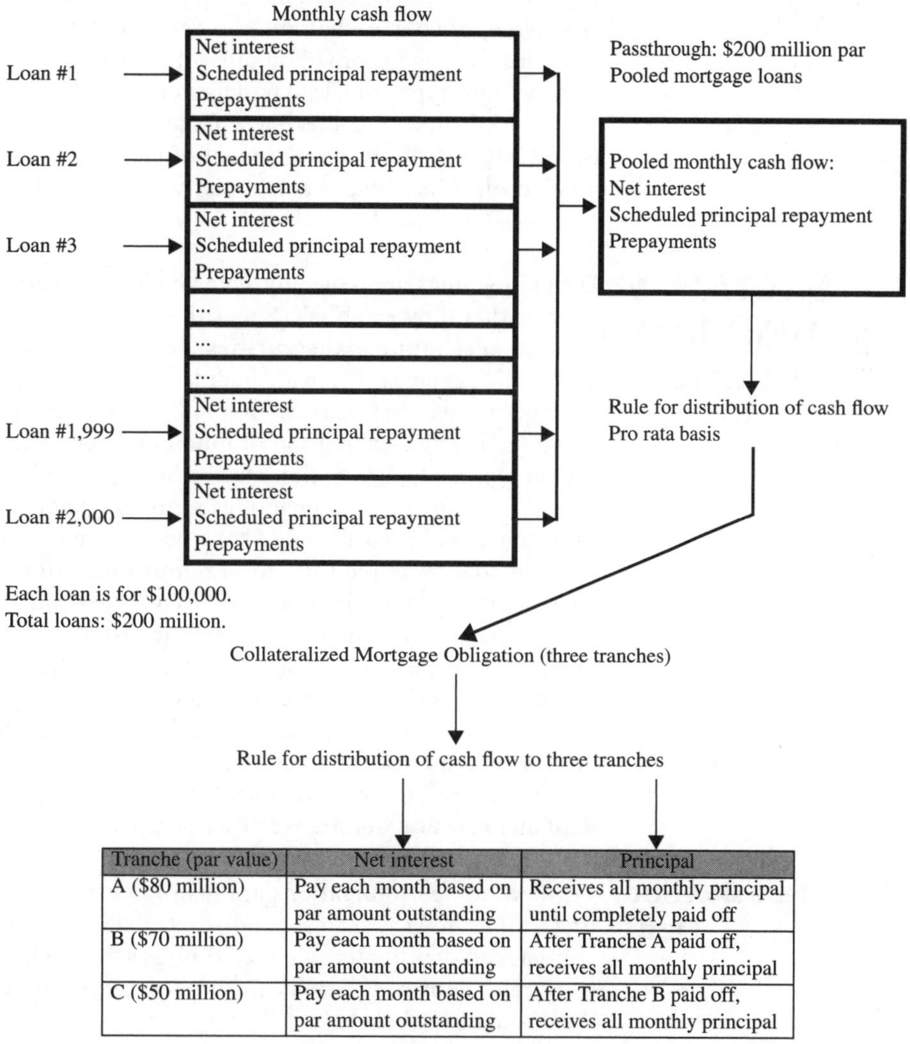

Tranche (par value)	Net interest	Principal
A ($80 million)	Pay each month based on par amount outstanding	Receives all monthly principal until completely paid off
B ($70 million)	Pay each month based on par amount outstanding	After Tranche A paid off, receives all monthly principal
C ($50 million)	Pay each month based on par amount outstanding	After Tranche B paid off, receives all monthly principal

Let's look now at what has been accomplished. Once again, the total prepayment risk for the CMO is the same as the total prepayment risk for the 2,000 mortgage loans. However, the prepayment risk has been distributed differently across the three tranches of the CMO. Tranche A absorbs prepayments first, then Tranche B, and then Tranche C. The result of this is that Tranche A effectively is a shorter term security than the other two tranches; Tranche C will have the longest maturity. Different institutional investors will be attracted to the different tranches, depending on the nature of their liabilities and the effective maturity of the CMO tranche. Moreover, there is less uncertainty about the maturity of each tranche of the CMO than there is about the maturity of the pool of passthroughs from which the CMO is created. Thus, redirection of the cash flow from the underlying mortgage pool creates tranches that satisfy the asset/liability objectives of certain institutional investors better than a passthrough. Stated differently, the rule for distributing principal repayments redistributes prepayment risk among the tranches.

The CMO we describe in Exhibit 5 has a simple set of rules for the distribution of the cash flow. Today, much more complicated CMO structures exist. The basic objective is to provide certain CMO tranches with less uncertainty about prepayment risk. Note, of course, that this can occur only if the reduction in prepayment risk for some tranches is absorbed by other tranches in the CMO structure. We will describe these various types of CMO tranches at Level II.

All three agencies have issued CMOs. Ginnie Mae was only authorized to issue CMO late in the development of the CMO market so the number and amount of CMO deals it has done is small relative to that of Fannie Mae and Freddie Mac.

SECTION V MUNICIPAL SECURITIES

Debt obligations are issued by state and local governments in the United States and by entities that they establish. Securities issued by any of these entities are popularly referred to as **municipal securities**, despite the fact that they are also issued by states and public agencies. There are both tax-exempt and taxable municipal securities. "Tax-exempt" means that interest on a municipal security is exempt from federal income taxation. The tax-exemption of municipal securities applies to interest income, not capital gains. The exemption may or may not extend to taxation at the state and local levels. Each state has its own rules as to how interest on municipal securities is taxed. Most municipal securities that have been issued are tax-exempt. Municipal securities are commonly referred to as **tax-exempt securities** despite the fact that there are taxable municipal securities that have been issued and are traded in the market.

Municipal securities expose investors to credit risk. The nationally recognized rating organizations rate municipal securities. In Level II, we look at the factors rating agencies consider in assessing credit risk.

Municipal bonds are traded in the over-the-counter market supported by municipal bond dealers across the country.

There are basically two types of municipal security structures: **tax-backed debt** and **revenue bonds**. We describe each type below, as well as variants.

A. Tax-Backed Debt

Tax-backed debt obligations are instruments issued by states, counties, special districts, cities, towns, and school districts that are secured by some form of tax revenue. Tax-backed debt includes **general obligation debt**, **appropriation-backed obligations**, and **debt obligations supported by public credit enhancement programs**. We discuss each below.

1. General Obligation Debt

The broadest type of tax-backed debt is general obligation debt. There are two types of general obligation pledges: unlimited and limited. An **unlimited tax general obligation debt** is the stronger form of general obligation pledge because it is secured by the issuer's unlimited taxing power. The tax revenue sources include corporate and individual income taxes, sales taxes, and property taxes. Unlimited tax general obligation debt is said to be secured by the full faith and credit of the issuer. A **limited tax general obligation debt** is a limited tax pledge because for such debt there is a statutory limit on tax rates that the issuer may levy to service the debt.

Certain general obligation bonds are secured not only by the issuer's general taxing powers to create revenues accumulated in a general fund, but also by certain identified fees, grants, and special charges, which provide additional revenues from outside the general fund. Such bonds are known as **double-barreled in security** because of the dual nature of the revenue sources. For example, the debt obligations issued by special purpose service systems may be secured by a pledge of property taxes, a pledge of special fees/operating revenue from the service provided, or a pledge of both property taxes and special fees/operating revenues. In the last case, they are double-barreled.

2. Appropriation-Backed Obligations

Agencies or authorities of several states have issued bonds that carry a potential state liability for making up shortfalls in the issuing entity's obligation. The appropriation of funds from the state's general tax revenue must be approved by the state legislature. However, the state's pledge is not binding. Debt obligations with this nonbinding pledge of tax revenue are called **moral obligation bonds**. Because a moral obligation bond requires legislative approval to appropriate the funds, it is classified as an appropriation-backed obligation. The purpose of the moral obligation pledge is to enhance the credit worthiness of the issuing entity. However, the investor must rely on the best-efforts of the state to approve the appropriation. (We'll explain how rating agencies treat moral obligation bonds at Level II.) Another type of appropriation-backed obligation is lease-backed debt.

3. Debt Obligations Supported by Public Credit Enhancement Programs

While a moral obligation is a form of credit enhancement provided by a state, it is not a legally enforceable or legally binding obligation of the state. There are entities that have issued debt that carries some form of public credit enhancement that is legally enforceable. This occurs when there is a guarantee by the state or a federal agency or when there is an obligation to automatically withhold and deploy state aid to pay any defaulted debt service by the issuing entity. Typically, the latter form of public credit enhancement is used for debt obligations of a state's school systems.

Some examples of state credit enhancement programs include Virginia's bond guarantee program that authorizes the governor to withhold state aid payments to a municipality and divert those funds to pay principal and interest to a municipality's general obligation holders in the event of a default. South Carolina's constitution requires mandatory withholding of state aid by the state treasurer if a school district is not capable of meeting its general obligation debt. Texas created the Permanent School Fund to guarantee the timely payment of principal and interest of the debt obligations of qualified school districts. The fund's income is obtained from land and mineral rights owned by the state of Texas.

More recently, states and local governments have issued increasing amounts of bonds where the debt service is to be paid from so-called "dedicated" revenues such as sales taxes, tobacco settlement payments, fees, and penalty payments. Many are structured to mimic the asset-backed bonds that are discussed later in this chapter (Section VII).

B. Revenue Bonds

The second basic type of security structure is found in a revenue bond. Revenue bonds are issued for enterprise financings that are secured by the revenues generated by the completed projects themselves, or for general public-purpose financings in which the issuers pledge to the bondholders the tax and revenue resources that were previously part of the general fund. This latter type of revenue bond is usually created to allow issuers to raise debt outside general obligation debt limits and without voter approval.

Revenue bonds can be classified by the type of financing. These include utility revenue bonds, transportation revenue bonds, housing revenue bonds, higher education revenue bonds, health care revenue bonds, sports complex and convention center revenue bonds, seaport revenue bonds, and industrial revenue bonds.

C. Special Bond Structures

Some municipal securities have special security structures. These include **insured bonds** and **prerefunded bonds**. We describe these three special security structures below.

1. Insured Bonds

Insured bonds, in addition to being secured by the issuer's revenue, are also backed by insurance policies written by commercial insurance companies. Insurance on a municipal bond is an agreement by an insurance company to pay the bondholder any bond principal and/or coupon interest that is due on a stated maturity date but that has not been paid by the bond issuer. Once issued, this municipal bond insurance usually extends for the term of the bond issue, and it cannot be canceled by the insurance company.

2. Prerefunded Bonds

Although originally issued as either revenue or general obligation bonds, municipals are sometimes prerefunded and called **prerefunded municipal bonds**. A prerefunding usually occurs when the original bonds are escrowed or collateralized by direct obligations guaranteed by the U.S. government. By this it is meant that a portfolio of securities guaranteed by the U.S. government is placed in a trust. The portfolio of securities is assembled such that the cash flows from the securities match the obligations that the issuer must pay. For example, suppose that a municipality has a 7% $100 million issue with 12 years remaining to maturity. The municipality's obligation is to make payments of $3.5 million every six months for the next 12 years and $100 million 12 years from now. If the issuer wants to prerefund this issue, a portfolio of U.S. government obligations can be purchased that has a cash flow of $3.5 million every six months for the next 12 years and $100 million 12 years from now.

Once this portfolio of securities whose cash flows match those of the municipality's obligation is in place, the prerefunded bonds are no longer secured as either general obligation or revenue bonds. The bonds are now supported by cash flows from the portfolio of securities held in an escrow fund. Such bonds, if escrowed with securities guaranteed by the U.S. government, have little, if any, credit risk. They are the safest municipal bonds available.

The escrow fund for a prerefunded municipal bond can be structured so that the bonds to be refunded are to be called at the first possible call date or a subsequent call date established in the original bond indenture. While prerefunded bonds are usually retired at their first or subsequent call date, some are structured to match the debt obligation to the maturity date. Such bonds are known as **escrowed-to-maturity bonds**.

D. Municipal Derivative Securities

In recent years, a number of municipal products have been created from the basic fixed-rate municipal bonds. This has been done by splitting up cash flows of newly issued bonds as well as bonds existing in the secondary markets. These products have been created by dividing the coupon interest payments and principal payments into two or more bond classes, or tranches. The resulting bond classes may have far different yield and price volatility characteristics than the underlying fixed-rate municipal bond from which they were created.

The name **municipal derivative securities** has been attributed to these bond classes because they derive their value from the underlying fixed-rate municipal bond. Much of the development in this market has paralleled that of the taxable market. An example of a municipal derivative security is the **municipal strip**. This security is created when a municipal bond is stripped — just as in the Treasury market described earlier in this chapter — resulting in zero-coupon instruments. The maturity value of each zero-coupon instrument created represents a cash flow of the underlying municipal bond issue that has been stripped.

SECTION VI CORPORATE DEBT INSTRUMENTS

Corporate debt instruments are financial obligations of a corporation that have a priority over the claims of common and preferred stockholders in the case of bankruptcy. Corporate issues can be public offered or privately placed. In the United States, one restriction imposed on privately placed securities is that they may not be resold for two years after acquisition. Thus, there is no liquidity in the market for that time period. However, **SEC Rule 144A** eliminates the 2-year holding period by permitting certain large institutions to trade securities acquired in a private placement among themselves without having to register these securities with the SEC.[5]

These securities include bonds, medium term notes, and commercial paper. Technically, asset-backed securities and mortgage-backed securities not issued by federal agencies are securities issued by corporations. (We provided a quick look at agency mortgage-backed in Section IV.) Before describing these debt instruments, we will discuss the rights of bondholders in a bankruptcy and factors considered by rating agencies in assigning a credit rating.

A. Bankruptcy and Bondholder Rights

The holder of a corporate debt instrument has priority over the equity owners in a bankruptcy proceeding. Moreover, there are creditors who have priority over other creditors. The law governing bankruptcy in the United States is the Bankruptcy Reform Act of 1978 as amended from time to time. One purpose of the act is to set forth the rules for a corporation to be either liquidated or reorganized.

The **liquidation** of a corporation means that all the assets will be distributed to the holders of claims of the corporation and no corporate entity will survive. In a **reorganization**, a new corporate entity will result. Some security holders of the bankrupt corporation will receive cash in exchange for their claims, others may receive new securities in the corporation that results from the reorganization, and others may receive a combination of both cash and new securities in the resulting corporation.

---

[5] Under Rule 144A, a large institution is defined as one holding at least $100 million of the security.

Another purpose of the bankruptcy act is to give a corporation time to decide whether to reorganize or liquidate and then the necessary time to formulate a plan to accomplish either a reorganization or liquidation. This is achieved because when a corporation files for bankruptcy, the act grants the corporation protection from creditors who seek to collect their claims. The petition for bankruptcy can be filed either by the company itself, in which case it is called a **voluntary bankruptcy**, or be filed by its creditors, in which case it is called an **involuntary bankruptcy**. A company that files for protection under the bankruptcy act generally becomes a "debtor-in-possession," and continues to operate its business under the supervision of the court.

The bankruptcy act is comprised of 15 chapters, each chapter covering a particular type of bankruptcy. Chapter 7 deals with the liquidation of a company; Chapter 11 deals with the reorganization of a company.

When a company is liquidated, creditors receive distributions based on the **absolute priority rule** to the extent assets are available. The absolute priority rule is the principle that senior creditors are paid in full before junior creditors are paid anything. For secured and unsecured creditors, the absolute priority rule guarantees their seniority to equity holders. In liquidations, the absolute priority rule generally holds. In contrast, there is a good body of literature that argues that strict absolute priority typically has not been upheld by the courts or the SEC in reorganizations.

B. Factors Considered in Assigning a Credit Rating

In the previous chapter we explained that there are companies that assign credit ratings to corporate issues based on the prospects of default. These companies are called rating agencies. In conducting a credit examination, each rating agency, as well as credit analysts employed by investment management companies, consider the four C's of credit — **character**, **capacity**, **collateral**, and **covenants**.

It is important to understand that a credit analysis can be for an entire company or a particular debt obligation of that company. Consequently, a rating agency may assign a different rating to the various issues of the same corporation depending on the level of seniority of the bondholders of each issue in the case of bankruptcy. For example, we will explain below that there is senior debt and subordinated debt. The latter has a better position in the case of a bankruptcy for a given issuer. So, a rating agency, for example, may assign a rating of "A" to the senior debt of a corporation and a lower rating, "BBB", to the subordinated debt of the same corporation.

Character analysis involves the analysis of the quality of management. In discussing the factors it considers in assigning a credit rating, Moody's Investors Service notes the following regarding the quality of management:

> Although difficult to quantify, management quality is one of the most important factors supporting an issuer's credit strength. When the unexpected occurs, it is a management's ability to react appropriately that will sustain the company's performance.[6]

In assessing management quality, the analysts at Moody's, for example, try to understand the business strategies and policies formulated by management. Following are factors that are considered: (1) strategic direction, (2) financial philosophy, (3) conservatism, (4) track record, (5) succession planning, and (6) control systems.[7]

---

[6] "Industrial Company Rating Methodology," *Moody's Investors Service: Global Credit Research* (July 1998), p. 6.
[7] "Industrial Company Rating Methodology," p. 7.

In assessing the ability of an issuer to pay, an analysis of the financial statements as discussed at Level II is undertaken. In addition to management quality, the factors examined by analysts at Moody's are (1) industry trends, (2) the regulatory environment, (3) basic operating and competitive position, (4) financial position and sources of liquidity, (5) company structure (including structural subordination and priority of claim), (6) parent company support agreements, and (7) special event risk.[8]

The third C, collateral, is looked at not only in the traditional sense of assets pledged to secure the debt, but also to the quality and value of those unpledged assets controlled by the issuer. In both senses the collateral is capable of supplying additional aid, comfort, and support to the debt and the debtholder. Assets form the basis for the generation of cash flow which services the debt in good times as well as bad. We discuss the various types of collateral used for a corporate debt issue and features that analysts should be cognizant of in looking at an investor's secured position later.

Covenants deal with limitations and restrictions on the borrower's activities. **Affirmative covenants** call upon the debtor to make promises to do certain things. **Negative covenants** are those which require the borrower not to take certain actions. Negative covenants are usually negotiated between the borrower and the lender or their agents. Borrowers want the least restrictive loan agreement available, while lenders should want the most restrictive, consistent with sound business practices. But lenders should not try to restrain borrowers from accepted business activities and conduct. A borrower might be willing to include additional restrictions (up to a point) if it can get a lower interest rate on the debt obligation. When borrowers seek to weaken restrictions in their favor, they are often willing to pay more interest or give other consideration. We will see examples of positive and negative covenants later in this chapter.

C. Corporate Bonds

In Chapter 1, we discussed the features of bonds including the wide range of coupon types, the provisions for principal repayments, provisions for early retirement, and other embedded options. So, we won't repeat these characteristics here. Also, in Chapter 2 we reviewed the various forms of credit risk and the ratings assigned by rating agencies. In our discussion of corporate bonds here, we will discuss secured and unsecured debt and information about default and recovery rates.

1. Secured Debt, Unsecured Debt, and Credit Enhancements

A corporate debt obligation may be secured or unsecured. By **secured debt** it is meant that there is some form of collateral which is pledged to ensure repayment of the debt. Take away the collateral and we have **unsecured debt**.

It is important to recognize that while a superior legal status will strengthen a bondholder's chance of recovery in case of default, it will not absolutely prevent bondholders from suffering financial loss when the issuer's ability to generate cash flow adequate to pay its obligations is seriously eroded. Claims against a weak lender are often satisfied for less than par value.

a. Secured Debt
Either **real property** or **personal property** may be pledged to offer security beyond that of the general credit standing of the issuer. With **mortgage debt**, the issuer has granted the bondholders a lien against the pledged assets. A lien is a legal right to sell mortgaged

[8] "Industrial Company Rating Methodology," p. 3.

property to satisfy unpaid obligations to bondholders. In practice, foreclosure and sale of mortgaged property is unusual. If a default occurs, there is usually a financial reorganization of the issuer in which provision is made for settlement of the debt to bondholders. The mortgage lien is important, though, because it gives the mortgage bondholders a strong bargaining position relative to other creditors in determining the terms of a reorganization.

Some companies do not own fixed assets or other real property and so have nothing on which they can give a mortgage lien to secure bondholders. Instead, they own securities of other companies; they are holding companies and the other companies are subsidiaries. To satisfy the desire of bondholders for security, the issuer grants investors a lien on stocks, notes, bonds or whatever other kind of financial asset they own. Bonds secured by such assets are called **collateral trust bonds**. The eligible collateral is periodically marked to market by the trustee to ensure that the market value has a liquidation value in excess of the amount needed to repay the entire outstanding bonds and accrued interest. If the collateral is insufficient, the issuer must, within a certain period, bring the value of the collateral up to the required amount. If the issuer is unable to do so, the trustee would then sell collateral and redeem bonds.

Mortgage bonds go by many different names. The following names have been used: **first mortgage bonds** (most common name), **first and general mortgage bonds**, **first refunding mortgage bonds**, and **first mortgage and collateral trust**. There are instances (excluding prior lien bonds as mentioned above) when a company might have two or more layers of mortgage debt outstanding with different priorities. This situation usually occurs because the companies cannot issue additional first mortgage debt (or the equivalent) under the existing indentures. Often this secondary debt level is called **general and refunding mortgage bonds** (G&R). In reality, this is mostly second mortgage debt. Some issuers may have third mortgage bonds.

Although an indenture may not limit the total amount of bonds that may be issued with the same lien, there are certain **issuance tests** that usually have to be satisfied before the company may sell more bonds. There is typically an **earnings test** that must be satisfied before additional bonds may be issued with the same lien.

b. Unsecured Debt

Unsecured debt is commonly referred to as **debenture bonds**. Although a debenture bond is not secured by a specific pledge of property, that does not mean that bondholders have no claim on property of issuers or on their earnings. Debenture bondholders have the claim of general creditors on all assets of the issuer not pledged specifically to secure other debt. And they even have a claim on pledged assets to the extent that these assets generate proceeds in liquidation that are greater than necessary to satisfy secured creditors. **Subordinated debenture bonds** are issues that rank after secured debt, after debenture bonds, and often after some general creditors in their claim on assets and earnings.

One of the important protective provisions for unsecured debt holders is the **negative pledge clause**. This provision, found in most senior unsecured debt issues and a few subordinated issues, prohibits a company from creating or assuming any lien to secure a debt issue without equally securing the subject debt issue(s) (with certain exceptions).

c. Credit Enhancements

Some debt issuers have other companies guarantee their loans. This is normally done when a subsidiary issues debt and the investors want the added protection of a **third-party guarantee**. The use of guarantees makes it easier and more convenient to finance special projects and affiliates, although guarantees are extended to operating company debt.

An example of a third-party (but related) guarantee was US West Capital Funding, Inc. 8% Guaranteed Notes that were due October 15, 1996 (guaranteed by US West, Inc.). The principal purpose of Capital Funding was to provide financing to US West and its affiliates through the issuance of debt guaranteed by US West. PepsiCo, Inc. has guaranteed the debt of its financing affiliate, PepsiCo Capital Resources, Inc., and The Standard Oil Company (an Ohio Corporation) has unconditionally guaranteed the debt of Sohio Pipe Line Company.

Another credit enhancing feature is the **letter of credit** (LOC) issued by a bank. A LOC requires the bank make payments to the trustee when requested so that monies will be available for the bond issuer to meet its interest and principal payments when due. Thus the credit of the bank under the LOC is substituted for that of the debt issuer. Specialized insurance companies also lend their credit standing to corporate debt, both new issues and outstanding secondary market issues. In such cases, the credit rating of the bond is usually no better than the credit rating of the guarantor.

While a guarantee or other type of credit enhancement may add some measure of protection to a debtholder, caution should not be thrown to the wind. In effect, one's job may even become more complex as an analysis of both the issuer and the guarantor should be performed. In many cases, only the latter is needed if the issuer is merely a financing conduit without any operations of its own. However, if both concerns are operating companies, it may very well be necessary to analyze both, as the timely payment of principal and interest ultimately will depend on the stronger party. A downgrade of the enhancer's claims paying ability reduces the value of the credit enhanced bonds.

2. Default Rates and Recovery Rates

Now we turn our attention to the various aspects of the historical performance of corporate issuers with respect to fulfilling their obligations to bondholders. Specifically, we will look at two aspects of this performance. First, we will look at the default rate of corporate borrowers. From an investment perspective, default rates by themselves are not of paramount significance: it is perfectly possible for a portfolio of bonds to suffer defaults and to outperform Treasuries at the same time, provided the yield spread of the portfolio is sufficiently high to offset the losses from default. Furthermore, because holders of defaulted bonds typically recover some percentage of the face amount of their investment, the **default loss rate** is substantially lower than the default rate. Therefore, it is important to look at default loss rates or, equivalently, **recovery rates**. This is the second aspect of historical performance we will examine.

a. Default Rates

A default rate can be measured in different ways. A simple way to define a default rate is to use the issuer as the unit of study. A default rate is then measured as the number of issuers that default divided by the total number of issuers at the beginning of the year. This measure — referred to as the **issuer default rate** — gives no recognition to the amount defaulted nor the total amount of issuance. Moody's, for example, uses this default rate statistic in its study of default rates. The rationale for ignoring dollar amounts is that the credit decision of an investor does not increase with the size of the issuer. The second measure — called the **dollar default rate** — is to define the default rate as the par value of all bonds that defaulted in a given calendar year, divided by the total par value of all bonds outstanding during the year. With either default rate statistic, one can measure the default for a given year or an average annual default rate over a certain number of years.

There have been several excellent studies of corporate bond default rates. We will not review each of these studies since the findings are similar. All of the studies found that the lower the credit rating, the greater the probability of a corporate issuer defaulting.

There have been extensive studies focusing on default rates for non-investment grade corporate bonds (i.e., speculative-grade issuer or high yield bonds). Studies by Edward Altman suggest that the annual default rate for speculative-grade corporate debt has been between 2.15% and 2.4% per year.[9] Asquith, Mullins, and Wolff, however, found that nearly one out of every three speculative-grade bonds defaults.[10] The large discrepancy arises because researchers use three different definitions of "default rate"; even if applied to the same universe of bonds (which they are not), the results of these studies could be valid simultaneously.[11]

Altman defines the default rate as the dollar default rate. His estimates (2.15% and 2.40%) are simple averages of the annual dollar default rates over a number of years. Asquith, Mullins, and Wolff use a cumulative dollar default rate statistic. While both measures are useful indicators of bond default propensity, they are not directly comparable. Even when restated on an annualized basis, they do not all measure the same quantity. The default statistics reported in both studies, however, are surprisingly similar once cumulative rates have been annualized. A majority of studies place the annual dollar default rates for all original issue high-yield bonds between 3% and 4%.

b. Recovery Rates

There have been several studies that have focused on recovery rates or default loss rates for corporate debt. Measuring the amount recovered is not a simple task. The final distribution to claimants when a default occurs may consist of cash and securities. Often it is difficult to track what was received and then determine the present value of any non-cash payments received.

Here we review recovery information as reported in a study by Moody's which uses the trading price at the time of default as a proxy for the amount recovered.[12] The recovery rate is the trading price at that time divided by the par value. Moody's found that the recovery rate was 38% for all bonds. Moreover, the study found that the higher the level of seniority, the greater the recovery rate.

D. Medium-Term Notes

A **medium-term note** (MTN) is a debt instrument, with the unique characteristic that notes are offered continuously to investors by an agent of the issuer. Investors can select from several maturity ranges: 9 months to 1 year, more than 1 year to 18 months, more than 18 months to 2 years, and so on up to 30 years. Medium-term notes are registered with the Securities and Exchange Commission under Rule 415 (the

---

[9] Edward I Altman and Scott A. Nammacher, *Investing in Junk Bonds* (New York: John Wiley, 1987) and Edward I. Altman, "Research Update: Mortality Rates and Losses, Bond Rating Drift," unpublished study prepared for a workshop sponsored by Merrill Lynch Merchant Banking Group, High Yield Sales and Trading, 1989.

[10] Paul Asquith, David W. Mullins, Jr., and Eric D. Wolff, "Original Issue High Yield Bonds: Aging Analysis of Defaults, Exchanges, and Calls," *Journal of Finance* (September 1989), pp. 923-952.

[11] As a parallel, we know that the mortality rate in the United States is currently less than 1% per year, but we also know that 100% of all humans (eventually) die.

[12] Moody's Investors Service, *Corporate Bond Defaults and Default Rates: 1970-1994*, Moody's Special Report, January 1995, p. 13.

shelf registration rule) which gives a borrower (corporation, agency, sovereign, or supranational) the maximum flexibility for issuing securities on a continuous basis.

The term "medium-term note" used to describe this debt instrument is misleading. Traditionally, the term "note" or "medium-term" was used to refer to debt issues with a maturity greater than one year but less than 15 years. Certainly this is not a characteristic of MTNs since they have been sold with maturities from nine months to 30 years, and even longer. For example, in July 1993, Walt Disney Corporation issued a security with a 100-year maturity off its medium-term note shelf registration. From the perspective of the borrower, the initial purpose of the MTN was to fill the funding gap between commercial paper and long-term bonds. It is for this reason that they are referred to as "medium term."

Borrowers have flexibility in designing MTNs to satisfy their own needs. They can issue fixed- or floating-rate debt. The coupon payments can be denominated in U.S. dollars or in a foreign currency. MTNs have been designed with the same features as corporate bonds.

As with corporate bonds, MTNs are rated by the nationally recognized statistical rating organizations.

1. The Primary Market

Medium-term notes differ from bonds in the manner in which they are distributed to investors when they are initially sold. Although some investment-grade corporate bond issues are sold on a "best-efforts basis" (i.e., the underwriter does not purchase the securities from the issuer but only agrees to sell them), typically they are underwritten by investment bankers. MTNs have been traditionally distributed on a best-efforts basis by either an investment banking firm or other broker/dealers acting as agents. Another difference between bonds and MTNs is that, when they are offered, MTNs are usually sold in relatively small amounts on either a continuous or an intermittent basis, while bonds are sold in large, discrete offerings.

What is an issuer more likely to issue, a corporate bond or a medium-term note? As noted by one market expert:

> In deciding whether to finance with MTNs or with bonds, a corporate borrower weighs the interest cost, flexibility, and other advantages of each security. The growth of the MTN market indicates that MTNs offer advantages that bonds do not. However, most companies that raise funds in the MTN market have also continued to issue corporate bonds, suggesting that each form of debt has advantages under particular circumstances.[13]

An entity that wants an MTN program will file a shelf registration with the SEC for the offering of securities. While the SEC registration for MTN offerings are between $100 million and $1 billion, once the total is sold, the issuer can file another shelf registration. The registration will include a list of the investment banking firms, usually two to four, that the borrower has arranged to act as agents to distribute the MTNs.

The issuer then posts rates over a range of maturities: for example, nine months to one year, one year to 18 months, 18 months to two years, and annually

---

[13] Leland E. Crabbe, "Medium-Term Notes and Structured Notes," Chapter 3 in Frank J. Fabozzi (ed.), *The Handbook of Corporate Debt Instruments* (New Hope, PA: Frank J. Fabozzi Associates, 1998), pp. 51-52.

thereafter. In an offering rate schedule an issuer will post rates as a spread over a Treasury security of comparable maturity. Rates will not be posted for maturity ranges that the issuer does not desire to sell.

The agents will then make the offering rate schedule available to their investor base interested in MTNs. An investor who is interested in the offering will contact the agent. In turn, the agent contacts the issuer to confirm the terms of the transaction. Since the maturity range in an offering rate schedule does not specify a specific maturity date, the investor can chose the final maturity subject to approval by the issuer. The minimum size that an investor can purchase an MTN offering typically ranges from $1 million to $25 million.

The rate offering schedule can be changed at any time by the issuer either in response to changing market conditions or because the issuer has raised the desired amount of funds at a given maturity. In the latter case, the issuer can either not post a rate for that maturity range or lower the rate.

2. Structured MTNs

At one time the typical MTN was a fixed-rate debenture that was noncallable. It is common today for issuers of MTNs to couple their offerings with transactions in the derivative markets (options, futures/forwards, swaps, caps, and floors) so as to create debt obligations with more complex risk/return features than are available in the corporate bond market. Specifically, an issue can have a floating-rate over all or part of the life of the security and the coupon formula can be based on a benchmark interest rate, equity index, individual stock price, foreign exchange rate, or commodity index. There are MTNs with an inverse floating coupon rate. MTNs can have various embedded options included.

MTNs created when the issuer simultaneously transacts in the derivative markets are called **structured notes**. The most common derivative instrument used in creating structured notes is a swap, an instrument described at Level II. By using the derivative markets in combination with an offering, borrowers are able to create investment vehicles that are more customized for institutional investors to satisfy their investment objectives, but who are forbidden from using swaps for hedging. Moreover, it allows institutional investors who are restricted to investing in investment grade debt issues the opportunity to participate in other asset classes such as the equity market. Hence, structured notes are sometimes referred to as "rule busters." For example, an investor who buys an MTN whose coupon rate is tied to the performance of the S&P 500 is participating in the equity market without owning common stock. If the coupon rate is tied to a foreign stock index, the investor is participating in the equity market of a foreign country without owning foreign common stock. In exchange for creating a structured note product, borrowers can reduce their funding costs.

E. Commercial Paper

Commercial paper is a short-term unsecured promissory note that is issued in the open market and represents the obligation of the issuing corporation. Typically, commercial paper is issued as a zero-coupon instrument.

In the United States, the maturity of commercial paper is typically less than 270 days and the most common maturity is 50 days or less. There are reasons for this. First, the Securities Act of 1933 requires that securities be registered with the SEC. Special provisions in the 1933 act exempt commercial paper from registration so long as the maturity does not exceed 270 days.

Exhibit 9: Moody's and S&P's Commercial Paper Ratings[*]

Category	Moody's	Standard & Poor's
Investment grade	P-1	A-1+
		A-1
	P-2	A-2
	P-3	A-3
Non-investment grade	NP (Not Prime)	B
		C
In default		D

* The definition of ratings varies by rating agency.
Source: Mitchell A. Post, "The Evolution of the U.S. Commercial Paper Market since 1980," *Federal Reserve Bulletin* (December 1992), p. 882.

To pay off holders of maturing paper, issuers generally use the proceeds obtained from selling new commercial paper. This process is often described as "rolling over" short-term paper. The risk that the investor in commercial paper faces is that the issuer will be unable to issue new paper at maturity. As a safeguard against this "roll-over risk," commercial paper is typically backed by unused bank credit lines.

There is very little secondary trading of commercial paper. Typically, an investor in commercial paper is an entity that plans to hold it until maturity. This is understandable since an investor can purchase commercial paper in a direct transaction with the issuer which will issue paper with the specific maturity the investor desires.

Corporate issuers of commercial paper can be divided into financial companies and nonfinancial companies. There are three types of financial companies: captive finance companies, bank-related finance companies, and independent finance companies. Captive finance companies are subsidiaries of equipment manufacturing companies. Their primary purpose is to secure financing for the customers of the parent company.

Commercial paper is classified as either **direct paper** or **dealer paper**. Direct paper is sold by the issuing firm directly to investors without the help of an agent or an intermediary. A large majority of the issuers of direct paper are financial companies. These entities require continuous funds in order to provide loans to customers. As a result, they find it cost-effective to establish a sales force to sell their commercial paper directly to investors. With dealer-placed commercial paper, the issuer uses the services of an agent to sell its paper.

The three nationally recognized statistical rating organizations that rate corporate bonds and medium-term notes also rate commercial paper. The ratings assigned by S&P and Moody's are shown in Exhibit 6. Commercial paper ratings, as with the ratings on other securities, are categorized as either investment grade or non-investment grade.

SECTION VII
ASSET-BACKED
SECURITIES

In **Section IV.B** we described how residential mortgage loans have been securitized. While residential mortgage loans is by far the largest type of asset that has been securitized, securities backed by other assets (consumer and business loans and receivables) have been securitized.

Our objective in this section is to provide a brief introduction to asset-backed securities. The details regarding the major types of asset-backed securities are discussed in much more detail at Level II where we also discuss credit analysis of these securities and the analytical techniques for evaluating them.

A. The Role of the Special Purpose Vehicle

The key question for investors first introduced to the asset-backed securities market is why doesn't a corporation simply issue a corporate bond or medium-term note rather than an asset-backed security? To understand why, consider a triple BBB rated corporation that manufactures construction equipment. We will refer to this corporation as XYZ Corp. Some of its sales are for cash and others are on an installment sales basis. The installment sales are assets on the balance sheet of XYZ Corp. shown as "installment sales receivables."

Suppose XYZ Corp wants to raise $75 million. If it issues a corporate bond, for example, XYZ Corp.'s funding cost would be whatever the benchmark Treasury yield is plus a yield spread for BBB issuers. Suppose, instead, that XYZ Corp. has installment sales receivables that are more than $75 million. XYZ Corp. can use the installment sales receivables as collateral for a bond issue. What will its funding cost be? It will probably be the same as if it issued a corporate bond. The reason is if XYZ Corp. defaults on any of its obligations, the creditors will go after all of its assets, including the installment sales receivables.

However, suppose that XYZ Corp. can create another corporation or legal entity and sell the installment sales receivables to that entity. We'll refer to this entity as SPV Corp. If the transaction is done properly, SPV Corp. owns the installment sales receivables, not XYZ Corp. This means that if XYZ Corp. is forced into bankruptcy, its creditors cannot go after the installment sales receivables because they are owned by SPV Corp. What are the implications?

Suppose that SPV Corp. sells securities backed by the installment sales receivables. Now creditors will evaluate the credit risk associated collecting the receivables independent of the credit rating of XYZ Corp. What credit rating will be received for the securities issued by SPV Corp.? Whatever SPV Corp. wants the rating to be! It may seem strange that the issuer (SPV Corp.) can get any rating it wants, but that is the case. The reason is that SPV Corp. will show the characteristics of the collateral for the security (i.e., the installment sales receivables) to a rating agency. In turn, the rating agency will evaluate the credit quality of the collateral and inform the issuer what must be done to obtain specific ratings.

More specifically, the issuer will be asked to "credit enhance" the securities. There are various forms of credit enhancement that we will review later. Basically, the rating agencies will look at the potential losses from the pool of installment sales receivables and make a determination of how much credit enhancement is needed for it to issue a specific rating. The higher the credit rating sought by the issuer, the greater the credit enhancement. Thus, XYZ Corp. which is BBB rated can obtain funding using its installment sales receivables as collateral to obtain a better credit rating for the securities issued. In fact, with enough credit enhancement it can issue a AAA rated security.

The key to a corporation issuing a security with a higher credit rating than the corporation's own credit rating is the SPV Corp. Actually, this legal entity that a corporation sells the assets to is called a **special purpose vehicle** or **special purpose corporation**. It plays a critical role in the ability to create a security — an asset-backed security — that separates the assets used as collateral from the corporation that is seeking financing.[14]

Why doesn't a corporation always seek the highest credit rating (AAA) for its securities backed by collateral? The answer is that credit enhancement does not come without a cost. As described later, there are credit enhancement mechanisms and they

---

[14] There are other advantages to the corporation having to do with financial accounting of the assets sold. We will not discuss this aspect of financing via asset securitization here since it is not significant for the investor.

increase the costs associated with a securitized borrowing via an asset-backed security. So, the corporation must monitor the trade-off when it is seeking a higher rating between the additional cost of credit enhancing the security versus the reduction in funding cost by issuing a security with a higher credit rating.

Additionally, if bankruptcy occurs, there is the risk that a bankruptcy judge may decide that the assets of the special purpose vehicle are assets that the creditors of the corporation seeking financing (XYZ Corp. in our example) may go after. This is an important but unresolved legal issue in the United States. Legal experts have argued that this is unlikely. In the prospectus of an asset-backed security there will be a legal opinion addressing this issue. This is the reason why special purpose vehicles in the United States are referred to as "bankruptcy remote" entities.

B. Credit Enhancement Mechanisms

In Level II, we will look at how rating agencies analyze the collateral in order to assign ratings. What is important to understand is that the amount of credit enhancement will be determined relative to a particular rating. There are two general types of credit enhancement structures: external and internal.

External credit enhancements come in the form of third-party guarantees. The most common forms of external credit enhancements are (1) a corporate guarantee, (2) a letter of credit, and (3) bond insurance. A corporate guarantee could be from the issuing entity seeking the funding (XYZ Corp. in our illustration above) or its parent company. Bond insurance provides the same function as in municipal bond structures and is referred to as an insurance "wrap."

A disadvantage of an external credit enhancement is that it is subject to the credit risk of the third-party guarantor. Should the third-party guarantor be downgraded, the issue itself could be subject to downgrade even if the structure is performing as expected. This is based on the "weak link" test followed by rating agencies. According to this test, when evaluating a proposed structure, the credit quality of the issue is only as good as the weakest link in credit enhancement regardless of the quality of the underlying loans. Basically, an external credit enhancement exposes the investor to event risk since the downgrading of one entity (the third-party guarantor) can result in a downgrade of the asset-backed security.

Internal credit enhancements come in more complicated forms than external credit enhancements. The most common forms of internal credit enhancements are reserve funds, over collateralization, and senior/subordinate structures. We discuss each of these at Level II.

SECTION VIII INTERNATIONAL BONDS

In this section we will look at international bonds. We highlight the debt obligations issued by central governments. The foreign exchange rate risk associated with investing in non-domestic denominated bonds was explained in Chapter 2. The motivation for investing in international bonds is left for Level III where we discuss portfolio strategies. A discussion of the analysis of the credit risk of international bonds is provided at Level II.

A. Types of International Bonds

International bonds can be classified into three categories: foreign bonds, Eurobonds, and global bonds. Within each classification these bonds can be classified by the currency in which the debt obligation is denominated. From the perspective of a U.S. investor, an international bond can be classified as either a **U.S.-pay bond** if it is denominated in U.S. dollars and a **non-U.S.-pay bond** if it is not denominated in U.S. dollars.

1. Foreign Bonds

A **foreign bond** is a bond issued in a country's national bond market by an issuer not domiciled in that country and where those bonds are subsequently traded. For example, in the United States a foreign bond is a bond issued by a non-U.S. entity and then subsequently traded in the U.S. bond market. Foreign bonds issued and then traded in the United States are nicknamed **Yankee bonds**. In Japan, a bond issued by a non-Japanese entity and subsequently traded in Japan's bond market is called a **Samurai bond**. Foreign bonds in the United Kingdom are referred to as **Bulldog bonds**, in the Netherlands **Rembrandt bonds**, and in Spain **Matador bonds**.

Regulatory authorities in the country where the bond is issued impose certain rules that govern the issuance of foreign bonds. These may include:

1. restrictions on the bond structures that may be issued (e.g., unsecured debt, zero-coupon bonds, convertible bonds, etc.)

2. restrictions on the minimum or maximum size of an issue and/or the frequency with which an issuer may come to market

3. a waiting period before an issuer can bring the issue to market (imposed to avoid an oversupply of issues)

4. a minimum quality standard (credit rating) for the issue or issuer

5. disclosure and periodic reporting requirements

6. restrictions on the types of financial institutions permitted to underwrite issues

Issuers of foreign bonds include national governments and their subdivisions, corporations (financial and nonfinancial), and supranationals. A **supranational** is an entity that is formed by two or more central governments through international treaties. The purpose for creating a supranational is to promote economic development for the member countries. Two examples of supranational institutions are the International Bank for Reconstruction and Development, popularly referred to as the World Bank, and the Inter-American Development Bank.

An investor in a foreign bond market must understand that country's conventions for quoting yields, calculating accrued interest, and rules for settlement. In some countries, coupon interest is paid semiannually while in others the payment is annual.

Foreign bonds can be denominated in any currency. For example, a foreign bond issued by an Australian corporation in the United States can be denominated in U.S. dollars, Australian dollars, or French francs. Foreign bonds can be publicly issued or privately placed. In many countries, foreign bonds have been privately placed.

2. Eurobonds

Eurobonds are bonds which generally have the following distinguishing features:

1. they are underwritten by an international syndicate
2. at issuance, they are offered simultaneously to investors in a number of countries

3. they are issued outside the jurisdiction of any single country

4. they are in unregistered form.

While a general characteristic of a Eurobond is that it is not regulated by the single country whose currency is used to pay bondholders, in practice only the United States and Canada do not place restrictions on U.S. dollar- or Canadian dollar-denominated issues sold outside their country. Regulators of other countries whose currencies are used in Eurobond issues have closely supervised such offerings. Their power to regulate Eurobond offerings comes from their ability to impose foreign exchange and/or capital restrictions.

While Eurobonds are said to be unregistered securities, they are typically registered on a national stock exchange, the most common being the Luxembourg, London, or Zurich exchanges. However, the bulk of all trading is in the over-the-counter market. Listing is purely to circumvent restrictions imposed on some institutional investors who are prohibited from purchasing securities that are not listed on an exchange. Some of the stronger issuers privately place issues with international institutional investors.

Eurobonds are classified based on the currency in which the issue is denominated. For example, when Eurobonds are denominated in U.S. dollars, they are referred to as Eurodollar bonds. Eurobonds denominated in Japanese yen are referred to as Euroyen bonds.

The Eurobond market has been characterized by new and innovative bond structures to accommodate particular needs of issuers and investors. There are the "plain vanilla," fixed-rate coupon bonds, referred to as **Euro straights**. Because these are issued on an unsecured basis, they are usually issued by high credit quality entities.

Coupon payments are made annually, rather than semiannually, because of the higher cost of distributing interest to geographically dispersed bondholders. There are also zero-coupon bond issues, deferred-coupon issues, and step-up issues, all of which were described in Chapter 1. There are also dual currency bonds, convertible bonds and bonds with warrants, and floating-rate notes.

3. Global Bonds

A **global bond** is a debt obligation that is issued and traded in *both* the U.S. Yankee bond market and the Eurobond market. The first global bond was issued in September 1989; the issue was a 10-year $1.5 billion dollar-denominated issue by the World Bank. A few corporations have since begun to issue global bonds. Since June 1990, Citicorp has had several global bond issues ranging from $1 to $1.5 billion. Each issue was backed by credit-card receivables and denominated in U.S. dollars. (This is a type of asset-backed security.) Two Canadian utility companies, Ontario-Hydro and Hydro-Quebec, have had several global bond offerings. The first global non-U.S. dollar issue was done by Ontario-Hydro in December 1990, denominated in Canadian dollars. Freddie Mac and Fannie Mae have issued global bonds (Freddie Mac's Reference Notes and Fannie Mae's Benchmark Notes).

In general, it is felt that the following three characteristics must be met for an entity to issue global bonds. First, the issuer must have a consistent demand for funds. Second, the amount of funds needed on a regular basis must be large. Today a global issue would probably exceed $3 billion. Finally, the issuer must have a high credit rating.

4. Sovereign Debt

In Section II, we covered the securities issued by the U.S. government. The central governments of other countries issue debt obligations which are referred to as **sovereign debt**. Many investors who first venture into the area of international bond investing restrict their holdings to foreign government securities, shunning nongovernment debt obligations by entities in the same country. The reasons for this are the lower credit risk, greater liquidity, and the simplicity of government securities relative to nongovernment debt obligations. While nongovernment markets ("semigovernment," local government, corporate, and mortgage bond markets) provide higher yields, generally they also have greater credit risks, and foreign investors may not be ready to accept alien credit risks and less liquidity.

The institutional settings for government bond markets throughout the world vary considerably, and these variations may affect liquidity and the ways in which strategies are implemented, or, more precisely, affect the tactics of investment strategies. For example, in the government bond market different primary market issuance practices may affect the liquidity and the price behavior of specific government bonds in a country. The nature of the secondary market affects the ease and cost of trading. The importance of the benchmark effect in various countries may influence which bonds to trade and hold. In addition, yields are calculated according to different methods in various countries, and these differences will affect the interpretation of yield spreads.

A country's tax authorities withhold tax on income derived in their country by nonresident entities. The withholding tax rate may vary, depending on the type of income (dividends or interest). Major trading countries often negotiate tax treaties to reduce the double taxation of income. Withholding tax practices also affect global investment strategies.

While the currency denomination of a government security is typically in the currency of the issuing country, a government can issue bonds that are payable in any currency.

a. Methods of Distribution of New Government Securities

A government can issue securities in its national bond market which are subsequently traded within that market. Or, a government can issue bonds in the Eurobond market or the foreign sector of another country's bond market. Consequently, a U.S. investor may be able to invest in a non-U.S. government bond of some country by buying a Yankee bond issued by that government, a Eurobond issued by that government, or that government's bond issued and traded within that country's domestic bond market. In addition to raising funds through the sale of securities, a government can raise funds by borrowing from a bank via a syndicated bank loan. This method of financing is most often used by governments of emerging market countries.

One of four methods have been used by central governments to distribute new securities that they issue: (1) regular auction cycle/multiple-price method, (2) regular auction cycle/single-price method, (3) ad hoc auction method, and (4) tap method.

With the **regular auction cycle/multiple-price method** there is a regular auction cycle and winning bidders are allocated securities at the yield (price) they bid. For the **regular auction cycle/single-price method** — the same method used by the U.S. Treasury — there is a regular auction cycle and all winning bidders are awarded securities at the highest yield accepted by the government (i.e, the stop-out yield). For example, if the highest yield or stop out yield for a single-price auction is 7.14% and someone bid 7.12%, that bidder would be awarded the securities at 7.14%. In contrast, with the multiple-price method that bidder would be awarded securities at 7.12%.

In the **ad hoc auction system**, governments announce auctions when prevailing market conditions appear favorable. It is only at the time of the auction that the amount to be auctioned and the maturity of the security to be offered is announced. This is one of the methods used by the Bank of England in distributing British government bonds. In a **tap system**, additional bonds of a previously outstanding bond issue are auctioned. The government announces periodically that it is adding this new supply. The tap system has been used in the United Kingdom and the Netherlands.

b. Credit Ratings

While U.S. government debt is not rated by any nationally recognized statistical rating organization, the debt of other national governments is rated. These ratings are referred to as sovereign ratings. Standard & Poor's and Moody's rate sovereign debt. We will discuss the factors considered in rating sovereign bonds in Level II.

The rating agencies assign two ratings to each national government. The first is a **local currency debt rating** and the second a **foreign currency debt rating**. The reason for distinguishing between the two types of debt is that historically, the default frequency differs by the currency denomination of the debt. Specifically, defaults have been greater on foreign currency denominated debt. The reason for the difference in default rates for local currency debt and foreign currency debt is that if a government is willing to raise taxes and control its domestic financial system, it can generate sufficient local currency to meet its local currency debt obligation. This is not the case with foreign currency denominated debt. A national government must purchase foreign currency to meet a debt obligation in that foreign currency and therefore has less control with respect to its exchange rate. Thus, a significant depreciation of the local currency relative to a foreign currency in which a debt obligation is denominated will impair a national government's ability to satisfy such obligation.

SECTION IX KEY POINTS

- ❑ *Treasury securities are backed by the full faith and credit of the U.S. government and viewed by market participants as having no credit risk.*

- ❑ *The Treasury issues two types of Treasury securities: discount securities and coupon securities (fixed rate and variable rate).*

- ❑ *Treasury discount securities are called bills and have a maturity of one year or less.*

- ❑ *A Treasury note is a coupon-bearing security which when issued has an original maturity between two and 10 years; a Treasury bond is a coupon-bearing security which when issued has an original maturity greater than 10 years.*

- ❑ *The Treasury issued inflation-protection securities (TIPS) whose principal and coupon payments are indexed to the Consumer Price Index.*

- ❑ *Treasury bills and coupon securities are auctioned on a regular basis.*

- ❑ *While there are outstanding Treasury bonds that are callable, the Treasury no longer issues callable bonds.*

❑ *Treasury securities are all issued on a competitive bid basis in a single-price auction.*

❑ *In a single-price auction, all winning bidders are awarded securities at the highest yield of accepted competitive tenders (i.e., the stop yield).*

❑ *The over-the-counter market for Treasury securities is the most liquid financial market in the world.*

❑ *The most recently auctioned Treasury issue for a maturity is referred to as the on-the-run issue or current coupon issue; off-the-run issues are issues auctioned prior to the current coupon issues and are not as liquid as an on-the-run issue for a given maturity.*

❑ *Zero-coupon Treasury instruments are created by dealers stripping the coupon payments and principal payment of a Treasury coupon security.*

❑ *Strips created from the coupon payments are called coupon strips; those created from the principal are called principal strips.*

❑ *A disadvantage of a taxable entity investing in Treasury strips is that accrued interest is taxed each year even though interest is not received.*

❑ *Federal agencies are categorized as either federally related institutions or government sponsored enterprises.*

❑ *Those federal agencies that provide credit for the housing market issue debentures and mortgage-backed securities.*

❑ *Federally related institutions are arms of the federal government and generally do not issue securities directly in the marketplace.*

❑ *Government sponsored enterprises (GSEs) are privately owned, publicly chartered entities that were created by Congress to reduce the cost of capital for certain borrowing sectors of the economy deemed to be important enough to warrant assistance.*

❑ *The five GSEs that issue debentures are the Federal Farm Credit System, Federal Home Loan Bank System, Federal National Mortgage Association, Federal Home Loan Bank Corporation, and Student Loan Marketing Association.*

❑ *With the exception of the securities issued by the Federal Farm Credit Financial Assistance Corporation, GSE securities are not backed by the full faith and credit of the U.S. government, and therefore expose investors to credit risk.*

❑ *In addition to debentures, Fannie Mae and Freddie Mac issue mortgage-backed securities, securities backed by a pool of residential mortgage loans.*

❑ *A mortgage loan is a loan secured by the collateral of some specified real estate property.*

❑ *Mortgage loan payments consist of interest, regularly scheduled principal, and prepayments.*

❑ *Prepayments are any payments in excess of the required monthly mortgage payment.*

❑ *Prepayment can be made at any time prior to the scheduled date and is repaid at par value.*

❑ *Prepayments made to pay off part of the outstanding balance is called a curtailment.*

❑ *Prepayment risk is the uncertainty about the cash flows due to prepayments.*

❏ *Loans included in an agency issued mortgage-backed security are conforming loans — loans that meet the underwriting standards established by the issuing entity.*

❏ *For a mortgage passthrough security the monthly payments are passed through to the certificate holders on a pro rata basis.*

❏ *In a collateralized mortgage obligation, there are rules for the payment of interest and principal (regularly scheduled and prepayments) to the bond class (tranches) in the deal.*

❏ *The payment rules in a CMO structure allow for the redistribution of prepayment risk to the tranches comprising the structure.*

❏ *Municipal securities are debt obligations issued by state governments, local governments, and entities created by local governments.*

❏ *There are both tax-exempt and taxable municipal securities, where "tax-exempt" means that interest on a municipal security is exempt from federal income taxation; most municipal securities that have been issued are tax-exempt.*

❏ *There are basically two types of municipal security structures: tax-backed debt and revenue bonds.*

❏ *Tax-backed debt obligations are instruments issued by states, counties, special districts, cities, towns, and school districts that are secured by some form of tax revenue.*

❏ *Tax-backed debt includes general obligation debt (the broadest type of tax-backed debt), appropriation-backed obligations, and debt obligations supported by public credit enhancement programs.*

❏ *A general obligation bond is said to be double-barreled when it is secured not only by the issuer's general taxing powers to create revenues accumulated in a general fund, but also by certain identified fees, grants, and special charges, which provide additional revenues from outside the general fund.*

❏ *Revenue bonds are issued for enterprise financings that are secured by the revenues generated by the completed projects themselves, or for general public-purpose financings in which the issuers pledge to the bondholders the tax and revenue resources that were previously part of the general fund.*

❏ *Revenue bonds include utility revenue bonds, transportation revenue bonds, housing revenue bonds, higher education revenue bonds, health care revenue bonds, sports complex and convention center revenue bonds, seaport revenue bonds, and industrial revenue bonds.*

❏ *Insured bonds, in addition to being secured by the issuer's revenue, are backed by insurance policies written by commercial insurance companies.*

❏ *Prerefunded bonds are no longer secured as either general obligation or revenue bonds but are supported by a portfolio of securities held in an escrow fund.*

❏ *If escrowed with securities guaranteed by the U.S. government, refunded bonds are the safest municipal bonds available.*

❏ *A prerefunded municipal bond is one in which the escrow fund is structured so that the bonds are to be called at the first possible call date or a subsequent call date established in the original bond indenture.*

❏ *Escrowed-to-maturity bonds are refunded bonds structured to match the debt obligation to the maturity date.*

❑ *The Bankruptcy Reform Act of 1978 governs the bankruptcy process in the United States.*

❑ *Chapter 7 of the bankruptcy act deals with the liquidation of a company; Chapter 11 of the bankruptcy act deals with the reorganization of a company.*

❑ *In theory, creditors should receive distributions based on the absolute priority rule to the extent assets are available; this rule means that senior creditors are paid in full before junior creditors are paid anything.*

❑ *Generally, the absolute priority rule holds in the case of liquidations and is typically violated in reorganizations.*

❑ *A credit analyst must consider the four C's of credit — character, capacity, collateral, and covenants.*

❑ *Character relates to the ethical reputation as well as the business qualifications and operating record of the board of directors, management, and executives responsible for the use of the borrowed funds and its repayment.*

❑ *Capacity deals with the ability of an issuer to repay its obligations.*

❑ *Collateral involves not only the traditional pledging of assets to secure the debt, but also the quality and value of those unpledged assets controlled by the issuer.*

❑ *Covenants are important because they impose restrictions on how management operates the company and conducts its financial affairs.*

❑ *A corporate debt issue is said to be secured debt if there is some form of collateral which is pledged to ensure repayment of the debt.*

❑ *Mortgage debt is debt secured by real property such as plant and equipment.*

❑ *Collateral trust debentures, bonds, and notes are secured by financial assets such as cash, receivables, other notes, debentures or bonds, and not by real property.*

❑ *Unsecured debt, like secured debt, comes in several different layers or levels of claim against the corporation's assets and subordination of the debt instrument might not be apparent from the issue's name.*

❑ *Some debt issues are credit enhanced by having other companies guarantee their loans.*

❑ *One of the important protective provisions for unsecured debt holders is the negative pledge clause which prohibits a company from creating or assuming any lien to secure a debt issue without equally securing the subject debt issue(s) (with certain exceptions).*

❑ *Investors in corporate bonds are interested in default rates and, more importantly, default loss rates or recovery rates.*

❑ *There is ample evidence to suggest that the lower the credit rating, the higher the probability of a corporate issuer defaulting.*

❑ *Medium-term notes are corporate debt obligations offered on a continuous basis and are offered through agents.*

❑ *The rates posted for medium-term notes are for various maturity ranges, with maturities as short as nine months to as long as 30 years.*

❑ *MTNs have been issued simultaneously with transactions in the derivatives market to create structured MTNs allowing issuers greater flexibility in creating MTNs that are attractive to investors who seek to hedge or undertake a market play that they might otherwise be prohibited from doing.*

❑ *Commercial paper is a short-term unsecured promissory note issued in the open market that represents the obligation of the issuing entity.*

❑ *Commercial paper is sold on a discount basis and the maturity of commercial paper is less than 270 days.*

❑ *There is little liquidity in the commercial paper market.*

❑ *Asset-backed securities are securities backed by a pool of loans or receivables.*

❑ *The motivation for issuers to issue an asset-backed security rather than a traditional debt obligation is that there is the opportunity to reduce funding cost by separating the credit rating of the issuer from the credit quality of the pool of loans or receivables.*

❑ *The separation of the pool of assets from the issuer is accomplished by means of a special purpose vehicle or special purpose corporation.*

❑ *In obtaining a credit rating for an asset-backed security, the rating agencies require that the issue be credit enhanced; the higher the credit rating sought, the greater the credit enhancement needed.*

❑ *There are two general types of credit enhancement structures: external and internal.*

❑ *International bonds can be classified into three categories: foreign bonds, Eurobonds, and global bonds.*

❑ *Within each classification international bonds can be classified by the currency in which the debt obligation is denominated.*

❑ *From the perspective of a U.S. investor, an international foreign bond can be classified as either a U.S.-pay bond if it denominated in U.S. dollars and a non-U.S.-pay bond if it not denominated in U.S. dollars.*

❑ *A foreign bond is a bond issued in a country's national bond market by an issuer not domiciled in that country and where those bonds are subsequently traded.*

❑ *Yankee bonds are foreign bonds issued and then traded in the U.S. bond market.*

❑ *Regulatory authorities in the country where the bond is issued impose rules governing the issuance of foreign bonds.*

❑ *Issuers of foreign bonds include national governments and their subdivisions, corporations, and supranationals.*

❑ *Eurobonds are bonds which generally have the following distinguishing features: (1) they are underwritten by an international syndicate, (2) at issuance they are offered simultaneously to investors in a number of countries, (3) they are issued outside the jurisdiction of any single country, and (4) they are in unregistered form.*

❑ *A global bond is a debt obligation that is issued and traded in both the U.S. Yankee bond market and the Eurobond market.*

❑ *Sovereign debt is the obligation of a country's central government.*

❑ *The institutional settings for government bond markets throughout the world vary considerably, and these variations may affect liquidity and the ways in which strategies are implemented.*

❑ *There are various methods of distribution that have been used by central governments when issuing securities: regular auction cycle/single-price system; the regular auction cycle/multiple-price system, ad hoc auction system, and the tap system.*

❑ *Sovereign credits are rated by Standard & Poor's and Moody's.*

❑ *There are two ratings assigned to each central government: a local currency debt rating and a foreign currency debt rating.*

❑ *Historically, defaults have been greater on foreign currency denominated debt.*

END OF CHAPTER QUESTIONS

1. Suppose a portfolio manager purchases $1 million of par value of a Treasury inflation protection security. The real rate (determined at the auction) is 3.2%.

    a. Assume that at the end of the first six months the CPI-U is 3.6% (annual rate). Compute the (i) inflation adjustment to principal at the end of the first six months, (ii) the inflation-adjusted principal at the end of the first six months, and (iii) the coupon payment made to the investor at the end of the first six months.

    b. Assume that at the end of the second six months the CPI-U is 4.0% (annual rate). Compute the (i) inflation adjustment to principal at the end of the second six months, (ii) the inflation-adjusted principal at the end of the second six months, and (iii) the coupon payment made to the investor at the end of the second six months.

2. a. What is the measure of the rate of inflation selected by the U.S. Treasury for determining the inflation adjustment for Treasury inflation protection securities?

    b. Suppose that there is deflation over the life of a Treasury inflation protection security resulting in an inflation-adjusted principal at the maturity date that is less than the initial par value. How much will the U.S. Treasury pay at the maturity date to redeem the principal?

    c. Why is it necessary for the U.S. Treasury to report a daily index ratio for each TIPS issue?

3. Below are quotes for Treasury coupon securities. Complete the following table for the price per $100 par value and the price for the par value indicated.

Price quote	Price per $100 par	Par value ($)	Price for par value ($)
104-9		100,000	
114-28+		300,000	
91-23		5,000,000	
95-30+		10,000,000	

4. What is the difference between a federally related agency and a government sponsored enterprise?

5. What is an agency debenture?

6. Suppose that a 15-year mortgage loan for $200,000 is obtained. The mortgage is a level-payment, fixed-rate, fully amortized mortgage. The mortgage rate is 7.0% and the monthly mortgage payment is $1,797.66.
    a. Compute an amortization schedule for the first six months.
    b. What will the mortgage balance be at the end of the 15th year?
    c. If an investor purchased this mortgage, what will the timing of the cash flow be assuming that the borrower does not default?

7. a. What is a prepayment?
    b. What do the monthly cash flows of a mortgage-backed security consist of?
    c. What is a curtailment?
    d. What is prepayment risk?

8. a. What is the difference between a mortgage passthrough security and a collateralized mortgage obligation?

   b. Why is a collateralized mortgage obligation created?

9. What federal agencies issue mortgage-backed securities?

10. What is the difference between a limited and unlimited general obligation bond?

11. What is a moral obligation bond?

12. a. What is prerefunded bond?

   b. Why does a properly structured prerefunded municipal bond have no credit risk?

13. What is an insured municipal bond?

14. a. What is the difference between a liquidation and a reorganization?

   b. What is the principle of absolute priority?

   c. Comment on the following statement: "An investor who purchases a mortgage bond issued by a corporation knows that should the corporation become bankrupt, mortgage bondholders will be paid in full before the stockholders receive any proceeds."

15. a. What is a subordinated debenture corporate bond?

   b. What is negative pledge clause?

16. a. Why is the default rate alone not an adequate measure of the potential performance of corporate bonds?

   b. One study of default rates for speculative grade corporate bonds has found that one-third of all such issues default. Other studies have found that the default rate is between 2.15% and 2.4% for speculative grade corporate bonds. Why is there such a difference in these findings for speculative grade corporate bonds?

   c. Comment on the following statement: "Most studies have found that recovery rates are less than 15% of the trading price at the time of default and the recovery rate does not vary with the level of seniority."

17. a. What is the difference between a medium-term note and a corporate bond?

   b. What is a structured note?

18. A financial corporation with a BBB rating has a consumer loan portfolio. An investment banker has suggested that this corporation consider issuing an asset-backed security where the collateral for the security is the consumer loan portfolio. What would be the advantage of issuing an asset-backed security rather than a straight offering of corporate bonds?

19. What is the role played by a special purpose vehicle in an asset-backed security structure?

20. a. What are the various forms of external credit enhancement for an asset-backed security?
    b. What is the disadvantage of using an external credit enhancement in an asset-backed security structure?

21. Why might a U.S. investor in non-U.S. bonds restrict their investments to the government bond sector?

22. When issuing bonds, a central government can select from several distribution methods.

    a. What is the difference between a single-price auction and a multiple-price auction?
    b. What is a tap system?

23. Why do rating agencies assign two ratings to the debt of a sovereign entity based on whether the debt is denominated in the local currency or a foreign currency?

SOLUTIONS TO END OF CHAPTER QUESTIONS

1. a. Since the inflation rate (as measured by the CPI-U) is 3.6%, the semiannual inflation rate for adjusting the principal is 1.8%.

   (i) The inflation adjustment to the principal is

   $1,000,000 × 0.018% = $18,000

   (ii) The inflation-adjusted principal is

   $1,000,000 + the inflation adjustment to the principal
   = $1,000,000 + $18,000 = $1,018,000

   (iii) The coupon payment is equal to

   inflation-adjusted principal × (real rate/2)
   = $1,018,000 × (0.032/2) = $16,288.00

   b. Since the inflation rate is 4.0%, the semiannual inflation rate for adjusting the principal is 2.0%.

   (i) The inflation adjustment to the principal is

   $1,018,000 × 0.02% = $20,360

   (ii) The inflation-adjusted principal is

   $1,018,000 + the inflation adjustment to the principal
   = $1,018,000 + $20,360 = $1,038,360

   (iii) The coupon payment is equal to

   inflation-adjusted principal × (real rate/2)
   = $1,038,360 × (0.032/2) =$16,613.76

2. a. The inflation rate selected is the non-seasonally adjusted U.S. City Average All Items Consumer Price Index for All Urban Consumers (denoted CPI-U).

   b. The Treasury has agreed that if the inflation-adjusted principal is less than the initial par value, the par value will be paid at maturity.

   c. When a TIPS issue is purchased between coupon payments, the price paid by the buyer has to be adjusted for the inflation up to the settlement date. That is why the Treasury reports a daily index ratio for an issue.

3.

Price quote	Price per $100 par	Par value ($)	Price for par value ($)
104-9	104.28125	100,000	104,281.25
114-28+	114.89063	300,000	344,671.88
91-23	91.71875	5,000,000	4,585,937.50
95-30+	95.953125	10,000,000	9,595,312.50

4. A federally related agency is an arm of the U.S. government. These agencies are also referred to as government owned agencies. With the exception of securities issued by the TVA and the Private Export Funding Corporation, securities issued by federally related agencies are guaranteed by the full faith and credit of the U.S. government.

In contrast, a government sponsored enterprise is a private corporation established by Congress to reduce the borrowing cost for certain sectors of the debt market. While there are exceptions, securities issued by GSEs do *not* carry the full faith and credit of the U.S. government. Consequently, the securities issued by GSEs expose investors to credit risk.

5. Agency debentures are securities issued by government sponsored enterprises that do not have any specific collateral backing the bond. The ability to repay bondholders depends on the ability of the issuing GSE to generate sufficient cash flow to satisfy the obligation.

6. a. Monthly mortgage payment = $1,797.66
   Monthly mortgage rate = 0.00583333 (0.07/12)

Month	Beginning of month Mortgage balance	Mortgage Payment	Interest	Scheduled principal Repayment	End of Morth Mortgage Balance
1	200,000.00	1,797.66	1,166.67	630.99	199,369.01
2	199,369.01	1,797.66	1,162.99	634.67	198,734.34
3	198,734.34	1,797.66	1,159.28	638.37	198,095.97
4	198,095.97	1,797.66	1,155.56	642.10	197,453.87
5	197,453.87	1,797.66	1,151.81	645.84	196,808.03
6	196,808.03	1,797.66	1,148.05	649.61	196,158.42

   b. In the last month (month 180), after the final monthly mortgage payment is made, the ending mortgage balance will be zero. That is, the mortgage will be fully repaid.

   c. The cash flow is unknown even if the borrower does not default. This is because the borrower has the right to prepay in whole or in part the mortgage balance at any time.

7. a. A prepayment is any amount paid by the borrower in excess of the monthly mortgage payment.

   b. The monthly cash flow of a mortgage-backed security is made up of three elements: (1) net interest (i.e., interest less servicing and other fees), (2) regularly scheduled principal repayments (amortization), and (3) prepayments.

   c. A curtailment is a form of prepayment. Rather than prepaying the entire outstanding mortgage balance, a curtailment is a pay off of only part of the outstanding balance — it shortens (or "curtails") the life of the loan.

   d. Prepayment risk is the uncertainty about the cash flows due to prepayments. Because of prepayments the investor does not know how the principal payments will be made even if borrowers do not default on their mortgage loan.

8. a. In a mortgage passthrough security, the monthly cash flow from the underlying pool of mortgages is distributed on a pro rata basis to all the certificate holders. In contrast, for a collateralized mortgage obligation, there are rules for the distribution of the interest (net interest) and the principal (regularly scheduled and prepayments) to different tranches.

   b. While not fully developed in this chapter (but it will be at Level II), the rules for the distribution of interest and rules for the distribution of principal to the different tranches in a CMO structure effectively redistributes prepayment risk among the tranches. The tranches created can provide a better match relative to an institution's liability structure than a mortgage passthrough security.

9. The federal agencies that issue mortgage-backed securities are Ginnie Mae (a federally related agency) and Fannie Mae and Freddie Mac (government sponsored enterprises).

10. An unlimited tax general obligation bond is a stronger form of a general obligation bond than a limited tax general obligation bond. The former is secured by the issuer's unlimited taxing power. The latter is a limited tax pledge because for such debt there is a statutory limit on tax rates that the issuer may levy to service the debt.

11. A moral obligation bond is a municipal bond that in the case of default of an issuer allows the state where the issuer is located to appropriate funds that are scheduled to be paid to the defaulted issuer and use those funds to meet the defaulted issuer's obligation. This is a nonbinding obligation that depends on the best-efforts of the state to appropriate the funds to satisfy the defaulted issuer's obligation.

12. a. A prerefunded bond is a municipal bond that may have originally been a general obligation bond or a revenue bond that is effectively refunded by creating a portfolio of Treasury securities that generates a cash flow equal to the amount of the payments that must be made on the issue.

    b. Regardless of the credit rating of the issue prior to prerefunding, after prerefunding the issue is effectively collateralized by a portfolio of Treasury obligations such that the cash flow of the Treasury portfolio matches the payments on the issue when they are due. Hence, a prerefunded issue has no credit risk if properly structured to match the obligation.

13. An insured municipal bond is an issue that is backed by an insurance policy written by a commercial insurance company such that the insurer agrees to pay the bondholders any principal and/or coupon interest that the municipal issuer fails to make.

14. a. In a liquidation, all the assets of a corporation will be distributed to the holders of claims and no corporate entity will survive. In a reorganization, a new corporate entity will be created and some security holders will receive in exchange for their claims cash and/or new securities in the new corporation.

    b. The absolute priority rule is the principle that senior creditors are paid in full before junior creditors are paid anything.

    c. The statement is true in a liquidation; however, this is not necessarily the case in a reorganization. In fact, studies suggest that the principle of absolute priority is the exception rather than the rule in a reorganization.

15. a. An unsecured bond is called a debenture. Subordinated debenture bonds are issues that rank after secured debt, after debenture bonds, and often after some general creditors in their claim on assets and earnings.

b. A negative pledge clause prohibits a corporation from creating or assuming any lien to secure a debt issue at the expense of existing creditors. This is an important provision for unsecured creditors.

16. a. The performance of corporate bond will depend not only on the default rate, but the recovery rate as well as the spread over Treasury securities.

b. The reason for the discrepancy is that these studies are measuring defaults over different periods. Studies that find that one-third default look at cumulative default rates over a period of time. The 2.15% to 2.4% figure is an annual default rate.

c. The comment is wrong for two reasons. First, studies have found that the recovery rate is about 38% of the trading price at the time of default. Second studies have found that the higher the level of seniority, the greater the recovery rate.

17. a. A medium-term note and corporate bond differ as to how they are distributed to investors when they are initially sold. For an MTN, an issuer offers securities on a continuous basis via an investment banking firm or a broker/dealer acting as an agent by posting rates daily as to the rate it is willing to pay for specific maturities. In contrast, a corporate bond is issued on a discrete basis – it is issued at a given point in time by an investment banker.

b. An issuer can couple a medium-term note offering with one or more positions in derivative instruments to create an instrument that has a coupon rate customized with respect to risk-return characteristics for an institutional investor. Such medium-term notes are called structured notes.

18. The advantage is that depending on the quality of the consumer loan portfolio, this BBB rated issuer may be able to issue an asset-backed security with a higher rating than BBB and thereby reduce its borrowing costs, net of the cost of credit enhancement.

19. A special purpose vehicle allows a corporation seeking funds to issue a security backed by collateral such that the security will be rated based on the credit quality of the collateral rather than the entity seeking funds. Effectively, the special purpose vehicle is the owner of the collateral so that the creditors of the entity seeking funds cannot get access to the collateral should the entity seeking funds default.

20. a. External credit enhancement includes corporate guarantees, a letter of credit, and bond insurance.
b. A disadvantage of an external credit enhancement is that it exposes the asset-backed security structure to a credit downgrading should the third-party guarantor be downgraded.

21. The reasons why U.S. investors might restrict their investments to the government bond sector are that they have lower credit risk than non-government bonds, they typically have greater liquidity relative to non-government bonds, and they typically have simpler structures than non-government bonds.

22. a. In a single-price auction, all winning bidders are awarded securities at the stop yield (highest yield bid). In a multiple-price auction, all winning bidders are awarded securities at the yield they bid.

b. In a tap system, a government issues additional bonds of a previously outstanding bond issue via an auction.

23. The reason for assigning two ratings is that historically the default frequency for government issues denominated in a foreign currency is different from that of government issues denominated in the local currency.

SOLUTIONS TO PRACTICE QUESTIONS

1. a. Since the inflation rate (as measured by the CPI-U) is 2.4%, the semiannual inflation rate for adjusting the principal is 1.2%.

(i) The inflation adjustment to the principal is

$10,000 × 0.012% = $120.00

(ii) The inflation-adjusted principal is

$10,000 + the inflation adjustment to the principal
= $10,000 + $120 = $10,120

(iii) The coupon payment is equal to

inflation-adjusted principal × (real rate/2) = $10,120 × (0.038/2) = $192.28

b. Since the inflation rate is 2.8%, the semiannual inflation rate for adjusting the principal is 1.4%.

(i) The inflation adjustment to the principal is

$10,120 × 0.014% = $141.68

(ii) The inflation-adjusted principal is

$10,120 + the inflation adjustment to the principal
= $10,120 + $141.68 = $10,261.68

(iii) The coupon payment is equal to

inflation-adjusted principal × (real rate/2) = $10,261.68 × (0.038/2) = $194.97

2.

Price quote	Price per $100 par	Par value ($)	Price for par value ($)
86-16	86.5000	10,000	8,650.00
97-27+	97.8594	100,000	97,859.38
106-11	106.3438	500,000	531,718.75
111-4+	111.1406	1,000,000	1,111,406.25

3. Monthly mortgage payment = $699.21
Monthly mortgage rate = 0.00625 (0.075/12)

Month	Beginning of Month Mortgage Balance	Mortgage Payment	Interest	Scheduled Principal Repayment	End of Month Mortgage Balance
1	100,000.00	699.21	625.00	74.21	99,925.79
2	99,925.79	699.21	624.54	74.68	99,851.11
3	99,851.11	699.21	624.07	75.15	99,775.96
4	99,775.96	699.21	623.60	75.61	99,700.35
5	99,700.35	699.21	623.13	76.09	99,624.26
6	99,624.26	699.21	622.65	76.56	99,547.70

Chapter 4

UNDERSTANDING YIELD SPREADS

LEARNING OUTCOME STATEMENTS

After reading this chapter you should be able to:

- identify the interest rate tools used by the Federal Reserve Board
- describe the risks associated with U.S. Treasury securities.
- explain what the Treasury yield curve is, the different shapes observed for it, and what securities are used to construct the Treasury yield curve.
- explain what a Treasury spot rate is.
- describe what the term structure of interest rates is.
- explain what is meant by a spread product and a spread sector.
- explain the different type of yield spread measures (absolute yield spread, relative yield spread, and yield ratio) and how to compute yield spread measures given the yield for two securities.
- explain why investors may find a relative yield spread to be a better measure of yield spread than the absolute yield spread.
- explain the difference between an intermarket and intramarket sector spread.
- describe what an issuer's on-the-run yield curve is.
- describe what a credit spread is and the suggested relationship between credit spreads and the economic well being of the economy.
- identify how embedded options affect yield spreads.
- explain what is meant by a nominal spread and its drawback as a measure of yield spread for bonds with embedded options.
- provide an intuitive explanation for what an option-adjusted spread is and why it is used as a yield spread measure for bonds with embedded options.
- explain how the liquidity of an issue affects its yield spread relative to Treasury securities and relative to other issues that are comparable in all other ways except for liquidity.
- describe the relationship that is argued to exist between the size of an issue, liquidity, and yield spread.
- explain the relationship between the yield on Treasury securities and tax-exempt municipal securities.
- compute the after-tax yield of a taxable security and the tax-equivalent yield of a tax-exempt security.
- explain what technical factor might affect the yield spread.
- explain why yield spread between non-U.S. government bonds and U.S. government bonds is a nominal spread.

SECTION I
INTRODUCTION

The interest rate offered on a particular bond issue depends on the interest rate that can be earned on risk-free instruments plus the perceived risks associated with the issue. We described these risks in the previous chapter. We refer to the interest rates on risk-free instruments as the "level of interest rates." The actions of the central bank influence the level of interest rates. In the United States, the level of interest rates depends on the state of the economy and the interest rate policies implemented by the Board of Governors of the Federal Reserve Board.

A casual examination of the financial press and dealer quote sheets shows a wide range of interest rates reported at a given point in time. Why are there differences in interest rates between debt instruments? We provided the information for that in Chapters 1 and 2. In Chapter 1 we explained the various features of a bond while in Chapter 2 we explained how those features affect the risk characteristics of a bond relative to other bonds that do not share that feature. A good example is the call feature of a bond.

In this chapter we look more closely at the difference in yields offered by bonds in different sectors of the bond market and within a sector of the bond market. We will continue to use the terms "interest rate" and "yield" interchangeably. We postpone until Chapter 6 an explanation of how the yield of a bond is computed and the different types of yield measures.

In Section II, we provide a brief overview of the role of the Federal Reserve in determining the level of interest rates. In Section III we look at benchmark interest rates in the U.S. financial market as reflected by the yields on U.S. Treasury securities. We covered Treasury securities in Chapter 3. In Section IV we discuss the interest rates on non-Treasury securities. In Section V, we look at the structure of interest rates in non-U.S. financial markets.

SECTION II
INTEREST RATE
DETERMINATION

Our focus in this chapter is on the relationship between interest rates offered on different bond issues at a snapshot in time and the relationship between interest rates offered in different sectors in the economy at a given point in time. We do not discuss what determines the general level of interest rates in an economy. It is not that this subject is not important to portfolio managers; rather, it is commonly reserved for a course in economics. So, we will not review the different economic theories of interest rate determination here. However, we will provide a brief discussion of the role of the U.S. Federal Reserve (the Fed), the policy making body whose interest rate policy tools directly influence short-term interest rates and indirectly influence long-term interest rates.

The Fed periodically announces its policy decisions. However, managers who pursue an active strategy of positioning a portfolio to take advantage of expected changes in interest rates will watch closely the key economic indicators that the Fed watches in order to anticipate what policy the Fed will announce and assess the expected impact on short-term interest rates. The indicators that are closely watched by the Fed include non-farm payrolls, industrial production, housing starts, motor vehicle sales, durable good orders, NAPM supplier deliveries, and commodity prices.[1]

Once a policy decision is made by the Fed, it is immediately announced in a statement issued at the close of its meeting. The Fed also communicates its future intentions via public speeches or its Chairman's Humphrey-Hawkins testimony before Congress.[2] To see the impact of the Fed Chairman's influence on interest rates as a result of

---

[1] For a further discussion, see David M. Jones and Ellen Rachlin, "Monetary Policy: How the Fed Sets, Implements, and Measures Policy Choices," Chapter 2 in Frank J. Fabozzi (ed.), *Handbook of Portfolio Management* (New Hope, PA: Frank J. Fabozzi Associates, 1998).

[2] The Fed's Chairman testifies semiannually in February and July before the Senate Banking Committee and the House Banking Committee.

testimony before the Senate Banking Committee, Exhibit 1 shows the movement of the U.S. Treasury yield for 2-year and 30-year issues the day before the testimony, the day of the testimony, and one month later. The one day movements between the day before the testimony and the day of the testimony are quite large relative to typical daily movements in rates for the 2-year and 30-year Treasury issues. Notice also that the direction of the one day change in yield appears to set the course for yields in the following month.

In implementing monetary policy, the Fed can use one of the following interest rate policy tools:

1. open market operations
2. the discount rate
3. bank reserve requirements
4. verbal persuasion to influence how bankers supply credit to businesses and consumers

Engaging in open market operations and changing the discount rate are the interest rate policy tools most often employed. Together these tools can raise or lower the cost of funds in the economy. Open market operations does this through the Fed's buying and selling U.S. Treasury securities. This action either adds funds to the market (when Treasury securities are purchased) or withdraws funds from the market (when Treasury securities are sold). Fed open market operations influence the federal funds rate. The federal funds rate is the rate at which banks borrow from each other. Because the discount rate is the interest rate at which banks can borrow on a collateralized basis at the Fed's discount window, increasing the discount rate makes the cost of funds more expensive for banks; the cost of funds is reduced when the discount rate is lowered. Changing bank reserve requirements is a less frequently used policy.

Exhibit 1: Humphrey-Hawkins Testimony and Changes in Treasury Yields

Testimony date	Closing Yield (%)			Change in Yield (bps)		
	Day before	Day of	Month later	Day of	Over month	Total change
2/22/95						
2-year Treasury	7.09	6.92	6.75	−17	−17	−34
30-year Treasury	7.61	7.54	7.46	−7	−8	−15
7/19/95						
2-year Treasury	5.77	5.89	6.07	+12	+18	+30
30-year Treasury	6.73	6.89	6.91	+16	+ 2	+18
2/20/96						
2-year Treasury	4.90	5.18	5.85	+28	+67	+95
30-year Treasury	6.23	6.39	6.70	+16	+31	+47
7/18/96						
2-year Treasury	6.23	6.16	5.95	−7	−21	−28
30-year Treasury	7.02	6.92	6.77	−10	−15	−25
2/26/97						
2-year Treasury	5.90	6.06	6.38	+16	+32	+48
30-year Treasury	6.66	6.80	7.00	+14	+20	+34
7/27/97						
2-year Treasury	5.94	5.90	5.98	−4	+8	+4
30-year Treasury	6.54	6.43	6.67	−11	+24	+13
2/24/98						
2-year Treasury	5.46	5.57	5.50	+11	−7	+4
30-year Treasury	5.91	5.97	5.88	+6	−9	−3

Source: Treasurys Exhibit 1, *Spread Talk*, A Fixed Income Research Publication, Prudential Securities, Inc. (July 20, 1998).

SECTION III
U.S. TREASURY
RATES

The securities issued by the U.S. Department of the Treasury are backed by the full faith and credit of the U.S. government. Consequently, market participants throughout the world view these securities as being "default-free" securities. However, there are risks associated with owning U.S. Treasury securities.

As explained in Chapter 3, the Treasury issues the following securities:

Treasury bills: Zero-coupon securities that have a maturity at issuance that is one year or less. The Treasury currently issues 3-month, 6-month, and 1-year bills.

Treasury notes: Fixed-rate coupon securities with a maturity at issuance that is greater than 1 year but not greater than 10 years. The Treasury currently issues 2-year, 5-year, and 10-year notes.

Treasury bonds: Fixed-rate coupon securities with a maturity at issuance that is greater than 10 years. The Treasury currently issues only 30-year Treasury bonds.

Inflation-protection securities: Coupon securities whose reference rate is the Consumer Price Index. The Treasury has issued both notes and bonds.

The most recently auctioned issue of Treasury notes and bonds of each maturity is called the **on-the-run issue** or **current issue**. Securities that are replaced by the on-the-run issue are called **off-the-run issues**. Issues that have been replaced by several on-the-run issues are said to be "well off-the-run issues."

The secondary market for Treasury securities is an over-the-counter market where a group of U.S. government securities dealers provides continuous bids and offers on specific outstanding Treasuries. This secondary market is the most liquid financial market in the world. Off-the-run issues are less liquid than on-the-run issues.

A. Risks of Treasury Securities

With this brief introduction to Treasury securities, let's look at their risks. We listed the risks in Chapter 2 and repeat them here: (1) interest rate risk, (2) call and prepayment risk, (3) yield curve risk, (4) reinvestment risk, (5) credit risk, (6) liquidity risk, (7) exchange-rate risk, (8) volatility risk, (9) inflation or purchasing power risk, and (10) event risk.

All fixed income securities expose investors to interest rate risk. So, Treasury securities expose investors to this risk. However, the degree of interest rate risk is not the same for all Treasury securities. The reason is that the maturity and coupon rate affect how much the price will change when rates change. The first approximation of a security's interest rate risk is its duration. Since Treasury securities will have different durations, Treasury securities are not only exposed to interest rate risk, they have different exposure as measured by duration.

As just noted, the Treasury no longer issues callable securities. However, there are callable Treasury bonds outstanding. These securities expose an investor to call risk. So, a comparison of the yield on noncallable Treasury securities and callable Treasury bonds must give recognition to the call risk associated with the latter.

Technically, yield curve risk and volatility risk are risks associated with Treasury securities. However, at this early stage of our understanding of fixed income analysis, we will not attempt to explain these risks. Moreover, it is not necessary to understand how in order to appreciate the material that follows in this section.

In Chapter 2 we said that there are different forms of reinvestment risk. For a callable Treasury security, there is obviously reinvestment risk. For a noncallable Treasury coupon security there is reinvestment risk because to realize the yield offered on the security, it is necessary to reinvest the coupon payments received at an interest rate equal to the computed yield. So, all Treasury coupon securities are exposed to reinvestment risk. Treasury bills are not exposed to reinvestment risk because they are zero-coupon instruments.

As for credit risk, the perception in the global financial community is that Treasury securities have no credit risk. Consequently, investing in Treasury securities does not expose investors to credit risk. In fact, when market participants and the popular press state that Treasury securities are "risk free," we can see from our discussion thus far that they are referring to credit risk.

As we noted in our description of the secondary market for Treasury securities, these securities are highly liquid. However, on-the-run and off-the-run Treasury securities trade with different degrees of liquidity. Consequently, the yield offered by on-the-run and off-the-run issues will reflect their different degrees of liquidity.

Since U.S. Treasury securities are dollar denominated, there is no exchange-rate risk to an investor whose domestic currency is the U.S. dollar. However, non-U.S. investors whose domestic currency is not the U.S. dollar are exposed to exchange-rate risk.

Fixed-rate Treasury securities are exposed to inflation risk. Treasury inflation protection securities have a coupon rate that is effectively adjusted for the rate of inflation and therefore have protection again inflation risk.

Finally, the yield on Treasury securities are impacted by a myriad of events that can be classified as political risk. The actions of monetary and fiscal policy in the United States, as well as the actions of other central banks and governments, can have an adverse impact on U.S. Treasury yields.

B. The Treasury Yield Curve

Given that Treasury securities do not expose investors to credit risk, market participants look at the interest rate or yield offered on an on-the-run Treasury security as the minimum interest rate required on a non-Treasury security with the same maturity. The relationship between the yield offered on the on-the-run Treasury securities for each maturity on July 23, 1999 is presented graphically in panel a of Exhibit 2 and in tabular form in panel b. The relationship shown in Exhibit 2 is called the Treasury yield curve — even though the "curve" can be expressed in tabular form as in panel b.

The Treasury yield curve on July 23, 1999 as shown in Exhibit 2 indicates that the longer the maturity the higher the yield. This shape or relationship for the yield curve is referred to an **upward sloping yield curve**. Since this is the most typical shape observed for the Treasury yield curve, it is also referred to as a **normal yield curve**. Other shapes have been observed. An **inverted yield curve** is one where the longer the maturity, the lower the yield. Panel a of Exhibit 3 shows the inverted yield curve that existed on March 3, 1989. A **flat yield curve** is one where the yield is almost the same regardless of maturity. Panel b of Exhibit 3 shows this relationship on December 28, 1989.

In drawing the yield curve, remember that there are only seven on-the-run securities available — 3 months, 6 months, 1 year, 2 years, 5 years, 10 years, and 30 years).[3] To get a yield for maturities where no on-the-run Treasury issue exists, it is

---

[3] Note that in Exhibit 3 the yield curves are shown for a maturity between 2-years and 30-years. At the time, there were on-the-run issues for additional maturities than shown in Exhibit 2. Specifically, in 1989 there were 3-year, 4-year, and 7-year Treasury notes auctioned.

necessary to interpolate from the yield of two on-the-run issues. Notice that there are only five on-the-run maturity points with yields that are available to draw the curve between 1 year and 30 years (1 year, 2 year, 5 year, 10 year, and 30 year). To fill in the yield for the 25 missing whole year maturities (3 year, 4 year, 6 year, 7 year, 8 year, 9 year, 11 year, and so on to the 29-year maturity), the yield for the 25 whole year maturities are interpolated from the yield on the surrounding maturities. The simplest interpolation, and the one most commonly used in practice, is simple linear interpolation.

For example, suppose that we want to fill in the gap for each one year of maturity. To determine the amount to add to the on-the-run yield as we go from the lower maturity to the higher maturity, the following formula is used:

$$\frac{\text{yield at higher maturity} - \text{yield at lower maturity}}{\text{number of years between two maturity points}}$$

The estimated on-the-run yield for all intermediate whole-year maturities is found by adding to the yield at the lower maturity the amount computed from the above formula.

Exhibit 2: Yield Curve for the On-the-Run (Current) Treasury Issues on July 23, 1999
Panel a: Yield curve graph

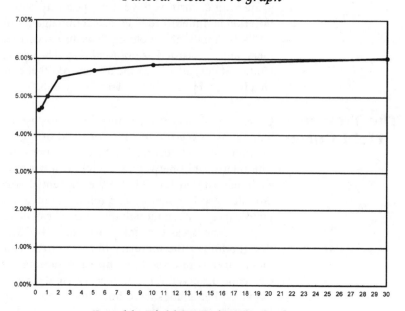

Panel b: Yield curve in tabular form

Issue (maturity)	Yield (%)
3 months	4.65
6 months	4.70
1 year	5.01
2 years	5.55
5 years	5.68
10 years	5.83
30 years	6.01

Source: *Global Relative Value*, Lehman Brothers, Fixed Income Research, July 26, 1999, p. T-2.

Exhibit 3: Inverted and Flat Yield Curves
Panel a: Inverted Yield Curve on 3/3/89

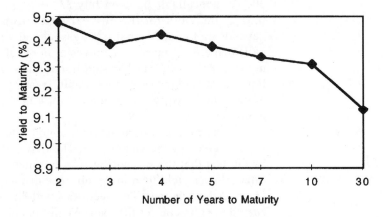

Panel b: Flat Yield Curve on 12/28/89

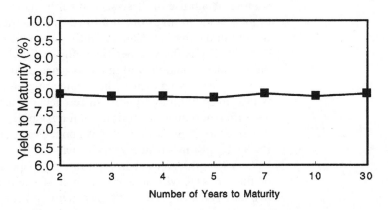

For example, from Exhibit 2 we see that on July 23, 1999 the 5-year yield is 5.68% and the 10-year yield is the 5.83%. Here is how the 6-year, 7-year, 8-year, and 9-year yields are estimated. First we calculate:

$$\frac{5.83\% - 5.68\%}{5} = 0.03\% \text{ (3 basis points)}$$

Then,

estimated 6-year yield = 5.68% + 0.03% = 5.71%
estimated 7-year yield = 5.71% + 0.03% = 5.74%
estimated 8-year yield = 5.74% + 0.03% = 5.77%
estimated 9-year yield = 5.77% + 0.03% = 5.80%

Thus, when market participants talk about a yield on the Treasury yield curve that is not one of the on-the-run maturities — for example, the 15-year yield — it is only an approximation. Notice that there is a large gap between the maturity points. This may result in misleading yields for the interim maturity points when estimated using the linear interpolation method.

We will be discussing the shape of the yield curve in much more detail at Level II. For now, what is critical to understand is that any non-Treasury bond or any off-the-run Treasury issue must offer a premium above the yield offered for the same-maturity on-the-run Treasury issue. For example, if a corporation wanted to offer a 30-year noncallable bond on July 23, 1999, the issuer must offer a yield greater than 6.01% (the yield for the 30-year on-the-run Treasury issue). How much greater depends on the additional risks associated with investing in the 30-year corporate issue that are not faced by an investor in the 30-year on-the-run Treasury issue. As we noted, even off-the-run Treasury issues must offer a premium to reflect differences in liquidity and, in the case of a callable Treasury, call risk. Exhibit 4 shows the yield for on-the-run Treasury issues and off-the-run Treasury (both noncallable and callable) issues on August 5, 1999.

There are two factors that complicate the relationship between maturity and yield as given by the yield curve. The first is that the yield for on-the-run is distorted by the fact that these securities can be financed at cheaper rates and as a result can offer a lower yield than in the absence of this financing advantage. To clarify, there are investors who purchase securities with borrowed funds and use the securities purchased as collateral for the loan. We discussed this type of collateralized borrowing in Chapter 1. It is called a repurchase agreement. Since dealers, for whatever reason, want to obtain use of these securities for their own trading activities, they are willing to loan funds to investors at a lower interest rate than is otherwise available for borrowing in the market. Consequently, impounded into the price of an on-the-run Treasury security is the cheaper financing available, resulting in a lower yield for an on-the-run than would prevail in the absence of attractive financeability.

The second factor when comparing on-the-run Treasury issues and off-the-run issues (in addition to liquidity differences) is that they have different interest rate risk and different reinvestment risk. So, for example, if the coupon rate for the 5-year on-the-run Treasury issue in July 1999 is about 5.68% and an off-the-run noncallable Treasury issue with just less than 5 years to maturity has a 6.5% coupon rate, the two bonds will have different degrees of interest rate risk. Specifically, as explained in Chapter 2, the on-the-run issue will have greater interest rate risk (duration) because of the lower coupon rate. However, it will have less reinvestment risk because the coupon rate is lower.

Exhibit 4: Treasury Yields for On-the-Run Issues and Off-the-Run Issues on August 5, 1999

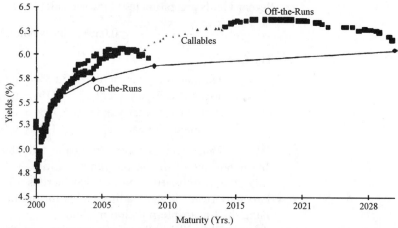

Source: Treasurys Exhibit 3: Treasury Yield Curve in Prudential Securities *Spread Talk*, A Fixed Income Research Publication (August 9, 1999), p. 6.

Because of this, when market participants talk about interest rates in the Treasury market and when they use these interest rates to value securities — which we will see in the next chapter — they look at another relationship in the Treasury market. This is the relationship between the yield on zero-coupon Treasury securities and maturity. But wait, we said that the Treasury only issues three securities that are zero-coupon securities — 3-month, 6-month, and 1-year Treasury bills. Where do we obtain the relationship between zero-coupon Treasury securities and maturity? We discuss this next.

PRACTICE QUESTION 1

The yield for the on-the-run Treasury on February 6, 1998 as reported by Lehman Brothers was as follows:

Issue (maturity)	Yield (%)
3 months	5.18
6 months	5.24
1 year	5.26
2 years	5.37
3 years	5.40
5 years	5.47
10 years	5.61
30 years	5.91

a. Which issues are Treasury notes?
b. Which issues are Treasury bills?
c. Which issues are Treasury bonds?
d. Which on-the-run Treasury reported above is no longer issued?
e. Compute using simple linear extrapolation the yield for the following maturities: 6 years, 7 years, 8 years, and 9 years.

C. Treasury Strips

The U.S. Department of the Treasury does not issue zero-coupon Treasury securities with a maturity greater than one year. However, government dealers synthetically create securities that are zero-coupon securities that are effectively guaranteed by the full faith and credit of the U.S. government. These securities are created by separating the coupon payments and the principal payment of a coupon Treasury security and selling them off separately. This process is referred to as **stripping a Treasury security** and the securities created are called **Treasury strips**. The Treasury strips created from coupon payments are called **Treasury coupon strips** and those created from the principal payment are called **Treasury principal strips**. We explained the process of creating Treasury strips in Chapter 3.

For now, what is important to understand is that the yield on Treasury strips for different maturities provide a superior relationship between yield and maturity than securities on the on-the-run Treasury yield curve. Recall that with a zero-coupon instrument there is no reinvestment risk. So, the problem we mentioned earlier is that comparing the yield on the Treasury yield curve with an off-the-run Treasury issue or a non-Treasury issue is biased by the difference in reinvestment risk for the securities being compared. Moreover, as we will see when we discuss duration in more detail in Chapter 7, the duration of a zero-coupon security is approximately equal to its maturity. Consequently, when comparing issues against Treasury strips, we can compare them on the basis of duration.

The yield on zero-coupon securities is given a special name. It is called the **spot rate**. In the case of Treasury securities, it is called **Treasury spot rates**. The relationship between maturity and Treasury spot rates is called the **term structure of interest rates**. Sometimes discussions get confusing when the conversation turns to the term structure of interest rates in the Treasury market. The Treasury yield curve and the Treasury term structure of interest rates are often used interchangeably. While there is a technical difference between the two, the context in which it is used should be understood.

Now it seems that it is simple to determine the term structure of interest rates in the Treasury market given the observed yields for the Treasury strips. This is not the case. There are problems with using the yield on the observed Treasury strips to construct the term structure of interest rates. We won't delve into the reasons here. What we will note is that there are several approaches to estimating the relationship. We will see how this is done at Level II.

SECTION IV YIELDS ON NON-TREASURY SECURITIES

Despite the imperfections of the Treasury yield curve as a benchmark for the minimum interest rate that an investor will require for investing in a non-Treasury security, it is commonplace to refer to the additional yield over the benchmark Treasury issue of the same maturity as the **yield spread**. In fact, since non-Treasury sectors of the fixed income market offer a yield spread to Treasury securities, non-Treasury sectors are commonly referred to as **spread sectors** and non-Treasury securities in these sectors are referred to as **spread products**.

A. Measuring Yield Spreads

While it is common to talk about spreads relative to a Treasury security of the same maturity, a yield spread between any two bond issues can be determined. In general, the yield spread between any two bond issues, bond A and bond B, is computed as follows:

$$\text{yield spread} = \text{yield on bond A} - \text{yield on bond B}$$

where bond B is considered the benchmark by which bond A is measured against.

When a yield spread is computed in this manner it is referred to as an **absolute yield spread** and is measured in basis points. For example, on July 16, 1999, the yield on the 10-year on- the-run Treasury issue was 5.83% and the yield on a 10-year industrial bond was 6.51%. Letting bond A be the 10-year industrial bond and bond B the 10-year on-the-run Treasury issue, the absolute yield spread was:

$$\text{yield spread} = 6.51\% - 5.83\% = 0.68\% \text{ or } 68 \text{ basis points}$$

Unless otherwise specified, yield spreads are typically measured in this way. Yield spreads can also be measured on a relative basis by taking the ratio of the yield spread to the yield level of the reference bond. This is called a **relative yield spread** and is computed as shown below assuming that the benchmark is bond B:

$$\text{relative yield spread} = \frac{\text{yield on bond A} - \text{yield on bond B}}{\text{yield on bond B}}$$

Sometimes bonds are compared in terms of a **yield ratio**, the quotient of two bond yields, as shown below:

$$\text{yield ratio} = \frac{\text{yield on bond A}}{\text{yield on bond B}}$$

Typically, when the various forms of yield spread are computed, bond B is the benchmark Treasury issue. In that case, the equations above for the yield spread are as follows:

$$\text{absolute yield spread} = \text{yield on bond A} - \text{yield of on-the-run Treasury}$$

$$\text{relative yield spread} = \frac{\text{yield on bond A} - \text{yield of on-the-run Treasury}}{\text{yield of on-the-run Treasury}}$$

$$\text{yield ratio} = \frac{\text{yield on bond A}}{\text{yield of on-the-run Treasury}}$$

For the above example comparing the yields on the 10-year industrial bond and the 10-year on-the-run Treasury, the relative yield spread and yield ratio are computed below:

$$\text{absolute yield spread} = 6.51\% - 5.83\% = 0.68\% = 68 \text{ basis points}$$

$$\text{relative yield spread} = \frac{6.51\% - 5.83\%}{5.83\%} = 0.117 = 11.7\%$$

$$\text{yield ratio} = \frac{6.51\%}{5.83\%} = 1.12$$

The reason for computing yield spreads in terms of a relative yield spread or a yield ratio is that the magnitude of the yield spread is affected by the level of interest rates. For example, in 1957 the yield on Treasuries was about 3%. At that time the absolute yield spread between triple B rated utility bonds and Treasuries was 40 basis points. This represented a relative yield spread of 13% (0.40% divided by 3%). However, when the yield on Treasuries exceeded 10% in 1985, an absolute yield spread of 40 basis points would have meant only a relative yield spread of 4% (0.40% divided by 10%). Consequently, in 1985 the absolute yield spread would have had to be greater than 40 basis points to produce a similar relative yield spread.

In our discussion in this chapter, we will focus on the yield spread as most commonly measured, the absolute yield spread. So, when we refer to yield spread, we mean absolute yield spread.

Whether we measure the yield spread as an absolute yield spread, a relative yield spread, or a yield ratio, the question is what causes the yield spread between two bond issues. Basically, active bond portfolio strategies involve assessing the factors that cause the yield spread, forecasting how that yield spread may change over an investment horizon, and taking a position to capitalize on expectations about how the yield spread will change.

PRACTICE QUESTION 2

Here is information for the 10-year Treasury yield and the estimated yield for 10-year bonds of two issuers as of March 19, 1999:

Issue	Yield
10-year on-run-Treasury issue:	5.16%
10-year approximate yield for GTE Corp. (Baa1/A)	6.11%
10-year approximate yield for IBM (A1/A)	5.93%

a. Compute the following yield spread measures between the 10-year GTE yield and the 10-year on-the-run Treasury yield: absolute yield spread, relative yield spread, and yield ratio.

b. Compute the following yield spread measures between the 10-year IBM yield and the 10-year on-the-run Treasury yield: absolute yield spread, relative yield spread, and yield ratio.

B. Intermarket Sector Spreads and Intramarket Spreads

The bond market is classified into sectors based on the type of issuer. In the United States, these sectors include the U.S. government sector, the U.S. government agencies sector, the municipal sector, the corporate sector, the mortgage sector, the asset-backed securities sector, and the foreign (sovereign, supranational, and corporate) sector. Different sectors are generally perceived to represent different risks and rewards.

The major market sectors are further subdivided into sub-sectors intended to reflect common economic characteristics. For example, within the corporate sector, the subsectors are: (1) industrial companies, (2) utility companies, (3) finance companies, and (4) banks. In the market for asset-backed securities, the sub-sectors are based on the type of collateral backing the security. The major types are securities backed by pools of (1) credit card receivables, (2) home equity loans, (3) automobile loans, (4) manufactured housing loans, and (5) student loans. Excluding the Treasury market sector, the other market sectors have a wide range of issuers, each with different abilities to satisfy their contractual obligations. Therefore, a key feature of a debt obligation is the nature of the issuer.

The yield spread between the interest rate offered in two sectors of the bond market with the same maturity is referred to as an **intermarket sector spread**. The most common intermarket sector spread calculated by market participants is the yield spread between Treasury securities and some sector of the non-Treasury market with the same maturity. The intermarket yield spread (in basis points) between selected corporate issuers and the benchmark Treasury issue of the same maturity on July 23, 1999 is shown in Exhibit 5.

The yield spread between two issues within a market sector is called an **intramarket sector spread**. For example, in Exhibit 5 we can see the difference between the yields on issues that differ by maturity. Notice that the yield spread for a given issuer increases as maturity increases. As with Treasury securities, a yield curve can be estimated for a given issuer. The yield spread typically increases with maturity. The yield spreads for a given issuer such as those reported in Exhibit 5 can be added to the yield for the corresponding maturity for the on-the-run Treasury issue. The resulting yield curve is then the **issuer's on-the-run yield curve.**

The factors that affect the intermarket and intramarket yield spreads in addition to maturity are (1) the relative credit risk of the two issues; (2) the presence of embedded options; (3) the liquidity of an issue; and, (4) the taxability of the interest received by investors. Each is discussed below.

Exhibit 5: Yield Spread Between Selected Corporate Issuers and Treasuries with the Same Maturity on July 23, 1999

Issuer	Rating*	2-year	5-year	7-year	10-year	30-year
Merrill Lynch	Aa3/AA-	90	115	125	148	167
Citigroup/Citicorp	Aa2/AA-	84	118	123	135	160
BankAmerica	Aa3/AA-	86	120	128	138	162
Time Warner Ent.	Baa3/BBB-	87	111	120	138	158
Philip Morris	A2/A	97	120	135	155	175
Sprint	Baa1/BBB+	85	105	116	140	158
MCI/Worldcom	A3/A-	74	95	106	119	136

* The first rating is the rating assigned by Moody's Investor Service and the second rating is the rating assigned by Standard & Poor's.

Source: Abstracted from *Global Relative Value*, Lehman Brothers, Fixed Income Research, July 26, 1999, p. T-8.

Exhibit 6: Credit Spreads in the Corporate Sector for 10-Year Issues on July 23, 1999

Sector	AAA	AA	A	BBB
Industrials	90	97	128	152
Utilities	88	94	110	137
Finance	94	120	134	158
Banks	—	120	130	145

Source: Abstracted from *Global Relative Value*, Lehman Brothers, Fixed Income Research, July 26, 1999, p. T-8.

C. Credit Spreads

The yield spread between Treasury securities and non-Treasury securities that are identical in all respects except for credit rating is referred to as a **credit spread** or **quality spread**. It is important to keep in mind by what is meant by "identical in all respects except for credit rating." This means that the maturities are the same and that there are no embedded options.

For example, Exhibit 6 shows the yield spread within the corporate sector by credit rating on July 23, 1999 for 10-year issues. Notice that the lower the credit rating, the higher the credit spread.

It is argued that credit spreads between corporates and Treasuries change systematically because of expected changes in economic prospects. Credit spreads widen (i.e., become larger) in a declining or contracting economy and narrow (i.e., become smaller) during economic expansion. The economic rationale is that in a declining or contracting economy, corporations experience a decline in revenue and reduced cash flow, making it difficult for corporate issuers to service their contractual debt obligations. To induce investors to hold spread products of lower quality issuers, the credit spread widens. The widening occurs as investors sell off corporates and invest the proceeds in Treasury securities (popularly referred to as a "flight to quality"). The converse is that during economic expansion and brisk economic activity, revenue and cash flow pick up, increasing the likelihood that corporate issuers will have the capacity to service their contractual debt obligations.

Some market observers use the yield spread between issuers in cyclical and non-cyclical industry sectors as a proxy for yield spreads due to expected economic conditions. The rationale is as follows. While both companies in cyclical and non-cyclical industries are adversely affected by expectations of a recession or contracting economy, the impact is expected to be greater for cyclical industries. As a result, the yield spread between issuers in non-cyclical and cyclical industry sectors will widen when there are expectations of a contracting economy. In contrast, in an expanding economy the yield spread should be small. For example, in a monthly publication analysts at Morgan Stanley Dean Witter comment on the yield spread between cyclical versus noncyclical industrials. Exhibit 7 shows this yield spread from 3/3/98 to 4/4/99. Notice how the yield spread jumped in August 1998 and remained considerably higher than the pre-August 1998 period. In its April 1999 publication, the following commentary accompanied the yield spread exhibit: "The steady march tighter of the cyclicals will continue to benefit from the ever-improving economic picture." That is, because economic prospects for the economy were favorable the yield spread between cyclical and non-cyclicals narrowed.

D. Inclusion of Embedded Options

It is not uncommon for a bond issue to include a provision that gives either the issuer and/or the bondholder an option to take some action against the other party. Such embedded options were discussed in Chapter 1. The most common type of option in a bond issue is the call provision that grants the issuer the right to retire the debt, fully or partially, before the scheduled maturity date.

The presence of an embedded option has an effect on the spread of an issue relative to a Treasury security and the spread relative to otherwise comparable issues that do not have an embedded option. In general, investors will require a larger spread to a comparable Treasury security for an issue with an embedded option that is favorable to the issuer (e.g. a call option) than for an issue without such an option. In contrast, market participants will require a smaller spread to a comparable Treasury security for an issue with an embedded option that is favorable to the investor (e.g., put option or conversion option). In fact, for a bond with an option favorable to an investor, the interest rate on this issue may be less than that on a comparable Treasury security.

Exhibit 7: Cyclical versus Noncyclical Industry Sector Yield Spreads

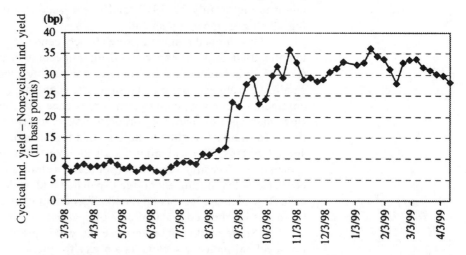

Source: Exhibit 3 in Morgan Stanley Dean Witter, *U.S. Portfolio Strategy*, Fixed Income Research (April 15, 1999), p. 43

Exhibit 8: Yield Spread on Fannie Mae Noncallable and Callable Issues on 6/30/99

Maturity	Call Provision	Yield Spread (bp)
5 years	Noncallable	50
5 years	Noncallable for 2 years	71
10 years	Noncallable	66
10 years	Noncallable for 3 years	114
10 years	Noncallable for 5 years	103

Source: Abstracted from *Spread Talk*, A Fixed Income Research Publication, Prudential Securities Inc., Volume 4, Number 24, July 26, 1999, Agency Exhibit 8.

Exhibit 9: Yield Spread on Callable Agency Securities by Deferred Call on 7/23/99

Maturity	No. of Years of Deferred Call	Yield Spread	Option-Adjusted Spread
5 years	3 months	130	53
5 years	6 months	123	45
5 years	1 year	118	53
5 years	2 years	105	53
5 years	3 years	90	56
10 years	1 year	160	49
10 years	3 years	140	65
10 years	5 years	123	76

Source: Abstracted from *Spread Talk*, A Fixed Income Research Publication, Prudential Securities Inc., Volume 4, Number 24, July 26, 1999, Agency Exhibit 11.

Exhibit 8 shows the yield spread on Fannie Mae (Federal National Mortgage Association or FNMA) — a government sponsored enterprise discussed in Chapter 3 — 5-year and 10-year issues with and without a call provision on June 30, 1999. The yield spread is based on the yield spread between the issue and the on-the-run Treasury issue. Notice that for both the 5-year and 10-year issues, the yield spread relative to the on-the-run Treasury is larger for a callable issue than for a noncallable. Also note that for the 10-year issues there are two callable issues — one with a deferred call of three years and the other with a deferred call for five years. The longer the deferred call, the lower the call risk. This is reflected in the yield spread in Exhibit 8. The yield spread for the 3-year deferred call issue is 114 basis points, while for the 5-year deferred call it is only 103 basis points.

This is further illustrated in Exhibit 9 which shows the yield spread on callable agency securities on July 23, 1999 for issues with 5 years and 10 years to maturity. Again, notice that the longer the deferred call period, the lower the yield spread.

A major part of the bond market is the mortgage market. There is a wide range of mortgage-backed securities that we discussed in Chapter 3 and will discuss in more detail at Level II. But these securities expose an investor to prepayment risk. Consequently, a yield spread between a mortgage-backed security and a comparable on-the-run Treasury security reflects prepayment risk. To see this, consider a basic mortgage-backed security called a Ginnie Mae passthrough security. This security is backed by the full faith and credit of the U.S. government. Consequently, the yield spread between a Ginnie Mae passthrough security and a comparable Treasury security is not due to credit risk. Rather, it is primarily due to prepayment risk. For example, on July 22, 1999 Prudential Securities reported that the yield on a 30-year Ginnie

Mae passthrough security was 7.38%. The question is what maturity on-the-run Treasury issue should this be benchmarked against in order to calculate a yield spread. The reason for this question is that a mortgage passthrough security is an amortizing security and therefore it repays principal over time rather than just at the stated maturity date (30 years in our illustration). Consequently, while the Ginnie Mae passthrough is stated to have a 30-year maturity it should not be compared to a 30-year on-the-run Treasury issue. Just which maturity Treasury issue it should be compared to will not be addressed here — but it will be at Level II. For now, we will simply state that it is compared to the 10-year on-the-run Treasury issue which at the time offered a yield of 5.77%. Thus the yield spread between the 30-year Ginnie Mae passthrough (7.38%) and the 10-year on-the-run Treasury issue (5.77%) is 1.61% or 161 basis points.

In general, when we cite the yield spread when an issue is callable, we recognize that part of the yield spread reflects the embedded option. As we develop analytical tools to value bonds with embedded options, we will see how to determine a yield spread that adjusts for the embedded option. This yield spread is referred to as the **option-adjusted spread**. We postpone discussion of this concept until Level II where models for valuing bonds with embedded options are covered. Here it is only important to recognize that yield spreads reported do not adjust for the embedded option that may be included in an issue. Sometimes these raw yield spreads are referred to as **nominal spreads** — nominal in the sense that the value of any embedded options has not been taken into consideration in computing the yield spread.

The last column of Exhibit 9 gives Prudential Securities estimate of the option-adjusted spread for the callable agencies shown in the exhibit. The nominal spread would be the yield spread shown in the next-to-the-last column. Notice that the option-adjusted spread is considerably less than the nominal spread. For example, for the 10-year issue with a 3-year deferred call, the nominal spread is 140 basis points. After adjusting for the embedded call option, the yield spread (i.e., the option-adjusted spread) is considerably less, 65 basis points.

Also, we said earlier that the yield spread (now we can call it the nominal spread) between the 30-year Ginnie Mae passthrough security and the 10-year on-the-run Treasury issue is 161 basis points. But this yield spread reflects prepayment risk. Prudential Securities estimated that the option-adjusted spread is 125 basis points. That is, after adjusting for the prepayment risk, the 30-year Ginnie Mae passthrough is offering a 125 basis point spread.

PRACTICE QUESTION 3

Below are the yield spreads estimated between 10-year federal agency securities and the 10-year on-the-run Treasury issue on June 30, 1998 as reported in the July 20, 1998 issue of *Spread Talk* published by Prudential Securities (p. 7):

noncallable	40 basis points
callable, 1 year deferred call	110
callable, 2 year deferred call	95
callable, 3 year deferred call	75

a. Why is the yield spread for the noncallable issue less than for the three callable issues?
b. Why is it that for the callable issues the longer the deferred call, the smaller the yield spread?

Exhibit 10: Off-the-Run versus On-the-Run Yield Spread in the Corporate Market (2/21/98 to 6/2/99)

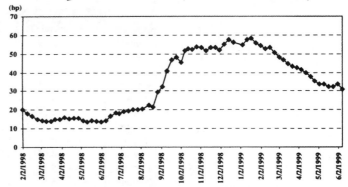

Source: Exhibit 3 in Morgan Stanley Dean Witter, *U.S. Portfolio Strategy*, Fixed Income Research (June 15, 1999), p. 46.

E. Liquidity   In Chapter 2 we discussed liquidity risk. In Section III we explained how even within the Treasury market there is a yield spread between off-the-run Treasury issues and on-the-run Treasury issues of similar maturity due to differences in liquidity and the effects of the repo market. Similarly, in the spread sectors, generic on-the-run yield curves can be estimated and the liquidity spread due to an off-the-run issue can be computed. Exhibit 10 shows this yield spread from 2/2/98 to 6/21/99. As can be seen, the off-the-run/on-the run yield spread can vary significantly — from just more than 10 basis points to almost 60 basis points in the time period shown in Exhibit 10.

As explained in Chapter 2, one factor that affects the liquidity of an issue is its size. Lehman Brothers has investigated the relationship between issue size and the value of liquidity as measured in terms of yield spread.[4] For example, the historical yield spreads between the following issues were examined:

> Ford Motor Credit 7½s of 2003 (A1/A): $500 million issue
>> versus
> Ford Motor Credit Global 6s of 2003 (A1/A): $1 billion issue
>
> Quebec 6½s of 2006 (A2/A+): $500 million Yankee issue
>> versus
> Quebec Global 5¾s (A2/A+): $1 billion issue
>
> Korean Development Bank 6¾s of 2005 (Baa3/BBB−): $200 million issue
>> versus
> Korean Development Bank 7¼s of 2006 (Baa3/BBB−): $750 million issue

The above comparisons are between global bonds (explained in Chapter 3) and smaller issue counterparts. For the Ford Motor Credit, the average yield spread between the smaller issue and the larger issue was 6 basis points from 6/30/98 and 6/25/99. For the 4-month period ending 6/25/99, the yield spread between the smaller Quebec issue and the larger issue was about 4 basis points. For the Korean Development Bank the yield spread over the period 6/30/98 and 6/25/99 averaged 18 basis points between the smaller and larger issues. These findings support the relationship between size and value.

---

[4] *Global Relative Value*, Lehman Brothers, Fixed Income Research, June 28,1999, COR-2 AND 3.

Exhibit 11: Yield Ratio for AAA General Obligation Municipal Bonds to U.S. Treasuries of the Same Maturity (August 16, 1999)

Maturity	Yield on		Yield Ratio
	AAA General Obligation	U.S. Treasury	
3 months	3.29	4.93	0.67
6 months	3.43	5.21	0.66
1 year	3.56	5.55	0.64
2 years	4.03	5.78	0.70
3 years	4.23	5.84	0.72
4 years	4.37	6.00	0.73
5 years	4.46	5.87	0.76
7 years	4.66	6.20	0.75
10 years	4.95	5.99	0.83
15 years	5.33	6.39	0.83
20 years	5.50	6.47	0.85
30 years	5.55	6.26	0.89

Copyright: Bloomberg Financial Markets

F. Taxability of Interest Income

In the United States unless exempted under the federal income tax code, interest income is taxable at the federal level. In addition to federal income taxes, there may be state and local taxes on interest income.

The federal tax code specifically exempts the interest income from *qualified* municipal bond issues from taxation at the federal level.[5] Because of the tax-exempt feature of municipal bonds, the yield on municipal bonds is less than that on Treasuries with the same maturity. Exhibit 11 shows this relationship on August 16, 1999 as reported by Bloomberg Financial Markets. The yield ratio shown for municipal bonds is that of AAA general obligation bonds (discussed in Chapter 3) to the same maturity on-the-run Treasury issue. (There are maturities for Treasury securities shown in the exhibit that are not on-the-run issues. These are estimates of the fair value for the market yields, just as we computed using the interpolation method in Section II.) A graph of the relationship is shown as Exhibit 12.

The difference in yield between tax-exempt securities and Treasury securities is typically measured not in terms of the absolute yield spread but as a yield ratio. More specifically, it is measured as the percentage of the yield on a tax-exempt security relative to a comparable Treasury security. This spread is popularly referred to as the "MOB spread." This is reported in Exhibit 11.

The yield ratio has changed over time. The higher the tax rate, the more attractive the tax-exempt feature and the lower the yield ratio. The yield ratio for 10-year AAA general obligation bonds and 10-year Treasury securities varied in the 1990s from a low of 0.72 on September 30, 1994 to a high of 0.94 on September 30, 1998.

1. After-Tax Yield and Taxable-Equivalent Yield

The yield on a taxable bond issue after federal income taxes are paid is called the **after-tax yield** and computed as follows:

$$\text{after-tax yield} = \text{pre-tax yield} \times (1 - \text{marginal tax rate})$$

---

[5] As explained in Chapter 3, there are also municipal bonds that are taxable.

Exhibit 12: Fair Market Yield Curves for U.S. Treasuries and AAA General Obligation Municipal Bonds (August 16, 1999)

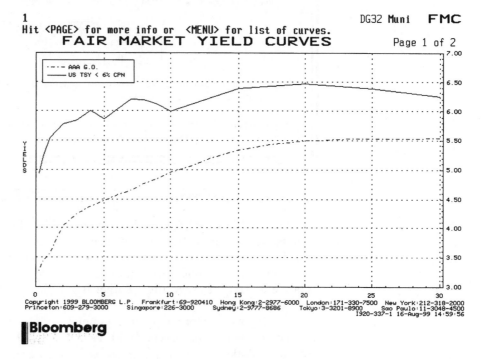

Copyright: Bloomberg Financial Markets

Of course, the marginal tax rate varies among investors. For example, suppose a taxable bond issue offers a yield of 5% and is acquired by an investor facing a marginal tax rate of 31%. The after-tax yield would then be:

$$\text{after-tax yield} = 0.05 \times (1 - 0.31) = 0.0345 = 3.45\%$$

Alternatively, we can determine the yield that must be offered on a taxable bond issue to give the same after-tax yield as a tax-exempt issue. This yield is called the **taxable-equivalent yield** or **tax-equivalent yield** and is computed as follows:

$$\text{taxable-equivalent yield} = \frac{\text{tax-exempt yield}}{(1 - \text{marginal tax rate})}$$

For example, consider an investor facing a 31% marginal tax rate who purchases a tax-exempt issue with a yield of 4%. The taxable-equivalent yield is then:

$$\text{taxable-equivalent yield} = \frac{0.04}{(1 - 0.31)} = 0.058 = 5.8\%$$

Notice that the higher the marginal tax rate, the higher the taxable equivalent yield. For example, in our previous example if the marginal tax rate is 40% rather than 31%, the taxable-equivalent yield would be 6.67% rather than 5.8%, as shown below:

$$\text{taxable-equivalent yield} = \frac{0.04}{(1 - 0.40)} = 0.0667 = 6.67\%$$

PRACTICE QUESTION 4

Following is information about two investor's: Ms. High and Mr. Low:

	Marginal tax bracket
Ms. High	40%
Mr. Low	15%

a. Suppose that these two investors are considering investing in a taxable bond that offers a yield of 6.8%. What is the after-tax yield for both investors?

b. Suppose that these two investors can purchase a tax-exempt security offering a yield of 4.8%. What is the taxable-equivalent yield for both investors?

---

2. Intramarket Yield Spreads and Benchmark Issues

As explained in Chapter 3, the U.S. municipal bond market is divided into two bond sectors: general obligation and revenue bonds. The revenue sector is further decomposed into the following sectors: (1) housing, (2) power, (3) hospitals, and (4) insured. For the tax-exempt bond market, the benchmark for calculating yield spreads is not relative to Treasury securities. Rather it is a generic AAA general obligation bond with a specified maturity.

Below is information on a sample of yield spreads relative to AAA general obligation bonds from November 30, 1993 to July 30, 1999 as reported by Bloomberg Financial Markets:

30-year generic BBB revenue bonds – 30-year AAA general obligation bonds	
Average	51 basis points
Low	29 basis points on 8/31/98
High	68 basis points on 1/31/96

20-year AAA hospital bonds – 20-year AAA general obligation bonds	
Average	23 basis points
Low	12 basis points on 2/26/99
High	41 basis points on 11/30/99

10-year New York City bonds – 10-year AAA general obligation bonds	
Average	76 basis points
Low	24 basis points on 9/29/95
High	121 basis points on 5/31/99

Notice that in the second panel above there is a difference between two triple A rated bonds with the same maturity. This may be surprising since it would seem that all triple A rated bonds with the same maturity and features should offer the same yield. This is not the case. Even within a sector of the bond market, such as the municipal bond market, sub-sectors will trade at different yields for a given credit rating and maturity to reflect different gradations of perceived credit risk. So, for example, within the corporate bond market which has sub-sectors there are yield spreads within a given credit rating. For example, noncallable industrial corporate bonds will trade at a different yield than utility corporate bonds with the same maturity and credit quality.

3. Impact of State and Local Taxes

State and local governments may tax interest income on bond issues that are exempt from federal income taxes. Some municipalities exempt interest income from all municipal issues from taxation, others do not. Some states exempt interest income from bonds issued by municipalities within the state, but tax the interest income from bonds issued by municipalities outside of the state. The implication is that two municipal securities of the same credit rating and the same maturity may trade at some yield spread because of the relative demand for bonds of municipalities in different states. For example, in a high income tax state such as New York, the demand for bonds of municipalities will drive down their yield relative to municipalities in a low income tax state such as Florida.

G. Technical Factors

There are times in the market where deviations from typical yield spreads are caused by temporary imbalances between supply and demand. For example, in the second quarter of 1999, issuers became concerned that the Fed would pursue a policy to increase interest rates. In response, there was record issuance of corporate securities. This resulted in an increase in the yield spread between corporates and Treasuries.

In the municipal market, yield spreads are affected by the temporary oversupply of issues within a market sector. For example, a substantial-new issue volume of high-grade state general obligation bonds may tend to decrease the yield spread between high-grade and low-grade revenue bonds. In a weak market environment, it is easier for high-grade municipal bonds to come to market than for weaker credits. So there are times when high grades flood weak markets at the same time that there is a relative scarcity of medium- and low-grade municipal bond issues.

Since technical factors cause temporary misalignments of the yield spread relationship, some investors look at the forward calendar for planned offerings to project the impact on future yield spreads. Some corporate analysts actually identify the risk of yield spread changes due to the supply of new issues when evaluating issuers or sectors. For example, analysts at Morgan Stanley Dean Witter assess this risk for individual companies and sectors — which they call "supply risk" — in terms of "positive," "negative," or "neutral."

SECTION V NON-U.S. INTEREST RATES

The same factors that affect yield spreads in the United States are responsible for yield spreads in other countries and between countries. Major non-U.S. bond markets have a government benchmark yield curve similar to that of the U.S. Treasury yield curve. Panel a of Exhibit 13 shows the government yield curve (2-year, 5-year, 10-year, and 30-year issues) for the G-7 countries on July 22, 1999. Panel b shows the nominal spread for each maturity between the yield in each G7 country relative to the U.S. Treasury yield. It is a "nominal spread" because it does not take into account exchange rate risk. Nor does it take into account the callability of issues of non-U.S. government bond issues.

Because of the important role of the German bond market, nominal spreads are typically computed relative to German government bonds (German **bunds)**. (The German bond market is the largest market for publicly issued bonds in Europe. The yields on German government bonds are viewed as benchmark interest rates in Europe.) This is shown in panel c of Exhibit 13 for the French, Italian, and U.K. government bonds.

Exhibit 13: Yields and Nominal Spreads on G-7 Government Benchmark Bonds on July 22, 1999

Panel a: Yield Curve (in percent)

Country	2-year	5-year	10-year	30-year
U.S.	5.51	5.64	5.78	5.96
Canada	5.26	5.39	5.46	5.49
Japan	0.28	0.95	1.74	2.63
Germany	3.21	3.93	4.60	5.34
France	3.30	4.02	4.71	5.40
Italy	3.37	4.16	4.84	5.58
U.K.	5.47	5.49	5.15	4.65

Panel b: Nominal Spread to U.S. Treasuries (in basis points)

Country	2-year	5-year	10-year	30-year
Canada	−25	−25	−32	−47
Japan	−523	−469	−404	−333
Germany	−230	−171	−118	−62
France	−221	−162	−107	−56
Italy	−214	−148	−94	−38
U.K.	−4	−15	−63	−131

Panel c: Nominal Spread to German Bunds (in basis points)

Country	2-year	5-year	10-year	30-year
France	9	9	11	6
Italy	16	23	24	24
UK	226	156	55	−69

Source: Abstracted from *Global Relative Value*, Lehman Brothers, Fixed Income Research, July 26, 1999, p. T-3.

There are also representative issues in different sectors of the global bond market that investors use to gauge nominal spreads relative to U.S. Treasury issues. Exhibit 14 shows nominal spreads on corporate issues relative to U.S. Treasuries on July 23, 1999. Panel a shows issues denominated in Euros and panel b issues denominated in British sterling. Exhibit 15 shows representative yield spreads for emerging market bond issues denominated in U.S. dollars relative to U.S. Treasuries.

With Monetary Union in Europe and the resulting increased supply of corporate bonds and improved liquidity, the European corporate bond market has developed clearer yield spread patterns. However, better known issuers tend to trade at a narrower yield spread than issuers that are not as well known. That is, there is a "name recognition" that continues to exist in the European corporate bond market. This is due to the bidding up of the prices of issues of better known issuers and thereby driving down their yield relative to issuers not as well know. This is also observed in the U.S. corporate bond market where there tends to be a wider yield spread on Yankee issues compared to U.S. issuers.[6]

---

[6] *Global Relative Value*, Lehman Brothers, May 17, 1999, COR-8-11. There are other reasons for some of the apparent yield spreads attributable to name recognition that are explained in this publication.

Exhibit 14: Nominal Spreads for Representative Corporate Issues Denominated in Euros and Sterling (July 23, 1999)
Panel a: Nominal Spreads (in basis points) for Euro-Denominated Issues

Issuer	Sector	Maturity	Rating	Nominal Spread
Deutsche Tele	Industrial	5/20/08	Aa2/AA-	48
Scottish Power	Industrial	8/20/08	Aa2/A+	73
Ford	Industrial	6/16/08	A1/A	75
Abbey National	Financial	7/12/04	Aa2AA	36
Merrill Lynch	Financial	1/4/09	Aa3/AA-	88
Fortis Finance	Financial	4/7/09	Aa3/A+	59

Panel b: Nominal Spreads (in basis points) for Sterling Denominated Issues

Issuer	Sector	Maturity	Rating	Nominal Spread
Yorkshire Water	Industrial	4/23/10	Aa3/AA	115
Coca Cola	Industrial	3/12/08	A3/A+	101
Abbey National	Financial	1/21/04	Aa2/AA	81
Frankfurter Hypo	Financial	2/4/08	Aaa/AAA	70

Source: Abstracted from *Global Relative Value*, Lehman Brothers, Fixed Income Research, July 26, 1999, p. T-9

Exhibit 15: Nominal Spreads for Representative U.S. Dollar-Denominated Emerging Markets Issues on July 23, 1999

		Coupon (%)	Maturity	Yield (%)	Nominal Spread (bp)
Argentina	ArgRep06	11.000	10/09/2006	13.01	698
	ArgRep27	9.750	09/19/2027	13.57	739
	FRB	5.938	03/31/2005	15.22	954
Brazil	BrzRep27	10.125	05/15/2027	14.48	829
	IDU	6.500	01/01/2001	12.37	708
Columbia	ColRep07	7.625	02/15/2007	12.77	673
	ColRep27	8.375	02/15/2027	12.17	597
Russia	Russia01	9.250	11/27/2001	27.02	2141
	Russia07	10.000	06/26/2007	24.93	1888
Venezuela	VenRep27	9.250	09/15/2027	14.86	868
	FLIRBA	6.000	03/31/2007	17.92	1213
	DCBDL	6.313	12/18/2007	16.90	1106

Source: Abstracted from *Global Relative Value*, Lehman Brothers, Fixed Income Research, July 26, 1999, p. T-10

SECTION VI KEY POINTS

❑ The interest rate offered on a particular bond issue depends on the interest rate that can be earned on risk-free instruments plus the perceived risks associated with the issue.

❑ The level of interest rates depends on the state of the economy and the interest rate policies implemented by the country's Central Bank.

❑ The structure of interest rates refers to the systematic reasons why the interest rate offered on one bond issue will differ from the interest rate offered on another bond issue at a snapshot in time.

❑ The U.S. Federal Reserve is the policy making body whose interest rate policy tools directly influence short-term interest rates and indirectly influence long-term interest rates in the United States.

❏ *The most frequently employed interest rate policy tools used by the Fed are open market operations (changing the federal funds rate) and changing the discount rate; less frequently used tools are changing bank reserve requirements and verbal persuasion to influence how bankers supply credit to businesses and consumers*

❏ *Because Treasury securities have no credit risk, market participants look at the interest rate or yield offered on an on-the-run Treasury security as the minimum interest rate required on a non-Treasury security with the same maturity.*

❏ *The Treasury yield curve shows the relationship between the yield on the on-the-run Treasury issues and maturity.*

❏ *The typical shape for the Treasury yield curve is upward sloping — yield increases with maturity — and is referred to as a normal yield curve.*

❏ *Historically, inverted yield curves — yield decreases with maturity — and flat yield curves — yield roughly the same regardless of maturity — have been observed for the Treasury yield curve.*

❏ *Two factors complicate the relationship between maturity and yield as given by the Treasury yield curve: (1) the yield for on-the-run issues is distorted by the fact that these securities can be financed at cheaper rates and as a result can offer a lower yield than in the absence of this financing advantage and (2) on-the-run Treasury issues and off-the-run issues have different interest rate risk and different reinvestment risk.*

❏ *The yield on Treasury strips for different maturities provides a superior relationship between yield and maturity than the on-the-run Treasury yield curve.*

❏ *The yield on zero-coupon or stripped Treasury securities is called the Treasury spot rate.*

❏ *The term structure of interest rates is the relationship between maturity and Treasury spot rates.*

❏ *There are problems with using the observed yield on Treasury strips to construct the term structure of interest rates.*

❏ *Despite the imperfections of the Treasury yield curve as a benchmark for the minimum interest rate that an investor will require for investing in a non-Treasury security, it is commonplace to refer to the additional yield over the on-the-run Treasury issue of the same maturity as the yield spread.*

❏ *The yield spread can be computed in one of three ways: (1) difference between the yield on two bonds or bond sectors (called the absolute yield spread), (2) the percentage of one yield relative to another (called the relative yield spread), and (3) the ratio of one yield to another yield (called the yield ratio).*

❏ *An intermarket yield spread is the yield spread between the interest rate offered in two sectors of the bond market with the same maturity.*

❏ *The most common intermarket sector spread calculated by market participants is the yield spread between Treasury securities and some sector of the non-Treasury market with the same maturity.*

❏ *An intramarket yield spread is the yield spread between two issues within a market sector.*

❏ *An issuer specific yield curve can be computed given the yield spread by maturity for an issuer and the yield for the on-the-run Treasury securities.*

❏ *The factors that affect the intermarket and intramarket yield spreads in addition to maturity are (1) the relative credit risk of the two issues; (2) the presence of embedded options; (3) the liquidity of an issue; and, (4) the taxability of the interest received by investors.*

❑   *A credit spread or quality spread is the yield spread between non-Treasury securities and Treasury securities that are identical in all respects except for credit*

❑   *There is a view that credit spreads between corporates and Treasuries change systematically because of expected changes in economic prospects — widening in a declining economy ("flight to quality") and narrowing in an expanding economy.*

❑   *Generally investors will require a larger spread to a comparable Treasury security for issues with an embedded option favorable to an issuer, and a smaller spread for an issue with an embedded option favorable to the investor.*

❑   *For mortgage-backed securities, one reason for the yield spread relative to a comparable Treasury security is due to the exposure to prepayment risk.*

❑   *The option-adjusted spread of a security seeks to measure the yield spread after adjusting for any embedded options.*

❑   *A yield spread exists due to the difference in the perceived liquidity of two issues.*

❑   *One factor that affects the liquidity of an issue (and therefore the yield spread) is the size of an issue — the larger the issue, the greater the liquidity relative to a smaller issue, and the higher the yield spread.*

❑   *Because of the tax-exempt feature of municipal bonds, the yield on municipal bonds is less than that on Treasuries with the same maturity.*

❑   *The difference in yield between tax-exempt securities and Treasury securities is typically measured in terms of a yield ratio — the percentage of the yield on a tax-exempt security relative to a comparable Treasury security.*

❑   *The after-tax yield is computed by multiplying the pre-tax yield by one minus the marginal tax rate.*

❑   *In the tax-exempt bond market, the benchmark for calculating yield spreads is a generic AAA general obligation bond with a specified maturity.*

❑   *Technical factors having to do with temporary imbalances between the supply of new issues and demand affect yield spreads.*

❑   *The same factors that affect yield spreads in the United States affect yield spreads in other countries and between countries.*

❑   *Major non-U.S. bond markets have a government benchmark yield curve similar to that of the U.S. Treasury yield curve.*

❑   *Because of the important role of the German bond market, nominal spreads in the European bond market are typically computed relative to German government bonds.*

END OF CHAPTER QUESTIONS

1. The following statement appears on page 2 of the August 2, 1999 issue of Prudential Securities' *Spread Talk*.

   > The market appears to be focusing all of its energy on predicting whether or not the Fed will raise rates again at the August and/or October FOMC [Federal Open Market Committee] meetings.

   What do market observers do to try to predict "whether or not the Fed will raise rates"?

2. The yield for the on-the-run Treasury issues on August 6, 1999 as reported by Lehman Brothers was as follows:

Issue (maturity)	Yield (%)
3 months	4.79
6 months	5.03
1 year	5.14
2 years	5.67
5 years	5.90
10 years	6.02
30 years	6.16

   Compute using simple linear extrapolation the Treasury yield for the following maturities: 3 years, 4 years, 6 years, 7 years, and 8 years.

3. The following information was abstracted from Lehman Brothers' *Global Relative Value* publication on August 9, 1999 pertaining to federal agency spreads on August 6, 1999:

Agency Spreads versus Benchmark Treasury (basis points)

	Yield spread	Last 12 months High	Low	Average
Noncallable				
3-year	70	70	28	44.1
5-year	80	80	32	55.4
10-year	95	95	45	71.2
Callable				
3-year (NC1)	107	107	50	80.2
5-year (NC1)	145	145	77	112.1
5-year (NC2)	132	132	65	96.9
5-year (NC3)	124	124	—	33.6
10-year (NC3)	178	178	99	132.9
10-year (NC5)	156	156	79	112.5
Callable OAS (volatility = 14%)				
3-year (NC1)	75	75	20	50.0
5-year (NC1)	100	100	20	63.8
5-year (NC2)	100	100	23	60.7
5-year (NC3)	100	100	29	59.6
10-year (NC3)	115	115	34	77.0
10-year (NC5)	115	115	36	77.4

Note: NCX = X-year deferred call

   a. Relative to the previous 12 months, what does the yield spread data above indicate about credit spreads?

   b. Explain what causes the yield spread relationship between callable and noncallable issues for a given maturity?

c. Explain what causes the yield spread relationship between the different callable issues for a given maturity?

d. Why are the yield spreads shown in the second panel referred to as nominal spreads?

e. Explain what causes the yield spread relationship between the callable yield spread and the callable OAS for a given maturity and given deferred call?

4. Following is a quote from the February 9, 1998 issue of Lehman Brothers' *Global Relative Value* publication (REL-4):

> The spread sectors have benefitted from this shift in market psychology. Last week was the best week of this young year for the investment-grade corporate and Eurobond asset classes. Our strong recommendation: keep riding the sector spread train during February. Spreads contracted by 5-7 bp along most parts of the curve in most sectors.

What is the impact of contracting sector spreads on the performance of spread sectors of the bond market?

5. The exhibit below (reprinted from Exhibit 5 on page 46 of Morgan Stanley Dean Witter, *U.S. Portfolio Strategies*, February 18, 1999) had the following commentary regarding the yield spread between cyclical and non-cyclical industry sectors:

> "The market is still pricing in a recession in the cyclical sectors despite GDP forecasts calling for strong growth."

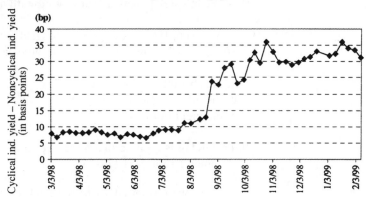

a. What is the yield spread between cyclical and non-cyclical industry sectors a proxy for?

b. Explain why the commentary is suggesting that a recession is being factored into the cyclical sector.

6. The following is an excerpt from the June 28, 1999 issue of Lehman Brothers' *Global Relative Value* (COR 10):

> Given the tough corporate environment during 2H 1998, the "exit strategy" or liquidity was one of the main concerns investors had at

the start of this year. But as the fundamental outlook improved during the onset of 1999, capital and corporate market sentiment recovered, and investors were rewarded for adding yield by giving up liquidity.

What is meant by "investors were rewarded for adding yield by giving up liquidity"?

7. Comment on the following statement by a representative of an investment management firm that is working with a client in selecting sectors in which the manager for the account will be permitted to invest:

Mortgage-backed securities give our managers the opportunity to increase yield because these securities offer a higher yield than comparable Treasury securities. In particular, our managers prefer Ginnie Mae mortgage-backed securities because they have no credit risk since they are backed by the full faith and credit of the U.S. government. Therefore, our managers can pickup additional yield with no additional credit risk. While Ginnie Mae mortgage-backed securities may not be as liquid as U.S. Treasury securities, the yield spread is more than adequate to compensate for the lesser liquidity.

8. a. Why is the yield spread between a bond with an embedded option and an otherwise comparable Treasury security referred to as a "nominal spread"?

b. What is an option-adjusted spread and why is it superior to a nominal spread as a yield spread measure for a bond with an embedded option?

9. On August 6, 1999, the approximate yield for MCI/Worldcom (A3/A−) was 7.25%. The 10-year on-the-run Treasury on the same date was 6.02%. Compute the following:

a. the absolute yield spread
b. the relative yield spread
c. the yield ratio

10. Following is a quote that appeared in the May 19, 1999 *Global Relative Value* by Lehman Brothers (COR-1):

As we have written in the past, percent yield spreads (spread as a percent of Treasury yields) are still cheap on an historical basis. As an illustration, the average single A 10-year industrial percent yield spread was 17% on April 30 compared to a 10 year monthly average of 12%.

a. What is another name for the yield spread measure cited in the quote?

b. Why would the analysts at Lehman Brothers focus on "percent yield spreads" rather than the absolute yield spread?

11. Using the Treasury yield curve on July 23, 1999 as shown in Exhibit 2 and the yield spreads shown for Sprint in Exhibit 5, what is the estimated on-the-run yield curve (2-year, 5-year, 7-year, 10-year, and 30-year) for Sprint on July 23, 1999.

12. If there are proposals being considered by Congress to reduce tax rates and the market views that this prospect of passage of such legislation is likely, what would you expect will happen to the yield on municipal bonds?

13. a. Why isn't the Treasury yield curve used as a benchmark in measuring yield spreads between different sectors of the municipal bond market?
    b. What benchmark is used?

14. a. What is the after-tax yield for an investor in the 40% tax bracket if the taxable yield is 5%?
    b. What is the taxable-equivalent yield for an investor in the 39% tax bracket if the tax-exempt yield on an investment is 3.1%.

15. Why is the yield spread between the yield on a non-U.S. government bond and a U.S. Treasury bond of the same maturity referred to as a "nominal spread"?

SOLUTIONS TO END OF CHAPTER QUESTIONS

1. Market participants will look at the key indicators watched by the Fed to try to predict how the Fed will react to the movement in the indicators.

2. Between the 2-year and 5-year issues the difference per year is

$$\frac{5.90\% - 5.67\%}{3} = 0.08\% = 8 \text{ basis points}$$

3-year yield = 5.67% + 0.08% = 5.75%
4 year yield = 5.75% + 0.08% = 5.82%

Between the 5-year and 10-year issues the difference per year is

$$\frac{6.02\% - 5.90\%}{5} = 0.02\% = 2 \text{ basis points}$$

6-year yield = 5.90% + 0.02% = 5.92%
7-year yield = 5.92% + 0,02% = 5.95%
8-year yield = 5.94% + 0.02% = 5.97%

3. a. The data clearly suggest that yield spreads are at their 12-month highs.

   b. A callable agency issue must offer a higher yield spread than a noncallable agency issue because of the call risk faced by investors in the former.

   c. For a given maturity, the longer the deferred call the lower the call risk. Hence, the yield spread for a callable issue is less the longer the deferred call.

   d. The yield spread between an agency security and a benchmark Treasury issue of a given maturity reflects credit risk, liquidity risk, and call risk. Because these yield spreads in the second panel include call risk, they are referred to as nominal spreads.

   e. The compensation for credit risk, liquidity risk, and call risk are lumped together in the nominal spreads (i.e., yield spreads shown in the second panel). The OAS is an estimate of the yield spread after taking out the call (or option) risk. So, the OAS is less than the nominal yield spread.

4. When the yield spread narrows (assuming Treasury yields do not increase), this means that the market requires a lower yield for a spread product (i.e., a non-Treasury security). By February 8, 1998, there was a considerable narrowing of the yield spread for all maturities so the spread sectors performed well relative to the Treasury sector.

5. a. Some market observers believe that this yield spread is a proxy for the market's expectations for future economic prospects. A widening of the yield spread suggests that the market expects the economy to contract; a narrowing of the yield spread suggests that the market economy expects good economic prospects ahead.

   b. A wide yield spread (on an historical basis) suggests that the market may be anticipating a recession and pricing cycles accordingly. In February 1999, the yield spread between cyclicals and non-cyclicals was considerably larger than in the first three quarter of 1998. Thus, the commentary suggests that despite the strong GDP forecasts, the yield spread is still wide and the market appears to believe a recession is ahead in the cyclical sector.

6. There is a component of yield spread attributable to liquidity. In the second half of 1998, that yield spread was particularly wide. That is, investors on a historical basis were being offered a large yield spread for accepting liquidity risk. Subsequently, the yield spread due to liquidity risk narrowed and investors benefited from price appreciation attributable to a narrowing yield spread.

7. While it is true that a Ginnie Mae mortgage-backed security has no credit risk and that part of the yield spread between a Ginnie Mae mortgage-backed security and a U.S. Treasury security is due to differences in liquidity, the major reason for the yield spread is the prepayment risk of a mortgage-backed security. This risk is ignored in the statement made by the representative of the investment management firm.

8. a. Part of the yield spread between a bond with an embedded option and a Treasury security (which is an option-free security) is due to the value of the embedded option granted to the issuer. For example, for a callable bond, the yield spread is larger than a noncallable non-Treasury security and a Treasury security for several reasons, one of which is the presence of the call option. Hence the yield spread is nominal because it fails to adjust the yield spread for compensation for accepting call risk that must be given to the bondholder of a callable bonds, whereas no such compensation is required by the bondholder of an otherwise comparable noncallable bond.

   b. The option-adjusted spread measure seeks to determine what part of the yield spread between a non-Treasury security and a Treasury security is attributable to the embedded option and adjusts the yield spread for the value of the option. So, the option-adjusted spread is less than the nominal spread.

9. a. absolute yield spread = 7.25% − 6.02% = 1.23% = 123 basis points

   b. relative yield spread = $\dfrac{7.25\% - 6.02\%}{6.02\%}$ = 0.204 = 20.4%

   c. yield ratio = $\dfrac{7.25\%}{6.02\%}$ = 1.20

10. a. The percent yield spread is the relative yield spread.

    b. Managers and analysts recognize that historical comparisons of the absolute yield spread for assessing how yield spreads are changing do not recognize the level of yields. For example, a 40 basis point absolute yield spread in a 5% interest rate environment is quite different than a 40 basis point absolute yield spread in a 10% yield environment.

11. To obtain an estimated on-the-run issue yield curve for Sprint on July 23, 1999, the yield spread shown in Exhibit 5 must be added to the corresponding maturity on-the-run Treasury issue in Exhibit 2. That is:

Maturity	Treasury yield (%)	Yield spread for Sprint (%)	Sprint on the run yield (%)
2	5.55	0.85	6.40
5	5.68	1.05	6.73
7*	5.74	1.16	6.90
10	5.83	1.40	7.23
30	6.01	1.58	7.59

* The 7-year yield using a simple linear extrapolation was computed in the chapter to be 5.74%.

12. Tax-exempt municipal securities offer a lower yield than Treasury securities because of the value of the tax-exempt feature. This feature is more attractive to high tax bracket investors than to low tax bracket investors. A proposal to reduce marginal tax rates makes the tax-exempt feature less attractive to investors. This requires that tax-exempt municipals offer a higher yield compared to the yield level prior to the proposal. In fact, when Congress was entertaining proposals for a flat tax (with a low tax rate), municipal yields did increase in the market.

13. a. Because of the tax exemption of municipals while Treasury issues are taxed at the federal level, yield spreads between the municipal market relative to Treasuries are affected by marginal tax rates.
    b. Yield spreads within the municipal market are calculated relative to the highest credit quality (AAA) issues of more actively traded issues (general obligation bonds).

14. a. The after-tax yield is

$$5\% \times (1 - 0.4) = 3\%$$

    b. The taxable-equivalent yield is

$$\frac{3.1\%}{(1 - 0.39)} = 5.08\%$$

15. The yield spread between a non-U.S. government bond and a same-maturity U.S. Treasury security does not reflect exchange rate risk between the currencies of the two countries. Therefore, the yield spread is a nominal spread. Moreover, if a non-U.S. government bond is callable, the yield spread is nominal because it does not take into account the portion of the yield spread attributable to the call option.

SOLUTIONS TO PRACTICE QUESTIONS

1 a. The 2-year, 3-year, 5-year, and 10-year issues are the Treasury notes.
   b. The 3-month, 6-month, and 1-year issues are the Treasury bills.
   c. There is only one Treasury bond, the 30-year issue.
   d. The U.S. Department of the Treasury no longer issues 3-year Treasury notes.
   e. Using linear extrapolation:

$$\frac{5.61\% - 5.47\%}{5} = 0.028\% = 2.8 \text{ basis points}$$

6-year maturity = 5.47% + 0.028% = 5.50%
7-year maturity = 5.50% + 0.028% = 5.53%
8-year maturity = 5.53% + 0.028% = 5.55%
9-year maturity = 5.56% + 0.028% = 5.58%

2. In the computation, we will treat the Treasury issue as bond B and the corporate issue as bond A.
   a. GTE versus Treasury

absolute yield spread = 6.11% − 5.16% = 0.95% = 95 basis points

$$\text{relative yield spread} = \frac{6.11\% - 5.16\%}{5.16\%} = 0.184 = 18.4\%$$

$$\text{yield ratio} = \frac{6.11\%}{5.16\%} = 1.18$$

   b. IBM versus Treasury

absolute yield spread = 5.93% − 5.16% = 0.77% = 77 basis points

$$\text{relative yield spread} = \frac{5.93\% - 5.16\%}{5.16\%} = 0.149 = 14.9\%$$

$$\text{yield ratio} = \frac{5.93\%}{5.16\%} = 1.15$$

3 a. Since the call feature is an unattractive feature to an investor and results in call risk, the callable issues must offer a higher yield spread.
   b. The longer the protection against the issue being called, the lower the call risk. Consequently, the greater the deferred call period, the lower the yield spread.

4. a.
   after-tax yield for Ms. High = 6.8% (1 − 0.40) = 4.08%
   after-tax yield for Mr. Low = 6.8% (1 − 0.15) = 5.78%
   b.

$$\text{taxable equivalent yield for Ms.High} = \frac{4.8\%}{1 - 0.40} = 0.0800 = 8.00\%$$

$$\text{taxable equivalent yield for Ms.High} = \frac{4.8\%}{1 - 0.15} = 0.0565 = 5.65\%$$

Chapter 5

INTRODUCTION TO THE VALUATION OF FIXED INCOME SECURITIES

LEARNING OUTCOME STATEMENTS

After reading this chapter you should be able to:

- describe the fundamental principle of bond valuation.
- explain the three steps in the valuation process: estimate expected cash flows, determine an appropriate discount rate or rates, and compute the present value of the cash flows.
- explain what is meant by a bond's cash flow.
- describe the difficulties of estimating the expected cash flows for some types of bonds.
- identify the bond types for which it is difficult to estimate the expected cash flows.
- compute the value of a bond given the expected cash flows and the appropriate discount rates.
- explain how the value of a bond changes if the discount rate increases and decreases.
- describe the relationship between the coupon rate, discount rate, and price of a bond relative to par value.
- explain how the price of a bond changes as it approaches its maturity date.
- compute the price of the bond given the term structure of default free spot rates and the term structure of credit spreads.
- compute the value of a zero-coupon bond.
- compute the value of a bond that is between coupon payments.
- compute the dirty price of a bond, accrued interest, and clean price of a bond.
- explain the deficiency of the traditional approach to valuation – approach whereby each cash flow is discounted at the same discount rate.
- explain the arbitrage-free valuation approach and the role of Treasury spot rates in the valuation process.
- explain how the process of stripping and reconstitution forces the price of a bond towards its arbitrage-free value so that no arbitrage profit is possible.
- demonstrate how a dealer can generate an arbitrage profit if the market price of a bond differs from its arbitrage-free value.
- explain the basic features of common to models that can be used to value bonds with embedded options.

SECTION I
INTRODUCTION

Valuation is the process of determining the fair value of a financial asset. The process is also referred to as "valuing" or "pricing" a financial asset. In this chapter we will explain the general principles of fixed income security valuation. We will limit our discussion in this chapter to the valuation of option-free bonds. While we mention the issues associated with valuing bonds with embedded options in the last section of this chapter, these models are the subject of Level II.

Yields and yield spreads are often cited in the market and used as a measure of relative value. We postpone our discussion of yields and yield spread measures until the next chapter where we discuss how they are calculated and their limitations as a measure of relative value.

SECTION II
GENERAL
PRINCIPLES OF
VALUATION

The fundamental principle of valuation is that the value of any financial asset is the present value of the expected cash flows. This principle applies regardless of the financial asset. Thus, the valuation of a financial asset involves the following three steps:

Step 1: Estimate the expected cash flows.
Step 2: Determine the appropriate interest rate or interest rates that should be used to discount the cash flows.
Step 3: Calculate the present value of the expected cash flows found in step 1 by the interest rate or interest rates determined in step 2.

A. Estimating Cash Flows

Cash flow is simply the cash that is expected to be received in the future from an investment. In the case of a fixed income security, it does not make any difference whether the cash flow is interest income or repayment of principal. The **cash flows** of a security are the collection of each period's cash flow. Holding aside the risk of default, the cash flows for only a few fixed income securities are simple to project. Noncallable U.S. Treasury securities have this feature. These securities have known cash flows. For Treasury coupon securities the cash flows are the coupon interest payments every six months up to and including the maturity date and the principal repayment at the maturity date.

Following are examples of when investors will find it difficult to estimate the cash flows when they purchase a fixed income security:

1. the issuer or the investor has the option to change the contractual due date of the repayment of the principal, or
2. the coupon payment is reset periodically based on a formula that depends on some value or values for reference rates, prices, or exchange rates, or
3. the investor has the choice to convert or exchange the security into common stock.

Callable bonds, putable bonds, mortgage-backed securities, and asset-backed securities are examples of (1). Floating-rate securities are an example of (2). Convertible bonds and exchangeable bonds are examples of (3).

For securities that fall into the first category, a key factor determining whether either the issuer of the security or the investor would exercise an option to alter the cash flows is the level of interest rates in the future relative to the security's coupon rate. Specifically, for a callable bond, if the prevailing market rate the issuer can realize by issuing a new security is sufficiently below the issue's coupon rate to justify the costs associated with refunding the issue, the issuer is likely to call the issue. Similarly, for a loan, if the prevailing refinancing rate available in the market is sufficiently below the loan's rate so that there will be savings by refinancing after considering the associated refinancing costs, then the borrower has an incentive to refinance. For a putable bond, if the interest rate on comparable securities rises such that the value of the putable bond falls below the value at which it must be repurchased by the issuer (i.e., the put price), then the investor will put the issue.

What this means is that to properly estimate the cash flows of a fixed income security it is necessary to incorporate into the analysis, how in the future, changes in interest rates and other factors affecting the embedded option may affect cash flows. As we will see at Level II, this is taken into consideration in valuation models by introducing a parameter that reflects the expected volatility of interest rates.

B. Determining the Appropriate Rate or Rates

Once the cash flows for a fixed income security are estimated, the next step is to determine the appropriate interest rate that should be used to discount a cash flow. As we did in the previous chapter, we will use the terms interest rate and yield interchangeably. The minimum interest rate that an investor should require is the yield available in the marketplace on a default-free cash flow. As explained in the previous chapter, in the United States this is the yield on a U.S. Treasury security. This is one of the reasons that the Treasury market is a closely watched market by market participants. At this point we can think of the minimum interest rate that investors want as the yield on the on-the-run Treasury security with the same maturity. We will qualify this shortly.

The premium over the yield on the on-the-run Treasury issue that investors will require reflects the additional risks the investor faces by acquiring a security that is not issued by the U.S. government. In Chapter 3 we discussed this premium which we called the yield spread.

For each cash flow estimated, the same interest rate can be used to calculate the present value. However, since each cash flow is unique, it is more appropriate to value each cash flow using an interest rate specific to that cash flow. In the traditional approach to valuation discussed in Section III, we will see that a single interest rate is used. In Section IV the proper approach to valuation using multiple interest rates is explained. In that section we will also demonstrate why this must be the case.

C. Discounting the Expected Cash Flows

Given the expected (estimated) cash flows and the appropriate interest rate or interest rates that should be used to discount the cash flows, the final step in the valuation process is to value the cash flows.

The value of a single cash flow to be received in the future is equal to the amount of money that must be invested today to generate that future value. The resulting value is called the **present value** of a cash flow. (It is also called the **discounted value**.) The present value of a cash flow will depend on when a cash flow will be received (i.e., the **timing** of a cash flow) and the interest rate used to calculate the present value. The interest rate used is called the **discount rate**.

A present value for each expected cash flow is first calculated. The sum of the present values for all of a security's expected cash flows is then the value of the security.

The present value of the expected cash flow to be received t years from now if a discount rate i can be earned on any sum invested today is:

$$\text{present value}_t = \frac{\text{expected cash flow in period } t}{(1 + i)^t}$$

The value of a financial instrument is then the sum of the present value of all the expected cash flows. That is, assuming that there are N expected cash flows:

$$\text{value} = \text{present value}_1 + \text{present value}_2 + ... + \text{present value}_N$$

To illustrate the present value formula, consider a simple bond that matures in four years, has a coupon rate of 10%, and has a maturity value of $100. For simplicity, let's assume for now that the bond pays interest annually and the same discount rate of 8% should be used to calculate the present value of each cash flow. Then the cash flow for this bond is:

Year	Cash Flow
1	$10
2	10
3	10
4	110

The present value of each cash flow is

$$\text{Year 1: present value}_1 = \frac{\$10}{(1.08)^1} = \$9.2593$$

$$\text{Year 2: present value}_2 = \frac{\$10}{(1.08)^2} = \$8.5734$$

$$\text{Year 3: present value}_3 = \frac{\$10}{(1.08)^3} = \$7.9383$$

$$\text{Year 4: present value}_4 = \frac{\$110}{(1.08)^4} = \$80.8533$$

The value of this security is then the sum of the present values of the four cash flows. That is, the present value is $106.6243 ($9.2593 + $8.5734 + $7.9383 + $80.8533).

PRACTICE QUESTION 1

a. What is the present value of a 5-year security with a coupon rate of 7% that pays annually assuming a discount rate of 5%.?

b. A 5-year amortizing security with a par value of $10,000 and a coupon rate of 5% has an expected cash flow of $2,309.75 per year assuming that there are no prepayments. The annual cash flow includes interest and principal repayment. What is the present value of this amortizing security assuming a discount rate of 6%?

---

1. Present Value Properties

An important property about the present value can be seen from the above illustration. For the first three years, the cash flow is the same ($10) and the discount rate is the same (8%). The present value is lower the further into the future the cash flow will be received. *This is an important property of the present value: for a given discount rate, the farther into the future a cash flow is received, the lower its present value.* This can be seen in the present value formula above. As t increases, present value$_t$ decreases.

Exhibit 1: Price/Discount Rate Relationship for an Option-Free Bond

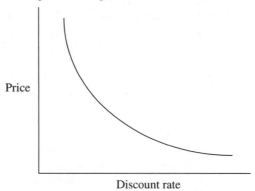

Suppose that instead of a discount rate of 8%, a 12% discount rate is used for each cash flow. Then, the present value of each cash flow is:

$$\textit{Year 1: present value}_1 = \frac{\$10}{(1.12)^1} = \$8.9286$$

$$\textit{Year 2: present value}_2 = \frac{\$10}{(1.12)^2} = \$7.9719$$

$$\textit{Year 3: present value}_3 = \frac{\$10}{(1.12)^3} = \$7.1178$$

$$\textit{Year 4: present value}_4 = \frac{\$110}{(1.12)^4} = \$69.9070$$

The value of this security is then $93.9253 ($8.9286 + $7.9719 + $7.1178 + $69.9070). The security's value is lower if a 12% discount rate is used compared to an 8% discount rate ($93.9253 versus $106.6243). This is a general property of present value. The higher the discount rate, the lower the present value. Since the value of a security is the present value of the expected cash flows, this property carries over to the value of a security: *the higher the discount rate, the lower a security's value*. The reverse is also true: *the lower the discount rate, the higher a security's value*.

Exhibit 1 shows for an option-free bond this inverse relationship between a security's value and the discount rate. The shape of the curve in Exhibit 1 is referred to as **convex**. By convex, it is meant the curve is bowed in from the origin. As we will see in Chapter 7, this convexity or bowed shape has implications for the price volatility of a bond when interest rates change. What is important to understand is that the relationship is not linear. In Chapter 7, we will see how the characteristics of an option-free bond (coupon and maturity) will affect the degree of the bowedness (convexity).

PRACTICE QUESTION 2

What is the present value of the cash flow of the 5-year 7% coupon security in Practice Question 1 assuming a discount rate of 4% rather than 5%?

2. Relationship between Coupon Rate, Discount Rate, and Price Relative to Par Value

In Chapter 2 we described the relationship between the coupon rate, the required market yield, and the price relative to par value (i.e., premium, discount, or par value). The required yield is the discount rate. We stated the following relationship:

coupon rate = yield required by market → price = par value
coupon rate < yield required by market → price < par value (discount)

coupon rate > yield required by market → price >par value (premium)

Now that we know how to value a bond, we can demonstrate the relationship. The coupon rate on our hypothetical bond is 10%. When an 8% discount rate is used, the bond's value is $106.6243. That is, the price is greater than par value (premium). This is because the coupon rate (10%) is greater than the required yield (the 8% discount rate). We also showed above that when the discount rate is 12% (i.e., greater than the coupon rate of 10%), the price of the bond is $93.9253. That is, the bond's value is less than par value when the coupon rate is less than the required yield (discount). When the discount rate is the same as the coupon rate, 10%, the bond's value is par value as shown below:

Year	Cash flow	Present value at 10%
1	$10	$9.0909
2	10	8.2645
3	10	7.5131
4	110	75.1315
Total		$100.0000

PRACTICE QUESTION 3

a. What is the value of a 5-year 7% coupon bond when the discount rate is (i) 6%, (ii) 7%, and (iii) 8%?

b. Show that the results obtained in part a are consistent with the relationship between the coupon rate, discount rate, and price relative to par value given in the text?

---

3. Change in a Bond's Value as it Moves Toward Maturity

As a bond moves closer to its maturity date, its value changes. More specifically, assuming that the discount rate does not change, a bond's value:

1. decreases over time if the bond is selling at a premium
2. increases over time if the bond is selling at a discount
3. is unchanged if the bond is selling at par value

At the maturity date, the bond's value is equal to its par value. So, over time as the bond moves toward its maturity date, its price will move to its par value — a characteristic sometimes referred to as a "pull to par value."

To illustrate what happens to a bond selling at a premium, consider once again the 4-year 10% coupon bond. When the discount rate is 8%, the bond's price is

106.6243. Suppose that one year later, the discount rate is still 8%. There are only three cash flows remaining since the bond is now a 3-year security. The cash flow and the present value of the cash flows are given below:

Year	Cash flow	Present value at 8%
1	$10	$9.2593
2	10	8.5734
3	110	87.3215
	Total	$105.1542

The price has declined from $106.6243 to $105.1542.

Now suppose that the bond's price is initially below par value. For example, if the discount rate is 12%, the 4-year 10% coupon bond's value would be $93.9253. Assuming the discount rate remains at 12%, one year later the cash flow and the present value of the cash flow would be as shown below:

Year	Cash flow	Present value at 12%
1	$10	$8.9286
2	10	7.9719
3	110	78.2958
	Total	$95.1963

The bond's price increases from $93.9253 to $95.1963.

To illustrate how the price of a bond changes as it moves towards maturity, consider the following three 20-year bonds for which the yield required by the market is 8%: a premium bond (10% coupon selling for 119.7928), a discount bond (6% coupon selling for 80.2072), and a par bond (8% coupon). To simplify the illustration, it is assumed that each bond pays interest annually. Exhibit 2 shows the price of each bond as it moves towards maturity assuming that the 8% yield required by the market does not change. Notice the pull downward to par value for the premium bond and the pull upward to par value for the discount bond.

In practice, over time the discount rate will change. So, the bond's value will change due to both the change in the discount rate and the change in the cash flow as the bond moves toward maturity. For example, suppose that the discount rate for the 4-year 10% coupon is 8% so that the bond is selling for $106.6243. One year later, suppose that the discount rate appropriate for a 3-year 10% coupon bond increases from 8% to 9%. Then the cash flow and present value of the cash flows are shown below:

Year	Cash flow	Present value at 9%
1	$10	$9.1743
2	10	8.4168
3	110	84.9402
	Total	$102.5313

The bond's price will decline from $106.6243 to $102.5313. If the discount rate did not increase, the price would have declined to only $105.1542. The price decline of $4.0930 ($106.6243 − $102.5313) can be decomposed as follows:

Price change attributable to moving to maturity (no change in discount rate)	$1.4701	(106.6243 − 105.1542)
Price change attribute to an increase in the discount rate from 8% to 9%	$2.6229	(105.1542 − 102.5313)
Total price change	$4.0930	

Exhibit 2: Movement of a Premium, Discount, and Par Bond as a Bond Moves Towards Maturity

Information about the three bonds:
All bonds mature in 20 years and the yield required by the market is 8%
Coupon payments are annual

Premium bond = 10% coupon selling for 119.7928
Discount bond = 6% coupon selling for 80.2072
Par bond = 8% coupon selling at par value

Assumption: The yield required by the market is unchanged over the life of the bond at 8%.

Time to maturity in years	Premium bond	Discount bond	Par bond
20	119.6363	80.3637	100.0000
19	119.2072	80.7928	100.0000
18	118.7438	81.2562	100.0000
17	118.2433	81.7567	100.0000
16	117.7027	82.2973	100.0000
15	117.1190	82.8810	100.0000
14	116.4885	83.5115	100.0000
13	115.8076	84.1924	100.0000
12	115.0722	84.9278	100.0000
11	114.2779	85.7221	100.0000
10	113.4202	86.5798	100.0000
9	112.4938	87.5062	100.0000
8	111.4933	88.5067	100.0000
7	110.4127	89.5873	100.0000
6	109.2458	90.7542	100.0000
5	107.9854	92.0146	100.0000
4	106.6243	93.3757	100.0000
3	105.1542	94.8458	100.0000
2	103.5665	96.4335	100.0000
1	101.8519	98.1481	100.0000
0	100.0000	100.0000	100.0000

D. Valuation Using Multiple Discount Rates

Thus far we have used one discount rate to compute the present value of each cash flow. As we will see shortly, the proper way to value the cash flows of a bond is to use a different discount rate that is unique to the time period in which a cash flow will be received. So, let's look at how we would value a security using a different discount rate for each cash flow.

Suppose that the appropriate discount rates are as follows

year 1   6.8%
year 2   7.2%
year 3   7.6%
year 4   8.0%

Then, for the 4-year 10% coupon bond, the present value of each cash flow is:

$$\text{Year 1: present value}_1 = \frac{\$10}{(1.068)^1} = \$9.3633$$

$$\text{Year 2: present value}_2 = \frac{\$10}{(1.072)^2} = \$8.7018$$

$$Year\ 3:\ present\ value_3 = \frac{\$10}{(1.076)^3} = \$8.0272$$

$$Year\ 4:\ present\ value_4 = \frac{\$110}{(1.080)^4} = \$80.8533$$

The present value of this security assuming the above set of discount rates is $106.9456.

PRACTICE QUESTION 4

Compute the value per $100 of par value of a 5-year 7% coupon bond assuming the payments are annual and the discount rate for each year is as follows:

Year	Discount rate (%)
1	3.5
2	3.9
3	4.2
4	4.5
5	5.0

E. Valuing Semiannual Cash Flows

In our illustrations, we assumed that the coupon payments are paid once per year. For most bonds, the payments are semiannual. This does not introduce any complexities into the calculation. The procedure is to simply adjust the coupon payments by dividing the annual coupon payment by 2 and adjust the discount rate by dividing the annual discount rate by 2. The time period t in the present value formula is treated in terms of 6-month periods rather than years.

For example, consider once again the 4-year 10% coupon bond with a maturity value of $100. The cash flow for the first 3.5 years is equal to $5 ($10/2). The last cash flow is equal to final coupon payment ($5) plus the maturity value ($100). So the last cash flow is $105.

Now the tricky part. If an annual discount rate of 8% is used, how do we obtain the semiannual discount rate? We will use one-half the annual rate, 4% (8%/2). The reader should have a problem with this: a 4% semiannual rate is not an 8% effective annual rate. That is correct. However, as we will see in the next chapter, the *convention* in the bond market is to quote annual interest rates that are just double semiannual rates. This will be explained more fully in the next chapter. Don't let this throw you off here. For now, just accept the fact that one-half an annual discount rate is used to obtain a semiannual discount rate in the balance of the chapter.

Given the cash flows and the semiannual discount rate of 4%, the present value of each cash flow is shown below:

$$Period\ 1:\ present\ value_1 = \frac{\$5}{(1.04)^1} = \$4.8077$$

$$Period\ 2:\ present\ value_2 = \frac{\$5}{(1.04)^2} = \$4.6228$$

$$Period\ 3:\ present\ value_3 = \frac{\$5}{(1.04)^3} = \$4.4450$$

$$\textit{Period 4}: \text{present value}_4 = \frac{\$5}{(1.04)^4} = \$4.2740$$

$$\textit{Period 5}: \text{present value}_5 = \frac{\$5}{(1.04)^5} = \$4.1096$$

$$\textit{Period 6}: \text{present value}_6 = \frac{\$5}{(1.04)^6} = \$3.9516$$

$$\textit{Period 7}: \text{present value}_7 = \frac{\$5}{(1.04)^7} = \$3.7996$$

$$\textit{Period 8}: \text{present value}_8 = \frac{\$105}{(1.04)^8} = \$76.7225$$

The security's value is equal to the sum of the present value of the 8 cash flows, $106.7327. Notice that this price is greater than the price when coupon payments are annual ($106.6243). This is because one-half the annual coupon payment is received six months sooner than when payments are annual. This produces a higher present value for the semiannual coupon payments relative to the annual coupon payments.

The value of a non-amortizing bond can be divided in two components: (1) the present value of the coupon payments and (2) the present value of the maturity value. For a fixed-rate coupon bond, the coupon payments represent an annuity. A short-cut formula for computing the value of a bond when a single discount rate is used is to compute the present value of the annuity and then add the present value of the maturity value.

The present value of an annuity is equal to:

$$\text{annuity payment} \times \left[\frac{1 - \dfrac{1}{(1 + r)^{\text{no. of periods}}}}{r} \right]$$

where r is the annual discount rate.

Applying this formula to a semiannual-pay bond, the annuity payment is one half the annual coupon payment and the number of periods is double the number of years to maturity. So, the present value of the coupon payments can be expressed as:

$$\text{semiannual coupon payment} \times \left[\frac{1 - \dfrac{1}{(1 + i)^{\text{no. of years} \times 2}}}{i} \right]$$

where i is the semiannual discount rate ($r/2$). Notice that in the formula, for the number of periods we use the number of years multiplied by 2 since a period in our illustration is six months.

The present value of the maturity value is equal to

$$\text{present value of maturity value} = \frac{\$100}{(1 + i)^{\text{no. of years} \times 2}}$$

To illustrate this computation, consider once again the 4-year 10% coupon bond and assume the annual discount rate is 8% and therefore the semiannual discount rate is one half this rate (4%) for the reason cited earlier. Then:

$$\text{semiannual coupon payment} \ = \ \$5$$
$$\text{semiannual discount rate } (i) \ = \ 4\%$$
$$\text{number of years} \ = \ 4$$

then the present value of the coupon payments is

$$\$5 \times \left[\frac{1 - \dfrac{1}{(1.04)^{4 \times 2}}}{0.04} \right] = \$33.6637$$

To determine the price, the present value of the maturity value must be added to the present value of the coupon payments. The present value of the maturity value is

$$\text{present value of maturity value} \ = \ \frac{\$100}{(1.04)^{4 \times 2}} = \$73.0690$$

The price is then $106.7327 ($33.6637 + $73.0690). This agrees with our previous calculation for the price of this bond.

PRACTICE QUESTION 5

What is the value of a 5-year 7% coupon bond that pays interest semiannually assuming that the annual discount rate is 5%?

F. Valuing a Zero-Coupon Bond

For a zero-coupon bond, there is only one cash flow — the maturity value. The value of a zero-coupon bond that matures N years from now is

$$\frac{\text{maturity value}}{(1 + i)^{\text{no. of years} \times 2}}$$

where i is the semiannual discount rate.

It may seem surprising that the number of periods is double the number of years to maturity. In computing the value of a zero-coupon bond, the number of 6-month periods (i.e., "no. of years $\times 2$") is used in the denominator of the formula. The rationale is that the pricing of a zero-coupon bond should be consistent with the pricing of a coupon bond. Therefore, the use of 6-month periods is required in order to have uniformity between the present value calculation of the maturity value for a coupon bond that pays semiannually and a zero-coupon bond.

To illustrate the application of the formula, the value of a 5-year zero-coupon bond with a maturity value of $100 discounted at an 8% interest rate is $67.5564, as shown below:

$$i = 0.04 \ (= 0.08/2)$$

$$N = 5$$

$$\frac{\$100}{(1.04)^{5 \times 2}} = \$67.5564$$

PRACTICE QUESTION 6

a. Complete the following table for a 10-year zero-coupon bond with a maturity value of $1,000 for each of the following *annual* discount rates.

Annual rate	Semiannual rate	Price
1%		
2%		
3%		
4%		
5%		
6%		
7%		
8%		
9%		
10%		
11%		
12%		
13%		
14%		

b. Given the prices for the bond in part a, draw a graph of the price/yield relationship. On the horizontal axis (x-axis) should be the annual rate and on the vertical axis (y-axis) should be the price.

G. Valuing a Bond between Coupon Payments

For coupon-paying bonds, a complication arises when we try to price a bond between coupon payments. The amount that the buyer pays the seller in such cases is the present value of the cash flow. But one of the cash flows, the very next cash flow, encompasses two components as shown below (assuming the buyer does not sell the bond prior to the next coupon payment date):

1. interest earned by the seller
2. interest earned by the buyer

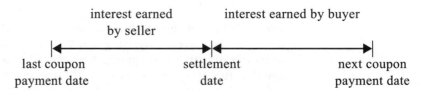

The interest earned by the seller is the interest that has accrued since the last coupon payment was made and the settlement date. This interest is called **accrued interest**. The buyer must compensate the seller for the accrued interest. The buyer recovers the accrued interest when the next coupon payment is received.

When the price of a bond is computed using the present value calculations described earlier, it is computed with accrued interest embodied in the price. This price is referred to as the **full price**. (Some market participants refer to it as the **dirty price**.) It is the full price that the buyer pays the seller. From the full price the accrued interest must be deducted to determine the **price** of the bond, sometimes referred to as the **clean price**.

Below we show how the present value formula is modified to compute the full price when a bond is purchased between coupon periods.

1. Computing the Full Price

To compute the full price it is first necessary to determine the fractional periods between the settlement date and the next coupon payment date. This is determined as follows:

$$w \text{ periods} = \frac{\text{days between settlement date and next coupon payment date}}{\text{days in coupon period}}$$

Then the present value of the expected cash flow to be received t periods from now using a discount rate i assuming the first coupon payment is w periods from now is:

$$\text{present value}_t = \frac{\text{expected cash flow}}{(1 + i)^{t-1+w}}$$

This procedure for calculating the present value when a security is purchased between coupon payments is called the "Street method."

To illustrate the calculation, suppose that there are five semiannual coupon payments remaining for a 10% coupon bond. Also assume the following:

  1. 78 days between the settlement date and the next coupon payment date
  2. 182 days in the coupon period

Then w is 0.4286 periods (= 78/182). The present value of each cash flow assuming that each is discounted at 8% annual discount rate is

$$\textit{Period 1: } \text{present value}_1 = \frac{\$5}{(1.04)^{0.4286}} = \$4.9167$$

$$\textit{Period 2: } \text{present value}_2 = \frac{\$5}{(1.04)^{1.4286}} = \$4.7276$$

$$\textit{Period 3: } \text{present value}_3 = \frac{\$5}{(1.04)^{2.4286}} = \$4.5457$$

$$\textit{Period 4: } \text{present value}_4 = \frac{\$5}{(1.04)^{3.4286}} = \$4.3709$$

$$\textit{Period 5: } \text{present value}_5 = \frac{\$105}{(1.04)^{4.4286}} = \$88.2584$$

The full price is the sum of the present value of the cash flows, which is $106.8192. Remember that the full price includes the accrued interest that the buyer is paying the seller.

PRACTICE QUESTION 7

Suppose that a bond is purchased between coupon periods. The days between the settlement date and the next coupon period is 58. There are 183 days in the coupon period. Suppose that the bond purchased has a coupon rate of 7% and there are 10 semiannual coupon payments remaining. What is the full price for this bond if a 5% annual discount rate is used?

2. Computing the Accrued Interest and the Clean Price

To find the price without accrued interest, called the **clean price** or simply **price**, the accrued interest must be computed. To determine the accrued interest, it is first necessary to determine the number of days in the accrued interest period. The number of days in the accrued interest period is determined as follows:

days in accrued interest period =
days in coupon period − days between settlement and next coupon payment

The percentage of the next semiannual coupon payment that the seller has earned as accrued interest is the found as follows:

$$\frac{\text{days in accrued interest period}}{\text{days in coupon period}}$$

So, for example, returning to our illustration where the full price was computed, since there are 182 days in the coupon period and there are 78 days from the settlement date to the next coupon payment, the days in the accrued interest period is 182 minus 78, or 104 days. Therefore, the percentage of the coupon payment that is accrued interest is:

$$\frac{104}{182} = 0.5714 = 57.14\%$$

This is the same percentage found by simply subtracting w from 1. In our illustration, w was 0.4286. Then $1 - 0.4286 = 0.5714$.

Given the value of w, the amount of accrued interest (AI) is equal to:

AI = semiannual coupon payment $\times (1 - w)$

So, for the 10% coupon bond whose full price we computed, since the semiannual coupon payment per $100 of par value is $5 and w is 0.4286, the accrued interest is:

$$\$5 \times (1 - 0.4286) = \$2.8571$$

The clean price is then:

full price − accrued interest

In our illustration, the clean price is[1]

$$\$106.8192 - \$2.8571 = \$103.9621$$

PRACTICE QUESTION 8

What is the accrued interest and the clean price for the bond whose full price is computed in Practice Question 7?

---

[1] Notice that in computing the full price the present value of the next coupon payment is computed. However, the buyer pays the seller the accrued interest now despite the fact that it will be recovered at the next coupon payment date.

3. Day Count Conventions

The accrued interest must be subtracted from the full price to get the clean price. The practice for calculating the number of days between two dates depends on day count conventions used in the bond market. The convention differs by the type of security. Day count conventions are also used to calculate the number of days in the numerator and denominator of the ratio w.

The accrued interest (AI) assuming semiannual payments is calculated as follows:

$$AI = \frac{annual\ coupon}{2} \times \frac{days\ in\ AI\ period}{days\ in\ coupon\ period}$$

In calculating the number of days between two dates, the actual number of days is not always the same as the number of days that should be used in the accrued interest formula. The number of days used depends on the day count convention for the particular security. Specifically, there are different day count *conventions* for Treasury securities than for government agency securities, municipal bonds, and corporate bonds.

For coupon-bearing Treasury securities, the day count convention used is to determine the actual number of days between two dates. This is referred to as the "actual/actual" day count convention. For example, consider a coupon-bearing Treasury security whose previous coupon payment was March 1. The next coupon payment would be on September 1. Suppose this Treasury security is purchased with a settlement date of July 17th. The actual number of days between July 17 (the settlement date) and September 1 (the date of the next coupon payment) is 46 days, as shown below:

July 17 to July 31	14 days
August	31 days
September 1	1 day
	46 days

Note that the settlement date (July 17) is not counted. The number of days in the coupon period is the actual number of days between March 1 and September 1, which is 184 days. The number of days between the last coupon payment (March 1) through July 17 is therefore 138 days (184 days − 46 days).

For coupon-bearing agency, municipal, and corporate bonds, a different day count convention is used. It is assumed that every month has 30 days, that any 6-month period has 180 days, and that there are 360 days in a year. This day count convention is referred to as "30/360." For example, consider once again the Treasury security purchased with a settlement date of July 17, the previous coupon payment on March 1, and the next coupon payment on September 1. If the security is an agency, municipal, or corporate bond, the number of days until the next coupon payment is 44 days as shown below:

July 17 to July 31	13 days
August	30 days
September 1	1 day
	44 days

Note that the settlement date, July 17, is not counted. Since July is treated as having 30 days, there are 13 days (30 days minus the first 17 days in July). The number of days from March 1 to July 17 is 136, which is the number of days in the accrued interest period.

Exhibit 3: Cash Flows for Three 10-Year Hypothetical Treasury Securities Per $100 of Par Value
Each period is six months

Period	Coupon Rate		
	12%	8%	0%
1-19	$6	$4	$0
20	106	104	100

SECTION III
TRADITIONAL APPROACH TO VALUATION

The traditional approach to valuation has been to discount every cash flow of a fixed income security by the same interest rate (or discount rate). For example, consider the three hypothetical 10-year Treasury securities shown in Exhibit 3: a 12% coupon bond, an 8% coupon bond, and a zero-coupon bond. The cash flows for each bond are shown in the exhibit. Since the cash flows of all three bonds are viewed as default free, the traditional practice is to use the same discount rate to calculate the present value of all three bonds and use the same discount rate for the cash flow for each period. The discount rate used is the yield for the on-the-run issue obtained from the Treasury yield curve. For example, suppose that the yield for the 10-year on-the-run Treasury issue is 10%. Then, the practice is to discount each cash flow of each bond using a discount rate of 10%.

For a non-Treasury security, a premium or yield spread is added to the on-the-run Treasury yield. The yield spread is the same regardless of when a cash flow is to be received in the traditional approach. For a 10-year non-Treasury security, suppose that 90 basis points is the appropriate yield spread. Then all cash flows would be discounted at the yield for the on-the-run 10-year Treasury issue of 10% plus 90 basis points.

SECTION IV
THE ARBITRAGE-FREE VALUATION APPROACH

The fundamental flaw of the traditional approach is that it views each security as the same package of cash flows. For example, consider a 10-year U.S. Treasury issue with an 8% coupon rate. The cash flows per $100 of par value would be 19 payments of $4 every six months and $104 twenty 6-month periods from now. The traditional practice would discount every cash flow using the same discount rate.

The proper way to view the 10-year 8% coupon Treasury issue is as a package of zero-coupon bonds whose maturity value is the amount of the cash flow and whose maturity date is the date that the cash flow is to be received. Thus, the 10-year 8% coupon Treasury issue should be viewed as 20 zero-coupon instruments. The reason this is the proper way to value a security is that it does not allow a market participant to realize an arbitrage profit by taking apart or "stripping" a security and selling off the stripped securities at a higher aggregate value than it would cost to purchase the security in the market. We'll illustrate this later. We refer to this approach to valuation as the **arbitrage-free valuation approach**.

By viewing any financial asset as a package of zero-coupon bonds, a consistent valuation framework can be developed. Viewing a financial asset as a package of zero-coupon bonds means that these two bonds would be viewed as different packages of zero-coupon bonds and valued accordingly.

The difference between the traditional valuation approach and the arbitrage-free approach is illustrated in Exhibit 4 which shows how the three bonds whose cash flows are depicted in Exhibit 3 should be valued. With the traditional approach, the interest rate for all three bonds is the yield on a 10-year U.S. Treasury security. With the arbitrage-free approach the interest rate for a cash flow is the theoretical rate that the U.S. Treasury would have to pay if it issued a zero-coupon bond with a maturity date equal to the maturity date of the cash flow.

Therefore, to implement the arbitrage-free approach it is necessary to determine the theoretical rate that the U.S. Treasury would have to pay on a zero-coupon Treasury security for each maturity. As explained in the previous chapter, the name given to the zero-coupon Treasury rate is the **Treasury spot rate**. In Chapter 6, we will explain how the Treasury spot rate can be calculated. The spot rate for a Treasury security of some maturity is the interest rate that should be used to discount a default-free cash flow with the same maturity. We call the value of a bond based on spot rates the **arbitrage-free value**.

A. Valuation Using Treasury Spot Rates

For the purposes of our discussion below, we will take the Treasury spot rate for each maturity as given. To illustrate how Treasury spot rates are used to compute the arbitrage-free value of a Treasury security, we will use the hypothetical Treasury spot rates shown in the third column of Exhibit 5 to value an 8% 10-year Treasury security. The present value of each period's cash flow is shown in the last column. The sum of the present values is the arbitrage-free value for the Treasury security. For the 8% 10-year Treasury it is $115.2619.

As a second illustration, suppose that a 4.8% coupon 10-year Treasury bond is being valued based on the Treasury spot rates shown in Exhibit 5. The arbitrage-free value of this bond is $90.8428 as shown in Exhibit 6.

Exhibit 4: Comparison of Traditional Approach and Arbitrage-Free Approach in Valuing a Treasury Security
Each period is six months

Period	Discount (Base Interest) Rate		Cash Flows For*		
	Traditional Approach	Arbitrage-Free Approach	12%	8%	0%
1	10-year Treasury rate	1-period Treasury spot rate	$6	$4	$0
2	10-year Treasury rate	2-period Treasury spot rate	6	4	0
3	10-year Treasury rate	3-period Treasury spot rate	6	4	0
4	10-year Treasury rate	4-period Treasury spot rate	6	4	0
5	10-year Treasury rate	5-period Treasury spot rate	6	4	0
6	10-year Treasury rate	6-period Treasury spot rate	6	4	0
7	10-year Treasury rate	7-period Treasury spot rate	6	4	0
8	10-year Treasury rate	8-period Treasury spot rate	6	4	0
9	10-year Treasury rate	9-period Treasury spot rate	6	4	0
10	10-year Treasury rate	10-period Treasury spot rate	6	4	0
11	10-year Treasury rate	11-period Treasury spot rate	6	4	0
12	10-year Treasury rate	12-period Treasury spot rate	6	4	0
13	10-year Treasury rate	13-period Treasury spot rate	6	4	0
14	10-year Treasury rate	14-period Treasury spot rate	6	4	0
15	10-year Treasury rate	15-period Treasury spot rate	6	4	0
16	10-year Treasury rate	16-period Treasury spot rate	6	4	0
17	10-year Treasury rate	17-period Treasury spot rate	6	4	0
18	10-year Treasury rate	18-period Treasury spot rate	6	4	0
19	10-year Treasury rate	19-period Treasury spot rate	6	4	0
20	10-year Treasury rate	20-period Treasury spot rate	106	104	100

* Per $100 of par value.

Exhibit 5: Determination of the Arbitrage-Free Value of an 8% 10-Year Treasury

Period	Years	Cash Flow ($)	Spot Rate (%)*	Present Value ($)**
1	0.5	4	3.0000	3.9409
2	1.0	4	3.3000	3.8712
3	1.5	4	3.5053	3.7968
4	2.0	4	3.9164	3.7014
5	2.5	4	4.4376	3.5843
6	3.0	4	4.7520	3.4743
7	3.5	4	4.9622	3.3694
8	4.0	4	5.0650	3.2747
9	4.5	4	5.1701	3.1791
10	5.0	4	5.2772	3.0828
11	5.5	4	5.3864	2.9861
12	6.0	4	5.4976	2.8889
13	6.5	4	5.6108	2.7916
14	7.0	4	5.6643	2.7055
15	7.5	4	5.7193	2.6205
16	8.0	4	5.7755	2.5365
17	8.5	4	5.8331	2.4536
18	9.0	4	5.9584	2.3581
19	9.5	4	6.0863	2.2631
20	10.0	104	6.2169	56.3828
			Total	$115.2619

* The spot rate is an annual discount rate. The convention to obtain a semiannual discount rate is to take one-half the annual discount rate. So, for period 6 (i.e., 3 years), the spot rate is 4.7520%. The semiannual discount rate is 2.376%.
** The present value for the cash flow is equal to:

$$\frac{\text{Cash flow}}{(1 + \text{Spot rate}/2)^{period}}$$

In the next chapter we discuss yield measures. The yield to maturity is a measure that would be computed for this bond. We won't show how it is computed in this chapter, but simply state the result. The yield is 6.033%. Notice that the spot rates are used to obtain the price and the price is then used to compute a conventional yield measure. *It is important to understand that there are an infinite number of spot rate curves that can generate the same price of $90.8428 and therefore the same yield.* We return to this point in the next chapter.

PRACTICE QUESTION 9

a. Using the Treasury spot rates shown in Exhibit 5, what is the arbitrage-free value of a 7.4% coupon 8-year Treasury security?

b. Using the Treasury spot rates shown in Exhibit 5, what is the arbitrage-free value of a 4% coupon 8-year Treasury security?

B. Reason for Using Treasury Spot Rates

Thus far we simply asserted that the value of a Treasury security should be based on discounting each cash flow using the corresponding Treasury spot rate. But what if market participants value a security using just the yield for the on-the-run Treasury with a maturity equal to the maturity of the Treasury security being valued? Let's see why a Treasury security will have to trade close to its arbitrage-free value.

Exhibit 6: Determination of the Arbitrage-Free Value of a 4.8% 10-Year Treasury

Period	Years	Cash Flow ($)	Spot Rate (%)*	Present Value ($)**
1	0.5	2.4	3.0000	2.3645
2	1.0	2.4	3.3000	2.3227
3	1.5	2.4	3.5053	2.2781
4	2.0	2.4	3.9164	2.2209
5	2.5	2.4	4.4376	2.1506
6	3.0	2.4	4.7520	2.0846
7	3.5	2.4	4.9622	2.0216
8	4.0	2.4	5.0650	1.9648
9	4.5	2.4	5.1701	1.9075
10	5.0	2.4	5.2772	1.8497
11	5.5	2.4	5.3864	1.7916
12	6.0	2.4	5.4976	1.7334
13	6.5	2.4	5.6108	1.6750
14	7.0	2.4	5.6643	1.6233
15	7.5	2.4	5.7193	1.5723
16	8.0	2.4	5.7755	1.5219
17	8.5	2.4	5.8331	1.4722
18	9.0	2.4	5.9584	1.4149
19	9.5	2.4	6.0863	1.3578
20	10.0	102.4	6.2169	55.5154
			Total	90.8428

* The spot rate is an annual discount rate. The convention to obtain a semiannual discount rate is to take one-half the annual discount rate. So, for period 6 (i.e., 3 years), the spot rate is 4.7520%. The semiannual discount rate is 2.376%.

** The present value for the cash flow is equal to:

$$\frac{\text{Cash flow}}{(1 + \text{Spot rate}/2)^{period}}$$

1. Stripping and the Arbitrage-Free Valuation

The key in the process is the existence of the Treasury strips market. As explained in Chapter 3, a dealer has the ability to take apart the cash flows of a Treasury coupon security (i.e., strip the security) and create zero-coupon securities. These zero-coupon securities, which we called Treasury strips, can be sold to investors. What interest rate or yield can these Treasury strips be sold to investors. They can be sold at the Treasury spot rates. If the market price of a Treasury security is less than its value using the arbitrage-free valuation approach, then a dealer can buy the Treasury security, strip it, and sell off the Treasury strips so as to generate greater proceeds than the cost of purchasing the Treasury security. The resulting profit is an arbitrage profit. Since, as we will see, the value determined by using the Treasury spot rates does not allow for the generation of an arbitrage profit, this is the reason why the approach is referred to as an "arbitrage-free" approach.

To illustrate this, suppose that the yield for the on-the-run 10-year Treasury issue is 6%. (We will see in Chapter 6 that the Treasury spot rate curve in Exhibit 5 was generated from a yield curve where the on-the-run 10-year Treasury issue was 6%.) Suppose that the 8% coupon 10-year Treasury issue is valued using the traditional approach based on 6%. Exhibit 7 shows the value based on discounting all the cash flows at 6% is $114.8775.

Exhibit 7: Price of an 8% 10-Year Treasury Valued at a 6% Discount Rate

Period	Years	Cash Flow ($)	Discount Rate (%)*	Present Value ($)**
1	0.5	4	6.0000	3.8835
2	1.0	4	6.0000	3.7704
3	1.5	4	6.0000	3.6606
4	2.0	4	6.0000	3.5539
5	2.5	4	6.0000	3.4504
6	3.0	4	6.0000	3.3499
7	3.5	4	6.0000	3.2524
8	4.0	4	6.0000	3.1576
9	4.5	4	6.0000	3.0657
10	5.0	4	6.0000	2.9764
11	5.5	4	6.0000	2.8897
12	6.0	4	6.0000	2.8055
13	6.5	4	6.0000	2.7238
14	7.0	4	6.0000	2.6445
15	7.5	4	6.0000	2.5674
16	8.0	4	6.0000	2.4927
17	8.5	4	6.0000	2.4201
18	9.0	4	6.0000	2.3496
19	9.5	4	6.0000	2.2811
20	10.0	104	6.0000	57.5823
			Total	114.8775

* The discount rate is an annual discount rate. The convention to obtain a semiannual discount rate is to take one-half the annual discount rate. So, since the discount rate for each period is 6%, the semiannual discount rate is 3%.
** The present value for the cash flow is equal to:

$$\frac{\text{Cash flow}}{(1.03)^{\text{period}}}$$

Consider what would happen if the market priced the security at $114.8775. The value based on the Treasury spot rates (Exhibit 5) is $115.2619. What can the dealer do? The dealer can buy the 8% 10-year issue for $114.8775, strip it, and sell the Treasury strips at the spot rates shown in Exhibit 5. By doing so, the proceeds that will be received by the dealer are $115.2619. This results in an arbitrage profit of $0.3844 (= $115.2619 − $114.8775). Dealers recognizing this arbitrage opportunity will bid up the price of the 8% 10-year Treasury issue in order to acquire it and strip it. At what point will the arbitrage profit disappear? When the security is priced at $115.2619, the value that we said is the arbitrage-free value.

To understand in more detail where this arbitrage profit is coming from, look at Exhibit 8.The third column shows how much each cash flow can be sold for by the dealer if it is stripped. The values in the third column are simply the present values in Exhibit 5 based on discounting the cash flows at the Treasury spot rates. The fourth column shows how much the dealer is effectively purchasing the cash flow if each cash flow is discounted at 6%. This is the last column in Exhibit 7. The sum of the arbitrage profit from each cash flow stripped is the total arbitrage profit.

2. Reconstitution and Arbitrage-Free Valuation

We have just demonstrated how coupon stripping of a Treasury issue will force the market value to be close to the value as determined by the arbitrage-free valuation approach when the market price is less than the arbitrage-free value. What happens when a Treasury issue's market price is greater than the arbitrage-free value? Obviously, a dealer will not want to strip the Treasury issue since the proceeds generated from stripping will be less than the cost of purchasing the issue.

When such situations occur, the dealer will follow a procedure called **reconstitution**. Basically, the dealer can purchase a package of Treasury strips so as to create a synthetic Treasury coupon security that is worth more than the same maturity and same coupon Treasury issue.

To illustrate this, consider the 4.8% 10-year Treasury issue whose arbitrage-free value was computed in Exhibit 6. The arbitrage-free value is $90.8428. Exhibit 9 shows the price assuming the traditional approach where all the cash flows are discounted at a 6% interest rate. The price is $91.0735. What the dealer can do is purchase the Treasury strip for each 6-month period at the prices shown in Exhibit 6 and sell short the 4.8% 10-year Treasury coupon issue whose cash flows are being replicated. By doing do, the dealer has the cash flow of a 4.8% coupon 10-year Treasury security at a cost of $90.8428, thereby generating an arbitrage profit of $0.2307 ($91.0735 – $90.8428). The cash flows from the package of Treasury strips purchased is used to make the payments for the Treasury coupon security shorted. Actually, in practice this can be done in an more efficient manner using a procedure for reconstitution provided for by the Department of the Treasury.

What forces the market price to the arbitrage-free value of $90.8428? As dealers sell short the Treasury coupon issue (4.8% 10-year issue), this drives down the price of the issue. When the price is driven down to $90.8428, the arbitrage profit is no longer exists.

This process of stripping and reconstitution assures that the price of a Treasury issue will not depart materially from its arbitrage-free value. In other countries, as governments permit the stripping and reconstitution of their issues, the value of non-U.S. government issues have also moved toward their arbitrage-free value.

Exhibit 8: Arbitrage Profit from Stripping the 8% 10-Year Treasury

Period	Years	Sell for	Buy for	Arbitrage profit
1	0.5	3.9409	3.8835	0.0574
2	1.0	3.8712	3.7704	0.1008
3	1.5	3.7968	3.6606	0.1363
4	2.0	3.7014	3.5539	0.1475
5	2.5	3.5843	3.4504	0.1339
6	3.0	3.4743	3.3499	0.1244
7	3.5	3.3694	3.2524	0.1170
8	4.0	3.2747	3.1576	0.1170
9	4.5	3.1791	3.0657	0.1134
10	5.0	3.0829	2.9764	0.1065
11	5.5	2.9861	2.8897	0.0964
12	6.0	2.8889	2.8055	0.0834
13	6.5	2.7916	2.7238	0.0678
14	7.0	2.7055	2.6445	0.0611
15	7.5	2.6205	2.5674	0.0531
16	8.0	2.5365	2.4927	0.0439
17	8.5	2.4536	2.4201	0.0336
18	9.0	2.3581	2.3496	0.0086
19	9.5	2.2631	2.2811	–0.0181
20	10.0	56.3828	57.5823	–1.1995
		115.2619	114.8775	0.3844

Exhibit 9: Price of a 4.8% 10-Year Treasury Valued at a 6% Discount Rate

Period	Years	Cash Flow ($)	Discount Rate (%)	Present Value ($)
1	0.5	2.4	6.0000	2.3301
2	1.0	2.4	6.0000	2.2622
3	1.5	2.4	6.0000	2.1963
4	2.0	2.4	6.0000	2.1324
5	2.5	2.4	6.0000	2.0703
6	3.0	2.4	6.0000	2.0100
7	3.5	2.4	6.0000	1.9514
8	4.0	2.4	6.0000	1.8946
9	4.5	2.4	6.0000	1.8394
10	5.0	2.4	6.0000	1.7858
11	5.5	2.4	6.0000	1.7338
12	6.0	2.4	6.0000	1.6833
13	6.5	2.4	6.0000	1.6343
14	7.0	2.4	6.0000	1.5867
15	7.5	2.4	6.0000	1.5405
16	8.0	2.4	6.0000	1.4956
17	8.5	2.4	6.0000	1.4520
18	9.0	2.4	6.0000	1.4097
19	9.5	2.4	6.0000	1.3687
20	10.0	102.4	6.0000	56.6964
			Total	91.0735

C. Credit Spreads and the Valuation of Non-Treasury Securities

The Treasury spot rates can be used to value any default-free security. For a non-Treasury security, the theoretical value is not as easy to determine. The value of a non-Treasury security is found by discounting the cash flows by the Treasury spot rates plus a yield spread to reflect the additional risks. This was discussed in Chapter 2 that are associated with investing in a non-Treasury security.

The spot rate used to discount the cash flow of a non-Treasury security can be the Treasury spot rate plus a constant credit spread. For example, suppose the 6-month Treasury spot rate is 3% and the 10-year Treasury spot rate is 6%. Also suppose that a suitable credit spread is 90 basis points. Then a 3.9% spot rate is used to discount a 6-month cash flow of a non-Treasury bond and a 6.9% discount rate to discount a 10-year cash flow. (Remember that when each semiannual cash flow is discounted, the discount rate used is one-half the spot rate — 1.95% for the 6-month spot rate and 3.45% for the 10-year spot rate.)

The drawback of this approach is that there is no reason to expect the credit spread to be the same regardless of when the cash flow is to be received. We actually observed this in the previous chapter when we saw how credit spreads increase with maturity. Consequently, it might be expected that the credit spread increases with the maturity of the bond. That is, there is a **term structure of credit spreads**.

Dealer firms typically estimate a term structure for credit spreads for each credit rating and market sector. Generally, the credit spread increases with maturity. This is a typical shape for the term structure of credit spreads. In addition, the shape of the term structure is not the same for all credit ratings. Typically, the lower the credit rating, the steeper the term structure of credit spreads.

When the credit spreads for a given credit rating and market sector are added to the Treasury spot rates, the resulting term structure is used to value the bonds of issuers with that credit rating in that market sector. This term structure is referred to as the **benchmark spot rate curve** or **benchmark zero-coupon rate curve**.

*Exhibit 10: Calculation of Arbitrage-Free Value of a
Hypothetical 8% 10-Year Non-Treasury Security Using
Benchmark Spot Rate Curve*

Period	Years	Cash flow ($)	Treasury spot rate (%)	Credit spread (%)	Benchmark spot (%)	Present value ($)
1	0.5	4	3.0000	0.20	3.2000	3.9370
2	1.0	4	3.3000	0.20	3.5000	3.8636
3	1.5	4	3.5053	0.25	3.7553	3.7829
4	2.0	4	3.9164	0.30	4.2164	3.6797
5	2.5	4	4.4376	0.35	4.7876	3.5538
6	3.0	4	4.7520	0.35	5.1020	3.4389
7	3.5	4	4.9622	0.40	5.3622	3.3237
8	4.0	4	5.0650	0.45	5.5150	3.2177
9	4.5	4	5.1701	0.45	5.6201	3.1170
10	5.0	4	5.2772	0.50	5.7772	3.0088
11	5.5	4	5.3864	0.55	5.9364	2.8995
12	6.0	4	5.4976	0.60	6.0976	2.7896
13	6.5	4	5.6108	0.65	6.2608	2.6794
14	7.0	4	5.6643	0.70	6.3643	2.5799
15	7.5	4	5.7193	0.75	6.4693	2.4813
16	8.0	4	5.7755	0.80	6.5755	2.3838
17	8.5	4	5.8331	0.85	6.6831	2.2876
18	9.0	4	5.9584	0.90	6.8584	2.1801
19	9.5	4	6.0863	0.95	7.0363	2.0737
20	10.0	104	6.2169	1.00	7.2169	51.1833
					Total	$108.4615

For example, Exhibit 10 reproduces the Treasury spot rate curve in Exhibit 5. Also shown in the exhibit is a hypothetical credit spread for a non-Treasury security. The resulting benchmark spot rate curve is in the next-to-the-last column. It is this spot rate curve that is used to value the securities of issuers that have the same credit rating and are in the same market sector. This is done in Exhibit 10 for a hypothetical 8% 10-year issue. The arbitrage-free value is $108.4615. Notice that the theoretical value is less than that for an otherwise comparable Treasury security. The arbitrage-free value for an 8% 10-year Treasury is $115.2619 (see Exhibit 5).

**SECTION V
VALUATION
MODELS**

A **valuation model** provides the fair value of a security. Thus far, the two approaches to valuation we have presented have dealt with the valuation of simple securities. By simple we mean that it assumes the securities do not have an embedded option. A Treasury security and an option-free non-Treasury security can be valued using the arbitrage-free valuation approach explained in Section IV.

More general valuation models handle securities with embedded options. In the fixed income area, two common models that are used are the **binomial model** and the **Monte Carlo simulation model**. The former model is used to value callable bonds, putable bonds, floating-rate notes, and structured notes in which the coupon formula is based on an interest rate. The Monte Carlo simulation model is used to value mortgage-backed securities and certain types of asset-backed securities.[2]

---

[2] The reason why Monte Carlo simulation model is used to value these products rather than the binomial model will be explained at Level II. For those who need to know why now, here is the reason: mortgage-backed securities and certain asset-backed securities are interest rate path dependent securities and the binomial model cannot handle such securities. If you don't know what an interest rate path dependent security is, you will at Level II, not here.

Here we will not delve into the details of these two models. What is critical to understand is that valuation models use the principles of valuation described earlier in this chapter. In very general terms, there are five features common to the binomial and Monte Carlo simulation valuation models. First, each model begins with the yields on the on-the-run Treasury securities and generates the Treasury spot rates. Second, each model makes an assumption about the expected volatility of short-term interest rates. This is a critical assumption in both models since it can significantly affect the value estimated. Third, based on the volatility assumption, different "branches" of an interest rate tree (in the case of the binomial model) and interest rate "paths" (in the case of the Monte Carlo model) are generated. Fourth, the model is calibrated to the Treasury market. This means that if an "on-the-run" Treasury issue is valued using the model, the model will produce the observed market price. Finally, rules are developed to determine when an issuer/borrower will exercise an option — a call rule for callable bonds and a prepayment model for mortgage-backed securities and certain asset-backed securities.

We repeat what we stated at the close of Chapter 1. The user of any valuation model is exposed to **modeling risk**. This is the risk that the output of the model is incorrect because the assumptions upon which it is based are incorrect. Consequently, it is imperative that the results of a valuation model be stress-tested for modeling risk by altering the assumptions.

SECTION VI KEY POINTS

❑ *Valuation is the process of determining the fair value of a financial asset.*

❑ *The fundamental principle of valuation is that the value of any financial asset is the present value of the expected cash flows, where a cash flow is the cash that is expected to be received at some time period.*

❑ *The valuation process involves three steps: (1) estimating the expected cash flows, (2) determining the appropriate interest rate or interest rates that should be used to discount the cash flows, and (3) calculating the present value of the expected cash flows.*

❑ *For any fixed income security in which neither the issuer nor the investor can alter the repayment of the principal before its contractual due date, the cash flows can easily be determined assuming that the issuer does not default.*

❑ *The difficulty in determining cash flows arises for securities where either the issuer or the investor can alter the cash flows or the coupon rate is reset by a formula that depends on the future value of some reference rate, price, or exchange rate.*

❑ *On-the-run Treasury yields are viewed as the starting point for the minimum interest rate that an investor should require when investing in a bond.*

❑ *The risk premium or yield spread over the interest rate on a Treasury security that investors will require reflects the additional risks the investor faces by acquiring a security that is not issued by the U.S. government.*

❑ *For a given discount rate, the present value of a single cash flow to be received in the future is the amount of money that must be invested today that will generate that future value.*

❑ *The present value of a cash flow will depend on when a cash flow will be received (i.e., the timing of a cash flow) and the discount rate (i.e., interest rate) used to calculate the present value*

❑ *The sum of the present values for a security's expected cash flows is the value of the security.*

❑ *The present value is lower the further into the future the cash flow will be received.*

❑ *The higher the discount rate, the lower a cash flow's present value and therefore since the value of a security is the present value of the cash flows, the higher the discount rate, the lower a security's value.*

❑ *The value of a bond is equal to the present value of the coupon payments plus the present value of the maturity value.*

❑ *The price/yield relationship for an option-free bond is convex.*

❑ *When a bond is purchased between coupon periods, the buyer pays a price that includes accrued interest, called the full price or dirty price.*

❑ *The clean price or simply price of a bond is the full price minus accrued interest.*

❑ *In computing accrued interest, day count conventions are used to determine the number of days in the coupon payment period and the number of days since the last coupon payment date.*

❑ *The traditional valuation methodology is to discount every cash flow of a security by the same interest rate (or discount rate), thereby incorrectly viewing each security as the same package of cash flows.*

❑ *The arbitrage-free approach values a bond as a package of cash flows, with each cash flow viewed as a zero-coupon bond and each cash flow discounted at its own unique discount rate.*

❑ *The theoretical Treasury zero-coupon rates are called Treasury spot rates.*

❑ *The Treasury spot rates are used to discount the cash flows.*

❑ *To value a security with credit risk, it is necessary to determine a term structure of credit rates.*

❑ *Adding a credit spread for an issuer to the Treasury spot rate curve gives the benchmark spot rate curve that should be used to value that issuer's security.*

❑ *Valuation models seek to estimate the fair or theoretical value of a bond and accommodate securities with embedded options.*

❑ *The common valuation models used to value bonds with embedded options are the binomial model and the Monte Carlo simulation model.*

❑ *The binomial model is used to value callable bonds, putable bonds, floating-rate notes, and structured notes in which the coupon formula is based on an interest rate.*

❑ *The Monte Carlo simulation model is used to value mortgage-backed securities.*

❑ *The user of a valuation model is exposed to modeling risk and should test the sensitivity of the model to alternative assumptions.*

END OF CHAPTER QUESTIONS

1. Compute the value of a 5-year 7.4% coupon bond that pays interest annually assuming that the appropriate discount rate is 5.6%.

2. A 5-year amortizing security with a par value of $100,000 and a coupon rate of 6.4% has an expected cash flow of $23,998.55 per year assuming no prepayments. The annual cash flow includes interest and principal repayment. What is the value of this amortizing security assuming no prepayments and a discount rate of 7.8%.

3. a. What is the value of a 5-year 6.2% coupon bond when the discount rate is (I) 4.5%, (ii) 6.2%, and (iii) 7.3%?
   b. Show that the results obtained in part a are consistent with the relationship between the coupon rate, discount rate, and price relative to par value.

4. A client is reviewing a year-end portfolio report. Since the beginning of the year, market yields have increased slightly. In comparing the beginning-of-the-year price for the bonds selling at a discount from par value to the end-of-year prices, the client observes that all the prices are higher. The client is perplexed since he expected that the price of all bonds should be lower since interest rates increased. Explain to the client why the prices of the bonds in the portfolio selling at discount have increased in value.

5. A 4-year 5.8% coupon bond is selling to yield 7%. The bond pays interest annually. One year later interest rates decrease from 7% to 6.2%.

   a. What is the price of the 4-year 5.8% coupon bond selling to yield 7%?
   b. What is the price of this bond one year later assuming the yield is unchanged at 7%?
   c. What is the price of this bond one year later if instead of the yield being unchanged the yield decreases to 6.2%?
   d. Complete the following:

   Price change attributable to moving to maturity
   (no change in discount rate) ....

   Price change attributable to a decrease in the
   yield from 7% to 6.2%% ....

   Total price change ....

6. What is the value of a 5-year 5.8% coupon bond if the appropriate discount rate for discounting each cash flow is as follows:

Year	Discount rate
1	5.90%
2	6.40%
3	6.60%
4	6.90%
5	7.30%

7. What is the value of a 5-year 7.4% coupon bond selling to yield 5.6% assuming the coupon payments are made semiannually?

8. What is the value of a zero-coupon bond that matures in 20 years, has a maturity of $1 million, and is selling to yield 7.6%

9. Suppose that a bond is purchased between coupon periods. The days between the settlement date and the next coupon period is 115. There are 183 days in the coupon period. Suppose that the bond purchased has a coupon rate of 7.4% and there are 10 semiannual coupon payments remaining.

   a. What is the dirty price for this bond if a 5.6% discount rate is used?
   b. What is the accrued interest for this bond?
   c. What is the clean price?

10. Suppose that the prevailing Treasury spot rate curve is the one shown in Exhibit 5.

    a. What is the value of a 7.4% 8-year Treasury issue?
    b. Suppose that the 7.4% 8-year Treasury issue is priced in the market based on the on-the-run 8-year Treasury yield. Assume further that yield is 5.65%, so that each cash flow is discounted at 5.65%. What is the price of the 7.4% 8-year Treasury issue based on a 5.65% discount rate?
    c. Given the arbitrage-free value found in part a and the price in part b, what action would a dealer take and what would the arbitrage profit be if the market priced the 7.4% 8-year Treasury issue at the price found in part b?
    d. What process assures that the market price will not differ materially from the arbitrage-free value?

11. Suppose that the prevailing Treasury spot rate curve is the one shown in Exhibit 5.

    a. What is the value of a 4% 8-year Treasury issue?
    b. Suppose that the 4% 8-year Treasury issue is priced in the market based on the on-the-run 8-year Treasury yield. Assume further that yield is 5.65%, so that each cash flow is discounted at 5.65%. What is the price of the 4% 8-year Treasury issue based on a 5.65% discount rate?
    c. Given the arbitrage-free value found in part a and the price in part b, what action would a dealer take and what would the arbitrage profit be if the market priced the 4% 8-year Treasury issue at the price found in part b?
    d. What process assures that the market price will not differ materially from the arbitrage-free value?

12. Why do valuation models that seek to value bonds with embedded options require the analysis of a security over possible future interest rate paths?

SOLUTIONS TO END OF CHAPTER QUESTIONS

1. The value is $107.6655 as shown below:

Year	Cash flow	PV at 5.6%
1	7.4	7.0076
2	7.4	6.6360
3	7.4	6.2841
4	7.4	5.9508
5	107.4	81.7871
	Total	107.6655

2. The value is $96,326.46 as shown below

Year	Cash flow	PV at 7.8%
1	$23,998.55	$22,262.10
2	23,998.55	20,651.30
3	23,998.55	19,157.05
4	23,998.55	17,770.92
5	23,998.55	16,485.08
	Total	96,326.46

3 a. The present value of the cash flows for the three discount rates is provided below:

Year	Cash flow	PV at 4.5%	Cash flow	PV at 6.2%	Cash flow	PV at 7.3%
1	$6.2	$5.9330	$6.2	$5.8380	$6.2	$5.7782
2	6.2	5.6775	6.2	5.4972	6.2	5.3851
3	6.2	5.4330	6.2	5.1763	6.2	5.0187
4	6.2	5.1991	6.2	4.8741	6.2	4.6773
5	106.2	85.2203	106.2	78.6144	106.2	74.6665
	Total	107.4630	Total	100.0000	Total	95.5258

b. The following relationship holds:

- When the coupon rate (6.2%) is greater than the discount rate (4.5%), the bond's value is a premium to par value ($107.4630).
- When the coupon rate is equal to the discount rate, the bond's value is par value.
- When the coupon rate (6.2%) is less than the discount rate (7.3%), the bond's value is a discount to par value ($95.5258).

4. A basic property of a discount bond is that its price increases as it moves toward maturity assuming that interest rates do not change. Over the one year that the portfolio is being reviewed, while market yields have increased slightly, the bonds selling at a discount at the beginning of the year can increase despite a slight increase in the market yield since the beginning of the year.

5. a. The price is $95.9353 as shown below:

Year	Cash flow	PV at 7%
1	5.8	5.4206
2	5.8	5.0659
3	5.8	4.7345
4	105.8	80.7143
	Total	$95.9353

b. The price of the 3-year 5.8% coupon bond assuming the yield is unchanged at 7% is $96.8508, as shown below.

Year	Cash flow	PV at 7%
1	5.8	5.4206
2	5.8	5.0659
3	105.8	86.3643
	Total	$96.8508

c. The price is $98.9347 as shown below:

Year	Cash flow	PV at 6%
1	5.8	5.4614
2	5.8	5.1426
3	105.8	88.3308
	Total	$98.9347

d.

Price change attributable to moving to maturity
(no change in discount rate) .... $0.9155 (96.8508 – 95.9353)
Price change attributable to a decrease in the
yield from 7% to 6.2%% .... $2.0839 (98.9347 – 96.8508)
Total price change $2.9994

6. The value is $94.2148 as shown below:

Year	Discount rate	Cash flow	PV
1	5.90%	5.8	5.4769
2	6.40%	5.8	5.1232
3	6.60%	5.8	4.7880
4	6.90%	5.8	4.4414
5	7.30%	105.8	74.3853
		Total	$94.2148

7. The value is $107.7561 as shown below:

Period	Discount rate	Cash flow	PV at 3.7%
1	0.028	3.7	3.5992
2	0.028	3.7	3.5012
3	0.028	3.7	3.4058
4	0.028	3.7	3.3131
5	0.028	3.7	3.2228
6	0.028	3.7	3.1350
7	0.028	3.7	3.0496
8	0.028	3.7	2.9666
9	0.028	3.7	2.8858
10	0.028	103.7	78.6770
		Total	107.7561

Alternatively, the short-cut formula can be used.

semiannual coupon payment = $3.70
semiannual discount rate   =   2.8%
number of years   =   5

then

$$\$3.70 \times \left[\frac{1 - \dfrac{1}{(1.028)^{5 \times 2}}}{0.028} \right] = \$31.8864$$

To determine the price, the present value of the maturity value must be added to the present value of the coupon payments. The present value of the maturity value is

$$\text{present value of maturity value} = \frac{\$100}{(1.028)^{5 \times 2}} = \$75.8698$$

The price is then $107.7561 ($31.8864 + $75.8698). This agrees with our previous calculation for the price of this bond.

8.

$$\frac{\$1,000,000}{(1.038)^{40}} = \$224,960.29$$

9. a. First, w must be calculated. We know that

Days between settlement date and next coupon payment   115
Days in the coupon period   183

Therefore,

$$w \text{ periods} = \frac{115}{183} = 0.6284$$

Since the discount rate is 5.6%, the semiannual rate is 2.8%. The present value of each cash flow is $108.8676 and is therefore the full price.

Period	Cash flow	PV at 2.8%
1	3.7	3.6363
2	3.7	3.5373
3	3.7	3.4410
4	3.7	3.3472
5	3.7	3.2561
6	3.7	3.1674
7	3.7	3.0811
8	3.7	2.9972
9	3.7	2.9155
10	103.7	79.4885
	Total	108.8676

b. The accrued interest is

AI = semiannual coupon payment $\times (1 - w)$

AI = $3.7 \times (1 - 0.6284) = 1.3749$

c. The clean price is

clean price = full price − accrued interest

$108.8676 − $1.3749 = $107.4927

10. a. The arbitrage-free value was found in Practice Question 9a to be $111.3322.

b. The price based on single discount rate of 5.65% is $111.1395 as shown below:

Period	Years	Cash Flow	PV at 2.825%
1	0.5	3.7	3.5983
2	1.0	3.7	3.4995
3	1.5	3.7	3.4033
4	2.0	3.7	3.3098
5	2.5	3.7	3.2189
6	3.0	3.7	3.1305
7	3.5	3.7	3.0445
8	4.0	3.7	2.9608
9	4.5	3.7	2.8795
10	5.0	3.7	2.8004
11	5.5	3.7	2.7234
12	6.0	3.7	2.6486
13	6.5	3.7	2.5758
14	7.0	3.7	2.5051
15	7.5	3.7	2.4362
16	8.0	103.7	66.4048
		Total	111.1395

c. Dealers would buy the 7.4% 8-year issue for $111.1395, strip it, and sell the Treasury strips for $111.3322. The arbitrage profit is $0.1927 ($111.3322 − $111.1395). The table below shows how that arbitrage profit is realized.

Period	Years	Sell for	Buy for	Arbitrage profit
1	0.5	3.6453	3.5983	0.0470
2	1.0	3.5809	3.4995	0.0814
3	1.5	3.5121	3.4033	0.1087
4	2.0	3.4238	3.3098	0.1140
5	2.5	3.3155	3.2189	0.0966
6	3.0	3.2138	3.1305	0.0833
7	3.5	3.1167	3.0445	0.0722
8	4.0	3.0291	2.9608	0.0683
9	4.5	2.9407	2.8795	0.0612
10	5.0	2.8516	2.8004	0.0513
11	5.5	2.7621	2.7234	0.0387
12	6.0	2.6723	2.6486	0.0237
13	6.5	2.5822	2.5758	0.0064
14	7.0	2.5026	2.5051	−0.0024
15	7.5	2.4240	2.4362	−0.0123
16	8.0	65.7595	66.4048	−0.6452
Total		111.3322	111.1395	0.1927

d. The process of bidding up the price of the 7.4% 8-year Treasury issue by dealers in order to strip it will increase the price until no material arbitrage profit is available — the arbitrage-free value of $111.3322.

11. a. The arbitrage-free value was found in Practice Question 9b to be $89.3154.

b. The price based on a single discount rate of 5.65% is as shown below to be $89.4971.

Period	Years	Cash Flow	Present value 2.825%
1	0.5	2	1.9451
2	1.0	2	1.8916
3	1.5	2	1.8396
4	2.0	2	1.7891
5	2.5	2	1.7399
6	3.0	2	1.6921
7	3.5	2	1.6457
8	4.0	2	1.6004
9	4.5	2	1.5565
10	5.0	2	1.5137
11	5.5	2	1.4721
12	6.0	2	1.4317
13	6.5	2	1.3923
14	7.0	2	1.3541
15	7.5	2	1.3169
16	8.0	102	65.3162
		Total	89.4971

c. The dealer will buy a package of Treasury strips such that the cash flow from the package will replicate the cash flow of a 4% 8-year Treasury issue and sell the overvalued Treasury issue. The cost of buying the package of Treasury strips is $89.3154. The value of the synthetic coupon Treasury created is $89.4971. The arbitrage profit is therefore $0.1817 ($89.4971 − $89.3154) per $100 par value.

d. The process of dealers selling the Treasury issue will drive down its prices until the market price is close to the arbitrage-free value of $89.3154.

12. Once there is an embedded option, the cash flow will depend on whether or not the option will be exercised by the issuer or investor. In turn, whether or not the option will be exercised will depend on the level of interest rates relative to the issue's coupon rate. Consequently, modeling how interest rates may change over time provides scenarios over which the cash flow can be projected and then valued.

SOLUTIONS TO PRACTICE QUESTIONS

1. a. The cash flow per $100 of par value for this security is:

Year	Cash flow
1	$7
2	7
3	7
4	7
5	107

The present value for each cash flow assuming a discount rate of 5% is:

Year 1: present value$_1$ = $\dfrac{\$7}{(1.05)^1}$ = $6.6667

Year 2: present value$_2$ = $\dfrac{\$7}{(1.05)^2}$ = $6.3492

Year 3: present value$_3$ = $\dfrac{\$7}{(1.05)^3}$ = $6.0469

Year 4: present value$_4$ = $\dfrac{\$7}{(1.05)^4}$ = $5.7589

Year 5: present value$_5$ = $\dfrac{\$107}{(1.05)^5}$ = $83.8373

The present value is the sum of the five present values above, $108.6590.

b. The cash flow for this security is $2,309.75 for each year. The present value of each cash flow assuming a discount rate of 6% is:

Year 1: present value$_1$ = $\dfrac{\$2,309.75}{(1.06)^1}$ = $2,179.0075

Year 2: present value$_2$ = $\dfrac{\$2,309.75}{(1.06)^2}$ = $2,055.6675

Year 3: present value$_3$ = $\dfrac{\$2,309.75}{(1.06)^3}$ = $1,939.3089

Year 4: present value$_4$ = $\dfrac{\$2,309.75}{(1.06)^4}$ = $1,829.5367

Year 5: present value$_5$ = $\dfrac{\$2,309.75}{(1.06)^5}$ = $1,725.9781

The present value of the five cash flows is $9,729.4988.

2. The present value for each cash flow assuming a discount rate of 4% is:

Year 1: present value$_1$ = $\dfrac{\$7}{(1.04)^1}$ = $6.7308

Year 2: present value$_2$ = $\dfrac{\$7}{(1.04)^2}$ = $6.4719

Year 3: present value$_3$ = $\dfrac{\$7}{(1.04)^3}$ = $6.2230

$$\text{Year 4: present value}_4 = \frac{\$7}{(1.05)^4} = \$5.9836$$

$$\text{Year 5: present value}_5 = \frac{\$107}{(1.05)^5} = \$87.9462$$

The present value is the sum of the five present values above, $113.3555. A 4% discount produced a present value of $113.3555 which is greater than the present value of $108.6590 when the higher discount rate of 5% is used.

3. a. The value of the bond for the three discount rates is provided below:

Year	Present value at 6%	Present value at 7%	Present value at 8%
1	$6.6038	$6.5421	$6.4815
2	6.2300	6.1141	6.0014
3	5.8773	5.7141	5.5568
4	5.5447	5.3403	5.1452
5	79.9566	76.2895	72.8224
	$104.2124	$100.0000	$96.0073

b. The following relationship holds:

- When the coupon rate is greater than the discount rate (7% versus 6%), the bond's value is a premium to par value ($104.2124).
- When the coupon rate is equal to the discount rate, the bond's value is par value.
- When the coupon rate is less than the discount rate (7% versus 8%), the bond's value is a discount to par value ($96.0073).

4. The cash flow per $100 of par value for this security is:

Year	Cash flow
1	$7
2	7
3	7
4	7
5	107

The present value of each cash flow is

$$\text{Year 1: present value}_1 = \frac{\$7}{(1.035)^1} = \$6.7633$$

$$\text{Year 2: present value}_2 = \frac{\$7}{(1.039)^2} = \$6.4844$$

$$\text{Year 3: present value}_3 = \frac{\$7}{(1.042)^3} = \$6.1872$$

$$\text{Year 4: present value}_4 = \frac{\$7}{(1.045)^4} = \$5.8699$$

$$\text{Year 5: present value}_5 = \frac{\$107}{(1.050)^5} = \$83.8373$$

The sum of the present values is $109.1421.

5. The semiannual cash flows for the first 9 six-month periods per $100 of par value is $3.50. For the last period, the cash flow is $103.50. The semiannual discount rate is 2.5%. The present value of each cash flow discounted at 2.5% is shown below:

$$\textit{Period 1: present value}_1 = \frac{\$3.5}{(1.025)^1} = \$3.4146$$

$$\textit{Period 2: present value}_2 = \frac{\$3.5}{(1.025)^2} = \$3.3314$$

$$\textit{Period 3: present value}_3 = \frac{\$3.5}{(1.025)^3} = \$3.2501$$

$$\textit{Period 4: present value}_4 = \frac{\$3.5}{(1.025)^4} = \$3.1708$$

$$\textit{Period 5: present value}_5 = \frac{\$3.5}{(1.025)^5} = \$3.0935$$

$$\textit{Period 6: present value}_6 = \frac{\$3.5}{(1.025)^6} = \$3.0180$$

$$\textit{Period 7: present value}_7 = \frac{\$3.5}{(1.025)^7} = \$2.9444$$

$$\textit{Period 8: present value}_8 = \frac{\$3.5}{(1.025)^8} = \$2.8726$$

$$\textit{Period 9: present value}_9 = \frac{\$3.5}{(1.025)^9} = \$2.8025$$

$$\textit{Period 10: present value}_{10} = \frac{\$103.5}{(1.025)^{10}} = \$80.8540$$

The value of this bond is the sum of the present values, $108.7521.

Alternatively, the short-cut formula can be used. The present value of the coupon payments is:

$$\$3.5 \times \left[\frac{1 - \frac{1}{(1.025)^{5 \times 2}}}{0.025} \right] = \$30.6322$$

The present value of the maturity value is

$$\text{present value of maturity value} = \frac{\$100}{(1.025)^{5 \times 2}} = \$78.1198$$

The price is then $108.7520 (= $30.6322 + $78.1198), the same value as computed above.

6. a. The value given the semiannual discount rate i (one-half the annual discount rate) is found by the following formula:

$$\frac{\$1,000}{(1 + i)^{20}}$$

The solutions follow:

Annual discount rate	Semiannual discount rate	Present value
1%	0.5%	905.0629
2%	1.0%	819.5445
3%	1.5%	742.4704
4%	2.0%	672.9713
5%	2.5%	610.2709
6%	3.0%	553.6758
7%	3.5%	502.5659
8%	4.0%	456.3869
9%	4.5%	414.6429
10%	5.0%	376.8895
11%	5.5%	342.7290
12%	6.0%	311.8047
13%	6.5%	283.7970
14%	7.0%	258.4190

b.

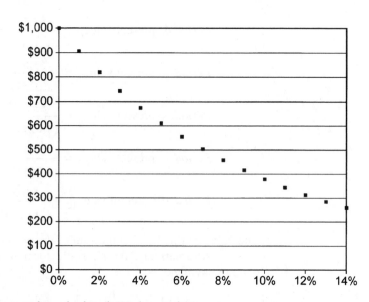

7. First, w must be calculated. We know that

Days between settlement date and next coupon payment	58
Days in the coupon period	183

Therefore,

$$w \text{ periods} = \frac{58}{183} = 0.3169$$

Since the discount rate is 5%, the semiannual rate is 2.5%. The present value of each cash flow is:

$$\textit{Period 1: } \text{present value}_1 = \frac{\$3.5}{(1.025)^{0.3169}} = \$3.4727$$

$$\textit{Period 2: } \text{present value}_2 = \frac{\$3.5}{(1.025)^{1.3169}} = \$3.3880$$

$$Period\ 3:\ \text{present value}_3 = \frac{\$3.5}{(1.025)^{2.3169}} = \$3.3054$$

$$Period\ 4:\ \text{present value}_4 = \frac{\$3.5}{(1.025)^{3.3169}} = \$3.2248$$

$$Period\ 5:\ \text{present value}_5 = \frac{\$3.5}{(1.025)^{4.3169}} = \$3.1461$$

$$Period\ 6:\ \text{present value}_6 = \frac{\$3.5}{(1.025)^{5.3169}} = \$3.0694$$

$$Period\ 7:\ \text{present value}_7 = \frac{\$3.5}{(1.025)^{6.3169}} = \$2.9945$$

$$Period\ 8:\ \text{present value}_8 = \frac{\$3.5}{(1.025)^{7.3169}} = \$2.9215$$

$$Period\ 9:\ \text{present value}_9 = \frac{\$3.5}{(1.025)^{8.3169}} = \$2.8502$$

$$Period\ 10:\ \text{present value}_{10} = \frac{\$103.5}{(1.025)^{9.3169}} = \$82.2293$$

The full price for this bond is the sum of the present values, $110.6019.

8. The value of w is 0.3169 and the coupon interest for the period is $2.50. Therefore, the accrued interest is:

$$AI = \$3.5 \times (1 - 0.3169) = \$2.3907$$

Since the full price is $110.6019, the clean price is

$$\text{clean price} = \$110.6019 - \$2.3907 = \$108.2112$$

9. a. The value for the 7.4% coupon 8-year Treasury security is $111.3322 as shown below:

Period	Years	Cash Flow ($)	Spot Rate (%)	Present Value ($)
1	0.5	3.7	3.0000	3.6453
2	1.0	3.7	3.3000	3.5809
3	1.5	3.7	3.5053	3.5121
4	2.0	3.7	3.9164	3.4238
5	2.5	3.7	4.4376	3.3155
6	3.0	3.7	4.7520	3.2138
7	3.5	3.7	4.9622	3.1167
8	4.0	3.7	5.0650	3.0291
9	4.5	3.7	5.1701	2.9407
10	5.0	3.7	5.2772	2.8516
11	5.5	3.7	5.3864	2.7621
12	6.0	3.7	5.4976	2.6723
13	6.5	3.7	5.6108	2.5822
14	7.0	3.7	5.6643	2.5026
15	7.5	3.7	5.7193	2.4240
16	8.0	103.7	5.7755	65.7595
	Total			111.3322

b. The value for the 4% coupon 8-year Treasury security is $89.3154 as shown below

Period	Years	Cash Flow ($)	Spot Rate (%)	Present Value ($)
1	0.5	2	3.0000	1.9704
2	1.0	2	3.3000	1.9356
3	1.5	2	3.5053	1.8984
4	2.0	2	3.9164	1.8507
5	2.5	2	4.4376	1.7922
6	3.0	2	4.7520	1.7372
7	3.5	2	4.9622	1.6847
8	4.0	2	5.0650	1.6373
9	4.5	2	5.1701	1.5895
10	5.0	2	5.2772	1.5414
11	5.5	2	5.3864	1.4930
12	6.0	2	5.4976	1.4445
13	6.5	2	5.6108	1.3958
14	7.0	2	5.6643	1.3528
15	7.5	2	5.7193	1.3103
16	8.0	102	5.7755	64.6815
			Total	89.3154

Chapter 6

YIELD MEASURES, SPOT RATES, AND FORWARD RATES

LEARNING OUTCOME STATEMENTS

After reading this chapter you should be able to:

- explain the sources of return from investing in a bond (coupon interest payments, capital gain/loss, and reinvestment income).
- compute the traditional yield measures for fixed-rate bonds (current yield, yield to maturity, yield to first call, yield to first par call date, yield to put, yield to worst, and cash flow yield).
- explain the assumptions underlying traditional yield measures and the limitations of the traditional yield measures
- explain the importance of reinvestment income in generating the yield computed at the time of purchase.
- explain the factors affecting reinvestment risk.
- calculate the reinvestment income that will be needed to generate the yield computed at the time of purchase.
- calculate the discount margin measure for a floater and explain the limitation of this measure.
- calculate the yield on a discount basis for a Treasury bill.
- explain the limitations of the yield on a discount basis for a Treasury bill.
- compute using the method of bootstrapping the theoretical Treasury spot rate curve given the Treasury par yield curve.
- explain the limitations of the nominal spread.
- describe what the zero-volatility spread is, why it is superior to the nominal spread, and how to compute it given a spot rate curve.
- explain why the zero-volatility spread will diverge from the nominal spread.
- explain what the option-adjusted spread for a bond with an embedded option is and what is meant by the option cost.
- illustrate why the nominal spread hides the option risk for bonds with embedded options.
- explain what a forward rate is.
- compute forward rates from spot rates.
- demonstrate the relationship between short-term forward rates and spot rates.
- explain why valuing a bond using spot rates and forward rates produces the same value.
- calculate the forward discount factor from forward rates.
- calculate the value of a bond given forward rates.

SECTION I
INTRODUCTION

In Chapter 5 we focused on the basic principles for valuing a fixed income security. Frequently, investors assess the relative value of a security by some yield or yield spread measure. There are various yield measures that are quoted in the market. These measures are based on assumptions that limit their use to gauge relative value. This chapter explains the various yield and yield spread measures and their limitations.

In Chapter 5 we also discussed how to compute the arbitrage-free value of an option-free bond given the Treasury spot rates. However, we did not discuss how to obtain the spot rates. In this chapter, we will see a basic approach to computing the spot rates from the on-the-run Treasury issues. We'll explain other approaches to constructing the spot rate curve at Level II.

We also discussed in earlier chapters the nominal spread between the yield on an issue and the yield on a comparable Treasury security. We will see the limitations of the nominal spread measure and explain two measures that overcome these limitations — zero-volatility spread and option-adjusted spread. While we don't use these two measures in the balance of the material at Level I, we will show how they are used in the analysis of bonds with embedded options at Level II. At Level II when we introduce valuation models, we will see how the option-adjusted spread is computed.

SECTION II
SOURCES OF
RETURN

When an investor purchases a fixed income security, he or she can expect to receive a dollar return from one or more of the following sources:

1. the coupon interest payments made by the issuer
2. any capital gain (or capital loss – a negative dollar return) when the security matures, is called, or is sold
3. income from reinvestment of the interim cash flows

Any yield measure that purports to measure the potential return from a fixed income security should consider all three sources of return described above.

A. Coupon Interest Payments

The most obvious source of return is the periodic coupon interest payments. For zero-coupon instruments, the return from this source is zero, despite the fact that the investor is effectively receiving interest by purchasing a security below its par value and realizing interest at the maturity date when the investor receives the par value.

B. Capital Gain or Loss

When the proceeds received when a bond matures, is called, or is sold are greater than the purchase price, a capital gain results. For a bond held to maturity, there will be a capital gain if the bond is purchased below its par value. For example, a bond purchased for $94.17 with a par value of $100 will generate a capital gain of $5.83 ($100 – $94.17) if held to maturity. For a callable bond, a capital gain results if the price at which the bond is called (i.e., the call price) is greater than the purchase price. For example, if the bond in our previous example is callable and subsequently called at $100.5, a capital gain of $6.33 ($100.50 – $94.17) will be realized. If the same bond is sold prior to its maturity or before it is called, a capital gain will result if the proceeds exceed the purchase price. So, if our hypothetical bond is sold prior to the maturity date for $103, the capital gain would be $8.83 ($103 – $94.17).

A capital loss is generated when the proceeds received when a bond matures, is called, or is sold are less then the purchase price. For a bond held to maturity, there will be a capital loss if the bond is purchased for more than its par value (i.e., purchased at a premium). For example, a bond purchased for $102.50 with a par value of $100 will generate a capital loss of $2.50 ($102.50 − $100) if held to maturity. For a callable bond, a capital loss results if the price at which the bond is called is less than the purchase price. For example, if the bond in our example is callable and subsequently called at $100.50, a capital loss of $2 ($102.50 − $100.50) will be realized. If the same bond is sold prior to its maturity or before it is called, a capital loss will result if the sale price is less than the purchase price. So, if our hypothetical bond is sold prior to the maturity date for $98.5, the capital loss would be $4 ($102.50 − $98.50).

C. Reinvestment Income

With the exception of zero-coupon instruments, fixed income securities make periodic payments of interest that can be reinvested until the security is removed from the portfolio. Amortizing securities (such as mortgage-backed securities and asset-backed securities) make periodic principal repayments which can be reinvested until the security is removed from the portfolio. The interest earned from reinvesting the interim cash flows (interest and/or principal payments) until the security is removed from the portfolio is called **reinvestment income**.

SECTION III TRADITIONAL YIELD MEASURES

There are several yield measures cited in the bond market. These include current yield, yield to maturity, yield to call, yield to put, yield to worst, and cash flow yield. These yield measures are expressed as a percent return rather than a dollar return. Below we explain how each measure is calculated and its limitations.

A. Current Yield

The **current yield** relates the annual dollar coupon interest to the market price. The formula for the current yield is:

$$\text{current yield} = \frac{\text{annual dollar coupon interest}}{\text{price}}$$

For example, the current yield for a 7% 8-year bond whose price is $94.17 is 7.43% as shown below:

annual dollar coupon interest = $0.07 \times \$100 = \$7$

price = $94.17

$$\text{current yield} = \frac{\$7}{\$94.17} = 0.0743 \text{ or } 7.43\%$$

The current yield will be greater than the coupon rate when the bond sells at a discount; the reverse is true for a bond selling at a premium. For a bond selling at par, the current yield will be equal to the coupon rate.

The drawback of the current yield is that it considers only the coupon interest and no other source that will impact an investor's return. No consideration is given to the capital gain that the investor will realize when a bond is purchased at a discount and held to maturity; nor is there any recognition of the capital loss that the investor will realize if a bond purchased at a premium is held to maturity. No consideration is given to reinvestment income.

B. Yield to Maturity

The most popular measure of yield in the bond market is the **yield to maturity**. The yield to maturity is the interest rate that will make the present value of the cash flows from a bond equal to its market price plus accrued interest. To find the yield to maturity, we first determine the expected cash flows. Then we search by trial and error for the interest rate that will make the present value of the cash flows equal to the market price plus accrued interest. (This is simply a special case of an **internal rate of return** (IRR) calculation where the cash flows used are those to be received if the bond is held to the maturity date.) In the illustrations presented in this chapter, we assume that the next coupon payment will be six months from now so that there is no accrued interest.

To illustrate, consider a 7% 8-year bond selling for $94.17. The cash flows for this bond are (1) 16 payments every 6-months of $3.50 and (2) a payment sixteen 6-month periods from now of $100. The present value using various *semiannual* discount (interest) rates is:

Semiannual interest rate	3.5%	3.6%	3.7%	3.8%	3.9%	4.0%
Present value	100.00	98.80	97.62	96.45	95.30	94.17

When a 4.0% interest rate is used, the present value of the cash flows is equal to $94.17, which is the price of the bond. Hence, 4.0% is the *semiannual* yield to maturity.

The market convention adopted to annualize the semiannual yield to maturity is to double it and call that the yield to maturity. Thus, the yield to maturity for the above bond is 8% (2 times 4.0%). The yield to maturity computed using this convention — doubling the semiannual yield — is called a **bond-equivalent yield**.

The following relationships between the price of a bond, coupon rate, current yield, and yield to maturity hold:

Bond selling at	Relationship				
par	coupon rate	=	current yield	=	yield to maturity
discount	coupon rate	<	current yield	<	yield to maturity
premium	coupon rate	>	current yield	>	yield to maturity

PRACTICE QUESTION 1

Determine whether the yield to maturity of a 6% 15-year bond selling for $84.25 is either 7.2%, 7.6%, or 7.8%.

---

1. The Bond-Equivalent Yield Convention

The *convention* that was developed in the bond market to move from a semiannual yield to an annual yield is to simply double the semiannual yield. As just noted, this is called the bond-equivalent yield. In general, when one doubles a semiannual yield (or a semiannual return) to obtain an annual measure, one is said to be computing the measure on a **bond-equivalent basis**.

Students of the bond market are troubled by this convention. The two questions most commonly asked are: First, why is the practice of simply doubling a semiannual yield followed? Second, wouldn't it be more appropriate to compute the effective annual yield by compounding the semiannual yield?[1]

The answer to the first question is that it is simply a convention. There is no danger with a convention unless you use it improperly. The fact is that market participants recognize that a yield (or return) is computed on a semiannual basis by convention and adjust accordingly when using the number. So, if the bond-equivalent yield

---

[1] By compounding the semiannual yield it is meant that the annual yield is computed as follows:

effective annual yield $= (1 + \text{semiannual yield})^2 - 1$

on a security purchased by an investor is 6%, the investor knows the semiannual yield is 3%. Given that, the investor can use that semiannual yield to compute an effective annual yield or any other annualized measure desired. For a manager comparing the yield on a security to a yield offered on a liability it is seeking to earn enough funds to satisfy, the yield number will be measured in a manner consistent with that of the yield offered on the liability.

The answer to the second question is that it is true that computing an effective annual yield would be better. But so what! Once we discover below the limitations of yield measures in general, we will question whether or not an investor should use a bond-equivalent yield measure or an effective annual yield measure in making investment decisions. That is, if we were to identify the major problems with yield measures, the doubling of a semiannual yield is the least of our problems.

So, don't lose any sleep over this convention. Just make sure that you don't use a bond-equivalent yield measure improperly.

2. Limitations of Yield-to-Maturity Measure

The yield to maturity considers not only the coupon income but any capital gain or loss that the investor will realize by holding the bond to maturity. The yield to maturity also considers the timing of the cash flows. *It does consider reinvestment income; however, it assumes that the coupon payments can be reinvested at an interest rate equal to the yield to maturity.* So, if the yield to maturity for a bond is 8%, for example, to earn that yield the coupon payments must be reinvested at an interest rate equal to 8%.

The illustrations below clearly demonstrate this. In the illustrations, the analysis will be cast in terms of dollars. Be sure you keep in mind the difference between the **total future dollars** which are equal to all the dollars that the investor expects to receive (including the recovery of the principal) and the **total dollar return** which is equal to the dollars the investor expects to realize from the three sources of return (coupon payments, capital gain/loss, and reinvestment income).

Suppose an investor has $94.17 and places the funds in a certificate of deposit that matures in 8 years. Let's suppose that the bank agrees to pay 4% interest every six months. This means that the bank is agreeing to pay 8% on a bond equivalent basis (i.e., doubling the semiannual yield). We can translate all of this into the total future dollars that will be generated by this investment at the end of 8 years. From the standard formula for the future value of a sum invested today, we can determine the total future dollars from this investment:

$$\$94.17 \times (1.04)^{16} = \$176.38$$

So, to an investor who invests $94.17 for 8 years at an 8% yield on a bond equivalent basis and interest is paid semiannually, this translates into an investment that will generate $176.38. Decomposing the total future dollars we see that:

Total future dollars	=	$176.38
Return of principal	=	$94.17
Total interest from CD	=	$82.21

Thus, any investment that promises a yield of 8% on a bond equivalent basis for 8 years on an investment of $94.17 must generate total future dollars of $176.38 or equivalently a return from all sources of $82.21. That is, if we look at the three sources of a bond return that offered an 8% yield with semiannual coupon payments and sold at a price of $94.17, the following would have to hold:

Coupon interest
+ Capital gain
+ Reinvestment income
= Total dollar return = Total interest from CD = $82.21

Now, instead of the certificate of deposit, suppose that an investor purchases a bond with a coupon rate of 7% that matures in 8 years. We know that the three sources of return are coupon income, capital gain/loss, and reinvestment income. Suppose that the price of this bond is $94.17. The yield to maturity for this bond (on a bond equivalent basis) is 8%. Notice that this is the same type of investment as the certificate of deposit — the bank offered an 8% yield on a bond equivalent basis for 8 years and made payments semiannually. So, what should the investor in this bond expect in terms of *total future dollars*? As we just demonstrated, an investment of $94.17 must generate $176.38 in order to say that it provided a yield of 8%. Or equivalently, the total dollar return that must be generated is $82.21. Let's look at what in fact is generated in terms of dollar return.

The coupon is $3.50 every six months. So the dollar return from the coupon interest is $3.50 for 16 six-month periods, or $56. When the bond matures, there is a capital gain of $5.83 ($100 − $94.17). Therefore, based on these two sources of return we have:

Coupon interest	= $56.00
Capital gain	= $ 5.83
Dollar return *without reinvestment income*	= $61.83

Something's wrong here. Only $61.83 is generated from the bond whereas $82.21 is needed in order to say that this bond provided an 8% yield. That is, there is a dollar return shortfall of $20.38 ($82.21 − $61.83). How is this dollar return shortfall going to be made up?

Recall that in the case of the certificate of deposit, the bank does the reinvesting of the principal and the yield at which it does the reinvesting is 4% every six month or 8% on a bond equivalent basis. In contrast, for the bond, the investor has to reinvest any coupon interest until the bond matures. It is the reinvestment income that must make up the dollar return shortfall of $20.38. But at what yield will the investor have to reinvest the coupon payments in order to generate the $20.38? The answer is: the yield to maturity.[2] That is, the reinvestment income will be the following if each

---

[2] This can be verified by using the future value of an annuity. The future of an annuity is given by the following formula:

$$\text{Annuity payment} = \left[\frac{(1+i)^n - 1}{i}\right]$$

where i is the interest rate and n is the number of periods.

In our example, i is 4%, n is 16, and the amount of the annuity is the semiannual coupon of $3.50. Therefore, the future value of the coupon payment is

$$\$3.50\left[\frac{(1.04)^{16} - 1}{0.04}\right] = \$76.38$$

Since the coupon payments are $56, the reinvestment income is $20.38 ($76.38 − $56). This is the amount that is necessary to produce the dollar return shortfall in our example.

semiannual coupon payment of $3.50 can be reinvested at a semiannual yield of 4% (one half the yield to maturity). The reinvestment income earned on a given coupon payment of $3.50 if it is invested from the time of receipt in period t to the maturity date (16 periods in our example) at a 4% semiannual rate is:

$$\$3.50 \, (1.04)^{16-t} - \$3.50$$

For example, the first coupon payment ($t = 1$) can be reinvested for 15 periods. Applying the formula above we would find that the reinvestment income that would be earned on the first coupon payment is:

$$\$3.50 \, (1.04)^{16-1} - \$3.50 = \$2.80$$

Similarly, the reinvestment income for all coupon payments is shown below:

Period	Periods reinvested	Coupon payment	Reinvestment income
1	15	$3.5	$2.80
2	14	3.5	2.56
3	13	3.5	2.33
4	12	3.5	2.10
5	11	3.5	1.89
6	10	3.5	1.68
7	9	3.5	1.48
8	8	3.5	1.29
9	7	3.5	1.11
10	6	3.5	0.93
11	5	3.5	0.76
12	4	3.5	0.59
13	3	3.5	0.44
14	2	3.5	0.29
15	1	3.5	0.14
16	0	3.5	0.00
		Total	$20.39

The total reinvestment income is $20.39 (differing from $20.38 due to rounding).

So, with the reinvestment income of $20.38 at 4% semiannually (i.e., one half the yield to maturity on a bond-equivalent basis), the total dollar return is

Coupon interest	=	$56.00
Capital gain	=	$ 5.83
Reinvestment income	=	$20.38
Total dollar return	=	$82.21

In our illustration, we used an investment in a certificate of deposit to show what the total future dollars will have to be in order to obtain a yield of 8% on an investment of $94.17 for 8 years when interest payments are semiannual. However, this holds for any type of investment, not just a certificate of deposit. For example, if an investor is told that he or she can purchase a debt instrument for $94.17 that offers an 8% yield (on a bond-equivalent basis) for 8 years and makes interest payments semiannually, then the investor should translate this yield into the following:

I should be receiving total future dollars of $176.38
I should be receiving a total dollar return of $82.21

It is always important to think in terms of dollars (or pound sterling, yen, or other currency) because "yield measures" are misleading.

We can also see that the reinvestment income can be a significant portion of the total dollar return. In our example, the total dollar return is $82.21 and the total dollar return from reinvestment income to make up the shortfall is $20.38. This means that reinvestment income is about 25% of the total dollar return.

This is such an important point that we should go through this one more time for another bond. Suppose an investor purchases a 15-year 8% coupon bond at par value ($100). The yield for this bond is simple to determine since the bond is trading at par. The yield is equal to the coupon rate, 8%. Let's translate this into dollars. We know that if an investor made an investment of $100 for 15 years that offered an 8% yield and the interest payments are semiannual, the total future dollars will be:

$$\$100 \times (1.04)^{30} = \$324.34$$

Decomposing the total future dollars we see that:

$$
\begin{array}{rcl}
\text{Total future dollars} & = & \$324.34 \\
\text{Return of principal} & = & \$100.00 \\
\text{Total dollar return} & = & \$224.34
\end{array}
$$

Without reinvestment income, the dollar return is:

$$
\begin{array}{lcl}
\text{Coupon interest} & = & \$120 \\
\text{Capital gain} & = & \$\ \ 0 \\
\text{Dollar return } \textit{without reinvestment income} & = & \overline{\$120}
\end{array}
$$

Note that the capital gain is $0 because the bond is purchased at par value.

The dollar return shortfall is therefore $104.34 ($224.34 − $120). This shortfall is made up if the coupon payments can be reinvested at a yield of 8% (the yield on the bond at the time of purchase). For this bond, the reinvestment income is 46.5% of the total dollar return needed to produce a yield of 8% ($104.34/$224.34).[3]

Clearly, the investor will only realize the yield to maturity that is stated at the time of purchase if the following two assumptions hold:

> *Assumption 1:* the coupon payments can be reinvested at the yield to maturity
> *Assumption 2:* the bond is held to maturity

With respect to the first assumption, the risk that an investor faces is that future interest rates will be less than the yield to maturity at the time the bond is purchased. That is, there is **reinvestment risk**. If the bond is not held to maturity, it may have to be sold for less than its purchase price, resulting in a return that is less than the yield to maturity. That is, there is **interest rate risk**.

So we can now see how the assumptions underlying the yield to maturity are related to the two risks discussed in earlier chapters — interest rate risk and reinvestment risk.

---

[3] The future value of the coupon payments of $4 for 30 six-month periods is:

$$\$4.00\left[\frac{(1.04)^{30} - 1}{0.04}\right] = \$224.34$$

Since the coupon payments are $120 and the capital gain is $0, the reinvestment income is $104.34. This is the amount that is necessary to produce the dollar return shortfall in our example.

PRACTICE QUESTION 2

a. Suppose that an investor purchases a 6% coupon bond with 20 years to maturity at a price of $89.32 per $100 par value. The yield to maturity for this bond is 7%. Determine the dollar return that must be generated from reinvestment income in order to generate a yield of 7% and the percentage of the reinvestment income relative to the total dollar return needed to generate a 7% yield.

b. Suppose that a zero-coupon bond that matures in 10 years is selling to yield 7%. Determine the dollar return that must be generated from reinvestment income in order to generate a yield of 7% and the percentage of the reinvestment income relative to the total dollar return needed to generate a 7% yield.

---

3. Factors Affecting Reinvestment Risk

There are two characteristics of a bond that affect the degree of reinvestment risk:

> *Characteristic 1.* For a given yield to maturity and a given non-zero coupon rate, the longer the maturity the more the bond's total dollar return is dependent on reinvestment income to realize the yield to maturity at the time of purchase. That is, the greater the reinvestment risk.

The implication is that the yield to maturity measure for long-term coupon bonds tells little about the potential return that an investor may realize if the bond is held to maturity. For long-term bonds, in high interest rate environments the reinvestment income component may be as high as 70% of the bond's potential total dollar return.

> *Characteristic 2.* For a given maturity and a given yield to maturity, for a coupon bond the higher the coupon rate, the more dependent the bond's total dollar return will be on the reinvestment of the coupon payments in order to produce the yield to maturity at the time of purchase.

This means that holding maturity and yield to maturity constant, bonds selling at a premium will be more dependent on reinvestment income than a bond selling at par. This is because the reinvestment income has to make up the capital loss that will be realized by holding the bond to maturity. In contrast, a bond selling at a discount will be less dependent on reinvestment income than a bond selling at par because a portion of the return is coming from the capital gain that will be realized from holding the bond to maturity. For zero-coupons bonds, none of the bond's total dollar return is dependent on reinvestment income. So, a zero-coupon bond has no reinvestment risk if held to maturity.

The dependence of the total dollar return on reinvestment income for bonds with different coupon rates and maturities is shown in Exhibit 1.

4. Comparing Semiannual-Pay and Annual-Pay Bonds

In our yield calculations we have been dealing with bonds that pay interest semiannually. A non-U.S. bond may pay interest annually rather than semiannually. This is the case for many government bonds in Europe and Eurobonds. In such instances, an adjustment is required to make a direct comparison between the yield to maturity on a U.S. fixed-rate bond and that on an annual-pay non-U.S. fixed-rate bond.

Given the yield to maturity on an annual-pay bond, its bond-equivalent yield is computed as follows:

Exhibit 1: Percentage of Total Dollar Return from Reinvestment Income for a Bond to Generate an 8% Yield (BEY)

	Years to maturity				
	2	3	5	8	15
Bond with a 7% coupon					
Price	98.19	97.38	95.94	94.17	91.35
% of total	5.2%	8.6%	15.2%	24.8%	44.5%
Bond with an 8% coupon					
Price	100.00	100.00	100.00	100.00	100.00
% of total	5.8%	9.5%	16.7%	26.7%	46.5%
Bond with a 12% coupon					
Price	107.26	110.48	116.22	122.30	134.58
% of total	8.1%	12.9%	21.6%	31.0%	51.8%

bond-equivalent yield of an annual-pay bond

$$= 2[(1 + \text{yield on annual-pay bond})^{0.5} - 1]$$

The term in the square brackets involves determining what semiannual yield when compounded produces the yield on an annual-pay bond. Doubling this semiannual yield (i.e., multiplying the term in the square brackets by 2), gives the bond-equivalent yield.

For example, suppose that the yield to maturity on an annual-pay bond is 6%. Then the bond-equivalent yield is:

$$2[(1.06)^{0.5} - 1] = 5.91\%$$

Notice that the bond-equivalent yield will always be less than the annual-pay bond's yield to maturity.

To convert the bond-equivalent yield of a U.S. bond issue to an annual-pay basis so that it can be compared to the yield on an annual-pay bond, the following formula can be used:

$$\text{yield on an annual-pay basis} = \left[\left(1 + \frac{\text{yield on a bond-equivalent basis}}{2}\right)^2 - 1\right]$$

By dividing the yield on a bond-equivalent basis by 2 in the above expression, the semiannual yield is computed. The semiannual yield is then compounded to get the yield on an annual-pay basis.

For example, suppose that the yield of a U.S. bond issue quoted on a bond-equivalent basis is 6%. The yield to maturity on an annual-pay basis would be:

$$[(1.03)^2 - 1] = 6.09\%$$

The yield on an annual-pay bond is always greater than the yield on a bond-equivalent basis because of compounding.

PRACTICE QUESTION 3

a. If the yield to maturity on an annual-pay bond is 4.8%, what is the bond-equivalent yield?

b. If the yield of a U.S. bond issue quoted on a bond-equivalent basis is 4.8%, what is the yield to maturity on an annual-pay basis?

Exhibit 2: Yield to Call for an 8-Year 7% Coupon Bond with a Maturity Value of $100, First Call Date is the End of Year 3, and Call Price of $103

Annual interest rate (%)	Semiannual interest rate (%)	Present value of 6 payments of $3.5	Present value of $103 6 periods from now	Present value of cash flows
5.0	2.5	$19.28	$88.82	$108.10
5.2	2.6	19.21	88.30	107.51
5.4	2.7	19.15	87.78	106.93
5.6	2.8	19.09	87.27	106.36

C. Yield to Call

When a bond is callable, the market convention has been to calculate a yield to call as well as a yield to maturity. As explained in Chapter 1, a callable bond may have a call schedule. The yield to call assumes that the issuer will call the bond at some assumed call date and the call price is then the call price specified in the call schedule. Typically, investors calculate a **yield to first call** and a **yield to first par call**.

The procedure for calculating the yield to call is the same as for any yield to maturity calculation: determine the interest rate that will make the present value of the expected cash flows equal to the market price plus accrued interest. In the case of yield to first call, the expected cash flows are the coupon payments to the first call date and the call price. For the yield to first par call, the expected cash flows are the coupon payments to the first date at which the issuer can call the bond at par.

To illustrate the computation, consider a 7% 8-year bond with a maturity value of $100 selling for $106.36. Suppose that the first call date is three years from now and the call price is $103. The cash flows for this bond if it is called in three years are (1) 6 coupon payments of $3.50 every six months and (2) $103 in six 6-month periods from now.

The process for finding the yield to first call is the same as for finding the yield to maturity. The present value for several semiannual interest rates is shown in Exhibit 2. Since a semiannual interest rate of 2.8% makes the present value of the cash flows equal to the price, 2.8% is the yield to first call. Therefore, the yield to first call on a bond-equivalent basis is 5.6%.

For our 7% 8-year callable bond suppose that the first par call date is 5 years from now. The cash flows for computing the first par call are then: (1) 10 coupon payments of $3.50 every six months and (2) $100 in ten 6-month periods. The yield to par call is 5.53%. Let's verify that this is the case. The semiannual yield is 2.765% (one half of 5.53%). The present value of the 10 coupon payments of $3.50 every six months when discounted at 2.765% is $30.22. The present value of $100 (the call price of par) at the end of five years (10 semiannual periods) is $76.13. The present value of the cash flow is then $106.35 (= $30.22 + $76.13). Since the price of the bond is $106.36 and since using a yield of 5.53% produces a value for this callable bond that differs from $106.36 by only 1 penny, 5.53% is the yield to first par call.

Let's take a closer look at the yield to call as a measure of the potential return of a security. The yield to call does consider all three sources of potential return from owning a bond. However, as in the case of the yield to maturity, it assumes that all cash flows can be reinvested at the yield to call until the assumed call date. As we just demonstrated, this assumption may be inappropriate. Moreover, the yield to call assumes that

Assumption 1: the investor will hold the bond to the assumed call date
Assumption 2: the issuer will call the bond on that date

These assumptions underlying the yield to call are unrealistic. Moreover, comparison of different yields to call with the yield to maturity are meaningless because the cash flows stop at the assumed call date. For example, consider two bonds, M and N. Suppose that the yield to maturity for bond M, a 5-year noncallable bond, is 7.5% while for bond N the yield to call assuming the bond will be called in three years is 7.8%. Which bond is better for an investor with a 5-year investment horizon? It's not possible to tell from the yields cited. If the investor intends to hold the bond for five years and the issuer calls bond N after three years, the total dollar return that will be available at the end of five years will depend on the interest rate that can be earned from investing funds from the call date to the end of the investment horizon.

PRACTICE QUESTION 4

Suppose that a 9% 10-year bond has the following call structure:
   not callable for the next 5 years
   first callable in 6 years (i.e., at the end of the fifth year) at $104.50
   first par call date is in 9 years (i.e., at the end of the eighth year)
The price of the bond is $123.04.
a. Is the yield to first call for this bond 4.4%, 4.6%, or 4.8%?
b. Is the yield to first par call for this bond 5.41%, 5.62%, or 5.75%?

D. Yield to Put

When a bond is putable, the yield to the first put date is calculated. The yield to put is the interest rate that will make the present value of the cash flows to the first put date equal to the price plus accrued interest. As with all yield measures (except the current yield), yield to put assumes that any interim coupon payments can be reinvested at the yield calculated. Moreover, the yield to put assumes that the bond will be put on the first put date.

For example, suppose that a 6.2% coupon bond maturing in 8 years is putable at par in 3 years. The price of this bond is $102.19. The cash flows for this bond if it is put in three years are: (1) 6 coupon payments of $3.10 every six months and (2) the $100 put price in six 6-month periods from now. The semiannual interest rate that will make the present value of the cash flows equal to the price of $102.19 is 2.7%. Therefore, 2.7% is the semiannual yield to put and 5.4% is the yield to put on a bond equivalent basis.

E. Yield to Worst

A yield can be calculated for every possible call date and put date. In addition, a yield to maturity can be calculated. The lowest of all these possible yields is called the **yield to worst**. For example, suppose that there are only four possible call dates for a callable bond and that a yield to call assuming each possible call date is 6%, 6.2%, 5.8%, and 5.7%, and that the yield to maturity is 7.5%. Then the yield to worst is the minimum of these yields, 5.7% in our example.

The yield to worst measure holds little meaning as a measure of potential return. It supposedly states that this is the worst possible yield that the investor will realize. However, as we have noted about any yield measure, it does not identify the potential return over some investment horizon. Moreover, the yield to worst does not recognize that each yield calculation used in determining the yield to worst has different exposures to reinvestment risk.

F. Cash Flow Yield

As we will explain at Level II, mortgage-backed securities and asset-backed securities are backed by a pool of loans or receivables. The cash flows for these securities include principal repayment as well as interest. The complication that arises is that the individual borrowers whose loans make up the pool typically can prepay their loan in whole or in part prior to the scheduled principal repayment date. Because of prepayments, in order to project the cash flows it is necessary to make an assumption about the rate at which prepayments will occur. This rate is called the **prepayment rate** or **prepayment speed**.

Given the cash flows based on an assumed prepayment rate, a yield can be calculated. The yield is the interest rate that will make the present value of the projected cash flows equal to the price plus accrued interest. The yield calculated is commonly referred to as a **cash flow yield**.[4]

1. Bond-Equivalent Yield

Typically, the cash flows for mortgage-backed and asset-backed securities are monthly. Therefore the interest rate that will make the present value of the projected principal repayment and interest payments equal to the market price plus accrued interest is a monthly rate. The monthly yield is then annualized as follows.

First, the semiannual effective yield is computed from the monthly yield by compounding it for six months as follows:

$$\text{effective semiannual yield} = (1 + \text{monthly yield})^6 - 1$$

Next, the effective semiannual yield is doubled to get the annual cash flow yield on a bond-equivalent basis. That is,

$$\text{cash flow yield} = 2 \times \text{effective semiannual yield}$$
$$= 2\,[(1 + \text{monthly yield})^6 - 1]$$

For example, if the monthly yield is 0.5%, then:

$$\text{cash flow yield on a bond-equivalent basis} = 2[(1.005)^6 - 1] = 6.08\%$$

The calculation of the cash flow yield may seem strange because it first requires the computing of an effective semiannual yield given the monthly yield and then doubling. This is simply a market convention. Of course, the student of the bond market can always ask the same two questions as with the yield to maturity: Why it is done? Isn't it better to just compound the monthly yield to get an effective annual yield? The answers are the same as given earlier for the yield to maturity. Moreover, as we will see next, this is the least of our problems in using a cash flow yield measure for an asset-backed and mortgage-backed security.

2. Limitations of Cash Flow Yield

As we have noted, the yield to maturity has two shortcomings as a measure of a bond's potential return: (1) it is assumed that the coupon payments can be reinvested

---

[4] Some firms such as Prudential Securities refer to this yield as yield to maturity rather than cash flow yield.

at a rate equal to the yield to maturity and (2) it is assumed that the bond is held to maturity. These shortcomings are equally present in application of the cash flow yield measure: (1) the projected cash flows are assumed to be reinvested at the cash flow yield and (2) the mortgage-backed or asset-backed security is assumed to be held until the final payoff of all the loans based on some prepayment assumption. The importance of reinvestment risk, the risk that the cash flows will be reinvested at a rate less than the cash flow yield, is particularly important for mortgage-backed and asset-backed securities since payments are typically monthly and include principal repayments (scheduled and prepayments), as well as interest. Moreover, the cash flow yield is dependent on realization of the projected cash flows according to some prepayment rate. If actual prepayments differ significantly from the prepayment rate assumed, the cash flow yield will not be realized.

G. Yield Spread Measures for Floating-Rate Securities

The coupon rate for a floating-rate security changes periodically according to a reference rate (such as LIBOR or a Treasury rate). Since the future value for the reference rate is unknown, it is not possible to determine the cash flows. This means that a yield to maturity cannot be calculated. Instead, there are several conventional measures used as margin or spread measures cited by market participants for floaters. These include **spread for life** (or **simple margin**), **adjusted simple margin**, **adjusted total margin**, and **discount margin**.

The most popular of these measures is discount margin, so we will discuss this measure and its limitations below.[5] This measure estimates the average margin over the reference rate that the investor can expect to earn over the life of the security. The procedure for calculating the discount margin is as follows:

Step 1. Determine the cash flows assuming that the reference rate does *not* change over the life of the security.

Step 2. Select a margin.

Step 3. Discount the cash flows found in Step 1 by the current value of the reference rate plus the margin selected in Step 2.

Step 4. Compare the present value of the cash flows as calculated in Step 3 to the price plus accrued interest. If the present value is equal to the security's price plus accrued interest, the discount margin is the margin assumed in Step 2. If the present value is not equal to the security's price plus accrued interest, go back to Step 2 and try a different margin.

For a security selling at par, the discount margin is simply the quoted margin in the coupon reset formula.

To illustrate the calculation, suppose that the coupon reset formula for a 6-year floating-rate security selling for $99.3098 is 6-month LIBOR plus 80 basis points. (We explained in Chapter 2 why a floater's price may be different from par value.) The coupon rate is reset every six months. Assume that the current value for the reference rate is 10%.

Exhibit 3 shows the calculation of the discount margin for this security. The second column shows the current value for 6-month LIBOR. The third column sets

---

[5] For a discussion of the other traditional measures, see Chapter 3 in Frank J. Fabozzi and Steven V. Mann, *Floating Rate Securities* (New Hope, PA; Frank J. Fabozzi Associates, 2000).

forth the cash flows for the security. The cash flows for the first 11 periods are equal to one-half the current 6-month LIBOR (5%) plus the semiannual assumed margin of 40 basis points multiplied by $100. At the maturity date (i.e., period 12), the cash flow is $5.4 plus the maturity value of $100. The top row of the last five columns shows the assumed margin. The rows below the assumed margin show the present value of each cash flow. The last row gives the total present value of the cash flows.

For the five assumed margins, the present value is equal to the price of the floating-rate security ($99.3098) when the assumed margin is 96 basis points. Therefore, the discount margin is 96 basis points. Notice that the discount margin is 80 basis points, the same as the quoted margin, when the security is selling at par.

There are two drawbacks of the discount margin as a measure of the potential return from investing in a floating-rate security. First, the measure assumes that the reference rate will not change over the life of the security. Second, if the floating-rate security has a cap or floor, this is not taken into consideration.

PRACTICE QUESTION 5

Suppose that the price of the floater in our illustration was 99.8269 rather than 99.3098. Without doing any calculation, determine what the discount margin would be.

Exhibit 3: Calculation of the Discount Margin for a Floating-Rate Security

Floating rate security:

Maturity = 6 years
Price = 99.3098
Coupon formula = LIBOR + 80 basis points
Reset every six months

Period	LIBOR (%)	Cash flow ($)*	80 bp	84 bp	88 bp	96 bp	100 bp
1	10	5.4	5.1233	5.1224	5.1214	5.1195	5.1185
2	10	5.4	4.8609	4.8590	4.8572	4.8535	4.8516
3	10	5.4	4.6118	4.6092	4.6066	4.6013	4.5987
4	10	5.4	4.3755	4.3722	4.3689	4.3623	4.3590
5	10	5.4	4.1514	4.1474	4.1435	4.1356	4.1317
6	10	5.4	3.9387	3.9342	3.9297	3.9208	3.9163
7	10	5.4	3.7369	3.7319	3.7270	3.7171	3.7122
8	10	5.4	3.5454	3.5401	3.5347	3.5240	3.5186
9	10	5.4	3.3638	3.3580	3.3523	3.3409	3.3352
10	10	5.4	3.1914	3.1854	3.1794	3.1673	3.1613
11	10	5.4	3.0279	3.0216	3.0153	3.0028	2.9965
12	10	105.4	56.0729	55.9454	55.8182	55.5647	55.4385
		Present value	100.0000	99.8269	99.6541	99.3098	99.1381

Present value ($) at assumed margin of**

* For periods 1-11: cash flow = $100 (0.5) (LIBOR + assumed margin)
  For period 12: cash flow = $100 (0.5) (LIBOR + assumed margin) + $100
** The discount rate is found as follows. To LIBOR of 10%, the assumed margin is added. Thus, for an 88 basis point assumed margin, the discount rate is 10.88%. This is an annual discount rate on a bond-equivalent basis. The semiannual discount rate is then half this amount, 5.44%. It is this discount rate that is used to compute the present value of the cash flows for an assumed margin of 88 basis points.

H. Yield on Treasury Bills

Treasury bills are zero-coupon instruments with a maturity of one year or less. The convention in the Treasury bill market is to calculate a bill's **yield on a discount basis**. This yield is determined by two variables:

1. the settlement price per \$1 of maturity value (denoted by p)
2. the number of days to maturity which is calculated as the number of days between the settlement date and the maturity date (denoted by N_{SM})

The yield on a discount basis (denoted by d) is calculated as follows:

$$d = (1 - p)\left(\frac{360}{N_{SM}}\right)$$

We will use two actual Treasury bills to illustrate the calculation of the yield on a discount basis assuming a settlement date in both cases of 8/6/97. The first bill has a maturity date of 1/8/98 and a price of 0.97769722. For this bill, the number of days from the settlement date to the maturity date, N_{SM}, is 155. Therefore, the yield on a discount basis is

$$d = (1 - 0.97769722)\left(\frac{360}{155}\right) = 5.18\%$$

For our second bill, the maturity date is 7/23/98 and the price is 0.9490075. Assuming a settlement date of 8/6/97, the number of days from the settlement date to the maturity date is 351. The yield on a discount basis for this bill is

$$d = (1 - 0.9490075)\left(\frac{360}{351}\right) = 5.23\%$$

Given the yield on a discount basis, the price of a bill (per \$1 of maturity value) is computed as follows:

$$p = 1 - d(N_{SM}/360)$$

For the 155-day bill selling for a yield on a discount basis of 5.18%, the price per \$1 of maturity value is

$$p = 1 - 0.0518\,(155/360) = 0.97769722$$

For the 351-day bill selling for a yield on a discount basis of 5.23%, the price per \$1 of maturity value is

$$p = 1 - 0.0523\,(351/360) = 0.9490075$$

The quoted yield on a discount basis is not a meaningful measure of the return from holding a Treasury bill for two reasons. First, the measure is based on a maturity value investment rather than on the actual dollar amount invested. Second, the yield is annualized according to a 360-day year rather than a 365-day year, making it difficult to compare yields on Treasury bills with Treasury notes and bonds which pay interest based on the actual number of days in a year. The use of 360 days for a year is a convention for money market instruments. Despite its shortcomings as a measure of return, this is the method dealers have adopted to quote Treasury bills.

Market participants recognize this limitation of yield on a discount basis and consequently make adjustments to make the yield quoted on a Treasury bill comparable to that on a Treasury coupon security. The formula for conversion is complex and beyond the scope of this chapter. For investors who want to compare the yield on Treasury bills to that of other money market instruments (i.e., debt obligations with a maturity that does not exceed one year), there is a formula to convert the yield on a discount basis to that of a money market yield. Again, the conversion formula will not be discussed in this chapter. The key point is that while the convention is to quote the yield on a Treasury bill in terms of a yield on a discount basis, no one uses that yield measure other than to compute the price given the quoted yield.

PRACTICE QUESTION 6

a. A Treasury bill with 115 days from settlement to maturity is selling for $0.9825 per $1 of maturity value. What is the yield on a discount basis?

b. A Treasury bill with 162 days from settlement to maturity is quoted as having a yield on a discount basis of 5.9%. What is the price of this Treasury bill?

SECTION IV
THEORETICAL
SPOT RATES

In Chapter 2, we explained the key role that theoretical spot rates play in valuation. Recall that a spot rate is a zero-coupon rate. The theoretical spot rates for Treasury securities represent the appropriate set of interest rates that should be used to value default-free cash flows. A default-free theoretical spot rate curve can be constructed from the observed Treasury yield curve. There are several approaches that are used in practice. The approach that we describe below for creating a theoretical spot rate curve is called **bootstrapping**. At Level II we will discuss other approaches.

A. Bootstrapping

Bootstrapping begins with the yield for the on-the-run Treasury issues. The on-the-run Treasury issues are used because it is believed that they are fairly priced, there is no credit risk, and there is no liquidity risk. In practice, however, the observed yields for the on-the-run Treasury coupon issues are not actually used. Instead, the coupon rate is adjusted so that the price of an issue would be par value. As explained in Chapter 4, the reason for this is that the observed price and yield may reflect cheap repo financing available from an issue. The adjusted on-the-run Treasury yield curve where the coupon issues are at par value and the coupon rate is therefore equal to the yield to maturity is called the **par yield curve**. The exception is for the 6-month and 1-year issues which are Treasury bills and therefore the yields for these two issues are already spot rates.

To illustrate bootstrapping, we will use the Treasury par yield curve shown in Exhibit 4. The par yield curve shown is for 20 Treasury securities and the longest maturity is 10 years. Our objective is to show how the values in the last column of the exhibit (labeled "Spot Rate") are obtained.

Throughout the analysis and illustrations to come, it is important to remember that the basic principle is that the value of the Treasury coupon security should be equal to the value of the package of zero-coupon Treasury securities that duplicates the coupon bond's cash flows. We saw this in Chapter 5 when we discussed arbitrage-free valuation.

Exhibit 4: Hypothetical Treasury Par Yield Curve

Period	Years	Annual Yield to Maturity (BEY) (%)*	Price	Spot Rate (BEY) (%)*
1	0.5	3.00	—	3.0000
2	1.0	3.30	—	3.3000
3	1.5	3.50	100.00	3.5053
4	2.0	3.90	100.00	3.9164
5	2.5	4.40	100.00	4.4376
6	3.0	4.70	100.00	4.7520
7	3.5	4.90	100.00	4.9622
8	4.0	5.00	100.00	5.0650
9	4.5	5.10	100.00	5.1701
10	5.0	5.20	100.00	5.2772
11	5.5	5.30	100.00	5.3864
12	6.0	5.40	100.00	5.4976
13	6.5	5.50	100.00	5.6108
14	7.0	5.55	100.00	5.6643
15	7.5	5.60	100.00	5.7193
16	8.0	5.65	100.00	5.7755
17	8.5	5.70	100.00	5.8331
18	9.0	5.80	100.00	5.9584
19	9.5	5.90	100.00	6.0863
20	10.0	6.00	100.00	6.2169

* The yield to maturity and the spot rate are annual rates. They are reported as bond-equivalent yields. To obtain the semiannual yield or rate, one half the annual yield or annual rate is used.

Consider the 6-month and 1-year Treasury securities in Exhibit 4. As we explained in Chapter 5, these two securities are called Treasury bills and they are issued as zero-coupon instruments. Therefore, the annualized yield (not the discount yield) of 3.00% for the 6-month Treasury security is equal to the 6-month spot rate.[6] Similarly, for the 1-year Treasury security, the cited yield of 3.30% is the 1-year spot rate. Given these two spot rates, we can compute the spot rate for a theoretical 1.5-year zero-coupon Treasury. The value of a theoretical 1.5-year Treasury should equal the present value of the three cash flows from the 1.5-year coupon Treasury, where the yield used for discounting is the spot rate corresponding to the time of receipt of the cash flow. Since all the coupon bonds are selling at par, as explained in the previous section, the yield to maturity for each bond is the coupon rate. Using $100 as par, the cash flows for the 1.5-year coupon Treasury are:

0.5 year	$0.035 \times \$100 \times 0.5$	$= \$1.75$
1.0 year	$0.035 \times \$100 \times 0.5$	$= \$1.75$
1.5 years	$0.035 \times \$100 \times 0.5 + 100$	$= \$101.75$

The present value of the cash flows is then:

$$\frac{1.75}{(1 + z_1)^1} + \frac{1.75}{(1 + z_2)^2} + \frac{101.75}{(1 + z_3)^3}$$

[6] We will assume that the annualized yield for the Treasury bill is computed on a bond-equivalent basis. Earlier in this chapter we saw how the yield on a Treasury bill is quoted. The quoted yield can be converted into a bond-equivalent yield. But, we assume that this has been done in Exhibit 4.

where

z_1 = one-half the annualized 6-month theoretical spot rate
z_2 = one-half the 1-year theoretical spot rate
z_3 = one-half the 1.5-year theoretical spot rate

Since the 6-month spot rate is 3% and the 1-year spot rate is 3.30%, we know that:

$$z_1 = 0.0150 \text{ and } z_2 = 0.0165$$

We can compute the present value of the 1.5-year coupon Treasury security as:

$$\frac{1.75}{(1+z_1)^1} + \frac{1.75}{(1+z_2)^2} + \frac{101.75}{(1+z_3)^3} = \frac{1.75}{(1.015)^1} + \frac{1.75}{(1.0165)^2} + \frac{101.75}{(1+z_3)^3}$$

Since the price of the 1.5-year coupon Treasury security is par value (see Exhibit 4), the following relationship must hold:[7]

$$\frac{1.75}{(1.015)^1} + \frac{1.75}{(1.0165)^2} + \frac{101.75}{(1+z_3)^3} = 100$$

We can solve for the theoretical 1.5-year spot rate as follows:

$$1.7241 + 1.6936 + \frac{101.75}{(1+z_3)^3} = 100$$

$$\frac{101.75}{(1+z_3)^3} = 96.5822$$

$$(1+z_3)^3 = \frac{101.75}{96.5822}$$

$$z_3 = 0.0175265 = 1.7527\%$$

Doubling this yield we obtain the bond-equivalent yield of 3.5053%, which is the theoretical 1.5-year spot rate. That rate is the rate that the market would apply to a 1.5-year zero-coupon Treasury security if, in fact, such a security existed. In other words, all Treasury cash flows to be received 1.5 years from now should be valued (i.e., discounted) at 3.5053%.

Given the theoretical 1.5-year spot rate, we can obtain the theoretical 2-year spot rate. The cash flows for the 2-year coupon Treasury in Exhibit 3 are:

0.5 year	$0.039 \times \$100 \times 0.5$	=	$1.95
1.0 year	$0.039 \times \$100 \times 0.5$	=	$1.95
1.5 years	$0.039 \times \$100 \times 0.5$	=	$1.95
2.0 years	$0.039 \times \$100 \times 0.5 + 100$	=	$101.95

The present value of the cash flows is then:

$$\frac{1.95}{(1+z_1)^1} + \frac{1.95}{(1+z_2)^2} + \frac{1.95}{(1+z_3)^3} + \frac{101.95}{(1+z_4)^4}$$

where z_4 = one-half the 2-year theoretical spot rate.

---

[7] If we had not been working with a par yield curve, the equation would have been set equal to whatever the market price for the 1.5-year issue is.

Since the 6-month spot rate, 1-year spot rate, and 1.5-year spot rate are 3.00%, 3.30%, and 3.5053%, respectively, then:

$$z_1 = 0.0150 \quad z_2 = 0.0165 \quad z_3 = 0.017527$$

Therefore, the present value of the 2-year coupon Treasury security is:

$$\frac{1.95}{(1.0150)^1} + \frac{1.95}{(1.0165)^2} + \frac{1.95}{(1.017527)^3} + \frac{101.95}{(1 + z_4)^4}$$

Since the price of the 2-year coupon Treasury security is par, the following relationship must hold:

$$\frac{1.95}{(1.0150)^1} + \frac{1.95}{(1.0165)^2} + \frac{1.95}{(1.017527)^3} + \frac{101.95}{(1 + z_4)^4} = 100$$

We can solve for the theoretical 2-year spot rate as follows:

$$\frac{101.95}{(1 + z_4)^4} = 94.3407$$

$$(1 + z_4)^4 = \frac{101.95}{94.3407}$$

$$z_4 = 0.019582 = 1.9582\%$$

Doubling this yield, we obtain the theoretical 2-year spot rate bond-equivalent yield of 3.9164%.

One can follow this approach sequentially to derive the theoretical 2.5-year spot rate from the calculated values of z_1, z_2, z_3, and z_4 (the 6-month-, 1-year-, 1.5-year-, and 2-year rates), and the price and coupon of the 2.5-year bond in Exhibit 4. Further, one could derive theoretical spot rates for the remaining 15 half-yearly rates.

The spot rates thus obtained are shown in the last column of Exhibit 4. They represent the term structure of default-free spot rate for maturities up to 10 years at the particular time to which the bond price quotations refer. In fact, it is the default-free spot rates shown in Exhibit 4 that were used in our illustrations in the previous chapter.

PRACTICE QUESTION 7

Show how the 2.5-year spot rate reported in Exhibit 4 is obtained.

B. Yield Spread Measures Relative to a Spot Rate Curve

Traditional analysis of the yield spread for a non-Treasury bond involves calculating the difference between the bond's yield and the yield to maturity of a benchmark Treasury coupon security. The latter is obtained from the Treasury yield curve. For example, consider the following 10-year bonds:

Issue	Coupon	Price	Yield to maturity
Treasury	6%	100.00	6.00%
Non-Treasury	8%	104.19	7.40%

The yield spread for these two bonds as traditionally computed is 140 basis points (7.4% minus 6%). We have referred to this traditional yield spread as the **nominal spread**.

The drawbacks of the nominal spread measure are

1. for both bonds, the yield fails to take into consideration the term structure of the spot rates and
2. in the case of callable and/or putable bonds, expected interest rate volatility may alter the cash flows of the non-Treasury bond.

Let's examine each of the drawbacks and alternative spread measures for handling them.

1. Zero-Volatility Spread

The **zero-volatility spread** or **Z-spread** is a measure of the spread that the investor would realize over the entire Treasury spot rate curve if the bond is held to maturity. It is not a spread off one point on the Treasury yield curve, as is the nominal spread. The Z-spread, also called the **static spread**, is calculated as the spread that will make the present value of the cash flows from the non-Treasury bond, when discounted at the Treasury spot rate plus the spread, equal to the non-Treasury bond's price. A trial-and-error procedure is required to determine the Z-spread.

To illustrate how this is done, let's use the non-Treasury bond in our previous illustration and the Treasury spot rate curve in Exhibit 4. These spot rates are repeated in Exhibit 5. The third column in Exhibit 5 shows the cash flows for the 8% 10-year non-Treasury issue. The goal is to determine the spread that, when added to all the Treasury spot rates, will produce a present value for the cash flows of the non-Treasury bond equal to its market price of $104.19.

Suppose we select a spread of 100 basis points. To each Treasury spot rate shown in the fourth column of Exhibit 5, 100 basis points are added. So, for example, the 5-year (period 10) spot rate is 6.2772% (5.2772% plus 1%). The spot rate plus 100 basis points is then used to calculate the present values as shown in the fifth column. The total present value of the fifth column is $107.5414. Because the present value is not equal to the non-Treasury issue's price ($104.19), the Z-spread is not 100 basis points. If a spread of 125 basis points is tried, it can be seen from the next-to-the-last column of Exhibit 5 that the present value is $105.7165; again, because this is not equal to the non-Treasury issue's price, 125 basis points is not the Z-spread. The last column of Exhibit 5 shows the present value when a 146 basis point spread is tried. The present value is equal to the non-Treasury issue's price. Therefore 146 basis points is the Z-spread, compared to the nominal spread of 140 basis points.

What does the Z-spread represent for this non-Treasury security? Since the Z-spread is measured relative to the Treasury spot rate curve, it represents a spread to compensate for the non-Treasury security's credit risk, liquidity risk, and any option risks (i.e., the risks associated with any embedded options).

PRACTICE QUESTION 8

Suppose the price of the non-Treasury issue in our example is 105.7165 instead of 104.2145. Without doing computations, what would the Z-spread be?

Exhibit 5: Determination of the Z-Spread for an 8%, 10-Year Non-Treasury Issue Selling at $104.19 to Yield 7.4%

Period	Years	Cash flow ($)	Spot rate (%)*	Present value ($) assuming a spread of**		
				100 bp	125 bp	146 bp
1	0.5	4.00	3.0000	3.9216	3.9168	3.9127
2	1.0	4.00	3.3000	3.8334	3.8240	3.8162
3	1.5	4.00	3.5053	3.7414	3.7277	3.7163
4	2.0	4.00	3.9164	3.6297	3.6121	3.5973
5	2.5	4.00	4.4376	3.4979	3.4767	3.4590
6	3.0	4.00	4.7520	3.3742	3.3497	3.3293
7	3.5	4.00	4.9622	3.2565	3.2290	3.2061
8	4.0	4.00	5.0650	3.1497	3.1193	3.0940
9	4.5	4.00	5.1701	3.0430	3.0100	2.9826
10	5.0	4.00	5.2772	2.9366	2.9013	2.8719
11	5.5	4.00	5.3864	2.8307	2.7933	2.7622
12	6.0	4.00	5.4976	2.7255	2.6862	2.6537
13	6.5	4.00	5.6108	2.6210	2.5801	2.5463
14	7.0	4.00	5.6643	2.5279	2.4855	2.4504
15	7.5	4.00	5.7193	2.4367	2.3929	2.3568
16	8.0	4.00	5.7755	2.3472	2.3023	2.2652
17	8.5	4.00	5.8331	2.2596	2.2137	2.1758
18	9.0	4.00	5.9584	2.1612	2.1148	2.0766
19	9.5	4.00	6.0863	2.0642	2.0174	1.9790
20	10.0	104.00	6.2169	51.1833	49.9638	48.9630
			Total	107.5414	105.7165	104.2145

* The spot rate is an annual rate.

** The discount rate used to compute the present value of each cash flow in the third column is found by adding the assumed spread to the spot rate and then dividing by 2. For example, for period 4 the spot rate is 3.9164%. If the assumed spread is 100 basis points, then 100 basis points is added to 3.9164% to give 4.9164%. Dividing this rate by 2 gives the semiannual rate of 2.4582%. The present value is then found as follows:

$$= \frac{\text{cash flow in period } t}{(1.024582)^t}$$

a. Divergence Between Z-Spread and Nominal Spread

Typically, for standard coupon-paying bonds with a bullet maturity (i.e., a single payment of principal) the Z-spread and the nominal spread will not differ significantly. In our example it is only 6 basis points. In general terms, the divergence is a function of the shape of the term structure of interest rates and the characteristics of the security (i.e., coupon rate, time to maturity, and type of principal repayment provision — non-amortizing versus amortizing).

For short-term issues, there is little divergence. The main factor causing any difference is the shape of the Treasury spot rate curve. The steeper the spot rate curve, the greater the difference. To illustrate this, consider the two spot rate curves shown in Exhibit 6. The yield for the longest maturity of both spot rate curves is 6%. The first curve is steeper than the one used in Exhibit 5; the second curve is flat, with the yield for all maturities is equal to 6%. It can be shown that for the first spot rate curve the Z-spread is 192. Thus, with this steeper spot rate curve, the difference between the Z-spread and the nominal spread is 52 basis points. For the flat curve the Z-spread is 140 basis points, the same as the nominal spread. This will always be the case because the nominal spread assumes that the same yield is used to discount each cash flow and with a flat yield curve the same yield is being used to discount each flow. Thus, the nominal yield spread and the Z-spread will produce the same value for this security.

The difference between the Z-spread and the nominal spread is greater for issues in which the principal is repaid over time rather than only at maturity. Thus the difference between the nominal spread and the Z-spread will be considerably greater for mortgage-backed securities and asset-backed securities in a steep yield curve environment. We can see this intuitively if we think in terms of a 10-year zero-coupon bond and a 10-year amortizing security with equal semiannual cash flows (that includes interest and principal repayment). The Z-spread for the zero-coupon bond will not be affected by the shape of the term structure but the amortizing security will be.

b. Z-Spread Relative to Any Benchmark

In the same way that a Z-spread relative to a Treasury spot rate curve can be calculated, a Z-spread to any benchmark spot rate curve can be calculated. To illustrate, suppose that a hypothetical non-Treasury security with a coupon rate of 8% and a 10-year maturity is trading at $105.5423. Assume that the *benchmark spot rate curve for this issuer* is the one given in Exhibit 10 of the previous chapter. The Z-spread relative to that issuer's benchmark spot rate curve is the spread that must be added to the spot rates shown in the next-to-last column of that exhibit that will make the present value of the cash flows equal to the market price. In our illustration, the Z-spread relative to this benchmark is 40 basis points.

What does the Z-spread mean when the benchmark is not the Treasury spot rate curve (i.e., default-free spot rate curve)? When the Treasury spot rate curve is the benchmark, we said that the Z-spread for a non-Treasury issue embodies credit risk, liquidity risk, and any option risks. When the benchmark is the spot rate curve for the issuer, the Z-spread is measuring the spread attributable to the liquidity risk of the issue and any option risks.

Exhibit 6: Two Hypothetical Spot Rate Curves

Period	Years	Steep curve (%)	Flat curve (%)
1	0.5	2.00	6.00
2	1.0	2.40	6.00
3	1.5	2.80	6.00
4	2.0	2.90	6.00
5	2.5	3.00	6.00
6	3.0	3.10	6.00
7	3.5	3.30	6.00
8	4.0	3.80	6.00
9	4.5	3.90	6.00
10	5.0	4.20	6.00
11	5.5	4.40	6.00
12	6.0	4.50	6.00
13	6.5	4.60	6.00
14	7.0	4.70	6.00
15	7.5	4.90	6.00
16	8.0	5.00	6.00
17	8.5	5.30	6.00
18	9.0	5.70	6.00
19	9.5	5.80	6.00
20	10.0	6.00	6.00

Thus, when a Z-spread is cited, it must be cited relative to some benchmark spot rate curve. This is necessary because it indicates the credit and sector risks that are being considered when the Z-spread was calculated. While Z-spreads are typically calculated using Treasury securities as the benchmark interest rates, this need not be the case. Vendors of analytical systems commonly allow the user to select a benchmark. Moreover, in non-U.S. markets, Treasury securities are typically not the benchmark. The key point is that an investor should always ask what benchmark was used in computing the Z-spread.

2. Option-Adjusted Spread

The Z-spread seeks to measure the spread over a spot rate curve. This overcomes the first problem of the traditional spread measure — the nominal spread — that we cited earlier. Now let's look at the second shortcoming — failure to take future interest rate volatility into account which could change the cash flows for bonds with embedded options.

What an investor seeks to do is to buy securities whose value is greater than their price. A valuation model allows an investor to estimate the value of a security, which at this point would be sufficient to determine the fairness of the security's price. That is, the investor can say that a bond is 1 point cheap or 2 points cheap, and so on.

A valuation model need not stop here, however. Instead, it can convert the divergence between the market price for the security and the value derived from the model into a yield spread measure. This step is necessary since most market participants find it more convenient to think about yield spread than about price differences.

The **option-adjusted spread** (OAS) was developed as a measure of the yield spread that can be used to convert dollar differences between value and market price. Thus, basically, the OAS is used to reconcile value with market price. *What is critical to understand is that the OAS is model dependent. That is, as explained further at Level II, the OAS computed depends on the valuation model used.* But what is it a "spread" over? The OAS is a spread over the Treasury spot rate curve or the issuer's benchmark used in the analysis. The spot rate curve itself is not a single curve, but a series of spot rate curves that allow for changes in interest rates.

The reason that the resulting spread is referred to as "option-adjusted" is because the cash flows of the security whose value we seek are adjusted to reflect the embedded option. In contrast, the Z-spread does not consider how the cash flows will change when interest rates change in the future. That is, the Z-spread assumes that interest rate volatility is zero. This is why the Z-spread is also referred to as the **zero-volatility OAS**.

The OAS is used by investors as a measure of relative value when comparing bonds. Prior to the introduction of the OAS measure, investors used the nominal spread as a measure of relative value despite the fact that it fails to take into consideration the effect of any embedded options when comparing the nominal spread on bonds. However, it must be emphasized when using OAS that it is a product of a valuation model and as we explained in the last section of the previous chapter, there are assumptions that underlie a valuation model. Consequently, these assumptions affect the calculated OAS. One critical assumption is interest rate volatility. Specifically, the higher the interest rate volatility assumed, the lower the OAS.

In comparing the OAS of dealer firms, it is critical to check on the volatility assumption made. Moreover, it is important to inquire as to the benchmark on-the-run yield curve used. Some dealers use the Treasury on-the-run issues. As a result, the

OAS also captures the credit spread. In contrast, some vendors and dealers use the issuer's on-the-run issue which reflects the issuer's credit risk.

a. Option Cost

The implied cost of the option embedded in any security can be obtained by calculating the difference between the OAS at the assumed interest rate or yield volatility and the Z-spread. That is,

option cost = Z-spread − OAS

The reason that the option cost is measured in this way is as follows. In an environment in which interest rates are assumed not to change, the investor would earn the Z-spread. When future interest rates are uncertain, the spread is different because of the embedded option(s); the OAS reflects the spread after adjusting for this option. Therefore, the option cost is the difference between the spread that would be earned in a static interest rate environment (the Z-spread, or equivalently, the zero-volatility OAS) and the spread after adjusting for the option (the OAS).

For callable bonds and most mortgage-backed and asset-backed securities, the option cost is positive. This is because the borrower's ability to alter the cash flows will result in an OAS that is less than the Z-spread. In the case of a putable bond, the OAS is greater than the Z-spread so that the option cost is negative. This occurs because of the investor's ability to alter the cash flows.

In general, when the option cost is positive, this means that the investor has sold an option to the issuer or borrower. This is true for callable bonds and most mortgage-backed and asset-backed securities. A negative value for the option cost means that the investor has purchased an option from the issuer or borrower. A putable bond is an example of this negative option cost. There are certain securities in the mortgage-backed securities market that also have an option cost that is negative.

b. Highlighting the Pitfalls of the Nominal Spread

We can use the concepts presented in this chapter to highlight the pitfalls of the nominal spread. First, we can recast the relationship between the option cost, Z-spread, and OAS as follows:

Z-spread = OAS + option cost

Next, recall that the nominal spread and the Z-spread may not diverge significantly. Suppose that the nominal spread is approximately equal to the Z-spread. Then, we can substitute nominal spread for Z-spread in the previous relationship giving:

nominal spread ≈ OAS + option cost

This relationship tells us that a high nominal spread could be hiding a high option cost. The option cost represents the portion of the spread that the investor has given to the issuer or borrower. Thus, while the nominal spread for a security that can be called or prepaid might be, say 200 basis points, the option cost may be 190 and the OAS only 10 basis points. But, an investor is only compensated for the OAS. An investor that relies on the nominal spread may not be adequately compensated for taking on the option risk associated with a security with an embedded option.

SECTION V FORWARD RATES

We just saw how a default-free theoretical spot rate curve can be extrapolated from the Treasury yield curve. Additional information useful to market participants can be extrapolated from the default-free theoretical spot rate curve: **forward rates**. Under certain assumptions, these rates can be viewed as the market's consensus of future interest rates.

Examples of forward rates that can be calculated from the default-free theoretical spot rate curve are the:

- 6-month forward rate six months from now
- 6-month forward rate three years from now
- 1-year forward rate one year from now
- 3-year forward rate two years from now
- 5-year forward rates three years from now

Since the forward rates are implicitly extrapolated from the default-free theoretical spot rate curve, these rates are sometimes referred to as **implicit forward rates**. We begin by showing how to compute the 6-month forward rates. Then we explain how to compute any forward rate.

A. Deriving 6-Month Forward Rates

To illustrate the process of extrapolating 6-month forward rates, we will use the yield curve and corresponding spot rate curve from Exhibit 4. We will use a very simple arbitrage principle as we did earlier in this chapter to derive the spot rates. Specifically, if two investments have the same cash flows and have the same risk, they should have the same value.

Consider an investor who has a 1-year investment horizon and is faced with the following two alternatives:

- buy a 1-year Treasury bill, or
- buy a 6-month Treasury bill, and when it matures in six months buy another 6-month Treasury bill.

The investor will be indifferent toward the two alternatives if they produce the same return over the 1-year investment horizon. The investor knows the spot rate on the 6-month Treasury bill and the 1-year Treasury bill. However, he does not know what yield will be available on a 6-month Treasury bill that will be purchased six months from now. That is, he does not know the 6-month forward rate six months from now. Given the spot rates for the 6-month Treasury bill and the 1-year Treasury bill, the forward rate on a 6-month Treasury bill is the rate that equalizes the dollar return between the two alternatives.

To see how that rate can be determined, suppose that an investor purchased a 6-month Treasury bill for $\$X$. At the end of six months, the value of this investment would be:

$$X(1 + z_1)$$

where z_1 is one-half the bond-equivalent yield (BEY) of the theoretical 6-month spot rate.

Let f represent one-half the forward rate (expressed as a BEY) on a 6-month Treasury bill available six months from now. If the investor were to rollover his investment by purchasing that bill at that time, then the future dollars available at the end of one year from the $\$X$ investment would be:

$$X(1 + z_1)(1 + f)$$

Exhibit 7: Graphical Depiction of the Six-Month Forward Rate Six Months from Now

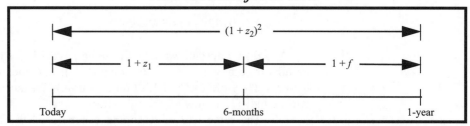

Now consider the alternative of investing in a 1-year Treasury bill. If we let z_2 represent one-half the BEY of the theoretical 1-year spot rate, then the future dollars available at the end of one year from the X investment would be:

$$X(1 + z_2)^2$$

The reason that the squared term appears is that the amount invested is being compounded for two periods. (Recall that each period is six months.)

The two choices are depicted in Exhibit 7. Now we are prepared to analyze the investor's choices and what this says about forward rates. The investor will be indifferent toward the two alternatives confronting him if he makes the same dollar investment (X) and receives the same future dollars from both alternatives at the end of one year. That is, the investor will be indifferent if:

$$X(1 + z_1)(1 + f) = X(1 + z_2)^2$$

Solving for f, we get:

$$f = \frac{(1 + z_2)^2}{(1 + z_1)} - 1$$

Doubling f gives the BEY for the 6-month forward rate six months from now.

We can illustrate the use of this formula with the theoretical spot rates shown in Exhibit 4. From that exhibit, we know that:

6-month bill spot rate = 0.030, therefore z_1 = 0.0150
1-year bill spot rate = 0.033, therefore z_2 = 0.0165

Substituting into the formula, we have:

$$f = \frac{(1.0165)^2}{(1.0150)} - 1 = 0.0180 = 1.8\%$$

Therefore, the 6-month forward rate six months from now is 3.6% (1.8% × 2) BEY.

Let's confirm our results. If X is invested in the 6-month Treasury bill at 1.5% and the proceeds then reinvested for six months at the 6-month forward rate of 1.8%, the total proceeds from this alternative would be:

$$X(1.015)(1.018) = 1.03327\,X$$

Investment of $\$X$ in the 1-year Treasury bill at one-half the 1-year rate, 1.0165%, would produce the following proceeds at the end of one year:

$$X(1.0165)^2 = 1.03327\,X$$

Both alternatives have the same payoff if the 6-month Treasury bill yield six months from now is 1.8% (3.6% on a BEY). This means that, if an investor is guaranteed a 1.8% yield (3.6% BEY) on a 6-month Treasury bill six months from now, he will be indifferent toward the two alternatives.

The same line of reasoning can be used to obtain the 6-month forward rate beginning at any time period in the future. For example, the following can be determined:

- the 6-month forward rate three years from now
- the 6-month forward rate five years from now

The notation that we use to indicate 6-month forward rates is $_1f_m$ where the subscript 1 indicates a 1-period (6-month) rate and the subscript m indicates the period beginning m periods from now. When m is equal to zero, this means the current rate. Thus, the first 6-month forward rate is simply the current 6-month spot rate. That is, $_1f_0 = z_1$.

The general formula for determining a 6-month forward rate is:

$$_1f_m = \frac{(1 + z_{m+1})^{m+1}}{(1 + z_m)^m} - 1$$

For example, suppose that the 6-month forward rate four years (eight 6-month periods) from now is sought. In terms of our notation, m is 8 and we seek $_1f_8$. The formula is then:

$$_1f_8 = \frac{(1 + z_9)^9}{(1 + z_8)^8} - 1$$

From Exhibit 4, since the 4-year spot rate is 5.065% and the 4.5-year spot rate is 5.1701%, z_8 is 2.5325% and z_9 is 2.58505%. Then,

$$_1f_8 = \frac{(1.0258505)^9}{(1.025325)^8} - 1 = 3.0064\%$$

Doubling this rate gives a 6-month forward rate four years from now of 6.01%

Exhibit 8 shows all of the 6-month forward rates for the Treasury yield curve and corresponding spot rate curve shown in Exhibit 4. The forward rates reported in Exhibit 8 are the annualized rates on a bond-equivalent basis. The set of these forward rates is called the **short-term forward-rate curve**.

PRACTICE QUESTION 9

Show how the 6-month forward rate 6.5 years (13 periods from now) reported in Exhibit 8 is computed?

Exhibit 8: Six-Month Forward Rates: The Short-Term Forward Rate Curve (Annualized Rates on a Bond-Equivalent Basis)

Notation	Forward Rate
$_1f_0$	3.00
$_1f_1$	3.60
$_1f_2$	3.92
$_1f_3$	5.15
$_1f_4$	6.54
$_1f_5$	6.33
$_1f_6$	6.23
$_1f_7$	5.79
$_1f_8$	6.01
$_1f_9$	6.24
$_1f_{10}$	6.48
$_1f_{11}$	6.72
$_1f_{12}$	6.97
$_1f_{13}$	6.36
$_1f_{14}$	6.49
$_1f_{15}$	6.62
$_1f_{16}$	6.76
$_1f_{17}$	8.10
$_1f_{18}$	8.40
$_1f_{19}$	8.72

B. Relationship between Spot Rates and Short-Term Forward Rates

Suppose an investor invests $\$X$ in a 3-year zero-coupon Treasury security. The total proceeds three years (six periods) from now would be:

$$X(1 + z_6)^6$$

The investor could instead buy a 6-month Treasury bill and reinvest the proceeds every six months for three years. The future dollars or dollar return will depend on the 6-month forward rates. Suppose that the investor can actually reinvest the proceeds maturing every six months at the calculated 6-month forward rates shown in Exhibit 8. At the end of three years, an investment of $\$X$ would generate the following proceeds:

$$X(1 + z_1)(1 + _1f_1)(1 + _1f_2)(1 + _1f_3)(1 + _1f_4)(1 + _1f_5)$$

Since the two investments must generate the same proceeds at the end of four years, the two previous equations can be equated:

$$X(1 + z_6)^6 = X(1 + z_1)(1 + _1f_1)(1 + _1f_2)(1 + _1f_3)(1 + _1f_4)(1 + _1f_5)$$

Solving for the 3-year (6-period) spot rate, we have:

$$z_6 = [(1 + z_1)(1 + _1f_1)(1 + _1f_2)(1 + _1f_3)(1 + _1f_4)(1 + _1f_5)]^{1/6} - 1$$

This equation tells us that the 3-year spot rate depends on the current 6-month spot rate and the five 6-month forward rates. In fact, the right-hand side of this equation is a geometric average of the current 6-month spot rate and the five 6-month forward rates.

Let's use the values in Exhibits 4 and 8 to confirm this result. Since the 6-month spot rate in Exhibit 4 is 3%, z_1 is 1.5% and therefore[8]

$$z_6 = [(1.015)(1.018)(1.0196)(1.02577)(1.0327)(1.03165)]^{1/6} - 1$$
$$= 0.023761 = 2.3761\%$$

Doubling this rate gives 4.7522%. This agrees with the spot rate shown in Exhibit 4.

In general, the relationship between a T-period spot rate, the current 6-month spot rate, and the 6-month forward rates is as follows:

$$z_T = [(1 + z_1)(1 + {}_1f_1)(1 + {}_1f_2) \dots (1 + {}_1f_{T-1})]^{1/T} - 1$$

Therefore, discounting at the forward rates will give the same present value as discounting at spot rates.

C. Valuation Using Forward Rates

Since a spot rate is simply a package of short-term forward rates, it will not make any difference whether we discount cash flows using spot rates or forward rates. That is, suppose that the cash flow in period T is $1. Then the present value of the cash flow can be found using the spot rate for period T as follows:

$$\text{PV of \$1 in } T \text{ periods } = \frac{1}{(1 + z_T)^T}$$

Alternatively, since we know that

$$z_T = [(1 + z_1)(1 + {}_1f_1)(1 + {}_1f_2) \cdots (1 + {}_1f_{T-1})]^{1/T} - 1$$

then, adding 1 to both sides of the equation,

$$(1 + z_T) = [(1 + z_1)(1 + {}_1f_1)(1 + {}_1f_2) \cdots (1 + {}_1f_{T-1})]^{1/T}$$

Raising both sides of the equation to the T-th power we get:

$$(1 + z_T)^T = (1 + z_1)(1 + {}_1f_1)(1 + {}_1f_2) \cdots (1 + {}_1f_{T-1})$$

Substituting the right-hand side of the above equation into the present value formula we get:

$$\text{PV of \$1 in } T \text{ periods } = \frac{1}{(1 + z_1)(1 + {}_1f_1)(1 + {}_1f_2) \dots (1 + {}_1f_{T-1})}$$

In practice, the present value of $1 in T periods is called the **forward discount factor for period T.**

For example, consider the forward rates shown in Exhibit 8. The forward discount rate for period 4 is found as follows:

$$z_1 = 3\%/2 = 1.5\% \qquad {}_1f_1 = 3.6\%/2 = 1.8\%$$
$$_1f_2 = 3.92\%/2 = 1.958\% \qquad {}_1f_3 = 5.15\%/2 = 2.577\%$$

$$\text{forward discount factor of \$1 in 4 periods } = \frac{\$1}{(1.015)(1.018)(1.01958)(1.02577)}$$
$$= 0.925369$$

---

[8] Actually, the semiannual forward rates are based on annual rates calculated to more decimal places. For example, $f_{1,3}$ is 5.15% in Exhibit 8 but based on the more precise value, the semiannual rate is 2.577%.

Exhibit 9: Calculation of the Forward Discount Factor for Each Period

Periods	Years	Notation	Forward Rate*	0.5 × Forward Rate**	1 + Forward Rate	Forward Discount Factor
1	0.5	$_1f_0$	3.00%	1.5000%	1.01500	0.985222
2	1.0	$_1f_1$	3.60%	1.8002%	1.01800	0.967799
3	1.5	$_1f_2$	3.92%	1.9583%	1.01958	0.949211
4	2.0	$_1f_3$	5.15%	2.5773%	1.02577	0.925362
5	2.5	$_1f_4$	6.54%	3.2679%	1.03268	0.896079
6	3.0	$_1f_5$	6.33%	3.1658%	1.03166	0.868582
7	3.5	$_1f_6$	6.23%	3.1139%	1.03114	0.842352
8	4.0	$_1f_7$	5.79%	2.8930%	1.02893	0.818668
9	4.5	$_1f_8$	6.01%	3.0063%	1.03006	0.794775
10	5.0	$_1f_9$	6.24%	3.1221%	1.03122	0.770712
11	5.5	$_1f_{10}$	6.48%	3.2407%	1.03241	0.746520
12	6.0	$_1f_{11}$	6.72%	3.3622%	1.03362	0.722237
13	6.5	$_1f_{12}$	6.97%	3.4870%	1.03487	0.697901
14	7.0	$_1f_{13}$	6.36%	3.1810%	1.03181	0.676385
15	7.5	$_1f_{14}$	6.49%	3.2450%	1.03245	0.655126
16	8.0	$_1f_{15}$	6.62%	3.3106%	1.03311	0.634132
17	8.5	$_1f_{16}$	6.76%	3.3778%	1.03378	0.613412
18	9.0	$_1f_{17}$	8.10%	4.0504%	1.04050	0.589534
19	9.5	$_1f_{18}$	8.40%	4.2009%	1.04201	0.565767
20	10.0	$_1f_{19}$	8.72%	4.3576%	1.04358	0.542142

* The rates in this column are rounded to two decimal places.
** The rates in this column used the forward rates in the previous column carried to four decimal places.

To see that this is the same present value that would be obtained using the spot rates, note from Exhibit 4 that the 2-year spot rate is 3.9164%. Using that spot rate we find:

$$z_4 = 3.9164\%/2 = 1.9582\%$$

$$\text{PV of \$1 in 4 periods} = \frac{\$1}{(1.019582)^4} = 0.925361$$

The answer is the same as the forward discount factor (the slight difference is due to rounding).

Exhibit 9 shows the computation of the forward discount factor for each period based on the forward rates in Exhibit 8. Let's show how both the forward rates and the spot rates can be used to value a 2-year 6% coupon Treasury bond. The present value for each cash flow is found as follows using spot rates:

$$\frac{\text{cash flow for period } t}{(1 + z_t)^t}$$

The following table uses the spot rates in Exhibit 4 to value this bond:

Period	Spot rate BEY (%)	Semiannual spot rate (%)	Cash flow	PV of cash flow
1	3.0000	1.50000	3	2.955665
2	3.3000	1.65000	3	2.903397
3	3.5053	1.75266	3	2.847633
4	3.9164	1.95818	103	95.312278
			Total	104.018973

Based on the spot rates, the value of this bond is $104.0190.

Using forward rates and the forward discount factors the present value of the cash flow in period t is found as follows:

cash flow in period t × discount factor for period t

The following table uses the forward rates and the forward discount factors in Exhibit 9 to value this bond:

Period	Semiann. forward rate	Forward discount factor	Cash flow	PV of cash flow
1	1.5000%	0.985222	3	2.955665
2	1.8002%	0.967799	3	2.903397
3	1.9583%	0.949211	3	2.847633
4	2.5773%	0.925362	103	95.312278
			Total	104.018973

The present value of this bond using forward rates is $104.0190.

So, it does not matter whether one discounts cash flows by spot rates or forward rates, the value is the same.

PRACTICE QUESTION 10

Compute the value of a 10% coupon 3-year bond using the forward rates in Exhibit 8.

D. Computing Any Forward Rate

Using spot rates, we can compute any forward rate. Using the same arbitrage arguments as used above to derive the 6-month forward rates, any forward rate can be obtained.

There are two elements to the forward rate. The first is when in the future the rate begins. The second is the length of time for the rate. For example, the 2-year forward rate 3 years from now means a rate three years from now for a length of two years. The notation used for a forward rate, f, will have two subscripts — one before f and one after f as shown below:

$$_t f_m$$

The subscript before f is t and is the length of time that the rate applies. The subscript after f is m and is when the forward rate begins. That is,

the length of time of the forward rate f when the forward rate begins

Remember our time periods are still 6-month periods. Given the above notation, here is what the following mean:

Notation	Interpretation for the forward rate
$_1f_{12}$	6-month (1-period) forward rate beginning 6 years (12 periods) from now
$_2f_8$	1-year (2-period) forward rate beginning 4 years (8 periods) from now
$_6f_4$	3-year (6-period) forward rate beginning 2 years (4 periods) from now
$_8f_{10}$	4-year (8-period) forward rate beginning 5 years (10 periods) from now

To see how the formula for the forward rate is derived, consider the following two alternatives for an investor who wants to invest for $m + t$ periods:

- buy a zero-coupon Treasury bond that matures in $m + t$ periods, or
- buy a zero-coupon Treasury bond that matures in m periods and invest the proceeds at the maturity date in a zero-coupon Treasury bond that matures in t periods.

The investor will be indifferent between the two alternatives if they produce the same return over the $m + t$ investment horizon.

For $100 invested in the first alternative, the proceeds for this investment at the horizon date assuming that the semiannual rate is z_{m+t} is

$$\$100 \, (1 + z_{m+t})^{m+t}$$

For the second alternative, the proceeds for this investment at the end of m periods assuming that the semiannual rate is z_m is

$$\$100 \, (1 + z_m)^m$$

When the proceeds are received in m periods, they are reinvested at the forward rate, $_tf_m$, producing a value for the investment at the end of $m + t$ periods of

$$\$100 \, (1 + z_m)^m \, (1 + {_tf_m})^t$$

For the investor to be indifferent to the two alternatives, the following relationship must hold:

$$\$100 \, (1 + z_{m+t})^{m+t} = \$100 \, (1 + z_m)^m \, (1 + {_tf_m})^t$$

Solving for $_tf_m$ we get:

$$_tf_m = \left[\frac{(1 + z_{m+t})^{m+t}}{(1 + z_m)^m} \right]^{1/t} - 1$$

Notice that if t is equal to 1, the formula reduces to the 1-period (6-month) forward rate.

To illustrate, for the spot rates shown in Exhibit 4 suppose that an investor wants to know the 2-year forward rate three years from now. In terms of the notation, t is equal to 4 and m is equal to 6. Substituting for t and m into the equation for the forward rate we have:

$$_4f_6 = \left[\frac{(1 + z_{10})^{10}}{(1 + z_6)^6} \right]^{1/4} - 1$$

This means that the following two spot rates are needed: z_6 (the 3-year spot rate) and z_{10} (the 5-year spot rate). From Exhibit 4 we know

$$z_6 \text{ (the 3-year spot rate)} = 4.752\%/2 = 0.02376$$
$$z_{10} \text{ (the 5-year spot rate)} = 5.2772\%/2 = 0.026386$$

then

$$_4f_6 = \left[\frac{(1.026386)^{10}}{(1.02376)^6}\right]^{1/4} - 1 = 0.030338$$

Therefore, $_4f_6$ is equal to 3.0338% and doubling this rate gives 6.0675% the forward rate on a bond-equivalent basis.

We can verify this result. Investing $100 for 10 periods at the spot rate of 2.6386% will produce the following value:

$$\$100 (1.026386)^{10} = \$129.7499$$

By investing $100 for 6 periods at 2.376% and reinvesting the proceeds for 4 periods at the forward rate of 3.030338% gives the same value

$$\$100 (1.02376)^6 (1.030338)^4 = \$129.75012$$

PRACTICE QUESTION 11

a. Given the spot rates in Exhibit 4, compute the 6-year forward rate 4 years from now.
b. Demonstrate that the forward rate computed in part a is correct.

SECTION VI
KEY POINTS

❑ *The sources of return from holding a bond to maturity are the coupon interest payments, any capital gain or loss, and reinvestment income.*

❑ *Reinvestment income is the interest income generated by reinvesting coupon interest payments and any principal repayments from the time of receipt to the bond's maturity.*

❑ *The current yield relates the annual dollar coupon interest to the market price and fails to recognize any capital gain or loss and reinvestment income.*

❑ *The yield to maturity is the interest rate that will make the present value of the cash flows from a bond equal to the price plus accrued interest.*

❑ *The market convention to annualize a semiannual yield is to double it and the resulting annual yield is referred to as a bond-equivalent yield.*

❑ *When market participants refer to a yield or return measure as computed on a bond-equivalent basis it means that a semiannual yield or return is doubled.*

❑ *The yield to maturity takes into account all three sources of return but assumes that the coupon payments and any principal repayments can be reinvested at an interest rate equal to the yield to maturity.*

❑ *The yield to maturity will only be realized if the interim cash flows can be reinvested at the yield to maturity and the bond is held to maturity.*

❑ *Reinvestment risk is the risk an investor faces that future reinvestment rates will be less than the yield to maturity at the time a bond is purchased.*

❑ *Interest rate risk is the risk that if a bond is not held to maturity, an investor may have to sell it for less than the purchase price.*

❑ *The longer the maturity and the higher the coupon rate, the more a bond's return is dependent on reinvestment income to realize the yield to maturity at the time of purchase.*

❑ *For callable bonds a yield to first call (which assumes the bond will be called on the first call date) and a yield to first par call (which assumes the bond will be called on the first date it is callable at par) are computed.*

❑ *The yield to call considers all three sources of potential return but assumes that all cash flows can be reinvested at the yield to call until the assumed call date, the investor will hold the bond to the assumed call date, and the issuer will call the bond on the assumed call date.*

❑ *For a putable bond a yield to put is computed assuming that the issue will be put on the first put date.*

❑ *The yield to worst is the lowest yield from among all possible yield to calls, yield to puts, and the yield to maturity.*

❑ *For mortgage-backed and asset-backed securities, the cash flow yield based on some prepayment rate is the interest rate that equates the present value of the projected principal and interest payments to the price plus accrued interest.*

❑ *The cash flow yield assumes that all cash flows (principal payments and interest payments) can be reinvested at the calculated yield and that the assumed prepayment rate will be realized over the security's life.*

❑ *For amortizing securities, reinvestment risk is greater than for standard coupon nonamortizing securities because payments are typically made monthly and include principal repayment as well as interest payments.*

❑ *For a floating-rate security the discount margin is the conventional measure that estimates the average spread over the reference rate that the investor can expect to earn over the life of the security.*

❑ *The discount margin assumes that the reference rate will not change over the life of the security and that there is no cap or floor restriction on the coupon rate.*

❑ *The theoretical spot rate is the interest rate that should be used to discount a default-free cash flow.*

❑ *Default-free spot rates can be derived from the Treasury par yield curve by a method called bootstrapping.*

❑ *The basic principle underlying the bootstrapping method is that the value of a Treasury coupon security should be equal to the value of the package of zero-coupon Treasury securities that duplicates the coupon bond's cash flows.*

❑ *The nominal spread is the difference between the yield for a non-Treasury bond and a comparable-maturity Treasury coupon security.*

❑ *The nominal spread fails to consider the term structure of the spot rates and the fact that, for bonds with embedded options, future interest rate volatility may alter the cash flows.*

❏ *The zero-volatility spread or Z-spread is a measure of the spread that the investor would realize over the entire Treasury spot rate curve if the bond is held to maturity, thereby recognizing the term structure of interest rates.*

❏ *Unlike the nominal spread, the Z-spread is not a spread off one point on the Treasury yield curve but is a spread over the entire spot rate curve.*

❏ *For bullet bonds, unless the yield curve is very steep, the nominal spread will not differ significantly from the Z-spread; for securities where principal is repaid over time rather than just at maturity there can be a significant difference, particularly in a steep yield curve environment.*

❏ *The option-adjusted spread (OAS) converts the cheapness or richness of a bond into a spread over the future possible spot rate curves.*

❏ *An OAS is said to be option adjusted because it allows for future interest rate volatility to affect the cash flows.*

❏ *The OAS is a product of a valuation model and, when comparing the OAS of dealer firms, it is critical to check on the volatility assumption (and other assumptions) employed in the valuation model.*

❏ *The cost of the embedded option is measured as the difference between the Z-spread and the OAS.*

❏ *Investors should not rely on the nominal spread for bonds with embedded options since it hides how the spread is split between the OAS and the option cost.*

❏ *OAS is used as a relative value measure to assist in the selection of bonds with embedded options.*

❏ *Using arbitrage arguments, forward rates can be extrapolated from the Treasury yield curve or the Treasury spot rate curve.*

❏ *The spot rate for a given period is related to the forward rates; specifically, the spot rate is a geometric average of the current 6-month spot rate and the subsequent 6-month forward rates.*

END OF
CHAPTER
QUESTIONS

1. What are the sources of return that any yield measure should incorporate?

2. a. Suppose a 10-year 9% coupon bond is selling for $112 with a par value of $100. What is the current yield for the bond?
   b. What is the limitation of the current yield measure?

3. Determine whether the yield to maturity of a 6.5% 20-year bond that pays interest semiannually and is selling for $90.68 is 7.2%. 7.4%, or 7.8%.

4. The following yields and prices were reported in the financial press. Are any of them incorrect assuming that the reported price and coupon rate are correct? If so, explain why? (No calculations are needed to answer this question.)

Bond	Price	Coupon rate	Current Yield	Yield to Maturity
A	100	6.0%	5.0%	6.0%
B	110	7.0%	6.4%	6.1%
C	114	7.5%	7.1%	7.7%
D	95	4.7%	5.2%	5.9%
E	75	5.6%	5.1%	4.1%

5. Comment on the following statement: "The yield to maturity measure is a useless measure because it doubles a semiannual yield (calling the annual yield a bond-equivalent yield) rather than computing an effective annual yield. This is the major shortcoming of the yield to maturity measure."

6. a. Suppose that an investor invests $108.32 in a 5-year certificate of deposit that pays 7% annually (on a bond-equivalent basis) or 3.5% semiannually and the interest payments are semiannual. What are the total future dollars of this investment at the end of 5 years (i.e., ten 6-month periods)?

   b. How much total interest is generated from the investment in this certificate of deposit?

   c. Suppose an investor can purchase any investment for $108.32 that offers a 7% yield on a bond-equivalent basis and pays interest semiannually. What is the total future dollars and the total dollar return from this investment?

   d. Suppose an investor can purchase a 5-year 9% coupon bond that pays interest semiannually and the price of this bond is $108.32. The yield to maturity for this bond is 7% on a bond-equivalent basis. What is the total future dollars and the total dollar return that will be generated from this bond if it is to yield 7%?

   e. Complete the following for this bond:

   coupon interest   =
   capital gain/loss   =
   reinvestment income = _____
   total dollar return =

   f. What percentage of the total dollar return is dependent on reinvestment income?

   g. How is the reinvestment income in part e realized?

7. a. Which of the following three bonds has the greatest dependence on reinvestment income to generate the computed yield? Assume that each bond is offering the same yield to maturity. (No computations are needed.)

Bond	Maturity	Coupon rate
X	25 years	0%
Y	20 years	7%
Z	20 years	8%

   b. Which of the three bonds in part a has the least dependence on reinvestment income to generate the computed yield? Assume that each bond is offering the same yield to maturity. (No computations are needed.)

8. What is the reinvestment risk and interest rate risk associated with a yield to maturity measure?

9. a. If the yield to maturity on an annual-pay bond is 5.6%, what is the bond-equivalent yield?

   b. If the yield of a U.S. bond issue quoted on a bond-equivalent basis is 5.6%, what is the yield to maturity on an annual-pay basis?

10. Suppose that a 10% 15-year bond has the following call structure:

    not callable for the next 5 years
    first callable in 5 year at $105
    first par call date is in 10 years

    The price of the bond is $127.5880.

    a. Is the yield to maturity for this bond 7.0%, 7.4%, or 7.8%?
    b. Is the yield to first call for this bond 4.55%, 4.65%, or 4.85?
    c. Is the yield to first par call for this bond 6.25%, 6.55%, or 6.75%?

11. Suppose a 5% coupon 6-year bond is selling for $105.2877 and can be put in four years at par value. The yield to maturity for this bond is 6%. Determine whether the yield to put is 3.38%, 3.44% or 3.57%.

12. Suppose that an amortizing security pays interest monthly. Based on the projected principal repayments and interest, suppose that the monthly interest rate that makes the present value of the cash flows equal to the price of the security is 0.41%. What is the cash flow yield on a bond-equivalent basis?

13. Two portfolio managers are discussing the investment characteristics of amortizing securities. Manager A believes that the advantage of these securities relative to nonamortizing securities is that since the periodic cash flows include principal repayments as well as coupon payments, the manager can generate greater reinvestment income. In addition, the payments are typically monthly so even greater reinvestment income can be generated. Manager B believes that the need to reinvest monthly and the need to invest larger amounts than just coupon interest payments make amortizing securities less attractive. Who do you agree with and why?

14. An investor is considering the purchase of a 5-year floating-rate note that pays interest semiannually. The coupon formula is equal to 6-month LIBOR plus 30 basis points. The current value for 6-month LIBOR is 5% (annual rate). The price of this note is 99.1360. Is the discount margin 40 basis points, 50 basis points, or 55 basis points?

15. How does the discount margin handle any cap on a floater and the fact that the reference rate may change over time?

16. a. A Treasury bill with 105 days from settlement to maturity is selling for $0.989 per $1 of maturity value. What is the yield on a discount basis?
    b. A Treasury bill with 275 days from settlement to maturity is quoted as having a yield on a discount basis of 3.68%. What is the price of this Treasury bill?

17. What are the problems with using the yield on a discount basis as measure of a Treasury bill's yield.

18. Suppose that the annual yield to maturity for the 6-month and 1-year Treasury bill is 4.6% and 5.0%, respectively. These yields represent the 6-month and 1-year spot rates. Also assume the following Treasury par yield curve (i.e., the price for each issue is $100) has been estimated for 6-month periods out to a maturity of 3 years:

Years to maturity	Annual yield to maturity (BEY)
1.5	5.4%
2.0	5.8%
2.5	6.4%
3.0	7.0%

Compute the 1.5-year, 2-year, 2.5-year, and 3-year spot rates.

19. Given the spot rates computed in the previous question and the 6-month and 1-year spot rates, compute the arbitrage-free value of a 3-year Treasury security with a coupon rate of 8%.

20. What are the two limitations of the nominal spread as a measure of relative value of two bonds?

21. Suppose that the Treasury spot rate curve is as follows:

Period	Years to maturity	Spot rate
1	0.5	5.0%
2	1.0	5.4
3	1.5	5.8
4	2.0	6.4
5	2.5	7.0
6	3.0	7.2
7	3.5	7.4
8	4.0	7.8

Suppose that the market price of a 4-year 6% coupon non-Treasury issue is $91.4083 Determine whether the zero-volatility spread (Z-spread) relative to the Treasury spot rate curve for this issue is 80 basis points, 90 basis points, or 100 basis points.

22. The Prestige Investment Management Company sent a report to its pension client. In the report, Prestige indicated that the yield curve is currently flat (i.e., the yield to maturity for each maturity is the same) and then discussed the nominal spread for the corporate bond issues in the client's portfolio. A trustee of the pension funds was concerned that Prestige focused on the nominal spread rather than the zero-volatility spread or option-adjusted spread for these bond issues. Joan Thomas is Prestige's employee who is the contact person for this account. She received a phone call from the trustee regarding his concern. How should she respond regarding the use of nominal spread rather than zero-volatility spread and option-adjusted spread as a spread measure for corporate bonds?

23. John Tinker is a a junior portfolio manager assigned to work for Laura Sykes, the manager of the corporate bond portfolio of a public pension fund. Ms. Sykes asked Mr. Tinker to construct a profile of the portfolio that she could use in her presentation to the trustees. One of the measures Ms. Sykes insisted that Mr. Tinker include in the portfolio's profile is the option-adjusted spread of each issue. In preparing the profile of the portfolio, Mr. Tinker encountered the following situations that he did not understand. Provide Mr. Tinker with an explanation.

   a. Mr. Tinker checked with several dealer firms to determine the option-adjusted spread for each issue. For several of the issues, there were substantially different option-adjusted spreads reported. For example, for one callable issue one dealer firm reported an OAS of 100 basis points, one dealer reported 170 basis points, and a third dealer 200 basis points. Mr. Tinker could not understand how dealers could have substantially different OAS values when in fact the yield to maturity and nominal spread values for each of the issues did not differ from dealer to dealer.

   b. The dealers that Mr. Tinker checked with furnished him with the nominal spread and the Z-spread for each issue in addition to the OAS. For all the bond issues where there were no embedded options, each dealer reported that the Z-spread was equal to the OAS. Mr. Tinker could not understand why.

   c. One dealer firm reported an option cost for each issue. There were positive, negative, and zero values reported. Mr. Tinker observed that for all the bond issues that were putable, the option cost was negative. For all the option-free bond issues, the reported value was zero. For most of the callable bond issues, the option cost was a positive value; however, there were some low coupon callable bond issues with a few years to maturity where a zero option cost was reported. Mr. Tinker could not understand why the option-free issues had a zero option cost, why the putable issues had a negative value, and why the callable issues had a positive value except for the zero value for the low coupon issues that had only a few years to maturity.

24. Max Dumas is considering the purchase of a callable corporate bond. He has available to him two analytical systems to value the bond. In one system, System A, the vendor uses the on-the-run Treasury issues to construct the theoretical spot rate and that benchmark is used to construct a model to compute the OAS. The other analytical system, System B, uses as its benchmark the on-the-run issue for the particular issuer in constructing a model to compute the OAS.

a. Suppose that using System A, Mr. Dumas finds that the OAS for the callable corporate bond being considered for acquisition is 50 basis points. How should he interpret this OAS value?

b. Suppose that using System B, Mr. Dumas finds that the OAS computed for the callable corporate bond is 15 basis points. How should he interpret this OAS value?

c. Suppose that a dealer firm shows Mr. Dumas another callable corporate bond of the same credit quality and duration with an OAS of 40 basis points. Should Mr. Dumas view that this bond is more attractive or less attractive than the issue he is considering for acquisition.

25. Assume the following Treasury spot rates:

Period	Years to maturity	Spot rate
1	0.5	5.0%
2	1.0	5.4
3	1.5	5.8
4	2.0	6.4
5	2.5	7.0
6	3.0	7.2
7	3.5	7.4
8	4.0	7.8

Compute the following forward rates:

a. the 6-month forward rate six months from now.
b. the 6-month forward rate one year from now.
c. the 6-month forward rate three years from now.
d. the 2-year forward rate one year from now.
e. the 1-year forward rate two years from now.

26. For the previous question, demonstrate that the 6-month forward rate six month from now is the rate that will produce at the end of one year the same future dollars as investing either (1) at the current 1-year spot rate of 5.4% or (2) at the 6-month spot rate of 5.0% and reinvesting at the 6-month forward rate six months from now.

27. Two sales people of analytical systems are making a presentation to you about the merits of their respective systems. One sales person states that in valuing bonds the system first constructs the theoretical spot rates and then discounts cash flows using these rates. The other sales person interjects that his firm takes a different approach. Rather than using spot rates, forward rates are used to value the cash flows and he believes this is a better approach to valuing bonds compared to using spot rates. How would you respond to the second sales person's comment about his firm's approach?

28. a. Given the following 6-month forward rates, compute the forward discount factor for each period

Period	Annual forward rate (BEY)
1	4.00%
2	4.40
3	5.00
4	5.60
5	6.00
6	6.40

b. Compute the value of a 3-year 8% coupon bond using the forward rates.

SOLUTIONS TO END OF CHAPTER QUESTIONS

1. The three sources are (1) coupon interest, (2) any capital gain (or loss, a reduction in return), and (3) reinvestment income.

2. a. The current yield for the bond is

$$\text{annual coupon payment} = 0.09 \times \$100 = \$9$$

$$\text{current yield} = \frac{\$9}{\$112} = 0.0804 = 8.04\%$$

   b. The current yield measure only considers coupon interest and ignores any capital gain or loss (a capital loss of $12 for the bond in our example), and reinvestment income.

3. The present value of the cash flows of a 6.5% 20-year semiannual-pay bond using the three discount rates is shown below:

Discount rate (annual BEY)	Semiannual rate (Half annual rate)	Present value of cash flows
7.2%	3.6%	92.64
7.4	3.7	90.68
7.8	3.8	86.94

Since 3.7% equates the present value of the cash flows to the price of 90.68, 3.7% is the semiannual yield to maturity. Doubling that rates gives a 7.4% yield to maturity on a bond-equivalent basis.

4. This question requires no calculations. (Note that the maturity of each bond is intentionally omitted.) The question tests for an understanding of the relationship between coupon rate, current yield, and yield to maturity for a bond trading at par, a discount, and a premium.

   • Bond A's current yield is incorrect. The current yield should be equal to the coupon rate.
   • Bond B is fine. That is, it has the expected relationship between coupon rate, current yield, and yield to maturity for a bond trading at a premium.
   • Bond C's yield to maturity is incorrect. Since the bond is a premium bond, the yield to maturity should be less than the coupon rate.
   • Bond D is fine. That is, it has the expected relationship between coupon rate, current yield, and yield to maturity for a bond trading at a discount.
   • Bond E is incorrect. Both the current yield and the yield to maturity should be greater than the coupon rate since the bond is trading at a discount.

5. The statement is misleading in that while it is true that the yield to maturity computed on a bond-equivalent basis is flawed, it is not the reason why the yield to maturity is limited. The major reason is that it assumes that the bond is held to maturity and the coupon payments are assumed to be reinvested at the computed yield to maturity.

6. a. The total future dollars are found as follows:

$$\$108.32 \, (1.035)^{10} = \$152.80$$

   b. Since the total future dollars are $152.80 and the investment is $108.32, the total interest from the CD is $44.48.

c. The answer is the same as for parts a and b. The total future dollars are $152.80. The total dollar return is the same as the total interest, $44.48.

d. The answer is the same as for part c:

total future dollars = $152.80
total dollar return   = $44.48

e.

coupon interest   = $45.00
capital gain/loss   = −$ 8.32
reinvestment income   = $ 7.80
total dollar return   = $44.48

f. The percentage of the total dollar return that must be generated from reinvestment income is 17.5% ($7.80/$44.48).

g. The $7.80 reinvestment income must be generated by reinvesting the semiannual coupon payments from the time of receipt to the maturity date at the semiannual yield to maturity, 3.5% in this example. The reinvestment income earned on a given coupon payment of $4.50 if it invested from the time of receipt in period t to the maturity date (10 periods in our example) at a 3.5% semiannual rate is:

$$\$4.50\,(1.035)^{10-t} - \$4.50$$

The reinvestment income for each coupon payment is shown below:

Period	Periods reinvested	Coupon payment	Reinvestment income at 3.5%
1	9	$4.5	$1.63
2	8	4.5	1.43
3	7	4.5	1.23
4	6	4.5	1.03
5	5	4.5	0.84
6	4	4.5	0.66
7	3	4.5	0.49
8	2	4.5	0.32
9	1	4.5	0.16
10	0	4.5	0.00
		Total	7.79

The reinvestment income totals $7.79 which differs from $7.80 due to rounding.

7. a. Bond X has no dependence on reinvestment income since it is a zero-coupon bond. So it is either Bond Y or Bond Z. The two bonds have the same maturity. Since they are both selling at the same yield, the one with the higher coupon rate is more dependent on reinvestment income.

b. As explained in part a, since Bond X is a zero-coupon bond, it has the least dependence (in fact, no dependence) on reinvestment income.

8. The reinvestment risk is that to generate the computed yield, it is necessary to reinvest the interim cash flows (i.e., coupon payments in the case of a nonamortizing security and principal plus coupon payments in the case of an amortizing security) at the computed yield. The interest rate risk comes into play because it is assumed that the security will be held to the maturity date. If it is not, the yield no longer applies because there is the risk of having to sell the security below its purchase price.

9. a. The bond-equivalent yield is

$$2[(1.056)^{0.5} - 1] = 0.0552 = 5.52\%$$

b. The annual yield is

$$[(1.028)^2 - 1] = 0.0568 = 5.68\%$$

10. a. The cash flows for this bond to the maturity date are (1) 30 coupon payments of $5 and (2) $100 at the maturity date. The table below shows the present values of the coupon payments and maturity value for the three interest rates in the question:

Annual interest rate (%)	Semiannual interest rate (%)	Present value of 30 payments of $5	Present value of $100 30 periods from now	Present value of cash flows
7.0	3.5	91.9602	35.6278	127.5880
7.4	3.7	89.6986	33.6231	123.3217
7.8	3.9	87.5197	31.7346	119.2543

Since a semiannual interest rate of 3.5% produces a present value equal to the price of the bond ($127.5880), the yield to maturity is 7% on a bond-equivalent basis.

b. The cash flows for this bond up to the first call date are (1) 10 coupon payments of $5 and (2) $105 ten 6-month periods from now. The table below shows the present values of the coupon payments and maturity value for the three interest rates in the question:

Annual interest rate (%)	Semiannual interest rate (%)	Present value of 10 payments of $5	Present value of $105 10 periods from now	Present value of cash flows
4.55	2.275	44.2735	83.8483	128.1218
4.65	2.325	44.1587	83.4395	127.5982
4.85	2.425	43.9304	82.6284	126.5588

Since of the three interest rates in the question, a semiannual interest rate of 2.325% makes the present value of the cash flows closest to the price of $127.5880, the yield to the first call date is 4.65% on a bond-equivalent basis.

c. The cash flows for this bond up to the first par call date are (1) 20 coupon payments of $5 and (2) $100 twenty 6-month periods from now. The table below shows the present values of the coupon payments and maturity value for the three interest rates in the question:

Annual interest rate (%)	Semiannual interest rate (%)	Present value of 20 payments of $5	Present value of $100 20 periods from now	Present value of cash flows
6.25	3.125	73.5349	54.0407	127.5756
6.55	3.275	72.5308	52.4923	125.0231
6.75	3.375	71.8725	51.4860	123.3585

Since of the three interest rates in the question, a semiannual interest rate of 3.125% makes the present value of the cash flows closest to the price of $127.5880, the yield to the first par call date is 6.25% on a bond-equivalent basis.

11. The cash flows to the put date are (1) 8 coupon payments of $2.50 and (2) $100 (the put price) eight 6-month periods from now. The table below shows the present values of the coupon payments and maturity value for the three interest rates in the question:

Annual interest rate (%)	Semiannual interest rate (%)	Present value of 8 payments of $2.5	Present value of $100 8 periods from now	Present value of cash flows
3.38	1.690	18.5609	87.4529	106.0136
3.44	1.720	18.5367	87.2467	105.7834
3.57	1.785	18.4846	86.8020	105.2866

Since of the three interest rates in the question, a semiannual interest rate of 1.785% makes the present value of the cash flows closest to the price of $105.2877, the yield to the put date is 3.57% on a bond-equivalent basis.

12. First, the semiannual effective yield is computed from the monthly yield by compounding it for six months as follows:

$$\text{effective semiannual yield} = (1.0041)^6 - 1 = 0.024854 = 2.4854\%$$

Next, the effective semiannual yield is doubled to get the annual cash flow yield on a bond-equivalent basis. Thus, the cash flow yield on a bond-equivalent basis is 4.97% (2 times 2.4854%).

13. The cash flow yield, as with any other yield measure such as the yield to maturity or any yield to call date, requires that the investor be able to reinvest any interim cash flows in order to realize the computed yield. A cash flow yield is even more dependent on reinvestment income because the interim cash flows are monthly coupon and principal, rather than simply semiannual coupon for a standard coupon bond. Consequently, the reinvestment risk is greater with an amortizing security.

14. The table below shows the present value using the three discount margins:

5-year floater
current LIBOR   5.00%
quoted margin   30 basis points

				Present value ($) at assumed margin of		
	LIBOR	Coupon	Cash flow	40	50	55
Period	(annual rate) (%)	rate (%)	($)	5.400%	5.500%	5.550%
1	5.00	5.300	2.65	2.5803	2.5791	2.5784
2	5.00	5.300	2.65	2.5125	2.5100	2.5088
3	5.00	5.300	2.65	2.4464	2.4429	2.4411
4	5.00	5.300	2.65	2.3821	2.3775	2.3752
5	5.00	5.300	2.65	2.3195	2.3139	2.3110
6	5.00	5.300	2.65	2.2585	2.2519	2.2486
7	5.00	5.300	2.65	2.1991	2.1917	2.1879
8	5.00	5.300	2.65	2.1413	2.1330	2.1289
9	5.00	5.300	2.65	2.0850	2.0759	2.0714
10	5.00	5.300	102.65	78.6420	78.2601	78.0700
			Total	99.5669	99.1360	98.9214

When a margin of 50 basis points is used, the present value of the cash flows is equal to the price ($99.1360).

15. The discount margin ignores both and hence is a limitation of this measure. The cap is not considered because the reference rate is assumed to be unchanged at the current value for the reference rate. The only way in which the cap is considered is in the special case where the current value for the reference rate is capped and in this case it assumes that the reference rate will not fall below the cap for the life of the floater.

16. a. The yield on a discount basis, d, is

$$(1 - 0.989)\left(\frac{360}{105}\right) = 0.0377 = 3.77\%$$

b. The price of this Treasury bill, p, per $1 dollar of maturity value is:

$$1 - 0.0368 \, (275/360) = 0.971889$$

17. The yield on a discount basis has two major shortcomings. First, it relates the interest return to the maturity or face value rather than the amount invested. Second, it is based on a 360-day year rather than 365-day year as used for Treasury coupon securities.

18. We will use the same notation as in the chapter. One-half the annualized spot rate for a 6-month period will be denoted by z_t. We know that the 6-month Treasury bill yield is 4.6% and the 1-year Treasury yield is 5.0%, so

$$z_1 = 4.6\%/2 = 2.3\% \quad \text{and} \quad z_2 = 5.0\%/2 = 2.5\%$$

Now we use the bootstrapping methodology. The 1.5-year Treasury yield from the par yield curve is selling to yield 5.4%. Since the price of the issue is its par value, the coupon rate is 5.4%. So, the cash flow for this issue is:

0.5 year	$0.054 \times \$100 \times 0.5$		=	$2.70
1.0 year	$0.054 \times \$100 \times 0.5$		=	$2.70
1.5 years	$0.054 \times \$100 \times 0.5$	$+ \$100$	=	$102.70

The present value of the cash flows is then:

$$\frac{2.7}{(1 + z_1)^1} + \frac{2.7}{(1 + z_2)^2} + \frac{102.7}{(1 + z_3)^3}$$

Substituting the first two spot rates we have:

$$\frac{2.7}{(1.023)^1} + \frac{2.7}{(1.025)^2} + \frac{102.7}{(1 + z_3)^3}$$

The goal is to find z_3. Since the value of this cash flow must be equal to the price of the 1.5-year issue which is par value, we can set the previous equation equal to 100:

$$\frac{2.7}{(1.023)^1} + \frac{2.7}{(1.025)^2} + \frac{102.7}{(1 + z_3)^3} = 100$$

We then solve for z_3 as follows:

$$2.639296 + 2.569899 + \frac{102.7}{(1 + z_3)^3} = 100$$

$$\frac{102.7}{(1 + z_3)^3} = 94.7908$$

$$z_3 = 0.027073 = 2.7073\%$$

Doubling this yield we obtain the bond-equivalent yield of 5.4146%.

The equation for obtaining the 2-year, 2.5-year, and 3-year spot rates are given below.

For the 2-year spot rate, the coupon rate from the par yield curve is 5.8%. So, the present value of the cash flow is:

$$\frac{2.9}{(1 + z_1)^1} + \frac{2.9}{(1 + z_2)^2} + \frac{2.9}{(1 + z_3)^3} + \frac{102.9}{(1 + z_4)^4}$$

Substituting: $z_1 = 2.3\%$ $z_2 = 2.5\%$ $z_3 = 2.7073\%$
and setting the present value equal to the price of the 2-year issue (100), we obtain:

$$\frac{2.9}{(1.023)^1} + \frac{2.9}{(1.025)^2} + \frac{2.9}{(1.027073)^3} + \frac{102.9}{(1 + z_4)^4} = 100$$

Solving the above equation we would find that z_4 is 2.9148%. Therefore, the 2-year spot rate on a bond-equivalent basis is 5.8297%.

For the 2.5-year spot rate, we use the 2.5-year issue from the par yield curve. The yield is 6.4% and therefore the coupon rate is 6.4%. The present value of the cash flow for this issue is then:

$$\frac{3.2}{(1 + z_1)^1} + \frac{3.2}{(1 + z_2)^2} + \frac{3.2}{(1 + z_3)^3} + \frac{3.2}{(1 + z_4)^4} + \frac{103.2}{(1 + z_5)^5}$$

Substituting: $z_1 = 2.3\%$ $z_2 = 2.5\%$ $z_3 = 2.7073\%$ $z_4 = 2.9148\%$
and setting the present value equal to the price of the 2.5-year issue (100), we obtain:

$$\frac{3.2}{(1.023)^1} + \frac{3.2}{(1.025)^2} + \frac{3.2}{(1.027073)^3} + \frac{3.2}{(1.029148)^4} + \frac{103.2}{(1 + z_5)^5} = 100$$

Solving the above equation we would find that z_5 is 3.2333%. Therefore, the 2.5-year spot rate on a bond-equivalent basis is 6.4665%.

For the 3-year spot rate, we use the 3-year issue from the par yield curve. The yield is 7.0% and therefore the coupon rate is 7.0%. The present value of the cash flow for this issue is then:

$$\frac{3.5}{(1 + z_1)^1} + \frac{3.5}{(1 + z_2)^2} + \frac{3.5}{(1 + z_3)^3} + \frac{3.5}{(1 + z_4)^4} + \frac{3.5}{(1 + z_5)^5} + \frac{103.5}{(1 + z_6)^6}$$

Substituting: $z_1 = 2.3\%$ $z_2 = 2.5\%$ $z_3 = 2.7073\%$ $z_4 = 2.9148\%$ $z_5 = 3.2333\%$
and setting the present value equal to the price of the 3-year issue (100), we obtain:

$$\frac{3.5}{(1.023)^1} + \frac{3.5}{(1.025)^2} + \frac{3.5}{(1.027073)^3} + \frac{3.5}{(1.029148)^4} + \frac{3.5}{(1.032333)^5} + \frac{103.5}{(1+z_6)^6} = 100$$

Solving the above equation we would find that z_6 is 3.5586%. Therefore, the 3-year spot rate on a bond-equivalent basis is 7.1173%.

To summarize the findings for the spot rates:

Period	Year	Annualized spot rate (BEY)	z_t
1	0.5	4.6000%	2.3000%
2	1.0	5.0000	2.5000
3	1.5	5.4146	2.7073
4	2.0	5.8297	2.9148
5	2.5	6.4665	3.2333
6	3.0	7.1173	3.5586

19. To obtain the arbitrage-free value of an 8% coupon 3-year Treasury bond, the cash flows for the bond are discounted at the spot rates in the previous question as shown below:

Period	Annual spot rate (%)	Semiannual spot rate (%)	Cash flow	PV of CF
1	4.6000	2.3000	$4.0	$3.9101
2	5.0000	2.5000	4.0	3.8073
3	5.4146	2.7073	4.0	3.6919
4	5.8297	2.9148	4.0	3.5657
5	6.4665	3.2333	4.0	3.4116
6	7.1173	3.5586	104.0	84.3171
			Total	$102.7037

The arbitrage-free value of this bond is $102.7037.

20. The nominal spread fails to take into consideration (1) the shape of the yield curve (and therefore spot rates) and (2) any option embedded in a bond.

21. The Z-spread relative to the Treasury spot rate curve is the spread that when added to all the Treasury spot rates will produce a present value for the cash flows equal to the market price. The present value using each of the three spreads in the question — 80, 90, and 100 basis points — is shown below:

Period	Years to maturity	Spot rate (BEY) (%)	Semiannual spot rate (%)	Cash flow	PV at assumed spread (bp) 80	90	100
1	0.5	5.0	2.50	$3	$2.9155	$2.9140	$2.9126
2	1.0	5.4	2.70	3	2.8223	2.8196	2.8168
3	1.5	5.8	2.90	3	2.7216	2.7176	2.7137
4	2.0	6.4	3.20	3	2.6042	2.5992	2.5942
5	2.5	7.0	3.50	3	2.4777	2.4717	2.4658
6	3.0	7.2	3.60	3	2.3709	2.3641	2.3573
7	3.5	7.4	3.70	3	2.2645	2.2569	2.2493
8	4.0	7.8	3.90	103	73.5466	73.2652	72.9849
				Total	91.7233	91.4083	91.0947

The last three columns in the table show the assumed spread. One-half of the spread is added to the column showing the semiannual spot rate. Then the cash flow is discounted used the semiannual spot rate plus one-half the assumed spread.

As can be seen, when a 90 basis point spread is used, the present value of the cash flow is equal to the price of the non-Treasury issue, $91.4083. Therefore, the Z-spread is 90 basis points.

22. When the yield curve is flat, all the cash flows are discounted at the same rate. Therefore, if Treasury securities are the benchmark, the nominal spread will be equal to the Z-spread. So, in the case of the corporate bond issues where there is no embedded option, using either measure is acceptable. In contrast, for corporate bonds issues in the portfolio with embedded options, the option-adjusted spread is more appropriate than either the nominal spread or the Z-spread regardless of the shape of the yield curve. Consequently, Joan Thomas would have to agree that the option-adjusted spread should be used for the corporate issues with embedded options.

23. a. There are several assumptions that are made in valuing bonds with embedded options. One important assumption is interest rate volatility. Because these assumptions differ from dealer to dealer, the OAS values may differ substantially.

   b. The relationship between the OAS, Z-spread, and option cost is as follows:

   option cost = Z-spread − OAS

   If a bond has no embedded option, then there is no option cost. That is, the option cost is zero. Substituting zero into the above equation, we have

   Z-spread = OAS

   That is, the Z-spread is equal to the OAS. This is the reason why Mr. Tinker observed that for the issues with no embedded options the OAS is the same as the Z-spread.

   c. A negative value for the option cost means that the investor has purchased an option from the issuer. A putable bond is an example of where the investor purchases an option. This explains why Mr. Tinker finds that a negative value for the option cost was reported for the putable bond issues. When there is no embedded option, the option cost is zero and that is why Mr. Tinker finds this value for issues with this characteristic. A positive value for the option cost means that the investor has sold an option to the issuer. This occurs for callable bond issues, as Mr. Tinker observes. However, low coupon issues with only a few years to maturity could have an option cost of zero. This is because it may be unattractive for the issuer to call such issues since they have only a few years to maturity and the coupon rate is low so that rates will have to be move lower in a few years (before the issue matures) in order for the issuer to call them. (In the parlance of the options industry, the option for such callable issues is deep out of the money.)

24. a. Because the Treasury securities are the benchmark, the OAS reflects a spread to compensate for credit risk and liquidity risk. (Remember that option risk has already been removed.)

b. Since the benchmark is the issuer's on-the-run yield curve, the spread already reflects credit risk. So, basically the OAS reflects compensation for liquidity risk. (Remember that option risk has already been removed.)

c. The answer depends on the benchmark interest rates used by the dealer firm. If the benchmark interest rates are Treasury rates, than the OAS is better for the issue that Mr. Dumas is considering. If the benchmark is the issuer's on-the-run yield curve, then the issue that the dealer is offering to Mr. Dumas is more attractive. However, the qualifier is that the answer also depends on the interest rate volatility assumed by the dealer and the interest rate volatility assumed by Mr. Dumas when analyzing the issue using System A and System B. Without knowing the assumed interest rate volatilities, no statement can be made about the relative value of these two issues.

25. We will use the notation in the chapter:

f will denote the forward rate

t will be the subscript before f and will indicate the length of time that the rate applies

m will be the subscript after f and will indicate when the forward rate begins

All periods are equal to six months.

The forward rate is then found as follows:

$$_{t}f_{m} = \left[\frac{(1 + z_{m+t})^{m+t}}{(1 + z_{m})^{m}} \right]^{1/t} - 1$$

a. For the 6-month forward rate six months from now, $t = 1$ and $m = 1$. Therefore,

$$_{1}f_{1} = \left[\frac{(1 + z_{1+1})^{1+1}}{(1 + z_{1})^{1}} \right]^{1/1} - 1$$

or

$$_{1}f_{1} = \left[\frac{(1 + z_{2})^{2}}{(1 + z_{1})^{1}} \right]^{1} - 1$$

Since

$z_{1} = 5.0\%/2 = 2.5\%$ and $z_{2} = 5.4\%/2 = 2.7\%$
then

$$_{1}f_{1} = \left[\frac{(1.027)^{2}}{(1.025)^{1}} \right]^{1} - 1 = 0.029004 = 2.9004\%$$

Then the annualized 6-month forward rate six months from now on a bond-equivalent basis is 5.8008%.

b. For the 6-month forward rate one year from now, $t = 1$ and $m = 2$. Therefore,

$$_{1}f_{2} = \left[\frac{(1 + z_{2+1})^{2+1}}{(1 + z_{2})^{2}} \right]^{1/1} - 1$$

or

$$_1f_2 = \left[\frac{(1+z_3)^3}{(1+z_2)^2}\right]^{1} - 1$$

Since

$$z_2 = 5.4\%/2 = 2.7\% \quad \text{and} \quad z_3 = 5.8\%/2 = 2.9\%$$

then

$$_1f_2 = \left[\frac{(1.029)^3}{(1.027)^2}\right]^{1} - 1 = 0.033012 = 3.3012\%$$

Then the annualized 6-month forward rate one year from now on a bond-equivalent basis is 6.6023%.

c. For the 6-month forward rate three years from now, $t = 1$ and $m = 6$. Therefore,

$$_1f_6 = \left[\frac{(1+z_{6+1})^{6+1}}{(1+z_6)^6}\right]^{1/1} - 1$$

or

$$_1f_6 = \left[\frac{(1+z_7)^7}{(1+z_6)^6}\right]^{1/1} - 1$$

Since

$$z_6 = 7.2\%/2 = 3.6\% \quad \text{and} \quad z_7 = 7.4\%/2 = 3.7\%$$

then

$$_1f_6 = \left[\frac{(1.037)^7}{(1.036)^6}\right]^{1/1} - 1 = 0.04302 = 4.302\%$$

Then the annualized 6-month forward rate three years from now on a bond-equivalent basis is 8.6041%.

d. For the 2-year forward rate one year from now, $t = 4$ and $m = 2$. Therefore,

$$_4f_2 = \left[\frac{(1+z_{4+2})^{4+2}}{(1+z_2)^2}\right]^{1/4} - 1$$

or

$$_4f_2 = \left[\frac{(1+z_6)^6}{(1+z_2)^2}\right]^{1/4} - 1$$

Since

$$z_2 = 5.4\%/2 = 2.7\% \quad \text{and} \quad z_6 = 7.2\%/2 = 3.6\%$$

then

$$_4f_2 = \left[\frac{(1.036)^6}{(1.027)^2}\right]^{1/4} - 1 = 0.04053 = 4.053\%$$

Then the annualized 2-year forward rate one year from now on a bond-equivalent basis is 8.1059%.

e. For the 2-year forward rate one year from now, $t = 2$ and $m = 4$. Therefore,

$$_2f_4 = \left[\frac{(1 + z_{2+4})^{2+4}}{(1 + z_4)^4}\right]^{1/2} - 1$$

or

$$_2f_4 = \left[\frac{(1 + z_6)^6}{(1 + z_4)^4}\right]^{1/2} - 1$$

Since

$$z_4 = 6.4\%/2 = 3.2\% \quad \text{and} \quad z_6 = 7.2\%/2 = 3.6\%$$

then

$$_2f_4 = \left[\frac{(1.036)^6}{(1.032)^4}\right]^{1/2} - 1 = 0.04405 = 4.405\%$$

Then the annualized 1-year forward rate two years from now on a bond-equivalent basis is 8.810%.

26. The 6-month forward rate six months from now as found in the previous question is 5.8008%. The two alternatives are:

Alternative 1: Invest $X at the 1-year spot rate of 5.4% for one year
Alternative 2: Invest $X today at the 6-month spot rate of 5.0% and reinvest at the end of six months the proceeds at the 6-month forward rate of 5.8008%

For Alternative 1, the amount at the end of one year will be:

$X $(1 + 0.054/2)^2 = 1.054729$ ($X)

For Alternative 2, the amount at the end of one year will be:

$X $(1 + 0.05/2)(1 + 0.058008/2) = 1.054729$ ($X)

Thus, the two alternatives produce the same future value if the 6-month forward rate six months from now is 5.8008%.

27. Discounting at spot rates and forward rates will produce the same value for a bond. This is because spot rates are nothing more than packages of short-term forward rates. So, the second sales person's comment are wrong about the superiority of forward rates for valuation compared to spot rates.

28. a. The forward discount factor for period T is computed as follows.

$$\frac{1}{(1 + z_1)(1 + {}_1f_1)(1 + {}_1f_2)...(1 + {}_1f_{T-1})}$$

Therefore,

Period	Annual forward rate (BEY)	Semiannual rate	Forward discount factor
1	4.00%	2.00%	0.980392
2	4.40	2.20	0.959288
3	5.00	2.50	0.935891
4	5.60	2.80	0.910399
5	6.00	3.00	0.883883
6	6.40	3.20	0.856476

b. The value is found by multiplying each cash flow by the forward discount factor for the period as shown below:

Period	Forward discount factor	Cash flow	PV of cash flow
1	0.980392	$4	$3.921569
2	0.959288	4	3.837151
3	0.935891	4	3.743562
4	0.910399	4	3.641598
5	0.883883	4	3.535532
6	0.856476	104	89.073470
		Total	$107.752881

The value of this bond is $107.752881.

SOLUTIONS TO PRACTICE QUESTIONS

1. The cash flow for this bond is 30 payments of $3 plus a maturity value of $100 thirty 6-month periods from now. Below is the present value of the cash flow when discounted at one-half the yields of 7.2%, 7.6%, and 7.8%. The short-cut formula given in Chapter 5 was used so the information is provided for the present value of the coupon payments and the present value of the maturity value.

Annual rate (BEY)	7.2%	7.6%	7.8%
Semiannual rate	3.6%	3.8%	3.9%
Present value of:			
Coupon payments	54.49	53.16	52.51
Maturity value	34.61	32.66	31.74
Total present value	89.10	85.82	84.25

Since the semiannual discount rate of 3.9% equates the present value of the cash flows to the price of $84.25, 3.9% is the semiannual yield to maturity. Doubling this yield gives a yield to maturity of 7.8% on a bond equivalent basis.

2. a. The total future dollars from an investment of $89.32 if the yield is 7% is:

$$\$89.32 \times (1.035)^{40} = \$353.64$$

Decomposing the total future dollars we see that:

Total future dollars   = $353.64
Return of principal = $ 89.32
Total dollar return = $264.32

Without reinvestment income, the dollar return is:

Coupon interest = $120.00
Capital gain   = $ 10.68
Dollar return   = $130.68

The dollar return shortfall is therefore $133.64 ($264.32 - $130.68). This shortfall is made up if the coupon payments can be reinvested at a yield of 7% (the yield on the bond at the time of purchase). For this bond, the reinvestment income is 51% of the total dollar return needed to produce a yield of 7% ($133.64/$264.32).

b. There are no coupon payments to reinvest because the coupon rate is 0%. Therefore, no portion of the dollar return of a zero-coupon bond comes from reinvestment income.

3. a. The bond-equivalent yield is

$$2[(1.048)^{0.5} - 1] = 4.74\%$$

b. The annual yield is

$$[(1.024)^2 - 1] = 4.86\%$$

4. a. The cash flows for this bond up to the first call date are (1) 10 coupon payments of $4.50 and (2) $104.50 ten 6-month periods from now. The table below shows the present values of the coupon payments and maturity value for the three interest rates in the question:

Annual interest rate (%)	Semiannual interest rate (%)	Present value of 10 payments of $4.5	Present value of $104.5 10 periods from now	Present value of cash flows
4.4	2.2	40.0019	84.0635	124.0654
4.6	2.3	39.7944	83.2453	123.0397
4.8	2.4	39.5886	82.4360	122.0246

Since a semiannual rate of 2.3% produces a present value for the cash flows of $123.0397 and the price is $123.04, 2.3% is the semiannual yield to put. Doubling this yield gives a 4.6% yield to put on a bond-equivalent basis.

b. The cash flows for this bond up to the first par call date are (1) 16 coupon payments of $4.50 and (2) $100 sixteen 6-month periods from now. The table below shows the present values of the coupon payments and maturity value for the three interest rates in the question:

Annual interest rate (%)	Semiannual interest rate (%)	Present value of 16 payments of $4.5	Present value of $100 16 periods from now	Present value of cash flows
5.41	2.705	57.8211	65.2431	123.0642
5.62	2.810	57.3548	64.1851	121.5399
5.75	2.875	57.0689	63.5393	120.6082

For the three semiannual interest rates used, the one that makes the present value of the cash flows to the first par call date closest to the price of $123.04 is 2.705%. Doubling this yield gives a 5.41% yield to first par call date on a bond-equivalent basis.

5. The discount margin is the margin that when added to LIBOR will make the present value of the cash flows (assuming LIBOR is unchanged over the life of the floater) equal to the price. When the price is 99.8269, it can be seen from Exhibit 3 that a margin of 84 basis points makes the present value of the cash flows equal to that price. Thus, if the floater's price is 99.8269, the discount margin is 84 basis points.

6. a. The yield on a discount basis, d, is

$$(1 - 0.9825)\left(\frac{360}{115}\right) = 0.0548 = 5.48\%$$

b. The price of this Treasury bill, p, per $1 dollar of maturity value is:

$$1 - 0.059\,(162/360) = 0.97345$$

7. From Exhibit 4, the coupon rate for the on-the-run issue is 4.4%. Thus, the semiannual coupon payment per $100 of par value is $2.20 (4.4%/2 times $100). The present value of the cash flow is:

$$\frac{2.2}{(1+z_1)^1} + \frac{2.2}{(1+z_2)^2} + \frac{2.2}{(1+z_3)^3} + \frac{2.2}{(1+z_4)^4} + \frac{102.2}{(1+z_5)^5}$$

where z_5 is one half of the 2.5-year theoretical spot rate.
Given the other four spot rates, we can write

$$\frac{2.2}{(1.0150)^1} + \frac{2.2}{(1.0165)^2} + \frac{2.2}{(1.017527)^3} + \frac{2.2}{(1.019582)^4} + \frac{102.2}{(1+z_5)^5}$$

Since the price of the 2.5-year coupon Treasury security is par, the present value must equal par. Therefore,

$$\frac{2.2}{(1.0150)^1} + \frac{2.2}{(1.0165)^2} + \frac{2.2}{(1.017527)^3} + \frac{2.2}{(1.019582)^4} + \frac{102.2}{(1+z_5)^5} = 100$$

Solving the above equation:

$$2.167488 + 2.129158 + 2.088261 + 2.035795 + \frac{102.20}{(1+z_5)^5} = 100$$

$$8.420702 + \frac{102.20}{(1+z_5)^5} = 100$$

$$\frac{102.20}{(1+z_5)^5} = 91.5793$$

$$(1+z_5)^5 = \frac{102.20}{91.5793}$$

$$z_5 = 0.022188 = 2.2188\%$$

Doubling the semiannual yield gives 4.4376% for the 2.5-year spot rate on a bond-equivalent basis. This rate agrees with the rate in Exhibit 4.

8. From Exhibit 5 it can be seen that if 125 basis points is added to each spot rate, the present value of the cash flow is 105.7165, the assumed price for the non-Treasury issue. Therefore, the Z-spread is 100 basis.

9. $_1f_{13}$ is found as follows:

$$_1f_{13} = \frac{(1+z_{14})^{14}}{(1+z_{13})^{13}} - 1$$

From Exhibit 4, the annual spot rates for z_{13} and z_{14} are reported. They are 5.6108% and 5.6643%, respectively. Therefore,

$$z_{13} = 0.056108/2 = 0.028054$$

$$z_{14} = 0.056643/2 = 0.028322$$

Substituting we get

$$_1f_{13} = \frac{(1.028322)^{14}}{(1.028054)^{13}} - 1 = 0.0318 = 3.18\%$$

Doubling this rate gives the annualized rate for $_1f_{13}$ on a bond-equivalent basis of 6.36% reported in Exhibit 8.

10. The value is $114.8195 as shown below:

Period	Semiann. forward rate (%)	Forward discount factor	Cash flow	PV of cash flow
1	1.500	0.985222	$5	$4.926108
2	1.800	0.967799	5	4.838996
3	1.958	0.949211	5	4.746055
4	2.577	0.925362	5	4.626810
5	3.268	0.896079	5	4.480396
6	3.166	0.868582	105	91.201111
			Total	$114.819476

11. a. The forward rate sought is $_{12}f_8$. The formula for this forward rate is therefore:

$$_{12}f_8 = \left[\frac{(1 + z_{20})^{20}}{(1 + z_8)^8} \right]^{1/12} - 1$$

The spot rates needed are z_8 (the 4-year spot rate) and z_{20} (the 10-year spot rate). From Exhibit 4 we know

z_8 (the 4-year spot rate) = 5.065%/2 = 0.025325
z_{20} (the 10-year spot rate) = 6.2169%/2 = 0.031085

then

$$_{12}f_8 = \left[\frac{(1.031085)^{20}}{(1.025325)^8} \right]^{1/12} - 1 = 0.034943$$

Therefore, $_{12}f_8$ is equal to 3.4943% and doubling this rate gives 6.9885% the forward rate on a bond-equivalent basis.

b. We can verify this result. Investing $100 for 20 periods at the spot rate of 3.1085% will produce the following value:

$$\$100 \, (1.031085)^{20} = \$184.4545$$

By investing $100 for 8 periods at 2.5325% and reinvesting the proceeds for 12 periods at the forward rate of 3.4942% gives the same value

$$\$100 \, (1.025325)^8 \, (1.034942)^{12} = \$184.4545$$

Chapter 7

INTRODUCTION TO THE MEASUREMENT OF INTEREST RATE RISK

LEARNING OUTCOME STATEMENTS

After reading this chapter you should be able to:

- distinguish between the full valuation approach and the duration/convexity approach for measuring interest rate risk.
- compute the interest rate risk exposure of a bond position or a bond portfolio for a given scenario regarding a change in interest rates.
- explain why it is difficult to apply the full valuation approach to a bond portfolio with a large number of positions especially if the portfolio includes bonds with embedded options.
- explain the advantage of using the full valuation approach compared to the duration/convexity approach.
- state the price volatility characteristics for option-free bonds when interest rates change (including the concept of "positive convexity").
- state the price volatility characteristics of callable bonds and prepayable securities (including the concept of "negative convexity").
- compute the duration of a bond given information about how the price will increase and decrease for a given shock in interest rates.
- compute the approximate percentage price change for a bond given its duration and a specified change in yield.
- explain why duration does an effective job of estimating price changes for small changes in rates but is not as effective for a large change in rates.
- draw a diagram of the relationship between price and yield for an option-free bond and use the graph to show why duration does an effective job of estimating price changes for small changes in rates but is not as effective for a large change in rates.
- draw a diagram of the relationship between price and yield for a callable and prepayable security and use the graph to explain what is meant by negative convexity.
- draw a diagram of the relationship between price and yield for a putable bond.
- explain how the rate shocks for interest rates used to compute duration may affect the duration calculation.
- explain the difference between modified duration and effective (or option-adjusted) duration.
- explain why effective duration should be used for bonds with embedded options rather than modified duration.
- explain the relationship between modified duration and Macaulay duration and the limitations of using either for measuring the interest rate risk for bonds with embedded options.
- describe the various ways that duration has been interpreted and why the best way to interpret duration is as a measure of the sensitivity of a bond or portfolio to changes in interest rates.
- compute the duration of a portfolio given the duration of the bonds comprising the portfolio and the limitations of portfolio duration.
- compute the convexity measure of a bond given information about how the price will increase and decrease for a given shock in interest rates.
- compute the convexity adjustment to the duration estimate of a bond's percentage price change given the convexity measure and a given change in interest rates.
- compute the estimate of a bond's percentage price change given its duration, convexity measure, and a given change in interest rates.
- explain why convexity measures will differ among dealers and venders of analytical services due to differences in scaling.
- explain the difference between modified convexity and effective convexity.
- compute the price value of a basis point ("dollar value of an 01") of a bond.
- state the relationship between duration and the price value of a basis point.
- explain the importance of yield volatility in measuring the exposure of a bond position to interest rate risk.

SECTION I
INTRODUCTION

In Chapter 2 we discussed the interest rate risk associated with investing in bonds. We know that the value of a bond changes in the opposite direction of the change in interest rates. A long bond position's value will decline if interest rates rise, resulting in a loss. For a short bond position, a loss will be realized if interest rates fall. However, a manager wants to know more than simply when a position will realize a loss. To control interest rate risk, a manager must be able to quantify what will result.

The key to measuring the interest rate risk is the accuracy of the estimate is of the value of the position after an adverse rate change. A valuation model is used to determine the value of a position after an adverse rate move. Consequently, if a reliable valuation model is not used, there is no way to properly measure interest rate risk exposure.

There are two approaches to measuring interest rate risk – the full valuation approach and the duration/convexity approach. In Section II, we discuss the full valuation approach. The balance of the chapter is devoted to the duration/convexity approach. As a background to the duration/convexity approach, we discuss the price volatility characteristics of option-free bonds and bonds with embedded options in Section III. In Section IV, we look at how duration can be used to estimate interest rate risk and distinguish between various duration measures (effective, modified, and Macaulay). In Section V, we show how a measure referred to as "convexity" can be used to improve the duration estimate of the price volatility of a bond to rate changes. In Section VI, we show the relationship between duration and another measure of price volatility used by managers, the price value of a basis point (or "dollar value of an 01"). In the last section of this chapter we discuss the importance of incorporating yield volatility in estimates of exposure to interest rate risk.

SECTION II
THE FULL
VALUATION
APPROACH

The most obvious way to measure the interest rate risk exposure of a bond position or a portfolio is to re-value it when interest rates change. The analysis is performed for a given scenario with respect to interest rate changes. For example, a manager may want to measure the interest rate exposure to a 50 basis point, 100 basis point, and 200 basis point instantaneous change in interest rates. This approach requires the re-valuation of a bond or bond portfolio for a given interest rate change scenario and is referred to as the **full valuation approach**. It is sometimes referred to as **scenario analysis** because it involves assessing the exposure to interest rate change scenarios.

To illustrate this approach, suppose that a manager has a $10 million par value position in a 9% coupon 20-year bond. The bond is option-free. The current price is 134.6722 for a yield (i.e., yield to maturity) of 6%. The market value of the position is $13,467,220 (134.6722% × $10 million). Since the manager owns the bond, she is concerned with a rise in yield since this will decrease the market value of the position. To assess the exposure to a rise in market yields, the manager decides to look at how the value of the bond will change if yields change instantaneously for the following three scenarios: (1) 50 basis point increase, (2) 100 basis point increase, and (3) 200 basis point increase. This means that the manager wants to assess what will happen to the bond position if the yield on the bond increases from 6% to (1) 6.5%, (2) 7%, and (3) 8%. Because this is an option-free bond, valuation is straightforward. We will assume that one yield is used to discount each of the cash flows. That is, we will assume a flat yield curve. The price of this bond per $100 par value and the market value of the $10 million par position is shown in Exhibit 1. Also shown is the change in the market value and the percentage change.

Exhibit 1: Illustration of Full Valuation Approach to Assess the Interest Rate Risk of a Bond Position for Three Scenarios

Current bond position: 9% coupon 20-year bond (option-free)
Price: 134.6722
Yield to maturity: 6%
Par value owned: $10 million
Market value of position: $13,467,220.00

Scenario	Yield change (bp)	New yield	New price	New market value ($)	Percentage change in market value (%)
1	50	6.5%	127.7606	12,776,060	−5.13%
2	100	7.0%	121.3551	12,135,510	−9.89%
3	200	8.0%	109.8964	10,989,640	−18.40%

Exhibit 2: Illustration of Full Valuation Approach to Assess the Interest Rate Risk of a Bond Portfolio for Three Scenarios Assuming a Parallel Shift in the Yield Curve

Two bond portfolio (both bonds are option-free bonds)

Panel a

Bond 1:   6% coupon 5-year bond   Par value: $5,000,000
Initial price: 104.3760   Market value: $5,218,800
Yield: 5%

Scenario	Yield change (bp)	New yield	New price	New market value ($)
1	50	5.5%	102.1600	5,108,000
2	100	6.0%	100.0000	5,000,000
3	200	7.0%	95.8417	4,792,085

Panel b

Bond 2:   9% coupon 20-year bond   Par value: $10,000,000
Initial price: 134.6722   Market value: $13,467,220
Yield: 6%

Scenario	Yield change (bp)	New yield	New price	New market value ($)
1	50	6.5%	127.7602	12,776,020
2	100	7.0%	121.3551	12,135,510
3	200	8.0%	109.8964	10,989,640

Panel c

Portfolio Market value: $18,686,020.00

Scenario	Yield change (bp)	Market Value of			Percentage change in market value (%)
		Bond 1 ($)	Bond 2 ($)	Portfolio ($)	
1	50	5,108,000	12,776,020	17,884,020	−4.29%
2	100	5,000,000	12,135,510	17,135,510	−8.30%
3	200	4,792,085	10,989,640	15,781,725	−15.54%

In the case of a portfolio, each bond is valued for a given scenario and then the total value of the portfolio is computed for the scenario. For example, suppose that a manager has a portfolio with the following two option-free bonds: (1) 6% coupon 5-year bond and (2) 9% coupon 20-year bond. For the shorter term bond, $5 million of par value is owned and the price is 104.3760 for a yield of 5%. For the longer term bond, $10 million of par value is owned and the price is 134.6722 for a yield of 6%. Suppose that the manager wants to assess the interest rate risk of this portfolio for a 50, 100, and 200 basis point increase in interest rates assuming both the 5-year yield and 20-year yield change by the same number of basis points. Exhibit 2 shows the exposure.

Panel a of the exhibit shows the market value of the 5-year bond for the three scenarios. Panel b does the same for the 20-year bond. Panel c shows the total market value of the portfolio and the percentage change in the market value for the three scenarios.

In the illustration in Exhibit 2, it is assumed that both the 5-year and the 20-year yields changed by the same number of basis points. The full valuation approach can also handle scenarios where the yield curve does not change in a parallel fashion. Exhibit 3 illustrates this for our portfolio that includes the 5-year and 20-year bonds. The scenario analyzed is a yield curve shift scenario combined with scenarios for shifts in the level of yields. In the illustration in Exhibit 3, the following yield changes for the 5-year and 20-year yields are assumed:

Scenario	Change in 5-year rate (bp)	Change in 20-year rate (bp)
1	50	10
2	100	50
3	200	100

The last panel in Exhibit 3 shows how the market value of the portfolio changes for each scenario.

The full valuation approach seems straightforward. If one has a good valuation model, assessing how the value of a portfolio or individual bond will change for different scenarios for parallel and nonparallel yield curve shifts measures the interest rate risk of a portfolio.

Exhibit 3: Illustration of Full Valuation Approach to Assess the Interest Rate Risk of a Bond Portfolio for Three Scenarios Assuming a Nonparallel Shift in the Yield Curve

Two bond portfolio (both bonds are option-free bonds)

Panel a

Bond 1:   6% coupon 5-year bond   Par value: $5,000,000
Initial price: 104.3760   Market value: $5,218,800
Yield: 5%

Scenario	Yield change (bp)	New yield	New price	New market value ($)
1	50	5.5%	102.1600	5,108,000
2	100	6.0%	100.0000	5,000,000
3	200	7.0%	95.8417	4,792,085

Panel b

Bond 2:   9% coupon 20-year bond   Par value: $10,000,000
Initial price: 134.6722   Market value: $13,467,220
Yield: 6%

Scenario	Yield change (bp)	New yield	New price	New market value ($)
1	10	6.1%	133.2472	13,324,720
2	50	6.5%	127.7605	12,776,050
3	100	7.0%	121.3551	12,135,510

Panel c

Portfolio Market value: $18,686,020.00

Scenario	Market Value of			Percentage change in market value (%)
	Bond 1 ($)	Bond 2 ($)	Portfolio ($)	
1	5,108,000	13,324,720	18,432,720	−1.36%
2	5,000,000	12,776,050	17,776,050	−4.87%
3	4,792,085	12,135,510	16,927,595	−9.41%

A common question that often arises when using the full valuation approach is which scenarios should be evaluated to assess interest rate risk exposure. For some regulated entities, there are specified scenarios established by regulators. For example, it is common for regulators of depository institutions to require entities to determine the impact on the value of their bond portfolio for a 100, 200, and 300 basis point instantaneous change in interest rates (up and down). (Regulators tend to refer to this as "simulating" interest rate scenarios rather than scenario analysis.) Risk managers and highly leveraged investors such as hedge funds tend to look at extreme scenarios to assess exposure to interest rate changes. This practice is referred to as **stress testing**.

Of course, in assessing how changes in the yield curve can affect the exposure of a portfolio, there are an infinite number of scenarios that can be evaluated. The state-of-the-art technology involves using a complex statistical procedure[1] to determine a likely set of yield curve shift scenarios from historical data.

It seems like the chapter should end right here. We can use the full valuation approach to assess the exposure of a bond or portfolio to interest rate changes to evaluate any scenario, assuming — and this must be repeated continuously — *that the manager has a good valuation model to estimate what the price of the bonds will be in each interest rate scenario*. However, we are not stopping here. In fact, the balance of this chapter is considerably longer than this section. Why? The reason is that while the full valuation approach is the recommended approach for assessing the position of a single bond or a portfolio of a few bonds, for a portfolio with a large number of bonds and with even a minority of those bonds being complex (i.e., having embedded options), the full valuation process is time consuming. Managers want one measure that they can use to get an idea of how a portfolio or a even a single bond will change if rates change in a parallel fashion rather than having to revalue a portfolio to obtain that answer. In Chapter 2, such a measure was introduced — duration. We will discuss this measure as well as a supplementary measure (convexity) in Sections IV and V, respectively. To build a foundation to understand the limitations of these measures, we describe the basic price volatility characteristics of bonds in Section III. The fact that there are limitations of using one or two measures to describe the interest rate exposure of a position or portfolio should not be surprising. What is important to understand is that these measures provide a starting point for assessing interest rate risk.

SECTION III PRICE VOLATILITY CHARACTERISTICS OF BONDS

In Chapter 2 we described the characteristics of a bond that affect its price volatility: (1) maturity, (2) coupon rate, and (3) presence of embedded options. We also explained how the level of yields affects price volatility. In this section, we will take a closer look at the price volatility characteristics of bonds.

A. Price Volatility Characteristics of Option-Free Bonds

Let's begin by focusing on option-free bonds (i.e., bonds that do not have embedded options). A fundamental characteristic of an option-free bond is that the price of the bond changes in the opposite direction from a change in the bond's required yield. Exhibit 4 illustrates this property for four hypothetical bonds assuming a par value of $100.

---

[1] The procedure used is principal component analysis.

Exhibit 4: Price/Yield Relationship for Four Hypothetical Option-Free Bonds

Yield (%)	Price ($)			
	6%/5 year	6%/20 year	9%/5 year	9%/20 year
4.00	108.9826	127.3555	122.4565	168.3887
5.00	104.3760	112.5514	117.5041	150.2056
5.50	102.1600	106.0195	115.1201	142.1367
5.90	100.4276	101.1651	113.2556	136.1193
5.99	100.0427	100.1157	112.8412	134.8159
6.00	100.0000	100.0000	112.7953	134.6722
6.01	99.9574	99.8845	112.7494	134.5287
6.10	99.5746	98.8535	112.3373	133.2472
6.50	97.8944	94.4479	110.5280	127.7605
7.00	95.8417	89.3225	108.3166	121.3551
8.00	91.8891	80.2072	104.0554	109.8964

Exhibit 5: Price/Yield Relationship for a Hypothetical Option-Free Bond

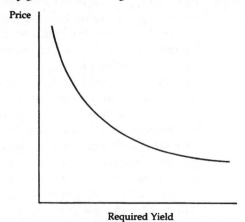

When the price/yield relationship for any option-free bond is graphed, it exhibits the shape shown in Exhibit 5. Notice that as the required yield increases, the price of an option-free bond declines. However, this relationship is not linear (i.e., not a straight line relationship). The shape of the price/yield relationship for any option-free bond is referred to as **convex**. This price/yield relationship is for an instantaneous change in the required yield.

The price sensitivity of a bond to changes in the required yield can be measured in terms of the dollar price change or the percentage price change. Exhibit 6 uses the four hypothetical bonds in Exhibit 4 to show the percentage change in each bond's price for various changes in yield, assuming that the initial yield for all four bonds is 6%. An examination of Exhibit 6 reveals the following properties concerning the price volatility of an option-free bond:

Property 1: Although the price moves in the opposite direction from the change in required yield, the percentage price change is not the same for all bonds.

Property 2: For small changes in the required yield, the percentage price change for a given bond is roughly the same, whether the required yield increases or decreases.

Exhibit 6: Instantaneous Percentage Price Change for Four Hypothetical Bonds
(Initial yield for all four bonds is 6%)

New Yield (%)	Percentage Price Change			
	6%/5 year	6%/20 year	9%/5 year	9%/20 year
4.00	8.98	27.36	8.57	25.04
5.00	4.38	12.55	4.17	11.53
5.50	2.16	6.02	2.06	5.54
5.90	0.43	1.17	0.41	1.07
5.99	0.04	0.12	0.04	0.11
6.01	−0.04	−0.12	−0.04	−0.11
6.10	−0.43	−1.15	−0.41	−1.06
6.50	−2.11	−5.55	−2.01	−5.13
7.00	−4.16	−10.68	−3.97	−9.89
8.00	−8.11	−19.79	−7.75	−18.40

Exhibit 7: Graphical Illustration of Properties 3 and 4 for an Option-Free Bond

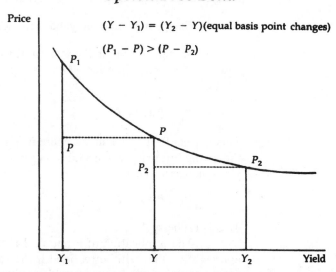

Property 3: For large changes in required yield, the percentage price change is not the same for an increase in required yield as it is for a decrease in required yield.

Property 4: For a given large change in basis points in the required yield, the percentage price increase is greater than the percentage price decrease.

While the properties are expressed in terms of percentage price change, they also hold for dollar price changes.

An explanation for these two properties of bond price volatility lies in the convex shape of the price/yield relationship. Exhibit 7 illustrates this. The following notation is used in the exhibit

Y = initial yield
Y_1 = lower yield
Y_2 = higher yield

$$P = \text{initial price}$$
$$P_1 = \text{price at lower yield } Y_1$$
$$P_2 = \text{price at higher yield } Y_2$$

What was done in the exhibit was to change the initial yield (Y) up and down by the same number of basis points. That is, in Exhibit 7, the yield is decreased from Y to Y_1 and increased from Y to Y_2 such that the amount of the change is the same:

$$Y - Y_1 = Y_2 - Y$$

Also, the amount of the change in yield is a large number of basis points.

The vertical distance from the horizontal axis (the yield) to the intercept on the graph shows the price. The change in the initial price (P) when the yield declines from Y to Y_1 is equal to the difference between the new price (P_1) and the initial price. That is,

$$\text{change in price when yield decreases} = P_1 - P$$

The change in the initial price (P) when the yield increases from Y to Y_2 is equal to the difference between the new price (P_2) and the initial price. That is,

$$\text{change in price when yield increases} = P - P_2$$

As can be seen in the exhibit, the change in price when yield decreases is not equal to the change in price when yield increases by the same number of basis points. That is,

$$P_1 - P \neq P - P_2$$

This is what Property 3 states. Moreover, a comparison of the price change shows that the change in price when yield decreases is greater than the change in price when yield increases. That is,

$$P_1 - P > P - P_2$$

This is Property 4.

The implication of Property 4 is that if an investor is long a bond, the price appreciation that will be realized if the required yield decreases is greater than the capital loss that will be realized if the required yield increases by the same number of basis points. For an investor who is short a bond, the reverse is true: the potential capital loss is greater than the potential capital gain if the yield changes by a given number of basis points.

To see how the convexity of the price/yield relationship impacts Property 4, look at Exhibits 8 and 9. Exhibit 8 shows a less convex price/yield relationship than Exhibit 7. That is, the price/yield relationship in Exhibit 8 is less bowed than the price/yield relationship in Exhibit 7. Because of the difference in the convexities, look at what happens when the yield increases and decreases by the same number of basis points and the yield change is a large number of basis points. We use the same notation in Exhibits 8 and 9 as in Exhibit 7. Notice that while the price gain when the required yield decreases is greater than the price decline when the required yield increases, the gain is not much greater than the loss. In contrast, Exhibit 9 has much greater convexity than the bonds in Exhibits 7 and 8 and the price gain is significantly greater than the loss for the bonds depicted in Exhibits 7 and 8.

Exhibit 8: Impact of Convexity on Property 4: Less Convex Bond

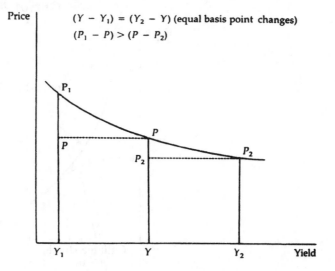

$(Y - Y_1) = (Y_2 - Y)$ (equal basis point changes)
$(P_1 - P) > (P - P_2)$

Exhibit 9: Impact of Convexity on Property 4: Highly Convex Bond

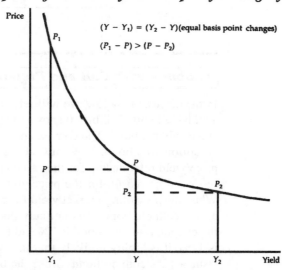

$(Y - Y_1) = (Y_2 - Y)$ (equal basis point changes)
$(P_1 - P) > (P - P_2)$

B. Price Volatility Characteristics of Bonds with Embedded Options

Now let's turn to the price volatility characteristics of bonds with embedded options. As explained in previous chapters, the price of a bond with an embedded option is comprised of two components. The first is the value of the same bond if it had no embedded option. That is, the price if the bond is option free. The second component is the value of the embedded option.

The two most common types of embedded options are call (or prepay) options and put options. As interest rates in the market decline, the issuer may call or prepay the debt obligation prior to the scheduled principal repayment date. The other type of option is a put option. This option gives the investor the right to require the issuer to purchase the bond at a specified price. Below we will examine the price/yield relationship for bonds with both types of embedded options (calls and puts) and implications for price volatility.

Exhibit 10: Price/Yield Relationship for a Callable Bond and an Option-Free Bond

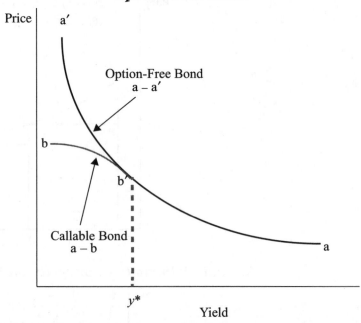

1. Bonds with Call and Prepay Options

In the discussion below, we will refer to a bond that may be called or is prepayable as a callable bond. Exhibit 10 shows the price/yield relationship for an option-free bond and a callable bond. The convex curve given by *a-a′* is the price/yield relationship for an option-free bond. The unusual shaped curve denoted by *a-b* in the exhibit is the price/yield relationship for the callable bond.

The reason for the price/yield relationship for a callable bond is as follows. When the prevailing market yield for comparable bonds is higher than the coupon rate on the callable bond, it is unlikely that the issuer will call the issue. For example, if the coupon rate on a bond is 7% and the prevailing market yield on comparable bonds is 12%, it is highly unlikely that the issuer will call a 7% coupon bond so that it can issue a 12% coupon bond. Since the bond is unlikely to be called, the callable bond will have a similar price/yield relationship as an otherwise comparable option-free bond. Consequently, the callable bond is going to be valued as if it is an option-free bond. However, since there is still some value to the call option, the bond won't trade exactly like an option-free bond.

As yields in the market decline, the concern is that the issuer will call the bond. The issuer won't necessarily exercise the call option as soon as the market yield drops below the coupon rate. Yet, the value of the embedded call option increases as yields approach the coupon rate from higher yield levels. For example, if the coupon rate on a bond is 7% and the market yield declines to 7.5%, the issuer will most likely not call the issue. However, market yields are at a level at which the investor is concerned that the issue may eventually be called if market yields decline further. Cast in terms of the value of the embedded call option, that option becomes more valuable to the issuer and therefore it reduces the price relative to an otherwise comparable option-free bond.[2] In Exhibit 10, the value of the embedded call option at a given yield can be measured by the difference between the price of an option-free bond (the price shown on the curve a-a′) and the price on the curve a-b. Notice that at low yield levels (below y* on the horizontal axis), the value of the embedded call option is high.

Let's look at the difference in the price volatility properties relative to an option-free bond given the price/yield relationship for a callable bond shown in Exhibit 10. Exhibit 11 blows up the portion of the price/yield relationship for the callable bond where the two curves in Exhibit 10 depart (segment b-b′ in Exhibit 10). We know from our discussion of the price/yield relationship that for a large change in yield of a given number of basis points, the price of an option-free bond increases by more than it decreases (Property 4 above). Is that what happens for a callable bond in the region of the price/yield relationship shown in Exhibit 11? No, it is not. In fact, as can be seen in the exhibit, the opposite is true! That is, for a given large change in yield, the price appreciation is less than the price decline.

The price volatility characteristic of a callable bond is important to understand. The characteristic of a callable bond — that its price appreciation is less than its price decline when rates change by a large number of basis points — is referred to as **negative convexity**.[3] But notice from Exhibit 10 that callable bonds don't exhibit this characteristic at every yield level. When yields are high (relative to the issue's coupon rate), the bond exhibits the same price/yield relationship as an option-free bond and therefore at high yield levels it also has the characteristic that the gain is greater than the loss. Because market participants have referred to the shape of the price/yield relationship shown in Exhibit 11 as negative convexity, market participants refer to the relationship for an option-free bond as **positive convexity**. Consequently, a callable bond exhibits negative convexity at low yield levels and positive convexity at high yield levels. This is depicted in Exhibit 12.

Exhibit 11: Negative Convexity Region of the Price/Yield Relationship for a Callable Bond

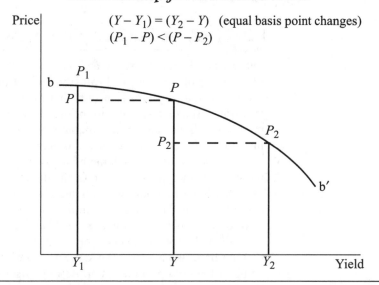

$$(Y - Y_1) = (Y_2 - Y) \quad \text{(equal basis point changes)}$$
$$(P_1 - P) < (P - P_2)$$

---

[2] For readers who are already familiar with option theory, this characteristic can be restated as follows: When the coupon rate for the issue is below the market yield, the embedded call option is said to be "out-of-the-money." When the coupon rate for the issue is above the market yield, the embedded call option is said to be "in-the-the money."
[3] Mathematicians refer to this shape as being "concave."

Exhibit 12: Negative and Positive Convexity Exhibited by a Callable Bond

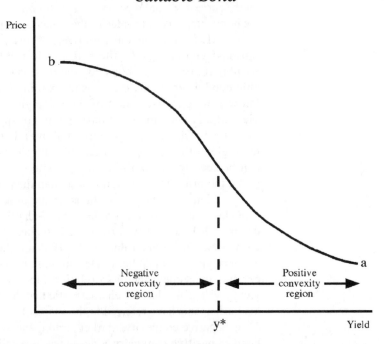

As can be seen from the exhibits, when a bond exhibits negative convexity, the bond compresses in price as rates decline. That is, at a certain yield level there is very little price appreciation when rates decline. When a bond enters this region, the bond is said to exhibit "price compression."

2. Bonds with Embedded Put Options

Putable bonds may be redeemed by the bondholder on the dates and at the put price specified in the indenture. Typically, the put price is par value. The advantage to the investor is that if yields rise such that the bond's value falls below the put price, the investor will exercise the put option. If the put price is par value, this means that if market yields rise above the coupon rate, the bond's value will fall below par and the investor will then exercise the put option.

The value of a putable bond is equal to the value of an option-free bond plus the value of the put option. Thus, the difference between the value of a putable bond and the value of an otherwise comparable option-free bond is the value of the embedded put option. This can be seen in Exhibit 13 which shows the price/yield relationship for a putable bond (the curve *a-b*) and an option-free bond (the curve *a-a'*).

At low yield levels (low relative to the issue's coupon rate), the price of the putable bond is basically the same as the price of the option-free bond because the value of the put option is small. As rates rise, the price of the putable bond declines, but the price decline is less than that for an option-free bond. The divergence in the price of the putable bond and an otherwise comparable option-free bond at a given yield level is the value of the put option. When yields rise to a level where the bond's price would fall below the put price, the price at these levels is the put price.

Exhibit 13: Price/Yield Relationship for a Putable Bond and an Option-Free Bond

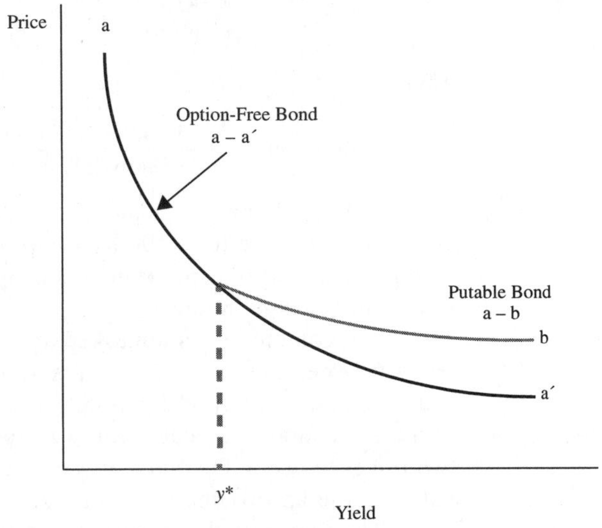

SECTION IV
DURATION

With the background about the price volatility characteristics of a bond, we can now turn to an alternate approach to full valuation: the duration/convexity approach. As explained in Chapter 2, *duration is a measure of the approximate sensitivity of a bond's value to rate changes*. More specifically, *it is the approximate percentage change in value for a 100 basis point change in rates*. We will see in this section that duration is the first approximation of the percentage price change. To improve the estimate provided by duration, a measure called "convexity" can be used. Hence, using duration combined with convexity to estimate the percentage price change of a bond to changes in interest rates is called the **duration/convexity approach**.

A. Calculating Duration

In Chapter 2 we explained that the duration of a bond is estimated as follows:

$$\frac{\text{price if yields decline} - \text{price if yields rise}}{2(\text{initial price})(\text{change in yield in decimal})}$$

If we let

$$\Delta y = \text{change in yield in decimal}$$
$$V_0 = \text{initial price}$$
$$V_- = \text{price if yields decline by } \Delta y$$
$$V_+ = \text{price if yields increase by } \Delta y$$

then duration can be expressed as

$$\text{duration} = \frac{V_- - V_+}{2(V_0)(\Delta y)} \tag{1}$$

For example, consider a 9% coupon 20-year option-free bond selling at 134.6722 to yield 6% (see Exhibit 4). Let's change (i.e., shock) the yield down and up by 20 basis points and determine what the new prices will be for the numerator. If the yield is decreased by 20 basis points from 6.0% to 5.8%, the price would increase to 137.5888. If the yield increases by 20 basis points, the price would decrease to 131.8439. Thus,

$$
\begin{aligned}
\Delta y &= 0.002 \\
V_0 &= 134.6722 \\
V_- &= 137.5888 \\
V_+ &= 131.8439
\end{aligned}
$$

Then,

$$
\text{duration} = \frac{137.5888 - 131.8439}{2 \times (134.6722) \times (0.002)} = 10.66
$$

As explained in Chapter 2, duration is interpreted as the approximate percentage change in price for a 100 basis point change in rates. Consequently, a duration of 10.66 means that the approximate change in price for this bond is 10.66% for a 100 basis point change in rates.

A common question asked about this interpretation of duration is the consistency between the yield change that is used to compute duration using equation (1) and the interpretation of duration. For example, recall that in computing the duration of the 9% coupon 20-year bond, we used a 20 basis point yield change to obtain the two prices to use in the numerator of equation (1). Yet, we interpret the duration computed as the approximate percentage price change for a 100 basis point change in yield. The reason is that regardless of the yield change used to estimate duration in equation (1), the interpretation is the same. If we used a 25 basis point change in yield to compute the prices used in the numerator of equation (1), the resulting duration is interpreted as the approximate percentage price change for a 100 basis point change in yield. Later we will use different changes in yield to illustrate the sensitivity of the computed duration.

PRACTICE QUESTION 1

a. Compute the duration of the 9% coupon 20-year option-free bond by changing the yield down and up by 10 basis points. (The relevant values can be found in Exhibit 4.)

b. Suppose a 6% coupon 20-year option-free bond is selling at par value and therefore offering a yield of 6%. Compute the duration by changing the yield down and up by 10 basis points. (The relevant values can be found in Exhibit 4.)

B. Approximating the Percentage Price Change Using Duration

In Chapter 2, an explanation of how to approximate the percentage price change for a given change in yield and a given duration was provided. Here we will express the process using the following formula:

$$
\text{approximate percentage price change} = -\text{duration} \times \Delta y \times 100 \tag{2}
$$

The reason for the negative sign on the right-hand side of equation (2) is due to the inverse relationship between price change and yield change.

For example, consider the 9% 20-year bond trading at 134.6722 whose duration we just showed is 10.66. The approximate percentage price change for a 10 basis point increase in yield (i.e., $\Delta y = +0.001$) is:

$$
\text{approximate percentage price change} = -10.66 \times (+0.001) \times 100 = -1.066\%
$$

How good is this approximation? The actual percentage price change is −1.06% (as shown in Exhibit 6 when yield increases to 6.10%). Duration, in this case, did an excellent job in estimating the percentage price change. We would come to the same conclusion if we used duration to estimate the percentage price change if the yield declined by 10 basis points (i.e., $\Delta y = -0.001$). In this case, the approximate percentage price change would be +1.066% (i.e., the direction of the estimated price change is the reverse but the magnitude of the change is the same). Exhibit 6 shows that the actual percentage price change is +1.07%.

In terms of estimating the new price, let's see how duration performed. The initial price is 134.6722. For a 10 basis point increase in yield, duration estimates that the price will decline by 1.066%. Thus, the price will decline to 133.2366 (found by multiplying 134.6722 by one minus 0.01066). The actual price from Exhibit 4 if the yield increases by 10 basis points is 133.2472. Thus, the price estimated using duration is close to the actual price. For a 10 basis point decrease in yield, the actual price from Exhibit 4 is 136.1193 and the estimated price using duration is 136.1078 (a price increase of 1.066%). Consequently, the new price estimated by duration is close to the actual price for a 10 basis point change in yield.

Let's look at how well duration does in estimating the percentage price change if the yield increases by 200 basis points instead of 10 basis points. In this case, Δy is equal to +0.02. Substituting into equation (2) we have

approximate percentage price change $= -10.66 \times (+0.02) \times 100 = -21.32\%$

How good is this estimate? From Exhibit 6 we see that the actual percentage price change when the yield increases by 200 basis points to 8% is −18.40%. Thus, the estimate is not as accurate as when we used duration to approximate the percentage price change for a change in yield of only 10 basis points. If we use duration to approximate the percentage price change when the yield decreases by 200 basis points, the approximate percentage price change in this scenario is +21.32%. The actual percentage price change as shown in Exhibit 6 is +25.40%.

Again, let's look at the use of duration in terms of estimating the new price. Since the initial price is 134.6722 and a 200 basis point increase in yield will decrease the price by 21.32%, the estimated new price using duration is 105.9601 (found by multiplying 134.6722 by one minus 0.2132). From Exhibit 4 the actual price if the yield is 8% is 109.8964. Consequently, the estimate is not as accurate as the estimate for a 10 basis point change in yield. The estimated new price using duration for a 200 basis point decrease in yield is 163.3843 compared to the actual price (from Exhibit 4) of 168.3887. Once again, the estimation of the price using duration is not as accurate as for a 10 basis point change. *Notice that whether the yield is increased or decreased by 200 basis points, duration underestimates what the new price will be.* We will see why shortly.

Let's summarize what we found in our application of duration to approximate the percentage price change:

Yield change (bp)	Initial price	New price		Percent price change		Comment
		Based on duration	Actual	Based on duration	Actual	
+10	134.6722	133.2366	133.2472	−1.066	−1.06	estimated price close to new price
−10	134.6722	136.1078	136.1193	+1.066	+1.07	estimated price close to new price
+200	134.6722	105.9601	109.8964	−21.320	−18.40	underestimates new price
−200	134.6722	163.3843	168.3887	+21.320	+25.40	underestimates new price

Should any of this be a surprise to you? No, not after reading Section III and evaluating equation (2) in terms of the properties for the price/yield relationship discussed in that section. Look again at equation (2). Notice that whether the change in yield is an increase or a decrease, the approximate percentage price change will be the same except that the sign is reversed. This violates Property 3 and Property 4 with respect to the price volatility of option-free bonds when yields change. Recall that Property 3 states that the percentage price change will not be the same for a large increase and decrease in yield by the same number of basis points. This is one reason why we see that the estimate is inaccurate for a 200 basis point yield change. Why did the duration estimate of the price change do a good job for a small change in yield of 10 basis points? Recall from Property 2 that the percentage price change will be approximately the same whether there is an increase or decrease in yield by a small number of basis points. We can also explain these results in terms of the graph of the price/yield relationship. We will do this next.

PRACTICE QUESTION 2

Using the duration for the 6% coupon 20-year bond found in part b of Practice Question 1, answer the following questions.

a. What is the approximate percentage price change if interest rates increase by 10 basis points?

b. Comment on the approximation compared to the actual price change as given in Exhibit 6.

c. What is the approximate percentage price change if interest rates decrease by 10 basis points?

d. Comment on the approximation compared to the actual price change as given in Exhibit 6.

e. What is the approximate percentage price change if interest rates increase by 200 basis points?

f. Comment on the approximation compared to the actual price change as given in Exhibit 6.

g. What is the approximate percentage price change if interest rates decrease by 200 basis points?

h. Comment on the approximation compared to the actual price change as given in Exhibit 6.

C. Graphical Depiction of Using Duration to Estimate Price Changes

In Section III we used the graph of the price/yield relationship to demonstrate the price volatility properties of bonds. We can use graphs to illustrate what we observed in our examples about how duration estimates the percentage price change, as well as some other noteworthy points.

The shape of the price/yield relationship for an option-free bond is convex. Exhibit 14 shows this relationship. In the exhibit a tangent line is drawn to the price/yield relationship at yield y^*. (For those unfamiliar with the concept of a tangent line, it is a straight line that just touches a curve at one point within a relevant (local) range. In Exhibit 14, the tangent line touches the curve at the point where the yield is equal to y^* and the price is equal to p^*.) The tangent line is used to *estimate* the new price if the yield changes. If we draw a vertical line from any yield (on the horizontal axis), as in Exhibit 14, the distance between the horizontal axis and the tangent line represents the price approximated by using duration starting with the initial yield y^*.

Exhibit 14: Price/Yield Relationship for an Option-Free Bond with a Tangent Line

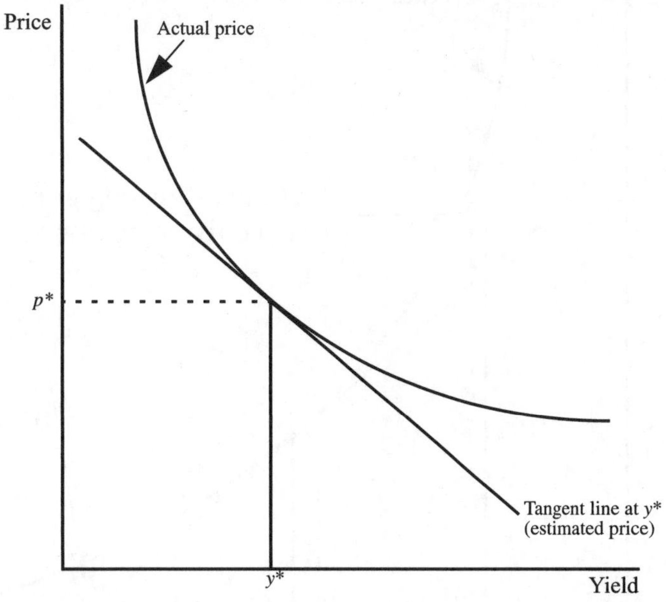

Now how is the tangent line, used to approximate what the new price will be if yields change, related to duration? The tangent line tells us the approximate new price of a bond if the yield changes. Given (1) the initial price and (2) the new price of a bond if the yield changes using the tangent line, the approximate percentage price change can be computed for a given change in yield. But this is precisely what duration (using equation (2)) gives us: the approximate percentage change for a given change in yield. Thus, using the tangent line one obtains the same approximate percentage price change as using equation (2).

This helps us understand why duration did an effective job of estimating the percentage price change, or equivalently the new price, when the yield changes by a small number of basis points. Look at Exhibit 15. Notice that for a small change in yield, the tangent line does not depart much from the price/yield relationship. Hence, when the yield changes up or down by 10 basis points, the tangent line does a good job of estimating the new price, as we found in our earlier numerical illustration.

Exhibit 15 also shows what happens to the estimate using the tangent line when the yield changes by a large number of basis points. Notice that the error in the estimate gets larger the further one moves from the initial yield. The estimate is less accurate the more convex the bond. This is illustrated in Exhibit 16.

Also note that regardless of the magnitude of the yield change, the tangent line always underestimates what the new price will be for an option-free bond because the tangent line is below the price/yield relationship. This explains why we found in our illustration that when using duration we underestimated what the actual price will be.

D. Rate Shocks and Duration Estimate

In calculating duration using equation (1), it is necessary to shock interest rates (yields) up and down by the same number of basis points to obtain the values for V_- and V_+. In our illustration, 20 basis points was arbitrarily selected. But how large should the shock be? That is, how many basis points should be used to shock the rate?

Exhibit 15: Estimating the New Price Using a Tangent Line

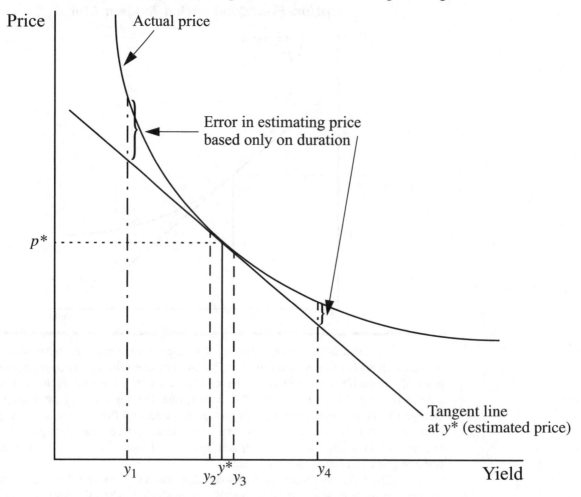

In Exhibit 17, the duration estimate for our four hypothetical bonds using equation (1) for rate shocks of 1 basis point to 200 basis points is reported. The duration estimates for the two 5-year bonds are not affected by the size of the shock. The two 5-year bonds are less convex than the two 20-year bonds. But even for the two 20-year bonds, for the size of the shocks reported in Exhibit 17, the duration estimates are not materially affected by the greater convexity.

Thus, it would seem that the size of the shock is unimportant. However, the results reported in Exhibit 17 are for option-free bonds. When we deal with more complicated securities, small rate shocks that do not reflect the types of rate changes that may occur in the market do not permit the determination of how prices can change because expected cash flows may change when dealing with bonds with embedded options. In comparison, if large rate shocks are used, we encounter the asymmetry caused by convexity. Moreover, large rate shocks may cause dramatic changes in the expected cash flows for bonds with embedded options that may be far different from how the expected cash flows will change for smaller rate shocks.

Exhibit 16: Estimating the New Price for a Large Yield Change for Bonds with Different Convexities

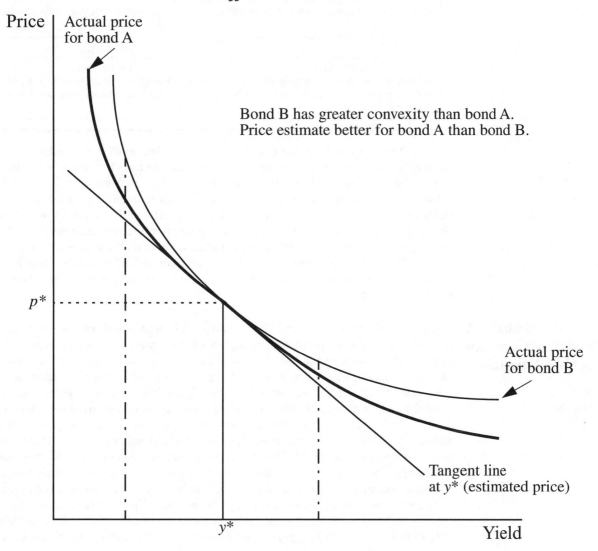

Exhibit 17: Duration Estimates for Different Rate Shocks

Assumption: Initial yield is 6%

Bond	1 bp	10 bps	20 bps	50 bps	100 bps	150 bps	200 bps
6% 5 year	4.27	4.27	4.27	4.27	4.27	4.27	4.27
6% 20 year	11.56	11.56	11.56	11.57	11.61	11.69	11.79
9% 5 year	4.07	4.07	4.07	4.07	4.07	4.08	4.08
9% 20 year	10.66	10.66	10.66	10.67	10.71	10.77	10.86

Exhibit 18: Modified Duration versus Effective Duration

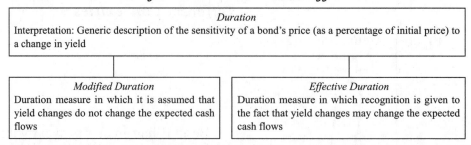

There is another potential problem with using small rate shocks for complicated securities. The prices that are inserted into the duration formula as given by equation (1) are derived from a valuation model. At Level II we will discuss various valuation models and their underlying assumptions. The duration measure depends crucially on a valuation model. If the rate shock is small and the valuation model used to obtain the prices for equation (1) is poor, dividing poor price estimates by a small shock in rates in the denominator will have a significant affect on the duration estimate.

What is done in practice by dealers and vendors of analytical systems? Each system developer uses rate shocks that they have found to be realistic based on historical rate changes.

E. Modified Duration versus Effective Duration

One form of duration that is cited by practitioners is **modified duration**. Modified duration is the approximate percentage change in a bond's price for a 100 basis point change in yield *assuming that the bond's expected cash flows do not change when the yield changes*. What this means is that in calculating the values of V_- and V_+ in equation (1), the same cash flows used to calculate V_0 are used. Therefore, the change in the bond's price when the yield is changed is due solely to discounting cash flows at the new yield level.

The assumption that the cash flows will not change when the yield is changed makes sense for option-free bonds such as noncallable Treasury securities. This is because the payments made by the U.S. Department of the Treasury to holders of its obligations do not change when interest rates change. However, the same cannot be said for bonds with embedded options (i.e., callable and putable bonds and mortgage-backed securities). For these securities, a change in yield may significantly alter the expected cash flows.

In Section III we showed the price/yield relationship for callable and prepayable bonds. Failure to recognize how changes in yield can alter the expected cash flows will produce two values used in the numerator of equation (1) that are not good estimates of how the price will actually change. The duration is then not a good number to use to estimate how the price will change.

When we discuss valuation models for bonds with embedded options at Level II, we will see how these models take into account how changes in yield will affect the expected cash flows. Thus, when V_- and V_+ are the values produced from these valuation models, the resulting duration takes into account both the discounting at different interest rates and how the expected cash flows may change. When duration is calculated in this manner, it is referred to as **effective duration** or **option-adjusted duration**. Exhibit 18 summarizes the distinction between modified duration and effective duration.

The difference between modified duration and effective duration for bonds with embedded options can be quite dramatic. For example, a callable bond could have a modified duration of 5 but an effective duration of only 3. For certain collateralized mortgage obligations, the modified duration could be 7 and the effective duration 20! Thus, using modified duration as a measure of the price sensitivity of a security with embedded options to changes in yield would be misleading. The more appropriate measure for any bond with an embedded option is effective duration.

F. Macaulay Duration and Modified Duration

It is worth comparing the relationship between modified duration to the another duration measure. Modified duration can also be written as:[4]

$$\frac{1}{(1+\text{yield}/k)}\left[\frac{1 \times \text{PVCF}_1 + 2 \times \text{PVCF}_2 + ... + n \times \text{PVCF}_n}{k \times \text{Price}}\right] \tag{3}$$

where

k = number of periods, or payments, per year (e.g., $k = 2$ for semiannual-pay bonds and $k = 12$ for monthly-pay bonds)

n = number of periods until maturity (i.e., number of years to maturity times k)

yield = yield to maturity of the bond

PVCF_t = present value of the cash flow in period t discounted at the yield to maturity where $t = 1, 2, ..., n$

We know that if duration tells us the approximate percentage price change for a bond if the yield changes.

The expression in the brackets of the modified duration formula given by equation (3) is a measure formulated in 1938 by Frederick Macaulay.[5] This measure is popularly referred to as **Macaulay duration**. Thus, modified duration is commonly expressed as:

$$\text{Modified duration} = \frac{\text{Macaulay duration}}{(1 + \text{yield}/k)}$$

The general formulation for duration as given by equation (1) provides a short-cut procedure for determining a bond's modified duration. Because it is easier to calculate the modified duration using the short-cut procedure, most vendors of analytical software will use equation (1) rather than equation (3) to reduce computation time.

However, it must be clearly understood that modified duration is a flawed measure of a bond's price sensitivity to interest rate changes for a bond with an embedded option and therefore so is Macaulay duration. The use of the formula for duration given by equation (3) *misleads* the user because it masks the fact that changes in the expected cash flows must be recognized for bonds with embedded options. Although equation (3) will give the same estimate of percent price change for an option-free bond as equation (1), equation (1) is still better because it acknowledges that cash flows and thus value can change due to yield changes.

G. Interpretations of Duration

Throughout this book the following definition was provided for duration: the approximate percentage change in price for a 100 basis point change in rates. That definition is the most relevant for what a manager or investor is attempting to use duration for. In fact, if you understand this definition, you will never need to use the equation for the approximate percentage price change given by equation (2) and you can easily calculate the change in a bond's value.

---

[4] More specifically, this is the formula for the modified duration of a bond on a coupon anniversary date.

[5] Frederick Macaulay, *Some Theoretical Problems Suggested by the Movement of Interest Rates, Bond Yields, and Stock Prices in the U.S. Since 1856* (New York: National Bureau of Economic Research, 1938).

For example, suppose we want to know the approximate percentage change in price for a 50 basis point change in yield for our hypothetical 9% coupon 20-year bond selling for 134.6722. Since the duration is 10.66, a 100 basis point change in yield would change the price by about 10.66%. For a 50 basis point change in yield the price will change by approximately 5.33% (= 10.66%/2). So, if the yield increases by 50 basis points, the price will decrease by about 5.33% from 134.6722 to 127.4942.

Now let's look at some other definitions or interpretations of duration that appear in publications and are cited in discussions by managers with their clients.

1. Duration is the "First Derivative"

Sometimes a market participant will refer to duration as the "first derivative of the price/ yield function" or simply the "first derivative." Wow! Sounds impressive. First, "derivative" here has nothing to do with "derivative instruments" (i.e., futures, swaps, options, etc.). A derivative as used in this context is obtained by differentiating a mathematical function. There are first derivatives, second derivatives, and so on. When market participants say that duration is the first derivative, here is what they mean. If it were possible to write a mathematical equation for a bond in closed form, the first derivative would be the result of differentiating that equation the first time. Even if you don't know how to do the process of differentiation to get the first derivative, it sounds like you are really smart since it suggests you understand calculus! While it is a correct interpretation of duration, it is an interpretation that in no way helps us understand what the interest rate risk is of a bond. That is, it is an operationally meaningless interpretation.

Why is it an operationally meaningless interpretation? Go back to the $10 million bond position with a duration of 6. Suppose a client is concerned with the exposure of the bond to changes in interest rates. Now, tell that client the duration is 6 and that it is the first derivative of the price function for that bond. What have you told the client? Not much. In contrast, tell that client that the duration is 6 and that duration is the approximate price sensitivity of a bond to a 100 basis point change in rates and you have told the client a great deal more with respect the bond's interest rate risk.

2. Duration is Some Measure of Time

When the concept of duration was originally introduced by Macaulay in 1938, he used it as a gauge of the time that the bond was outstanding. More specifically, Macaulay defined duration as the weighted average of the time to each coupon and principal payment of a bond. Subsequently, duration has too often been thought of in temporal terms, i.e., years. This is most unfortunate for two reasons.

First, in terms of dimensions, there is nothing wrong with expressing duration in terms of years because that is the proper dimension of this value. But the proper interpretation is that duration is the price volatility of a zero-coupon bond with that number of years to maturity. So, when a manager says a bond has a duration of 4 years, it is not useful to think of this measure in terms of time, but that the bond has the price sensitivity to rate changes of a 4-year zero-coupon bond.

Second, thinking of duration in terms of years makes it difficult for managers and their clients to understand the duration of some complex securities. Here are a few examples. For a mortgage-backed security that is an interest-only security (i.e., receives coupons but not principal repayment) discussed at Level II, the duration is negative. What does a negative number of, say, −4 mean? In terms of our interpretation as a percentage price change, it means that when rates change by 100 basis points, the price of the bond changes by about 4% but the change is in the same direction as the change in rates.

As a second example, consider an inverse floater created in the CMO market. (This CMO product was introduced in Chapter 3 and will be discussed in more detail at Level II.) The underlying collateral for such a security might be loans with 25 years to final maturity. However, an inverse floater can have a duration that easily exceeds 25. This does not make sense to a manager or client who uses a temporal definition for duration.

As a final example, consider derivative instruments. We will discuss the duration of these instruments at Level II. Consider the duration of an option that expires in one year. Suppose that it is reported that its duration is 60. What does that mean? To someone who interprets duration in terms of time, does that mean 60 years, 60 days, 60 seconds? It doesn't mean any of these. It simply means that the option tends to have the price sensitivity to rate changes of a 60-year zero-coupon bond.

3. Forget First Derivatives and Temporal Definitions

The bottom line is that one should not care if it is technically correct to think of duration in terms of years (volatility of a zero-coupon bond) or in terms of first derivatives. There are even some who interpret duration in terms of the "half life" of a security. Subject to the limitations that we will describe as we proceed in this book, duration is used as a measure of the sensitivity of a security's price to changes in yield. We will fine tune this definition as we move along.

Users of this interest rate risk measure are interested in what it tells them about the price sensitivity of a bond (or a portfolio) to changes in rates. Duration provides the investor with a feel for the dollar price exposure or the percentage price exposure to potential rate changes. Try the following definitions on a client who has a portfolio with a duration of 4 and see which one the client finds most useful for understanding the interest rate risk of the portfolio when rates change:

> *Definition 1*: The duration of 4 for your portfolio indicates that the portfolio's value will change by approximately 4% if rates change by 100 basis points.
> *Definition 2*: The duration of 4 for your portfolio is the first derivative of the price function for the bonds in the portfolio.
> *Definition 3*: The duration of 4 for your portfolio is the weighted average number of years to receipt of the present value of the cash flows of the portfolio.

It would be ridiculous to expect clients to understand the last two definitions better than the first.

Moreover, interpreting duration in terms of a measure of price sensitivity to rate changes allows a manager to make comparisons between bonds regarding their interest rate risk under certain assumptions.

H. Portfolio Duration A portfolio's duration can be obtained by calculating the weighted average of the duration of the bonds in the portfolio. The weight is the proportion of the portfolio that a security comprises. Mathematically, a portfolio's duration can be calculated as follows:

$$w_1 D_1 + w_2 D_2 + w_3 D_3 + \ldots + w_K D_K$$

where

w_i = market value of bond i/market value of the portfolio
D_i = duration of bond i
K = number of bonds in the portfolio

To illustrate this calculation, consider the following 3-bond portfolio in which all three bonds are option free:

Bond	Price ($)	Yield (%)	Par amount owned	Market value	Duration
10% 5-year	100.0000	10	$4 million	$4,000,000	3.861
8% 15-year	84.6275	10	5 million	4,231,375	8.047
14% 30-year	137.8586	10	1 million	1,378,586	9.168

In this illustration, it is assumed that the next coupon payment for each bond is exactly six months from now (i.e., there is no accrued interest). The market value for the portfolio is $9,609,961. Since each bond is option free, modified duration can be used. The market price per $100 par value of each bond, its yield, and its duration are given below:

In this illustration, K is equal to 3 and:

$$w_1 = \$4,000,000/\$9,609,961 = 0.416 \quad D_1 = 3.861$$
$$w_2 = \$4,231,375/\$9,609,961 = 0.440 \quad D_2 = 8.047$$
$$w_3 = \$1,378,586/\$9,609,961 = 0.144 \quad D_3 = 9.168$$

The portfolio's duration is:

$$0.416\,(3.861) + 0.440\,(8.047) + 0.144\,(9.168) = 6.47$$

A portfolio duration of 6.47 means that for a 100 basis point change in the yield for each of the three bonds, the market value of the portfolio will change by approximately 6.47%. But keep in mind, the yield for each of the three bonds must change by 100 basis points for the duration measure to be useful. This is a *critical assumption* and its importance cannot be overemphasized. We introduced this assumption in Chapter 2.

An alternative procedure for calculating the duration of a portfolio is to calculate the dollar price change for a given number of basis points for each security in the portfolio and then add up all the price changes. Dividing the total of the price changes by the initial market value of the portfolio produces a percentage price change that can be adjusted to obtain the portfolio's duration.

For example, consider the 3-bond portfolio shown above. Suppose that we calculate the dollar price change for each bond in the portfolio based on its respective duration for a 50 basis point change in yield. We would then have:

Bond	Market value	Duration	Change in value for 50 bp yield change
10% 5-year	$4,000,000	3.861	$77,220
8% 15-year	4,231,375	8.047	170,249
14% 30-year	1,378,586	9.168	63,194
		Total	$310,663

Thus, a 50 basis point change in all rates changes the market value of the 3-bond portfolio by $310,663. Since the market value of the portfolio is $9,609,961, a 50 basis point change produced a change in value of 3.23% ($310,663 divided by $9,609,961). Since duration is the approximate percentage change for a 100 basis point change in rates, this means that the portfolio duration is 6.46 (found by doubling 3.23). This is the same value for the portfolio's duration as found earlier.

SECTION V CONVEXITY

The duration measure indicates that regardless of whether interest rates increase or decrease, the approximate percentage price change is the same. However, as we noted earlier, this is not consistent with Property 3 of a bond's price volatility. Specifically, while for small changes in yield the percentage price change will be the same for an increase or decrease in yield, for large changes in yield this is not true. This suggests that duration is only a good approximation of the percentage price change for small changes in yield.

We demonstrated this property earlier using a 9% 20-year bond selling to yield 6% with a duration of 10.66. For a 10 basis point change in yield, the estimate was accurate for both an increase or decrease in yield. However, for a 200 basis point change in yield the approximate percentage price change was off considerably.

The reason for this result is that duration is in fact a first (linear) approximation for a small change in yield.[6] The approximation can be improved by using a second approximation. This approximation is referred to as "convexity." *The use of this term in the industry is unfortunate since the term convexity is also used to describe the shape or curvature of the price/yield relationship.* The **convexity measure** of a security can be used to approximate the change in price that is not explained by duration.

A. Convexity Measure

The convexity measure of a bond is approximated using the following formula:

$$\text{convexity measure} = \frac{V_+ + V_- - 2V_0}{2V_0(\Delta y)^2} \tag{4}$$

where the notation is the same as used earlier for duration as given by equation (4).

For our hypothetical 9% 20-year bond selling to yield 6%, we know that for a 20 basis point change in yield ($\Delta y = 0.002$):

$$V_0 = 134.6722, \quad V_- = 137.5888, \quad \text{and} \quad V_+ = 131.8439$$

Substituting these values into the convexity measure given by equation (7):

$$\text{Convexity measure} = \frac{131.8439 + 137.5888 - 2(134.6722)}{2(134.6722)(0.002)^2} = 81.96$$

We'll see how to use this convexity measure shortly. Before doing so, there are three points that should be noted. First, there is no simple interpretation of the convexity measure as there is for duration. Second, it is more common for market participants to refer to the value computed in equation (4) as the "convexity of a bond" rather than the "convexity measure of a bond." Finally, the convexity measure reported by dealers and vendors will differ for an option-free bond. The reason is that the value obtained from equation (4) is often scaled for the reason explained after we demonstrate how to use the convexity measure.

---

[6] The reason it is a linear approximation can be seen in Exhibit 15 where the tangent line is used to estimate the new price. That is, a straight line is being used to approximate a non-linear (i.e., convex) relationship.

PRACTICE QUESTION 3

What is the convexity measure for a 6% coupon 20-year option-free selling at 100 to yield 6% using an interest rate shock of 10 basis points?

B. Convexity Adjustment to Percentage Price Change

Given the convexity measure, the approximate percentage price change adjustment due to the bond's convexity (i.e., the percentage price change not explained by duration) is:

$$\text{Convexity adjustment to percentage price change} = \text{Convexity measure} \times (\Delta y)^2 \times 100 \qquad (5)$$

For example, for the 9% coupon bond maturing in 20 years, the convexity adjustment to the percentage price change based on duration if the yield increases from 6% to 8% is

$$81.96 \times (0.02)^2 \times 100 = 3.28\%$$

If the yield decreases from 6% to 4%, the convexity adjustment to the approximate percentage price change based on duration would also be 3.28%.

The approximate percentage price change based on duration and the convexity adjustment is found by adding the two estimates. So, for example, if yields change from 6% to 8%, the estimated percentage price change would be:

Estimated change using duration	= −21.32%
Convexity adjustment	= +3.28%
Total estimated percentage price change	= −18.04%

The actual percentage price change is −18.40%.

For a decrease of 200 basis points, from 6% to 4%, the approximate percentage price change would be as follows:

Estimated change using duration	= +21.32%
Convexity adjustment	= +3.28%
Total estimated percentage price change	= +24.60%

The actual percentage price change is +25.04%. Thus, duration combined with the convexity adjustment does a better job of estimating the sensitivity of a bond's price change to large changes in yield.

Notice that when the convexity measure is positive, we have the situation described earlier that the gain is greater than the loss for a given large change in rates. That is, the bond exhibits positive convexity. We can see this in the example above. However, if the convexity measure is negative, we have the situation where the loss will be greater than the gain. For example, suppose that a callable bond has an effective duration of 4 and a convexity measure of −30. This means that the approximate percentage price change for a 200 basis point change is 8%. The convexity adjustment for a 200 basis point change in rates is then

$$-30 \times (0.02)^2 \times 100 = -1.2$$

The convexity adjustment is -1.2% and therefore the bond exhibits the negative convexity property illustrated in Exhibit 10. The approximate percentage price change after adjusting for convexity is:

Estimated change using duration $= -8.0\%$
Convexity adjustment $= -1.2\%$
Total estimated percentage price change $= \overline{-9.2\%}$

For a decrease of 200 basis points, the approximate percentage price change would be as follows:

Estimated change using duration $= +8.0\%$
Convexity adjustment $= -1.2\%$
Total estimated percentage price change $= \overline{+6.8\%}$

Notice that the loss is greater than the gain — a property called negative convexity that we discussed in Section III and illustrated in Exhibit 10.

PRACTICE QUESTION 4

Using the convexity measure for the 6% coupon 20-year option free bond selling at 100 to yield 6% found in Practice Question 3, complete the following:

a. For a 10 basis point increase in interest rates:
   Estimated change using duration   = _____ %
   Convexity adjustment   = _____ %
   Total estimated percentage price change = _____ %

   Actual percentage price change   = _____ %

b. For a 10 basis point decrease in interest rates:
   Estimated change using duration   = _____ %
   Convexity adjustment   = _____ %
   Total estimated percentage price change = _____ %

   Actual percentage price change   = _____ %

c. For a 200 basis point increase in interest rates:
   Estimated change using duration   = _____ %
   Convexity adjustment   = _____ %
   Total estimated percentage price change = _____ %

   Actual percentage price change   = _____ %

d. For a 200 basis point decrease in interest rates:
   Estimated change using duration   = _____ %
   Convexity adjustment   = _____ %
   Total estimated percentage price change = _____ %

   Actual percentage price change   = _____ %

C. Scaling the Convexity Measure

The convexity measure as given by equation (4) means nothing in isolation. It is the substitution of the computed convexity measure into equation (5) that provides the estimated adjustment for convexity that is meaningful. Therefore, it is possible to scale the convexity measure in any way as long as the same convexity adjustment is obtained.

For example, in some books the convexity measure is defined as follows:

$$\text{Convexity measure} = \frac{V_+ + V_- - 2V_0}{V_0(\Delta y)^2} \qquad (6)$$

Equation (6) differs from equation (4) since it does not include 2 in the denominator. Thus, the convexity measure computed using equation (6) will be double the convexity measure using equation (4). So, for our earlier illustration, since the convexity measure using equation (4) is 81.96, the convexity measure using equation (6) would be 163.92.

Which is correct, 81.96 or 163.92? The answer is both. The reason is that the corresponding equation for computing the convexity adjustment would not be given by equation (5) if the convexity measure is obtained from equation (6). Instead, the corresponding convexity adjustment formula would be:

$$\begin{array}{l} \text{Convexity adjustment to percentage price change} \\ = (\text{Convexity measure}/2) \times (\Delta y)^2 \times 100 \end{array} \qquad (7)$$

Equation (7) differs from equation (5) in that the convexity measure is divided by 2. Thus, the convexity adjustment will be the same whether one uses equation (4) to get the convexity measure and equation (5) to get the convexity adjustment or one uses equation (6) to compute the convexity measure and equation (7) to determine the convexity adjustment.

Some dealers and vendors scale in a different way. One can also compute the convexity measure as follows:

$$\text{Convexity measure} = \frac{V_+ + V_- - 2V_0}{2V_0(\Delta y)^2(100)} \qquad (8)$$

Equation (8) differs from equation (4) by the inclusion of 100 in the denominator. In our illustration, the convexity measure would be 0.8196 rather than 81.96 using equation (4). The convexity adjustment formula corresponding to the convexity measure given by equation (8) is then

$$\begin{array}{l} \text{Convexity adjustment to percentage price change} \\ = \text{Convexity measure} \times (\Delta y)^2 \times 10,000 \end{array} \qquad (9)$$

Similarly, one can express the convexity measure as shown in equation (10):

$$\text{Convexity measure} = \frac{V_+ + V_- - 2V_0}{V_0(\Delta y)^2(100)} \qquad (10)$$

For the bond we have been using in our illustrations, the convexity measure is 1.6392. The corresponding convexity adjustment is:

$$\begin{array}{l} \text{Convexity adjustment to percentage price change} \\ = (\text{Convexity measure}/2) \times (\Delta y)^2 \times 10,000 \end{array} \qquad (11)$$

Consequently, the convexity measure (or just simply "convexity" as it is referred to by some market participants) that could be reported for this option-free bond are 81.96, 163.92, 0.8196, or 1.6392. All of these values are correct, but they mean nothing in isolation. To use them to obtain the convexity adjustment to the price change estimated by duration requires knowing how they are computed so that the correct convexity adjustment formula is used. *It is the convexity adjustment that is important – not the convexity measure in isolation.*

It is also important to understand this when comparing the convexity measures reported by dealers and vendors. For example, if one dealer shows a manager Bond A with a duration of 4 and a convexity measure of 50, and a second dealer shows the manager Bond B with a duration of 4 and a convexity measure of 80, which bond has the greater percentage price change response to changes in interest rates? Since the duration of the two bonds is identical, the bond with the larger convexity measure will change more when rates decline. However, not knowing how the two dealers computed the convexity measure means that the manager does not know which bond will have the greater convexity adjustment. If the first dealer used equation (4) while the second dealer used equation (6), then the convexity measures must be adjusted in terms of either equation. For example, the convexity measure of 80 computed using equation (6) is equal to a convexity measure of 40 based on equation (4).

D. Modified Convexity and Effective Convexity

The prices used in equation (4) to calculate convexity can be obtained by either assuming that when the yield changes the expected cash flows either do not change or they do change. In the former case, the resulting convexity is referred to as **modified convexity**. (Actually, in the industry, convexity is not qualified by the adjective "modified.") In contrast, **effective convexity** assumes that the cash flows do change when yields change. This is the same distinction made for duration.

As with duration, there is little difference between modified convexity and effective convexity for option-free bonds. However, for bonds with embedded options there can be quite a difference between the calculated modified convexity and effective convexity measures. In fact, for all option-free bonds, either convexity measure will have a positive value. For bonds with embedded options, the calculated effective convexity measure can be negative when the calculated modified convexity measure is positive.

SECTION VI PRICE VALUE OF A BASIS POINT

Some managers use another measure of the price volatility of a bond to quantify interest rate risk – the **price value of a basis point** (PVBP). This measure, also called the **dollar value of an 01** (DV01), is the absolute value of the change in the price of a bond for a 1 basis point change in yield. That is,

PVBP = | initial price – price if yield is changed by 1 basis point |

Does it make a difference if the yield is increased or decreased by 1 basis point? It does not because of Property 2 — the change will be about the same for a small change in basis points.

To illustrate the computation, let's use the values in Exhibit 4. If the initial yield is 6%, we can compute the PVBP by using the prices for either the yield at 5.99% or 6.01%. The PVPB for both for each bond is shown below:

Coupon	6.0%	6.0%	9.0%	9.0%
Maturity	5	20	5	20
Initial price	$100.0000	$100.0000	$112.7953	$134.6722
Price at 5.99%	100.0427	100.1157	112.8412	134.8159
PVBP at 5.99%	$0.0427	$0.1157	$0.0459	$0.1437
Price at 6.01%	99.9574	99.8845	112.7494	134.5287
PVPB at 6.01%	$0.0426	$0.1155	$0.0459	$0.1435

The PVBP is related to duration. In fact, PVBP is simply a special case of dollar duration described in Chapter 2. We know that the duration of a bond is the approximate percentage price change for a 100 basis point change in interest rates. We also know how to compute the approximate percentage price change for any number of basis points given a bond's duration using equation (2). Given the initial price and the approximate percentage price change for 1 basis point, we can compute the change in price for a 1 basis point change in rates.

For example, consider the 9% 20-year bond. The duration for this bond is 10.66. Using equation (2), the approximate percentage price change for a 1 basis point increase in interest rates (i.e., $\Delta y = 0.0001$) ignoring the negative sign in equation (2) is:

$$10.66 \times (0.0001) \times 100 = 0.1066\%$$

Given the initial price of 134.6722, the dollar price change estimated using duration is

$$0.1066\% \times 134.6722 = \$0.1435$$

This is the same price change as shown above for a PVPB for this bond. Below is (1) the PVPB based on a 1 basis point increase for each bond and (2) the estimated price change using duration for a 1 basis point increase for each bond:

Coupon	6.0%	6.0%	9.0%	9.0%
Maturity	5	20	5	20
PVBP for 1 bp increase	$0.0426	$0.1155	$0.0459	$0.1435
Duration of bond	4.2700	11.5600	4.0700	10.6600
Duration estimate	$0.0427	$0.1156	$0.0459	$0.1436

SECTION VII
THE
IMPORTANCE
OF YIELD
VOLATILITY

What we have not considered thus far is the volatility of interest rates. For example, as we explained in Chapter 2, all other factors equal, the higher the coupon rate, the lower the price volatility of a bond to changes in interest rates. In addition, the higher the level of yields, the lower the price volatility of a bond to changes in interest rates. This is illustrated in Exhibit 19 which shows the price/yield relationship for an option-free bond. When the yield level is high (Y_H in the exhibit) a change in interest rates does not produce a large change in the initial price (P_H in the exhibit). However, when the yield level is low (Y_L in the exhibit) a change in interest rates of the same number of basis points as shown when the yield is high does produce a large change in the initial price (P_L in the exhibit).

This can also be cast in terms of duration properties: the higher the coupon, the lower the duration; and the higher the yield level the lower the duration. Given these two properties, a 10-year non-investment grade bond has a lower duration than a current coupon 10-year Treasury note since the former has a higher coupon rate and trades at a higher yield level. Does this mean that a 10-year non-investment grade bond has less interest rate risk than a current coupon 10-year Treasury note? Consider also that a 10-year Swiss government bond has a lower coupon rate than a current coupon 10-year U.S. Treasury note and trades at a lower yield level. Therefore, a 10-year Swiss government bond will have a higher duration than a current coupon 10-year Treasury note. Does this mean that a 10-year Swiss government bond has greater interest rate risk than a current coupon 10-year U.S. Treasury note? The missing link is the relative volatility of rates which we shall refer to as **yield volatility** or **interest rate volatility**.

Exhibit 19: The Effect of Yield Level on Price Volatility

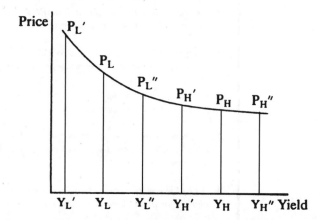

$$(Y_H' - Y_H) = (Y_H - Y_H'') = (Y_L' - Y_L) = (Y_L - Y_L'')$$
$$(P_H - P_H') < (P_L - P_L') \text{ and}$$
$$(P_H - P_H'') < (P_L - P_L'')$$

The greater the expected yield volatility, the greater the interest rate risk for a given duration and current value of a position. In the case of non-investment grade bonds, while their durations are less than current coupon Treasuries of the same maturity, the yield volatility of non-investment grade bonds is greater than that of current coupon Treasuries. For the 10-year Swiss government bond, while the duration is greater than for a current coupon 10-year U.S. Treasury note, the yield volatility of 10-year Swiss bonds is considerably less than that of 10-year U.S. Treasury notes.

Consequently, to measure the exposure of a portfolio or position to rate changes it is necessary to measure yield volatility. This requires an understanding of the fundamental principles of probability distributions. The measure of yield volatility is the standard deviation of yield changes. At Level II, we show how to estimate yield volatility. As we will see, depending on the underlying assumptions, there could be a wide range for the yield volatility estimate.

A framework that ties together the price sensitivity of a bond position to rate changes and yield volatility is the **value-at-risk (VaR) framework**. Risk in this framework is defined as the maximum estimated loss in market value of a given position that is expected to happen with a specified probability. We will discuss the VaR framework at Level III.

SECTION VIII
KEY POINTS

❏ *To control interest rate risk, a manager must be able to quantify what will result from an adverse change in interest rates.*

❏ *A valuation model is used to determine the value of a position after a rate movement and therefore if a reliable valuation model is not used there is no way to measure interest rate risk exposure.*

❏ *There are two approaches to measure interest rate risk: full valuation approach and duration/convexity approach.*

❏ *The full valuation approach involves revaluing a bond position (every position in the case of a portfolio) for a scenario of interest rate changes.*

❏ *The advantage of the full valuation approach is its accuracy with respect to interest rate exposure for a given interest rate change scenario — accurate relative to the valuation model used — but its disadvantage for a large portfolio is having to revalue each bond for each scenario.*

❏ *The characteristics of a bond that affect its price volatility are (1) maturity, (2) coupon rate, and (3) presence of any embedded options.*

❏ *The price sensitivity of a bond to changes in the required yield can be measured in terms of the dollar price change or percentage price change.*

❏ *One property of an option-free bond is that although the price moves in the opposite direction from the change in required yield, the percentage price change is not the same for all bonds.*

❏ *A second property of an option-free bond is that for small changes in the required yield, the percentage price change for a given bond is roughly the same whether the required yield increases or decreases.*

❏ *A third property of an option-free bond is that for a large change in yield, the percentage price change for an increase in yield is not the same as for a decrease in yield.*

❏ *A fourth property of an option-free bond is that for a large change in yield of a given number of basis points, the price of an option-free bond increases by more than it decreases.*

❏ *The shape of the price/yield relationship for an option-free bond is convex.*

❏ *Option-free bonds exhibit positive convexity.*

❏ *Positive convexity means that for a large change in interest rates, the amount of the price appreciation is greater than the amount of the price depreciation.*

❏ *A callable bond exhibits positive convexity at high yield levels and negative convexity at low yield levels where "high" and "low" yield levels are relative to the issue's coupon rate.*

❏ *Negative convexity means that for a large change in interest rates, the amount of the price appreciation is less than the amount of the price depreciation.*

❏ *At low yield levels (low relative to the issue's coupon rate), the price of a putable bond is basically the same as the price of an option-free bond because the value of the put option is small; as rates rise, the price of a putable bond declines, but the price decline is less than that for an option-free bond.*

❏ *Duration is a first approximation of a bond's price or a portfolio's value to rate changes.*

❏ *To improve the estimate provided by duration, a convexity measure can be used.*

❏ *Using duration combined with a convexity measure to estimate the percentage price change of a bond to changes in interest rates is called the duration/convexity approach to interest rate risk measurement.*

❏ *Duration does a good job of estimating the percentage price change for a small change in interest rates but the estimation becomes poorer the larger the change in interest rates.*

❏ *In calculating duration, it is necessary to shock interest rates (yields) up and down by the same number of basis points to obtain the values when rates change.*

❏ *For option-free bonds the size of the shock is unimportant for reasonable changes in yield.*

❑ *For bonds with embedded options, the problem with using a small shock to estimate duration is that divergences between actual and estimated price changes are magnified by dividing by a small change in rate in the denominator of the duration formula; in addition, small rate shocks that do not reflect the types of rate changes that may occur in the market do not permit the determination of how prices can change because expected cash flows may change.*

❑ *For bonds with embedded options, if large rate shocks are used the asymmetry caused by convexity is encountered; in addition, large rate shocks may cause dramatic changes in the expected cash flows for bonds with embedded options that may be far different from how the expected cash flows will change for smaller rate shocks.*

❑ *Modified duration is the approximate percentage change in a bond's price for a 100 basis point change in yield assuming that the bond's expected cash flows do not change when the yield changes.*

❑ *In calculating the values to be used in the numerator of the duration formula, for modified duration the cash flows are not assumed to change and therefore, the change in the bond's price when the yield is changed is due solely to discounting at the new yield level.*

❑ *Effective duration is the approximate percentage change in a bond's price for a 100 basis point change in yield assuming that the bond's expected cash flows do change when the yield changes.*

❑ *Modified duration is appropriate for option-free bonds; effective duration should be used for bonds with embedded options.*

❑ *The difference between modified duration and effective duration for bonds with an embedded option can be quite dramatic.*

❑ *Macaulay duration is mathematically related to modified duration and is therefore a flawed measure of the duration of a bond with an embedded option.*

❑ *Interpretations of duration in temporal terms (i.e.s, some measure of time) or calculus terms (i.e., first derivative of the price/yield relationship) are operationally meaningless and should be avoided.*

❑ *The duration for a portfolio is equal to the market-value weighted duration of each bond in the portfolio.*

❑ *In applying portfolio duration to estimate the sensitivity of a portfolio to changes in interest rates, it is assumed that the yield for all bonds in the portfolio change by the same number of basis points.*

❑ *The duration measure indicates that regardless of whether interest rates increase or decrease, the approximate percentage price change is the same; however, this is not a property of a bond's price volatility for large changes in yield.*

❑ *A convexity measure can be used to improve the estimate of the percentage price change obtained using duration, particularly for a large change in yield.*

❑ *As with duration, the convexity measure is computed by shocking rates up and down by the same number of basis points.*

❑ *Given the convexity measure, the convexity adjustment to the duration estimate can be computed; the convexity adjustment is just the amount that should be added to the duration estimate for the percentage price change.*

❑ *The convexity measure can be scaled in different ways, so the convexity measure by itself can vary; however, the formula for the convexity adjustment will be scaled accordingly so that the same estimate for the convexity adjustment will result regardless of how the convexity measure is scaled.*

❑ *The same distinction made between modified duration and effective duration applies to modified convexity and effective convexity.*

❑ *For a bond with an embedded that exhibits negative convexity at some yield level, the convexity measure will be negative.*

❑ *The price value of a basis point (or dollar value of an 01) is the change in the price of a bond for a 1 basis point change in yield.*

❑ *The price value of a basis point is the same as the estimated price change using duration for a 1 basis point change in yield.*

❑ *Yield volatility must be recognized in estimating the interest rate risk of a bond and a portfolio.*

❑ *Value-at-risk is a measure that ties together the duration of a bond and yield volatility.*

END OF CHAPTER QUESTIONS

1. Explain why you agree or disagree with the following statement:

   The disadvantage of the full valuation approach to measuring interest rate risk is that it requires a revaluation of each bond in the portfolio for each interest rate scenario. Consequently, you need a valuation model. In contrast, for the duration/convexity approach there is no need for a valuation model because the duration and convexity measures can be obtained without a valuation model.

2. Explain why you agree or disagree with the following statement:

   The problem with both the full valuation approach and the duration/convexity approach is that they fail to take into account how the change in the yield curve can affect a portfolio's value.

3. Explain why you agree or disagree with the following statement:

   If two bonds have the same duration, then the percentage change in price of the two bonds will be the same for a given change in interest rates.

4. James Smith and Donald Robertson are assistant portfolio managers for Micro Management Partners. In a review of the interest rate risk of a portfolio, Smith and Robertson discussed the riskiness of two Treasury securities. Following is the information about these two Treasuries:

Bond	Price	Modified duration
A	90	4
B	50	6

   Smith noted that Treasury bond B is the more price volatile bond because of its higher modified duration. Robertson disagreed noting that Treasury bond A is the more price volatile despite its lower modified duration. Which manager is correct?

5. At its quarterly meeting, the trustees of the National Baggage Handlers Pension Fund reviewed the status of its bond portfolio. The portfolio is managed by William Renfro of Wiser and Wiser Management Company. The portfolio consists of 20% Treasury bonds, 10% corporate bonds that are noncallable for the life of the bonds, 30% callable corporate bonds, and 40% mortgage-backed securities. The report provided by Wiser and Wiser includes the following information for each bond in the portfolio: (1) modified duration, (2) effective duration, and (3) effective convexity. The portfolio's modified duration and effective duration were reported to be 5 and 3, respectively. Renfro attended the board meeting to answer any questions that the trustees might have. Nancy Weston, one of the trustee for the fund, prepared the following list of questions:

   a. What does the duration of a bond mean and how should the board interpret the portfolio duration?
   b. Why is the modified duration and effective duration for each Treasury bond and noncallable corporate bond the same?
   c. What is the appropriate duration measure, effective duration or modified duration?
   d. How were the effective duration measures obtained?
   e. What are the limitations in using duration?

The minutes of the board meeting indicated the following response by Mr. Renfro to each of these questions:

a. Duration is a measure of the approximate weighted average life of a bond or a bond portfolio. For example, a portfolio duration of 5 means that the fund will realize the return of the amount invested (in present value terms) in about 5 years.

b. Because the Treasury bonds in the portfolio are noncallable, modified duration is the same as effective duration. The same is true for the corporate bonds that are noncallable for life.

c. The appropriate measure is the effective duration since it takes into account the option embedded in the bonds held in the portfolio.

d. We obtained the effective duration from various sources — dealers firms and commercial vendors. There is a standard formula that all of these sources use to obtain the effective duration. Sometimes, a source may provide an effective duration that is not logical and we override the value by using the modified duration. For example, for some of the collateralized mortgage obligations, one vendor reported an effective duration of 40. This value was obviously wrong since the underlying collateral is 30-year loans; therefore, the duration cannot exceed 30. Moreover, for some of the CMOs, the duration is negative and this is obviously wrong. Again, in such instances we use the modified duration.

e. Duration is only a good measure for small changes in yield and assumes that the yield curve will shift in a parallel fashion. However, if these assumptions are satisfied, two portfolio with the same duration will perform in exactly the same way.

You are employed by Pension Consultants, a consultant to the labor union. You have been given the minutes of the meeting of the board of trustees with the responses of Mr. Renfro to the questions of Ms. Weston. Prepare a report indicating whether you agree or disagree with Mr. Renfro's responses.

6. Lewis Marlo, an assistant portfolio manager, was reviewing a potential buy list of corporate bonds. The list provided information on the effective duration and effective convexity for each corporate bond on the list. The senior portfolio manager, Jane Zorick, noticed that Mr. Marlo crossed out each bond with a convexity that is negative. When Mr. Marlo was questioned as to why, he responded that a negative value meant that the particular corporate bond was unattractive. How do you think Ms. Zorick should respond?

7. A client is reviewing information about the portfolio. For one of the issues in the portfolio the client sees the following:

Issue	Maturity	Duration
X	10 years	13

The client has questioned you as to whether or not the reported duration of 13 is correct. The client's concern is that he has heard that duration is some measure of time for a bond and as such cannot exceed the maturity of the security. Yet, the duration of Issue X exceeds its maturity. What explanation do you give to the client?

8. A portfolio manager is reviewing information provided by two dealers for a noncallable Treasury bond, bond W. Dealer 1 reported a convexity measure for bond W of

142. For the same bond Dealer 2 reported a value of 0.71. The portfolio manager is confused as to why the dealers have reported two significantly different values for the convexity measure. Why would the two dealers report such different values?

9. Suppose that you are given the following information about two callable bonds of the same issuer that can be called immediately:

| | Estimated percentage change in price if interest rates change by 100: | |
	−50 basis points	+ 50 basis points
Bond ABC	+2%	−5%
Bond XYZ	+11%	−8%

You are told that both bonds have about the same maturity and the coupon rate of one bond is 7% and the other 13%. Suppose that the yield curve for this issuer is flat at 8%. Based on this information, which bond is the lower coupon bond and which is the higher coupon bond? Explain why.

10. a. Why is modified duration an inappropriate measure for a high-coupon callable bond?
   b. What would be a better measure than modified duration?

11. Suppose that a 7% coupon corporate bond is immediately callable. Also suppose that if this issuer issued new bonds the coupon rate would be 12%. Why would the modified duration be a good approximation of the effective duration for this bond?

Questions 12-16 are based on the following price information for four bonds and assuming that all four bonds are trading to yield 5%:

Yield	Coupon Maturity	5.0% 4	5.0% 25	8.0% 4	8.0% 25
3.00%		107.4859	134.9997	118.7148	187.4992
4.00%		103.6627	115.7118	114.6510	162.8472
4.50%		101.8118	107.4586	112.6826	152.2102
4.75%		100.9011	103.6355	111.7138	147.2621
4.90%		100.3593	101.4324	111.1374	144.4042
5.00%		100.0000	100.0000	110.7552	142.5435
5.10%		99.6423	98.5959	110.3746	140.7175
5.25%		99.1085	96.5416	109.8066	138.0421
5.50%		98.2264	93.2507	108.8679	133.7465
6.00%		96.4902	87.1351	107.0197	125.7298
7.00%		93.1260	76.5444	103.4370	111.7278

Percentage price based on an initial yield of 5%

Yield	Coupon Maturity	5.0% 4	5.0% 25	8.0% 4	8.0% 25
3.00%		7.49%	35.00%	7.19%	31.54%
4.00%		3.66%	15.71%	3.52%	14.24%
4.50%		1.81%	7.46%	1.74%	6.78%
4.75%		0.90%	3.64%	0.87%	3.31%
4.90%		0.36%	1.43%	0.35%	1.31%
5.00%		0.00%	0.00%	0.00%	0.00%
5.10%		−0.36%	−1.40%	−0.34%	−1.28%
5.25%		−0.89%	−3.46%	−0.86%	−3.16%
5.50%		−1.77%	−6.75%	−1.70%	−6.17%
6.00%		−3.51%	−12.86%	−3.37%	−11.80%
7.00%		−6.87%	−23.46%	−6.61%	−21.62%

12. Assuming all four bonds are selling to yield 5%, compute the following for each bond:

    a. duration based on a 25 basis point rate shock
    b. duration based on a 50 basis point rate shock

13. Assuming all four bonds are selling to yield 5%, compute the convexity measure for each bond using a 25 basis point rate shock.

14. a. Using the duration computed in question 12a, compute the approximate percentage price change using duration for the two 8% coupon bonds assuming that the yield changes by 10 basis points.
    b. How does the estimated percentage price change compare to the actual percentage price change?

15. a. Using the duration computed in question 12a, compute the approximate percentage price change using duration for the two 8% coupon bonds assuming that the yield changes by 200 basis points.
    b. How does the estimated percentage price change compare to the actual percentage price change?

16. a. Using the convexity measure computed in question 13, compute the convexity adjustment for the two 25-year bonds assuming that the yield changes by 200 basis points.
    b. Compute the estimated percentage price change using duration (as computed in question 12a) and convexity measure (as computed in question 13) if yield changes by 200 basis points.
    c. How does the estimated percentage price change using duration and convexity compare to the actual percentage price change for a 200 basis point change in yield?

17. a. Given the information below for a 6.2% 18-year bond compute the price value of a basis point:

    price = 114.1338   yield = 5%   price if yield is 5.01% = 114.0051

    b. If the duration of the 6.2% 18-year bond is 11.28, what is the estimated price change for a 1 basis point change in yield.

18. Why is information about a bond's duration and convexity measure insufficient to quantity interest rate risk exposure?

SOLUTIONS TO END OF CHAPTER QUESTIONS

1. While it is true that a disadvantage of the full valuation approach is that it requires revaluing the bonds in the portfolio, it not true that the duration/convexity approach does not require a valuation model. A valuation model is required in order to obtain the prices when rates are shocked that are used in the duration and convexity measure formulas.

2. The duration/convexity approach does not take into consideration how the yield curve can shift. However, this is not correct for the full valuation approach since yield curve scenarios can be assessed.

3. The statement is not correct. While two bonds may have the same duration, they can have different convexities.

4. The problem here is in the definition of price volatility. It can be measured in terms of dollar price change or percentage price change. Smith is correct that there is greater price volatility for bond B because of its higher modified duration — that is, a higher percentage price change. Robertson is correct that bond A has greater price volatility but in terms of dollar price change. Specifically, for a 100 basis point change in rates, bond A will change by $3.60 (4% times 90); for bond B the dollar price change will be $3 (6% times 50) for a 100 basis point rate change.

5. a. Mr. Renfro's definition is a temporal definition and it is best not to use such an interpretation. Duration is related to the percentage price change of a bond when interest rates change.

   b. Mr. Renfro's response is correct.

   c. Mr. Renfro's response is correct.

   d. The computation of effective duration and convexity measures requires a valuation model to determine what the new prices will be when rates change. These models are based on assumptions. When duration and convexity measures are taken from different sources, there is no consistency of assumptions. There is, in fact, no standard formula that all sources use. While it is true that there is a formula for computing duration once the new prices for the bond are determined from a valuation model when rates are shocked, there is no simple valuation formula for bonds with embedded options.

   Mr. Renfro incorrectly overrode duration measures. It is possible — and it does occur in practice — to have a duration for a bond that is greater than the maturity of the bond. A negative duration does occur for some securities. For example, certain mortgage-backed securities have a negative duration. A negative duration of –3, for example, would mean that if interest rates increased by 100 basis points, the price of the bond will increase by approximately 3%. That is, the price of the bond moves in the same direction as the change in rates. In fact, for the types of bonds that have a duration longer than maturity and a negative duration, modified duration is not what the manager would want to use.

   e. The first part of the statement is correct. However, the second part is not true. Two bonds can have the same duration but perform differently when rates change because they have different convexity measures.

6. A negative convexity measure simply means that the price appreciation will be less than the price decline for a large number of basis points. Whether or not a bond with negative convexity is attractive depends on its price and expectations about future interest rate changes.

7. If one interprets duration as some measure of time, it is difficult to understand why a bond will have a duration greater than its maturity. Duration is the approximate percentage change of the price of a bond for a 100 basis point change in rates. It is possible to have a security with a maturity of 10 years and a duration of 13.

8. Computing the convexity measure is the first step in adjusting the duration estimate for the convexity of a bond. Once the convexity measure is computed, there is a relationship between the convexity measure and the yield change that is used to compute the convexity adjustment. The convexity measure can be scaled in any way desired. What is critical is that the convexity adjustment formula be scaled accordingly.

   For example, suppose the formula for the convexity measure as given by equation (6) in the chapter is used by Dealer 1:

$$\text{Convexity measure} = \frac{V_+ + V_- - 2V_0}{V_0(\Delta y)^2}$$

   If Dealer 1 used equation (6) to obtain a convexity measure, then the corresponding convexity adjustment to the percentage price change would be given by equation (7) in the chapter:

   Convexity adjustment to percentage price change
   $$= (\text{Convexity measure}/2) \times (\Delta y)^2 \times 100$$

   Now, suppose instead of using equation (6), Dealer 2 used equation (8) in the chapter to obtain the convexity measure:

$$\text{Convexity measure} = \frac{V_+ + V_- - 2V_0}{2V_0(\Delta y)^2(100)}$$

   Then the corresponding formula for the convexity adjustment to the percentage price change given by equation (9) in the chapter is:

   Convexity adjustment to percentage price change
   $$= \text{Convexity measure} \times (\Delta y)^2 \times 10{,}000$$

   Both alternatives would give the same convexity adjustment to the percentage price change but would have a different convexity measure. Specifically, using equation (6) Dealer 1 could have obtained a convexity measure of 142. However, using equation (8) the convexity measure would have been one half the value divided by 100, or 0.71.

9. Bond ABC exhibits negative convexity — for a 100 basis point change in rates, the gain is less than the loss; Bond XYZ exhibits positive convexity. A high coupon bond will exhibit negative convexity. A low coupon bond will exhibit positive convexity. Therefore, bond ABC is probably the high coupon bond while bond XYZ is probably the low coupon bond.

10. a. Modified duration is an inappropriate duration measure for a high coupon callable bond because it fails to recognize that as interest rates change, the expected cash flows will change.

   b. A better measure for a high-coupon callable bond is effective or option-adjusted duration.

11. Because the issue's coupon rate is substantially below the prevailing rate at which the issue can be refunded (500 basis points below), this issue is not likely to be called. Basically, if rates are shocked up and down, the expected cash flows are not likely to change because the coupon rate is so far below the market rate. Thus, modified duration — which assumes that the expected cash flow will not change when rates are changed — will be a good approximation for effective duration.

12. a. For a 25 basis point rate shock, the duration formula is:

$$\text{duration} = \frac{V_- - V_+}{2V_0(0.0025)}$$

		5%, 4 year	5%, 25 year	8%, 4 year	8%, 25 year
Initial value	V_0	100.0000	100.0000	110.7552	142.5435
Value at 4.75%	V_-	100.9011	103.6355	111.7138	147.2621
Value at 5.25%	V_+	99.1085	96.5416	109.8066	138.0421
Duration		3.59	14.19	3.44	12.94

   b. For a 50 basis point rate shock, the duration formula is:

$$\text{duration} = \frac{V_- - V_+}{2V_0(0.0050)}$$

		5%, 4 year	5%, 25 year	8%, 4 year	8%, 25 year
Initial value	V_0	100.0000	100.0000	110.7552	142.5435
Value at 4.50%	V_-	101.8118	107.4586	112.6826	152.2102
Value at 5.50%	V_+	98.2264	93.2507	108.8679	133.7465
Duration		3.59	14.21	3.44	12.95

13. For a 25 basis point rate shock, the convexity measure formula is:

$$\text{convexity measure} = \frac{V_+ + V_- - 2V_0}{2V_0(0.0025)^2}$$

		5%, 4 year	5%, 25 year	8%, 4 year	8%, 25 year
Initial value	V_0	100.0000	100.0000	110.7552	142.5435
Value at 4.75%	V_-	100.9011	103.6355	111.7138	147.2621
Value at 5.25%	V_+	99.1085	96.5416	109.8066	138.0421
Convexity measure		7.64	141.74	7.23	121.93

14. a. For a 10 basis point change:

$$\text{duration for 8\% 4-year bond} = 3.44$$
$$\text{duration for 8\% 25-year bond} = 12.94$$
$$\Delta y = 0.0010$$

For the 8% 4-year bond: approximate percentage price change for 10 basis point shock:

10 basis point increase:
approximate percentage price change = $-3.44 \times (0.0010) \times 100 = -0.34\%$

10 basis point decrease:
approximate percentage price change = $-3.44 \times (-0.0010) \times 100 = +0.34\%$

For the 8% 25-year bond: approximate percentage price change for 10 basis point shock:

10 basis point increase:
approximate percentage price change = $-12.94 \times (0.0010) \times 100 = -1.29\%$
10 basis point decrease:
approximate percentage price change = $-12.94 \times (-0.0010) \times 100 = +1.29\%$

b. For the 4-year bond, the estimated percentage price change using duration is excellent for a 10 basis point change, as shown below:

	duration estimate	actual change
10 bp increase	−0.34%	−0.34%
10 bp decrease	+0.34%	+0.35%

For the 25-year bond, the estimated percentage price change using duration is excellent for a 10 basis point change, as shown below:

	duration estimate	actual change
10 bp increase	−1.29%	−1.28%
10 bp decrease	+1.29%	+1.31%

15. a. For a 200 basis point change:

$$
\begin{aligned}
\text{duration for 8\% 4-year bond} &= 3.44 \\
\text{duration for 8\% 25-year bond} &= 12.94 \\
\Delta y &= 0.02
\end{aligned}
$$

For the 8% 4-year bond: approximate percentage price change for 200 basis point shock:

200 basis point increase:
approximate percentage price change = $-3.44 \times (0.02) \times 100 = -6.89\%$

200 basis point decrease:
approximate percentage price change = $-3.44 \times (-0.02) \times 100 = +6.89\%$

For the 8% 25-year bond: approximate percentage price change for 200 basis point shock:
200 basis point increase:
approximate percentage price change = $-12.94 \times (0.02) \times 100 = -25.87\%$

200 basis point decrease:
approximate percentage price change = $-12.94 \times (-0.02) \times 100 = +25.87\%$

b. For the 4-year bond, the estimated percentage price change using duration is very good despite a 200 basis point change, as shown below:

	duration estimate	actual change
200 bp increase	−6.89%	−6.61%
200 bp decrease	+6.89%	+7.19%

For the 25-year bond, the estimated percentage price change using duration is poor for a 200 basis point change, as shown below:

	duration estimate	actual change
200 bp increase	−25.87%	−21.62%
200 bp decrease	+25.87%	+31.54%

16. a. The convexity adjustment for the two 25-year bonds is:

For the 5% 25-year bond:

$$\text{convexity measure} = 141.74$$
$$\Delta y = 0.02$$

convexity adjustment to percentage price change $= 141.74 \times (0.02)^2 \times 100 = 5.67\%$

For the 8% 25-year bond:

$$\text{convexity measure} = 121.93$$

convexity adjustment to percentage price change $= 121.93 \times (0.02)^2 \times 100 = 4.88\%$

b. Estimated price change using duration and convexity adjustment.

For the 5% 25 year bond:

$$\text{duration} = 14.21$$
$$\Delta y = 0.02$$

approximate percentage price change based on duration
$$= -14.21 \times 0.02 \times 100 = -28.38\%$$

convexity adjustment $= 5.67\%$

Therefore,

Yield change	+200 bps
Estimated change using duration	−28.38%
Convexity adjustment	5.67%
Total estimated percentage price change	−22.71%

Yield change	−200 bps
Estimated change using duration	28.38%
Convexity adjustment	5.67%
Total estimated percentage price change	34.05%

For the 8% 25-year bond:

$$\text{duration} = 12.94$$
$$\Delta y = 0.02$$

approximate percentage price change based on duration
$$= -12.94 \times 0.02 \times 100 = -25.87\%$$

convexity adjustment $= 4.88\%$

Yield change	+200 bps
Estimated change using duration	−25.87%
Convexity adjustment	4.88%
Total estimated percentage price change	−21.00%

Yield change	−200 bps
Estimated change using duration	25.87%
Convexity adjustment	4.88%
Total estimated percentage price change	30.75%

c. For a large change in rates of 200 basis points, duration with the convexity adjustment does a pretty good job of estimating the actual percentage price change, as shown below.

	duration/convexity estimate	actual change
For 5% 25-year bond		
200 bp increase	−22.71%	−23.46%
200 bp decrease	+34.05%	+35.00%
For 8% 25-year bond		
200 bp increase	−21.00%	−21.62%
200 bp decrease	+30.75%	+31.54%

17. a. The price value of a basis point is

$$\$114.1338 - \$114.0051 = \$0.1287$$

b. Using equation (2), the approximate percentage price change for a 1 basis point increase in interest rates (i.e., $\Delta y = 0.0001$) ignoring the negative sign in equation (2) is:

$$11.28 \times (0.0001) \times 100 = 0.1128\%$$

Given the initial price of 114.1338, the dollar price change estimated using duration is

$$0.1128\% \times 114.1338 = \$0.1287$$

18. Duration even after adjusting for convexity indicates that if interest rates change what the exposure of a bond or bond portfolio will be. However, to capture fully the interest rate exposure, it is necessary to know how volatile interest rates are. For example, in comparing duration of government bonds in different countries, the duration only indicates the sensitivity of the price to changes in interest rates by a given number of basis points. It does not consider the volatility of rates. In a country with little volatility in rates but where the government bonds have a high duration, just looking at duration misleads the investor as to the interest rate risk exposure.

SOLUTIONS TO PRACTICE QUESTIONS

1. a. From Exhibit 4 we know that

V_- (price at 5.9% yield) = 136.1193
V_+ (price at 6.1% yield) = 133.2472

and

$\Delta y = 0.001$
$V_0 = 134.6722$

$$\text{duration} = \frac{136.1193 - 133.2472}{2(134.6722)(0.001)} = 10.66$$

Note that this is the same value computed for duration when a 20 basis point rate shock was used. Duration is therefore the same for this bond regardless of whether the yield change used is 20 basis points or 10 basis points.

b. From Exhibit 4 we know that

V_- (price at 5.9% yield) = 101.1651
V_+ (price at 6.1% yield) = 98.8535

and

$\Delta y = 0.001$
$V_0 = 100$

$$\text{duration} = \frac{101.1651 - 98.8535}{2(100)(0.001)} = 11.56$$

2. a. The duration for this bond is 11.56. The approximate percentage price change for a 10 basis point increase in interest rates is

$$= -11.56 \times 0.0010 \times 100 = -1.156\%$$

b. The actual percentage price change from Exhibit 6 is −1.15%. Therefore the estimate is good.

c. The approximate percentage price change for a 10 basis point decrease in interest rates is

$$= -11.56 \times (-0.0010) \times 100 = 1.156\%$$

d. The actual percentage price change from Exhibit 6 is 1.17%. Therefore the estimate is good.

e. The approximate percentage price change for a 200 basis point increase in interest rates is

$$= -11.56 \times 0.02 \times 100 = -23.12\%$$

f. The actual percentage price change from Exhibit 6 is −19.79%. Therefore duration provides a poor estimate and underestimates the new price.

g. The approximate percentage price change for a 200 basis point decrease in interest rates is

$$= -11.56 \times (-0.02) \times 100 = 23.12\%$$

h. The actual percentage price change from Exhibit 6 is 27.36%. Therefore duration provides a poor estimate and underestimates the new price.

3. The convexity measure is

$$\text{convexity measure} = \frac{101.1651 + 98.8535 - 2(100)}{2(100)(0.001)^2} = 93.00$$

4.

a. For a 10 basis point increase in interest rates

Estimated change using duration	−1.16%
Convexity adjustment	0.0093%
Total estimated percentage price change	−1.15%
Actual percentage price change	−1.15%

b. For a 10 basis point decrease in interest rates

Estimated change using duration	1.16%
Convexity adjustment	0.0093%
Total estimated percentage price change	1.17%
Actual percentage price change	1.17%

c. For a 200 basis point increase in interest rates

Estimated change using duration	−23.12%
Convexity adjustment	3.72%
Total estimated percentage price change	−19.40%
Actual percentage price change	−19.79%

d. For a 200 basis point decrease in interest rates

Estimated change using duration	23.12%
Convexity adjustment	3.72%
Total estimated percentage price change	26.84%
Actual percent price change	27.36%

LEVEL II

Chapter 1

THE TERM STRUCTURE AND THE VOLATILITY OF INTEREST RATES

LEARNING OUTCOME STATEMENTS

After reading this chapter you should be able to:

- describe the different shapes that have been observed for the Treasury yield curve.
- explain what is meant by the slope of the yield curve.
- explain what is meant by a parallel and nonparallel shift in the yield curve.
- explain what is meant by a yield curve twist and change in the curve of the yield curve (i.e., butterfly shift).
- describe the factors that have been observed to drive Treasury returns and the importance of each factor.
- explain the various universes of Treasury securities that are used to construct the theoretical spot rate curve.
- identify the reasons why market participants may not want to use Treasury coupon strips to construct the spot rate curve.
- explain the theories of the term structure of interest rates (including the expectations theory and the market segmentation theory).
- explain the various forms of the expectations theory (pure expectations theory, liquidity theory, and preferred habitat theory) and the implications of each theory for the shape of the yield curve.
- interpret forward rates in the context of the theories of the term structure.
- identify two interpretations of forward rates based on arbitrage arguments.
- describe how to measure the yield curve risk of a security or a portfolio using rate duration.
- compute the yield volatility given historical yields.
- explain the issues associated with calculating yield volatility (i.e., the number of observations to use and the annualizing of daily yield volatility).
- explain the difference between historical yield volatility and implied yield volatility.
- explain how yield volatility is forecasted.

SECTION I
INTRODUCTION

At Level I we discussed the reasons why market participants pay close attention to yields on Treasury securities. We saw that an analysis of these yields is critical because they are used to derive interest rates which are used to value securities. Also, they are benchmarks used to measure the minimum yields that investors want when investing in a non-Treasury security. In Level I we distinguished between the on-the-run Treasury yield curve and the term structure of interest rates. The on-the-run Treasury yield curve shows the relationship between the yield for on-the-run Treasury issues and maturity. The term structure of interest rates is the relationship between the theoretical yield on zero-coupon Treasury securities and maturity. The yield on a zero-coupon Treasury security is called the Treasury spot rate.

At Level I (Chapter 6) we demonstrated how to derive the Treasury spot rate curve from the on-the-run Treasury issues using the method of bootstrapping and then how to obtain an arbitrage-free value for an option-free bond. In this chapter we will describe other methods to derive the Treasury spot rates. In Level I (Chapter 6), we introduced the concept of forward rates. In this chapter, we will discuss economic theories of the term structure of interest rates and the meaning of forward rates within the context of these theories.

At Level I we also mentioned the role of interest rate volatility or yield volatility in valuing securities and in measuring interest rate exposure of a bond. In the analytical chapters in Level II we will continue to see the importance of this measure. Specifically, we will see the role of interest rate volatility in valuing bonds with embedded options, valuing mortgage-backed and certain asset-backed securities, and valuing derivatives. (We will see how interest rate volatility is used in controlling the interest rate risk of a portfolio at Level III.) Consequently, in this first chapter to Level II, we will explain how interest rate volatility is estimated and the issues associated with computing this measure. Much of what we say here about interest rate volatility applies to measuring volatility in the stock market.

In the opening sections of this chapter we provide some historical information about the Treasury yield curve. In addition, we set the stage for understanding bond returns by looking at empirical evidence on some of the factors that drive returns.

SECTION II
HISTORICAL LOOK AT THE TREASURY YIELD CURVE

The yields offered on Treasury securities represent the base interest rate or minimum interest rate that investors demand if they purchase a non-Treasury security. For this reason market participants continuously monitor the yields on Treasury securities, particularly the yields of the on-the-run issues. In this chapter we will discuss the historical relationship that has been observed between the yields offered on on-the-run Treasury securities and maturity (i.e., the yield curve).

A. Shape of the Yield Curve

Exhibit 1 shows the yield for the on-the-run Treasury issues for three days: 10/24/94, 12/28/89, and 3/3/89. In Exhibit 2, this relationship is drawn for the three days whose yields are reported in Exhibit 1.

Historically, three shapes have been observed for the yield curve. Exhibit 2 shows these three shapes for the yields reported in Exhibit 1. The most common relationship is a yield curve in which the longer the maturity, the higher the yield. That is, investors are rewarded for holding longer maturity Treasuries in the form of a higher potential yield. This shape is referred to as a **normal** or **positively sloped yield curve**.

The yield curve on 10/24/94 was an example. A **flat yield curve** is one in which the yield for all maturities is approximately equal. The yield curve on 12/28/89 was an example. There have been times when the relationship between maturities and yields were such that the longer the maturity the lower the yield. Such a downward sloping yield curve is referred to as an **inverted** or a **negatively sloped yield curve**. On 3/3/89 the yield curve exhibited this characteristic.

Exhibit 1: Yields on On-the-Run Treasury Issues for Three Days

Maturity (years)	Yields on		
	10/24/94	12/28/89	3/3/89
2	6.81%	7.96%	9.48%
3	7.12	7.88	9.39
4	not issued	7.91	9.43
5	7.51	7.86	9.38
7	not issued	7.95	9.34
10	7.84	7.91	9.31
30	8.04	7.96	9.13

Source: Ryan Labs, Inc.

Exhibit 2: Treasury Yield Curve Shape on Three Days
Yields on 10/24/94 — Normal

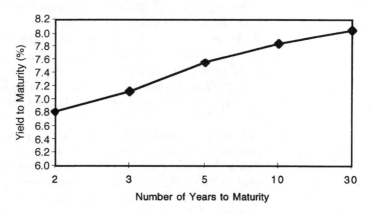

Yields on 12/28/89 — Flat

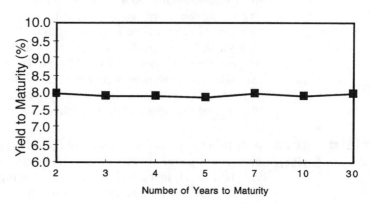

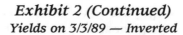

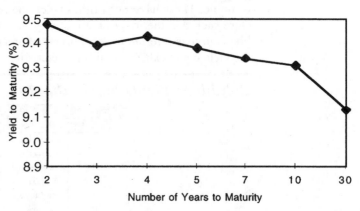

Exhibit 2 (Continued)
Yields on 3/3/89 — Inverted

Market participants talk about the difference between long-term Treasury yields and short-term Treasury yields. The spread between these yields for two maturities is referred to as the **steepness** or **slope of the yield curve**. There is no industry-wide accepted definition of the maturity used for the long-end and the maturity for the short-end of the yield curve. Some market participants define the slope of the yield curve as the difference between the 30-year yield and the 3-month yield — that is, the difference between the longest and shortest Treasury securities issued. Other market participants define the slope of the yield curve as the difference between the 30-year yield and the 2-year yield.

The slope of the yield curve varies over time. For example, over the period 1989 to 1999, the slope of the yield curve as measured by the difference between the 30-year Treasury yield and the 2-year Treasury yield was steepest at 348 basis points in September and October 1992. It was negative — that is, the 2-year Treasury yield was greater than the 30-year Treasury yield — for most of 1989. In March 1989, the 2-year Treasury yield exceeded the 30-year Treasury yield by 51 basis points (i.e., the slope of the yield curve was −51 basis points).

Market participants sometimes break the yield curve down into a short end and long end and look at the slope of the short end and long end of the yield curve. It is common for market participants to refer to the short end of the yield curve as up to the 10-year maturity and the long as from the 10-year maturity to the 30-year maturity. Using the 2-year as the shortest maturity, the slope of the short end of the yield curve is then the difference between the 10-year Treasury yield and the 2-year Treasury yield. The slope of the long end of the yield curve is the difference between the 30-year Treasury yield and the 10-year Treasury yield. Historically, the long end of the yield curve has been flatter than the short-end of the yield curve. For example, in October 1992 when the slope of the yield curve was the greatest at 348 basis points, the slope of the long end of the yield curve was only 95 basis points.

B. Yield Curve Shifts

A shift in the yield curve refers to the relative change in the yield for each Treasury maturity. A **parallel shift in the yield curve** refers to a shift in which the change in the yield for all maturities is the same. A **nonparallel shift in the yield curve** means that the yield for all maturities does not change by the same number of basis points.

Historically, two types of nonparallel yield curve shifts have been observed: (1) a twist in the slope of the yield curve and (2) a change in the humpedness or curvature of the yield curve. All of these shifts are graphically portrayed in Exhibit 3. A **twist in the slope of the yield curve** refers to a flattening or steepening of the yield curve. A **flattening of the yield curve** means that the slope of the yield curve (i.e., the spread between the yield on a long-term and short-term Treasury) has decreased; a **steepening of the yield curve** means that the slope of the yield curve has increased. This is depicted in panel b of Exhibit 3.

The other type of nonparallel shift is a change in the curvature or humpedness of the yield curve. This type of shift involves the relative movement of yields at the short maturity and long maturity sectors of the yield curve relative to the intermediate maturity sector of the yield curve. Such nonparallel shifts in the yield curve that change its curvature are referred to as **butterfly shifts**. The reason is that the three maturity sectors (short, intermediate, and long) can be viewed as three parts of a butterfly. Specifically, the intermediate maturity sector is viewed as the body of the butterfly and the short maturity and long maturity sectors are viewed as the wings of the butterfly.

A **positive butterfly** means that the yield curve becomes less humped (i.e., has less curvature). This means that if yields increase, for example, the yields in the short maturity and long maturity sectors increase more than the yields in the intermediate maturity sector. If yields decrease, the yields in the short and long maturity sectors decrease less than the intermediate maturity sector. A **negative butterfly** means the yield curve becomes more humped (i.e., has more curvature). So, if yields increase, for example, yields in the intermediate maturity sector will increase more than yields in the short maturity and long maturity sectors. If, instead, yields decrease, a negative butterfly occurs when yields in the intermediate maturity sector decrease less than the short maturity and long maturity sectors. Butterfly shifts are depicted in panel c of Exhibit 3.

Historically, these three types of shifts in the yield curve have not been found to be independent. The two most common types of shifts have been (1) a downward shift in the yield curve combined with a steepening of the yield curve and (2) an upward shift in the yield curve combined with a flattening of the yield curve. Positive butterfly shifts tend to be associated with an upward shift in yields and negative butterfly shifts with a downward shift in yields.

SECTION III TREASURY RETURNS RESULTING FROM YIELD-CURVE MOVEMENTS

As we discussed in Level I (Chapter 6), a yield measure is a promised return if certain assumptions are satisfied. As explained in Chapter 6, the total return is a more appropriate measure of the potential return from investing in a Treasury security. The potential return for a short investment horizon depends critically on how interest rates change; that is, it is a function of how the yield curve changes.

There have been several published and unpublished studies of how changes in the shape of the yield curve affect the total return on Treasury securities. The first such study by two researchers at Goldman Sachs (Robert Litterman and José Scheinkman) was published in 1991.[1] The results reported in more recent studies support the findings of the Litterman-Scheinkman study so we will just discuss their findings. Litterman and Scheinkman found that three factors explained historical returns. The first factor was changes in the level of rates, the second factor was changes in the slope of the yield curve, and the third factor was changes in the curvature of the yield curve.

---

[1] Robert Litterman and José Scheinkman, "Common Factors Affecting Bond Returns," *Journal of Fixed Income* (June 1991), pp. 54-61.

Exhibit 3: Types of Yield Curve Shifts
(a) Parallel shifts

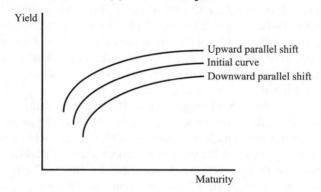

(b) Nonparallel shifts: Twists (steepening and flattening)

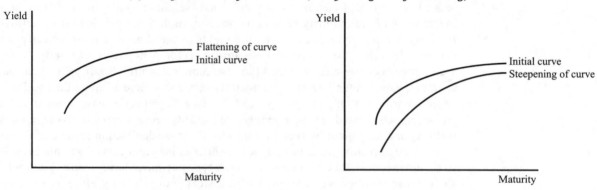

(c) Nonparallel shifts: Butterfly shifts (positive and negative)

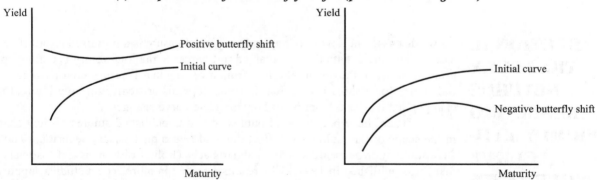

Exhibit 4: Factors Explaining Treasury Returns

Factor 1: Changes in the level of interest rates
Factor 2: Changes in the yield curve slope
Factor 3: Changes in the curvature of the yield curve

Zero Coupon Maturity	Variance of Total Returns Explained	Proportion of Total Explained Variance Accounted for by		
		Factor 1 Level	Factor 2 Slope	Factor 3 Curvature
6 months	99.5%	79.5%	17.2%	3.3%
1 year	99.4	89.7	10.1	0.2
2 years	98.2	93.4	2.4	4.2
5 years	98.8	98.2	1.1	0.7
8 years	98.7	95.4	4.6	0.0
10 years	98.8	92.9	6.9	0.2
14 years	98.4	86.2	11.5	2.2
18 years	95.3	80.5	14.3	5.2
Average	98.4	89.5	8.5	2.0

Source: Adapted from Robert Litterman and José Scheinkman, "Common Factors Affecting Bond Returns," *Journal of Fixed Income* (June 1991), p. 58. This copyrighted material is reprinted from Institutional Investor, Inc., *Journal of Fixed Income*, 488 Madison Avenue, New York, New York 10022.

Litterman and Scheinkman employed regression analysis to determine the relative contribution of these three factors in explaining the returns on zero-coupon Treasury securities of different maturities. Exhibit 4 summarizes their results. The second column of the exhibit shows the coefficient of determination, popularly referred to as the "R^2," for each zero-coupon maturity. In general, the R^2 measures the percentage of the variance in the dependent variable (i.e., the total return on the zero-coupon Treasury security) explained by the independent variables (i.e., the three factors). For example, an R^2 of 0.8 means that 80% of the variation of the return on a zero-coupon Treasury security is explained by the three factors. Therefore, 20% of the variation of the return is not explained by these three factors. The R^2 will have a value between 0% and 100%. As can be seen in the second column, the R^2 was very high for all maturities, meaning that the three factors had a very strong predictive or explanatory power.

The last three columns show the relative contribution that each of the three factors had in explaining the return on the zero-coupon Treasury security of a given maturity. For example, let's look at the 18-year zero. The second column indicates that 95% of the variance of the return in the 18-year zero is explained by the three factors. The first factor represents changes in the level of rates, holding all other factors constant (in particular, yield curve slope) and contributes about 81% of the explanatory power. This factor has the greatest explanatory power for all the maturities, averaging about 90%. The implication is that the most important factor that a manager of a Treasury portfolio should control for is exposure to changes in the level of interest rates. For this reason it is important to have a way to measure or quantify this risk. Duration is in fact the measure used to quantify exposure to a parallel shift in the yield curve.

The second factor, changes in the yield curve slope, is the second largest contributing factor. For the 18-year zero-coupon Treasury, the relative contribution is about 14.3%. The average relative contribution for all maturities is 8.5%. Thus, changes in the yield curve slope are, on average, about one tenth as significant as changes in the level of rates. While the relative contribution is only 8.5%, this can still have a significant impact on the return for a Treasury portfolio and a portfolio manager must control for this risk. We briefly explained in Level I (Chapter 2) how a manager can do this using key rate duration.

The third factor, changes in the curvature of the yield curve, contributes relatively little to explaining historical returns.

SECTION IV CONSTRUCTING THE THEORETICAL SPOT RATE CURVE FOR TREASURIES

At Level I (Chapter 5) we explained the importance of constructing a default-free theoretical spot rate curve. This curve can be constructed from the yield on Treasury securities. The Treasury issues that are candidates for inclusion are:

1. on-the-run Treasury issues
2. on-the-run Treasury issues and selected off-the-run Treasury issues
3. all Treasury coupon securities and bills
4. Treasury coupon strips

Once the securities that are to be included in the construction of the theoretical spot rate curve are selected, the methodology for constructing the curve must be determined. The methodology depends on the securities included. If Treasury coupon strips are used, the procedure is simple since the observed yields are the spot rates. If the on-the-run Treasury issues with or without selected off-the-run Treasury issues are used, then the methodology of bootstrapping is used. When *all* Treasury coupon securities and bills are used, then elaborate statistical techniques are used.

A. On-the-Run Treasury Issues

The on-the-run Treasury issues are the most recently auctioned issues of a given maturity. These issues include the 3-month, 6-month, and 1-year Treasury bills, the 2-year, 5-year, and 10-year Treasury notes, and the 30-year Treasury bond. Treasury bills are zero-coupon instruments; the notes and the bond are coupon securities.[2]

There is an observed yield for each of the on-the-run issues. For the coupon issues, these yields are not the yields used in the analysis when the issue is not trading at par. Instead, for each on-the-run coupon issue, the estimated yield necessary to make the issue trade at par is used. The resulting on-the-run yield curve is called the *par coupon curve*. The reason for using securities with a price of par is to eliminate the effect of the tax treatment for securities selling at a discount or premium.

At Level I (Chapter 6) we explained how bootstrapping is used to construct the spot rate curve. Exhibit 5 shows in table form and Exhibit 6 in graphical form the theoretical spot rate curve estimated on August 13, 1996 by applying the bootstrapping methodology to on-the-run issues. Also shown in the two exhibits are the rates based on the coupon strips. Note the significant divergence between the coupon strips and the rates generated from bootstrapping after the 6-year maturity point.

B. On-the-Run Treasury Issues and Selected Off-the-Run Treasury Issues

One of the problems with using just the on-the-run issues is the large gap between maturities, particularly after five years. To mitigate this problem, some dealers and vendors use selected off-the-run Treasury issues. Typically, the issues used are the 20-year issue and 25-year issue.[3] Given the par coupon curve including any off-the-run selected issues, the linear interpolation method described at Level I (Chapter 6) is used to fill in the gaps for the other maturities. The bootstrapping method is then used to construct the theoretical spot rate curve.

[2] At one time, the Department of the Treasury issued 3-year notes, 7-year notes, 15-year bonds, and 20-year bonds.
[3] See, for example, Philip H. Galdi and Shenglin Lu, *Analyzing Risk and Relative Value of Corporate and Government Securities*, Merrill Lynch & Co., Global Securities Research & Economics Group, Fixed Income Analytics, 1997, p. 11.

Exhibit 5: Comparison of Theoretical Annual Spot Rates Using Bootstrapping Methodology, Merrill Lynch Exponential Spline Methodology, and Coupon Strips on August 13, 1996

Years to Maturity	Bootstrapping using on-the-run issues	Bootstrapping Using On-the-Run Issues + 20-Year and 25-Year Issues	All Treasury Securities*	Coupon Strips
1	5.62	5.62	5.69	5.60
2	5.98	5.98	6.00	5.98
3	6.17	6.17	6.18	6.17
4	6.27	6.27	6.29	6.27
5	6.36	6.36	6.37	6.35
6	6.42	6.42	6.44	6.42
7	6.47	6.47	6.51	6.51
8	6.53	6.53	6.58	6.60
9	6.59	6.59	6.65	6.68
10	6.66	6.66	6.71	6.74
11	6.66	6.68	6.77	6.79
12	6.67	6.72	6.83	6.84
13	6.68	6.75	6.89	6.90
14	6.69	6.78	6.94	6.94
15	6.71	6.82	6.98	6.98
16	6.72	6.86	7.02	7.03
17	6.73	6.89	7.06	7.06
18	6.75	6.94	7.09	7.07
19	6.77	6.98	7.12	7.10
20	6.78	7.02	7.14	7.11
21	6.80	7.04	7.16	7.13
22	6.82	7.04	7.16	7.14
23	6.84	7.05	7.16	7.14
24	6.86	7.05	7.15	7.13
25	6.88	7.06	7.12	7.10
26	6.90	7.01	7.08	7.06
27	6.92	6.96	7.02	6.98
28	6.95	6.91	6.95	6.95
29	6.98	6.86	6.85	6.88
30	7.00	6.81	6.74	6.85**

* The methodology used by Merrill Lynch for obtaining the theoretical spot rates when all Treasury securities are used is exponential spline fitting. The model is described in Arnold Shapiro, *et al.*, *Merrill Lynch Exponential Spline Model*, Merrill Lynch & Co., Global Securities Research & Economics Group, Fixed Income Analytics, August 8, 1994.
** 29.5 yrs

Source: The data points were provided by Philip H. Galdi, First Vice President at Merrill Lynch, and Shenglin Lu, Vice President at Merrill Lynch. These data were used to construct the spot rate curves in Exhibits 4 and 5 in this chapter and which appear in Philip H. Galdi and Shenglin Lu, *Analyzing Risk and Relative Value of Corporate and Government Securities*, Merrill Lynch & Co., Global Securities Research & Economics Group, Fixed Income Analytics, 1997. Copyright ©1997 Merrill Lynch, Pierce, Fenner & Smith Incorporated.

Exhibit 6: Comparison of Theoretical Spot Rates Using the Bootstrapping Methodology and Based on Coupon Strips (August 13, 1996)

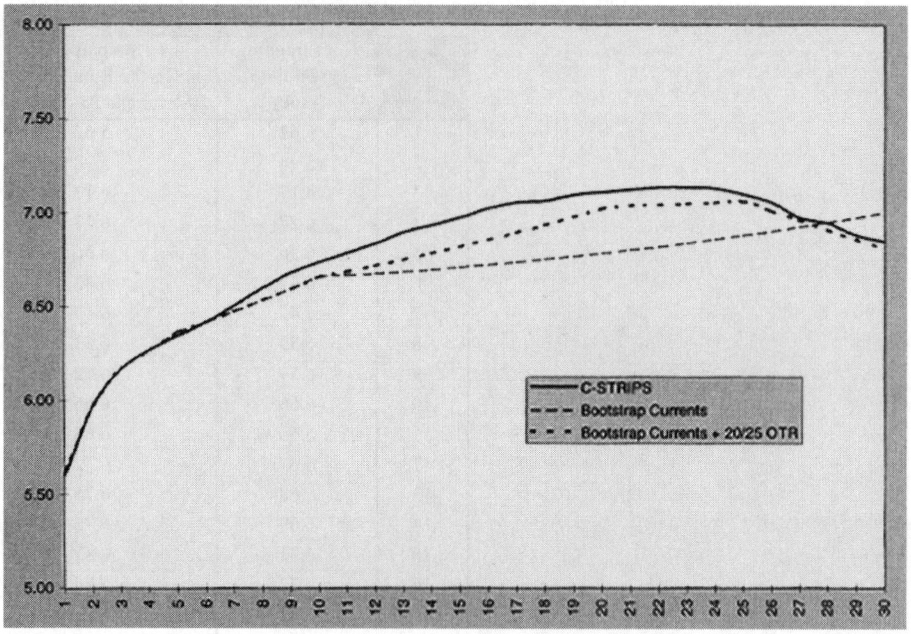

Source: Figure 7 in Philip H. Galdi and Shenglin Lu, *Analyzing Risk and Relative Value of Corporate and Government Securities*, Merrill Lynch & Co., Global Securities Research & Economics Group, Fixed Income Analytics, 1997, p. 11. Copyright ©1997 Merrill Lynch, Pierce, Fenner & Smith Incorporated.

Exhibit 5 compares in table form the theoretical annual spot rates on August 13, 1996 using the bootstrapping methodology applied to (1) the on-run-issues and (2) the on-the-run issues plus the 20-year and 25-year off-the-run issues.[4] The exhibit also includes the coupon strip rates. Exhibit 6 compares the first two curves to the coupon strips curve. Notice how much closer the theoretical spot rate curve comes to the coupon strips curve when the on-the-run issues are supplemented with the 20-year and 25-year off-the-run issues.

C. All Treasury Coupon Securities and Bills

Using only on-the-run issues, even when extended to include a few off-the-run issues, fails to recognize the information embodied in Treasury prices that are not included in the analysis. Thus, it is argued that it is more appropriate to use all Treasury coupon securities and bills to construct the theoretical spot rate curve. Some practitioners do not use callable Treasury bonds. Moreover, a common practice is to filter the Treasury securities universe to eliminate securities that are on special in the repo market.[5]

When all coupon securities and bills are used, methodologies must be employed to construct the theoretical spot rate curve rather than bootstrapping since there may be more than one yield for each maturity. There are various methodologies for fitting a curve to the points when all the Treasury securities are used. The method-

---

[4] At Level I (Chapter 6) we saw how to compute the yields for maturities in the gap between maturity levels using linear interpolation.

[5] This is explained in Chapter 6.

ologies make an adjustment for the effect of taxes and for call features on U.S. Treasury bonds.[6] A discussion of the various methodologies is beyond the scope this book.

The drawback of using all Treasury securities is that real-time information is not available for all issues.[7] To deal with this problem, Merrill Lynch, for example, has developed a real time spline model. This model uses only the on-the-run issues (and in some cases the previous on-the-run issues).

Exhibit 5 provides a comparison of the theoretical spot rate constructed on August 13, 1996 using coupon strips with those of the exponential spline methodology and the bootstrapping methodology. Exhibit 7 compares in graphical form the spot rates constructed from bootstrapping the on-the-run issues plus the 20-year and 25-year off-the-run issues, the Merrill Lynch spline methodology, and the coupon strips. Notice how close the spot rates based on the spline methodology are to the coupon strips, particularly after the 6-year maturity point.

D. Treasury Coupon Strips

In Level I (Chapter 3) we described Treasury coupon strips. It would seem logical that the observed yield on strips could be used to construct an actual spot rate curve rather than go through the procedures we described above. There are three problems with using the observed rates on Treasury strips. First, the liquidity of the strips market is not as great as that of the Treasury coupon market. Thus, the observed rates on strips reflect a premium for liquidity.

Exhibit 7: Comparison of Theoretical Spot Rates Using the Bootstrapping Methodology, the Merrill Lynch Exponential Spline Methodology, and Based on Coupon Strips (August 13, 1996)

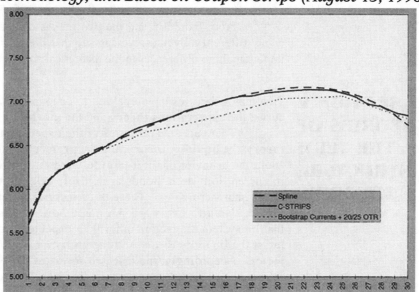

Source: Figure 8 in Philip H. Galdi and Shenglin Lu, *Analyzing Risk and Relative Value of Corporate and Government Securities*, Merrill Lynch & Co., Global Securities Research & Economics Group, Fixed Income Analytics, 1997, p. 12. Copyright ©1997 Merrill Lynch, Pierce, Fenner & Smith Incorporated.

[6] See, Oldrich A. Vasicek and H. Gifford Fong, "Term Structure Modeling Using Exponential Splines," *Journal of Finance* (May 1982), pp. 339-358. For an example of a dealer model, see Arnold Shapiro *et al.*, *Merrill Lynch Exponential Spline Model,* Merrill Lynch & Co., Global Securities Research & Economics Group, Fixed Income Analytics, August 8, 1994.

[7] Galdi and Lu, *Analyzing Risk and Relative Value of Corporate and Government Securities*, p. 11.

Exhibit 8: Term Structure Theories

```
                    ┌─────────────────────────┐              ┌──────────────┐
                    │   Expectations Theory   │              │    Market    │
                    └─────────────────────────┘              │ Segmentation │
                      ╱                 ╲                     │    Theory    │
                     ╱                   ╲                    └──────────────┘
        ┌──────────────────────┐   ┌──────────────────┐
        │ Pure Expectations    │   │ Biased Expectations │
        │ Theory               │   │ Theory              │
        │ Two Interpretations  │   └──────────────────┘
        └──────────────────────┘        ╱        ╲
           ╱            ╲               ╱          ╲
    ┌────────────┐ ┌────────────┐ ┌──────────┐ ┌──────────┐
    │ Broadest   │ │ Local      │ │ Liquidity│ │ Preferred│
    │Interpretation│ │ Expectations│ │ Theory  │ │ Habitat  │
    └────────────┘ └────────────┘ └──────────┘ │ Theory   │
                                                └──────────┘
```

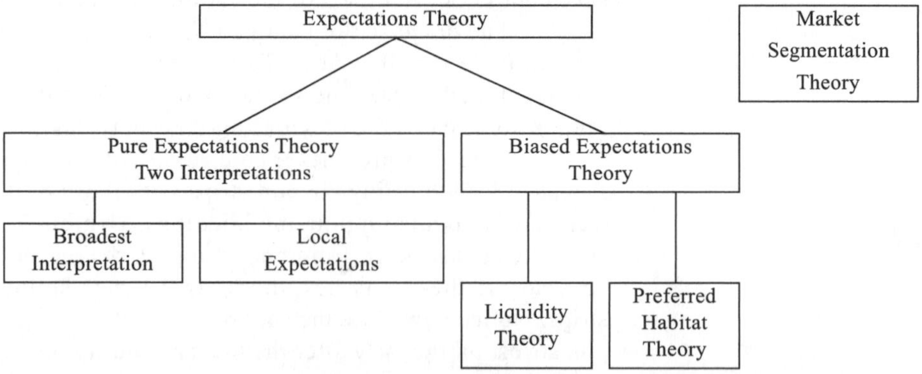

Second, the tax treatment of strips is different from that of Treasury coupon securities. Specifically, the accrued interest on strips is taxed even though no cash is received by the investor. Thus they are negative cash flow securities to taxable entities, and, as a result, their yield reflects this tax disadvantage.

Finally, there are maturity sectors where non-U.S. investors find it advantageous to trade off yield for tax advantages associated with a strip. Specifically, certain foreign tax authorities allow their citizens to treat the difference between the maturity value and the purchase price as a capital gain and tax this gain at a favorable tax rate. Some will grant this favorable treatment only when the strip is created from the principal rather than the coupon. For this reason, those who use Treasury strips to represent theoretical spot rates restrict the issues included to coupon strips.

From Exhibit 5 and the two graphs comparing the theoretical spot rate curves using different universes, we can see that there will be differences in the curve. How important those differences in the theoretical spot rates are depends on the application.

SECTION V THEORIES OF THE TERM STRUCTURE THEORIES

Two major theories have evolved to account for these observed shapes of the yield curve: the **expectations theory** and the **market segmentation theory.**

There are several forms of the expectations theory — the **pure expectations theory**, the **liquidity theory**, and the **preferred habitat theory**. All share a hypothesis about the behavior of short-term forward rates and also assume that the forward rates in current long-term bonds are closely related to the market's expectations about future short-term rates.[8] These three theories differ, however, on whether or not other factors also affect forward rates, and how. The pure expectations theory postulates that no systematic factors other than expected future short-term rates affect forward rates; the liquidity theory and the preferred habitat theory assert that there are other factors. Accordingly, the last two forms of the expectations theory are sometimes referred to as **biased expectations theories**. The relationship among the various theories is described below and summarized in Exhibit 8.

A. The Pure Expectations Theory

According to the pure expectations theory, forward rates exclusively represent expected future spot rates. Thus, the entire term structure at a given time reflects the market's current expectations of the family of future short-term rates. Under this view, a rising term structure must indicate that the market expects short-term rates to rise

---

[8] For a review of forward rates, see Level I (Chapter 6).

throughout the relevant future. Similarly, a flat term structure reflects an expectation that future short-term rates will be mostly constant, while a falling term structure must reflect an expectation that future short-term rates will decline.

1. Drawbacks of the Theory

The pure expectations theory suffers from one shortcoming, which, qualitatively, is quite serious. It neglects the risks inherent in investing in bonds. If forward rates were perfect predictors of future interest rates, then the future prices of bonds would be known with certainty. The return over any investment period would be certain and independent of the maturity of the instrument acquired. However, with the uncertainty about future interest rates and, therefore, about future prices of bonds, these instruments become risky investments in the sense that the return over some investment horizon is unknown.

There are two risks that cause uncertainty about the return over some investment horizon. The first is the uncertainty about the price of the bond at the end of the investment horizon. For example, an investor who plans to invest for five years might consider the following three investment alternatives:

Alternative 1: Invest in a 5-year zero-coupon bond and hold it for five years.
Alternative 2: Invest in a 12-year zero-coupon bond and sell it at the end of five years.
Alternative 3: Invest in a 30-year zero-coupon bond and sell it at the end of five years.

The return that will be realized in Alternatives 2 and 3 is not known because the price of each of these bonds at the end of five years is unknown. In the case of the 12-year bond, the price will depend on the yield on 7-year bonds five years from now; and the price of the 30-year bond will depend on the yield on 25-year bonds five years from now. Since forward rates implied in the current term structure for a 7-year bond five years from now and a 25-year bond five years from now are not perfect predictors of the actual future rates, there is uncertainty about the price for both bonds five years from now. Thus, there is interest rate risk; that is, the price of the bond may be lower than currently expected at the end of the investment horizon due to an increase in interest rates. As explained in Level I, an important feature of interest rate risk is that it increases with the length of the bond's maturity.

The second risk involves the uncertainty about the rate at which the proceeds from a bond that matures prior to the end of the investment horizon can be reinvested until the maturity date, that is, reinvestment risk. For example, an investor who plans to invest for five years might consider the following three alternative investments:

Alternative 1: Invest in a 5-year zero-coupon bond and hold it for five years.
Alternative 2: Invest in a 6-month zero-coupon instrument and, when it matures, reinvest the proceeds in 6-month zero-coupon instruments over the entire 5-year investment horizon.
Alternative 3: Invest in a 2-year zero-coupon bond and, when it matures, reinvest the proceeds in a 3-year zero-coupon bond.

The risk for Alternatives 2 and 3 is that the return over the 5-year investment horizon is unknown because rates at which the proceeds can be reinvested until the end of the investment horizon are unknown.

2. Interpretations of the Theory

There are several interpretations of the pure expectations theory that have been put forth by economists. These interpretations are not exact equivalents nor are they consistent with each other, in large part because they offer different treatments of the two risks associated with realizing a return that we have just explained.[9]

a. Broadest Interpretation

The broadest interpretation of the pure expectations theory suggests that investors expect the return for any investment horizon to be the same, regardless of the maturity strategy selected.[10] For example, consider an investor who has a 6-month investment horizon. According to this theory, it makes no difference if a 5-year, 12-year, or 30-year bond is purchased and held for five years since the investor expects the return from all three bonds to be the same over the 6-month investment horizon. A major criticism of this very broad interpretation of the theory is that, because of price risk associated with investing in bonds with a maturity greater than the investment horizon, the expected returns from these three very different investments should differ in significant ways.[11]

b. Local Expectations Form of the Pure Expectations Theory

A second interpretation, referred to as the **local expectations form of the pure expectations theory**, suggests that the return will be the same over a short-term investment horizon starting today. For example, if an investor has a 6-month investment horizon, buying a 1-year, 5-year or 10-year bond will produce the same 6-month return.

To illustrate this, we will use the hypothetical yield curve shown in Exhibit 9. At Level I (Chapter 6), we used the yield curve in Exhibit 9 to show how to compute spot rates and forward rates. Exhibit 10 shows all the 6-month forward rates. We will focus on the 1-year, 5-year, and 10-year issues.

Our objective is to look at what happens to the total return over a 6-month investment horizon for the 1-year, 5-year, and 10-year issues if all the 6-month forward rates are realized. Look first at panel a in Exhibit 11. This shows the total return for the 1-year issue. At the end of 6 months, this issue is a 6-month issue. The 6-month forward rate is 3.6%. This means that if the forward rate is realized, the 6-month yield 6 months from now will be 3.6%. Given a 6-month issue that must offer a yield of 3.6% (the 6-month forward rate), the price of this issue will decline from 100 (today) to 99.85265 six months from now. The price must decline because if the 6-month forward rate is realized 6 months from now, the yield increases from 3.3% to 3.6%. The total dollars realized over the 6 months are coupon interest adjusted for the decline in the price. The total return for the 6 months is 3%.

What the local expectations theory asserts is that over the 6-month investment horizon even the 5-year and the 10-year issues will generate a total return of 3% if forward rates are realized. Panels b and c show this to be the case. We need only explain the computation for one of the two issues. Let's use the 5-year issue. The 6-month forward rates are shown in the third column of panel b. Now we apply a few principles discussed at Level I (Chapter 6). We demonstrated that to value a security each cash flow should be discounted at the spot rate with the same maturity. We also

---

[9] These formulations are summarized by John Cox, Jonathan Ingersoll, Jr., and Stephen Ross, "A Re-examination of Traditional Hypotheses About the Term Structure of Interest Rates," *Journal of Finance* (September 1981), pp. 769-799.

[10] F. Lutz, "The Structure of Interest Rates," *Quarterly Journal of Economics* (1940-41), pp. 36-63.

[11] Cox, Ingersoll and Ross, pp. 774-775.

demonstrated that 6-month forward rates can also be used to value the cash flows of a security and that the results will be identical using the forward rates to value a security. For example, consider the cash flow in period 3 for the 5-year issue. The cash flow is $2.60. The 6-month forward rates are 3.6%, 3.92%, and 5.15%. These are annual rates. So, half these rates are 1.8%, 1.96%, and 2.575%. The present value of $2.60 using the 6-month forward is:

$$\frac{\$2.60}{(1.018)(1.0196)(1.02575)} = \$2.44205$$

This is the present value shown in the third column of panel b. In a similar manner, all of the other present values in the third column are computed. The arbitrage-free value for this 5-year issue 6 months from now (when it is a 4.5-year issue) is 98.89954. The total return (taking into account the coupon interest and the loss due to the decline in price from 100) is 3%.

Exhibit 9: Hypothetical Treasury Par Yield Curve

Period	Years	Annual Yield to Maturity (BEY) (%)[*]	Price	Spot Rate (BEY) (%)[*]
1	0.5	3.00	—	3.0000
2	1.0	3.30	—	3.3000
3	1.5	3.50	100.00	3.5053
4	2.0	3.90	100.00	3.9164
5	2.5	4.40	100.00	4.4376
6	3.0	4.70	100.00	4.7520
7	3.5	4.90	100.00	4.9622
8	4.0	5.00	100.00	5.0650
9	4.5	5.10	100.00	5.1701
10	5.0	5.20	100.00	5.2772
11	5.5	5.30	100.00	5.3864
12	6.0	5.40	100.00	5.4976
13	6.5	5.50	100.00	5.6108
14	7.0	5.55	100.00	5.6643
15	7.5	5.60	100.00	5.7193
16	8.0	5.65	100.00	5.7755
17	8.5	5.70	100.00	5.8331
18	9.0	5.80	100.00	5.9584
19	9.5	5.90	100.00	6.0863
20	10.0	6.00	100.00	6.2169

[*] The yield to maturity and the spot rate are annual rates. They are reported as bond-equivalent yields. To obtain the semiannual yield or rate, one half the annual yield or annual rate is used.

Exhibit 10: Six-Month Forward Rates: The Short-Term Forward Rate Curve (Annualized Rates on a Bond-Equivalent Basis)

Notation	Forward Rate	Notation	Forward Rate
$_1f_0$	3.00	$_1f_{10}$	6.48
$_1f_1$	3.60	$_1f_{11}$	6.72
$_1f_2$	3.92	$_1f_{12}$	6.97
$_1f_3$	5.15	$_1f_{13}$	6.36
$_1f_4$	6.54	$_1f_{14}$	6.49
$_1f_5$	6.33	$_1f_{15}$	6.62
$_1f_6$	6.23	$_1f_{16}$	6.76
$_1f_7$	5.79	$_1f_{17}$	8.10
$_1f_8$	6.01	$_1f_{18}$	8.40
$_1f_9$	6.24	$_1f_{19}$	8.72

Exhibit 11: Total Return Over 6-Month Investment Horizon if 6-Month Forward Rates are Realized

a: Total return on 1-year issue if forward rates are realized

Period	Cash flow ($)	Six-month forward rate (%)	Price at horizon ($)
1	101.650	3.60	99.85265
Price at horizon: 99.85265	Total proceeds: 101.5027		
Coupon: 1.65	Total return: 3.00%		

b: Total return on 5-year issue if forward rates are realized

Period	Cash flows ($)	Six-month forward rate (%)	Present value ($)
1	2.600	3.60	2.55403
2	2.600	3.92	2.50493
3	2.600	5.15	2.44205
4	2.600	6.54	2.36472
5	2.600	6.33	2.29217
6	2.600	6.23	2.22293
7	2.600	5.79	2.16039
8	2.600	6.01	2.09736
9	102.600	6.24	80.26096
		Total:	98.89954
Price at horizon: 98.89954	Total proceeds: 101.4995		
Coupon: 2.60	Total return: 3.00%		

c: Total return on 10-year issue if forward rates are realized

Period	Cash flows ($)	Six-month forward rate (%)	Present value ($)
1	3.000	3.60	2.94695
2	3.000	3.92	2.89030
3	3.000	5.15	2.81775
4	3.000	6.54	2.72853
5	3.000	6.33	2.64482
6	3.000	6.23	2.56492
7	3.000	5.79	2.49275
8	3.000	6.01	2.42003
9	3.000	6.24	2.34681
10	3.000	6.48	2.27316
11	3.000	6.72	2.19927
12	3.000	6.97	2.12520
13	3.000	6.36	2.05970
14	3.000	6.49	1.99497
15	3.000	6.62	1.93105
16	3.000	6.76	1.86791
17	3.000	8.10	1.79521
18	3.000	8.40	1.72285
19	103.000	8.72	56.67989
		Total:	98.50208
Price at horizon: 98.50208	Total proceeds: 101.5021		
Coupon: 3.00	Total return: 3.00%		

Thus, if the 6-month forward rates are realized, all three issues provide a short-term (6-month) return of 3%. It has been demonstrated that the local expectations formulation, which is narrow in scope, is the only interpretation of the pure expectations theory that can be sustained in equilibrium.[12]

c. Forward Rates and Market Consensus

We first introduced forward rates at Level I (Chapter 6). We saw how various types of forward rates can be computed. That is, we saw how to compute the forward rate for any length of time beginning at any future period of time. So, it is possible to compute the 2-year forward rate beginning 5 years from now or the 3-year forward rate beginning 8 years from now. We showed how, using arbitrage arguments, forward rates can be derived from spot rates.

At Level I, no interpretation was given to the forward rates. The focus was just on how to compute them from spot rates based on arbitrage arguments. Let's provide two interpretations now with a simple illustration. Suppose that an investor has a 1-year investment horizon and has a choice of investing in either a 1-year Treasury bill or a 6-month Treasury bill and rolling over the proceeds from the maturing 6-month issue in another 6-month Treasury bill. Since the Treasury bills are zero-coupon securities, the rates on them are spot rates and can be used to compute the 6-month forward rate six months from now. For example, if the 6-month Treasury bill rate is 5% and the 1-year Treasury bill rate is 5.6%, then the 6-month forward rate six months from now is 6.2%. To verify this, suppose an investor invests $100 in a 1-year investment. The $100 investment in a zero-coupon instrument will grow at a rate of 2.8% (one half 5.6%) for two 6-month periods to:

$$\$100 \, (1.028)^2 = \$105.68$$

If $100 is invested in a six month zero-coupon instrument at 2.5% (one-half 5%) and the proceeds reinvested at the 6-month forward rate of 3.1% (one-half 6.2%), the $100 will grow to:

$$\$100 \, (1.025)(1.031) = \$105.68$$

Thus, the 6-month forward rate generates the same future dollars for the $100 investment at the end of 1 year.

One interpretation of the forward rate is that it is a "break-even rate." That is, a forward rate is the rate that will make an investor indifferent between investing for the full investment horizon and part of the investment horizon and rolling over the proceeds for the balance of the investment horizon. So, in our illustration, the forward rate of 6.2% can be interpreted as the break-even rate that will make an investment in a 6-month zero-coupon instrument with a yield of 5% rolled-over into another 6-month zero-coupon instrument equal to the yield on a 1-year zero-coupon instrument with a yield of 5.6%.

Similarly, a 2-year forward rate beginning four years from now can be interpreted as the break-even rate that will make an investor indifferent between investing in (1) a 4-year zero-coupon instrument at the 4-year spot rate and rolling over the investment for two more years in a zero-coupon instrument and (2) investing in a 6-year zero-coupon instrument at the 6-year spot rate.

A second interpretation of the forward rate is that it is a rate that allows the investor to lock in a rate for some future period. For example, consider once again our

---

[12] Cox, Ingersoll, and Ross.

1-year investment. If an investor purchases this instrument rather than the 6-month instrument, the investor has locked in a 6.2% rate six months from now regardless of how interest rates change six months from now. Similarly, in the case of a 6-year investment, by investing in a 6-year zero-coupon instrument rather than a 4-year zero-coupon instrument, the investor has locked in the 2-year zero-coupon rate four years from now. That locked in rate is the 2-year forward rate four years from now. The 1-year forward rate five years from now is the rate that is locked in by buying a 6-year zero-coupon instrument rather than investing in a 5-year zero-coupon instrument and reinvesting the proceeds at the end of five years in a 1-year zero-coupon instrument.

There is another interpretation of forward rates. Proponents of the pure expectations theory argue that forward rates reflect the "market's consensus" of future interest rates. They argue that forward rates can be used to predict future interest rates. A natural question about forward rates is then how well they do at predicting future interest rates. Studies have demonstrated that forward rates do not do a good job at predicting future interest rates.[13] Then, why is it so important to understand forward rates? The reason is that forward rates indicate how an investor's expectations must differ from the "break-even rate" or the "lock-in rate" when making an investment decision.

Thus, even if a forward rate may not be realized, forward rates can be highly relevant in deciding between two alternative investments. Specifically, if an investor's expectation about a rate in the future is less than the corresponding forward rate, then he would be better off investing now to lock in the forward rate.

B. Biased Expectations Theories

There are two forms of the biased expectations theory: the liquidity theory and the preferred habitat theory.

1. The Liquidity Theory

We have explained that the drawback of the pure expectations theory is that it does not consider the risks associated with investing in bonds. We know from Level I (Chapter 7) that the interest rate risk associated with holding a bond for one period is greater the longer the maturity of a bond. (Recall that duration increases with maturity.)

Given this uncertainty, and considering that investors typically do not like uncertainty, some economists and financial analysts have suggested a different theory. This theory states that investors will hold longer-term maturities if they are offered a long-term rate higher than the average of expected future rates by a risk premium that is positively related to the term to maturity.[14] Put differently, the forward rates should reflect both interest rate expectations and a "liquidity" premium (really a risk premium), and the premium should be higher for longer maturities.

According to this theory, which is called the **liquidity theory of the term structure**, forward rates will not be an unbiased estimate of the market's expectations of future interest rates because they embody a liquidity premium. Thus, an upward-sloping yield curve may reflect expectations that future interest rates either (1) will rise, or (2) will be unchanged or even fall, but with a liquidity premium increasing fast enough with maturity so as to produce an upward-sloping yield curve. That is, any shape for either the yield curve or the term structure of interest rates can be explained by the biased expectations theory.

[13] Eugene F. Fama, "Forward Rates as Predictors of Future Spot Rates," *Journal of Financial Economics* Vol. 3, No. 4, 1976, pp. 361-377.
[14] John R. Hicks, *Value and Capital* (London: Oxford University Press, 1946), second ed., pp. 141-145.

2. The Preferred Habitat Theory

Another theory, known as the **preferred habitat theory**, also adopts the view that the term structure reflects the expectation of the future path of interest rates as well as a risk premium. However, the preferred habitat theory rejects the assertion that the risk premium must rise uniformly with maturity.[15] Proponents of the preferred habitat theory say that the latter conclusion could be accepted if all investors intend to liquidate their investment at the shortest possible date while all borrowers are anxious to borrow long. This assumption can be rejected since institutions have holding periods dictated by the nature of their liabilities.

The preferred habitat theory asserts that if there is an imbalance between the supply and demand for funds within a given maturity range, investors and borrowers will not be reluctant to shift their investing and financing activities out of their preferred maturity sector to take advantage of any imbalance. However, to do so, investors must be induced by a yield premium in order to accept the risks associated with shifting funds out of their preferred sector. Similarly, borrowers can only be induced to raise funds in a maturity sector other than their preferred sector by a sufficient cost savings to compensate for the corresponding funding risk.

Thus, this theory proposes that the shape of the yield curve is determined by both expectations of future interest rates and a risk premium, positive or negative, to induce market participants to shift out of their preferred habitat. Clearly, according to this theory, yield curves that slope up, down, or flat are all possible.

C. Market Segmentation Theory

The **market segmentation theory** also recognizes that investors have preferred habitats dictated by the nature of their liabilities. This theory also proposes that the major reason for the shape of the yield curve lies in asset/liability management constraints (either regulatory or self-imposed) and/or creditors (borrowers) restricting their lending (financing) to specific maturity sectors.[16] However, the market segmentation theory differs from the preferred habitat theory in that it assumes that neither investors nor borrowers are willing to shift from one maturity sector to another to take advantage of opportunities arising from differences between expectations and forward rates. Thus, for the segmentation theory, the shape of the yield curve is determined by the supply of and demand for securities within each maturity sector. As with the biased expectations theory, any shape for either the yield curve or the term structure of interest rates can be explained by the theory.

SECTION VI MEASURING YIELD CURVE RISK

At Level I (Chapter 2) we introduced yield curve risk. We also explained an approach to its measurement by changing the spot rate for a particular key maturity and determining the sensitivity of a security or portfolio to this change holding the spot rate for the other key maturities constant. The sensitivity of the change in value to a particular change in spot rate is called **rate duration**. There is a rate duration for every point on the spot rate curve. Consequently, there is not one rate duration, but a vector of durations representing each maturity on the spot rate curve. The total change in value if all

---

[15] Franco Modigliani and Richard Sutch, "Innovations in Interest Rate Policy," *American Economic Review* (May 1966), pp. 178-197.

[16] This theory was suggested in J.M. Culbertson, "The Term Structure of Interest Rates," *Quarterly Journal of Economics* (November 1957), pp. 489-504.

rates change by the same number of basis points is simply the duration of a security or portfolio to a parallel shift in rates.

This approach was first suggested by Donald Chambers and Willard Carleton in 1988[17] who called it "duration vectors." Robert Reitano suggested a similar approach in a series of papers and referred to these durations as "partial durations."[18] The most popular version of this approach is that developed by Thomas Ho in 1992.[19]

Ho's approach focuses on 11 key maturities of the spot rate curve. These rate durations are called **key rate durations**. The specific maturities on the spot rate curve for which a key rate duration is measured are 3 months, 1 year, 2 years, 3 years, 5 years, 7 years, 10 years, 15 years, 20 years, 25 years, and 30 years. Changes in rates between any two key rates are calculated using a linear approximation.

The impact of any type of yield curve shift can be quantified using key rate durations. A level shift can be quantified by changing all key rates by the same number of basis points and determining, based on the corresponding key rate durations, the effect on the value of a portfolio. The impact of a steepening of the yield curve can be found by (1) decreasing the key rates at the short end of the yield curve and determining the positive change in the portfolio's value using the corresponding key rate durations, and (2) increasing the key rates at the long end of the yield curve and determining the negative change in the portfolio's value using the corresponding key rate durations.

To illustrate the key rate duration methodology, suppose that instead of a set of 11 key rates, there are only three key rates — 2 years, 16 years, and 30 years.[20] The duration of a zero-coupon security is approximately the number of years to maturity. Thus, the three key rate durations are 2, 16, and 30. Consider the following two $100 portfolios comprised of 2-year, 16-year, and 30-year issues:

Portfolio	2-year issue	16-year issue	30-year issue
I	$50	$0	$50
II	$0	$100	$0

To simplify the illustration, we are going to use only three points on the curve and the key rate durations for these three points will be denoted by $D(1)$, $D(2)$, and $D(3)$ and defined as follows:

$D(1)$ = key rate duration for the 2-year part of the curve
$D(2)$ = key rate duration for the 16-year part of the curve
$D(3)$ = key rate duration for the 30-year part of the curve

The key rate durations for the three issues and the duration are as follows:

Issue	$D(1)$	$D(2)$	$D(3)$	Duration
2-year	2	0	0	2
16-year	0	16	0	16
30-year	0	0	30	30

---

[17] Donald Chambers and Willard Carleton, "A Generalized Approach to Duration," *Research in Finance* 7(1988).

[18] See, for example, Robert R. Reitano, "Non-Parallel Yield Curve Shifts and Durational Leverage," *Journal of Portfolio Management* (Summer 1990), pp. 62-67, and "A Multivariate Approach to Duration Analysis," *ARCH* 2(1989).

[19] Thomas S.Y. Ho, "Key Rate Durations: Measures of Interest Rate Risk," *The Journal of Fixed Income* (September 1992), pp. 29-44.

[20] This is the numerical example used by Ho, "Key Rate Durations," p. 33.

A portfolio's key rate duration is the weighted average of the key rate durations of the securities in the portfolio. The key rate duration and the duration for each portfolio are calculated below:

Portfolio I
$$D(1) = (50/100) \times 2 + (0/100) \times 0 + (50/100) \times 0 = 1$$
$$D(2) = (50/100) \times 0 + (0/100) \times 16 + (50/100) \times 0 = 0$$
$$D(3) = (50/100) \times 0 + (0/100) \times 0 + (50/100) \times 30 = 15$$

Effective duration $= (50/100) \times 2 + (0/100) \times 16 + (50/100) \times 30 = 16$

Portfolio II
$$D(1) = (0/100) \times 2 + (100/100) \times 0 + (0/100) \times 0 = 0$$
$$D(2) = (0/100) \times 0 + (100/100) \times 16 + (0/100) \times 0 = 16$$
$$D(3) = (0/100) \times 0 + (100/100) \times 0 + (0/100) \times 30 = 0$$

Effective duration $= (0/100) \times 2 + (100/100) \times 16 + (0/100) \times 30 = 16$

Thus, the key rate durations differ for the two portfolios. However, the effective duration for each portfolio is the same. Despite the same duration, the performance of the two portfolios will not be the same for a nonparallel shift in the spot rates. Consider the following three scenarios:

Scenario 1: All spot rates shift down 10 basis points.
Scenario 2: The 2-year key rate shifts up 10 basis points and the 30-year rate shifts down 10 basis points.
Scenario 3: The 2-year key rate shifts down 10 basis points and the 30-year rate shifts up 10 basis points.

Let's illustrate how to compute the estimated total return based on the key rate durations for Portfolio I for scenario 1. The 2-year key rate duration [D(1)] for Portfolio I is 1. For a 100 basis point increase in the 2-year key rate, the portfolio's value will decrease by approximately 1%. For a 10 basis point increase (as assumed in scenario 1), the portfolio's value will decrease by approximately 0.1%. Now let's look at the change in the 30-year key rate in scenario 1. The 30-year key rate duration [D(3)] is 15. For a 100 basis point decrease in the 30-year key rate, the portfolio's value will increase by approximately 15%. For a 10 basis point decrease (as assumed in scenario 1), the increase in the portfolio's value will be approximately 1.5%. Consequently, for Portfolio I in scenario 1 we have:

change in portfolio's value due to 2-year key rate change	−0.1%
change in portfolio's value due to 30-year key rate change	+1.5%
change in portfolio value	+1.4%

In the same way, the total return for both portfolios can be estimated for the three scenarios. The estimated total returns are shown below:

Portfolio	Scenario 1	Scenario 2	Scenario 3
I	1.6%	1.4%	−1.4%
II	1.6%	0%	0%

Thus, only for the parallel yield curve shift (scenario 1) do the two portfolios have identical performance based on their durations.

Let's look at three actual Treasury portfolios to make the concept of key rate duration more concrete. Exhibit 12 shows three Treasury portfolios as of April 23, 1997. The first portfolio has 11 Treasury securities with approximately equal dollar amounts in each maturity. This portfolio is a **ladder portfolio**. By a ladder portfolio it is meant the distribution of securities across the maturity spectrum is roughly equal. The second portfolio is a **barbell portfolio**. A barbell portfolio is where there is considerably greater weights given to the shorter and longer maturity bonds than the intermediate maturity bonds. The third portfolio is a **bullet portfolio**. For this portfolio, the maturities of the issues included in the portfolio are concentrated in the intermediate maturity relative to the shorter and longer maturities. The duration for each Treasury portfolio is 4.7.

Exhibit 12 shows the key rate durations for each security and the key rate durations for each portfolio. The key rate duration profile for each portfolio is graphed in Exhibit 13. As can be seen, the ladder portfolio has roughly the same key rate duration for all the key maturities from year 2 on. For the barbell portfolio, the key rate durations are much greater for the 5-year and 20-year key maturities and much smaller for the other key maturities. For the bullet portfolio, the key rate duration is substantially greater for the 10-year maturity than the duration for other key maturities.

SECTION VII
YIELD
VOLATILITY
AND
MEASUREMENT

In several chapters at Level I we mentioned yield volatility but did not explain what it means nor how it is estimated. Measuring volatility is critical for two reasons. First, it is a critical input into a valuation model. We will see this in Chapters 2 and 5 when we explain how an assumption of yield volatility is needed to value bonds with embedded options and structured products. Also, in Chapter 8, we will see that the same measure is also needed in valuing some interest rate derivatives (i.e., options, caps, and floors). In addition, in measuring the interest rate risk of a position, duration alone is not sufficient. Duration simply indicates if rates change, how a security or portfolio will change in value. A key element in determining the interest rate exposure of a security or portfolio is to combine duration with yield volatility.

In this section, we look at how to measure yield volatility and discuss some techniques used to estimate it. Volatility is measured in terms of the standard deviation or variance. We will see how yield volatility as measured by the daily percentage change in yields is calculated from historical yields. We will see that there are several issues confronting an investor in measuring historical yield volatility. Then we turn to modeling and forecasting yield volatility.

A. Measuring Historical Yield Volatility

Market participants seek a measure of yield volatility. The measure used is the standard deviation or variance. Here we will see how to compute yield volatility using historical data.

The variance of a random variable using historical data is calculated using the following formula:

$$\text{variance} = \frac{\displaystyle\sum_{t=1}^{T} (X_t - \bar{X})^2}{T-1} \tag{1}$$

Exhibit 12: Key Rate and Effective Durations for Three Treasury Portfolios (April 23, 1997): Ladder, Barbell, and Bullet

LADDER PORTFOLIO

Bond	Code	Cusip	Coupon	Maturity	Description		Size	KEY RATE DURATIONS											Eff Dur
								3Mo	1yr	2yr	3yr	5yr	7yr	10yr	15yr	20yr	25yr	30yr	
1	TB	912810EW	6.000	2/15/26	TB 2/26	6.000	4,057,595	0.02	0.06	0.12	0.26	0.47	0.73	1.33	1.69	1.57	1.45	4.60	12.31
2	TN	912827X4	6.375	3/31/01	TN 3/01	6.375	11,679,547	0.01	0.06	0.11	1.79	1.45	0.00	0.00	0.00	0.00	0.00	0.00	3.42
3	TB	912810ET	7.625	2/15/25	TB 2/25	7.625	11,124,914	0.02	0.06	0.12	0.27	0.49	0.76	1.38	1.76	1.62	2.32	2.81	11.63
4	TC	912810BR	8.500	5/15/99	TC 599	8.500	2,987,478	0.06	0.00	0.00	0.00	0.00	0.00	0.00	0.00	0.00	0.00	0.00	0.06
5	TB	912810EG	8.750	8/15/20	TB 8/20	8.750	5,348,333	0.02	0.06	0.12	0.28	0.50	0.78	1.42	1.81	2.80	2.74	0.00	10.56
6	TB	912810DS	10.625	8/15/15	TB 8/15	10.625	1,944,533	0.02	0.07	0.13	0.30	0.53	0.83	1.50	3.01	2.77	0.00	0.00	9.16
7	TC	912810CM	11.750	2/15/10	TC 2/10	11.750	7,323,250	0.02	0.08	0.15	0.36	0.62	3.10	1.03	0.01	0.00	0.00	0.00	5.36
8	TC	912810DL	12.500	8/15/14	TC 8/14	12.500	1,212,780	0.02	0.07	0.14	0.33	0.59	0.91	3.19	1.86	0.01	0.00	0.00	7.13
9	TN	912820AQ	0.000	5/15/99	599	0.000	37,154,780	0.00	0.00	0.86	0.00	0.00	0.00	0.00	0.00	0.00	0.00	0.00	1.52
10	TN	912820AT	0.000	5/15/99	599	0.000	10,840,357	0.00	0.00	1.54	0.70	0.00	0.00	0.00	0.00	0.00	0.00	0.00	2.24
11	TN	912820BA	0.000	5/15/99	599	0.000	8,472,702	0.00	0.00	0.00	1.84	2.09	0.00	0.00	0.00	0.00	0.00	0.00	3.93
Total Portfolio								0.01	0.25	0.49	0.50	0.49	0.50	0.50	0.50	0.50	0.50	0.50	4.75

BARBELL PORTFOLIO

Bond	Code	Cusip	Coupon	Maturity	Description		Size	KEY RATE DURATIONS											Eff Dur
								3Mo	1yr	2yr	3yr	5yr	7yr	10yr	15yr	20yr	25yr	30yr	
1	TN	9128272P	6.625	3/31/02	3/02	6.625	86,528,320	0.12	0.06	0.12	0.34	3.62	0.00	0.00	0.00	0.00	0.00	0.00	4.14
2	TC	912810BR	8.500	5/15/99	599	8.500	69,853,088	0.07	0.00	0.00	0.00	0.00	0.00	0.00	0.00	0.00	0.00	0.00	0.07
3	TB	912810DY	8.750	5/15/17	5/17	8.750	63,761,372	0.01	0.06	0.12	0.28	0.50	0.78	1.41	1.80	4.69	0.06	0.00	9.73
Total Portfolio								0.03	0.04	0.08	0.22	1.49	0.25	0.46	0.59	1.53	0.02	0.00	4.71

BULLET PORTFOLIO

Bond	Code	Cusip	Coupon	Maturity	Description		Size	KEY RATE DURATIONS											Eff Dur
								3Mo	1yr	2yr	3yr	5yr	7yr	10yr	15yr	20yr	25yr	30yr	
1	TN	9128272H	5.875	2/15/00	2/00	5.875	2,388,518	0.01	0.05	0.52	1.94	0.00	0.00	0.00	0.00	0.00	0.00	0.00	2.53
2	TN	912827V4	6.125	9/30/00	9/00	6.125	3,949,212	0.01	0.05	0.11	2.26	0.61	0.00	0.00	0.00	0.00	0.00	0.00	3.04
3	TN	9128272J	6.250	2/15/07	2/07	6.250	26,670,542	0.02	0.06	0.11	0.25	0.45	1.00	5.20	0.00	0.00	0.00	0.00	7.08
4	TB	912810BQ	6.250	8/15/23	8/23	6.250	7,015,242	0.02	0.06	0.12	0.27	0.48	0.74	1.34	1.71	1.58	3.99	1.51	11.82
5	TN	9128272J	7.125	9/30/99	9/99	7.125	1,146,557	0.01	0.06	1.23	0.90	0.00	0.00	0.00	0.00	0.00	0.00	0.00	2.20
6	TB	912810EM	7.250	8/15/22	8/22	7.250	1,059,479	0.02	0.06	0.12	0.27	0.49	0.76	1.37	1.75	1.62	4.51	0.32	11.30
7	TB	912810DX	7.500	11/15/16	11/16	7.500	2,360,381	0.01	0.06	0.12	0.27	0.48	0.75	1.36	2.12	4.74	0.00	0.00	9.93
8	TC	912810BR	8.500	5/15/99	599	8.500	33,761,656	0.06	0.00	0.00	0.00	0.00	0.00	0.00	0.00	0.00	0.00	0.00	0.06
9	TB	222655P9	8.750	11/15/08	11/08	8.750	18,540,286	0.01	0.06	0.13	0.29	0.51	0.80	3.98	1.45	0.00	0.00	0.00	7.24
Total Portfolio								0.03	0.04	0.10	0.30	0.30	0.51	2.34	0.50	0.24	0.30	0.10	4.75

Source: BARRA

Exhibit 13: Key Rate Duration Profile for Three Treasury
Portfolios (April 23, 1997): Ladder, Barbell, and Bullet
(a) Ladder Portfolio

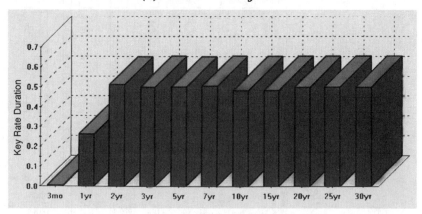

(b) Barbell Portfolio

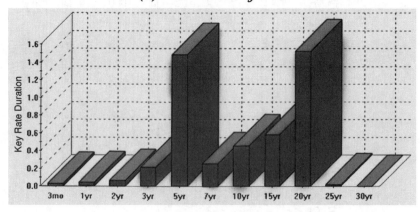

(c) Bullet Portfolio

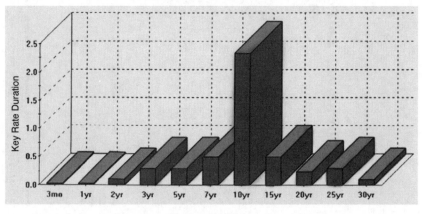

Source: BARRA

and then

$$\text{standard deviation } = \sqrt{\text{variance}}$$

where

$$X_t = \text{observation } t \text{ of variable } X$$
$$\overline{X} = \text{the sample mean for variable } X$$
$$T = \text{the number of observations in the sample}$$

Our focus is on yield volatility. More specifically, we are interested in the change in the daily yield relative to the previous day's yield. So, for example, the yield on a 30-year zero-coupon Treasury bond on 10/18/95 was 6.555% and 6.593% on 10/19/95. The relative change in yield was:

$$\frac{6.593\% - 6.555\%}{6.555\%} = 0.005797$$

This means if the yield is 6.555% on 10/18/95 and grows by 0.00597 in one day, the yield on 10/19/95 will be:

$$6.555\% \, (1.005797) = 6.593\%$$

If instead of assuming simple compounding it is assumed that there is continuous compounding, the relative change in yield can be computed as the natural logarithm of the ratio of the yield for two days. That is, the relative yield change can be computed as follows:

$$\text{Ln } (6.593\%/6.555\%) = 0.0057804$$

There is not much difference between the relative change of daily yields computed assuming simple compounding and continuous compounding. In practice, continuous compounding is used. Multiplying the natural logarithm of the ratio of the two yields by 100 scales the value to a percentage change in daily yields.

Therefore, letting y_t be the yield on day t and y_{t-1} be the yield on day $t-1$, the percentage change in yield, X_t, is found as follows:

$$X_t = 100[\text{Ln}(y_t/y_{t-1})]$$

In our example, y_t is 6.593% and y_{t-1} is 6.555%. Therefore,

$$X_t = 100[\text{Ln}(6.593/6.555)] = 0.57804$$

To illustrate how to calculate a daily standard deviation from historical data, consider the data in Exhibit 14 which show the yield on Treasury 30-year zeros from 10/8/95 to 11/12/95 in Column (3). From the 26 observations, 25 days of percentage yield changes are calculated in Column (4). The last column shows the square of the deviations of the observations from the mean. The bottom of Exhibit 14 shows the calculation of the daily mean for 25 yield changes, the variance, and the standard deviation. The daily standard deviation is 0.6360%.

Exhibit 14: Calculation of Daily Standard Deviation Based on 26 Daily Observations for 30-Year Treasury Zeros (October 8, 1995 to November 12, 1995)

(1) t	(2) Date	(3) y_t	(4) $X_t = 100[Ln(y_t/y_{t-1})]$	(5) $(X_t - \bar{X})^2$
0	08-Oct-95	6.6945		
1	09-Oct-95	6.699	0.06720	0.02599
2	10-Oct-95	6.710	0.16407	0.06660
3	11-Oct-95	6.675	−0.52297	0.18401
4	12-Oct-95	6.555	−1.81411	2.95875
5	15-Oct-95	6.583	0.42625	0.27066
6	16-Oct-95	6.569	−0.21290	0.01413
7	17-Oct-95	6.583	0.21290	0.09419
8	18-Oct-95	6.555	−0.42625	0.11038
9	19-Oct-95	6.593	0.57804	0.45164
10	22-Oct-95	6.620	0.40869	0.25270
11	23-Oct-95	6.568	−0.78860	0.48246
12	24-Oct-95	6.575	0.10652	0.04021
13	25-Oct-95	6.646	1.07406	1.36438
14	26-Oct-95	6.607	−0.58855	0.24457
15	29-Oct-95	6.612	0.07565	0.02878
16	30-Oct-95	6.575	−0.56116	0.21823
17	31-Oct-95	6.552	−0.35042	0.06575
18	01-Nov-95	6.515	−0.56631	0.22307
19	02-Nov-95	6.533	0.27590	0.13684
20	05-Nov-95	6.543	0.15295	0.06099
21	06-Nov-95	6.559	0.24424	0.11441
22	07-Nov-95	6.500	−0.90360	0.65543
23	08-Nov-95	6.546	0.70520	0.63873
24	09-Nov-95	6.589	0.65474	0.56063
25	12-Nov-95	6.539	−0.76173	0.44586
	Total		−2.35020	9.7094094

$$\text{sample mean} = \bar{X} = \frac{-2.35025}{25} = -0.09401\%$$

$$\text{variance} = \frac{9.7094094}{25-1} = 0.4045587$$

$$\text{std dev} = \sqrt{0.4045587} = 0.6360493\%$$

The daily standard deviation will vary depending on the 25 days selected. For example, when the daily yields from 8/20/95 to 9/24/95 were used to generate 25 daily percentage yield changes, the computed daily standard deviation was 0.8453%. For the 25-day period 10/8/95 to 11/12/95, the daily standard deviation is less, 0.6360%. Therefore, it is important to understand that the daily standard deviation is dependent on the period selected, a point we return to later in this chapter.

PRACTICE QUESTION 1

a. The daily yield for the each day of the 25-day period 8/20/95 to 9/24/95 are given below. Compute the daily percentage change in yield for each day assuming continuous compounding.

t	Date	y_t
0	20-Aug-95	7.17400
1	21-Aug-95	7.19400
2	22-Aug-95	7.21800
3	23-Aug-95	7.15100
4	24-Aug-95	7.02500
5	27-Aug-95	7.02400
6	28-Aug-95	7.03000
7	29-Aug-95	7.02000
8	30-Aug-95	6.96400
9	31-Aug-95	6.90400
10	03-Sep-95	6.89671
11	04-Sep-95	6.85300
12	05-Sep-95	6.87100
13	06-Sep-95	6.88300
14	07-Sep-95	6.87500
15	10-Sep-95	6.87800
16	11-Sep-95	6.80400
17	12-Sep-95	6.84300
18	13-Sep-95	6.79500
19	14-Sep-95	6.79500
20	17-Sep-95	6.85400
21	18-Sep-95	6.81000
22	19-Sep-95	6.77300
23	20-Sep-95	6.86700
24	21-Sep-95	6.88700
25	24-Sep-95	6.88100

b. Verify that the daily standard deviation for the 25-day period 8/20/95 to 9/24/95 is 0.67436%.

1. Determining the Number of Observations

In our illustration, we used 25 observations for the daily percentage change in yield. The appropriate number of observations depends on the situation at hand. For example, traders concerned with overnight positions might use the 10 most recent trading days (i.e., two weeks). A bond portfolio manager who is concerned with longer term volatility might use 25 trading days (about one month).

The selection of the number of observations can have a significant effect on the calculated daily standard deviation. This can be seen in Exhibit 15 which shows the daily standard deviation for the Treasury 30-year zero, Treasury 10-year zero, and Treasury 5-year zero using 60 days, 25 days, 10 days, and 683 days ending 11/12/95.

Exhibit 15: Comparison of Daily and Annual Volatility for a Different Number of Observations (Ending Date November 12, 1995) for Various Treasury Zeros

Number of observations	Daily standard deviation (%)	Annualized standard deviation (%)		
		250 days	260 days	365 days
Treasury 30-Year Zero				
683	0.4901505	7.75	7.90	9.36
60	0.6282858	9.93	10.13	12.00
25	0.6360493	10.06	10.26	12.15
10	0.6242041	9.87	10.06	11.93
Treasury 10-Year Zero				
683	0.7497844	11.86	12.09	14.32
60	0.7408469	11.71	11.95	14.15
25	0.7091771	11.21	11.44	13.55
10	0.7458877	11.79	12.03	14.25
Treasury 5-Year Zero				
683	1.0413025	16.46	16.79	19.89
60	0.8267317	13.07	13.33	15.79
25	0.7224093	11.42	11.65	13.80
10	0.8345784	13.20	13.46	15.94

2. Annualizing the Standard Deviation

The daily standard deviation can be annualized by multiplying it by the square root of the number of days in a year.[21] That is,

$$\text{daily standard deviation} \times \sqrt{\text{number of days in a year}}$$

Market practice varies with respect to the number of days in the year that should be used in the annualizing formula above. Some investors and traders use the number of days in the year, 365 days, to annualize the daily standard deviation. Some investors and traders use only either 250 days or 260 days to annualize. The latter is simply the number of trading days in a year based on five trading days per week for 52 weeks. The former reduces the number of trading days of 260 for 10 non-trading holidays.

Thus, in calculating an annual standard deviation, the investor must decide on:

1. the number of daily observations to use
2. the number of days in the year to use to annualize the daily standard deviation.

Exhibit 15 shows the difference in the annual standard deviation for the daily standard deviation based on a different number of observations and using 250 days, 260 days, and 365 days to annualize. Exhibit 16 compares the 25-day annual standard deviation for two different time periods for the 30-year zero, 10-year zero, and 5-year zero.

Now keep in mind that all of these decisions regarding the number of days to use in the daily standard deviation calculation, which set of days to use, and the number of days to use to annualize are not merely an academic exercise. Eventually, the daily

---

[21] For any probability distribution, it is important to assess whether the value of a random variable in one period is affected by the value that the random variable took on in a prior period. Casting this in terms of yield changes, it is important to know whether the yield today is affected by the yield in a prior period. The term *serial correlation* is used to describe the correlation between the yield in different periods. Annualizing the daily yield by multiplying the daily standard deviation by the square root of the number of days in a year assumes that serial correlation is not significant.

standard deviation will be used in either the valuation of a security or in the measurement of risk exposure. So, for example, if the 10-year yield volatility for Treasuries is being used in the valuation of a bond with an embedded option (just how we will see in the next chapter), from the second panel in Exhibit 15 a portfolio manager or trader could justify a volatility assumption of anywhere between 11.21% and 14.32%. This can lead to a significant difference in the value computed for a bond with an embedded option.

3. Interpreting the Standard Deviation

What does it mean if the annual standard deviation for the 30-year zero is 12%? It means that if the prevailing yield is 8%, then the annual standard deviation is 96 basis points (12% times 8%).

Assuming that the yield volatility is approximately normally distributed, we can use the normal distribution to construct an interval or range for what the future yield will be.[22] For example, we know that there is a 68.3% probability that the yield will be between *one* standard deviation below and above the expected value. The expected value is the prevailing yield. If the annual standard deviation is 96 basis points and the prevailing yield is 8%, then there is a 68.3% probability that the yield next year will be between 7.04% (8% minus 96 basis points) and 8.96% (8% plus 96 basis points). For *three* standard deviations below and above the prevailing yield, there is a 99.7% probability that the yield next year will be in this interval. Using the numbers above, three standard deviations is 288 basis points (3 times 96 basis points). The interval is then 5.12% (8% minus 288 basis points) and 10.88% (8% plus 288 basis points).

The interval or range constructed is called a "confidence interval."[23] Our first interval of 7.04% to 8.96% is a 68.3% confidence interval. Our second interval of 5.12% to 10.88% is a 99.7% confidence interval. A confidence interval with any probability can be constructed.

B. Historical versus Implied Volatility

Market participants estimate yield volatility in one of two ways. The first way is by estimating historical yield volatility. This is the method that we have thus far described in this chapter. The resulting volatility is called **historical volatility**. The second way is to estimate yield volatility based on the observed prices of interest rate options and caps. Yield volatility calculated using this approach is called **implied volatility**.

Exhibit 16: Comparison of Daily Standard Deviation Calculated for Two 25-Day Periods

Dates		Daily standard deviation(%)	Annualized standard deviation(%)		
From	To		250 days	260 days	365 days
Treasury 30-Year Zero					
10/8/95	11/12/95	0.6360493	10.06	10.26	12.15
8/20/95	9/24/95	0.8452714	13.36	13.63	16.15
Treasury 10-Year Zero					
10/8/95	11/12/95	0.7091771	11.21	11.44	13.55
8/20/95	9/24/95	0.9044855	14.30	14.58	17.28
Treasury 5-Year Zero					
10/8/95	11/12/95	0.7224093	11.42	11.65	13.80
8/20/95	9/24/95	0.8145416	12.88	13.13	15.56

[22] See Chapter 4 in Richard A. DeFusco and David E. Runkle, *Quantitative Methods for Investment Analysis* (Charlottesville, VA: Association for Investment Management and Research, 2000).

[23] See Chapter 6 in DeFusco and Runkle, *Quantitative Methods for Investment Analysis*.

The implied volatility is based on some option pricing model. As will be explained in Chapter 8, one of the inputs to any option pricing model in which the underlying is a Treasury security or Treasury futures contract is expected yield volatility. If the observed price of an option is assumed to be the fair price and the option pricing model is assumed to be the model that would generate that fair price, then the implied yield volatility is the yield volatility that, when used as an input into the option pricing model, would produce the observed option price.

There are several problems with using implied volatility. First, it is assumed the option pricing model is correct. Second, option pricing models typically assume that volatility is constant over the life of the option. Therefore, interpreting an implied volatility becomes difficult.[24]

C. Forecasting Yield Volatility

As can be seen, the yield volatility as measured by the standard deviation can vary based on the time period selected and the number of observations. Now we turn to the issue of forecasting yield volatility. There are several methods. Before describing these methods, let's address the question of what mean should be used in the calculation of the forecasted standard deviation.

Suppose at the end of 10/24/95 a trader was interested in a forecast for volatility using the 10 most recent days of trading and updating that forecast at the end of each trading day. What mean value should be used?

The trader can calculate a 10-day moving average of the daily percentage yield change. Exhibit 14 shows the daily percentage change in yield for the Treasury 30-year zero from 10/9/95 to 11/12/95. To calculate a moving average of the daily percentage yield change on 10/24/95, the trader would use the 10 trading days from 10/11/95 to 10/24/95. At the end of 10/25/95, the trader will calculate the 10-day average by using the percentage yield change on 10/25/95 and would exclude the percentage yield change on 10/11/95. That is, the trader will use the 10 trading days from 10/12/95 to 10/25/95.

Exhibit 17 shows the 10-day moving average calculated from 10/24/95 to 11/12/95. Notice the considerable variation over this period. The 10-day moving average ranged from −0.20324% to 0.07902%. For the period from 4/15/93 to 11/12/95, the 10-day moving average ranged from −0.61705% to 0.60298%.

Thus far, it is assumed that the moving average is the appropriate value to use for the expected value of the change in yield. However, there are theoretical arguments that suggest it is more appropriate to assume that the expected value of the change in yield will be zero.[25] That is, in the equation for the variance given by equation (1), instead of using for $\overline{X}$ the moving average, the value of zero is used. If zero is substituted into equation (1), the equation for the variance becomes:

$$\text{variance} = \frac{\sum_{t=1}^{T} X_t^2}{T-1} \qquad (2)$$

---

[24] For a further discussion, see Frank J. Fabozzi and Wai Lee, "Measuring and Forecasting Yield Volatility," Chapter 16 in Frank J. Fabozzi (ed.), *Perspectives on Interest Rate Risk Management for Money Managers and Traders* (New Hope, PA: Frank J. Fabozzi Associates, 1998).

[25] Jacques Longerstacey and Peter Zangari, *Five Questions about RiskMetrics^{TM}*, JP Morgan Research Publication 1995.

Exhibit 17: 10-Day Moving Average of Daily Yield Change for Treasury 30-Year Zero

10-Trading Days Ending	Daily Average (%)
24-Oct-95	−0.20324
25-Oct-95	−0.04354
26-Oct-95	0.07902
29-Oct-95	0.04396
30-Oct-95	0.00913
31-Oct-95	−0.04720
01-Nov-95	−0.06121
02-Nov-95	−0.09142
05-Nov-95	−0.11700
06-Nov-95	−0.01371
07-Nov-95	−0.11472
08-Nov-95	−0.15161
09-Nov-95	−0.02728
12-Nov-95	−0.11102

Exhibit 18: Moving Averages of Daily Standard Deviations Based on 10 Days of Observations

10-Trading Days Ending	Moving Average Daily Standard Deviation (%)
24-Oct-95	0.75667
25-Oct-95	0.81874
26-Oct-95	0.58579
29-Oct-95	0.56886
30-Oct-95	0.59461
31-Oct-95	0.60180
01-Nov-95	0.61450
02-Nov-95	0.59072
05-Nov-95	0.57705
06-Nov-95	0.52011
07-Nov-95	0.59998
08-Nov-95	0.53577
09-Nov-95	0.54424
12-Nov-95	0.60003

There are various methods for forecasting daily volatility. The daily standard deviation given by equation (2) assigns an equal weight to all observations. So, if a trader is calculating volatility based on the most recent 10 days of trading, each day is given a weight of 10%.

For example, suppose that a trader is interested in the daily volatility of the Treasury 30-year zero yield and decides to use the 10 most recent trading days. Exhibit 18 reports the 10-day volatility for various days using the data in Exhibit 14 and the standard deviation derived from the formula for the variance given by equation (2). For the period 4/15/93 to 11/12/95, the 10-day volatility ranged from 0.16370% to 1.33006%.

There is reason to suspect that market participants give greater weight to recent movements in yield or price when determining volatility. To give greater importance to more recent information, observations farther in the past should be given less weight. This can be done by revising the variance as given by equation (2) as follows:

$$\text{variance} = \frac{\sum\limits_{t=1}^{T} W_t X_t^2}{T-1} \tag{3}$$

where W_t is the weight assigned to observation t such that the sum of the weights is equal to 1 (i.e., $\sum W_t = 1$) and the farther the observation is from today, the lower the weight. The weights should be assigned so that the forecasted volatility reacts faster to a recent major market movement and declines gradually as we move away from any major market movement.

Finally, a times series characteristic of financial assets suggests that a period of high volatility is followed by a period of high volatility. Furthermore, a period of relative stability in returns appears to be followed by a period that can be characterized in the same way. This suggests that volatility today may depend upon recent prior volatility. This can be modeled and used to forecast volatility. The statistical model used to estimate this time series property of volatility is called an autoregressive conditional heteroskedasticity (ARCH) model.[26] The term "conditional" means that the value of the variance depends on or is conditional on the value of the random variable. The term heteroskedasticity means that the variance is not equal for all values of the random variable. The foundation for ARCH models is beyond the scope of this book.[27]

SECTION VIII
KEY POINTS

- ❑ *Historically, three shapes have been observed for the yield curve: (1) normal or positively sloped (i.e., the longer the maturity, the higher the yield), (2) flat (i.e., the yield for all maturities is approximately equal), and (3) inverted or negatively sloped (i.e., the longer the maturity, the lower the yield).*

- ❑ *The spread between long-term Treasury yields and short-term Treasury yields is referred to as the steepness or slope of the yield curve.*

- ❑ *Some investors define the slope as the spread between the 30-year yield and the 3-month yield and others as the spread between the 30-year yield and the 2-year yield.*

- ❑ *A shift in the yield curve refers to the relative change in the yield for each Treasury maturity.*

- ❑ *A parallel shift in the yield curve refers to a shift in which the change in the yield for all maturities is the same; a nonparallel shift in the yield curve means that the yield for all maturities does not change by the same number of basis points.*

- ❑ *Historically, the two types of nonparallel yield curve shifts that have been observed are a twist in the slope of the yield curve and a change in the curvature of the yield curve.*

- ❑ *A flattening of the yield curve means that the slope of the yield curve has decreased; a steepening of the yield curve means that the slope has increased.*

- ❑ *A butterfly shift is the other type of nonparallel shift — a change in the curvature or humpedness of the yield curve.*

[26] See Robert F. Engle, "Autoregressive Conditional Heteroskedasticity with Estimates of Variance of U.K. Inflation," *Econometrica* 50 (1982), pp. 987-1008.

[27] See Chapter 9 in Defusco and Runkle, *Quantitative Methods for Investment Analysis.*

❑ *Historically, the factors that have been observed to drive Treasury returns are a (1) shift in the level of interest rates, (2) a change in the slope of the yield curve, and (3) a change in the curvature of the yield curve.*

❑ *The most important factor driving Treasury returns is a shift in the level of interest rates.*

❑ *The universe of Treasury issues that can be used to construct the theoretical spot rate curve is (1) on-the-run Treasury issues, (2) on-the-run Treasury issues and selected off-the-run Treasury issues, (3) all Treasury coupon securities and bills, and (4) Treasury strips.*

❑ *There are three methodologies that have been used to derive the theoretical spot rate curve: (1) bootstrapping when the universe is on-the-run Treasury issues (with and without selected off-the-run issues), (2) econometric modeling for all Treasury coupon securities and bills, and (3) simply the observed yields on Treasury coupon strips.*

❑ *The problem with using Treasury coupon strips is that the observed yields may be biased due to a liquidity premium or an unfavorable tax treatment.*

❑ *The three forms of the expectations theory (the pure expectations theory, the liquidity theory, and the preferred habitat theory) assume that the forward rates in current long-term bonds are closely related to the market's expectations about future short-term rates.*

❑ *The three forms of the expectations theory differ on whether or not other factors also affect forward rates, and how.*

❑ *The pure expectations theory postulates that no systematic factors other than expected future short-term rates affect forward rates.*

❑ *Because forward rates are not perfect predictors of future interest rates, the pure expectations theory neglects the risks (interest rate risk and reinvestment risk) associated with investing in Treasury securities.*

❑ *The broadest interpretation of the pure expectations theory suggests that investors expect the return for any investment horizon to be the same, regardless of the maturity strategy selected.*

❑ *The local expectations form of the pure expectations theory suggests that the return will be the same over a short-term investment horizon starting today and it is this narrow interpretation that economists have demonstrated is the only interpretation that can be sustained in equilibrium.*

❑ *Two interpretations of forward rates based on arbitrage arguments are that they are (1) "break-even rates" and (2) rates that can be locked in.*

❑ *Advocates of the pure expectations theory argue that forward rates are the market's consensus of future interest rates.*

❑ *Forward rates have not been found to be good predictors of futures interest rates; however, an understanding of forward rates is still extremely important because of their role as break-even rates and rates that can be locked in.*

❑ *The liquidity theory and the preferred habitat theory assert that there are other factors that affect forward rates and these two theories are therefore referred to as biased expectations theories.*

❑ *The liquidity theory states that investors will hold longer-term maturities only if they are offered a risk premium and therefore forward rates should reflect both interest rate expectations and a liquidity risk premium.*

❑ *The preferred habitat theory, in addition to adopting the view that forward rates reflect the expectation of the future path of interest rates as well as a risk premium, argues that the yield premium need not reflect a liquidity risk but instead reflects the demand and supply of funds in a given maturity range.*

❑ *The market segmentation theory recognizes that investors have preferred maturity sectors dictated by the nature of their liabilities but it goes further than the preferred habitat theory by assuming that neither investors nor borrowers are willing to shift from one maturity sector to another to take advantage of opportunities arising from differences between expectations and forward rates.*

❑ *A common approach to measure yield curve risk is to change the yield for a particular maturity of the yield curve and determine the sensitivity of a security or portfolio to this change holding all other key rates constant.*

❑ *Key rate duration is the sensitivity of the change in a portfolio's value to a particular key rate.*

❑ *The most popular version of key rate duration uses 11 key maturities of the spot rate curve (3 months, 1, 2, 3, 5, 7, 10, 15, 20, 25, and 30 years).*

❑ *Variance is a measure of the dispersion of a random variable around its expected value.*

❑ *The standard deviation is the square root of the variance and is a commonly used measure of volatility.*

❑ *Yield volatility can be estimated from daily yield observations.*

❑ *The observation used in the calculation of the daily standard deviation is the natural logarithm of the percentage change in yield between two days.*

❑ *The selection of the number of observations and the time period can have a significant effect on the calculated daily standard deviation.*

❑ *A daily standard deviation is annualized by multiplying it by the square root of the number of days in a year.*

❑ *Typically, either 250 days, 260 days, or 365 days are used to annualize the daily standard deviation.*

❑ *Implied volatility can also be used to estimate yield volatility based on some option pricing model.*

❑ *In forecasting volatility, it is more appropriate to use an expectation of zero for the mean value.*

❑ *The simplest method for forecasting volatility is weighting all observations equally.*

❑ *A forecasted volatility can be obtained by assigning greater weight to more recent observations.*

❑ *Autoregressive conditional heteroskedasticity (ARCH) models can be used to capture the time series characteristic of yield volatility in which a period of high volatility is followed by a period of high volatility and a period of relative stability appears to be followed by a period that can be characterized in the same way.*

END OF CHAPTER QUESTIONS

1. What are the three types of shapes observed for the yield curve?

2. a. How is the slope of the yield curve defined and measured?
   b. How is the slope of the short end and long end of the yield curve measured?

3. a. In June 1990 the spread between the 30-year Treasury yield and the 2-year Treasury yield was 9 basis points. One year later, June 1991, the spread between these two Treasury yields increased to 157 basis points. What happened to the shape of the yield curve between June 1990 and June 1991?
   b. In January 1989 the spread between the 30-year Treasury yield and the 2-year Treasury yield was −25 basis points. What does that indicate was the shape of the yield curve in January 1989?

4. Historically, how has the slope of the long end of the yield curve differed from that of the short end of the yield curve at a given point in time?

5. a. What are the three factors that have empirically been observed to affect Treasury returns?
   b. What has been observed to be the most important factor in affecting Treasury returns?
   c. Given the most important factor identified in part b, justify the use of duration as a measure of interest rate risk.
   d. What has been observed to be the second most important factor in affecting Treasury returns?
   e. Given the most second important factor identified in part d, justify the use of a measure of interest rate risk in addition to duration.

6. a. What are the limitations of using just the on-the-run Treasury issues to construct the theoretical spot rate curve?
   b. Why if all Treasury bills and Treasury coupon securities are used to construct the theoretical spot rate curve is it not possible to use the bootstrapping method?

7. a. What are the problems with using the yield on Treasury strips to construct the theoretical spot rate curve?
   b. Why even if a practitioner decides to use the yield on Treasury strips to construct the theoretical spot rate curve despite the problems identified in part a will the practitioner restrict the analysis to Treasury coupon strips?

8. a. What is the pure expectations theory?
   b. What are the shortcomings of the pure expectations theory?

9. Based on the broadest interpretation of the pure expectations theory, what would be the difference in the 4-year total return if an investor purchased a 7-year zero-coupon bond or a 15-year zero-coupon bond?

10. Based on the local expectations form of the pure expectations theory, what would be the difference in the 6-month total return if an investor purchased a 5-year zero-coupon bond or a 2-year zero-coupon bond?

11. Comment on the following statement made by a portfolio manager to a client:

> Proponents of the unbiased expectations theory argue that the forward rates built into the term structure of interest rates are the market's consensus of future interest rates. We disagree with the theory because studies suggest that forward rates are poor predictors of future interest rates. Therefore, the position that our investment management firm takes is that forward rates are irrelevant and provide no information to our managers in managing a bond portfolio.

12. Based on arbitrage arguments give two interpretations for each of the following three forward rates:

a. The 1-year forward rate seven years from now is 6.4%.
b. The 2-year forward rate one year from now is 6.2%.
c. The 8-year forward rate three years from now is 7.1%.

13. There are two forms of the "biased" expectations theory. Why are these two forms referred to as "biased" expectations?

14. You are the financial consultant to a Taft Hartley pension fund. After your presentation to the trustees of the fund, you asked the trustees if they have any questions. You receive the two questions below. Answer each one.

a. "The yield curve is upward-sloping today. Doesn't this suggest that the market consensus is that interest rates are expected to increase in the future and therefore you should reduce the interest rate risk exposure for the portfolio that you are managing for us?"

b. "I am looking over one of the pages in your presentation that shows spot rates and I am having difficulty in understanding it. The spot rates at the short end (up to three years) are increasing with maturity. For maturities greater than three years but less than eight years, the spot rates are declining with maturity. finally, for maturities greater than eight years the spot rates are virtually the same for each maturity. There is simply no theory that would explain that type of shape for the term structure of interest rates. Is this market simply unstable?"

15. Below are the key rate durations for three portfolios of U.S. Treasury securities all with the same duration for a parallel shift in the yield curve.

a. For each portfolio describe the type of portfolio (barbell, ladder, or bullet).

Key rate maturity	Portfolio A	Portfolio B	Portfolio C
3-month	0.04	0.04	0.03
1-year	0.06	0.29	0.07
2-year	0.08	0.67	0.31
3-year	0.28	0.65	0.41
5-year	0.38	0.65	1.90
7-year	0.65	0.64	0.35
10-year	3.38	0.66	0.41
15-year	0.79	0.67	0.70
20-year	0.36	0.64	1.95
25-year	0.12	0.62	0.06
30-year	0.06	0.67	0.01

b. Which portfolio will benefit the most if the spot rate for the 10-year decreases by 50 basis points while the spot rate for all other key maturities change very little?

c. What is the duration for a parallel shift in the yield curve for the three portfolios?

16. Compute the daily standard deviation of the percentage change in yield assuming continuous compounding using the daily yield for the 5-year zero-coupon Treasury from October 29, 1995 to November 12, 1995.

t	Date	y_t
0	29-Oct-95	5.854
1	30-Oct-95	5.843
2	31-Oct-95	5.774
3	01-Nov-95	5.719
4	02-Nov-95	5.726
5	05-Nov-95	5.761
6	06-Nov-95	5.797
7	07-Nov-95	5.720
8	08-Nov-95	5.755
9	09-Nov-95	5.787
10	12-Nov-95	5.759

17. For the daily yield volatility computed in the previous question, what is the annual yield volatility assuming the following number of days in the year:

a. 250 days?
b. 260 days?
c. 365 days?

18. Comment on the following statement: "Two portfolio managers with the same set of daily yields will compute the same historical annual volatility."

19. Suppose that the annualized standard deviation of the 2-year Treasury yield based on daily yields is 7% and the current level of the 2-year Treasury yield is 5%. Assuming that the probability distribution for the percentage change in 2-year Treasury yields is approximately normally distributed, how would you interpret the 7% annualized standard deviation?

20. a. What is implied volatility?
    b. What are the problems associated with using implied volatility as a measure of yield volatility?

21. a. In forecasting yield volatility, why would a manager not want to weight each daily yield change equally?
    b. In forecasting yield volatility, what is recommended for the sample mean in the formula for the variance or standard deviation?

SOLUTIONS TO END OF CHAPTER QUESTIONS

1. Historically, three shapes have been observed for the yield curve. A positively sloping or normal yield curve is where the longer the maturity, the higher the yield. A flat yield curve is where the yield for all maturities is approximately the same. A negatively sloped or inverted yield curve is where yield decreases as maturity increases.

2. a. The slope of the yield curve is measured by the difference between long-term Treasury yields and short-term Treasury yields. While there is no industrywide accepted definition of the maturity used for the long-end and the maturity for the short-end of the yield curve, some market participants define the slope of the yield curve as the difference between the 30-year yield and the 3-month yield while other market participants define the slope of the yield curve as the difference between the 30-year yield and the 2-year yield.

   b. The slope of the short end of the yield curve is defined as the difference between either (1) the 10-year Treasury yield and the 3-month Treasury yield or (2) the 10-year Treasury yield and the 2-year Treasury yield. The slope of the long-end of the yield is typically the difference between the 30-year Treasury yield and the 10-year Treasury yield.

3. a. Because the slope of the yield increased between June 1990 and June 1991, this means that the yield curve steepened.
   b. Because of the negative slope in January 1989, the yield curve was inverted.

4. Historically, the slope of the long end of the yield curve has been flatter than the slope of the short end of the yield curve.

5. a. Studies have shown that there have been three factors that affect Treasury returns: (1) changes in the level of yields, (2) changes in the slope of the yield curve, and (3) changes in the curvature of the yield curve.

   b. The most important factor is the change in the level of interest rates.

   c. The implication is that the manager of a Treasury portfolio should control for its exposure to changes in the level of interest rates. For this reason it is important to have a measure such as duration to quantify exposure to a parallel shift in the yield curve.

   d. The second most important factor is changes in the yield curve slope.

   e. The implication is that a measure such as duration must be supplemented with information about a portfolio's exposure to changes in the slope of the yield — a measure such as key rate duration.

6. a. One limitation is that there is a large gap between maturities for the on-the-run issues and a linear extrapolation is used to get the yield for maturities between the on-the-runs. A second limitation is that information is lost about the yield on other Treasury securities. Finally, one or more of the on-the-run issues may be on special in the repo market and thereby distort the true yield for these issues.

   b. Since there may be more than one Treasury issue for a given maturity and since there are callable securities and securities trading at a price different from par (leading to tax issues), a methodology for handling these problems must be used. The bootstrapping methodology does not deal with such problems.

7. a. There are three problems with using the observed rates on Treasury strips (1) there is a liquidity premium for the observed yields in the strips market because strips are not as liquid as Treasury coupon securities; (2) the tax treatment of strips is different from that of Treasury coupon securities — the accrued interest on strips is taxed even though no cash is received by the investor — resulting in the yield on strips reflecting this tax disadvantage; and, (3) there are maturity sectors where non-U.S. investors find it advantageous to trade off yield for tax advantages in their country that are associated with a strip.

b. A practitioner may restrict the use of Treasury strips to construct the theoretical spot rate curve to coupon strips because of the tax aspect mentioned in part a. Specifically, certain foreign tax authorities allow their citizens to treat the difference between the maturity value and the purchase price as a capital gain and tax this gain at a favorable tax rate. Some will grant this favorable treatment only when the strip is created from the principal rather than the coupon. Any such bias can be avoided by just using coupon strips.

8. a. The pure expectations theory postulates that no systematic factors other than expected future short-term rates affect forward rates. According to the pure expectations theory, forward rates exclusively represent expected future rates. Thus, the entire term structure at a given time reflects the market's current expectations of the family of future short-term rates.

b. The pure expectations theory neglects the risks inherent in investing in bonds. If forward rates were perfect predictors of future interest rates, then the future prices of bonds would be known with certainty. The return over any investment period would be certain and independent of the maturity of the instrument acquired. However, with the uncertainty about future interest rates and, therefore, about future prices of bonds, these instruments become risky investments in the sense that the return over some investment horizon is unknown.

9. The broadest interpretation of the pure expectations theory asserts that there is no difference in the 4-year total return if an investor purchased a 7-year zero-coupon bond or a 15-year zero-coupon bond.

10. The local expectations form of the pure expectations theory asserts that the total return over a 6-month horizon for a 5-year zero-coupon bond would be the same as for a 2-year zero-coupon bond.

11. The first sentence of the statement is correct. Moreover, it is correct that studies have shown that forward rates are poor predictors of future interest rates. However, the last sentence of the statement is incorrect. Forward rates should not be ignored because they indicate break-even rates and rates that can be locked in. So, they play an important role in investment decisions.

12. The two interpretations of forward rates are that they are break-even rates and they are rates that can be locked in.

a. For the 1-year forward rate seven years from now of 6.4% the two interpretations are as follows:

(i) 6.4% is the rate that will make an investor indifferent between buying an 8-year zero-coupon bond or investing in a 7-year zero-coupon bond and when it matures reinvesting in a zero-coupon bond that matures in one year, and

(ii) 6.4% is the rate that can be locked in today by buying an 8-year zero-coupon bond rather than investing in a 7-year zero-coupon bond and when it matures reinvesting in a zero-coupon bond that matures in one year.

b. For the 2-year forward rate one year from now of 6.2% the two interpretations are as follows:

(i) 6.2% is the rate that will make an investor indifferent between buying a 3-year zero-coupon bond or investing in a 1-year zero-coupon bond and when it matures reinvesting in a zero-coupon bond that matures in two years, and

(ii) 6.2% is the rate that can be locked in today by buying a 3-year zero-coupon bond rather than investing in a 1-year zero-coupon bond and when it matures reinvesting in a zero-coupon bond that matures in two years.

c. For the 8-year forward rate three years from now of 7.1% the two interpretations are as follows:

(i) 7.1% is the rate that will make an investor indifferent between buying an 11-year zero-coupon bond or investing in a 3-year zero-coupon bond and when it matures reinvesting in a zero-coupon bond that matures in eight years, and

(ii) 7.1% is the rate that can be locked in today by buying an 11-year zero-coupon bond rather than investing in a 3-year zero-coupon bond and when it matures reinvesting in a zero-coupon bond that matures in eight years.

13. All expectations theories — the pure expectations theory, the liquidity theory, and the preferred habitat theory — share a hypothesis about the behavior of short-term forward rates and also assume that the forward rates in current long-term bonds are closely related to the market's expectations about future short-term rates. While the pure expectations theory postulates that no systematic factors other than expected future short-term rates affect forward rates, the liquidity theory and the preferred habitat theory postulate that there are other factors and therefore are referred to as biased expectations theories. The liquidity theory asserts that investors demand a liquidity premium for extending maturity so that the forward rates are biased by this premium. The preferred habitat theory asserts that investors must be induced by a yield premium in order to accept the risks associated with shifting funds out of their preferred sector and forward rates embody the premium for this inducement.

14. a. Proponents of the pure expectations theory would assert that an upward sloping yield curve is a market's forecast of a rise in interest rates. If that is correct, an expected rise in interest rates would mean that the manager should shorten or reduce the duration (i.e., interest rate risk) of the portfolio. However, the pure expectations has serious pitfalls and the forward rates are not good predictors of future interest rates.

b. The preferred habitat form of the biased expectations theory and the market segmentation theory are both consistent with the shape of the spot rate curve observed. The preferred habitat theory asserts that if there is an imbalance between the supply and demand for funds within a given maturity sector, market participants (i.e., borrowers and investors) will agree to shift their financing and investing activities out of their preferred maturity sector to take advantage of any such imbalance. However, participants will demand compensation for shifting out of their preferred maturity sector in the form of a yield premium. Consequently, any shape for the spot rate curve (and yield curve) can result, such as the one observed in the question.

The market segmentation theory asserts that when there are supply and demand imbalances within a maturity sector, market participants will not shift out of their preferred maturity sector. Consequently, different maturity sectors reflect supply and demand imbalances within each sector and the type of yield curve observed in the question is possible.

Therefore, the trustee's statement is incorrect.

15. a. Portfolio A is the bullet portfolio because its 10-year key rate duration dominates by far the key rate duration for the other maturities. Portfolio B is the laddered portfolio because the key rate durations after year 2 are roughly equal. Portfolio C is the barbell portfolio with the short end of the barbell at 5 years and the long end of the barbell at 20 years.

b. The bullet portfolio has the highest 10-year key rate duration and will therefore increase the most if the 10-year spot rate increases while the key rates for the other maturities do not change much.

c. Adding up the key rate durations for each portfolio gives 6.2. This is the duration of all three portfolios if the spot rate for all key maturities changes by the same number of basis points – that is, a parallel shift in the spot rate for the key maturities.

16. The information for computing the daily standard deviation for yield volatility is shown below:

t	Date	y_t	$X_t = 100[\text{Ln}(y_t/y_{t-1})]$	$(X_t - \bar{X})^2$
0	29-Oct-95	5.854		
1	30-Oct-95	5.843	−0.18808	0.00060
2	31-Oct-95	5.774	−1.18793	1.04922
3	01-Nov-95	5.719	−0.95711	0.62964
4	02-Nov-95	5.726	0.12232	0.08176
5	05-Nov-95	5.761	0.60939	0.59753
6	06-Nov-95	5.797	0.62295	0.61868
7	07-Nov-95	5.720	−1.33717	1.37724
8	08-Nov-95	5.755	0.61002	0.59851
9	09-Nov-95	5.787	0.55450	0.51568
10	12-Nov-95	5.759	−0.48502	0.10330
	Total		−1.63613	5.57216825

sample mean $= \bar{X} = \dfrac{-1.63613}{10} = -0.163613$

variance $= \dfrac{5.57216825}{10-1} = 0.6191298$

std dev $= \sqrt{0.6191298} = 0.786848\%$

17. a. Using 250 days: $\sqrt{250}\ (0.786848) = 12.44\%$

b. Using 260 days: $\sqrt{260}\ (0.786848) = 12.69\%$

c. Using 365 days: $\sqrt{365}\ (0.786848) = 15.03\%$

18. This is not necessarily the case because with the same data there are still choices that the managers must make that may result in quite different estimates of historical volatility. These choices include the number of days to use and the annualization of the daily standard deviation.

19. Since the current level of the 2-year Treasury yield is 5%, then the annual standard deviation of 7% translates into a 35 basis point (5% times 7%) standard deviation. Assuming that yield volatility is approximately normally distributed, we can use the normal distribution to construct an interval or range for what the future yield will be. There is a 68.3% probability that the yield will be between one standard deviation below and above the expected value. The expected value is the prevailing yield. If the annual standard deviation is 35 basis points and the prevailing yield is 5%, then there is a 68.3% probability that the yield next year will be between 4.65% (5% minus 35 basis points) and 5.35% (5% plus 35 basis points). There is a 99.7% probability that the yield next year will be within three standard deviations. In our case, three standard deviations is 105 basis points. Therefore there is a 99.7% probability that the yield will be between 3.95% (5% minus 105 basis points) and 6.05% (5% plus 105 basis points).

20. a. Yield volatility can be estimated from the observed prices of interest rate options and caps. A yield volatility estimated in this way is called implied volatility and is based on some option pricing model. An input to any option pricing model in which the underlying is a Treasury security or Treasury futures contract is expected yield volatility. If the observed price of an option is assumed to be the fair price and the option pricing model is assumed to be the model that would generate that fair price, then the implied yield volatility is the yield volatility that when used as an input into the option pricing model would produce the observed option price.

b. The problems with using implied volatility are that (1) it is assumed the option pricing model is correct, and (2) since option pricing models typically assume that volatility is constant over the life of the option interpreting an implied volatility becomes difficult.

21. a. There are reasons to believe that market participants give greater weight to recent movements in yield when determining volatility. To incorporate this belief into the estimation of historical volatility, different weights can be assigned to the observed changes in daily yields. More specifically, observations further in the past should be given less weight.

b. Some market practitioners argue that in forecasting volatility the expected value or mean that should be used in the formula for the variance is zero.

SOLUTIONS TO PRACTICE QUESTIONS

1. a. The daily percentage change in yield for each trading day is shown below in the next to the last column:

t	Date	y_t	$X_t = 100[Ln(y_t/y_{t-1})]$	$(X_t - \bar{X})^2$
0	20-Aug-95	7.17400		
1	21-Aug-95	7.19400	0.27840	0.19820
2	22-Aug-95	7.21800	0.33306	0.24985
3	23-Aug-95	7.15100	−0.93257	0.58641
4	24-Aug-95	7.02500	−1.77770	2.59500
5	27-Aug-95	7.02400	−0.01424	0.02328
6	28-Aug-95	7.03000	0.08538	0.06360
7	29-Aug-95	7.02000	−0.14235	0.00060
8	30-Aug-95	6.96400	−0.80092	0.40211
9	31-Aug-95	6.90400	−0.86531	0.48792
10	03-Sep-95	6.89671	−0.10565	0.00374
11	04-Sep-95	6.85300	−0.63580	0.21996
12	05-Sep-95	6.87100	0.26231	0.18414
13	06-Sep-95	6.88300	0.17449	0.11648
14	07-Sep-95	6.87500	−0.11630	0.00255
15	10-Sep-95	6.87800	0.04363	0.04428
16	11-Sep-95	6.80400	−1.08172	0.83709
17	12-Sep-95	6.84300	0.57156	0.54517
18	13-Sep-95	6.79500	−0.70392	0.28850
19	14-Sep-95	6.79500	0.00000	0.02782
20	17-Sep-95	6.85400	0.86454	1.06365
21	18-Sep-95	6.81000	−0.64403	0.22775
22	19-Sep-95	6.77300	−0.54480	0.14289
23	20-Sep-95	6.86700	1.37832	2.38739
24	21-Sep-95	6.88700	0.29082	0.20942
25	24-Sep-95	6.88100	−0.08716	0.00634
		Total	−4.16994	10.91412

b. The daily standard is computed as follows:

$$\text{sample mean} = \bar{X} = \frac{-4.16994}{25} = -0.166798$$

$$\text{variance} = \frac{10.91412}{25 - 1} = 0.4547550$$

$$\text{std dev} = \sqrt{0.4547550} = 0.67436\%$$

Chapter 2

VALUING BONDS WITH EMBEDDED OPTIONS

LEARNING OUTCOME STATEMENTS

After reading this chapter you should be able to:

- explain what an interest rate model is.
- explain what is meant by an interest rate tree.
- explain the backward induction valuation methodology within the binomial interest rate tree framework.
- compute the value of an option-free bond using an interest rate tree.
- compute the value of a callable bond from an interest rate tree given the call schedule and the rule for calling a bond.
- explain how the value of an embedded call option is determined.
- explain how an option-adjusted spread is calculated using the binomial model.
- describe how effective duration and effective convexity are calculated using the binomial model.
- compute the value of a putable bond using an interest rate tree.
- explain how the binomial model can accommodate multiple embedded options.
- explain how the binomial model can be used to value a step-up callable note.
- describe how the binomial model can be used to value a capped floater.
- describe the basic features of a convertible bond.
- compute and explain the meaning of the following for a convertible bond: conversion value, straight value, market conversion price, market conversion premium per share, market conversion premium ratio, premium payback period, and premium over straight value.
- identify the factors that complicate the valuation of a convertible bond.
- identify the type of model used by practitioners to value convertible bonds.
- describe the risk/return characteristics of a convertible bond versus the ownership of the underlying common stock.

SECTION I
INTRODUCTION

At Level I (Chapter 5) we explained how an option-free bond (i.e., a bond that is not callable, putable, or convertible) is valued using Treasury spot rates. Once embedded options must be considered, the valuation becomes more complicated. There are numerous models that have been proposed to value bonds with embedded options. Of interest to us are those models that provide an "arbitrage-free value" for a security.

At Level I, we saw that an arbitrage-free value for an option-free bond was obtained by first generating the spot rates (or forward rates). The spot rates are the rates that would produce a value for each on-the-run Treasury issue that is equal to its observed market price. In developing the interest rates that should be used to value a bond with an embedded option, the same principle must be maintained. That is, no matter how complex the valuation model, when each on-the-run Treasury issue is valued using the model, the value produced should be equal to the on-the-run issue's market price.[1] This is because it is assumed that the on-the-run issues are fairly priced.

The first complication in building a model to value bonds with embedded options is that the future cash flows will depend on what happens to interest rates in the future. This means that future interest rates must be considered. This is incorporated into a valuation model by considering how interest rates can change based on some assumed interest rate volatility. In the previous chapter we explained what interest rate volatility is and how it is estimated. Given the assumed interest rate volatility, an interest rate "tree" representing possible future interest rates consistent with the volatility assumption can be constructed. It is from the interest rate tree that two important elements in the valuation process are obtained. First, the interest rates on the tree are used to generate the cash flows taking into account the embedded option. Second, the interest rates on the tree are used to compute the present value of the cash flows.

For a given interest rate volatility, there are several interest rate models that have been used in practice to construct an interest rate tree. An **interest rate model** is a probabilistic description of how interest rates can change over the life of the bond. An interest rate model does this by making an assumption about the relationship between the level of short-term interest rates and the interest rate volatility as measured by the standard deviation. A discussion of the various interest rate models that have been suggested in the finance literature and that are used by practitioners in developing valuation models is beyond the scope of this chapter.[2] What is important to understand is that the interest rate models commonly used are based on how short-term interest rates can evolve (i.e., change) over time. Consequently, these interest rate models are referred to as **one-factor models**, where "factor" means only one interest rate is being modeled over time. More complex models would consider how more than one interest rate changes over time. For example, an interest rate model can specify how the short-term interest rate and the long-term interest rate can change over time. Such a model is called a **two-factor model**.

Given an interest rate model and an interest rate volatility assumption, it can be assumed that interest rates can realize one of two possible rates in the next period. A valuation model that makes this assumption in creating an interest rate tree is called a **binomial model**. There are valuation models that assume that interest rates can take on three possible rates in the next period and these models are called **trinomial models**. There are even more complex models that assume in creating an interest rate tree that more than three possible rates in the next period can be realized. Regardless of

---

[1] Market participants also refer to this characteristic of a model as one that "calibrates to the market."

[2] An excellent source for further explanation of many of these models is Gerald W. Buetow Jr. and James Sochacki, *Term Structure Models Using Binomial Trees: Demystifying the Process* (Charlottesville, VA: Association of Investment Management and Research, 2000).

the assumption about how many possible rates can be realized in the next period, the interest rate tree generated must produce a value for the on-the-run Treasury issue that is equal to its observed market price — that is, it must produce an arbitrage-free value. Moreover, the intuition and the methodology for using the interest rate tree (i.e., the backward induction methodology described later) are the same.

Once an interest rate tree is generated that (1) is consistent with both the interest rate volatility assumption and the interest rate model, and (2) generates the observed market price for each on-the-run issue, the next step is to use the interest rate tree to value a bond with an embedded option. The complexity here is that a set of rules must be introduced to determine, for any period, when the embedded option will be exercised. For a callable bond, these rules are called the "call rules." The rules vary from model builder to model builder.

At this stage, all of this sounds terribly complicated. While the building of a model to value bonds with embedded options is more complex than building a model to value option-free bonds, the basic principles are the same. In the case of valuing an option-free bond, the model that is built is simply a set of spot rates that are used to value cash flows. The spot rates will produce an arbitrage-free value. For a model to value a bond with embedded options, the interest rate tree is used to value future cash flows and the interest rate tree is combined with the call rules to generate the future cash flows. Again, the interest rate tree will produce an arbitrage-free value.

Let's move from theory to practice. Only a few practitioners will develop their own model to value bonds with embedded options. Instead, it is typical for a portfolio manager or analyst to use a model developed by either a dealer firm or a vendor of analytical systems. A fair question is then: Why bother covering a valuation model that is readily available from a third-party? The answer is that a valuation model should not be a black box to portfolio managers and analysts. *The models in practice share all of the principles described in this chapter, but differ with respect to certain assumptions that can produce quite different results.* The reasons for these differences in valuation must be understood. Moreover, third-party models give the user a choice of changing the assumptions. A user who has not "walked through" a valuation model has no appreciation of the significance of these assumptions and therefore how to assess the impact of these assumptions on the value produced by the model. In Level I, we discussed "modeling risk" in our introduction to fixed income. This is the risk that the underlying assumptions of a model may be incorrect. Understanding a valuation model permits the user to effectively determine the significance of an assumption.

An example of understanding the assumptions of a model is the volatility used. Suppose that the market price of a bond is $89. Suppose further that a valuation model produces a value for a bond with an embedded option of $90 based on a 12% interest rate volatility assumption. Then, according to the valuation model, this bond is cheap by one point. However, suppose that the same model produces a value of $87 if a 15% volatility is assumed. This tells the portfolio manager or analyst that the bond is two points rich. Which is correct?

In this chapter, we will use the binomial model to demonstrate all of the issues and assumptions associated with valuing a bond with embedded options. This model is available on Bloomberg, as well as from other commercial vendors and several dealer firms.[3] We begin by reviewing how to value an option-free bond given the spot rates

---

[3] The model described in this chapter was presented in Andrew J. Kalotay, George O. Williams, and Frank J. Fabozzi, "A Model for the Valuation of Bonds and Embedded Options," *Financial Analysts Journal* (May-June 1993), pp. 35-46.

and forward rates. We then show how to create an interest rate tree (more specifically, a binomial interest rate tree) given a volatility assumption and how the interest rate tree can be used to value an option-free bond. Given the interest rate tree, we then show how to value several types of bonds with an embedded option — a callable bond, a putable bond, a stepped-up note, and a floating-rate note with a cap. Along the way we will see how the option-adjusted spread is derived from the binomial model and how the values used in the effective duration and convexity measures are obtained from the binomial model. We postpone until Chapter 5 an explanation of why the binomial model is not used to value mortgage-backed and asset-backed securities. The binomial model is used to value options, caps, and floors as will be explained in Chapter 8.

Once again, it must be emphasized that while the binomial model is used in this chapter to demonstrate how to value bonds with embedded options, other models that allow for more than one interest rate in the next period all follow the same principles — they begin with on-the-run yields, they produce an interest rate tree that generates an arbitrage-free value obtained using a backward induction methodology, and they depend on assumptions regarding the volatility of interest rates and rules for when an embedded option will be exercised.

At the end of this chapter we will discuss the valuation of convertibles. The complexity here is that these bonds are typically callable and may be putable. Thus, the valuation process must take into account not only embedded options that depend on future interest rates (i.e., the call and the put options on the bond) but also the future price movement of the common stock (i.e., the call option on the common stock).

SECTION II REVIEW OF HOW TO VALUE AN OPTION-FREE BOND

At Level I (Chapter 5) we explained how to compute an arbitrage-free value for an option-free bond using spot rates. At Level I (Chapter 6) we also showed the relationship between spot rates and forward rates, and then how forward rates can be used to derive the same arbitrage-free value as using spot rates.

Let's review the valuation of option-free bonds. We must determine the on-the-run yield curve for the particular *issuer* whose bond we want to value. We refer to the on-the-run yield curve used for any valuation process as the **benchmark interest rates**. It is critical in any valuation that the benchmark interest rates be clearly defined. In the United States, the starting point for constructing the on-the-run yield curve for the issuer is the on-the-run Treasury issues. To obtain a particular issuer's on-the-run yield curve, an appropriate credit spread is added to each on-the-run Treasury issue. The credit spread need not be constant for all maturities. For example, as explained at Level I (Chapter 5), the credit spread may increase with maturity.

Outside of the United States, in some countries the benchmark interest rates are the recently auctioned or most actively traded securities issued by the central government. In other countries where the government market is not well developed, the benchmark interest rates are those of the highest credit quality issuers in the country. So, the principles presented in this chapter apply equally to the valuation of bonds with embedded options anywhere in the world. However, the valuation can only be interpreted relative to the benchmark interest rates used.

In our illustration, we use the following hypothetical on-the-run issue for an *issuer*:

Maturity	Yield to maturity	Market Price
1 year	3.5%	100
2 years	4.2%	100
3 years	4.7%	100
4 years	5.2%	100

Each bond is trading at par value (100) so the coupon rate is equal to the yield to maturity. We will simplify the illustration by assuming annual-pay bonds.

Using the bootstrapping methodology explained at Level I (Chapter 6), the spot rates are given below:

Year	Spot Rate
1	3.5000%
2	4.2147%
3	4.7345%
4	5.2707%

The corresponding one-year forward rates are:

Current 1-year forward rate	3.500%
1-year forward rate one year from now	4.935%
1-year forward rate two years from now	5.784%
1-year forward rate three years from now	6.893%

Now consider an option-free bond with four years remaining to maturity and a coupon rate of 6.5%. The value of this bond can be calculated in one of two ways, both producing the same value. First, the cash flows can be discounted at the spot rates as shown below:

$$\frac{\$6.5}{(1.035)^1} + \frac{\$6.5}{(1.042147)^2} + \frac{\$6.5}{(1.047345)^3} + \frac{\$100 + \$6.5}{(1.052707)^4} = \$104.643$$

The second way is to discount by the 1-year forward rates as shown below:

$$\frac{\$6.5}{(1.035)} + \frac{\$6.5}{(1.035)(1.04935)} + \frac{\$6.5}{(1.035)(1.04935)(1.05784)}$$

$$+ \frac{\$100 + \$6.5}{(1.035)(1.04935)(1.05784)(1.06893)} = \$104.643$$

SECTION III THE BINOMIAL MODEL

As explained in Section I, there are various models that have been developed to value a bond with embedded options. The one that we will use to illustrate the issues and assumptions associated with valuing bonds with embedded options is the binomial model. The interest rates that are used in the valuation process are obtained from a **binomial interest rate tree**. We'll explain the general characteristics of this tree first. Then we see how to value a bond using the binomial interest rate tree. We will then see how to construct this tree from an on-the-run yield curve. Basically, the derivation of a binomial interest rate tree is the same in principle as deriving the spot rates using the bootstrapping method described at Level I (Chapter 6) — that is, there is no arbitrage.

A. Binomial Interest Rate Tree

As explained in Section I, once we allow for embedded options, consideration must be given to interest rate volatility. This can be done by introducing a binomial interest rate tree. This tree is nothing more than a graphical depiction of the one-period or short-term interest rates over time based on some assumption about interest rate volatility. How this tree is constructed is illustrated below. This overview is presented to give the reader an "appreciation" only about the characteristics of the binomial interest rate tree.

Exhibit 1 provides an example of a binomial interest rate tree. In this tree, each node (i.e., dot) represents a time period that is equal to one year from the node to the left. One year is selected purely to illustrate the key principles. The methodology is the same for smaller time periods. In fact, in practice the selection of the length of the time period is critical but we need not be concerned with this nuance here.

Each node is labeled with an N, representing, of course, node. There is a subscript at all the nodes except for the very first node. L represents the lower of the two 1-year rates and H represents the higher of the two 1-year rates. For example, node N_{HH} means that to get to that node the following path for 1-year rates occurred: the 1-year rate realized is the higher of the two rates in the first year and then the higher of the two rates in the second year.

How about N_{HL} in Exhibit 1? This means that the higher of the two 1-year rates is realized in the first year and the lower of the two 1-year rates is realized in the second year. However, we would get to the same node as N_{HL} if instead the lower of the two 1-year rates is realized in the first year and the higher of the two 1-year rates is realized in the second year. That is, if we let the subscripts denote the path of interest rates, N_{HL} would be equal to N_{LH}. Why weren't both N_{HL} and N_{LH} shown in Exhibit 1, not just N_{HL}? This was done to avoid cluttering up the tree with notation. It would get particularly messy as we move out further along the tree. For example, at the node identified as N_{HHL} in Exhibit 1, three paths for the 1-year rate can get to that node: HHL, HLH, and LHH. Only N_{HHL} was arbitrarily selected for Exhibit 1.

Look at the point denoted by just N in Exhibit 1. This is the root of the tree and is nothing more than the current 1-year spot rate, or equivalently the current 1-year rate, which we denote by r_0. What we have assumed in creating this tree is that the 1-year rate can take on two possible values the next year and the two rates have the same probability of occurring. One rate will be higher than the other.

We use the following notation to describe the tree in the first year. Let

σ = assumed volatility of the 1-year rate
$r_{1,L}$ = the lower 1-year rate one year from now
$r_{1,H}$ = the higher 1-year rate one year from now

Exhibit 1: Four-Year Binomial Interest Rate Tree

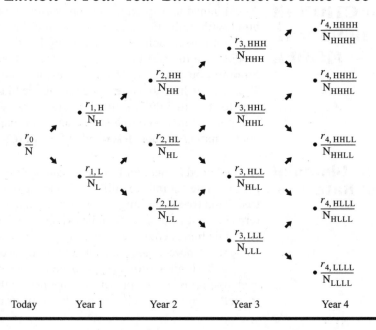

| Today | Year 1 | Year 2 | Year 3 | Year 4 |

The relationship between $r_{1,L}$ and $r_{1,H}$ is as follows:[4]

$$r_{1,H} = r_{1,L}(e^{2\sigma})$$

where e is the base of the natural logarithm, 2.71828.

For example, suppose that $r_{1,L}$ is 4.4448% and σ is 10% per year, then:

$$r_{1,H} = 4.4448\%(e^{2 \times 0.10}) = 5.4289\%$$

In the second year, there are three possible values for the 1-year rate, which we will denote as follows:

$r_{2,LL}$ = 1-year rate in second year assuming the lower rate in the first year and the lower rate in the second year

$r_{2,HH}$ = 1-year rate in second year assuming the higher rate in the first year and the higher rate in the second year

$r_{2,HL}$ = 1-year rate in second year assuming the higher rate in the first year and the lower rate in the second year or equivalently the lower rate in the first year and the higher rate in the second year

The relationship between $r_{2,LL}$ and the other two 1-year rates is as follows:

$$r_{2,HH} = r_{2,LL}(e^{4\sigma}) \quad \text{and} \quad r_{2,HL} = r_{2,LL}(e^{2\sigma})$$

So, for example, if $r_{2,LL}$ is 4.6958%, then assuming once again that σ is 10%, then

$$r_{2,HH} = 4.6958\%(e^{4 \times 0.10}) = 7.0053\%$$

and

$$r_{2,HL} = 4.6958\%(e^{2 \times 0.10}) = 5.7354\%$$

In the third year there are four possible values for the 1-year rate, which are denoted as follows: $r_{3,HHH}$, $r_{3,HHL}$, $r_{3,HLL}$, and $r_{3,LLL}$, and whose first three values are related to the last as follows:

$$r_{3,HHH} = r_{3,LLL}(e^{6\sigma})$$
$$r_{3,HHL} = r_{3,LLL}(e^{4\sigma})$$
$$r_{3,HLL} = r_{3,LLL}(e^{2\sigma})$$

Exhibit 1 shows the notation for a 4-year binomial interest rate tree. We can simplify the notation by letting r_t be the 1-year rate t years from now for the lower rate since all the other short rates t years from now depend on that rate. Exhibit 2 shows the interest rate tree using this simplified notation.

The interest rates shown in the binomial interest rate tree are actually forward rates. Basically, they are the one-period rates starting in period t. At Level I (Chapter 6) we used notation to describe forward rates. Specifically, we used two subscripts to describe forward rates — the subscript before f (to denote forward rate) is when the forward rate starts and the subscript after f indicates the length of time of the investment. This notation is shown in Exhibit 2. Of course, since the length of time is one period, all the subscripts following f are 1. Notice that there is not one forward rate for each year but a set of forward rates.

---

[4] It is assumed that the 1-year rate can evolve over time based on a random process called a lognormal random walk with a known volatility.

Exhibit 2: Four-Year Binomial Interest Rate Tree with One-Year Rates*

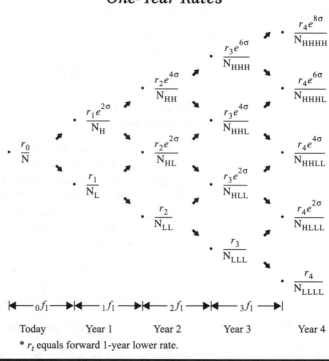

$$\begin{array}{c}\leftarrow\!\!\!\!\!\!-\,{}_0f_1\,-\!\!\!\!\!\!\rightarrow\!\!\!\!\!\!\leftarrow\!\!\!\!\!\!-\,{}_1f_1\,-\!\!\!\!\!\!\rightarrow\!\!\!\!\!\!\leftarrow\!\!\!\!\!\!-\,{}_2f_1\,-\!\!\!\!\!\!\rightarrow\!\!\!\!\!\!\leftarrow\!\!\!\!\!\!-\,{}_3f_1\,-\!\!\!\!\!\!\rightarrow\end{array}$$

| Today | Year 1 | Year 2 | Year 3 | Year 4 |

* r_t equals forward 1-year lower rate.

Thus, in valuing an option-free bond we know that it is valued using forward rates and we have illustrated this by using 1-period forward rates. For each period, there is a unique forward rate. When we value bonds with embedded options, we will see that we continue to use forward rates but there is not just one forward rate for a given period but a set of forward rates.

B. Determining the Value at a Node

To find the value of the bond at a node, we first calculate the bond's value at the high and low nodes to the right of the node we are interested in. For example, in Exhibit 2, suppose we want to determine the bond's value at node N_H. The bond's value at node N_{HH} and N_{HL} must be determined. Hold aside for now how we get these two values because, as we will see, the process involves starting from the last year in the tree and working backwards to get the final solution we want. Because the procedure for solving for the final solution in any interest rate tree involves moving backwards, the methodology is known as **backward induction**.

Effectively what we are saying is that if we are at some node, then the value at that node will depend on the future cash flows. In turn, the future cash flows depend on (1) the coupon payment one year from now and (2) the bond's value one year from now. The former is known. The bond's value depends on whether the rate is the higher or lower rate reported at the two nodes to the right of the node that is the focus of our attention. So, the cash flow at a node will be either (1) the bond's value if the 1-year rate is the higher rate plus the coupon payment, or (2) the bond's value if the 1-year rate is the lower rate plus the coupon payment. Let's return to the bond's value at node N_H. The cash flow will be either the bond's value at N_{HH} plus the coupon payment, or the bond's value at N_{HL} plus the coupon payment.

Exhibit 3: Calculating a Value at a Node

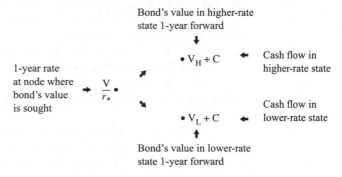

In general, to get the bond's value at a node we follow the fundamental rule for valuation: the value is the present value of the expected cash flows. The appropriate discount rate to use is the 1-year rate at the node where we are computing the value. Now there are two present values in this case: the present value if the 1-year rate is the higher rate and one if it is the lower rate. Since it is assumed that the probability of both outcomes is equal (i.e., there is a 50% probability for each), an average of the two present values is computed. This is illustrated in Exhibit 3 for any node assuming that the 1-year rate is r_* at the node where the valuation is sought and letting:

V_H = the bond's value for the higher 1-year rate
V_L = the bond's value for the lower 1-year rate
C = coupon payment

Using our notation, the cash flow at a node is either:

$V_H + C$ for the higher 1-year rate
$V_L + C$ for the lower 1-year rate

The present value of these two cash flows using the 1-year rate at the node, r_*, is:

$$\frac{V_H + C}{(1 + r_*)} = \text{present value for the higher 1-year rate}$$

$$\frac{V_L + C}{(1 + r_*)} = \text{present value for the lower 1-year rate}$$

Then, the value of the bond at the node is found as follows:

$$\text{Value at a node} = \frac{1}{2}\left[\frac{V_H + C}{(1 + r_*)} + \frac{V_L + C}{(1 + r_*)}\right]$$

C. Constructing the Binomial Interest Rate Tree

The construction of any interest rate tree is complicated, although the principle is simple to understand. This applies to the binomial interest rate tree or a tree based on more than two future rates in the next period. *The fundamental principle is that when a tree is used to value an on-the-run issue, the resulting value should be arbitrage free.* That is, the tree should generate a value for an on-the-run issue equal to its observed market value. Moreover, the interest rate tree should be consistent with the interest rate volatility assumed.

Here is a brief overview of the process for constructing the interest rate tree. Don't look for details. The interest rate at the first node (i.e., the root of the tree) is the one year interest rate for the on-the-run issue. (This is because in our simplified illustration we are assuming that the length of the time between nodes is one year.) The tree is grown just the same way that the spot rates were obtained using the bootstrapping method based on arbitrage arguments.

The interest rates for year 1 (there are two of them and remember they are effectively forward rates) are obtained from the following information:

1. the coupon rate for the 2-year on-the-run issue
2. the interest rate volatility assumed
3. the interest rate at the root of the tree (i.e., the current 1-year on-the-run rate)

Given the above, a *guess* is then made of the lower rate at node N_L, which is $r_{1,L}$. The upper rate, $r_{1,H}$, is not guessed at. Instead, it is determined by the assumed volatility of the 1-year rate ($r_{1,L}$). The formula for determining $r_{1,H}$ given $r_{1,L}$ was illustrated in Section III.A of this chapter. Using the $r_{1,L}$ that was guessed and the corresponding $r_{1,H}$, the 2-year on-the-run issue can be valued. If the resulting value computed using the backward induction method is not equal to the market value of the 2-year on-the-run issue, then the $r_{1,L}$ that was tried is not the rate that should be used in the tree. If the value is too high, then a higher rate guess should be tried; if the value is too low, then a lower rate guess should be tried. The process continues in an iterative (i.e., trial and error) process until a value for $r_{1,L}$ and the corresponding $r_{1,H}$ produce a value for the 2-year on-the-run issue equal to its market value.

After this stage, we have the rate at the root of the tree and the two rates for year 1 — $r_{1,L}$ and $r_{1,H}$. Now we need the three rates for year 2 — $r_{2,LL}$, $r_{2,HL}$, and $r_{2,HH}$. These rates are determined from the following information:

1. the coupon rate for the 3-year on-the-run issue
2. the interest rate volatility assumed
3. the interest rate at the root of the tree (i.e., the current 1-year on-the-run rate)
4. the two 1-year rates (i.e., $r_{1,L}$ and $r_{1,H}$)

A guess is made for $r_{2,LL}$. In Section III.A we showed how to obtain $r_{2,HL}$, and $r_{2,HH}$ given $r_{2,LL}$ and the assumed volatility for the 1-year rate. This gives the rates in the interest rate tree that are needed to value the 3-year on-the-run issue. The 3-year on-the-run issue is then valued. If the value generated is not equal to the market value of the 3-year on-the-run issue, then the $r_{2,LL}$ value tried is not the rate that should be used in the tree. At iterative process is again followed until a value for $r_{2,LL}$ produces rates for year 2 that will make the value of the 3-year on-the-run issue equal to its market value.

The tree is grown using the same procedure as described above to get $r_{1,L}$ and $r_{1,H}$ for year 1 and $r_{2,LL}$, $r_{2,HL}$, and $r_{2,HH}$ for year 2. Exhibit 4 shows the binomial interest rate tree for this issuer for valuing issues up to four years of maturity assuming volatility for the 1-year rate of 10%. Exhibit 5 verifies that the rates on the binomial interest rate tree up to year 2 are the correct values by showing that when the 3-year on-the-run issue is valued using the backward induction method the value is 100, which is the market value of the 3-year on-the-run issue.

Exhibit 4: Binomial Interest Rate Tree for Valuing an Issuer's Bond with a Maturity Up to 4 Years (10% Volatility Assumed)

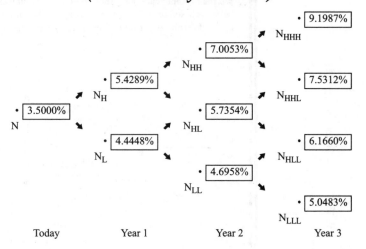

| | Today | Year 1 | Year 2 | Year 3 |

Exhibit 5: Demonstration that the Binomial Interest Rate Tree in Exhibit 4 Correctly Values the 3-Year 4.7% On-the-Run Issue

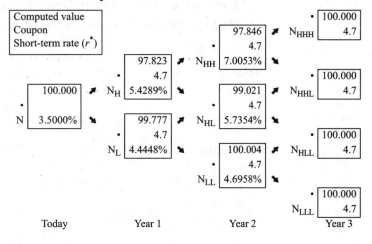

PRACTICE QUESTION 1

For the hypothetical issuer whose on-the-run yield was given in Section II, the binomial interest rate tree below is based on 20% volatility. Using the 4-year on-the-run issue, show that the binomial interest tree below does produce a value equal to the price of the 4-year issue (i.e., par value).

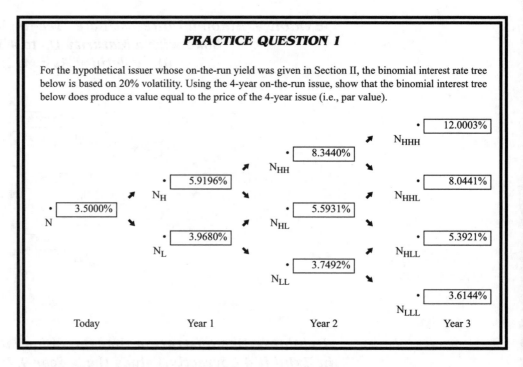

Exhibit 6: Valuing an Option-Free Bond with Four Years to Maturity and a Coupon Rate of 6.5% (10% Volatility Assumed)

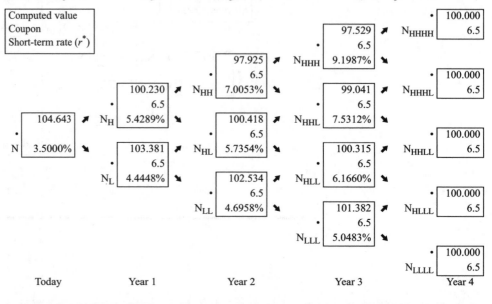

D. Valuing an Option-Free Bond with the Tree

To illustrate how to use the binomial interest rate tree shown in Exhibit 5, consider a 6.5% option-free bond with four years remaining to maturity. Also assume that the issuer's on-the-run yield curve is the one given earlier and hence the appropriate binomial interest rate tree is the one in Exhibit 5. Exhibit 6 shows the various values in the discounting process, and produces a bond value of $104.643.

It is important to note that this value is identical to the bond value found earlier when we discounted at either the spot rates or the 1-year forward rates. We should expect to find this result since our bond is option free. This clearly demonstrates that the valuation model is consistent with the arbitrage-free valuation model for an option-free bond.

PRACTICE QUESTION 2

Show that the value of an option-free bond with four years to maturity and a coupon rate of 6.5% is $104.643 if volatility is assumed to be 20%.

SECTION IV VALUING AND ANALYZING A CALLABLE BOND

Now we will demonstrate how the binomial interest rate tree can be applied to value a callable bond. The valuation process proceeds in the same fashion as in the case of an option-free bond, but with one exception: when the call option may be exercised by the issuer, the bond value at a node must be changed to reflect the lesser of its values if it is not called (i.e., the value obtained by applying the backward induction method described above) and the call price.

For example, consider a 6.5% bond with four years remaining to maturity that is callable in one year at $100. Exhibit 7 shows two values at each node of the binomial interest rate tree. The discounting process explained above is used to calculate the first of the two values at each node. The second value is the value based on whether the issue will be called. For simplicity, let's assume that this issuer calls the issue if it exceeds the call price.

In Exhibit 8 two portions of Exhibit 7 are highlighted. Panel a of the exhibit shows nodes where the issue is not called (based on the simple call rule used in the illustration) in year 2 and year 3. The values reported in this case are the same as in the valuation of an option-free bond. Panel b of the exhibit shows some nodes where the issue is called in year 2 and year 3. Notice how the methodology changes the cash flows. In year 3, for example, at node N_{HLL} the backward induction method produces a value (i.e., cash flow) of 100.315. However, given the simplified call rule, this issue would be called. Therefore, 100 is shown as the second value at the node and it is this value that is then used in the backward induction methodology. From this we can see how the binomial method changes the cash flow based on future interest rates and the embedded option.

The root of the tree, shown in Exhibit 7, indicates that the value for this callable bond is $102.899.

The question that we have not addressed in our illustration, which is nonetheless important, is the circumstances under which the issuer will actually call the bond. A detailed explanation of the call rule is beyond the scope of this chapter. Basically, it involves determining when it would be economical for the issuer on an after-tax basis to call the issue.

Suppose instead that the call price schedule is 102 in year 1, 101 in year 2, and 100 in year 3. Also assume that the bond will not be called unless it exceeds the call price for that year. Exhibit 9 shows the value at each node and the value of the callable bond. The call price schedule results in a greater value for the callable bond, $103.942 compared to $102.899 when the call price is 100 in each year.

Exhibit 7: Valuing a Callable Bond with Four Years to Maturity, a Coupon Rate of 6.5%, and Callable in One Year at 100 (10% Volatility Assumed)

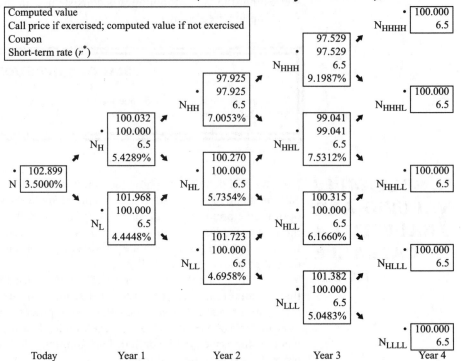

| Computed value |
| Call price if exercised; computed value if not exercised |
| Coupon |
| Short-term rate (r^*) |

Today — Year 1 — Year 2 — Year 3 — Year 4

Exhibit 8: Highlighting Nodes in Years 2 and 3 for a Callable Bond

a. Nodes where call option is not exercised

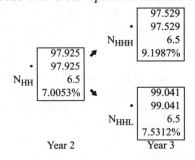

Year 2 — Year 3

b. Selected nodes where the call option is exercised

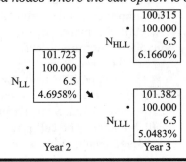

Year 2 — Year 3

Exhibit 9: Valuing a Callable Bond with Four Years to Maturity, a Coupon Rate of 6.5%, and with a Call Price Schedule (10% Volatility Assumed)

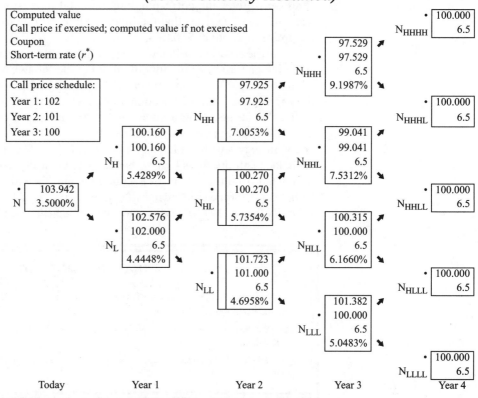

| | Today | Year 1 | Year 2 | Year 3 | Year 4 |

A. Determining the Call Option Value

As explained at Level I (Chapter 2), the value of a callable bond is equal to the value of an option-free bond minus the value of the call option. This means that:

value of a call option = value of an option-free bond − value of a callable bond

We have just seen how the value of an option-free bond and the value of a callable bond can be determined. The difference between the two values is therefore the value of the call option.

In our illustration, the value of the option-free bond is $104.643. If the call price is $100 in each year and the value of the callable bond is $102.899 assuming 10% volatility for the 1-year rate, the value of the call option is $1.744 (= $104.634 − $102.899).

B. Volatility and the Arbitrage-Free Value

In our illustration, interest rate volatility was assumed to be 10%. The volatility assumption has an important impact on the arbitrage-free value. More specifically, the higher the expected volatility, the higher the value of an option. The same is true for an option embedded in a bond. Correspondingly, this affects the value of a bond with an embedded option.

For example, for a callable bond, a higher interest rate volatility assumption means that the value of the call option increases and, since the value of the option-free bond is not affected, the value of the callable bond must be lower.

We can see this using the on-the-run yield curve in our previous illustrations. In the previous illustrations, we assumed interest rate volatility of 10%. To show the effect of higher volatility, we will assume volatility of 20%. The solution to Practice Question 1 gives the corresponding binomial interest rate tree. The solution to Practice Question 2 verifies that the binomial interest rate tree provides the same value for the option-free bond, $104.643.

The solution to Practice Question 3 shows the calculation for the callable bond assuming interest rate volatility of 20%. For the callable bond it is assumed that the issue is callable at par beginning in year 1. The value of the callable bond is $102.108 if volatility is assumed to be 20% compared to $102.899 if volatility is assumed to be 10%. Notice that at the higher assumed volatility (20%), the callable bond has a lower value than at the lower assumed volatility (10%). The reason for this is that the value of an option increases with the higher assumed volatility. So, at 20% volatility the value of the embedded call option is higher than at 10% volatility. But the embedded call option is subtracted from the option-free value to obtain the value of the callable bond. Since a higher value for the embedded call option is subtracted from the option-free value at 20% volatility than at 10% volatility, the value of the callable bond is lower at 20% volatility.

PRACTICE QUESTION 3

Suppose that the volatility assumption is 20% rather than 10% and therefore the binomial interest rate tree is the one shown in Practice Question 1.

a. Compute the arbitrage-free value for the 4-year 6.5% coupon bond callable at par beginning Year 1 based on 20% volatility.

b. Compare the arbitrage-free value for this bond based on 20% volatility and 10% volatility as computed in Exhibit 7.

C. Option-Adjusted Spread

Suppose the market price of the 4-year 6.5% callable bond is $102.218 and the theoretical value assuming 10% volatility is $102.899. This means that this bond is cheap by $0.681 according to the valuation model. Bond market participants prefer to think not in terms of a bond's price being cheap or expensive in dollar terms but rather in terms of a yield spread — a cheap bond trades at a higher yield spread and an expensive bond at a lower yield spread.

The **option-adjusted spread** is the constant spread that when added to all the 1-year rates on the binomial interest rate tree that will make the arbitrage-free value (i.e., the value produced by the binomial model) equal to the market price. In our illustration, if the market price is $102.218, the OAS would be the constant spread added to every rate in Exhibit 4 that will make the arbitrage-free value equal to $102.218. The solution in this case would be 35 basis points. This can be verified in Exhibit 10 which shows the value of this issue by adding 35 basis points to each rate.

As with the value of a bond with an embedded option, the OAS will depend on the volatility assumption. For a given bond price, the higher the interest rate volatility assumed, the lower the OAS for a callable bond. For example, if volatility is 20% rather than 10%, the OAS would be −6 basis points. This illustration clearly demonstrates the importance of the volatility assumption. Assuming volatility of 10%, the OAS is 35 basis points. At 20% volatility, the OAS declines and, in this case is negative and therefore the bond is overvalued relative to the model.

Exhibit 10: Demonstration that the Option-Adjusted Spread is 35 Basis Points For a 6.5% Callable Bond Selling at 102.218 (Assuming 10% Volatility)

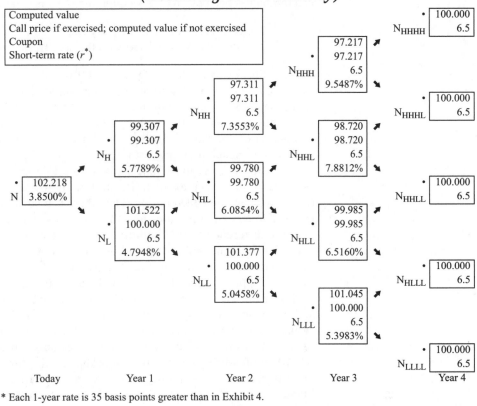

Today   Year 1   Year 2   Year 3   Year 4

* Each 1-year rate is 35 basis points greater than in Exhibit 4.

How do we interpret the OAS? At Level I (Chapter 6) we addressed this but did not demonstrate how the value was computed using a valuation model. In general, a nominal spread between two yields reflects differences in the:

1. credit risk of the two issues
2. liquidity risk of the two issues
3. option risk of the two issues

For example, if one of the issues is a non-U.S. Treasury issue with an embedded option and the benchmark interest rates are the rates for the U.S. Treasury on-the-run securities, then the nominal spread is a measure of the difference due to the:

1. credit risk of the non-Treasury issue
2. liquidity risk associated with the non-Treasury issue
3. option risk associated with the non-Treasury issue that is not present in Treasury issues

What the OAS seeks to do is remove from the nominal spread the amount that is due to the option risk. The measure is called an OAS because (1) it is a spread and (2) it adjusts the cash flows for the option when computing the spread to the benchmark interest rates. The second point can be seen from Exhibits 7 and 8. Notice that at each node the value obtained from the backward induction method is adjusted based on the call option and the call rule. Thus, the resulting spread is "option adjusted."

Thus, if the Treasury on-the-run issues are used as the benchmark, because the call option has been taken into account, the OAS is measuring the compensation for the:

1. credit risk of the non-Treasury issue
2. liquidity risk associated with the non-Treasury issue

So, for example, an OAS of 160 basis points for a callable BBB industrial issue would mean that based on the valuation model (including the volatility assumption), the OAS is compensation for the credit risk and the lower liquidity of the industrial issue relative to the Treasury benchmark issues. The OAS has removed the compensation for the call feature present in the industrial issue that is not present in the Treasury benchmark interest rates.

However, suppose that the benchmark interest rates are the on-the-run interest rates for the issuer, as in our illustration of how to use the binomial model to value a bond with an embedded option. Then there is no difference in the credit risk between the benchmark interest rates and the non-Treasury issue. That is, the OAS reflects only the difference in the liquidity of an issue relative to the on-the-run issues. The valuation has removed the spread due to the option risk and using the issuer's own benchmark interest rates removes the credit risk.

Suppose instead that the benchmark interest rates used are not of that particular issuer but the on-the-run issues for issuers in the same sector of the bond market and the same credit rating of the issue being analyzed. For example, suppose that the callable bond issue being analyzed is that issued by the XYZ Manufacturing Company, a BBB industrial company. An on-the-run yield curve can be estimated for the XYZ Manufacturing Company. Using that on-the-run yield curve, the OAS reflects the difference in the liquidity risk between the particular callable bond of the XYZ Manufacturing Company analyzed and the on-the-run issues of the XYZ Manufacturing Company. However, if instead the benchmark interest rates used to value the callable bond of the XYZ Manufacturing Company are those of a generic BBB industrial company, the OAS reflects (1) the difference between the liquidity risk of the XYZ Manufacturing Company's callable bond and that of a generic BBB industrial company and (2) differences between event risk/credit risk specific to XYZ Manufacturing Company's issue beyond generic BBB credit risk.

Consequently, we know that an OAS is a spread after adjusting for the embedded option. But we know nothing else until the benchmark interest rates are identified. Without knowing the benchmark used — Treasury on-the-run yield curve, an issuer's on-the-run yield curve, or a generic on-the-run yield curve for issuers in the same sector of the bond market and of the same credit rating — we cannot interpret what the OAS is providing compensation for. Some market participants might view this as unrealistic since most of the time the on-the-run Treasury yield curve is used and therefore the OAS reflects credit risk and liquidity risk. However, vendors of analytical system and most dealer models allow an investor to specify the benchmark interest rates to be used. The default feature in these systems (i.e., what the model uses as the benchmark interest rates if the investor does not specify the benchmark) is the Treasury on-the-run yield curve.

So, once an investor is told what the OAS is of a particular bond, the first question should be: Relative to what benchmark interest rates? This is particularly important in non-U.S. markets where the OAS concept is beginning to be used with greater frequency. It also means that comparing OAS values across global markets is difficult because different benchmark interest rates are being used and therefore the OAS is capturing different risks.

Today "funded" investors — that is, investors who borrow funds and seek to earn a spread over their funding costs — use the London interbank offered rate (LIBOR) as their benchmark interest rates. Most funded investors borrow funds at a spread over LIBOR. Consequently, if a yield curve for LIBOR is used as the benchmark interest rates, the OAS reflects a spread relative to their funding cost. The OAS reflects credit risk relative to the credit risk associated with LIBOR and liquidity risk of the issue. So, if a callable bond has an OAS of 80 basis points and the LIBOR yield curve is the benchmark, then the OAS is compensation relative to LIBOR after adjusting for the embedded call option. A funded investor will then compare the OAS to the spread it must pay over its funding costs. So, if an investor's funding cost is 25 basis points over LIBOR, then a callable bond with an OAS of 80 basis points would be acceptable. Whether or not a funded investor would purchase the callable bond depends on whether or not the credit risk and the liquidity risk are acceptable and whether or not the compensation for these risks (as measured by the OAS) in the opinion of the investor is adequate.

Finally, let's take a closer look at the interpretation of the OAS as a spread relative to benchmark interest rates. This does *not* mean that it is a spread over one maturity for the benchmark interest rates. For example, consider the 35 basis point OAS for the 4-year 6.5% callable issue. The yield for the 4-year on-the-run issue is 5.2%. An OAS of 35 basis points does *not* mean that this callable issue is offering an option-adjusted *yield* of 5.55% (5.2% plus 35 basis points). Rather, to understand how it is spread off the benchmark interest rates, look at Exhibit 10.

First, the benchmark interest rates are used to construct the interest rate at each node of the interest rate tree. Next, recall that the rate at each node in the interest rate tree is the 1-year forward rate. (In general, they are the 1-period forward rates). Now, to get the OAS we must determine the spread that must be added to each of the 1-year forward rates in the interest rate tree so that the backward induction method will produce a value equal to the market value. So, while it is often stated that the OAS is a spread relative to the benchmark interest rates, strictly speaking, it is a spread over the 1-period forward rates in the interest rate tree that are constructed from the benchmark interest rates.

PRACTICE QUESTION 4

Show that if 20% volatility is assumed the OAS is −6 basis points.

D. Effective Duration and Effective Convexity

At Level I (Chapter 7), we explained the meaning of duration and convexity measures and explained how these two measures can be computed. Specifically, duration is the approximate percentage change in the value of a security for a 100 basis point change in interest rates (assuming a parallel shift in the yield curve). The convexity measure allows for an adjustment to the estimated price change obtained by using duration. The formula for duration and convexity are repeated below:

$$\text{duration} = \frac{V_- - V_+}{2V_0(\Delta y)}$$

$$\text{convexity} = \frac{V_+ + V_- - 2V_0}{2V_0(\Delta y)^2}$$

where

$$\Delta y = \text{change in rate used to calculate new values}$$
$$V_+ = \text{estimated value if yield is increased by } \Delta y$$
$$V_- = \text{estimated value if yield is decreased by } \Delta y$$
$$V_0 = \text{initial price (per \$100 of par value)}$$

We also made a distinction at Level I between "modified" duration and convexity and "effective" duration and convexity (see Exhibit 18 in Chapter 7 of Level I). Modified duration and convexity do not allow for the fact that the cash flows for a bond with an embedded option may change due to the exercise of the option. In contrast, effective duration and convexity do take into consideration how changes in interest rates in the future may alter the cash flows due to the exercise of the option. But, we did not demonstrate how to compute effective duration and convexity because they require a model for valuing bonds with embedded options and we did not introduce such models until this chapter.

So, let's see how effective duration and convexity are computed using the binomial model. With effective duration and convexity, the values V_- and V_+ are obtained from the binomial model. Recall that in using the binomial model, the cash flows at a node are adjusted for the embedded call option as was demonstrated in Exhibit 7 and highlighted in the lower panel of Exhibit 8.

The procedure for calculating the value of V_+ is as follows:

Step 1: Given the market price of the issue calculate its OAS using the procedure described earlier.

Step 2: Shift the on-the-run yield curve up by a small number of basis points (Δy).

Step 3: Construct a binomial interest rate tree based on the new yield curve in Step 2.

Step 4: To each of the 1-year rates in the binomial interest rate tree, add the OAS to obtain an "adjusted tree." That is, the calculation of the effective duration and convexity assumes that the OAS will not change when interest rates change.

Step 5: Use the adjusted tree found in Step 4 to determine the value of the bond, which is V_+.

To determine the value of V_-, the same five steps are followed except that in Step 2, the on-the-run yield curve is shifted down by a small number of basis points (Δy).

To illustrate how V_+ and V_- are determined in order to calculate effective duration and effective convexity, we will use the same on-the-run yield curve that we have used in our previous illustrations assuming a volatility of 10%. The 4-year callable bond with a coupon rate of 6.5% and callable at par selling at 102.218 will be used in this illustration. The OAS for this issue is 35 basis points.

Exhibit 11 shows the adjusted tree by shifting the yield curve up by an arbitrarily small number of basis points, 25 basis points, and then adding 35 basis points (the OAS) to each 1-year rate. The adjusted tree is then used to value the bond. The resulting value, V_+, is 101.621. Exhibit 12 shows the adjusted tree by shifting the yield curve down by 25 basis points and then adding 35 basis points to each 1-year rate. The resulting value, V_-, is 102.765.

*Exhibit 11: Determination of V$_+$ for Calculating Effective Duration and Convexity**

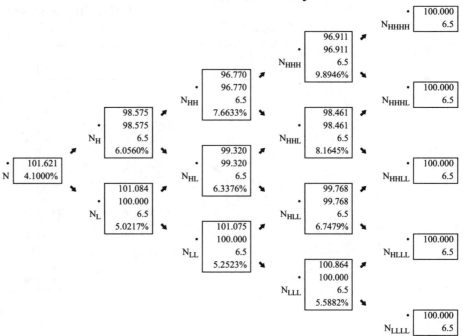

* +25 basis point shift in on-the-run yield curve.

*Exhibit 12: Determination of V$_-$ for Calculating Effective Duration and Convexity**

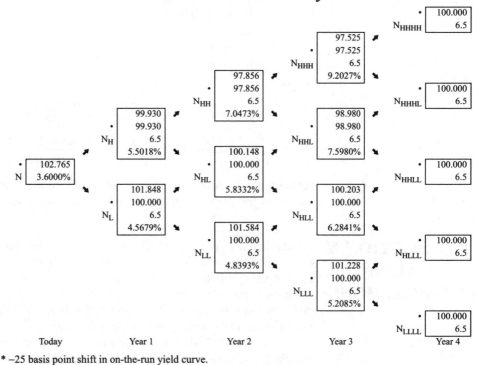

* −25 basis point shift in on-the-run yield curve.

Exhibit 13: Valuing a Putable Bond with Four Years to Maturity, a Coupon Rate of 6.5%, and Putable in One Year at 100 (10% Volatility Assumed)

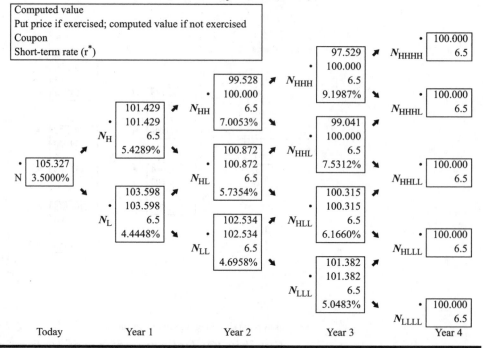

The results are summarized below:

$$\Delta y = 0.0025$$
$$V_+ = 101.621$$
$$V_- = 102.765$$
$$V_0 = 102.218$$

Therefore,

$$\text{effective duration} = \frac{102.765 - 101.621}{2(102.218)(0.0025)} = 2.24$$

$$\text{effective convexity} = \frac{101.621 + 102.765 - 2(102.218)}{2(102.218)(0.0025)^2} = -39.1321$$

Notice that this callable bond exhibits negative convexity. The characteristic of negative convexity for a bond with an embedded option was explained at Level I (Chapter 7).

SECTION V
VALUING A
PUTABLE BOND

A putable bond is one in which the bondholder has the right to force the issuer to pay off the bond prior to the maturity date. To illustrate how the binomial model can be used to value a putable bond, suppose that a 6.5% bond with four years remaining to maturity is putable in one year at par ($100). Also assume that the appropriate binomial interest rate tree for this issuer is the one in Exhibit 4 and the bondholder exercises the put if the bond's price is less than par.

Exhibit 13 shows the binomial interest rate tree with the values based on whether or not the investor exercises the option at a node. Exhibit 14 highlights selected nodes for year 2 and year 3 just as we did in Exhibit 8. The lower part of the exhibit shows the nodes where the put option is not exercised and therefore the value at each node is the same as when the bond is option free. In contrast, the upper part of the exhibit shows where the value obtained from the backward induction method is overridden and 100 is used because the put option is exercised.

The value of the putable bond is $105.327, a value that is greater than the value of the corresponding option-free bond. The reason for this can be seen from the following relationship:

value of a putable bond = value of an option-free bond + value of the put option

The reason for adding the value of the put option is that the investor has purchased the put option.

We can rewrite the above relationship to determine the value of the put option:

value of the put option = value of a putable bond − value of an option-free bond

In our example, since the value of the putable bond is $105.327 and the value of the corresponding option-free bond is $104.643, the value of the put option is −$0.684. The negative sign indicates the issuer has sold the option, or equivalently, the investor has purchased the option.

We have stressed that the value of a bond with an embedded option is affected by the volatility assumption. Unlike a callable bond, the value of a putable bond increases if the assumed volatility increases. It can be demonstrated that if a 20% volatility is assumed the value of this putable bond increases from 105.327 at 10% volatility to 106.010.

Exhibit 14: Highlighting Nodes in Years 2 and 3 for a Putable Bond

(a) Selected nodes where put option is exercised

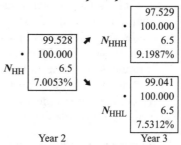

Year 2   Year 3

(b) Nodes where put option is not exercised

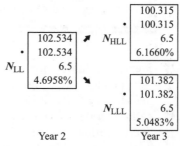

Year 2   Year 3

Exhibit 15: Valuing a Putable/Callable Issue
(10% Volatility Assumed)

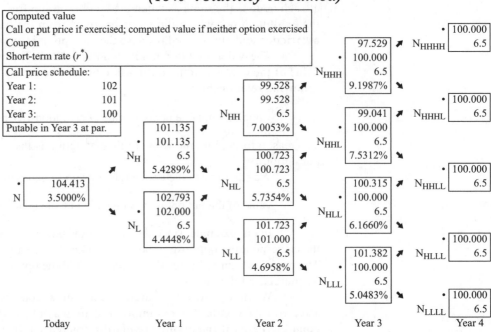

Suppose that a bond is both putable and callable. The procedure for valuing such a structure is to adjust the value at each node to reflect whether the issue would be put or called. To illustrate this, consider the 4-year callable bond analyzed earlier that had a call schedule. The valuation of this issue is shown in Exhibit 9. Suppose the issue is putable in year 3 at par value. Exhibit 15 shows how to value this callable/putable issue. At each node there are two decisions about the exercising of an option that must be made. First, given the valuation from the backward induction method at a node, the call rule is invoked to determine whether the issue will be called. If it is called, the value at the node is replaced by the call price. The valuation procedure then continues using the call price at that node. Second, if the call option is not exercised at a node, it must be determined whether or not the put option is exercised. If it is exercised, then the value from the backward induction method is overridden and the put price is substituted at that node and is used in subsequent calculations.

PRACTICE QUESTION 5

Using the binomial interest rate tree based on 20%, show that the value of this putable bond is 106.010.

SECTION VI
VALUING A
STEP-UP
CALLABLE NOTE

Step-up callable notes are callable instruments whose coupon rate is increased (i.e., "stepped up") at designated times. When the coupon rate is increased only once over the security's life, it is said to be a **single step-up callable note**. A **multiple step-up callable note** is a step-up callable note whose coupon is increased more than one time over the life of the security. Valuation using the binomial model is similar to that for valuing a callable bond except that the cash flows are altered at each node to reflect the coupon changing characteristics of a step-up note.

To illustrate how the binomial model can be used to value step-up callable notes, let's begin with a single step-up callable note. Suppose that a 4-year step-up callable note pays 4.25% for two years and then 7.5% for two more years. Assume that this note is callable at par at the end of Year 2 and Year 3. We will use the binomial interest rate tree given in Exhibit 4 to value this note.

Exhibit 16 shows the value of a corresponding single step-up *noncallable* note. The valuation procedure is identical to that performed in Exhibit 7 except that the coupon in the box at each node reflects the step-up terms. The value is $102.082. Exhibit 17 shows that the value of the single step-up callable note is $100.031. The value of the embedded call option is equal to the difference in the step-up noncallable note value and the step-up callable note value, $2.051.

The procedure is the same for a multiple step-up callable note. Suppose that a multiple step-up callable note has the following coupon rates: 4.2% in Year 1, 5% in Year 2, 6% in Year 3, and 7% in Year 4. Also assume that the note is callable at the end of Year 1 at par. Exhibit 18 shows that the value of this note if it noncallable is $101.012. The value of the multiple step-up callable note is $99.996 as shown in Exhibit 19. Therefore, the value of the embedded call option is $1.016 (= 101.012 − 99.996).

SECTION VII VALUING A CAPPED FLOATER

The valuation of a floating-rate note with a cap (i.e., a capped floater) using the binomial model requires that the coupon rate be adjusted based on the 1-year rate (which is assumed to be the reference rate). Exhibit 20 shows the binomial tree and the relevant values at each node for a floater whose coupon rate is the 1-year rate flat (i.e., no margin over the reference rate) and in which there are no restrictions on the coupon rate.

What is important to recall about floaters is that the coupon rate is set at the beginning of the period but paid at the end of the period (i.e., beginning of the next period). That is, the coupon interest is paid in arrears. We discussed this feature of floaters at Level I (Chapter 1).

The valuation procedure is identical to that for the other structures described above except that an adjustment is made for the characteristic of a floater that the coupon rate is set at the beginning of the year and paid in arrears. Here is how the payment in arrears characteristic affects the backward induction method. Look at the top node for year 2 in Exhibit 20. The coupon rate shown at that node is 7.0053% as determined by the 1-year rate at that node. Since the coupon payment will not be made until year 3 (i.e., paid in arrears), the value of 100 shown at the node is determined using the backward induction method but discounting the coupon rate shown at the node. For example, let's see how we get the value of 100 in the top box in year 2. The procedure is to calculate the average of the two present values of the bond value and coupon. Since the bond values and coupons are the same, the present value is simply:

$$\frac{100 + 7.0053}{1.070053} = 100$$

Suppose that the floater has a cap of 7.25%. Exhibit 21 shows how this floater would be valued. At each node where the 1-year rate exceeds 7.25%, a coupon of $7.25 is substituted. The value of this capped floater is 99.724. Thus, the cost of the cap is the difference between par and 99.724. If the cap for this floater was 7.75% rather than 7.25%, it can be shown that the value of this floater would be 99.858. That is, the higher the cap, the closer the capped floater will trade to par.

Exhibit 16: Valuing a Single Step-Up Noncallable Note with Four Years to Maturity (10% Volatility Assumed)

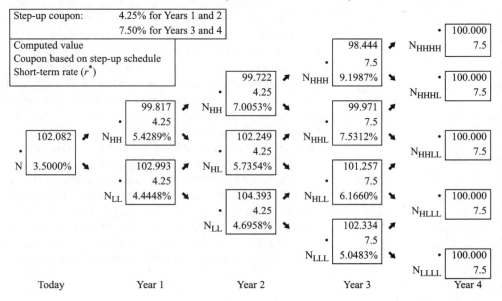

Exhibit 17: Valuing a Single Step-Up Callable Note with Four Years to Maturity, Callable in Two Years at 100 (10% Volatility Assumed)

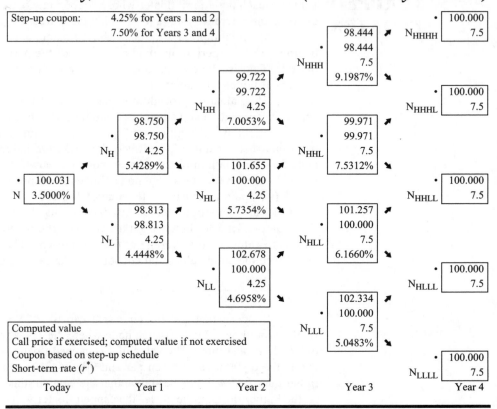

Exhibit 18: Valuing a Multiple Step-Up Noncallable Note with Four Years to Maturity (10% Volatility Assumed)

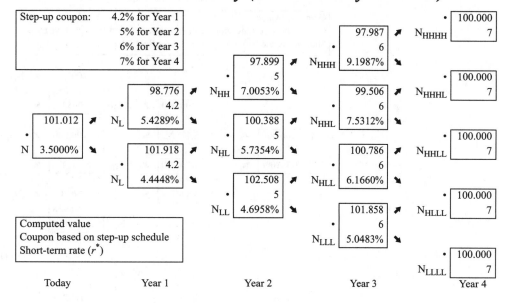

Exhibit 19: Valuing a Multiple Step-Up Callable Note with Four Years to Maturity, and Callable in One Year at 100 (10% Volatility Assumed)

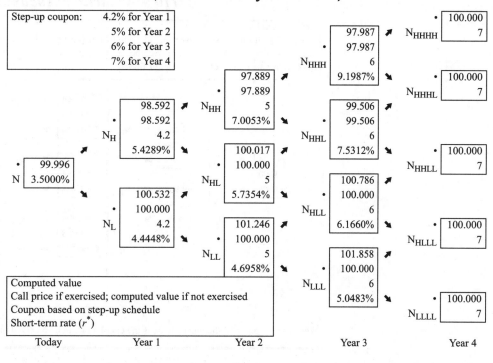

Exhibit 20: Valuing a Floater with No Cap
(10% Volatility Assumed)

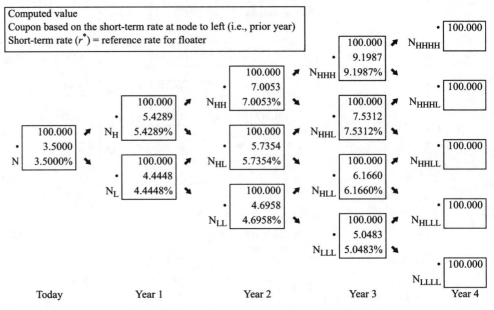

Today   Year 1   Year 2   Year 3   Year 4

Note: The coupon rate shown at a node is the coupon rate to be received in the next year.

Exhibit 21: Valuing a Floating Rate Note with a 7.25% Cap
(10% Volatility Assumed)

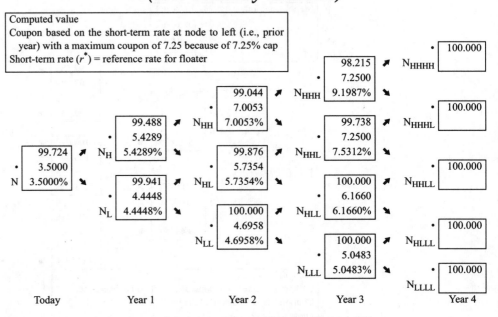

Today   Year 1   Year 2   Year 3   Year 4

Note: The coupon rate shown at a node is the coupon rate to be received in the next year.

Thus, it is important to emphasize that the valuation mechanics are being modified slightly only to reflect the characteristics of the floater's cash flow. All of the other principles regarding valuation of bonds with embedded options are the same. For a capped floater there is a rule for determining whether or not to override the cash flow at a node based on the cap. Since as explained at Level I (Chapter 1) a cap embedded in a floater is effectively an option granted by the investor to the issuer, it should be no surprise that the valuation model described in this chapter can be used to value a capped floater.

SECTION VIII ANALYSIS OF CONVERTIBLE BONDS

A convertible bond is a security that can be converted into common stock at the option of the investor. Hence, it is a bond with an embedded option where the option is granted to the investor. Moreover, since a convertible bond may be callable and putable, it is a complex bond because the value of the bond will depend on both how interest rates change (which affects the value of the call and any put option) *and* how changes in the market price of the stock affects the value of the option to convert to common stock.

A. Basic Features of Convertible Securities

The conversion provision of a convertible security grants the securityholder the right to convert the security into a predetermined number of shares of common stock of the issuer. A convertible security is therefore a security with an embedded call option to buy the common stock of the issuer. An **exchangeable security** grants the securityholder the right to exchange the security for the common stock of a firm *other* than the issuer of the security. For example, some Ford Motor Credit convertible bonds are exchangeable for the common stock of the parent company, Ford Motor Company. Throughout this chapter we use the term convertible security to refer to both convertible and exchangeable securities.

In illustrating the calculation of the various concepts described below, we will use the General Signal Corporation (ticker symbol "GSX") 5¾% convertible issue due June 1, 2002. Information about the issue and the stock of this issuer is provided in Exhibit 22 as of 10/7/93.

The number of shares of common stock that the securityholder will receive from exercising the call option of a convertible security is called the **conversion ratio**. The conversion privilege may extend for all or only some portion of the security's life, and the stated conversion ratio may change over time. It is always adjusted proportionately for stock splits and stock dividends. For the GSX convertible issue, the conversion ratio is 25.32 shares. This means that for each $1,000 of par value of this issue the securityholder exchanges for GSX common stock, he will receive 25.32 shares.

At the time of issuance of a convertible bond, the effective price at which the buyer of the convertible bond will pay for the stock can be determined as follows. The prospectus will specify the number of shares that the investor will receive by exchanging the bond for the common stock. The number of shares is called the **conversion ratio**. So, for example, assume the conversion ratio is 20. If the investor converts the bond for stock the investor will receive 20 shares of common stock. Now, suppose that the par value for the convertible bond is $1,000 and is sold to investors at issuance at that price. Then effectively by buying the convertible bond for $1,000 at issuance, investors are purchasing the common stock for $50 per share ($1,000/20 shares). This price is referred to in the prospectus as the **conversion price** and some investors refer to it as the **stated conversion price**. For a bond not issued at par (for example, a zero-coupon bond), the conversion price is determined by dividing the issue price per $1,000 of par value by the conversion ratio.

Exhibit 22: Information About General Signal Corporation Convertible Bond 5¾% Due June 1, 2002 and Common Stock

Convertible bond

Market price (as of 10/7/93):	$106.50	Issue date:	6/1/92
Issue proceeds:	$100 million	Maturity date:	6/1/02
Non-call until 6/1/95			

Call price schedule	
6/1/95	103.59
6/1/96	102.88
6/1/97	102.16
6/1/98	101.44
6/1/99	100.72
6/1/00	100.00
6/1/01	100.00

Coupon rate: 5¾%

Conversion ratio: 25.320 shares of GSX shares per $1,000 par value

Rating: A3/A−

GSX common stock

Expected volatility:	17%	Dividend yield (as of 10/7/93):	2.727%
Dividend per share:	$0.90 per year	Stock price:	$33

The GSX convertible was issued for $1,000 per $1,000 of par value and the conversion ratio is 25.32. Therefore, the conversion price at issuance for the GSX convertible issue is $39.49 ($1,000/25.32 shares).

Almost all convertible issues are callable. The GSX convertible issue had a non-call period at issuance of three years. The call price schedule for the GSX convertible issue is shown in Exhibit 22. There are some issues that have a provisional call feature that allows the issuer to call the issue during the non-call period if the price of the stock reaches a certain price.

Some convertible bonds are putable. Put options can be classified as "hard" puts and "soft" puts. A **hard put** is one in which the convertible security must be redeemed by the issuer for cash. In the case of a **soft put**, while the investor has the option to exercise the put, the *issuer* may select how the payment will be made. The issuer may redeem the convertible security for cash, common stock, subordinated notes, or a combination of the three.

B. Traditional Analysis of Convertible Securities

Traditional analysis of convertible bonds relies on measures that do not attempt to directly value the embedded call, put, or common stock options. We present and illustrate these measures below and later discuss an option-based approach to valuation of convertible bonds.

1. Minimum Value of a Convertible Security

The **conversion value** or **parity value** of a convertible security is the value of the security if it is converted immediately.[5] That is,

conversion value = market price of common stock × conversion ratio

---

[5] Technically, the standard textbook definition of conversion value given here is theoretically incorrect because as bondholders convert, the price of the stock will decline. The theoretically correct definition for the conversion value is that it is the product of the conversion ratio and the stock price *after* conversion.

The minimum price of a convertible security is the greater of

1. Its conversion value, or
2. Its value as a security without the conversion option — that is, based on the convertible security's cash flows if not converted (i.e., a plain vanilla security). This value is called its **straight value** or **investment value**. The straight value is found by using the valuation model described earlier in this chapter because almost all issues are callable.

If the convertible security does not sell for the greater of these two values, arbitrage profits could be realized. For example, suppose the conversion value is greater than the straight value, and the security trades at its straight value. An investor can buy the convertible security at the straight value and immediately convert it. By doing so, the investor realizes a gain equal to the difference between the conversion value and the straight value. Suppose, instead, the straight value is greater than the conversion value, and the security trades at its conversion value. By buying the convertible at the conversion value, the investor will realize a higher yield than a comparable straight security.

Consider the GSX convertible issue. Suppose that the straight value of the bond is $98.19 per $100 of par value on 10/7/93. Since the market price per share of common stock on that date was $33, the conversion value per $1,000 of par value was:

$$\text{conversion value} = \$33 \times 25.32 = \$835.56$$

Consequently, the conversion value is 83.556% of par value. Per $100 of par value the conversion value is $83.556. Since the straight value is $98.19 and the conversion value is $83.556, the minimum value for the GSX convertible on 10/7/93 had to be $98.19.

2. Market Conversion Price

The price that an investor effectively pays for the common stock if the convertible bond is purchased and then converted into the common stock is called the **market conversion price** or **conversion parity price**. It is found as follows:

$$\text{market conversion price} = \frac{\text{market price of convertible security}}{\text{conversion ratio}}$$

The market conversion price is a useful benchmark because once the actual market price of the stock rises above the market conversion price, any further stock price increase is certain to increase the value of the convertible bond by at least the same percentage. Therefore, the market conversion price can be viewed as a break-even price.

An investor who purchases a convertible bond rather than the underlying stock, effectively pays a premium over the current market price of the stock. This premium per share is equal to the difference between the market conversion price and the current market price of the common stock. That is,

$$\text{market conversion premium per share}$$
$$= \text{market conversion price} - \text{current market price}$$

The market conversion premium per share is usually expressed as a percentage of the current market price as follows:

$$\text{market conversion premium ratio} = \frac{\text{market conversion premium per share}}{\text{market price of common stock}}$$

Why would someone be willing to pay a premium to buy the stock? Recall that the minimum price of a convertible security is the greater of its conversion value or its straight value. Thus, as the common stock price declines, the price of the convertible bond will not fall below its straight value. The straight value therefore acts as a floor for the convertible security's price.

Viewed in this context, the market conversion premium per share can be seen as the price of a call option. As explained in Chapter 7, the buyer of a call option limits the downside risk to the option price. In the case of a convertible bond, for a premium, the securityholder limits the downside risk to the straight value of the bond. The difference between the buyer of a call option and the buyer of a convertible bond is that the former knows precisely the dollar amount of the downside risk, while the latter knows only that the most that can be lost is the difference between the convertible bond's price and the straight value. The straight value at some future date, however, is unknown; the value will change as market interest rates change or if the issuer's credit quality changes.

The calculation of the market conversion price, market conversion premium per share, and market conversion premium ratio for the GSX convertible issue based on market data as of 10/7/93 is shown below:

$$\text{market conversion price} = \frac{\$1,065}{25.32} = \$42.06$$

Thus, if the investor purchased the convertible and then converted it to common stock, the effective price that the investor paid per share is $42.06.

$$\text{market conversion premium per share} = \$42.06 - \$33 = \$9.06$$

The investor is effectively paying a premium per share of $9.06 by buying the convertible rather than buying the stock for $33.

$$\text{market conversion premium ratio} = \frac{\$9.06}{\$33} = 0.275 = 27.5\%$$

The premium per share of $9.06 means that the investor is paying 27.5% above the market price of $33 by buying the convertible.

3. Current Income of Convertible Bond versus Common Stock

As an offset to the market conversion premium per share, investing in the convertible bond rather than buying the stock directly, generally means that the investor realizes higher current income from the coupon interest from a convertible bond than would be received from common stock dividends based on the number of shares equal to the conversion ratio. Analysts evaluating a convertible bond typically compute the time it takes to recover the premium per share by computing the **premium payback period** (which is also known as the **break-even time**). This is computed as follows:

$$\text{premium payback period} = \frac{\text{market conversion premium per share}}{\text{favorable income differential per share}}$$

where the favorable income differential per share is equal to the following:

$$\frac{\text{coupon interest} - (\text{conversion ratio} \times \text{common stock dividend per share})}{\text{conversion ratio}}$$

The numerator of the formula is the difference between the coupon interest for the issue and the dividends that would be received if the investor converted the issue into common stock. Since the investor would receive the number of shares specified by the conversion ratio, then multiplying the conversion ratio by the dividend per share of common stock gives the total dividends that would be received if the investor converted. Dividing the difference between the coupon interest and the total dividends that would be received if the issue is converted by the conversion ratio gives the favorable income differential on a per share basis by owning the convertible rather than the common stock.

Notice that the premium payback period does *not* take into account the time value of money.

For the GSX convertible issue, the market conversion premium per share is $9.06. The favorable income differential per share is found as follows:

$$\text{coupon interest from bond} = 0.0575 \times \$1,000 = \$57.50$$

$$\text{conversion ratio} \times \text{dividend per share} = 25.32 \times \$0.90 = \$22.79$$

Therefore,

$$\text{favorable income differential per share} = \frac{\$57.50 - \$22.79}{25.32} = \$1.37$$

and

$$\text{premium payback period} = \frac{\$9.06}{\$1.37} = 6.6 \text{ years}$$

Without considering the time value of money, the investor would recover the market conversion premium per share assuming unchanged dividends in about 6.6 years.

4. Downside Risk with a Convertible Bond

Unfortunately, investors usually use the straight value as a measure of the downside risk of a convertible security, because it is assumed that the price of the convertible cannot fall below this value. Thus, some investors view the straight value as the floor for the price of the convertible bond. The downside risk is measured as a percentage of the straight value and computed as follows:

$$\text{premium over straight value} = \frac{\text{market price of convertible bond}}{\text{straight value}} - 1$$

The higher the premium over straight value, all other factors constant, the less attractive the convertible bond.

Despite its use in practice, this measure of downside risk is flawed because the straight value (the floor) changes as interest rates change. If interest rates rise (fall), the straight value falls (rises) making the floor fall (rise). Therefore, the downside risk changes as interest rates change.

For the GSX convertible issue, since the market price of the convertible issue is 106.5 and the straight value is 98.19, the premium over straight value is

$$\text{premium over straight value} = \frac{\$106.50}{\$98.19} - 1 = 0.085 = 8.5\%$$

5. The Upside Potential of a Convertible Security

The evaluation of the upside potential of a convertible security depends on the prospects for the underlying common stock. Thus, the techniques for analyzing common stocks discussed in books on equity analysis should be employed.

C. Investment Characteristics of a Convertible Security

The investment characteristics of a convertible bond depend on the common stock price. If the price is low, so that the straight value is considerably higher than the conversion value, the security will trade much like a straight security. The convertible security in such instances is referred to as a **fixed income equivalent** or a **busted convertible**.

When the price of the stock is such that the conversion value is considerably higher than the straight value, then the convertible security will trade as if it were an equity instrument; in this case it is said to be a **common stock equivalent**. In such cases, the market conversion premium per share will be small.

Between these two cases, fixed income equivalent and common stock equivalent, the convertible security trades as a **hybrid security**, having the characteristics of both a fixed income security and a common stock instrument.

D. An Option-Based Valuation Approach

In our discussion of convertible bonds, we did not address the following questions:

1. What is a fair value for the conversion premium per share?
2. How do we handle convertible bonds with call and/or put options?
3. How does a change in interest rates affect the stock price?

Consider first a noncallable/nonputable convertible bond. The investor who purchases this security would be effectively entering into two separate transactions: (1) buying a noncallable/nonputable straight security and (2) buying a call option (or warrant) on the stock, where the number of shares that can be purchased with the call option is equal to the conversion ratio.

The question is: What is the fair value for the call option? The fair value depends on the factors to be discussed in Chapter 8 that affect the price of a call option. While the discussion in that chapter will focus on options where the underlying is a fixed income instrument, the principles apply also to options on common stock. One key factor is the expected price volatility of the stock: the higher the expected price volatility, the greater the value of the call option. The theoretical value of a call option can be valued using the Black-Scholes option pricing model. This model will be discussed in Chapter 8 and is explained in more detail in investment textbooks. As a first approximation to the value of a convertible bond, the formula would be:

convertible security value = straight value + value of the call option on the stock

The value of the call option is added to the straight value because the investor has purchased a call option on the stock.

Now let's add in a common feature of a convertible bond: the issuer's right to call the issue. Therefore, the value of a convertible bond that is callable is equal to:

convertible bond value = straight value + value of the call option on the stock
− value of the call option on the bond

Consequently, the analysis of convertible bonds must take into account the value of the issuer's right to call. This depends, in turn, on (1) future interest rate volatility and (2) economic factors that determine whether or not it is optimal for the issuer to call the security. The Black-Scholes option pricing model cannot handle this situation.

Let's add one more wrinkle. Suppose that the callable convertible bond is also putable. Then the value of such a convertible would be equal to:

convertible bond value = straight value + value of the call option on the stock
− value of the call option on the bond
+ value of the put option on the bond

Once again, the Black-Scholes option pricing model cannot handle multiple options involving options that depend on future interest rates.

To link interest rates and stock prices together (the third question we raise above), statistical analysis of historical movements of these two variables must be estimated and incorporated into the model.

Valuation models based on an option pricing approach have been suggested by several researchers.[6] These models can generally be classified as one-factor or multi-factor models. By "factor" we mean the stochastic (i.e., random) variables that are assumed to drive the value of a convertible or bond. The obvious candidates for factors are the price movement of the underlying common stock and the movement of interest rates. According to Mihir Bhattacharya and Yu Zhu, the most widely used convertible valuation model has been the one-factor model and the factor is the price movement of the underlying common stock.[7]

E. The Risk/Return Profile of a Convertible Security

Let's use the GSX convertible issue and the valuation model to look at the risk/return profile by investing in a convertible issue or the underlying common stock.

Suppose on 10/7/93 an investor is considering the purchase of either the common stock of GSX or the 5¾% convertible issue due 6/1/02. The stock can be purchased in the market for $33. By buying the convertible bond, the investor is effectively purchasing the stock for $42.06 (the market conversion price per share). Exhibit 23 shows the total return for both alternatives one year later assuming (1) the stock price does not change, (2) it changes by ±10%, and (3) it changes by ±25%. The convertible's theoretical value is based on the Merrill Lynch valuation model.

If the GSX's stock price is unchanged, the stock position will underperform the convertible position despite the fact that a premium was paid to purchase the stock by acquiring the convertible issue. The reason is that even though the convertible's theoretical value decreased, the income from coupon more than compensates for the capital loss. In the two scenarios where the price of GSX stock declines, the convertible position outperforms the stock position because the straight value provides a floor for the convertible.

---

[6] See, for example: Michael Brennan and Eduardo Schwartz, "Convertible Bonds: Valuation and Optimal Strategies for Call and Conversion," *Journal of Finance* (December 1977), pp. 1699-1715; Jonathan Ingersoll, "A Contingent-Claims Valuation of Convertible Securities," *Journal of Financial Economics* (May 1977), pp. 289-322; Michael Brennan and Eduardo Schwartz, "Analyzing Convertible Bonds," *Journal of Financial and Quantitative Analysis* (November 1980), pp. 907-929; and, George Constantinides, "Warrant Exercise and Bond Conversion in Competitive Markets," *Journal of Financial Economics* (September 1984), pp. 371-398.

[7] Mihir Bhattacharya and Yu Zhu, "Valuation and Analysis of Convertible Securities," Chapter 42 in Frank J. Fabozzi (ed.), *The Handbook of Fixed Income Securities* (Chicago: Irwin Professional Publishing).

Exhibit 23: Comparison of 1-Year Return for GSX Stock and Convertible Issue for Assumed Changes in Stock Price

Beginning of horizon: 10/7/93
End of horizon: 10/07/94
Price of GSX stock on 10/7/93: $33.00
Assumed volatility of GSX stock return: 17%

Stock price change (%)	GSX stock return (%)	Convertible's theoretical value	Convertible's return (%)
−25	−22.27	100.47	−0.26
−10	−7.27	102.96	2.08
0	2.73	105.27	4.24
10	12.73	108.12	6.92
25	27.73	113.74	12.20

One of the critical assumptions in this analysis is that the straight value does not change except for the passage of time. If interest rates rise, the straight value will decline. Even if interest rates do not rise, the perceived creditworthiness of the issuer may deteriorate, causing investors to demand a higher yield. The illustration clearly demonstrates that there are benefits and drawbacks of investing in convertible securities. The disadvantage is the upside potential give-up because a premium per share must be paid. An advantage is the reduction in downside risk (as determined by the straight value).

Keep in mind that the major reason for the acquisition of the convertible bond is the potential price appreciation due to the increase in the price of the stock. An analysis of the growth prospects of the issuer's earnings and stock price is beyond the scope of this book but is described in all books on equity analysis.

SECTION IX
KEY POINTS

❏ *A valuation model must produce arbitrage-free values; that is, a valuation model must produce a value for each on-the-run issue that is equal to its observed market price.*

❏ *There are several arbitrage-free models that can be used to value bonds with embedded options but they all follow the same principle — they generate a tree of interest rates based on some interest rate volatility assumption, they require rules for determining when any of the embedded options will be exercised, and they employ the backward induction methodology.*

❏ *A valuation model involves generating an interest rate tree based on (1) an issuer's on-the-run yield curve, (2) an assumed interest rate model, and (3) an assumed interest rate volatility.*

❏ *The assumed volatility of interest rates incorporates the uncertainty about future interest rates into the analysis.*

❏ *The interest rate tree is constructed using a process that is similar to bootstrapping but requires an iterative procedure to determine the interest rates that will produce a value for the on-the-run issues equal to their market value.*

❏ *At each node of the tree there are interest rates and these rates are effectively forward rates; thus, there is a set of forward rates for each year.*

❏ *Using the interest rate tree the arbitrage-free value of any bond can be determined.*

❏ *In valuing a callable bond using the interest rate tree, the cash flows at a node are modified to take into account the call option.*

❏ *The value of the embedded call option is the difference between the value of an option-free bond and the value of the callable bond.*

❏ *The volatility assumption has an important impact on the arbitrage-free value.*

❏ *The option-adjusted spread is the constant spread that when added to the short rates in the binomial interest rate tree will produce a valuation for the bond (i.e., arbitrage-free value) equal to the market price of the bond.*

❏ *The interpretation of the OAS, or equivalently, what the OAS is compensating an investor for, depends on what benchmark interest rates are used.*

❏ *The benchmark interest rates can be the (1) on-the-run Treasury rates, (2) the on-the-run rates for the particular issuer, or (3) the on-the-run rates for issuers in the same sector of the bond market and with the same credit rating as the issue being evaluated.*

❏ *Funded investors can use LIBOR as the benchmark interest rates.*

❏ *Outside of the United States, the benchmark interest rates can be those offered on securities issued by the central government or those of highly rated private issuers.*

❏ *In general, a nominal spread captures (1) credit risk, (2) option risk, and (3) liquidity risk.*

❏ *The option-adjusted spread is a spread after adjusting for the option risk.*

❏ *Depending on the benchmark interest rates used to generate the interest rate tree, the option-adjusted spread may or may not capture credit risk.*

❏ *The option-adjusted spread is not a spread off of one maturity of the benchmark interest rates; rather, it is a spread over the forward rates in the interest rate tree that were constructed from the benchmark interest rates.*

❏ *The required values for calculating effective duration and effective convexity are found by shifting the on-the-run yield curve, calculating a new binomial interest rate tree, and then determining the required values after adjusting the tree by adding the OAS to each short rate.*

❏ *For a bond with any embedded option or options, application of the binomial model requires that the value at each node of the tree be adjusted based on whether or not the option will be exercised; the binomial model can be used to value bonds with multiple or interrelated embedded options by determining at each node of the tree whether or not one of the options will be exercised.*

❏ *With a putable bond, the option will be exercised if the value at a node is less than the price at which the bondholder can put the bond to the issuer.*

❏ *The value of a putable bond is greater than the value of an otherwise option-free bond.*

❏ *The binomial model can be used to value a single step-up callable note or a multiple step-up callable note.*

❏ *To value a floating-rate note that has a cap, the coupon at each node of the tree is adjusted by determining whether or not the cap is reached at a node; if the rate at a node does exceed the cap, the rate at the node is the capped rate rather than the rate determined by the floater's coupon formula.*

❏ *For a floating-rate note, the binomial method must be adjusted to account for the fact that a floater pays in arrears; that is, the coupon payment is determine in a period but not paid until the next period.*

❏ *Convertible and exchangeable securities can be converted into shares of common stock.*

❏ *The conversion ratio is the number of common stock shares for which a convertible security may be converted.*

❏ *Almost all convertible securities are callable and some are putable.*

❏ *The conversion value is the value of the convertible bond if it is immediately converted into the common stock.*

❏ *The market conversion price is the price that an investor effectively pays for the common stock if the convertible security is purchased and then converted into the common stock.*

❏ *The premium paid for the common stock is measured by the market conversion premium per share and market conversion premium ratio.*

❏ *The straight value or investment value of a convertible security is its value if there was no conversion feature.*

❏ *The minimum value of a convertible security is the greater of the conversion value and the straight value.*

❏ *A fixed income equivalent (or a busted convertible) refers to the situation where the straight value is considerably higher than the conversion value so that the security will trade much like a straight security.*

❏ *A common stock equivalent refers to the situation where the conversion value is considerably higher than the straight value so that the convertible security trades as if it were an equity instrument.*

❏ *A hybrid equivalent refers to the situation where the convertible security trades with characteristics of both a fixed income security and a common stock instrument.*

❏ *While the downside risk of a convertible security usually is estimated by calculating the premium over straight value, the limitation of this measure is that the straight value (the floor) changes as interest rates change.*

❏ *An advantage of buying the convertible rather than the common stock is the reduction in downside risk.*

❏ *The disadvantage of a convertible relative to the straight purchase of the common stock is the upside potential give-up because a premium per share must be paid.*

❏ *An option-based valuation model is a more appropriate approach to value convertible securities because of the multiple embedded options.*

❏ *There are various option-based valuation models: one-factor and multiple-factor models.*

❏ *The most common convertible bond valuation model is the one-factor model in which the one factor is the stock price movement.*

END OF CHAPTER QUESTIONS

1. Comment on the following statement:

> "There are several arbitrage-free models for valuing callable bonds. These models differ significantly in terms of how interest rates may change in the next period. There are models that allow the rate in the next period to take on only one of two values. Such a model is called a binomial model. There are models that allow the rate in the next period to take on more than two possible values. For example, there is model that allows the rate in the next period to take on three possible values. Such a model is called a trinomial model. All these models represent a significantly different approach to valuation and involve different procedures for obtain the arbitrage-free value."

2. In discussing the approach taken by its investment management firm in valuing bonds, a representative of the firm made the following statement:

> "Our managers avoid the use of valuation methodologies such as the binomial model or other fancier models because of the many assumptions required to determine the value. Instead, our managers are firm believers in the concept of option-adjusted spread."

Comment on this statement.

3. A portfolio manager must mark a bond position to market. One issue, a callable issue, has not traded in the market recently. So to obtain a price that can be used to mark a position to market, the manager requested a bid from both a dealer and a pricing service. The dealer bid's price was 92. The pricing service indicated a bid price of 93. The manager could not understand the reason for the 1 point difference in the bid prices.

Upon questioning the trader at the dealer firm that gave a bid of 92, the manager found that the trader based the price on the dealer's valuation model. The model used is the binomial model and the benchmark interest rates the model uses is the on-the-run Treasury issues. The manager then contacted a representative from the pricing service and asked what type of valuation model it used. Again, the response was that the binomial model is used and that the on-the-run Treasury issues are used as the benchmark interest rates.

The manager is puzzled why there is a 1 point difference even though the dealer and the pricing service used the same model and the same benchmark interest rates. The manager has asked you to explain why. Provide an explanation to the manager.

4. The manager of an emerging market bond portfolio is approached by a broker about purchasing a new corporate bond issue in Brazil. The issue is callable and the broker's firm estimates that the option-adjusted spread is 220 basis points. What questions would you ask the broker with respect to the 220 basis points OAS?

5. In discussing the option-adjusted spread to a client, a manager stated the following: "The option-adjusted spread measures the yield spread using the Treasury on-the-run yield curve as benchmark interest rates." Comment on this statement.

6. Why is the procedure for valuing a bond with an embedded option called "backward induction"?

7. Why is the value produced by a binomial model and any similar models referred to as an "arbitrage-free model"?

8. a. When valuing an option-free bond, short-term forward rates can be used. When valuing a bond with an embedded option, there is not one forward rate for a period but a set of forward rates for a given period. Explain why.
   b. Explain why the set of forward rates for a given period depend on the assumed interest rate volatility.

9. The on-the-run issue for the Inc.Net Company is shown below:

Maturity (years)	Yield to maturity (%)	Market price
1	7.5	100
2	7.6	100
3	7.7	100

Using the bootstrapping methodology, the spot rates are:

Maturity (years)	Spot rate (%)
1	7.500
2	7.604
3	7.710

Assuming an interest rate volatility of 10% for the 1-year rate, the binomial interest rate tree for valuing a bond with a maturity of up to three years is shown below:

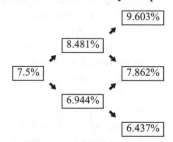

a. Demonstrate using the 2-year on-the-run issue that the binomial interest rate tree above is in fact an arbitrage-free tree.
b. Demonstrate using the 3-year on-the-run issue that the binomial interest rate tree above is in fact an arbitrage-free tree.
c. Using the spot rates given above, what is the arbitrage-free value of a 3-year 8.5% coupon issue of Inc.Net Company?
d. Using the binomial tree, determine the value of an 8.5% 3-year option-free bond.
e. Suppose that the 3-year 8.5% coupon issue is callable starting in Year 1 at par (100) (that is, the call price is 100). Also assume that the following call rule is used: if the price exceeds 100 the issue will be called. What is the value of this 3-year 8.5% coupon callable issue?
f. What is the value of the embedded call option for the 3-year 8.5% coupon callable issue?

10. a. Explain why the greater the assumed interest rate volatility the lower the value of a callable bond?

b. Explain why the greater the assumed interest rate volatility the higher the value of a putable bond?

11. An assistant portfolio manager described the process for valuing a bond that is both callable and putable using the binomial model as follows:

> "The process begins by first valuing one of the embedded options, say the call option. Then the model is used to value the put option. The value of the corresponding option-free bond is then computed. Given the value of the call option, the value of the put option, and the value of the option-free bond, the value of the bond that is callable and putable is found by adding to the value of the option-free bond the value of the put option and then subtracting the value of the call option."

Explain why you agree or disagree with this assistant portfolio manager's description of the process for valuing a bond that is both callable and putable.

12. Explain why when the binomial model is used to obtain the values to be used in the formula for computing duration and convexity, the measures computed are an effective duration and effective convexity.

13. An assistant portfolio manager is trying to find the duration of a callable bond of FeedCo Corp. One vendor of analytical systems reported that the duration for the issue is 5.4. A dealer firm reported that the duration is 4.5. The assistant portfolio manager was confused by the difference in the reported durations for the FeedCo Corp. issue. He discussed the situation with the senior portfolio manager. In the discussion, the assistant portfolio manager commented: "I don't understand how such a difference could occur. After all, there is a standard formula for computing any duration." How should the senior portfolio manager respond?

14. In computing the effective duration and convexity of a bond with an embedded option, what assumption is made about the option-adjusted spread when rates change?

15. Four portfolio managers are discussing the meaning of option-adjusted spread. Here is what each asserted:

Manager 1: "The option-adjusted spread is a measure of the value of the option embedded in the bond. That is, it is the compensation for accepting option risk."

Manager 2: "The option-adjusted spread is a measure of the spread relative to the Treasury on-the-run yield curve and reflects compensation for credit risk."

Manager 3: "The option-adjusted spread is a measure of the spread relative to the Treasury on-the-run yield curve and reflects compensation for credit risk and liquidity risk."

Manager 4: "The option-adjusted spread is a measure of the spread relative to the issuer's on-the-run yield curve and reflects compensation for credit risk and liquidity risk."

Comment on each manager's interpretation of OAS.

16. Suppose that a callable bond is valued using as the benchmark interest rates the on-the-run yield curve of the issuer and that the yield for the 10-year issue is 6%. Suppose further that the option-adjusted spread computed for a 10-year callable bond of this issuer is 20 basis points. Is it proper to interpret the OAS as meaning that the 10-year callable bond is offering a spread of 20 basis point over the 6% yield on the 10-year on-the-run-issue? If not, what is the proper interpretation of the 20 basis point OAS?

17. In valuing a floating rate note, it is necessary to make a modification to the backward induction method.

    a. Why is the adjustment necessary?
    b. What adjustment made?
    c. If the floating rate note has a cap, how is that handled by the backward induction method?

18. a. Why does a convertible bond typically have multiple embedded options?
    b. Why is it complicated to value a convertible bond?

19. In the October 26, 1992 prospectus summary of The Staples 5% convertible subordinated debentures due 1999 the offering stated: "Convertible into Common Stock at a conversion price of $45 per share..." Since the par value is $1,000, what is the conversion ratio?

20. Consider the convertible bond by Miser Electronics:

par value = $1,000
coupon rate = 8.5%
market price of convertible bond = $900
conversion ratio = 30
estimated straight value of bond = $700

Assume that the price of Miser Electronics common stock is $25 and that the dividend per share is $1 per annum.

Calculate each of the following:

    a. conversion value
    b. market conversion price
    c. conversion premium per share
    d. conversion premium ratio
    e. premium over straight value
    f. yield advantage of bond
    g. premium payback period

21. Suppose that the price of the common stock of Miser Electronics whose convertible bond was described in the previous question increases from $25 to $54.

    a. What will be the approximate return realized from investing in the convertible bond if an investor had purchased the convertible for $900?
    b. What would be the return realized if $25 had been invested in the common stock?

c. Why would the return be higher by investing in the common stock directly rather than by investing in the convertible bond?

22. Suppose that the price of the common stock declines from $25 to $10.

    a. What will be the approximate return realized from investing in the convertible bond if an investor had purchased the convertible for $900 *and* the straight value does not change?

    b. What would be the return realized if $25 had been invested in the common stock?

    c. Why would the return be higher by investing in the convertible bond rather than by investing in the common stock directly?

23. The following excerpt is taken from an article entitled "Caywood Looks for Convertibles," that appeared in the January 13, 1992 issue of *BondWeek*, p. 7:

> Caywood Christian Capital Management will invest new money in its $400 million high-yield portfolio in "busted convertibles," double-and triple-B rated convertible bonds of companies whose stock ...., said James Caywood, ceo. Caywood likes these convertibles as they trade at discounts and are unlikely to be called, he said.

    a. What is a "busted convertible"?

    b. What is the premium over straight value that these bonds would trade?

    c. Why does Mr. Caywood seek convertibles with higher investment grade ratings?

    d. Why is Mr. Caywood interested in call protection?

24. Explain the limitation of using premium over straight value as a measure of the downside risk of a convertible bond?

25. a. The valuation of a convertible bond using an options approach requires a two-factor model. What is meant by a two-factor model and what are the factors?

    b. In practice, is a two-factor model used to value a convertible bond?

SOLUTIONS TO END OF CHAPTER QUESTIONS

1. This statement is incorrect. While there are different models such as the binomial and trinomial models, the basic features of all these models are the same. They all involve assessing the cash flow at each node in the interest rate tree and determining whether or not to adjust the cash flow based on the embedded options. All these models require a rule for calling the issue and all require an assumption about the volatility of interest rates. The backward induction method is used for all these models.

2. The statement is wrong. The option-adjusted spread is a byproduct (i.e., is obtained from) of a valuation model. Any assumptions that must be made in a valuation model to obtain the arbitrage-value of a bond also apply to the option-adjusted spread. For example, if a valuation model assumes that interest rate volatility is x%, then the OAS is based on a volatility of x%.

3. Despite the fact that both the dealer and the pricing service used the same model and same benchmark, there are other inputs to the model that could cause a 1 point difference. The major reason is probably that the two may have used a different volatility assumption. A second reason is that the call rule by the two may have be quite different.

4. One of the first questions should be what is the benchmark that the spread is relative to. The other key question is what is the interest rate volatility assumed.

5. This statement is not necessarily correct. An OAS can be computed based on any benchmark interest rates. For example, the on-the-run rates for the issuer or the on-the-run rates for issuers in the same bond sector and the same credit rating can be used.

6. The procedure for determining the value of a bond with an embedded option starts at the maturity date on the interest rate tree(i.e., the end of the tree) and values the bond moving backward to the root of the tree — which is today's value. Hence the procedure is called backward induction.

7. The reason is that in constructing the interest rate tree the on-the-run issues are used and interest rates on the tree must be such that if the on-the-run issue is valued using the tree, the model will produce the market value of the on-the-run issue. When a model produces the market value of the on-the-run issues it is said to be "calibrated to the market" or "arbitrage free."

8. a. In the interest rate tree, the forward rates for a given period are shown at each node. (In the illustrations in the chapter, each period is one year.) Since there is more than one node for each period (after the root of the tree), there is not one forward rate for a given period but several forward rates.

   b. The binomial interest rate tree is constructed based on an assumption about interest rate volatility. If a different volatility assumption is made, a new interest rate tree is constructed and therefore there are different interest rates at the nodes for a given period and therefore a different set of forward rates.

9. a.

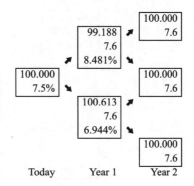

b.

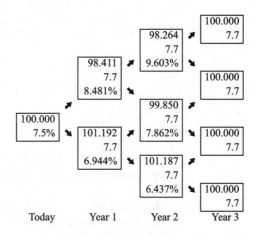

c. The value of an 8.5% coupon 3-year bond using the spot rates is as follows:

$$\frac{8.5}{(1.07500)} + \frac{8.5}{(1.07604)^2} + \frac{108.5}{(1.07710)^3} = \$102.076$$

d.

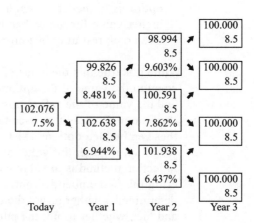

e. The value of this callable bond is 100.722.

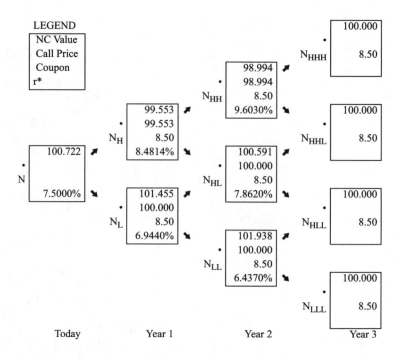

f. The value of the embedded call option is $1.354 which is equal to the value of the option-free bond ($126.076) minus the value of the callable bond ($100.722).

10. a. The value of a callable bond is equal to the value of an otherwise option-free bond minus the value of the embedded call option. The value of the embedded call option is higher the greater the assumed interest rate volatility. Therefore, a higher value for the embedded call option is subtracted from the value of the option-free bond, resulting in a lower value for the callable bond.

   b. The value of a putable bond is equal to the value of an otherwise option-free bond plus the value of the embedded put option. The value of the embedded put option is higher the greater the assumed interest rate volatility. Therefore, a higher value for the embedded put option is added to the value of the option-free bond, resulting in a higher value of the putable bond.

11. While it is true that the value of a bond that is callable and putable is conceptually equal to the value of the option-free bond adjusted for the value of the put option and the value of the call option, this is not the procedure used in a model such as the binomial model that uses the backward induction method. The reason is that these embedded options exist simultaneously so that the exercise of one option would extinguish the value of the other option. What is done in the backward induction method is to value the callable/putable bond by simultaneously considering the two embedded options. The way this works is at each node it will be determined whether or not the call option will be exercised based on the call rule and then whether or not the put option will be exercised. If either option is exercised, the corresponding exercise value for the bond is used in subsequent calculations in the backward induction process.

12. There are two types of duration and convexity — modified and effective. Modified forms of duration and convexity assume that when interest rates change the cash flows do not change. In contrast, the effective forms assume that when interest rates change the cash flows may change. When the binomial model is used to determine the values when rates are increased and decreased, the new values reflect how the cash flows may change. That is, the cash flow at each node of the binomial interest tree when rates are shifted up and down are allowed to change depending on the rules for when an option will be exercised. Thus, the resulting duration and convexity are effective duration and convexity.

13. It is true that there is a standard formula for computing duration by shocking (i.e., changing) interest rates and substituting the values computed in the duration formula. However, for a bond with an embedded option, such as a callable bond, it is necessary to have a valuation model (such as the binomial model) to determine the value of the bond when interest rates are changed. Valuation models can give different values for the same bond depending on the assumptions used. For example, suppose that the vendor and the dealer use the same valuation model but employ (1) a different volatility assumption, (2) different benchmark interest rates, and (3) a different call rule. The values produced by the two models that are substituted into the (effective) duration formula can result in the difference of 5.4 versus 4.5.

14. It is assumed that the option-adjusted spread is constant when interest rates change.

15. The starting point is defining what the benchmark interest rates are that the spread is being measured relative to. It is based on the benchmark that one interprets what the option-adjusted spread is compensation for.

    Manager 1 is wrong. The option-adjusted spread is adjusting any spread for the option risk. That is, it is netting out from the spread the option risk.

    Manager 2 is partially correct. If the benchmark interest rates are the on-the-run Treasury issues, then the option-adjusted spread is indicating compensation for credit risk. But it also captures liquidity risk. Moreover, it is not necessarily true that the benchmark interest rates are the on-the-run Treasury rates.

    Manager 3 is correct if the benchmark interest rates are the on-the-run Treasury issues. However, other benchmark interest rates have been used and in such cases Manager 3's interpretation would be incorrect.

    Manager 4 is incorrect. Even if the benchmark interest rates are the rates for the issuer's on-the-run issues, the spread would not reflect compensation for credit risk.

16. It is incorrect to state that the 20 basis point OAS is a spread over the issuer's 10-year on-the-run issue. That is, it is not a spread over one point on the yield curve. Rather, from the issuer's on-the-run yield curve, the rates at each node on the interest rate tree are determined. These rates are the one-period forward rates. The

OAS is the spread that when added to all these forward rates will produce a value for the callable bond equal to the market price of the bond. So, it is a spread over the forward rates in the interest rate tree which are in turn generated from the benchmark interest rates.

17. a. The coupon rate on a floater is paid in arrears. This means that for a floater the rate determined in the current period is not paid until the end of the period (or beginning of the next period). This requires that an adjustment be made to the backward induction method.

b. The adjustment is made to the backward induction method by discounting the coupon payment to be made in the next period for a floater based on the beginning of the period reference rate.

c. A cap on a floater is handled by determining at each node if the cap is reached. At a node where the coupon rate exceeds the cap, the coupon rate is replaced by the capped rate.

18. a. A convertible bond grants the investor the option to call the common stock of the issuer. Thus, a convertible bond has an embedded call option on the common sock. However, most convertible bonds are callable. That is, there is an embedded call option granting the issuer the right to retire the bond.

b. The complication that arises is that one of the options, the call on the common stock granted to the investor, depends on the future price of the common stock. However, the call on the bond granted to the issuer depends on future interest rates. Thus, valuing a callable convertible bond requires including in one valuation model both future stock price movements and future interest rate movements.

19. The conversion ratio is found by dividing the par value of $1,000 by the conversion price stated in the prospectus of $45 per share. The conversion ratio is then 22.22 ($1,000/$45).

20. a. conversion value = market price of common stock × conversion ratio
$$= \$25 \times 30 = \$750$$

b. market conversion price $= \dfrac{\text{market price of convertible bond}}{\text{conversion ratio}} = \dfrac{\$900}{30} = \$30$

c. conversion premium per share
$$= \text{market conversion price} - \text{market price of common stock}$$
$$= \$30 - \$25 = \$5$$

d. conversion premium ratio $= \dfrac{\text{conversion premium per share}}{\text{market price of common stock}} = \dfrac{\$5}{\$25} = 20\%$

e. premium over straight value $= \dfrac{\text{market price of convertible bond}}{\text{straight value}} - 1$

$$= \dfrac{\$900}{\$700} - 1 = 28.6\%$$

f. favorable income differential per share =

$$= \frac{\text{coupon interest from bond} - \text{conversion ratio} \times \text{dividend per share}}{\text{conversion ratio}}$$

$$= \frac{\$85 - (30 \times \$1)}{30} = \$1.833$$

g. premium payback period $= \dfrac{\text{market conversion premium per share}}{\text{favorable income differential per share}}$

$$= \frac{\$5}{\$1.833} = 2.73 \text{ years}$$

21. a. If the price increases to $54, the conversion value will be

conversion value = $54 × 30 = $1,620

Assuming that the convertible bond's price does not exceed the conversion value (that is why the question asked for an approximate return), then the return on the $900 investment in the convertible bond is:

$$\frac{\$1,620}{\$900} - 1 = 0.8 = 80\%$$

b. The return realized if $25 had been invested in the common stock is equal to:

$$\frac{\$54 - \$25}{\$25} = 1.16 = 116\%$$

c. The reason for the lower return by buying the convertible bond rather than the stock directly is that the investor has effectively paid $5 more for the stock.

22. a. If the price decreases to $10, the conversion value will be

conversion value = $10 × 30 = $300

However, it is assumed in the question that the straight value is unchanged at $700. The convertible bond will trade at the greater of the straight value and the conversion value. In this case, it is $700. The return is then:

$$\frac{\$700}{\$900} - 1 = -0.22 = -22\%$$

b. The return realized if $25 had been invested in the common stock is equal to:

$$\frac{\$10 - \$25}{\$25} = -0.6 = -60\%$$

c. The return is greater for convertible bond because of the assumption made that the straight value did not change. If the straight value did decline, the loss would be greater than −22% but it would still be probably less than the loss on the direct purchase of the stock. The key here is that the floor (straight value) is what cushion's the decline — but it is moving floor.

23. a. If the stock price is low so that the straight value is considerably higher than the conversion value, the bond will trade much like a straight bond. The convertible in such instances is referred to as a "busted convertible."

b. Since the market value of a busted convertible is very close to that of a straight bond, the premium over straight value would be very small.

c. By restricting the convertible bonds in which Mr. Caywood would invest to higher investment grade ratings, he is reducing credit risk.

d. By seeking bonds not likely to be called, Mr. Caywood is reducing call risk that would result in a forced conversion to the common stock.

24. The measure assumes that the straight value does not decline.

25. a. A "factor" it is the stochastic (or random) variable that is assumed to affect the value of a security. The two factors in valuing a convertible bond are the price movement of the underlying common stock (which affects the value of the embedded call option on the common stock) and the movement of interest rates (which affects the value of the embedded call option on the bond).

b. In practice, models used to value convertible bonds have been one-factor models with the factor included being the price movement of the underlying common stock.

SOLUTIONS TO PRACTICE QUESTIONS

1.

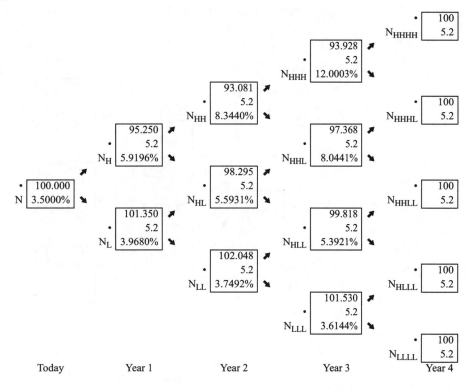

2. The binomial interest rate tree is the one in Practice Question 1. Below is the tree with the values completed at each node. As can be seen, the root of the tree is 104.643, the arbitrage-free value found in the chapter for this option-free bond.

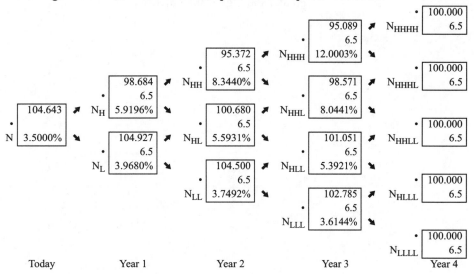

3. a. The root of the binomial interest rate tree below shows that the arbitrage-free value of this bond is 102.108.

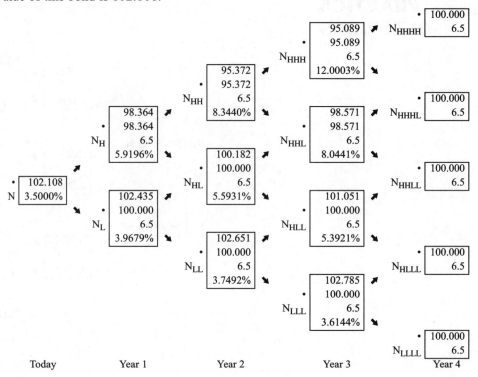

| Today | Year 1 | Year 2 | Year 3 | Year 4 |

b. The arbitrage-free value at 20% is less than the arbitrage-free value at 10% (102.108 versus 102.899). This is because the value of the embedded call option is greater the higher the volatility.

4. The tree below shows that the OAS is –6 basis points for the 6.5% callable bond assuming 20% volatility. (Each 1-year rate is 6 basis points less than in Practice Question 1.)

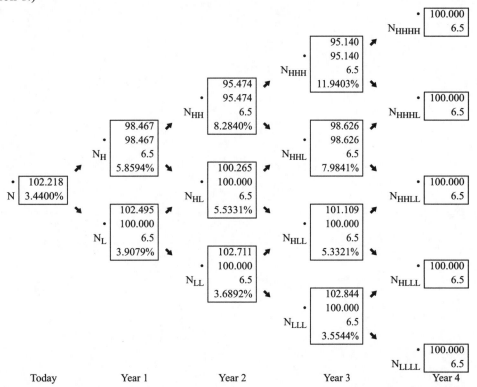

5. The tree below shows the arbitrage-free value for a putable bond with four years to maturity, a coupon rate of 6.5%, and putable in one year at 100 assuming a 20% volatility is 106.010.

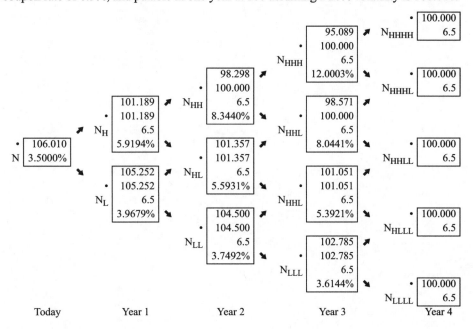

Chapter 3

MORTGAGE-BACKED SECURITIES

LEARNING OUTCOME STATEMENTS

After reading this chapter you should be able to:

- explain what a mortgage loan is.
- describe the cash flow characteristics of a fixed-rate, level payment, fully amortized mortgage loan.
- describe what prepayments are and how they result in prepayment risk.
- identify the factors that affect prepayments.
- explain the investment characteristics of mortgage passthrough securities.
- identify the issuers of agency mortgage-backed securities.
- explain what a TBA trade is.
- compute the amount paid by the buyer of a mortgage-backed security
- explain the importance of prepayments to the estimation of the cash flow of a mortgage-backed security.
- compute the weighted average coupon and weighted average maturity of a mortgage pool.
- explain what a conditional prepayment rate is and calculate the single monthly mortality rate given the conditional prepayment rate.
- describe the PSA prepayment benchmark and its relationship to the conditional prepayment rate.
- calculate the prepayment amount for a month given the single monthly mortality rate.
- explain what contraction and extension prepayment risks are and why they occur.
- explain why the average life of a mortgage-backed security is used rather than the security's maturity.
- explain what stripped mortgage-backed securities (principal only securities and interest only securities) are.
- explain the investment characteristics of principal-only and interest-only mortgage strips.
- explain why and how a collateralized mortgage obligation is created and the different types of CMO structures (including sequential-pay tranches, accrual tranches, floater tranches, inverse floater tranches, planned amortization class tranches, support tranches, and support tranches with schedules).
- describe how a CMO distributes prepayment risk among tranches so as to create products that provide a better matching of assets and liabilities for institutional investors
- explain for planned amortization class tranches what is meant by the initial PAC collar and the effective collar.
- explain why the support tranches have the greatest substantial prepayment risk in a CMO structure.
- explain what a nonagency mortgage-backed security is.
- explain the types of loans backing a nonagency mortgage-backed security.
- explain why a nonagency mortgage-backed security must be credit enhanced.

SECTION I
INTRODUCTION

In this chapter and the next we will discuss securities backed by a pool of loans or receivables — mortgage-backed securities and asset-backed securities. We described these securities briefly at Level I (Chapter 3). Mortgage-backed securities are backed by a pool of traditional residential mortgage loans and are issued in the United States by federal agencies (one federally related institution and two government sponsored enterprises) and private entities. The former securities are called **agency mortgage-backed securities** and the latter **nonagency mortgage-backed securities.** Securities backed by loans other than traditional residential mortgage loans and backed by receivables are referred to as **asset-backed securities**. There is a long and growing list of loans and receivables that have been used as collateral for these securities.

In this chapter, our focus will be on mortgage-backed securities. Many countries have developed mortgage-backed securities. However, we look at only those issued in the United States. We begin with this product because as we will see, credit risk does not exist for mortgage-backed securities issued by a federally related institution and is viewed as minimal for securities issued by a government sponsored enterprise. The significant risk is prepayment risk and there are ways to redistribute prepayment risk among the different bond classes created. Historically, it is important to note that the agency mortgage-backed securities market developed first. The technology developed for agency mortgage-backed security was then transferred to other types of loans and receivables. In transferring the technology to create securities that expose investors to credit risk, mechanisms had to be developed to create securities that could receive investment grade credit ratings sought by the issuer. In the next chapter, we will discuss these mechanisms. We postpone a discussion of how to value and estimate the interest rate risk of both mortgage-backed and asset-backed securities until Chapter 5.

Mortgage-backed securities include: (1) mortgage passthrough securities, (2) collateralized mortgage obligations, and (3) stripped mortgage-backed securities. The latter two mortgage-backed securities are referred to as **derivative mortgage-backed securities** because they are created from mortgage passthrough securities.

SECTION II
MORTGAGES

A **mortgage** is a loan secured by the collateral of some specified real estate property which obliges the borrower to make a predetermined series of payments. The mortgage gives the lender the right if the borrower defaults to "foreclose" on the loan and seize the property in order to ensure that the debt is paid off. The interest rate on the mortgage loan is called the **mortgage rate** or **contract rate**. Our focus in this section is on residential mortgage loans.

When the lender makes the loan based on the credit of the borrower and on the collateral for the mortgage, the mortgage is said to be a **conventional mortgage**. The lender may require that the borrower obtain mortgage insurance to guarantee the fulfillment of the borrower's obligations. Some borrowers can qualify for mortgage insurance which is guaranteed by one of three U.S. government agencies: the Federal Housing Administration (FHA), the Veteran's Administration (VA), and the Rural Housing Service (RHS). There are also private mortgage insurers. The cost of mortgage insurance is paid by the borrower in the form of a higher mortgage rate.

There are many types of **mortgage designs** used throughout the world. A mortgage design is a specification of the interest rate, term of the mortgage, and the manner in which the borrowed funds are repaid. In the United States, the alternative mortgage designs include (1) fixed rate, level-payment fully amortized mortgages, (2) adjustable-rate mortgages, (3) balloon mortgages, (4) growing equity mortgages, (5) reverse mortgages, and (6) tiered payment mortgages. Other countries have developed mortgage designs unique to their housing finance market. Some of these mortgage designs relate the mortgage payment to the country's rate of inflation. Below we will look at the most common mortgage design in the United States — the fixed-rate, level-payment, fully amortized mortgage. All of the principles we need to know regarding the risks associated with investing in mortgage-backed securities and the difficulties associated with their valuation can be understood by just looking at this mortgage design.

A. Fixed-Rate, Level-Payment, Fully Amortized Mortgage

The basic idea behind the design of the **fixed-rate, level-payment, fully amortized mortgage** is that the borrower pays equal installments over the term of the mortgage. The payments include principal repayment and interest. The payments are such that at the end of the term of the mortgage, the loan has been fully amortized. The frequency of payment is typically monthly.

Each monthly mortgage payment for this mortgage design is due on the first of each month and consists of:

1. interest of $\frac{1}{12}$ of the fixed annual interest rate times the amount of the outstanding mortgage balance at the beginning of the previous month, and
2. a repayment of a portion of the outstanding mortgage balance (principal).

The difference between the monthly mortgage payment and the portion of the payment that represents interest equals the amount that is applied to reduce the outstanding mortgage balance. The monthly mortgage payment is designed so that after the last scheduled monthly mortgage payment is made, the amount of the outstanding mortgage balance is zero (i.e., the mortgage is fully repaid).

To illustrate this mortgage design, consider a 30-year (360-month), $100,000 mortgage with an 8.125% mortgage rate. The monthly mortgage payment would be $742.50. Exhibit 1 shows for selected months how each monthly mortgage payment is divided between interest and scheduled principal repayment. At the beginning of month 1, the mortgage balance is $100,000, the amount of the original loan. The mortgage payment for month 1 includes interest on the $100,000 borrowed for the month. Since the interest rate is 8.125%, the monthly interest rate is 0.0067708 (0.08125 divided by 12). Interest for month 1 is therefore $677.08 ($100,000 times 0.0067708). The $65.41 difference between the monthly mortgage payment of $742.50 and the interest of $677.08 is the portion of the monthly mortgage payment that represents the scheduled principal repayment. It is also referred to as the **scheduled amortization** and we shall use the terms scheduled principal repayment and scheduled amortization interchangeably throughout this chapter. This $65.41 in month 1 reduces the mortgage balance.

The mortgage balance at the end of month 1 (beginning of month 2) is then $99,934.59 ($100,000 minus $65.41). The interest for the second monthly mortgage payment is $676.64, the monthly interest rate (0.0067708) times the mortgage balance at the beginning of month 2 ($99,934.59). The difference between the $742.50 monthly mortgage payment and the $676.64 interest is $65.86, representing the amount of the mortgage balance paid off with that monthly mortgage payment. Notice that the mortgage payment in month 360 — the final payment — is sufficient to pay off the remaining mortgage balance.

As Exhibit 1 clearly shows, *the portion of the monthly mortgage payment applied to interest declines each month and the portion applied to principal repayment increases.* The reason for this is that as the mortgage balance is reduced with each monthly mortgage payment, the interest on the mortgage balance declines. Since the monthly mortgage payment is a fixed dollar amount, an increasingly larger portion of the monthly payment is applied to reduce the mortgage balance outstanding in each subsequent month.

1. Servicing Fee

Every mortgage loan must be serviced. Servicing of a mortgage loan involves collecting monthly payments and forwarding proceeds to owners of the loan; sending payment notices to mortgagors; reminding mortgagors when payments are overdue; maintaining records of principal balances; administering an escrow balance for real estate taxes and insurance purposes; initiating foreclosure proceedings if necessary; and, furnishing tax information to borrowers (i.e., mortgagors) when applicable.

Exhibit 1: Amortization Schedule for a Level-Payment, Fixed-Rate, Fully Amortized Mortgage

Mortgage loan: $100,000   Monthly payment: $742.50
Mortgage rate: 8.125%   Term of loan: 30 years (360 months)

Month	Beginning of Month Mortgage Balance	Mortgage Payment	Interest	Scheduled Repayment	End of Month Mortgage Balance
1	$100,000.00	$742.50	$677.08	$65.41	$99,934.59
2	99,934.59	742.50	676.64	65.86	99,868.73
3	99,868.73	742.50	676.19	66.30	99,802.43
4	99,802.43	742.50	675.75	66.75	99,735.68
...	...	...	...	...	...
25	98,301.53	742.50	665.58	76.91	98,224.62
26	98,224.62	742.50	665.06	77.43	98,147.19
27	98,147.19	742.50	664.54	77.96	98,069.23
...	...	...	...	...	...
74	93,849.98	742.50	635.44	107.05	93,742.93
75	93,742.93	742.50	634.72	107.78	93,635.15
76	93,635.15	742.50	633.99	108.51	93,526.64
...	...	...	...	...	...
141	84,811.77	742.50	574.25	168.25	84,643.52
142	84,643.52	742.50	573.11	169.39	84,474.13
143	84,474.13	742.50	571.96	170.54	84,303.59
...	...	...	...	...	...
184	76,446.29	742.50	517.61	224.89	76,221.40
185	76,221.40	742.50	516.08	226.41	75,994.99
186	75,994.99	742.50	514.55	227.95	75,767.04
...	...	...	...	...	...
233	63,430.19	742.50	429.48	313.02	63,117.17
234	63,117.17	742.50	427.36	315.14	62,802.03
235	62,802.03	742.50	425.22	317.28	62,484.75
...	...	...	...	...	...
289	42,200.92	742.50	285.74	456.76	41,744.15
290	41,744.15	742.50	282.64	459.85	41,284.30
291	41,284.30	742.50	279.53	462.97	40,821.33
...	...	...	...	...	...
321	25,941.42	742.50	175.65	566.85	25,374.57
322	25,374.57	742.50	171.81	570.69	24,803.88
323	24,803.88	742.50	167.94	574.55	24,229.32
...	...	...	...	...	...
358	2,197.66	742.50	14.88	727.62	1,470.05
359	1,470.05	742.50	9.95	732.54	737.50
360	737.50	742.50	4.99	737.50	0.00

The servicing fee is a portion of the mortgage rate. If the mortgage rate is 8.125% and the servicing fee is 50 basis points, then the investor receives interest of 7.625%. The interest rate that the investor receives is said to be the **net interest** or **net coupon**. The servicing fee is commonly called the **servicing spread**.

The dollar amount of the servicing fee declines over time as the mortgage amortizes. This is true for not only the mortgage design that we have just described, but for all mortgage designs.

2. Prepayments and Cash Flow Uncertainty

Our illustration of the cash flow from a level-payment, fixed-rate, fully amortized mortgage assumes that the homeowner does not pay off any portion of the mortgage balance prior to the scheduled due date. But homeowners do pay off all or part of their mortgage balance prior to the maturity date. A payment made in excess of the monthly mortgage payment is called a **prepayment**. The prepayment could be to pay off the entire outstanding balance or a partial paydown of the mortgage balance. When a prepayment is not for the entire outstanding balance it is called a **curtailment**.

The effect of prepayments is that the amount and timing of the cash flow from a mortgage loan are not known with certainty. This risk is referred to as **prepayment risk**. For example, all that the investor in a $100,000, 8.125% 30-year mortgage knows is that as long as the loan is outstanding and the borrower does not default, interest will be received and the principal will be repaid at the scheduled date each month; then at the end of the 30 years, the investor would have received $100,000 in principal payments. What the investor does not know — the uncertainty — is for how long the loan will be outstanding, and therefore what the timing of the principal payments will be. This is true for all mortgage loans, not just the level-payment, fixed-rate, fully amortized mortgage. Factors affecting prepayments will be discussed later in this chapter.

Most mortgages have no prepayment penalty. That is, the outstanding loan balance can be repaid at par. In 1996, mortgages with prepayment penalties were originated. The purpose of the penalty is to deter prepayment when interest rates decline. A prepayment penalty mortgage has the following structure. There is a period of time over which if the loan is prepaid in full or in excess of a certain amount of the outstanding balance, there is a prepayment penalty. This period is referred to as the **lock-out period** or **penalty period.** During the penalty period, the borrower may prepay up to a specified amount of the outstanding balance without a penalty. The amount of the penalty is specified in terms of the number of months of interest that must be paid.

SECTION III MORTGAGE PASSTHROUGH SECURITIES

A **mortgage passthrough security** is a security created when one or more holders of mortgages form a collection (pool) of mortgages and sell shares or participation certificates in the pool. A pool may consist of several thousand or only a few mortgages. When a mortgage is included in a pool of mortgages that is used as collateral for a mortgage passthrough security, the mortgage is said to be **securitized**.

A. Cash Flow Characteristics

The cash flow of a mortgage passthrough security depends on the cash flow of the underlying pool of mortgages. As we explained in the previous section, the cash flow consists of monthly mortgage payments representing interest, the scheduled repayment of principal, and any prepayments.

Payments are made to security holders each month. However, neither the amount nor the timing of the cash flow from the pool of mortgages is identical to that of the cash flow passed through to investors. The monthly cash flow for a passthrough is less than the monthly cash flow of the underlying pool of mortgages by an amount equal to servicing and other fees. The other fees are those charged by the issuer or guarantor of the passthrough for guaranteeing the issue (discussed later). The coupon rate on a passthrough, called the **passthrough coupon rate**, is less than the mortgage rate on the underlying pool of mortgages by an amount equal to the servicing and guaranteeing fees.

The timing of the cash flow is also different. The monthly mortgage payment is due from each mortgagor on the first day of each month, but there is a delay in passing through the corresponding monthly cash flow to the security holders. The length of the delay varies by the type of passthrough security.

Not all of the mortgages that are included in a pool of mortgages that are securitized have the same mortgage rate and the same maturity. Consequently, when describing a passthrough security, a weighted average coupon rate and a weighted average maturity are determined. A **weighted average coupon rate**, or WAC, is found by weighting the mortgage rate of each mortgage loan in the pool by the percentage of the mortgage outstanding relative to the amount of all the mortgages in the pool. A **weighted average maturity**, or WAM, is found by weighting the remaining number of months to maturity for each mortgage loan in the pool by the amount of the outstanding mortgage balance.

For example, suppose a mortgage pool has just five loans and the outstanding mortgage balance, mortgage rate, and months remaining to maturity of each loan are as follows:

Loan	Outstanding mortgage balance	Weight in pool	Mortgage rate	Months remaining
1	$125,000	22.12%	7.50%	275
2	$85,000	15.04%	7.20%	260
3	$175,000	30.97%	7.00%	290
4	$110,000	19.47%	7.80%	285
5	$70,000	12.39%	6.90%	270
Total	$565,000	100.00%		

The WAC for this mortgage pool is:

$$0.2212\,(7.5\%) + 0.1504\,(7.2\%) + 0.3097\,(7.0\%) + 0.1947\,(7.8\%)$$
$$+ 0.1239\,(6.90\%) = 7.28\%$$

The WAM for this mortgage pool is

$$0.2212\,(275) + 0.1504\,(260) + 0.3097\,(290) + 0.1947\,(285)$$
$$+ 0.1239\,(270) = 279 \text{ months (rounded)}$$

B. Types of Mortgage Passthrough Securities

The three major types of passthrough securities are guaranteed by agencies created by Congress to increase the supply of capital to the residential mortgage market. Those agencies are the Government National Mortgage Association ("Ginnie Mae"), the Federal Home Loan Mortgage Corporation ("Freddie Mac"), and the Federal National Mortgage Association ("Fannie Mae").

While Freddie Mac and Fannie Mae are commonly referred to as "agencies" of the U.S. government, both are corporate instrumentalities of the U.S. government. That is, they are government sponsored enterprises; therefore, their guarantee does not carry the full faith and credit of the U.S. government. In contrast, Ginnie Mae is a federally related institution; it is part of the Department of Housing and Urban Development. As such, its guarantee carries the full faith and credit of the U.S. government. The securities associated with these three entities are known as **agency passthrough securities**. More than 90% of all passthrough securities are agency passthrough securities.

The name of the passthrough issued by Ginnie Mae and Fannie Mae is a *Mortgage-Backed Security* or *MBS*. So, when a market participant refers to a Ginnie Mae MBS or Fannie Mae MBS, it is meant the passthrough issued by these two entities. The name of the passthrough issued by Freddie Mac is a *Participation Certificate* or *PC*. So, when a market participant refers to a Freddie Mac PC, it is meant the passthrough issued by Freddie Mac. Every agency has different "programs" under which passthroughs are issued with different types of mortgage pools (e.g., 30-year fixed-rate mortgages, 15-year fixed-rate mortgages, adjustable-rate mortgages). We will not review the different programs here.

In order for a loan to be included in a pool of loans backing an agency security, it must meet specified underwriting standards. These standards set forth the maximum size of the loan, the loan documentation required, the maximum loan-to-value ratio, and whether or not insurance is required. If a loan satisfies the underwriting standards for inclusion as collateral for an agency mortgage-backed security, it is called a **conforming mortgage**. If a loan fails to satisfy the underwriting standards, it is called a **nonconforming mortgage**. Loans that fail to qualify as a conforming mortgage because they exceed the maximum loan size are called **jumbo mortgages**. Loans that fail to qualify because of documentation are called either "no doc" or "low doc" mortgages, the former indicating that the lender did not require documentation to verify the borrower's income and the latter that there was only limited documentation to verify the borrower's income.

Nonconforming mortgages used as collateral for mortgage passthrough securities are privately issued. These securities are called **nonagency mortgage passthrough securities**. These securities are issued by thrifts, commercial banks, and private conduits. Private conduits may purchase nonconforming mortgages, pool them, and then sell passthrough securities whose collateral is the underlying pool of nonconforming mortgages. Nonagency passthrough securities are rated by the nationally recognized statistical rating organizations. These securities are supported by credit enhancements so that they can obtain an investment grade rating. We shall describe these securities in the next chapter.

C. Trading and Settlement Procedures

Agency passthrough securities are identified by a pool prefix and pool number provided by the agency. The prefix indicates the type of passthrough. For example, a pool prefix of 20 for a Freddie Mac PC means that the underlying pool consists of conventional mortgages with an original maturity of 15 years. The pool number indicates the specific mortgages underlying the passthrough and the issuer of the passthrough.

There are specific rules established by the Public Securities Association for the trading and settlement of mortgage-backed securities. Many trades occur while a pool is still unspecified, and therefore no pool information is known at the time of the trade. This kind of trade is known as a **TBA trade (to be announced trade)**. In a TBA trade the two parties agree on the agency type, the agency program, the coupon rate, the face value, the price, and the settlement date. The actual pools of mortgage loans underlying the agency passthrough are not specified in a TBA trade. However, this information is provided by the seller to the buyer before delivery. There are trades where more specific requirements are established for the securities to be delivered. For example, a Freddie Mac with a coupon rate of 8.5% and a WAC between 9.0% and

9.2%. There are also specified pool trades wherein the actual pool numbers to be delivered are specified.

Passthroughs are quoted in the same manner as U.S. Treasury coupon securities. A quote of 94-05 means 94 and 5 32nds of par value, or 94.15625% of par value. The price that the buyer pays the seller is the agreed upon sale price plus accrued interest. Given the par value, the dollar price (excluding accrued interest) is affected by the amount of the pool mortgage balance outstanding. The **pool factor** indicates the percentage of the initial mortgage balance still outstanding. So, a pool factor of 90 means that 90% of the original mortgage pool balance is outstanding. The pool factor is reported by the agency each month.

The dollar price paid for just the principal is found as follows given the agreed upon price, par value, and the month's pool factor provided by the agency:

$$\text{price} \times \text{par value} \times \text{pool factor}$$

For example, if the parties agree to a price of 92 for $1 million par value for a passthrough with a pool factor of 0.85, then the dollar price paid by the buyer in addition to accrued interest is:

$$0.92 \times \$1,000,000 \times 0.85 = \$782,000$$

There are many seasoned issues of the same agency with the same coupon rate outstanding at a given point in time. For example, in early 2000 there were more than 30,000 pools of 30-year Ginnie Mae MBSs outstanding with a coupon rate of 9%. One passthrough may be backed by a pool of mortgage loans in which all the properties are located in California, while another may be backed by a pool of mortgage loans in which all the properties are in Minnesota. Yet another may be backed by a pool of mortgage loans in which the properties are from several regions of the country. So which pool are dealers referring to when they talk about Ginnie Mae 9s? They are not referring to any specific pool but instead to a generic security, despite the fact that the prepayment characteristics of passthroughs with underlying pools from different parts of the country are different. Thus, the projected prepayment rates for passthroughs reported by dealer firms (discussed later) are for generic passthroughs. A particular pool purchased may have a materially different prepayment rate from the generic. Moreover, when an investor purchases a passthrough without specifying a pool number, the seller has the option to deliver the worst-paying pools as long as the pools delivered satisfy good delivery requirements.

D. Prepayment Conventions and Cash Flow

In order to value a passthrough security, it is necessary to project its cash flow. The difficulty is that the cash flow is unknown because of prepayments. The only way to project a cash flow is to make some assumption about the prepayment rate over the life of the underlying mortgage pool.

Estimating the cash flow from a passthrough requires making an assumption about future prepayments. Two conventions have been used as a benchmark for prepayment rates — conditional prepayment rate and Public Securities Association prepayment benchmark.

1. Conditional Prepayment Rate

One convention for describing the pattern of prepayments and the cash flow of a passthrough assumes that some fraction of the remaining principal in the pool is prepaid each month for the remaining term of the mortgage. The prepayment rate assumed for a pool, called the **conditional prepayment rate** (CPR), is based on the characteristics of the pool (including its historical prepayment experience) and the current and expected future economic environment.

The CPR is an annual prepayment rate. To estimate monthly prepayments, the CPR must be converted into a monthly prepayment rate, commonly referred to as the **single-monthly mortality rate** (SMM). The following formula is used to calculate the SMM for a given CPR:[1]

$$\text{SMM} = 1 - (1 - \text{CPR})^{1/12} \tag{1}$$

For example, suppose that the CPR is 6%. The corresponding SMM is:

$$\text{SMM} = 1 - (1 - 0.06)^{1/12} = 1 - (0.94)^{0.08333} = 0.005143$$

An SMM of $w\%$ means that approximately $w\%$ of the remaining mortgage balance at the beginning of the month, less the scheduled principal payment, will prepay that month. That is,

$$\begin{aligned} \text{prepayment for month } t = \text{SMM} \times (&\text{beginning mortgage balance for month } t \\ &- \text{scheduled principal payment for month } t) \end{aligned} \tag{2}$$

That is, the prepayment for a month is found by first determining the amount that is available to be prepaid. This amount is equal to the outstanding balance at the beginning of the month less the amount of the scheduled principal repayment for that month. It is to this adjusted amount that the SMM is applied to obtain the prepayment for the month.

For example, suppose that an investor owns a passthrough in which the remaining mortgage balance at the beginning of some month is $290 million. Assuming that the SMM is 0.5143% and the scheduled principal payment is $3 million, the estimated prepayment for the month is:

$$0.005143 \times (\$290,000,000 - \$3,000,000) = \$1,476,041$$

2. PSA Prepayment Benchmark

The **Public Securities Association (PSA) prepayment benchmark** is expressed as a monthly series of CPRs. The PSA benchmark assumes that prepayment rates are low for newly originated mortgages and then will speed up as the mortgages become seasoned. The PSA benchmark assumes the following prepayment rates for 30-year mortgages: (1) a CPR of 0.2% for the first month, increased by 0.2% per year per month for the next 30 months until it reaches 6% per year, and (2) a 6% CPR for the remaining months.

This benchmark, referred to as "100% PSA" or simply "100 PSA," is graphically depicted in Exhibit 2. Mathematically, 100 PSA can be expressed as follows:

if $t < 30$ then CPR = 6% $(t/30)$
if $t \geq 30$ then CPR = 6%

where t is the number of months since the mortgages were originated.

---

[1] The reason why the SMM is not found by simply dividing the CPR by 12 is that there are scheduled principal repayments that are occurring.

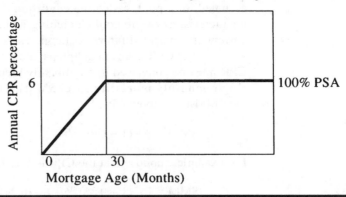

Exhibit 2: Graphical Depiction of 100 PSA

Slower or faster speeds are then referred to as some percentage of PSA. For example, "50 PSA" means one-half the CPR of the PSA prepayment benchmark; "150 PSA" means 1.5 times the CPR of the PSA prepayment benchmark; "300 PSA" means three times the CPR of the prepayment benchmark. A prepayment rate of 0 PSA means that no *prepayments* are assumed. While there are no prepayments at 0 PSA, there are scheduled principal repayments.

In constructing a schedule for monthly prepayments, the CPR (an annual rate) must be converted into a monthly prepayment rate (an SMM). The conversion is done using equation (1). For example, the SMMs for month 5, month 20, and months 31 through 360 assuming 100 PSA are calculated as follows:

for month 5:

$$CPR = 6\% \ (5/30) = 1\% = 0.01$$
$$SMM = 1 - (1 - 0.01)^{1/12} = 1 - (0.99)^{0.083333} = 0.000837$$

for month 20:

$$CPR = 6\% \ (20/30) = 4\% = 0.04$$
$$SMM = 1 - (1 - 0.04)^{1/12} = 1 - (0.96)^{0.083333} = 0.003396$$

for months 31-360:

$$CPR = 6\%$$
$$SMM = 1 - (1 - 0.06)^{1/12} = 1 - (0.94)^{0.083333} = 0.005143$$

The SMMs for month 5, month 20, and months 31 through 360 assuming 165 PSA are computed as follows:

for month 5:

$$CPR = 6\% \ (5/30) = 1\% = 0.01$$
$$165 \ PSA = 1.65 \ (0.01) = 0.0165$$
$$SMM = 1 - (1 - 0.0165)^{1/12} = 1 - (0.9835)^{0.08333} = 0.001386$$

for month 20:

$$CPR = 6\% \ (20/30) = 4\% = 0.04$$
$$165 \ PSA = 1.65 \ (.04) = 0.066$$
$$SMM = 1 - (1 - 0.066)^{1/12} = 1 - (0.934)^{0.08333} = 0.005674$$

for months 31-360:

$$\text{CPR} = 6\%$$
$$165 \text{ PSA} = 1.65 \, (0.06) = 0.099$$
$$\text{SMM} = 1 - (1 - 0.099)^{1/12} = 1 - (0.901)^{0.08333} = 0.008650$$

Notice that the SMM assuming 165 PSA is not just 1.65 times the SMM assuming 100 PSA. It is the CPR that is a multiple of the CPR assuming 100 PSA.

Again, it is necessary to convert the CPR to an SMM in order to compute monthly prepayments. The SMMs for month 5, month 20, and months 31 through 360 assuming 50 PSA are as follows:

for month 5:

$$\text{CPR} = 6\% \, (5/30) = 1\% = 0.01$$
$$50 \text{ PSA} = 0.5 \, (0.01) = 0.005$$
$$\text{SMM} = 1 - (1 - 0.005)^{1/12} = 1 - (0.995)^{0.08333} = 0.000418$$

for month 20:

$$\text{CPR} = 6\% \, (20/30) = 4\% = 0.04$$
$$50 \text{ PSA} = 0.5 \, (0.04) = 0.02$$
$$\text{SMM} = 1 - (1 - 0.02)^{1/12} = 1 - (0.98)^{0.08333} = 0.001682$$

for months 31-360:

$$\text{CPR} = 6\%$$
$$50 \text{ PSA} = 0.5 \, (0.06) = 0.03$$
$$\text{SMM} = 1 - (1 - 0.03)^{1/12} = 1 - (0.97)^{0.08333} = 0.002535$$

It is also important to note that the CPRs and corresponding SMMs apply to a mortgage pool *based on the number of months since origination.* For example, if a mortgage pool has loans that were originally 30-year (360-month) mortgage loans and the WAM is currently 357 months, this means that the mortgage pool is seasoned three months. So, in determining prepayments for the next month, the CPR and SMM that are applicable are those for month 4.

The PSA benchmark is commonly referred to as a prepayment model, suggesting that it can be used to estimate prepayments. Characterization of this benchmark as a prepayment model is wrong. It is simply a market convention regarding the expected pattern of prepayments.

---

3. Illustration of Monthly Cash Flow Construction

We now show how to construct a monthly cash flow for a hypothetical passthrough given a PSA assumption. For the purpose of this illustration, the underlying mortgages for this passthrough are assumed to be fixed-rate, level-payment, fully amortized mortgages with a weighted average coupon (WAC) rate of 8.125%. It will be assumed that the passthrough rate is 7.5% with a weighted average maturity (WAM) of 357 months.

Exhibit 3: Monthly Cash Flow for a $400 Million Passthrough with a 7.5% Passthrough Rate, a WAC of 8.125%, and a WAM of 357 Months Assuming 100 PSA

Months from Now (1)	Months Seasoned* (2)	Outstanding Balance (3)	SMM (4)	Mortgage Payment (5)	Net Interest (6)	Scheduled Principal (7)	Prepayment (8)	Total Principal (9)	Cash Flow (10)
1	4	$400,000,000	0.00067	$2,975,868	$2,500,000	$267,535	$267,470	$535,005	$3,035,005
2	5	399,464,995	0.00084	2,973,877	2,496,656	269,166	334,198	603,364	3,100,020
3	6	398,861,631	0.00101	2,971,387	2,492,885	270,762	400,800	671,562	3,164,447
4	7	398,190,069	0.00117	2,968,399	2,488,688	272,321	467,243	739,564	3,228,252
5	8	397,450,505	0.00134	2,964,914	2,484,066	273,843	533,493	807,335	3,291,401
6	9	396,643,170	0.00151	2,960,931	2,479,020	275,327	599,514	874,841	3,353,860
7	10	395,768,329	0.00168	2,956,453	2,473,552	276,772	665,273	942,045	3,415,597
8	11	394,826,284	0.00185	2,951,480	2,467,664	278,177	730,736	1,008,913	3,476,577
9	12	393,817,371	0.00202	2,946,013	2,461,359	279,542	795,869	1,075,410	3,536,769
10	13	392,741,961	0.00219	2,940,056	2,454,637	280,865	860,637	1,141,502	3,596,140
11	14	391,600,459	0.00236	2,933,608	2,447,503	282,147	925,008	1,207,155	3,654,658
27	30	364,808,016	0.00514	2,766,461	2,280,050	296,406	1,874,688	2,171,094	4,451,144
28	31	362,636,921	0.00514	2,752,233	2,266,481	296,879	1,863,519	2,160,398	4,426,879
29	32	360,476,523	0.00514	2,738,078	2,252,978	297,351	1,852,406	2,149,758	4,402,736
30	33	358,326,766	0.00514	2,723,996	2,239,542	297,825	1,841,347	2,139,173	4,378,715
100	103	231,249,776	0.00514	1,898,682	1,445,311	332,928	1,187,608	1,520,537	2,965,848
101	104	229,729,239	0.00514	1,888,917	1,435,808	333,459	1,179,785	1,513,244	2,949,052
102	105	228,215,995	0.00514	1,879,202	1,426,350	333,990	1,172,000	1,505,990	2,932,340
103	106	226,710,004	0.00514	1,869,538	1,416,938	334,522	1,164,252	1,498,774	2,915,712
104	107	225,211,230	0.00514	1,859,923	1,407,570	335,055	1,156,541	1,491,596	2,899,166
105	108	223,719,634	0.00514	1,850,357	1,398,248	335,589	1,148,867	1,484,456	2,882,703
200	203	109,791,339	0.00514	1,133,751	686,196	390,372	562,651	953,023	1,639,219
201	204	108,838,316	0.00514	1,127,920	680,239	390,994	557,746	948,740	1,628,980
202	205	107,889,576	0.00514	1,122,119	674,310	391,617	552,863	944,480	1,618,790
203	206	106,945,096	0.00514	1,116,348	668,407	392,241	548,003	940,243	1,608,650
300	303	32,383,611	0.00514	676,991	202,398	457,727	164,195	621,923	824,320
301	304	31,761,689	0.00514	673,510	198,511	458,457	160,993	619,449	817,960
302	305	31,142,239	0.00514	670,046	194,639	459,187	157,803	616,990	811,629
303	306	30,525,249	0.00514	666,600	190,783	459,918	154,626	614,545	805,328
352	355	3,034,311	0.00514	517,770	18,964	497,226	13,048	510,274	529,238
353	356	2,524,037	0.00514	515,107	15,775	498,018	10,420	508,437	524,213
354	357	2,015,600	0.00514	512,458	12,597	498,811	7,801	506,612	519,209
355	358	1,508,988	0.00514	509,823	9,431	499,606	5,191	504,797	514,228
356	359	1,004,191	0.00514	507,201	6,276	500,401	2,591	502,992	509,269
357	360	501,199	0.00514	504,592	3,132	501,199	0	501,199	504,331

*Since the WAM is 357 months, the underlying mortgage pool is seasoned an average of three months, and therefore based on 100 PSA, the CPR is 0.8% in month 1 and the pool seasons at 6% in month 27.

Exhibit 3 shows the cash flow for selected months assuming 100 PSA. The cash flow is broken down into three components: (1) interest (based on the passthrough rate), (2) the regularly scheduled principal repayment (i.e., scheduled amortization), and (3) prepayments based on 100 PSA.

Let's walk through Exhibit 3 column by column.

Column 1: This is the number of months from now when the cash flow will be received.

Column 2: This is the number of months of seasoning. Since the WAM for this mortgage pool is 357 months, this means that the loans are seasoned an average of 3 months (360 months − 357 months) now.

Column 3: This column gives the outstanding mortgage balance at the beginning of the month. It is equal to the outstanding balance at the beginning of the previous month reduced by the total principal payment in the previous month.

Column 4: This column shows the SMM based on the number of months the loans are seasoned — the number of months shown in Column (2). For example, for the first month shown in the exhibit, the loans are seasoned three months going into that month. Therefore, the CPR used is the CPR that corresponds to four months. From the PSA benchmark, the CPR is 0.8% (4 times 0.2%). The corresponding SMM is 0.00067. The mortgage pool becomes fully seasoned in Column (1) corresponding to month 27 because by that time the loans are seasoned 30 months. When the loans are fully seasoned the CPR at 100 PSA is 6% and the corresponding SMM is 0.00514.

Column 5: The total monthly mortgage payment is shown in this column. Notice that the total monthly mortgage payment declines over time as prepayments reduce the mortgage balance outstanding. There is a formula to determine what the monthly mortgage balance will be for each month given prepayments.[2]

Column 6: The *net* monthly interest (i.e., amount available to pay bondholders after the servicing fee) is found in this column. This value is determined by multiplying the outstanding mortgage balance at the beginning of the month by the passthrough rate of 7.5% and then dividing by 12.

Column 7: This column gives the scheduled principal repayment (i.e., scheduled amortization). This is the difference between the total monthly mortgage payment [the amount shown in Column (5)] and the gross coupon interest for the month. The gross coupon interest is found by multiplying 8.125% by the outstanding mortgage balance at the beginning of the month and then dividing by 12.

Column 8: The prepayment for the month is reported in this column. The prepayment is found by using equation (2). For example, in month 100, the beginning mortgage balance is $231,249,776, the scheduled principal payment is $332,928, and the SMM at 100 PSA is 0.00514301 (only 0.00514 is shown in the exhibit to save space), so the prepayment is:

$$0.00514301 \times (\$231,249,776 - \$332,928) = \$1,187,608$$

Column 9: The total principal payment, which is the sum of columns (7) and (8), is shown in this column.

Column 10: The projected monthly cash flow for this passthrough is shown in this last column. The monthly cash flow is the sum of the interest paid [Column (6)] and the total principal payments for the month [Column (9)].

---

[2] The formula is presented in Chapter 19 of Frank J. Fabozzi, *Fixed Income Mathematics* (Chicago: Irwin Professional Publishing, 1997).

Exhibit 4: Monthly Cash Flow for a $400 Million Passthrough with a 7.5% Passthrough Rate, a WAC of 8.125%, and a WAM of 357 Months Assuming 165 PSA

Month (1)	Months Seasoned* (2)	Outstanding Balance (3)	SMM (4)	Mortgage Payment (5)	Net Interest (6)	Scheduled Principal (7)	Prepayment (8)	Total Principal (9)	Cash Flow (10)
1	4	$400,000,000	0.00111	$2,975,868	$2,500,000	$267,535	$442,389	$709,923	$3,209,923
2	5	399,290,077	0.00139	2,972,575	2,495,563	269,048	552,847	821,896	3,317,459
3	6	398,468,181	0.00167	2,968,456	2,490,426	270,495	663,065	933,560	3,423,986
4	7	397,534,621	0.00195	2,963,513	2,484,591	271,873	772,949	1,044,822	3,529,413
5	8	396,489,799	0.00223	2,957,747	2,478,061	273,181	882,405	1,155,586	3,633,647
6	9	395,334,213	0.00251	2,951,160	2,470,839	274,418	991,341	1,265,759	3,736,598
7	10	394,068,454	0.00279	2,943,755	2,462,928	275,583	1,099,664	1,375,246	3,838,174
8	11	392,693,208	0.00308	2,935,534	2,454,333	276,674	1,207,280	1,483,954	3,938,287
9	12	391,209,254	0.00336	2,926,503	2,445,058	277,690	1,314,099	1,591,789	4,036,847
10	13	389,617,464	0.00365	2,916,666	2,435,109	278,631	1,420,029	1,698,659	4,133,769
11	14	387,918,805	0.00393	2,906,028	2,424,493	279,494	1,524,979	1,804,473	4,228,965
27	30	347,334,116	0.00865	2,633,950	2,170,838	282,209	3,001,955	3,284,164	5,455,002
28	31	344,049,952	0.00865	2,611,167	2,150,312	281,662	2,973,553	3,255,215	5,405,527
29	32	340,794,737	0.00865	2,588,581	2,129,967	281,116	2,945,400	3,226,516	5,356,483
30	33	337,568,221	0.00865	2,566,190	2,109,801	280,572	2,917,496	3,198,067	5,307,869
100	103	170,142,350	0.00865	1,396,958	1,063,390	244,953	1,469,591	1,714,544	2,777,933
101	104	168,427,806	0.00865	1,384,875	1,052,674	244,478	1,454,765	1,699,243	2,751,916
102	105	166,728,563	0.00865	1,372,896	1,042,054	244,004	1,440,071	1,684,075	2,726,128
103	106	165,044,489	0.00865	1,361,020	1,031,528	243,531	1,425,508	1,669,039	2,700,567
104	107	163,375,450	0.00865	1,349,248	1,021,097	243,060	1,411,075	1,654,134	2,675,231
105	108	161,721,315	0.00865	1,337,577	1,010,758	242,589	1,396,771	1,639,359	2,650,118
200	203	56,746,664	0.00865	585,990	354,667	201,767	489,106	690,874	1,045,540
201	204	56,055,790	0.00865	580,921	350,349	201,377	483,134	684,510	1,034,859
202	205	55,371,280	0.00865	575,896	346,070	200,986	477,216	678,202	1,024,273
203	206	54,693,077	0.00865	570,915	341,832	200,597	471,353	671,950	1,013,782
300	303	11,758,141	0.00865	245,808	73,488	166,196	100,269	266,465	339,953
301	304	11,491,677	0.00865	243,682	71,823	165,874	97,967	263,841	335,664
302	305	11,227,836	0.00865	241,574	70,174	165,552	95,687	261,240	331,414
303	306	10,966,596	0.00865	239,485	68,541	165,232	93,430	258,662	327,203
352	355	916,910	0.00865	156,460	5,731	150,252	6,631	156,883	162,614
353	356	760,027	0.00865	155,107	4,750	149,961	5,277	155,238	159,988
354	357	604,789	0.00865	153,765	3,780	149,670	3,937	153,607	157,387
355	358	451,182	0.00865	152,435	2,820	149,380	2,611	151,991	154,811
356	359	299,191	0.00865	151,117	1,870	149,091	1,298	150,389	152,259
357	360	148,802	0.00865	149,809	930	148,802	0	148,802	149,732

* Since the WAM is 357 months, the underlying mortgage pool is seasoned an average of three months, and therefore based on 165 PSA, the CPR is 0.8% × 1.65 in month 1 and the pool seasons at 6% × 1.65 in month 27.

Let's look at what happens to the cash flows for this passthrough if a different PSA assumption is made. Suppose that instead of 100 PSA, 165 PSA is assumed. That is, prepayments are assumed to be faster. Exhibit 4 shows the cash flow for this passthrough based on 165 PSA. Notice that the cash flows are greater in the early years compared to Exhibit 3 because prepayments are higher. The cash flows in later years are less for 165 PSA compared to 100 PSA because of the higher prepayments in the earlier years.

E. Factors Affecting Prepayment Behavior

The factors that affect prepayment behavior are:

1. prevailing mortgage rate
2. characteristics of the underlying mortgage pool
3. seasonal factors
4. general economic activity

1. Prevailing Mortgage Rate

The current mortgage rate affects prepayments in three ways. First, the spread between the prevailing mortgage rate in the market and the rate paid by the home-owner affects the **incentive to refinance**. Second, the path of mortgage rates since the loan was originated affects prepayments through a phenomenon referred to as **refinancing burnout**. Both the spread and path of mortgage rates affect prepayments that are the product of refinancing. The third way in which the prevailing mortgage rate affects prepayments is through its effect on the affordability of housing and **housing turnover**. The level of mortgage rates affects housing turnover to the extent that a lower rate increases the affordability of homes.

The single most important factor affecting prepayments because of refinancing is the current level of mortgage rates relative to the borrower's contract rate. The greater the difference between the two, the greater the incentive to refinance the mortgage loan. For refinancing to make economic sense, the interest savings must be greater than the costs associated with refinancing the mortgage. These costs include legal expenses, origination fees, title insurance, and the value of the time associated with obtaining another mortgage loan. Some of these costs — such as title insurance and origination points — will vary proportionately with the amount to be financed. Other costs such as the application fee and legal expenses are typically fixed.

Historically it had been observed that mortgage rates had to decline by between 250 and 350 basis points below the contract rate in order to make it worth-while for borrowers to refinance. However, the creativity of mortgage originators in designing mortgage loans such that the refinancing costs are folded into the amount borrowed has changed the view that mortgage rates must drop dramatically below the contract rate to make refinancing economic. Moreover, mortgage originators now do an effective job of advertising to make homeowners cognizant of the economic bene-fits of refinancing.

The historical pattern of prepayments and economic theory suggests that it is not only the level of mortgage rates that affects prepayment behavior but also the path that mortgage rates take to get to the current level. To illustrate why, suppose the underlying contract rate for a pool of mortgage loans is 11% and that three years after origination, the prevailing mortgage rate declines to 8%. Let's consider two possible paths of the mortgage rate in getting to the 8% level. In the first path, the mortgage rate declines to 8% at the end of the first year, then rises to 13% at the end of the sec-ond year, and then falls to 8% at the end of the third year. In the second path, the mort-gage rate rises to 12% at the end of the first year, continues its rise to 13% at the end of the second year, and then falls to 8% at the end of the third year.

If the mortgage rate follows the first path, those who can benefit from refinanc-ing will more than likely take advantage of this opportunity when the mortgage rate drops to 8% in the first year. When the mortgage rate drops again to 8% at the end of the third year, the likelihood is that prepayments because of refinancing will not surge;

those who want to benefit by taking advantage of the refinancing opportunity will have done so already when the mortgage rate declined for the first time. This is the prepayment behavior referred to as the refinancing burnout (or simply, burnout) phenomenon.

In contrast, the expected prepayment behavior when the mortgage rate follows the second path is quite different. Prepayment rates are expected to be low in the first two years. When the mortgage rate declines to 8% in the third year, refinancing activity and therefore prepayments are expected to surge. Consequently, the burnout phenomenon is related to the path of mortgage rates.

2. Characteristics of the Underlying Mortgage Loans

The following characteristics of the underlying mortgage loans affect prepayments: (1) the contract rate, (2) whether the loans are FHA/VA/RHS-guaranteed or conventional, (3) the amount of seasoning, (4) the type of loan (e.g., a 30-year level payment mortgage, 5-year balloon mortgage, etc.), and (4) the geographical location of the underlying properties.

3. Seasonal Factors

There is a well-documented **seasonal pattern** in prepayments. A seasonal pattern is related to activity in the primary housing market, with home buying activity increasing in the spring, and gradually reaching a peak[3] in the late summer. Home buying activity declines in the fall and winter. Mirroring this activity are the prepayments that result from the turnover of housing as home buyers sell their existing homes and purchase new ones. Prepayments are low in the winter months and begin to rise in the spring, reaching a peak in the summer months. However, probably because of delays in passing through prepayments, the peak in prepayments on mortgage passthrough securities may not be observed until early fall.

4. General Economic Activity

Economic theory would suggest that general economic activity affects prepayment behavior through its effect on housing turnover. The link is as follows: a growing economy results in a rise in personal income and in opportunities for worker migration; this increases family mobility and as a result increases housing turnover. The opposite holds for a weak economy.

F. Extension Risk and Contraction Risk

An investor who owns passthrough securities does not know what the cash flow will be because that depends on actual prepayments. As we noted earlier, this risk is called prepayment risk.

To understand the significance of prepayment risk, suppose an investor buys a 9% coupon passthrough security at a time when mortgage rates are 10%. Let's consider what will happen to prepayments if mortgage rates decline to, say, 6%. There will be two adverse consequences. First, a basic property of fixed income securities is that the price of an option-free bond will rise. But in the case of a passthrough security, the rise in price will not be as large as that of an option-free bond because a fall in

---

[3] Do not get confused between "seasoning" and "seasonal." Seasoning refers to the amount of time since the mortgage pool was originated. For example, a mortgage pool underlying a passthrough originated 13 months ago is said to be 13 months seasoned. Seasonal refers to the season of the year (fall, winter, spring, and summer).

interest rates will give the borrower an incentive to prepay the loan and refinance the debt at a lower rate. This results in the same adverse consequence faced by holders of callable bonds. As in the case of those instruments, the upside price potential of a passthrough security is compressed because of prepayments. (This is the negative convexity characteristic explained at Level I (Chapter 7.) The second adverse consequence is that the cash flow must be reinvested at a lower rate. Basically, the faster prepayments due to a decline in interest rates that causes these two adverse consequences are due to the passthrough shortening in terms of the timing of its cash flows. Later we will see that by "shortening" we mean that its "average life" declines. Consequently, the two adverse consequences from a decline in interest rates for a passthrough security are referred to as **contraction risk**.

Now let's look at what happens if mortgage rates rise to 15%. The price of the passthrough, like the price of any bond, will decline. But again it will decline more because the higher rates will tend to slow down the rate of prepayment, in effect increasing the amount invested at the coupon rate, which is lower than the market rate. Prepayments will slow down, because homeowners will not refinance or partially prepay their mortgages when mortgage rates are higher than the contract rate of 10%. Of course this is just the time when investors want prepayments to speed up so that they can reinvest the prepayments at the higher market interest rate. Basically, the slower prepayments associated with a rise in interest rates that causes this adverse consequences are due to the passthrough lengthening in terms of the timing of its cash flows. Later we will see that by "lengthening" we mean that its "average life" increases. Consequently, the adverse consequence from a rise in interest rates for a passthrough security is referred to as **extension risk**.

Therefore, prepayment risk encompasses contraction risk and extension risk. Prepayment risk makes passthrough securities unattractive for certain financial institutions to hold from an asset/liability perspective. Some institutional investors are concerned with extension risk and others with contraction risk when they purchase a passthrough security. This applies even for assets supporting specific types of insurance contracts. Is it possible to alter the cash flow of a passthrough so as to reduce the contraction risk or extension risk for institutional investors? This can be done, as we shall see, when we describe collateralized mortgage obligations.

G. Average Life

The stated maturity of a mortgage passthrough security is not a useful measure. Instead, market participants calculate the **average life** (or **weighted average life**) of a mortgage-backed security. This is the average time to receipt of principal payments (scheduled principal payments and projected prepayments). Mathematically, the average life is expressed as follows:

$$\text{Average life} = \sum_{t=1}^{T} \frac{t \times \text{Projected principal received at time } t}{12 \times \text{Total principal}}$$

where T is the number of months.

The average life of a passthrough depends on the prepayment assumption. To see this, the average life is shown below for different prepayment speeds for the pass-through we used to illustrate the cash flow for 100 PSA and 165 PSA in Exhibits 3 and 4:

PSA speed	50	100	165	200	300	400	500	600	700
Average life (years)	15.11	11.66	8.76	7.68	5.63	4.44	3.68	3.16	2.78

SECTION IV COLLATERALIZED MORTGAGE OBLIGATIONS

As we noted, there is prepayment risk associated with investing in a mortgage passthrough security. Some institutional investors are concerned with extension risk and others with contraction risk. This problem can be mitigated by redirecting the cash flows of mortgage-related products (passthrough securities or a pool of loans) to different bond classes, called **tranches**, so as to create securities that have different exposure to prepayment risk and therefore different risk/return patterns than the mortgage-related product from which they are created.

When the cash flows of mortgage-related products are redistributed to different bond classes, the resulting securities are called **collateralized mortgage obligations** (CMO). The creation of a CMO cannot eliminate prepayment risk; it can only distribute the various forms of this risk among different classes of bondholders. The CMO's major financial innovation is that the securities created more closely satisfy the asset/ liability needs of institutional investors, thereby broadening the appeal of mortgage-backed products.

There is a wide range of CMO structures.[4] We review the major ones below.

A. Sequential-Pay Tranches

The first CMO was structured so that each class of bond would be retired sequentially. Such structures are referred to as **sequential-pay** CMOs.

To illustrate a sequential-pay CMO, we discuss FJF-01, a hypothetical deal made up to illustrate the basic features of the structure. The collateral for this hypothetical CMO is a hypothetical passthrough with a total par value of $400 million and the following characteristics: (1) the passthrough coupon rate is 7.5%, (2) the weighted average coupon (WAC) is 8.125%, and (3) the weighted average maturity (WAM) is 357 months. This is the same passthrough that we used in Section III to describe the cash flow of a passthrough based on some PSA assumption.

From this $400 million of collateral, four bond classes or tranches are created. Their characteristics are summarized in Exhibit 5. The total par value of the four tranches is equal to the par value of the collateral (i.e., the passthrough security).[5] In this simple structure, the coupon rate is the same for each tranche and also the same as the coupon rate on the collateral. There is no reason why this must be so, and, in fact, typically the coupon rate varies by tranche.

Now remember that a CMO is created by redistributing the cash flow — interest and principal — to the different tranches based on a set of payment rules. The payment rules at the bottom of Exhibit 5 describe how the cash flow from the passthrough (i.e., collateral) is to be distributed to the four tranches. There are separate rules for the distribution of the coupon interest and the payment of principal (the principal being the total of the regularly scheduled principal payment and any prepayments).

While the payment rules for the disbursement of the principal payments are known, the precise amount of the principal in each month is not. This will depend on the cash flow, and therefore principal payments, of the collateral, which depends on the actual prepayment rate of the collateral. An assumed PSA speed allows the cash flow to be projected. Exhibit 6 shows the cash flow (interest, regularly scheduled principal repayment, and prepayments) assuming 165 PSA. Assuming that the collateral does prepay at 165 PSA, the cash flow available to all four tranches of FJF-01 will be precisely the cash flow shown in Exhibit 6.

---

[4] The issuer of a CMO wants to be sure that the trust created to pass through the interest and principal payments is not treated as a taxable entity. A provision of the Tax Reform Act of 1986, called the Real Estate Mortgage Investment Conduit (REMIC), specifies the requirements that an issuer must fulfill so that the legal entity created to issue a CMO is not taxable. Most CMOs today are created as REMICs. While it is common to hear market participants refer to a CMO as a REMIC, not all CMOs are REMICs.

[5] Actually, a CMO is backed by a pool of passthrough securities.

Exhibit 5: FJF-01 — A Hypothetical 4-Tranche Sequential-Pay Structure

Tranche	Par Amount ($)	Coupon Rate (%)
A	194,500,000	7.5
B	36,000,000	7.5
C	96,500,000	7.5
D	73,000,000	7.5
Total	400,000,000	

Payment rules:

1. *For payment of monthly coupon interest:* Disburse monthly coupon interest to each tranche on the basis of the amount of principal outstanding for each tranche at the beginning of the month.

2. *For disbursement of principal payments:* Disburse principal payments to tranche A until it is completely paid off. After tranche A is completely paid off, disburse principal payments to tranche B until it is completely paid off. After tranche B is completely paid off, disburse principal payments to tranche C until it is completely paid off. After tranche C is completely paid off, disburse principal payments to tranche D until it is completely paid off.

Exhibit 6: Monthly Cash Flow for Selected Months for FJF-01 Assuming 165 PSA

Month	Tranche A Balance ($)	Principal ($)	Interest ($)	Tranche B Balance ($)	Principal ($)	Interest ($)
1	194,500,000	709,923	1,215,625	36,000,000	0	225,000
2	193,790,077	821,896	1,211,188	36,000,000	0	225,000
3	192,968,181	933,560	1,206,051	36,000,000	0	225,000
4	192,034,621	1,044,822	1,200,216	36,000,000	0	225,000
5	190,989,799	1,155,586	1,193,686	36,000,000	0	225,000
6	189,834,213	1,265,759	1,186,464	36,000,000	0	225,000
7	188,568,454	1,375,246	1,178,553	36,000,000	0	225,000
8	187,193,208	1,483,954	1,169,958	36,000,000	0	225,000
9	185,709,254	1,591,789	1,160,683	36,000,000	0	225,000
10	184,117,464	1,698,659	1,150,734	36,000,000	0	225,000
11	182,418,805	1,804,473	1,140,118	36,000,000	0	225,000
12	180,614,332	1,909,139	1,128,840	36,000,000	0	225,000
75	12,893,479	2,143,974	80,584	36,000,000	0	225,000
76	10,749,504	2,124,935	67,184	36,000,000	0	225,000
77	8,624,569	2,106,062	53,904	36,000,000	0	225,000
78	6,518,507	2,087,353	40,741	36,000,000	0	225,000
79	4,431,154	2,068,807	27,695	36,000,000	0	225,000
80	2,362,347	2,050,422	14,765	36,000,000	0	225,000
81	311,926	311,926	1,950	36,000,000	1,720,271	225,000
82	0	0	0	34,279,729	2,014,130	214,248
83	0	0	0	32,265,599	1,996,221	201,660
84	0	0	0	30,269,378	1,978,468	189,184
85	0	0	0	28,290,911	1,960,869	176,818
95	0	0	0	9,449,331	1,793,089	59,058
96	0	0	0	7,656,242	1,777,104	47,852
97	0	0	0	5,879,138	1,761,258	36,745
98	0	0	0	4,117,879	1,745,550	25,737
99	0	0	0	2,372,329	1,729,979	14,827
100	0	0	0	642,350	642,350	4,015
101	0	0	0	0	0	0

Exhibit 6 (Continued)

Month	Tranche C Balance ($)	Principal ($)	Interest ($)	Tranche D Balance ($)	Principal ($)	Interest ($)
1	96,500,000	0	603,125	73,000,000	0	456,250
2	96,500,000	0	603,125	73,000,000	0	456,250
3	96,500,000	0	603,125	73,000,000	0	456,250
4	96,500,000	0	603,125	73,000,000	0	456,250
5	96,500,000	0	603,125	73,000,000	0	456,250
6	96,500,000	0	603,125	73,000,000	0	456,250
7	96,500,000	0	603,125	73,000,000	0	456,250
8	96,500,000	0	603,125	73,000,000	0	456,250
9	96,500,000	0	603,125	73,000,000	0	456,250
10	96,500,000	0	603,125	73,000,000	0	456,250
11	96,500,000	0	603,125	73,000,000	0	456,250
12	96,500,000	0	603,125	73,000,000	0	456,250
95	96,500,000	0	603,125	73,000,000	0	456,250
96	96,500,000	0	603,125	73,000,000	0	456,250
97	96,500,000	0	603,125	73,000,000	0	456,250
98	96,500,000	0	603,125	73,000,000	0	456,250
99	96,500,000	0	603,125	73,000,000	0	456,250
100	96,500,000	1,072,194	603,125	73,000,000	0	456,250
101	95,427,806	1,699,243	596,424	73,000,000	0	456,250
102	93,728,563	1,684,075	585,804	73,000,000	0	456,250
103	92,044,489	1,669,039	575,278	73,000,000	0	456,250
104	90,375,450	1,654,134	564,847	73,000,000	0	456,250
105	88,721,315	1,639,359	554,508	73,000,000	0	456,250
175	3,260,287	869,602	20,377	73,000,000	0	456,250
176	2,390,685	861,673	14,942	73,000,000	0	456,250
177	1,529,013	853,813	9,556	73,000,000	0	456,250
178	675,199	675,199	4,220	73,000,000	170,824	456,250
179	0	0	0	72,829,176	838,300	455,182
180	0	0	0	71,990,876	830,646	449,943
181	0	0	0	71,160,230	823,058	444,751
182	0	0	0	70,337,173	815,536	439,607
183	0	0	0	69,521,637	808,081	434,510
184	0	0	0	68,713,556	800,690	429,460
185	0	0	0	67,912,866	793,365	424,455
350	0	0	0	1,235,674	160,220	7,723
351	0	0	0	1,075,454	158,544	6,722
352	0	0	0	916,910	156,883	5,731
353	0	0	0	760,027	155,238	4,750
354	0	0	0	604,789	153,607	3,780
355	0	0	0	451,182	151,991	2,820
356	0	0	0	299,191	150,389	1,870
357	0	0	0	148,802	148,802	930

Note: The cash flow for a tranche in each month is the sum of the principal and interest.

To demonstrate how the payment rules for FJF-01 work, Exhibit 6 shows the cash flow for selected months assuming the collateral prepays at 165 PSA. For each tranche, the exhibit shows: (1) the balance at the end of the month, (2) the principal paid down (regularly scheduled principal repayment plus prepayments), and (3) interest. In month 1, the cash flow for the collateral consists of a principal payment of

$709,923 and an interest payment of $2.5 million (0.075 times $400 million divided by 12). The interest payment is distributed to the four tranches based on the amount of the par value outstanding. So, for example, tranche A receives $1,215,625 (0.075 times $194,500,000 divided by 12) of the $2.5 million. The principal, however, is all distributed to tranche A. Therefore, the cash flow for tranche A in month 1 is $1,925,548. The principal balance at the end of month 1 for tranche A is $193,790,076 (the original principal balance of $194,500,000 less the principal payment of $709,923). No principal payment is distributed to the three other tranches because there is still a principal balance outstanding for tranche A. This will be true for months 2 through 80. The cash flow for tranche A for each month is found by adding the amounts shown in the "Principal" and "Interest" columns. So, for tranche A, the cash flow in month 8 is $1,483,954 plus $1,169,958, or $2,653,912. The cash flow from months 82 on is zero based on 165 PSA.

After month 81, the principal balance will be zero for tranche A. For the collateral, the cash flow in month 81 is $3,318,521, consisting of a principal payment of $2,032,197 and interest of $1,286,325. At the beginning of month 81 (end of month 80), the principal balance for tranche A is $311,926. Therefore, $311,926 of the $2,032,196 of the principal payment from the collateral will be disbursed to tranche A. After this payment is made, no additional principal payments are made to this tranche as the principal balance is zero. The remaining principal payment from the collateral, $1,720,271, is distributed to tranche B. Based on an assumed prepayment speed of 165 PSA, tranche B then begins receiving principal payments in month 81. The cash flow for tranche B for each month is found by adding the amounts shown in the "Principal" and "Interest" columns. For months 1 though 80, the cash flow is just the interest. There is no cash flow after month 100 for Tranche B.

Exhibit 6 shows that tranche B is fully paid off by month 100, when tranche C begins to receive principal payments. Tranche C is not fully paid off until month 178, at which time tranche D begins receiving the remaining principal payments. The maturity (i.e., the time until the principal is fully paid off) for these four tranches assuming 165 PSA would be 81 months for tranche A, 100 months for tranche B, 178 months for tranche C, and 357 months for tranche D. The cash flow for each month for tranches C and D is found by adding the principal and the interest for the month.

The **principal pay down window** for a tranche is the time period between the beginning and the ending of the principal payments to that tranche. So, for example, for tranche A, the principal pay down window would be month 1 to month 81 assuming 165 PSA. For tranche B it is from month 81 to month 100. The window is also specified in terms of the length of the time from the beginning of the principal pay down window to the end of the principal pay down window. For tranche A, the window would be stated as 81 months, for tranche B 20 months. In confirmation of trades involving CMOs, the principal pay down window is specified in terms of the initial month that principal is expected to be received to the final month that principal is expected to be received.

Let's look at what has been accomplished by creating the CMO. Earlier we saw that the average life for of the passthrough is 8.76 years assuming a prepayment speed of 165 PSA. Exhibit 7 reports the average life of the collateral and the four tranches assuming different prepayment speeds. Notice that the four tranches have average lives that are both shorter and longer than the collateral, thereby attracting investors who have a preference for an average life different from that of the collateral.

Exhibit 7: Average Life for the Collateral and the Four Tranches of FJF-01

Prepayment Speed (PSA)	Average life (in years) for				
	Collateral	Tranche A	Tranche B	Tranche C	Tranche D
50	15.11	7.48	15.98	21.02	27.24
100	11.66	4.90	10.86	15.78	24.58
165	8.76	3.48	7.49	11.19	20.27
200	7.68	3.05	6.42	9.60	18.11
300	5.63	2.32	4.64	6.81	13.36
400	4.44	1.94	3.70	5.31	10.34
500	3.68	1.69	3.12	4.38	8.35
600	3.16	1.51	2.74	3.75	6.96
700	2.78	1.38	2.47	3.30	5.95

There is still a major problem: there is considerable variability of the average life for the tranches. We'll see how this can be handled later on. However, there is some protection provided for each tranche against prepayment risk. This is because prioritizing the distribution of principal (i.e., establishing the payment rules for principal) effectively protects the shorter-term tranche A in this structure against extension risk. This protection must come from somewhere, so it comes from the three other tranches. Similarly, tranches C and D provide protection against extension risk for tranches A and B. At the same time, tranches C and D benefit because they are provided protection against contraction risk, the protection coming from tranches A and B.

B. Accrual Bonds

In FJF-01, the payment rules for interest provide for all tranches to be paid interest each month. In many sequential-pay CMO structures, at least one tranche does not receive current interest. Instead, the interest for that tranche would accrue and be added to the principal balance. Such a tranche is commonly referred to as an **accrual tranche** or a **Z bond**. The interest that would have been paid to the accrual tranche is then used to pay off the principal balance of earlier tranches.

To see this, consider FJF-02, a hypothetical CMO structure with the same collateral as FJF-01 and with four tranches, each with a coupon rate of 7.5%. The difference is in the last tranche, Z, which is an accrual tranche. The structure for FJF-02 is shown in Exhibit 8.

Exhibit 9 shows cash flows for selected months for tranches A and B. Let's look at month 1 and compare it to month 1 in Exhibit 6. Both cash flows are based on 165 PSA. The principal payment from the collateral is $709,923. In FJF-01, this is the principal paydown for tranche A. In FJF-02, the interest for tranche Z, $456,250, is not paid to that tranche but instead is used to pay down the principal of tranche A. So, the principal payment to tranche A in Exhibit 9 is $1,166,173, the collateral's principal payment of $709,923 plus the interest of $456,250 that was diverted from tranche Z.

The expected final maturity for tranches A, B, and C has shortened as a result of the inclusion of tranche Z. The final payout for tranche A is 64 months rather than 81 months; for tranche B it is 77 months rather than 100 months; and, for tranche C it is 113 months rather than 178 months.

The average lives for tranches A, B, and C are shorter in FJF-02 compared to FJF-01 because of the inclusion of the accrual tranche. For example, at 165 PSA, the average lives are as follows:

Structure	Tranche A	Tranche B	Tranche C
FJF-02	2.90	5.86	7.87
FJF-01	3.48	7.49	11.19

Exhibit 8: FJF-02 — A Hypothetical 4-Tranche Sequential-Pay Structure with an Accrual Bond Class

Tranche	Par Amount ($)	Coupon Rate (%)
A	194,500,000	7.5
B	36,000,000	7.5
C	96,500,000	7.5
Z (Accrual)	73,000,000	7.5
Total	400,000,000	

Payment rules:

1. *For payment of monthly coupon interest:* Disburse monthly coupon interest to tranches A, B. and C on the basis of the amount of principal outstanding for each tranche at the beginning of the month. For tranche Z, accrue the interest based on the principal plus accrued interest in the previous month. The interest for tranche Z is to be paid to the earlier tranches as a principal paydown.

2. *For disbursement of principal payments:* Disburse principal payments to tranche A until it is completely paid off. After tranche A is completely paid off, disburse principal payments to tranche B until it is completely paid off. After tranche B is completely paid off, disburse principal payments to tranche C until it is completely paid off. After tranche C is completely paid off, disburse principal payments to tranche Z until the original principal balance plus accrued interest is completely paid off.

Exhibit 9: Monthly Cash Flow for Selected Months for Tranches A and B for FJF-02 Assuming 165 PSA

Month	Tranche A			Tranche B		
	Balance ($)	Principal ($)	Interest ($)	Balance ($)	Principal ($)	Interest ($)
1	194,500,000	1,166,173	1,215,625	36,000,000	0	225,000
2	193,333,827	1,280,997	1,208,336	36,000,000	0	225,000
3	192,052,829	1,395,531	1,200,330	36,000,000	0	225,000
4	190,657,298	1,509,680	1,191,608	36,000,000	0	225,000
5	189,147,619	1,623,350	1,182,173	36,000,000	0	225,000
6	187,524,269	1,736,446	1,172,027	36,000,000	0	225,000
7	185,787,823	1,848,875	1,161,174	36,000,000	0	225,000
8	183,938,947	1,960,543	1,149,618	36,000,000	0	225,000
9	181,978,404	2,071,357	1,137,365	36,000,000	0	225,000
10	179,907,047	2,181,225	1,124,419	36,000,000	0	225,000
11	177,725,822	2,290,054	1,110,786	36,000,000	0	225,000
12	175,435,768	2,397,755	1,096,474	36,000,000	0	225,000
60	15,023,406	3,109,398	93,896	36,000,000	0	225,000
61	11,914,007	3,091,812	74,463	36,000,000	0	225,000
62	8,822,195	3,074,441	55,139	36,000,000	0	225,000
63	5,747,754	3,057,282	35,923	36,000,000	0	225,000
64	2,690,472	2,690,472	16,815	36,000,000	349,863	225,000
65	0	0	0	35,650,137	3,023,598	222,813
66	0	0	0	32,626,540	3,007,069	203,916
67	0	0	0	29,619,470	2,990,748	185,122
68	0	0	0	26,628,722	2,974,633	166,430
69	0	0	0	23,654,089	2,958,722	147,838
70	0	0	0	20,695,367	2,943,014	129,346
71	0	0	0	17,752,353	2,927,508	110,952
72	0	0	0	14,824,845	2,912,203	92,655
73	0	0	0	11,912,642	2,897,096	74,454
74	0	0	0	9,015,546	2,882,187	56,347
75	0	0	0	6,133,358	2,867,475	38,333
76	0	0	0	3,265,883	2,852,958	20,412
77	0	0	0	412,925	412,925	2,581
78	0	0	0	0	0	0
79	0	0	0	0	0	0
80	0	0	0	0	0	0

Exhibit 10: FJF-03 — A Hypothetical 5-Tranche Sequential-Pay Structure with Floater, Inverse Floater, and Accrual Bond Classes

Tranche	Par Amount ($)	Coupon Rate (%)
A	194,500,000	7.50
B	36,000,000	7.50
FL	72,375,000	1-month LIBOR + 0.50
IFL	24,125,000	28.50 − 3 × (1-month LIBOR)
Z (Accrual)	73,000,000	7.50
Total	400,000,000	

Payment rules:

1. *For payment of monthly coupon interest:* Disburse monthly coupon interest to tranches A, B, FL, and IFL on the basis of the amount of principal outstanding at the beginning of the month. For tranche Z, accrue the interest based on the principal plus accrued interest in the previous month. The interest for tranche Z is to be paid to the earlier tranches as a principal paydown. The maximum coupon rate for FL is 10%; the minimum coupon rate for IFL is 0%

2. *For disbursement of principal payments:* Disburse principal payments to tranche A until it is completely paid off. After tranche A is completely paid off, disburse principal payments to tranche B until it is completely paid off. After tranche B is completely paid off, disburse principal payments to tranches FL and IFL until they are completely paid off. The principal payments between tranches FL and IFL should be made in the following way: 75% to tranche FL and 25% to tranche IFL. After tranches FL and IFI are completely paid off, disburse principal payments to tranche Z until the original principal balance plus accrued interest are completely paid off.

The reason for the shortening of the non-accrual tranches is that the interest that would be paid to the accrual tranche is being allocated to the other tranches. Tranche Z in FJF-02 will have a longer average life than tranche D in FJF-01 because in tranche Z the interest payments are being diverted to tranches A, B, and C.

Thus, shorter-term tranches and a longer-term tranche are created by including an accrual tranche in FJF-02 compared to FJF-01. The accrual tranche has appeal to investors who are concerned with reinvestment risk. Since there are no coupon payments to reinvest, reinvestment risk is eliminated until all the other tranches are paid off.

C. Floating-Rate Tranches

A floating-rate tranche can be created from a fixed-rate tranche by creating a floater and an inverse floater combination. We will illustrate the creation of a **floating-rate tranche** and an **inverse floating-rate tranche** using the hypothetical CMO structure FJF-02 — the 4-tranche sequential-pay structure with an accrual tranche. We can select any of the tranches from which to create a floating-rate and inverse floating-rate tranche. In fact, we can create these two securities for more than one of the four tranches or for only a portion of one tranche.

In this case, we create a floater and an inverse floater from tranche C. The par value for this tranche is $96.5 million, and we create two tranches that have a combined par value of $96.5 million. We refer to this CMO structure with a floater and an inverse floater as FJF-03. It has five tranches, designated A, B, FL, IFL, and Z, where FL is the floating-rate tranche and IFL is the inverse floating-rate tranche. Exhibit 10 describes FJF-03. Any reference rate can be used to create a floater and the corresponding inverse floater. The reference rate for setting the coupon rate for FL and IFL in FJF-03 is 1-month LIBOR.

The amount of the par value of the floating-rate tranche will be some portion of the $96.5 million. There are an infinite number of ways to slice up the $96.5 million between the floater and inverse floater, and final partitioning will be driven by the demands of investors. In the FJF-03 structure, we made the floater from $72,375,000 or 75% of the $96.5 million. The coupon formula for the floater is 1-month LIBOR plus 50 basis points. So, for example, if LIBOR is 3.75% at the reset date, the coupon rate on the floater is 3.75% + 0.5%, or 4.25%. There is a cap on the coupon rate for the floater (discussed later).

Unlike a floating-rate note in the corporate bond market whose principal is unchanged over the life of the instrument, the floater's principal balance declines over time as principal payments are made. The principal payments to the floater are determined by the principal payments from the tranche from which the floater is created. In our CMO structure, this is tranche C.

Since the floater's par value is $72,375,000 of the $96.5 million, the balance is par value for the inverse floater. Assuming that 1-month LIBOR is the reference rate, the coupon formula for the inverse floater takes the following form:

$$K - L \times (1\text{-month LIBOR})$$

In FJF-03, K is set at 28.50% and L at 3. Thus, if 1-month LIBOR is 3.75%, the coupon rate for the month is:

$$28.50\% - 3 \times (3.75\%) = 17.25\%$$

K is the cap or maximum coupon rate for the inverse floater. In FJF-03, the cap for the inverse floater is 28.50%. The determination of the inverse floater's cap rate is based on (1) the amount of interest that would have been paid to the tranche from which the floater and the inverse floater were created, tranche C in our hypothetical deal, and (2) the coupon rate for the floater if 1-month LIBOR is zero. Let's see how the 28.5% for the inverse floater is determined.

The total interest to be paid to tranche C if it was not split into the floater and the inverse floater is the principal of $96,500,000 times 7.5%, or $7,237,500. The maximum interest for the inverse floater occurs if 1-month LIBOR is zero. In that case, the coupon rate for the floater is

$$1\text{-month LIBOR} + 0.5\% = 0.5\%$$

Since the floater receives 0.5% on its principal of $72,375,000, the floater's interest is $361,875. The remainder of the interest of $7,237,500 from tranche C goes to the inverse floater. That is, the inverse floater's interest is $6,875,625 (= $7,237,500 − $361,875). Since the inverse floater's principal is $24,125,000, the cap rate for the inverse floater is

$$\frac{\$6,875,625}{\$24,125,000} = 28.5\%$$

In general, the formula for the cap rate on the inverse floater, K, is

$$K = \frac{\text{inverse floater interest when reference rate for floater is zero}}{\text{principal for inverse floater}}$$

The *L* or multiple in the coupon formula to determine the coupon rate for the inverse floater is called the *leverage*. The higher the leverage, the more the inverse floater's coupon rate changes for a given change in 1-month LIBOR. For example, a coupon leverage of 3 means that a 1-basis point change in 1-month LIBOR will change the coupon rate on the inverse floater by 3 basis points.

As in the case of the floater, the principal paydown of an inverse floater will be a proportionate amount of the principal paydown of tranche C.

Because 1-month LIBOR is always positive, the coupon rate paid to the floater cannot be negative. If there are no restrictions placed on the coupon rate for the inverse floater, however, it is possible for its coupon rate to be negative. To prevent this, a floor, or minimum, is placed on the coupon rate. In most structures, the floor is set at zero. Once a floor is set for the inverse floater, a cap or ceiling is imposed on the floater.

In FJF-03, a floor of zero is set for the inverse floater. The floor results in a cap or maximum coupon rate for the floater of 10%. This is determined as follows. If the floor for the inverse floater is zero, this means that the inverse floater receives no interest. All of the interest that would have been paid to tranche C, $7,237,500, would then be paid to the floater. Since the floater's principal is $72,375,000, the cap rate on the floater is $7,237,500/$72,375,000, or 10%.

In general, the cap rate for the floater *assuming a floor of zero for inverse floater* is determined as follows:

$$\text{cap rate for floater} = \frac{\text{collateral tranche interest}}{\text{principal for floater}}$$

The cap for the floater and the inverse floater, the floor for the inverse floater, the leverage, and the floater's spread are not determined independently. Any cap or floor imposed on the coupon rate for the floater and the inverse floater must be selected so that the weighted average coupon rate does not exceed the collateral tranche's coupon rate.

D. Structured Interest-Only Tranches

CMO structures can be created so that a tranche receives only interest. Interest only (IO) tranches in a CMO structure are commonly referred to as **structured IOs** to distinguish them from IO mortgage strips that we will describe later in this chapter. Let's look at how a structured IO is created.

Thus far, we used a simple CMO structure in which all the tranches have the same coupon rate (7.5%) and that coupon rate is the same as the collateral. A structured IO is created from a CMO structure where the coupon rate for at least one tranche is different from the collateral's coupon rate. This is seen in FJF-04 shown in Exhibit 11. In this structure, notice that the coupon interest rate for each tranche is less than the coupon interest rate for the collateral. That means that there is excess interest from the collateral that is not being paid to all the tranches. At one time, all of that excess interest not paid to the tranches was paid to a bond class called a "residual." Eventually (due to changes in the tax law that do not concern us here), structurers of CMO began allocating the excess interest to the tranche that receives only interest. This is tranche IO in FJF-04.

Notice that for this structure the par amount for the IO tranche is shown as $52,566,667 and the coupon rate is 7.5%. Since this is an IO tranche there is no par amount. The amount shown is the amount upon which the interest payments will be determined, not the amount that will be paid to the holder of this tranche. Therefore, it is called a **notional amount**. The resulting IO is called a **notional IO**.

Exhibit 11: FJF-04: A Hypothetical Five Tranche Sequential Pay with an Accrual Tranche, an Interest-Only Tranche, and a Residual Class

Tranche	Par amount	Coupon rate (%)
A	$194,500,000	6.00
B	36,000,000	6.50
C	96,500,000	7.00
Z	73,000,000	7.25
IO	52,566,667 (Notional)	7.50
Total	$400,000,000	

Payment rules:

1. *For payment of monthly coupon interest:* Disburse monthly coupon interest to tranches A, B, and C on the basis of the amount of principal outstanding for each class at the beginning of the month. For tranche Z, accrue the interest based on the principal plus accrued interest in the previous month. The interest for tranche Z is to be paid to the earlier tranches as a principal pay down. Disburse periodic interest to the IO tranche based on the notional amount for all tranches at the beginning of the month.

2. *For disbursement of principal payments:* Disburse monthly principal payments to tranche A until it is completely paid off. After tranche A is completely paid off, disburse principal payments to tranche B until it is completely paid off. After tranche B is completely paid off, disburse principal payments to tranche C until it is completely paid off. After tranche C is completely paid off, disburse principal payments to tranche Z until the original principal balance plus accrued interest is completely paid off.

3. *No principal is to be paid to the IO tranche:* The notional amount of the IO tranche declines based on the principal payments to all other tranches.

Let's look at how the notional amount is determined. Consider tranche A. The par value is $194.5 million and the coupon rate is 6%. Since the collateral's coupon rate is 7.5%, the excess interest is 150 basis points (1.5%). Therefore, an IO with a 1.5% coupon rate and a notional amount of $194.5 million can be created from tranche A. But this is equivalent to an IO with a notional amount of $38.9 million and a coupon rate of 7.5%. Mathematically, this notional amount is found as follows:

$$\text{notional amount for 7.5\% IO} = \frac{\text{original tranche's par value} \times \text{excess interest}}{0.075}$$

where

$$\text{excess interest} = \text{collateral tranche's coupon rate} - \text{tranche coupon rate}$$

For example, for tranche A:

$$\text{excess interest} = 0.075 - 0.060 = 0.015$$

$$\text{tranche's par value} = \$194,500,000$$

$$\text{notional amount for 7.5\% IO} = \frac{\$194,500,000 \times 0.015}{0.075} = \$38,900,000$$

Similarly, from tranche B with a par value of $36 million, the excess interest is 100 basis points (1%) and therefore an IO with a coupon rate of 1% and a notional amount of $36 million can be created. But this is equivalent to creating an IO with a notional amount of $4.8 million and a coupon rate of 7.5%. This procedure is shown in Exhibit 12 for all four tranches.

Exhibit 12: Creating a Notional IO

Tranche	Par amount	Excess interest (%)	Notional amount for a 7.5% coupon rate IO
A	$194,500,000	1.50	$38,900,000
B	36,000,000	1.00	4,800,000
C	96,500,000	0.50	6,433,333
Z	73,000,000	0.25	2,433,333
Notional amount for 7.5% IO = $52,566,667			

E. Planned Amortization Class Tranches

The CMO structures discussed above attracted many institutional investors who had previously either avoided investing in mortgage-backed securities or allocated only a nominal portion of their portfolio to this sector of the bond market. While some traditional corporate bond buyers shifted their allocation to CMOs, a majority of institutional investors remained on the sidelines, concerned about investing in an instrument they continued to perceive as posing significant prepayment risk. This concern was based on the substantial average life variability, despite the innovations designed to mitigate prepayment risk.

In 1987, several structures came to market that shared the following characteristic: if the prepayment speed is within a specified band over the collateral's life, the cash flow pattern is known. The greater predictability of the cash flow for these classes of bonds, now referred to as **planned amortization class (PAC) bonds**, occurs because there is a principal repayment schedule that must be satisfied. PAC bondholders have priority over all other classes in the CMO structure in receiving principal payments from the collateral. The greater certainty of the cash flow for the PAC bonds comes at the expense of the non-PAC tranches, called the **support tranches** or **companion tranches**. It is these tranches that absorb the prepayment risk. Because PAC tranches have protection against both extension risk and contraction risk, they are said to provide **two-sided prepayment protection**.

To illustrate how to create a PAC bond, we will use as collateral the $400 million passthrough with a coupon rate of 7.5%, an 8.125% WAC, and a WAM of 357 months. The creation requires the specification of two PSA prepayment rates — a *lower PSA prepayment assumption* and an *upper PSA prepayment assumption*. In our illustration the lower PSA prepayment assumption will be 90 PSA and the upper PSA prepayment assumption will be 300 PSA. A natural question is: How does one select the lower and upper PSA prepayment assumptions? These are dictated by market conditions. For our purpose here, how it is determined is not important. The lower and upper PSA prepayment assumptions are referred to as the **initial PAC collar** or the **initial PAC band**. In our illustration the initial PAC collar is 90-300 PSA.

The second column of Exhibit 13 shows the principal payment (regularly scheduled principal repayment plus prepayments) for selected months assuming a prepayment speed of 90 PSA, and the next column shows the principal payments for selected months assuming that the passthrough prepays at 300 PSA.

The last column of Exhibit 13 gives the minimum principal payment if the collateral prepays at 90 PSA or 300 PSA for months 1 to 349. (After month 349, the outstanding principal balance will be paid off if the prepayment speed is between 90 PSA and 300 PSA.) For example, in the first month, the principal payment would be $508,169.52 if the collateral prepays at 90 PSA and $1,075,931.20 if the collateral prepays at 300 PSA. Thus, the minimum principal payment is $508,169.52, as reported in the last column of Exhibit 13. In month 103, the minimum principal payment is also the amount if the prepayment speed is 90 PSA, $1,446,761, compared to $1,458,618.04 for 300 PSA. In month 104, however, a prepayment speed of 300 PSA would produce a principal payment of $1,433,539.23, which is less than the principal payment of $1,440,825.55 assuming 90 PSA. So, $1,433,539.23 is reported in the last column of Exhibit 13. From month 104 on, the minimum principal payment is the one that would result assuming a prepayment speed of 300 PSA.

Exhibit 13: Monthly Principal Payment for $400 Million, 7.5% Coupon Passthrough with an 8.125% WAC and a 357 WAM Assuming Prepayment Rates of 90 PSA and 300 PSA

Month	At 90% PSA ($)	At 300% PSA	Minimum Principal Payment Available to PAC Investors — the PAC Schedule ($)
1	508,169.52	1,075,931.20	508,169.52
2	569,843.43	1,279,412.11	569,843.43
3	631,377.11	1,482,194.45	631,377.11
4	692,741.89	1 683,966.17	692,741.89
5	753,909.12	1,884,414.62	753,909.12
6	814,850.22	2,083,227.31	814,850.22
7	875,536.68	2,280,092.68	875,536.68
8	935,940.10	2,474,700.92	935,940.10
9	996,032.19	2,666,744.77	996,032.19
10	1,055,784.82	2,855,920.32	1,055,784.82
11	1,115,170.01	3,041,927.81	1,115,170.01
12	1,174,160.00	3,224,472.44	1,174,160.00
13	1,232,727.22	3,403,265.17	1,232,727.22
14	1,290,844.32	3,578,023.49	1,290,844.32
15	1,348,484.24	3,748,472.23	1,348,484.24
16	1,405,620.17	3,914,344.26	1,405,620.17
17	1,462,225.60	4,075,381.29	1,462,225.60
18	1,518,274.36	4,231,334.57	1,518,274.36
101	1,458,719.34	1,510,072.17	1,458,719.34
102	1,452,725.55	1,484,126.59	1,452,725.55
103	1,446,761.00	1,458,618.04	1,446,761.00
104	1,440,825.55	1,433,539.23	1,433,539.23
105	1,434,919.07	1,408,883.01	1,408,883.01
211	949,482.58	213,309.00	213,309.00
212	946,033.34	209,409.09	209,409.09
213	942,601.99	205,577.05	205,577.05
346	618,684.59	13,269.17	13,269.17
347	617,071.58	12,944.51	12,944.51
348	615,468.65	12,626.21	12,626.21
349	613,875.77	12,314.16	3,432.32
350	612,292.88	12,008.25	0
351	610,719.96	11,708.38	0
352	609,156.96	11,414.42	0
353	607,603.S4	11,126.28	0
354	606,060.57	10,843.85	0
355	604,527.09	10,567.02	0
356	603,003.38	10,295.70	0
357	601,489.39	10,029.78	0

Exhibit 14: FJF-05 — CMO Structure with One PAC Tranche and One Support Tranche

Tranche	Par amount ($)	Coupon Rate (%)
P (PAC)	243,800,000	7.5
S (Support)	156,200,000	7.5
Total	400,000,000	

Payment rules:

1. *For payment of monthly coupon interest:* Disburse monthly coupon interest to each tranche on the basis of the amount of principal outstanding for each tranche at the beginning of the month.

2. *For disbursement of principal payments:* Disburse principal payments to tranche P based on its schedule of principal repayments. Tranche P has priority with respect to current and future principal payments to satisfy the schedule. Any excess principal payments in a month over the amount necessary to satisfy the schedule for tranche P are paid to tranche S. When tranche S is completely paid off, all principal payments are to be made to tranche P regardless of the schedule.

In fact, if the collateral prepays at any one speed between 90 PSA and 300 PSA over its life, the minimum principal payment would be the amount reported in the last column of Exhibit 13. For example, if we had included principal payment figures assuming a prepayment speed of 200 PSA, the minimum principal payment would not change: from month 1 through month 103, the minimum principal payment is that generated from 90 PSA, but from month 104 on, the minimum principal payment is that generated from 300 PSA.

This characteristic of the collateral allows for the creation of a PAC tranche, assuming that the collateral prepays over its life at a speed between 90 PSA to 300 PSA. A schedule of principal repayments that the PAC bondholders are entitled to receive before any other tranche in the CMO structure is specified. The monthly schedule of principal repayments is as specified in the last column of Exhibit 13, which shows the minimum principal payment. That is, it is this minimum principal payment in each month that is the principal repayment schedule (i.e., planned amortization schedule) for investors in the PAC tranche. While there is no assurance that the collateral will prepay at a constant speed between these two speeds over its life, a PAC tranche can be structured to assume that it will.

Exhibit 14 shows a CMO structure, FJF-05, created from the $400 million, 7.5% coupon passthrough with a WAC of 8.125% and a WAM of 357 months. There are just two tranches in this structure: a 7.5% coupon PAC tranche created assuming 90 to 300 PSA with a par value of $243.8 million, and a support tranche with a par value of $156.2 million.

Exhibit 15 reports the average life for the PAC tranche and the support tranche in FJF-05 assuming various *actual* prepayment speeds. Notice that between 90 PSA and 300 PSA, the average life for the PAC bond is stable at 7.26 years. However, at slower or faster PSA speeds, the schedule is broken, and the average life changes, extending when the prepayment speed is less than 90 PSA and contracting when it is greater than 300 PSA. Even so, there is much greater variability for the average life of the support tranche.

1. Creating a Series of PAC Tranches

Most CMO PAC structures have more than one class of PAC tranches. A sequence of six PAC tranches (i.e., PAC tranches paid off in sequence as specified by a principal schedule) is shown in Exhibit 16 and is called FJF-06. The total par value of the six PAC tranches is equal to $243.8 million, which is the amount of the single PAC tranche in FJF-05. The schedule of principal repayments for selected months for each PAC bond is shown in Exhibit 17.

Exhibit 15 shows the average life for the six PAC tranches and the support tranche in FJF-06 at various prepayment speeds. From a PAC bond in FJF-05 with an average life of 7.26, six tranches have been created with an average life as short as 2.58 years (P-A) and as long as 16.92 years (P-F) if prepayments stay within 90 PSA and 300 PSA.

Exhibit 15: Average Life for PAC Tranche and Support Tranche in FJF-05 Assuming Various Prepayment Speeds (Years)

Prepayment rate (PSA)	PAC Bond (P)	Support Bond (S)
0	15.97	27.26
50	9.44	24.00
90	7.26	20.06
100	7.26	18.56
150	7.26	12.57
165	7.26	11.16
200	7.26	8.38
250	7.26	5.37
300	7.26	3.13
350	6.56	2.51
400	5.92	2.17
450	5.38	1.94
500	4.93	1.77
700	3.70	1.37

Exhibit 16: FJF-06: CMO Structure with Six PAC Tranches and a Support Tranche

Tranche	Par amount	Coupon rate (%)
P-A	$85,000,000	7.5
P-B	8,000,000	7.5
P-C	35,000,000	7.5
P-D	45,000,000	7.5
P-E	40,000,000	7.5
P-F	30,800,000	7.5
S	156,200,000	7.5
Total	$400,000,000	

Payment rules:

1. For payment of monthly coupon interest: Disburse monthly coupon interest to each tranche on the basis of the amount of principal outstanding of each tranche at the beginning of the month.

2. For disbursement of principal payments: Disburse monthly principal payments to tranches P-A to P-F based on their respective schedules of principal repayments. Tranche P-A has priority with respect to current and future principal payments to satisfy the schedule. Any excess principal payments in a month over the amount necessary to satisfy the schedule for tranche P-A are paid to tranche S. Once tranche P-A is completely paid off, tranche P-B has priority, then tranche P-C, etc. When tranche S is completely paid off, all principal payments are to be made to the remaining PAC tranches in order of priority regardless of the schedule.

Exhibit 17: Mortgage Balance for Selected Months
for FJF-06 Assuming 165 PSA

Month	A	B	C	D	E	F	Support
							Tranche
1	85,000,000	8,000,000	35,000,000	45,000,000	40,000,000	30,800,000	156,200,000
2	84,491,830	8,000,000	35,000,000	45,000,000	40,000,000	30,800,000	155,998,246
3	83,921,987	8,000,000	35,000,000	45,000,000	40,000,000	30,800,000	155,746,193
4	83,290,609	8,000,000	35,000,000	45,000,000	40,000,000	30,800,000	155,444,011
5	82,597,868	8,000,000	35,000,000	45,000,000	40,000,000	30,800,000	155,091,931
6	81,843,958	8,000,000	35,000,000	45,000,000	40,000,000	30,800,000	154,690,254
7	81,029,108	8,000,000	35,000,000	45,000,000	40,000,000	30,800,000	154,239,345
8	80,153,572	8,000,000	35,000,000	45,000,000	40,000,000	30,800,000	153,739,635
9	79,217,631	8,000,000	35,000,000	45,000,000	40,000,000	30,800,000	153,191,621
10	78,221,599	8,000,000	35,000,000	45,000,000	40,000,000	30,800,000	152,595,864
11	77,165,814	8,000,000	35,000,000	45,000,000	40,000,000	30,800,000	151,952,989
12	76,050,644	8,000,000	35,000,000	45,000,000	40,000,000	30,800,000	151,263,687
13	74,876,484	8,000,000	35,000,000	45,000,000	40,000,000	30,800,000	150,528,708
52	5,170,458	8,000,000	35,000,000	45,000,000	40,000,000	30,800,000	109,392,664
53	3,379,318	8,000,000	35,000,000	45,000,000	40,000,000	30,800,000	108,552,721
54	1,595,779	8,000,000	35,000,000	45,000,000	40,000,000	30,800,000	107,728,453
55	0	7,819,804	35,000,000	45,000,000	40,000,000	30,800,000	106,919,692
56	0	6,051,358	35,000,000	45,000,000	40,000,000	30,800,000	106,126,275
57	0	4,290,403	35,000,000	45,000,000	40,000,000	30,800,000	105,348,040
58	0	2,536,904	35,000,000	45,000,000	40,000,000	30,800,000	104,584,824
59	0	790,826	35,000,000	45,000,000	40,000,000	30,800,000	103,836,469
60	0	0	34,052,132	45,000,000	40,000,000	30,800,000	103,102,817
61	0	0	32,320,787	45,000,000	40,000,000	30,800,000	102,383,711
62	0	0	30,596,756	45,000,000	40,000,000	30,800,000	101,678,995
78	0	0	3,978,669	45,000,000	40,000,000	30,800,000	92,239,836
79	0	0	2,373,713	45,000,000	40,000,000	30,800,000	91,757,440
80	0	0	775,460	45,000,000	40,000,000	30,800,000	91,286,887
81	0	0	0	44,183,878	40,000,000	30,800,000	90,828,046
82	0	0	0	42,598,936	40,000,000	30,800,000	90,380,792
83	0	0	0	41,020,601	40,000,000	30,800,000	89,944,997
108	0	0	0	3,758,505	40,000,000	30,800,000	82,288,542
109	0	0	0	2,421,125	40,000,000	30,800,000	82,030,119
110	0	0	0	1,106,780	40,000,000	30,800,000	81,762,929
111	0	0	0	0	39,815,082	30,800,000	81,487,234
112	0	0	0	0	38,545,648	30,800,000	81,203,294
113	0	0	0	0	37,298,104	30,800,000	80,911,362
153	0	0	0	0	1,715,140	30,800,000	65,030,732
154	0	0	0	0	1,107,570	30,800,000	64,575,431
155	0	0	0	0	510,672	30,800,000	64,119,075
156	0	0	0	0	0	30,724,266	63,661,761
157	0	0	0	0	0	30,148,172	63,203,587
158	0	0	0	0	0	29,582,215	62,744,644

Exhibit 17 (Continued)

Month	A	B	C	D	E	F	Support
347	0	0	0	0	0	29,003	1,697,536
348	0	0	0	0	0	16,058	1,545,142
349	0	0	0	0	0	3,432	1,394,152
350	0	0	0	0	0	0	1,235,674
351	0	0	0	0	0	0	1,075,454
352	0	0	0	0	0	0	916,910
353	0	0	0	0	0	0	760,026
354	0	0	0	0	0	0	604,789
355	0	0	0	0	0	0	451,182
356	0	0	0	0	0	0	299,191
357	0	0	0	0	0	0	148,801

Exhibit 18: Average Life for the Six PAC Tranches in FJF-06 Assuming Various Prepayment Speeds

Prepayment rate (PSA)	PAC Bonds					
	P-A	P-B	P-C	P-D	P-E	P-F
0	8.46	14.61	16.49	19.41	21.91	23.76
50	3.58	6.82	8.36	11.30	14.50	18.20
90	2.58	4.72	5.78	7.89	10.83	16.92
100	2.58	4.72	5.78	7.89	10.83	16.92
150	2.58	4.72	5.78	7.89	10.83	16.92
165	2.58	4.72	5.78	7.89	10.83	16.92
200	2.58	4.72	5.78	7.89	10.83	16.92
250	2.58	4.72	5.78	7.89	10.83	16.92
300	2.58	4.72	5.78	7.89	10.83	16.92
350	2.58	4.72	5.44	6.95	9.24	14.91
400	2.57	4.37	4.91	6.17	8.33	13.21
450	2.50	3.97	4.44	5.56	7.45	11.81
500	2.40	3.65	4.07	5.06	6.74	10.65
700	2.06	2.82	3.10	3.75	4.88	7.51

As expected, the average lives are stable if the prepayment speed is between 90 PSA and 300 PSA. Notice that even outside this range the average life is stable for several of the PAC tranches. For example, the PAC P-A tranche is stable even if prepayment speeds are as high as 400 PSA. For the PAC P-B, the average life does not vary when prepayments are in the initial collar until prepayments are greater than 350 PSA. Why is it that the shorter the PAC, the more protection it has against faster prepayments?

To understand this phenomenon, remember there are $156.2 million in support tranches that are protecting the $85 million of PAC P-A. Thus, even if prepayments are faster than the initial upper collar, there may be sufficient support tranches to assure the satisfaction of the schedule. In fact, as can be seen from Exhibit 18, even if prepayments are 400 PSA over the life of the collateral, the average life is unchanged.

Now consider PAC P-B. The support tranches provide protection for both the $85 million of PAC P-A and $93 million of PAC P-B. As can be seen from Exhibit 18, prepayments could be 350 PSA and the average life is still unchanged. From Exhibit 18 it can be seen that the degree of protection against extension risk increases the shorter the PAC. Thus, while the initial collar may be 90 to 300 PSA, the **effective collar** is wider for the shorter PAC tranches.

2. PAC Window

The length of time over which expected principal repayments are made is referred to as the window. For a PAC tranche it is referred to as the **PAC window**. A PAC window can be wide or narrow. The narrower a PAC window, the more it resembles a corporate bond with a bullet payment. For example, if the PAC schedule calls for just one principal payment in month 120 and only interest payments up to month 120, this PAC tranche would resemble a 10-year (120-month) corporate bond.

PAC buyers appear to prefer tight windows, although institutional investors facing a liability schedule are generally better off with a window that more closely matches their liabilities. Investor demand dictates the PAC windows that dealers will create. Investor demand in turn is governed by the nature of investor liabilities.

3. Effective Collars and Actual Prepayments

As we have emphasized several times, the creation of a mortgage-backed security cannot make prepayment risk disappear. This is true for both a passthrough and a CMO. Thus, the reduction in prepayment risk (both extension risk and contraction risk) that a PAC offers investors must come from somewhere.

Where does the prepayment protection come from? It comes from the support tranches. It is the support tranches that defer principal payments if the collateral prepayments are slow; support tranches do not receive any principal until the PAC tranches receive the scheduled principal repayment. This reduces the risk that the PAC tranches will extend. Similarly, it is the support tranches that absorb any principal payments in excess of the scheduled principal payments that are made. This reduces the contraction risk of the PAC tranches. Thus, the key to the prepayment protection offered by a PAC tranche is the amount of support tranches outstanding. If the support tranches are paid off quickly because of faster-than-expected prepayments, then there is no longer any protection for the PAC tranches. *In fact, in FJF-06, if the support tranche is paid off, the structure effectively becomes a sequential-pay CMO.*

The support tranches can be thought of as bodyguards for the PAC bondholders. When the bullets fly — i.e., prepayments occur — it is the bodyguards that get killed off first. The bodyguards are there to absorb the bullets. Once all the bodyguards are killed off (i.e., the support tranches paid off with faster-than-expected prepayments), the PAC tranches must fend for themselves: they are exposed to all the bullets. A PAC tranche in which all the support tranches have been paid off is called a **busted PAC** or **broken PAC**.

With the bodyguard metaphor for the support tranches in mind, let's consider two questions asked by investors in PAC tranches:

1. Will the schedule of principal repayments be satisfied if prepayments are faster than the initial upper collar?
2. Will the schedule of principal repayments be satisfied as long as prepayments stay within the initial collar?

a. Actual Prepayments Greater than the Initial Upper Collar

Let's address the first question. The initial upper collar for FJF-06 is 300 PSA. Suppose that actual prepayments are 500 PSA for seven consecutive months. Will this disrupt the schedule of principal repayments? The answer is: It depends!

There are two pieces of information we will need to answer this question. First, when does the 500 PSA occur? Second, what has been the actual prepayment experience up to the time that prepayments are 500 PSA? For example, suppose six years from now is when the prepayments reach 500 PSA, and also suppose that for the past six years the actual prepayment speed has been 90 PSA every month. What this means is that there are more bodyguards (i.e., support tranches) around than were expected when the PAC was structured at the initial collar. In establishing the schedule of principal repayments, it is assumed that the bodyguards would be killed off at 300 PSA. (Recall that 300 PSA is the upper collar prepayment assumption used in creating FJF-06.) But the actual prepayment experience results in them being killed off at only 90 PSA. Thus, six years from now when the 500 PSA is assumed to occur, there are more bodyguards than expected. In turn, a 500 PSA for seven consecutive months may have no effect on the ability of the schedule of principal repayments to be met.

In contrast, suppose that the actual prepayment experience for the first six years is 300 PSA (the upper collar of the initial PAC collar). In this case, there are no extra bodyguards around. As a result, any prepayment speeds faster than 300 PSA, such as 500 PSA in our example, jeopardize satisfaction of the principal repayment schedule and increase contraction risk. This does not mean that the schedule will be "busted" — the term used in the CMO market when the support tranches are fully paid off. What it does mean is that the prepayment protection is reduced.

It should be clear from these observations that the initial collars are not particularly useful in assessing the prepayment protection for a seasoned PAC tranche. This is most important to understand, as it is common for CMO buyers to compare prepayment protection of PACs in different CMO structures and conclude that the greater protection is offered by the one with the wider initial collar. This approach is inadequate because it is actual prepayment experience that determines the degree of prepayment protection, as well as the expected future prepayment behavior of the collateral.

The way to determine this protection is to calculate the **effective collar** for a seasoned PAC bond. An effective collar for a seasoned PAC is the lower and the upper PSA that can occur in the future and still allow maintenance of the schedule of principal repayments.

The effective collar changes every month. An extended period over which actual prepayments are below the upper range of the initial PAC collar will result in an increase in the upper range of the effective collar. This is because there will be more bodyguards around than anticipated. An extended period of prepayments slower than the lower range of the initial PAC collar will raise the lower range of the effective collar. This is because it will take faster prepayments to make up the shortfall of the scheduled principal payments not made plus the scheduled future principal payments.

b. Actual Prepayments within the Initial Collar

The PAC schedule may not be satisfied even if the actual prepayments never fall outside of the initial collar. This may seem surprising since our previous analysis indicated that the average life would not change if prepayments are at either extreme of the initial collar. However, recall that all of our previous analysis has been based on a single PSA speed for the life of the structure.

The table below shows for FJF-05 what happens to the effective collar if prepayments are 300 PSA for the first 24 months but another prepayment speed for the balance of the life of the structure:

PSA from year 2 on	Average Life
95	6.43
105	6.11
115	6.01
120	6.00
125	6.00
300	6.00
305	5.62

Notice that the average life is stable at six years if the prepayments for the subsequent months are between 115 PSA and 300 PSA. That is, the effective PAC collar is no longer the initial collar. Instead, the lower collar has shifted upward. This means that the protection from year 2 on is for 115 to 300 PSA, a narrower band than initially (90 to 300 PSA), even though the earlier prepayments did not exceed the initial upper collar.

F. Support Tranches

The support tranches are the bonds that provide prepayment protection for the PAC tranches. Consequently, support tranches expose investors to the greatest level of prepayment risk. Because of this, investors must be particularly careful in assessing the cash flow characteristics of support tranches to reduce the likelihood of adverse portfolio consequences due to prepayments.

The support tranche typically is divided into different tranches. All the tranches we have discussed earlier are available, including sequential-pay support tranches, floater and inverse floater support tranches, and accrual support tranches.

The support tranche can even be partitioned to create support tranches with a schedule of principal payments. That is, support tranches that are PAC tranches can be created. In a structure with a PAC tranche and a support tranche with a PAC schedule of principal payments, the former is called a **PAC I tranche** or **Level I PAC tranche** and the latter a **PAC II tranche** or **Level II PAC tranche** or **scheduled tranche** (denoted SCH in a prospectus). While PAC II tranches have greater prepayment protection than the support tranches without a schedule of principal repayments, the prepayment protection is less than that provided PAC I tranches.

The support tranche without a principal repayment schedule can be used to create any type of tranche. In fact, a portion of the non-PAC II support tranche can be given a schedule of principal repayments. This tranche would be called a **PAC III tranche** or a **Level III PAC tranche**. While it provides protection against prepayments for the PAC I and PAC II tranches and is therefore subject to considerable prepayment risk, such a tranche has greater protection than the support tranche without a schedule of principal repayments.

G. An Actual CMO Structure

Thus far we have presented some hypothetical CMO structures in order to demonstrate the characteristics of the different types of tranches. Now let's look at an actual CMO structure, one that we will look at further in Chapter 5 when we discuss how to analyze a CMO deal.

The CMO structure we will discuss is the Freddie Mac (FHLMC) Series 1706 issued in early 1994. The collateral for this structure is Freddie Mac 7% coupon passthroughs. A summary of the deal is provided in Exhibit 19.

There are 17 tranches in this structure: 10 PAC tranches, three scheduled tranches, two TAC support tranches, a floating-rate support tranche, and an inverse floating-rate support tranche.[6] Let's look at these tranches.

---

[6] Actually there were two other tranches, R and RS, called "residuals." These tranches were not described in the chapter. They receive any excess cash flows remaining after the payment of all the tranches. The residual is actually the equity part of the deal.

Exhibit 19: Summary of Federal Home Loan Mortgage Corporation — Multiclass Mortgage Participation Certificates (Guaranteed), Series 1706

Total Issue: $300,000,000   Original Settlement Date: 3/30/94
Issue Date: 2/18/94

Tranche	Original Balance ($)	Coupon (%)	Average Life (yrs)
A (PAC Bond)	24,600,000	4.50	1.3
B (PAC Bond)	11,100,000	5.00	2.5
C (PAC Bond)	25,500,000	5.25	3.5
D (PAC Bond)	9,150,000	5.65	4.5
E (PAC Bond)	31,650,000	6.00	5.8
G (PAC Bond)	30,750,000	6.25	7.9
H (PAC Bond)	27,450,000	6.50	10.9
J (PAC Bond)	5,220,000	6.50	14.4
K (PAC Bond)	7,612,000	7.00	18.8
LA (SCH Bond)	26,673,000	7.00	3.5
LB (SCH Bond)	36,087,000	7.00	3.5
M (SCH Bond)	18,738,000	7.00	11.2
O (TAC Bond)	13,348,000	7.00	2.5
OA (TAC Bond)	3,600,000	7.00	7.2
IA (IO, PAC Bond)	30,246,000	7.00	7.1
PF (FLTR, Support Bond)	21,016,000	6.75*	17.5
PS (INV FLTR, Support Bond)	7,506,000	7.70*	17.5

* Coupon at issuance.

Structural Features

Cash Flow Allocation: Commencing on the first principal payment date of the Class A Bonds, principal equal to the amount specified in the Prospectus will be applied to the Class A, B, C, D, E, G, H, J, K, LA, LB, M, O, OA, PF, and PS Bonds. After all other Classes have been retired, any remaining principal will be used to retire the Class O, OA, LA, LB, M, A, B, C, D, E, G, H, J, and K Bonds. The Notional Class IA Bond will have its notional principal amount retired along with the PAC Bonds.

Other: The PAC Range is 95% to 300% PSA for the A - K Bonds, 190% to 250% PSA for the LA, LB, and M Bonds, and 225% PSA for the O and OA Bonds.

First, we know what a PAC tranche is. There are 10 of them: tranches A, B, C, D, E, G, H, J, K, and IA. The initial collar used to create the PAC tranches was 95 PSA to 300 PSA. The PAC tranches except for tranche IA are simply PACs that pay off in sequence. Tranche IA is structured such that the underlying collateral's interest not allocated to the other PAC tranches is paid to the IO tranche. This is a notional IO tranche and we described earlier in this section how it is created. In this deal the tranches from which the interest is stripped are the PAC tranches. So, tranche IA is referred to as a **PAC IO**. (As of the time of this writing, tranches A and B had already paid off all of their principal.)

As we have explained earlier in this section, the prepayment protection for the PAC bonds is provided by the support tranches. The support tranches in this deal are tranches LA, LB, M, O, OA, PF, and PS. Notice that the support tranches have been carved up in different ways. First, there are scheduled (SCH) tranches. These are what we have called the PAC II tranches earlier in this section. The scheduled tranches are LA, LB, and M. The initial PAC collar used to create the scheduled tranches was 190 PSA to 250 PSA.

There are two support tranches that are designed such that they are created with a schedule that provides protection against contraction risk but not against extension. We did not discuss these tranches in this chapter. They are called **target amortization class** (TAC) **tranches**. The support tranches O and OA are TAC tranches. The schedule of principal payments is created by using just a single PSA. In this structure the single PSA is 225 PSA.

Finally, the support tranche without a schedule (that must provide support for the scheduled bonds and the PACs) was carved into two tranches — a floater (tranche PF) and an inverse floater (tranche PS). The procedure for splitting a tranche into a floater and inverse floater was explained earlier in this section. In this structure the creation of the floater and inverse floater was from a support tranche.

Now that we know what all these tranches are, the next step is to analyze them in terms of their relative value and their price volatility characteristics when rates change. We will do this in Chapter 5.

SECTION V STRIPPED MORTGAGE-BACKED SECURITIES

A mortgage passthrough security divides the cash flow from the underlying pool of mortgages on a pro rata basis to the certificate holders. A **stripped mortgage-backed security** is created by altering that distribution of principal and interest from a pro rata distribution to an unequal distribution. The result is that the securities created will have a price/yield relationship that is different from the price/ yield relationship of the underlying passthrough security.

In the most common type of stripped mortgage-backed securities all the interest is allocated to one class (called the **interest only** or **IO class**) and all the principal to the other class (called the **principal only** or **PO class**). The IO class receives no principal payments. These securities are also referred to as **mortgage strips**. The POs are called **principal-only mortgage strips** and the IOs are called **interest-only mortgage strips**.

A. Principal-Only Strips

A principal-only mortgage strip is purchased at a substantial discount from par value. The return an investor realizes depends on the speed at which prepayments are made. The faster the prepayments, the higher the investor's return. For example, suppose that a pool of 30-year mortgages has a par value of $400 million and the market value of the pool of mortgages is also $400. Suppose further that the market value of just the principal payments is $175 million. The dollar return from this investment is the difference between the par value of $400 million that will be repaid to the investor in the principal mortgage strip and the $175 million paid. That is, the dollar return is $225 million.

Since there is no interest that will be paid to the investor in a principal-only mortgage strip, the investor's return is determined solely by the speed at which he or she receives the $225 million. In the extreme case, if all homeowners in the underlying mortgage pool decide to prepay their mortgage loans immediately, PO investors will realize the $225 million immediately. At the other extreme, if all homeowners decide to remain in their homes for 30 years and make no prepayments, the $225 million will be spread out over 30 years, which would result in a lower return for PO investors.

Let's look at how the price of the PO would be expected to change as mortgage rates in the market change. When mortgage rates decline below the contract rate, prepayments are expected to speed up, accelerating payments to the PO investor. Thus, the cash flow of a PO improves (in the sense that principal repayments are received earlier). The cash flow will be discounted at a lower interest rate because the mortgage rate in the market has declined. The result is that the PO price will increase when mortgage rates decline. When mortgage rates rise above the contract rate, prepayments are expected to slow down. The cash flow deteriorates (in the sense that it takes longer to recover principal repayments). Couple this with a higher discount rate, and the price of a PO will fall when mortgage rates rise.

Exhibit 20 shows the relationship between the price of a principal-only mortgage strip when interest rates change and compares it to the relationship for the underlying passthrough from which it is created.

B. Interest-Only Strips

An interest-only mortgage strip has no par value. In contrast to the PO investor, the IO investor wants prepayments to be slow. The reason is that the IO investor receives interest only on the amount of the principal outstanding. When prepayments are made, less dollar interest will be received as the outstanding principal declines. In fact, *if prepayments are too fast, the IO investor may not recover the amount paid for the IO even if the security is held to maturity.*

Let's look at the expected price response of an IO to changes in mortgage rates. If mortgage rates decline below the contract rate, prepayments are expected to accelerate. This would result in a deterioration of the expected cash flow for an IO. While the cash flow will be discounted at a lower rate, the net effect typically is a decline in the price of an IO. If mortgage rates rise above the contract rate, the expected cash flow improves, but the cash flow is discounted at a higher interest rate. The net effect may be either a rise or fall for the IO.

Thus, we see an interesting characteristic of an IO: its price tends to move in the same direction as the change in mortgage rates (1) when mortgage rates fall below the contract rate and (2) for some range of mortgage rates above the contract rate. Both POs and IOs exhibit substantial price volatility when mortgage rates change. The greater price volatility of the IO and PO compared to the passthrough from which they were created is due to the fact that the combined price volatility of the IO and PO must be equal to the price volatility of the passthrough.

Exhibit 20 shows the relationship between the price of an interest-only mortgage strip when interest rates change and compares it to the relationship for the corresponding principal-only mortgage strip and underlying passthrough from which it is created.

Exhibit 20: Relationship between Price and Mortgage Rates for a Passthrough, PO, and IO

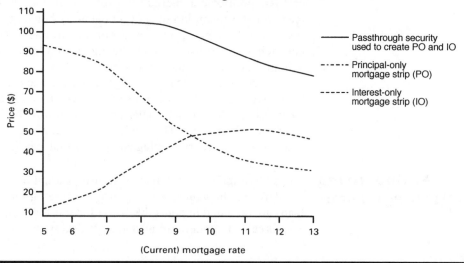

An average life for a PO can be calculated based on some prepayment assumption. However, an IO receives no principal payments, so technically an average life cannot be computed. Instead, for an IO a **cash flow average life** is computed, using the projected interest payments in the average life formula instead of principal.

C. Trading and Settlement Procedures

The trading and settlement procedures for stripped mortgage-backed securities are similar to those set by the Public Securities Association for agency passthroughs described in Section III.C. IOs and POs are extreme premium and discount securities and consequently are very sensitive to prepayments, which are driven by the specific characteristics (WAC, WAM, geographic concentration, average loan size) of the underlying loans. Therefore, almost all secondary trades in IOs and POs are on a specified pool basis rather than on a TBA basis.

All IOs and POs are given a trust number. For instance, FNMA Trust 1 is a IO/PO trust backed by specific pools of FNMA 9% mortgages. FNMA Trust 2 is backed by FNMA 10% mortgages. FNMA Trust 23 is another IO/PO trust backed by FNMA 10% mortgages. Therefore, a portfolio manager must specify which trust he or she is buying.

The total proceeds of a PO trade are calculated the same way as with a passthrough trade except that there is no accrued interest. The market trades IOs based on notional principal. The proceeds include the price on the notional amount and the accrued interest.

SECTION VI NONAGENCY MORTGAGE-BACKED SECURITIES

In the previous sections we looked at agency mortgage-backed securities in which the underlying mortgages are 1- to 4-single family residential mortgages. The mortgage-backed securities market includes other types of securities. These securities are called **nonagency mortgage-backed securities** (referred to as **nonagency securities** hereafter).

The underlying mortgage loans for nonagency securities can be for any type of real estate property. There are securities backed by 1- to 4-single family residential mortgages with a first lien on the mortgaged property. There are nonagency securities backed by other types of single family residential loans. These include home equity loan-backed securities and manufactured housing-loan backed securities. Commercial mortgage-backed securities are nonagency securities in which the underlying collateral is a pool of commercial mortgage loans. Commercial mortgage loans include loans for apartment buildings (multi-family housing), shopping centers, office buildings, warehouses, hotels, and nursing homes. Our focus in this section is on nonagency securities in which the underlying loans are first-lien mortgages for 1- to 4-single-family residential properties.

As with an agency mortgage-backed security, the servicer is responsible for the collection of interest and principal, which is passed along to the trustee. The servicer also handles delinquencies and foreclosures. Typically, there will be a master servicer and subservicers. The servicer plays a key role. In fact, in assessing the credit risk of a nonagency security, rating companies look carefully at the quality of the servicers.

A. Underlying Mortgage Loans

The underlying loans for agency securities are those that conform to the underwriting standards of the agency issuing or guaranteeing the issue. That is, only conforming loans are included in pools that are collateral for an agency mortgage-backed security. The three main underwriting standards deal with

1. the maximum loan-to-value ratio
2. the maximum payment-to-income ratio
3. the maximum loan amount

A **nonconforming mortgage loan** is one that does not conform to the underwriting standards established by any of the agencies.

Typically, the loans for a nonagency security are nonconforming mortgage loans that fail to qualify for inclusion because the amount of the loan exceeds the limit established by the agencies. Such loans are referred to as jumbo loans. Jumbo loans do not necessarily have greater credit risk than conforming mortgages.

Loans that fail to qualify because of the first two underwriting standards expose the lender to greater credit risk. In general, lenders classify borrowers by credit quality. Borrowers are classified as A borrowers, B borrowers, C borrowers, and D borrowers. A borrowers are those that are viewed as having the best credit record. Such borrowers are referred to as **prime borrowers**. Borrowers rated below A are viewed as **subprime borrowers**. However, there is no industry-wide classification system for prime and subprime borrowers.

B. Differences Between Agency and Nonagency Securities

Nonagency securities can be either passthroughs or CMOs. In the agency market, CMOs are created from pools of passthrough securities. In the nonagency market, a CMO can be created from either a pool of passthroughs or unsecuritized mortgage loans. It is uncommon for nonconforming mortgage loans to be securitized as passthroughs and then a pool of passthroughs is carved up to create a CMO. Instead, in the nonagency market a CMO is typically carved out of mortgage loans that have not been securitized as passthroughs. Since a mortgage loan not securitized as a passthrough is called a whole loan, nonagency CMOs are commonly referred to as **whole-loan CMOs**.

The major difference between agency and nonagency securities has to do with guarantees. With a nonagency security there is no explicit or implicit government guarantee of payment of interest and principal as there is with an agency security. The absence of any such guarantee means that the investor in a nonagency security is exposed to credit risk. The nationally recognized statistical rating organizations rate nonagency securities.

Because of the credit risk, all nonagency securities are **credit enhanced**. By credit enhancement it means that additional support against defaults must be obtained. The amount of credit enhancement needed is determined relative to a specific rating desired for a security rating agency. There are two general types of credit enhancement mechanisms: external and internal. We describe each of these types of credit enhancement in the next chapter where we cover asset-backed securities.

SECTION VII KEY POINTS

❑ *The basic mortgage-backed security is the mortgage passthrough security created from a pool of mortgage loans.*

❑ *Agency passthrough securities are those issued/guaranteed by Ginnie Mae, Fannie Mae, and Freddie Mac.*

❑ *The cash flow of a passthrough includes net interest, scheduled principal repayments (i.e., scheduled amortization), and prepayments.*

❑ *Any amount paid in excess of the required monthly mortgage payment is a prepayment; the cash flow of a mortgage-backed security is unknown because of prepayments.*

❑ *A projection of prepayments is necessary to project the cash flow of a passthrough security.*

❑ *The four factors that affect prepayments are (1) the prevailing mortgage rate, (2) characteristics of the underlying mortgage pool, (3) seasonal factors, and (4) general economic activity.*

❑ *The PSA prepayment benchmark is a series of conditional prepayment rates and is simply a market convention that describes in general the pattern of prepayments.*

❑ *A measure commonly used to estimate the life of a passthrough is its average life.*

❑ *The prepayment risk associated with investing in mortgage passthrough securities can be decomposed into contraction risk and extension risk.*

❑ *Prepayment risk makes passthrough securities unattractive for certain financial institutions to hold from an asset/liability perspective.*

❑ *Collateralized mortgage obligations are bond classes created by redirecting the interest and principal from a pool of passthroughs or whole loans.*

❑ *The creation of a CMO cannot eliminate prepayment risk; it can only transfer the various forms of this risk among different classes of bonds called tranches.*

❑ *From a fixed-rate CMO tranche, a floating-rate tranche and an inverse floating-rate tranche can be created.*

❑ *A notional interest-only tranche (also called a structured IO) can be created from the excess interest available from other tranches in the structure; excess interest is the difference between the collateral's coupon rate and a tranche's coupon rate.*

❑ *The amortization schedule for a planned amortization class is structured based on a lower PSA prepayment assumption and an upper PSA prepayment assumption — called the initial PAC collar.*

❑ *A planned amortization class (PAC) tranche has reduced average life variability, the better prepayment protection provided by the support tranches.*

❑ *If the collateral from which a PAC bond is created pays at a constant PSA rate that is anywhere within the initial PAC collar, the amortization schedule will be satisfied.*

❑ *Over time, the prepayment collar that will be able to support the PAC tranches (i.e., provide the prepayment protection) changes as the amount of the support tranches change.*

❑ *The effective collar is the lower and upper PSA prepayment rates that can occur in the future and still be able to satisfy the amortization schedule for the PAC tranche.*

❑ *The key to the prepayment protection for the PAC tranches is the support tranches.*

❑ *The support tranches are exposed to the greatest prepayment risk of all the tranches in a CMO structure and greater prepayment risk than the collateral (i.e., passthrough securities) from which a deal is created.*

❑ *Support tranches with a PAC schedule can be created from the support tranches; these tranches are still support tranches but they have better prepayment protection than other support tranches in the structure that do not have a schedule.*

❑ *A stripped mortgage-backed security is a derivative mortgage-backed security that is created by redistributing the interest and principal payments to two different classes.*

❑ *A principal-only mortgage strip (PO) benefits from declining interest rates and fast prepayments.*

❑ *An interest-only mortgage strip (IO) benefits from rising interest rates and a slowing of prepayments; if rates fall instead, the investor in an interest-only security may not realize the amount invested even if the security is held to maturity.*

❑ *Nonagency securities are not backed by any federal government agency guarantee.*

❑ *The underlying loans for nonagency securities are nonconforming mortgage loans – loans that do not qualify for inclusion in mortgage pools that underlie agency mortgage-backed securities.*

❑ *Credit enhancement is needed to support nonagency mortgage-backed securities.*

❑ *Credit enhancement levels are determined relative to a specific rating desired for a security and there are two general types of credit enhancement structures — external and internal.*

END OF CHAPTER QUESTIONS

1. a. Complete the following schedule for a 30-year fully amortizing mortgage loan with a mortgage rate of 7.25% where the amount borrowed is $150,000. The monthly mortgage payment is $1,023.26.

Month	Beginning Mortgage	Mortgage Payment	Interest	Sch. Prin Repayment	End of month balance
1	150,000.00	1,023.26			
2		1,023.26			
3		1,023.26			
4		1,023.26			
5		1,023.26			
6		1,023.26			
7		1,023.26			
8		1,023.26			
9		1,023.26			
10		1,023.26			
11		1,023.26			
12		1,023.26			
13		1,023.26			
14		1,023.26			

b. Complete the following schedule for the mortgage loan in part a given the following information:

Month	Beginning Mortgage	Mortgage Payment	Interest	Sch. Prin Repayment	End of month balance
357	4,031.97	1,023.26			
358		1,023.26			
359		1,023.26			
360		1,023.26			

2. a. Suppose that the servicing fee for a mortgage loan is 0.5%. Complete the following schedule for the mortgage loan in the previous question. The column labeled "Servicing Fee" is the dollar amount of the servicing fee for the month. The column labeled "Net Interest" is the monthly interest after the servicing fee for the month.

Month	Beginning Mortgage	Mortgage Payment	Servicing Fee	Net Interest	Sch. Prin Repayment	End of month Balance
1						
2						
3						
4						
5						
6						

b. Determine for the first six months the cash flow for an investor who purchases this mortgage loan after the servicing fee is paid.

3. Explain why you agree or disagree with the following statement: "Since mortgage passthrough securities issued by Ginnie Mae are guaranteed by the full faith and credit of the U.S. government, there is no uncertainty about the cash flow for the security."

4. Consider the following mortgage pool.

Loan	Outstanding mortgage balance	Mortgage rate	Months remaining
1	$215,000	6.75%	200
2	$185,000	7.75%	185
3	$125,000	7.25%	192
4	$100,000	7.00%	210
5	$200,000	6.50%	180
Total	$825,000		

a. What is the weighted average coupon rate for this mortgage pool?
b. What is the weighted average maturity for this mortgage pool?

5. Using the Public Securities Association Prepayment benchmark, complete the following table:

Month	PSA	CPR	SMM
5	100		
15	80		
20	175		
27	50		
88	200		
136	75		
220	225		

6. Explain why 30 months after the origination of a mortgage pool, discussing prepayments in terms of one CPR and a PSA are identical.

7. Suppose that in month 140 the mortgage balance for a mortgage pool underlying a passthrough security is $537 million and that the scheduled principal repayment for month 140 is $440,000. Assuming 175 PSA, what is the amount of the prepayment for month 140?

8. Comment on the following statement: "The PSA model is a prepayment model."

9. Robert Reed is an assistant portfolio manager who has been recently given the responsibility of assisting Joan Soprano, the portfolio manager for the mortgage-backed securities portfolio. Ms. Soprano gave Mr. Reed a copy of the a Prudential Securities publication for November 1999 entitled *Mortgage and Asset-Backed Prepayment and Issuance*. An excerpt from the publication is given below:

GNMA 30 YEAR		PROJECTED PSA			One YEAR	Long TERM
		DEC	JAN	FEB		
6.0	1998	73	68	60	60	65
6.5	1998	113	102	92	91	90
7.0	1998	154	137	124	126	116
7.5	1993	181	166	150	155	138
8.0	1996	220	211	181	185	159
8.5	1994	283	272	223	205	173
9.0	1986	269	263	232	209	195

The mortgage rate at the time of the report was 8.13%.

Mr. Reed asks the following questions about the information in the above excerpt. Respond to each question.

   a. What does "GNMA 30 YEAR" mean?
   b. What does "8.5 1994" mean?
   c. What do the numbers under "PROJECTED" mean?
   d. Do the prepayment rates for "7.5 1993" apply to all GNMA issues in the market?
   e. Why are the projected prepayments for "one year" and "long term" such that they increase with the coupon rate?

10. In the November 1999 Prudential Securities report cited in the previous question, the following statement was made in the summary section of the report:

   Agency aggregate prepayment speeds slowed in November, reflecting both a seasonal slowdown and the stabilization of mortgage rates in the last coupon of months.

   a. What does "Agency aggregate prepayments speeds slowed" mean?
   b. What is meant that the slow down in prepayment speeds reflected a "seasonal slowdown"?

11. Suppose that you are analyzing prepayments of a passthrough security that was issued more than 15 years ago. The weighted average coupon (WAC) for the underlying mortgage pool was 13%. Suppose that the mortgage rate over the year of the analysis declined from 8% to 7% but prepayments for this mortgage pool you are analyzing did not increase. Explain why there is no increase in prepayments despite the lower mortgage rate relative to 13% being paid by borrowers and the decline in the mortgage rates over the year.

12. What type of prepayment risk is an investor interested in a short-term security concerned with when purchasing a mortgage-backed security?

13. Suppose that a portfolio manager is considering a collateralized mortgage obligation structure KMF-01. This structure has three tranches. The deal is a simple sequential pay and was issued several years ago. The tranches are A, B, and C with a coupon rate paid to each tranche each month and principal payments are made first to tranche A, then to tranche B, and finally to tranche C. Here is the status of the deal as of the time of the analysis:

Tranche	Coupon rate	Par amount outstanding
A	6%	$3 million
B	7%	8 million
C	8%	30 million

Based on some prepayment rate, the projected principal payments (prepayments plus regularly schedule principal repayment) for the next four years for the collateral underlying this deal are as follows:

Month	Sch. Principal Repayment + Prepayments
1	520,000
2	510,000
3	490,000
4	450,000
5	448,000
6	442,000
7	410,000
8	405,000
9	400,000
10	396,000
11	395,000
12	390,000
13	388,000
14	385,000
15	380,000
16	377,000
17	375,000
18	370,000
19	369,000
20	366,000
21	300,000
22	298,000
23	292,000
24	290,000
25	287,000
26	285,000
27	283,000
28	280,000
29	278,000
30	275,000
31	271,000
32	270,000
33	265,000
34	260,000
35	255,000
36	252,000
37	250,000
38	245,000
39	240,000
40	210,000
41	200,000
42	195,000
43	190,000
44	185,000
45	175,000
46	170,000
47	166,000
48	164,000

a. Compute the principal, interest, and cash flow for tranche A for the 48 months.
b. Compute the principal, interest, and cash flow for tranche B for the 48 months.
c. Compute the principal, interest, and cash flow for tranche C for the 48 months.
d. Compute the average life for tranche A.

14. Suppose that in the previous CMO structure, KMF-01, that tranche C is an accrual tranche a tranche that pays coupon interest monthly. We will refer to this new CMO structure as KMF-02.

   a. What is the principal repayment, interest, and cash flow for tranche A in KMF-02?
   b. What is the principal balance for tranche C for the first five months?
   c. What is the average life for tranche A in KMF-02 and contrast this with the average life for tranche A in KMF-01?

15. Explain why it is necessary to have a cap for the floater when a fixed-rate tranche is split into a floater and an inverse floater.

16. Suppose that a tranche from which a floater and an inverse floater are created has an average life of six years. What will be the average life of the floater and the inverse floater?

17. How does a CMO alter the cash flow from mortgages so as to redistribute the prepayment risk across various tranches in a deal?

18. "By creating a CMO, an issuer eliminates the prepayment risk associated with the underlying mortgages loans." Explain why you agree or disagree with this statement?

19. Ellen Morgan received a phone call from the trustee of a pension fund. Ms. Morgan is the portfolio manager for the pension fund's bond portfolio. The trustee expressed concerns about the inclusion of CMOs in the portfolio. The trustee's concern arose after reading several articles in the popular press where the CMO market was characterized as the sector of the mortgage-backed securities market with the greatest prepayment risk and the passthrough sector as the safest sector in terms of prepayment risk. What should Ms. Morgan say to this trustee regarding such statements made in the popular press?

20. What is the role of a support tranche in a CMO structure?

21. Suppose that the manager of a savings & loan association portfolio has decided to invest in mortgage-backed securities and is considering the following two securities: (i) a Fannie Mae passthrough security with a WAM of 310 months or (ii) a PAC tranche of a Fannie Mae CMO issue with an average life of 2 years. Which mortgage-backed security would probably be better from an asset/liability perspective?

22. Suppose that a PAC bond is created using prepayment speeds of 90 PSA and 240 PSA and the average life is 5 years. Will the average life for this PAC tranche be shorter than, longer than, or equal to 5 years if the collateral pays at 140 PSA over its life? Explain your answer.

23. Suppose that $1 billion of passthroughs are used to create a CMO structure, KMF-05. This structure includes a PAC tranche with a par value of $650 million and a support tranche with a par value of $350 million.

a. Which of the following will have the least average life variability: (i) the collateral, (ii) the PAC tranche, or (iii) the support tranche? Why?

b. Which of the following will have the greatest average life variability: (i) the collateral, (ii) the PAC tranche, or (iii) the support tranche? Why?

24. Suppose that the $1 billion of collateral in the CMO structure KMF-05 in the previous question was divided into a PAC tranche with a par value of $800 million and a support tranche with a par value of $200 million (instead of $650 million and $350 million). The new structure is KMF-06. Will the PAC tranche in KMF-06 have more or less protection than the PAC tranche in KMF-05?

25. Suppose that $500 million of passthroughs are used to create a CMO structure with a PAC tranche with a par value of $350 million (PAC I), a support tranche with a schedule (PAC II) with a par value of $100 million, and a support tranche without a schedule with a par value of $200 million.

a. Will the PAC I or PAC II have less average life variability? Why?

b. Will the support tranche without a schedule or the PAC II have the greater average life variability? Why?

26. In a CMO structure with several PAC tranches that pay off sequentially, explain what the structure effectively becomes once all the support tranches are paid off.

27. Suppose that for the first four years of a CMO, prepayments are well below the initial upper PAC collar and within the initial lower PAC collar. What will happen to the effective upper collar?

28. Consider the following CMO structure backed by 8% collateral:

Tranche	Par amount	Coupon rate
A	$400,000,000	6.25%
B	$200,000,000	6.75%
C	$225,000,000	7.50%
D	$175,000,000	7.75%

Suppose that the structurer of this CMO wants to create a notional IO tranche with a coupon rate of 8%. Calculate the notional amount for this notional IO tranche.

29. An issuer is considering the following two CMO structures:

Structure I:

Tranche	Par amount	Coupon rate
A	$150 million	6.50%
B	100 million	6.75%
C	200 million	7.25%
D	150 million	7.75%
E	100 million	8.00%
F	500 million	8.50%

Tranches A-E are a sequence of PAC Is and F is the support tranche.

Structure II:

Tranche	Par amount	Coupon rate
A	$150 million	6.50%
B	100 million	6.75%
C	200 million	7.25%
D	150 million	7.75%
E	100 million	8.00%
F	200 million	8.25%
G	300 million	?????

Tranches A-E are a sequence of PAC Is, F is a PAC II, and G is a support tranche without a schedule.

    a. In Structure II tranche G is created from tranche F in Structure I. What is the coupon rate for tranche G assuming that the combined coupon rate for tranches F and G in Structure II should be 8.5%?

    b. What is the effect on the value and average life of tranches A-E by including the PAC II in Structure II?

    c. What is the difference in the average life variability of tranche G in Structure II and tranche F in Structure I?

30. What is a broken or busted PAC?

31. Assume that in FJF-04 in the chapter, tranche C had been split to create a floater with a principal of $80,416,667 and an inverse floater with a principal of $16,083,333.

    a. What would be the cap rate for the inverse floater if the coupon rate for the floater is 1-month LIBOR plus 1%?

    b. Assuming that (1) the coupon formula for the floater is 1-month LIBOR plus 1% and (2) a floor is imposed on the inverse floater of zero, what would be the cap rate on the floater?

32. a. What is a principal-only mortgage strip and an interest-only mortgage strip?

    b. How does an interest-only mortgage strip differ with respect to the certainty about the cash flow from a Treasury strip created from the coupon interest?

    c. How is the price of an interest-only mortgage strip expected to change when interest rates change?

33. a. An investor purchased $10 million par value of a 7% Ginnie Mae passthrough security agreeing to pay 102. The pool factor is 0.72. How much does the investor pay to the seller?

    b. Why would an investor who wants to purchase a principal-only mortgage strip not want to do so on a TBA basis?

34. Why can't all residential mortgage loans be securitized by either Ginnie Mae, Fannie Mae, or Freddie Mac?

35. Why is credit enhancement needed for a nonagency mortgage-backed security?

SOLUTIONS TO END OF CHAPTER QUESTIONS

1. a.

Month	Beginning Mortgage	Mortgage Payment	Interest	Sch. Prin Repayment	End of month balance
1	150,000.00	1,023.26	906.25	117.01	149,882.99
2	149,882.99	1,023.26	905.54	117.72	149,765.26
3	149,765.26	1,023.26	904.83	118.43	149,646.83
4	149,646.83	1,023.26	904.12	119.15	149,527.68
5	149,527.68	1,023.26	903.40	119.87	149,407.82
6	149,407.82	1,023.26	902.67	120.59	149,287.22
7	149,287.22	1,023.26	901.94	121.32	149,165.90
8	149,165.90	1,023.26	901.21	122.05	149,043.85
9	149,043.85	1,023.26	900.47	122.79	148,921.06
10	148,921.06	1,023.26	899.73	123.53	148,797.52
11	148,797.52	1,023.26	898.99	124.28	148,673.25
12	148,673.25	1,023.26	898.23	125.03	148,548.21
13	148,548.21	1,023.26	897.48	125.79	148,422.43
14	148,422.43	1,023.26	896.72	126.55	148,295.88

b.

Month	Beginning Mortgage	Mortgage Payment	Interest	Sch. Prin Repayment	End of month balance
357	4,031.97	1,023.26	24.36	998.90	3,033.07
358	3,033.07	1,023.26	18.32	1,004.94	2,028.13
359	2,028.13	1,023.26	12.25	1,011.01	1,017.12
360	1,017.12	1,023.26	6.15	1,017.12	0.00

2. a. The monthly servicing fee is found by dividing the servicing fee of 0.005 (50 basis points) by 12. The monthly servicing fee is therefore 0.0004167. Multiplying the monthly servicing fee by the beginning mortgage balance gives the servicing fee for the month.

Month	Beginning Mortgage	Mortgage Payment	Servicing Fee	Net Interest	Sch. Prin Repayment	End of month Balance
1	150,000.00	1,023.26	62.50	843.75	117.01	149,882.99
2	149,882.99	1,023.26	62.45	843.09	117.72	149,765.26
3	149,765.26	1,023.26	62.40	842.43	118.43	149,646.83
4	149,646.83	1,023.26	62.35	841.76	119.15	149,527.68
5	149,527.68	1,023.26	62.30	841.09	119.87	149,407.82
6	149,407.82	1,023.26	62.25	840.42	120.59	149,287.22

b. The investor's cash flow is the sum of the net interest and the scheduled principal repayment.

Month	Net Interest	Sch. Prin Repayment	Investor cash flow
1	843.75	117.01	960.76
2	843.09	117.72	960.81
3	842.43	118.43	960.86
4	841.76	119.15	960.91
5	841.09	119.87	960.96
6	840.42	120.59	961.01

3. The statement is incorrect. While the guarantee by the U.S. government means that there will not be a loss of principal and that interest payments will be made in full, there is uncertainty about the timing of the principal repayments because the borrower may prepay at any time, in whole or in part.

4. a and b. The weighted average coupon (WAC) and weighted average maturity (WAM) for the mortgage pool are computed below:

Loan	Outstanding mortgage balance	Weight in pool	Mortgage rate	Months remaining	WAC	WAM
1	$215,000	26.06%	6.75%	200	1.7591%	52.12
2	$185,000	22.42%	7.75%	185	1.7379%	41.48
3	$125,000	15.15%	7.25%	192	1.0985%	29.09
4	$100,000	12.12%	7.00%	210	0.8485%	25.45
5	$200,000	24.24%	6.50%	180	1.5758%	43.64
Total	$825,000	100.00%			7.02%	191.79

WAC = 7.02%   WAM = 192 (rounded)

5. The CPR and SMM for each month are shown below:

Month	PSA	CPR	SMM
5	100	0.010	0.000837
15	80	0.024	0.002022
20	175	0.070	0.006029
27	50	0.027	0.002278
88	200	0.120	0.010596
136	75	0.045	0.003829
220	225	0.135	0.012012

6. According to the PSA prepayment benchmark, after month 30 the CPR is constant over the life of the security. Specifically, it is equal to

$$CPR = 6\% \times (PSA/100)$$

So, for example, if the assumed PSA is 225, the CPR for the life of the security is

$$CPR = 6\% \times (225/100) = 13.5\%$$

Thus, the statement is correct that one CPR can be used to describe the PSA 30 months after the origination of the mortgages.

7. The amount of the prepayment for the month is determined as follows:

$$(\text{Beginning mortgage balance} - \text{regularly scheduled principal payment}) \times SMM$$

We know that

$$(\$537,000,000 - \$440,000) \times SMM$$

The CPR for month 140 assuming 175 PSA is

$$CPR = 6\% \times (175/100) = 10.5\%$$

The SMM is then

$$SMM = 1 - (1 - 0.105)^{0.08333} = 0.009201$$

Therefore, the prepayment in month 140 is

$$(\$537,000,000 - \$440,000) \times 0.009201 = \$4,936,889 \text{ (rounded)}$$

(Note: You will get a slightly different answer if you carried the SMM to more decimal places.)

8. The PSA model, or PSA prepayment benchmark, is not a prepayment model in that it does not predict prepayments for a mortgage-backed security. It is a generic benchmark that hypothesizes about what the pattern of prepayments will be over the life of a mortgage-backed security — that there is a prepayment ramp (that increases linearly) for 30 months, after which when the CPR is assumed to be constant for the life of the security.

9. a. GNMA refers to passthrough securities issued by the Government National Mortgage Association. "30-YEAR" indicates that the mortgage loans were originated with 30-year terms.

   b. This means GNMA 30-year passthrough securities with a coupon rate of 8.5% that were originated in 1994.

   c. These are the prepayment rates that are projected for various periods. The prepayment rates are expressed in term of the PSA prepayment benchmark. There is a prepayment rate projection for each of the subsequent three months, a prepayment rate projection for one year, and a long-term prepayment rate.

   d. First, the prepayments is only for 7.5% coupon GNMA issues originated in 1993. But there are many 7.5% coupon GNMA issues that were issued in 1993. The prepayments are for a generic issue. This means that when a specific Ginnie Mae 7.5% coupon originated in 1993 is delivered to the buyer, it can realize a prepayment rate quite different from the generic prepayment rate in the report, but on average, 1993 GNMA 7.5%s are projected to have this prepayment rate.

   e. One factor that affects prepayments is the prevailing mortgage rate relative to the rate that borrowers are paying on the underlying mortgages. As noted in the question, the mortgage rate at the time was 8.13%. The higher the coupon rate, the higher the rate that the borrowers in the underlying mortgage pool are paying and the greater the incentive to prepay. So, as the coupon rate increases, prepayments are expected to be greater because of the incentive to prepay.

10. a. Agency refers to Ginnie Mae, Fannie Mae, and Freddie Mac mortgage pools. Prepayments slowing down means that the prepayment rates decreased.

   b. One of the factors that affects prepayment is the season of the year. Prepayments tend to be faster during the late summer and early fall reflecting prepayments due to borrowers selling their home in the summer. By November, prepayments return to a more normal level after the seasonal pick up in the late summer and early fall.

11. Since the mortgage passthrough being analyzed has been outstanding for more than 15 years, there have been probably several opportunities for borrowers in the underlying mortgage pool to refinance at a lower rate than they are paying. Consequently, the low mortgage rate of 8% relative to 13% may not result in an increase in prepayments and the same is true for a further decline over the year to 7%. This characteristic of prepayments is referred to as "prepayment burnout."

12. An investor in a short-term security is concerned with extension risk. This is the risk that the security's average life will increase.

13. a. For tranche A:

Month	Sch. Principal repayment + prepayments	Beginning principal	Tranche A principal repayment	Interest at 6%	Cash flow
1	520,000	3,000,000	520,000	15,000	535,000
2	510,000	2,480,000	510,000	12,400	522,400
3	490,000	1,970,000	490,000	9,850	499,850
4	450,000	1,480,000	450,000	7,400	457,400
5	448,000	1,030,000	448,000	5,150	453,150
6	442,000	582,000	442,000	2,910	444,910
7	410,000	140,000	140,000	700	140,700
		Total	3,000,000		

From months 8 through 48, the principal repayment, interest, and cash flow are zero.

b. For tranche B:

Month	Sch. Principal repayment + prepayments	Beginning principal	Tranche B principal repayment	Interest at 7%	Cash flow
1	520,000	8,000,000	0	46,667	46,667
2	510,000	8,000,000	0	46,667	46,667
3	490,000	8,000,000	0	46,667	46,667
4	450,000	8,000,000	0	46,667	46,667
5	448,000	8,000,000	0	46,667	46,667
6	442,000	8,000,000	0	46,667	46,667
7	410,000	8,000,000	270,000	46,667	316,667
8	405,000	7,730,000	405,000	45,092	450,092
9	400,000	7,325,000	400,000	42,729	442,729
10	396,000	6,925,000	396,000	40,396	436,396
11	395,000	6,529,000	395,000	38,086	433,086
12	390,000	6,134,000	390,000	35,782	425,782
13	388,000	5,744,000	388,000	33,507	421,507
14	385,000	5,356,000	385,000	31,243	416,243
15	380,000	4,971,000	380,000	28,998	408,998
16	377,000	4,591,000	377,000	26,781	403,781
17	375,000	4,214,000	375,000	24,582	399,582
18	370,000	3,839,000	370,000	22,394	392,394
19	369,000	3,469,000	369,000	20,236	389,236
20	366,000	3,100,000	366,000	18,083	384,083
21	300,000	2,734,000	300,000	15,948	315,948
22	298,000	2,434,000	298,000	14,198	312,198
23	292,000	2,136,000	292,000	12,460	304,460
24	290,000	1,844,000	290,000	10,757	300,757
25	287,000	1,554,000	287,000	9,065	296,065
26	285,000	1,267,000	285,000	7,391	292,391
27	283,000	982,000	283,000	5,728	288,728
28	280,000	699,000	280,000	4,078	284,078
29	278,000	419,000	278,000	2,444	280,444
30	275,000	141,000	141,000	823	141,823
		Total	8,000,000		

For months 31 through 48 the principal payment, interest, and cash flow are zero.

c. For tranche C:

Month	Sch. Principal repayment + prepayments	Beginning principal	Tranche C principal repayment	Interest at 8%	Cash flow
1	520,000	30,000,000	0	200,000	200,000
2	510,000	30,000,000	0	200,000	200,000
3	490,000	30,000,000	0	200,000	200,000
4	450,000	30,000,000	0	200,000	200,000
5	448,000	30,000,000	0	200,000	200,000
6	442,000	30,000,000	0	200,000	200,000
7	410,000	30,000,000	0	200,000	200,000
8	405,000	30,000,000	0	200,000	200,000
9	400,000	30,000,000	0	200,000	200,000
10	396,000	30,000,000	0	200,000	200,000
11	395,000	30,000,000	0	200,000	200,000
12	390,000	30,000,000	0	200,000	200,000
13	388,000	30,000,000	0	200,000	200,000
14	385,000	30,000,000	0	200,000	200,000
15	380,000	30,000,000	0	200,000	200,000
16	377,000	30,000,000	0	200,000	200,000
17	375,000	30,000,000	0	200,000	200,000
18	370,000	30,000,000	0	200,000	200,000
19	369,000	30,000,000	0	200,000	200,000
20	366,000	30,000,000	0	200,000	200,000
21	300,000	30,000,000	0	200,000	200,000
22	298,000	30,000,000	0	200,000	200,000
23	292,000	30,000,000	0	200,000	200,000
24	290,000	30,000,000	0	200,000	200,000
25	287,000	30,000,000	0	200,000	200,000
26	285,000	30,000,000	0	200,000	200,000
27	283,000	30,000,000	0	200,000	200,000
28	280,000	30,000,000	0	200,000	200,000
29	278,000	30,000,000	0	200,000	200,000
30	275,000	30,000,000	134,000	200,000	334,000
31	271,000	29,866,000	271,000	199,107	470,107
32	270,000	29,595,000	270,000	197,300	467,300
33	265,000	29,325,000	265,000	195,500	460,500
34	260,000	29,060,000	260,000	193,733	453,733
35	255,000	28,800,000	255,000	192,000	447,000
36	252,000	28,545,000	252,000	190,300	442,300
37	250,000	28,293,000	250,000	188,620	438,620
38	245,000	28,043,000	245,000	186,953	431,953
39	240,000	27,798,000	240,000	185,320	425,320
40	210,000	27,558,000	210,000	183,720	393,720
41	200,000	27,348,000	200,000	182,320	382,320
42	195,000	27,148,000	195,000	180,987	375,987
43	190,000	26,953,000	190,000	179,687	369,687
44	185,000	26,763,000	185,000	178,420	363,420
45	175,000	26,578,000	175,000	177,187	352,187
46	170,000	26,403,000	170,000	176,020	346,020
47	166,000	26,233,000	166,000	174,887	340,887
48	164,000	26,067,000	164,000	173,780	337,780

d. The average life for tranche A is computed as follows:

Month	Tranche A principal repayment	Month × principal repayment
1	520,000	520,000
2	510,000	1,020,000
3	490,000	1,470,000
4	450,000	1,800,000
5	448,000	2,240,000
6	442,000	2,652,000
7	140,000	980,000
Total	3,000,000	10,682,000

$$\text{Average life} = \frac{\$10,682,000}{12(\$3,000,000)} = 0.30$$

14. a. The coupon interest that would be paid to tranche C is diverted as principal repayment to tranche A. In the table below, the total principal paid to tranche A is tranche A's principal repayment as in KMF-01 plus the interest diverted from tranche C.

Month	Beginning principal for tranche A	Principal repayment before C int*	Interest at 6%	Principal for Tranche C	Tranche C diverted to Tranche A	Principal repayment for Tranche A	Cash flow
1	3,000,000	520,000	15,000	30,000,000	200,000	720,000	735,000
2	2,280,000	510,000	11,400	30,200,000	201,333	711,333	722,733
3	1,568,667	490,000	7,843	30,401,333	202,676	692,676	700,519
4	875,991	450,000	4,380	30,604,009	204,027	654,027	658,407
5	221,964	448,000	1,110	30,808,036	205,387	221,964	223,074
					Total	3,000,000	

* This is the amount before the accrued interest from Tranche C is allocated to Tranche A.

b. The principal balance for tranche C is increased each month by the amount of interest diverted from tranche C to tranche A. The principal balance for the first five months is shown in the fifth column of the schedule for part a.

c.

Month	Principal repayment for tranche A	Month × principal
1	720,000	720,000
2	711,333	1,422,667
3	692,676	2,078,027
4	654,027	2,616,107
5	221,964	1,109,822
	3,000,000	7,946,622

$$\text{Average life} = \frac{\$7,946,622}{12(\$3,000,000)} = 0.22$$

The average life is shorter for tranche A in KMF-02 relative to KMF-01 due to the presence of the accrual tranche.

15. There is typically a floor placed on an inverse floater to prevent the coupon rate from being negative. In order to fund this floor, the floater must be capped.

16. The principal payments that would have gone to the tranche used to create the floater and inverse floater are distributed proportionately to the floater and inverse floater based on their percentage of the par value. That is, if the floater's par value is 80% of the tranche from which it is created and the inverse floater 20%, then if $100 is received in principal payment $80 is distributed to the floater and $20 to the inverse floater. The effect is that the average life for the floater and the inverse floater will be the same as the tranche from which they are created, six years in this example.

17. A CMO redistributes prepayment risk by using rules for the distribution of principal payments and interest payments from the collateral.

18. By creating any mortgage-backed security, prepayment risk cannot never be eliminated. Rather, the character of prepayment risk can be altered. Specifically, prepayment risk consists of contraction risk and extension risk. A CMO alters but does not eliminate the prepayment risk of the underlying mortgage loans. Therefore, the statement is incorrect.

19. Ms. Morgan should inform the trustee that the statement about the riskiness of the different sectors of the mortgage-backed securities market in terms of prepayment risk is incorrect. There are CMO tranches that expose an investor to less prepayment risk — in terms of extension or contraction risk — than the mortgage passthrough securities from which the CMO was created. There are CMO tranche types such as planned amortization classes that have considerably less prepayment risk than the mortgage passthrough securities from which the CMO was created. However, in order to create CMO tranches such as PACs, it is necessary to create tranches where there is considerable prepayment risk — prepayment risk that is greater than the underlying mortgage passthrough securities. These tranches are called support tranches.

20. A support tranche is included in a structure in which there are PAC tranches. The sole purpose of the support tranche is to provide prepayment protection for the PAC tranches. Consequently, support tranches are exposed to substantial prepayment risk.

21. The manager of an S&L portfolio is concerned with prepayment risk but more specifically extension risk. Moreover, to better match the average life of the investment to that of the S&L's funding cost, the manager will seek a shorter term investment. With the Fannie Mae PAC issue with an average life of 2 years the manager is buying a shorter term security and one with some protection against extension risk. In contrast, the Fannie Mae passthrough is probably a longer term average life security because of its WAM of 310 months and it will expose the S&L to substantial extension risk. Therefore, the Fannie Mae PAC tranche is probably a better investment from an asset/liability perspective.

22. Since the prepayments are assumed to be at a constant prepayment rate over the PAC tranche's life at 140 PSA which is within the PSA collar in which the PAC was created, the average life will be equal to five years.

23. a. The PAC tranche will have the least average life variability. This is because the PAC tranche is created to provide protection against extension risk and contraction risk — the support tranches providing the protection.

b. The support tranche will have the greatest average life variability. This is because it is designed to absorb the prepayment risk to provide protection for the PAC tranche.

24. The PAC structure in KMF-06 will have less prepayment protection than in KMF-05 because the support tranche is smaller ($200 million in KMF-06 versus $350 for KMF-05).

25. a. The PAC II is a support tranche and as a result will have more average life variability than the PAC I tranche. Consequently, PAC I has the less average life variability.

b. The support tranche without a schedule must provide prepayment protection for both the PAC I and the PAC II. Therefore, the support tranche without a schedule will have greater average life variability than the PAC II.

26. In a PAC tranche structure in which the PAC tranches are paid off in sequence, the support tranches absorb any excess prepayments above the scheduled amount. Once the support tranches are paid off, any prepayments must go to the PAC tranche that is currently receiving principal payments. Thus, the structure effectively becomes a typical (plain vanilla) sequential-pay structure.

27. If the prepayments are well below the initial upper PAC collar this means that there will be more support tranches available four years after the deal is structured than if prepayments were actually at the initial upper PAC collar. This means that there will be more support tranches to absorb prepayments. Hence, the effective upper collar will increase.

28. The notional amount of an 8% IO tranche is computed below:

Tranche	Par amount	Coupon rate	Excess interest	Excess dollar interest	Notional amount for an 8% coupon rate IO
A	$400,000,000	6.25%	1.75%	$7,000,000	$87,500,000
B	$200,000,000	6.75%	1.25%	$2,500,000	$31,250,000
C	$225,000,000	7.50%	0.50%	$1,125,000	$14,062,500
D	$175,000,000	7.75%	0.25%	$437,500	$5,468,750
				Notional amount for 8% IO	$138,281,250

29. a. The coupon rate for tranche G is found as follows:

$$\text{coupon interest for tranche F in Structure I} = \$500,000,000 \times 0.085$$
$$= \$42,500,000$$

$$\text{coupon interest for tranche F in Structure II} = \$200,000,000 \times 0.0825$$
$$= \$16,500,000$$

coupon interest available to tranche G in Structure II
$$= \$42,500,000 - \$16,500,000 = \$26,000,000$$

$$\text{coupon rate for tranche G} = \frac{\$26,000,000}{\$300,000,000} = 0.0867 = 8.67\%$$

b. There is no effect on the average life of the PAC tranches because the inclusion of the PAC II only impacts the support tranche in Structure I compared to Structure II.

c. There is greater average life variability for tranche G in Structure II than tranche F in Structure I because tranche G must provide prepayment protection in Structure II for not only the PACs but also tranche F.

30. A broken or busted PAC is a structure where all of the support tranches (the tranches that provide prepayment support for the PAC tranches in a structure) are completely paid off.

31. a. The formula for the cap rate on the inverse floater

$$\frac{\text{inverse floater interest when reference rate for floater is zero}}{\text{principal for inverse floater}}$$

The total interest to be paid to tranche C if it was not split into the floater and the inverse floater is the principal of $96,500,000 times 7.5%, or $7,237,500. The maximum interest for the inverse floater occurs if 1-month LIBOR is zero. In that case, the coupon rate for the floater is

1-month LIBOR + 1% = 1%

Since the floater receives 1% on its principal of $80,416,667, the floater's interest is $804,167. The remainder of the interest of $7,237,500 from tranche C goes to the inverse floater. That is, the inverse floater's interest is $6,433,333 (= $7,237,500 − $804,167). Since the inverse floater's principal is $16,083,333.33, the cap rate for the inverse floater is

$$\frac{\$6,433,333}{\$16,083,333} = 40.0\%$$

b. Assuming a floor of zero for inverse floater, the cap rate is determined as follows:

$$\text{cap rate for floater} = \frac{\text{collateral tranche interest}}{\text{principal for floater}}$$

The collateral tranche interest is $7,237,500. The floater principal is $80,416,667. Therefore,

$$\text{cap rate for floater} = \frac{\$7,237,500}{\$80,416,667} = 9\%$$

32. a. Mortgage strips are created when the principal (both scheduled principal repayments plus prepayments) and the coupon interest are allocated to different bond

classes. The tranche that is allocated the principal payments is called the principal-only mortgage strip and the tranche that is allocated the coupon interest is called the interest-only mortgage strip.

b. With an interest-only mortgage strip, there is no specific amount that will be received over time since the coupon interest payments depend on how prepayments occur over the security's life. In contrast, for a Treasury strip created from the coupon interest, the amount and the timing of the single cash flow is known with certainty.

c. Because prepayments increase when interest rates decrease and prepayments decrease when interest rates increase, the expected cash flow changes in the same direction as the change in interest rates. Thus, when interest rates increase, prepayments are expected to decrease and there will be an increase in the expected coupon interest payments since more of the underlying mortgages are expected to be outstanding. This will typically increase the value of an interest-only mortgage strip because the increase in the expected cash flow more than offsets the higher discount rates used to discount the cash flow. When interest rates decrease, the opposite occurs. So, an interest-only mortgage strip's value is expected to change in the same direction as the change in interest rates.

33. a. The purchase price per $100 par value is 1.02. Therefore

$$1.02 \times \$10,000,000 \times 0.72 = \$7,344,000$$

The investor pays $7,344,000 plus accrued interest.

b. Because the value and characteristics of a principal-only mortgage strip are highly sensitive to the underlying mortgage pool, an investor would not want the seller to have the option of which specific trust to deliver. If the trade is done on a TBA basis, the seller has the choice of the trust to deliver. To avoid this, a trade is done by the buyer specifying the trust that he or she is purchasing.

34. Ginnie Mae, Fannie Mae, and Freddie Mac have underwriting standards that must be met in order for a mortgage loan to qualify for inclusion in a mortgage pool underlying an agency mortgage-backed security. Mortgage loans that do qualify are called conforming loans. A loan may fail to be conforming because the loan balance exceeds the maximum permitted by the underwriting standard or the loan-to-value ratio is too high, or the payment-to-income ratio is too high. Loans that do not qualify are called nonconforming loans.

35. Since there is no implicit or explicit government guarantee for a nonagency mortgage-backed security, a mechanism is needed to reduce credit risk for bondholders when there are defaults. That is, there is a need to "enhance" the credit of the securities issued. These mechanisms are called credit enhancements of which there are two types, internal and external.

Chapter 4

ASSET-BACKED SECURITIES

LEARNING OUTCOME STATEMENTS

After reading this chapter you should be able to:

- explain the difference between amortizing assets and non-amortizing assets and why the former may have prepayments.
- explain the difference between an external and internal credit enhancement.
- explain the different types of external credit enhancements (corporate guarantees, letter of credit, and bond insurance) and the concerns with enhancing with third-party guarantors.
- explain the different types of internal credit enhancements (reserve accounts, overcollateralization, and senior-subordinated structures).
- describe what a shifting interest mechanism is in a senior-subordinated structure and explain what the purpose of this mechanism is.
- distinguish between a passthrough structure and a pay through structure.
- describe the cash flow for securities backed by closed-end home equity loans, open-end home equity loans, manufactured housing loans, student loans, SBA loans, and credit card receivables.
- explain what a prospectus prepayment curve is for home equity loan-backed securities.
- explain why there is an available funds cap when securities are backed by adjustable-rate home equity loans.
- describe what a non-accelerating senior tranche and a planned amortization class tranche are in a home equity loan-backed structure.
- explain why prepayments due to refinancing may not be significant for manufactured housing-backed securities and automobile loan-backed securities.
- explain what an absolute prepayment speed and a conditional prepayment rate are.
- explain the structure of a credit card receivable-backed security and what is meant by the lock-out period and the principal-amortization period.
- explain what the early amortization trigger for a credit card receivable-backed security is.
- identify the types of bonds used as collateral for a collateralized bond obligation.
- describe the basic structure of a collateralized bond obligation and the types of tranches.
- explain why it is necessary for the manager of a collateralized bond obligation to use interest rate derivatives.
- explain the different periods in the life of a collateralized bond obligation: start-up phase, reinvestment phase, and pay down phase.

SECTION I
INTRODUCTION

While the securitization of residential mortgage loans is by far the largest type of asset that has been securitized, securities backed by other assets (consumer and business loans and receivables) have been securitized. The largest sectors of the asset-backed securities market in the United States are securities backed by credit card receivables, auto loans, home equity loans, manufactured housing loans, student loans, Small Business Administration loans, and collateralized bond obligations. Since home equity loans and manufactured housing loans are backed by real estate property, the securities backed by them are referred to as **real estate-backed asset-backed securities**. Other asset-backed securities include securities backed by home improvement loans, health care receivables, agricultural equipment loans, equipment leases, commercial mortgage loans, music royalty receivables, movie royalty receivables, and municipal parking ticket receivables. The list is continually expanding.

In this chapter, we will discuss the basic features of asset-backed securities. Collectively, these products are **credit-sensitive structured products**. The issuer must structure the transaction so as to deal with both credit risk and prepayment risk. In Chapter 9, we will discuss the factors considered by rating agencies when assigning a credit rating to an asset-backed security. In Chapter 5 we discuss the models for valuing these products. At Level I (Chapter 3) we explained the motivation for a corporation to use an asset-backed security rather than a straight corporate bond offering.

SECTION II
FEATURES OF
AN ABS

Before we discuss the major types of asset-backed securities, let's first look at the general features of the underlying collateral and the structure.

A. Amortizing versus Nonamortizing Assets

The collateral for an asset-backed security can be classified as either amortizing or non-amortizing assets. **Amortizing assets** are loans in which the borrower's periodic payment consists of scheduled principal and interest payments over the life of the loan. The schedule for the repayment of the principal is called an **amortization schedule**. The standard residential mortgage loan falls into this category. Auto loans and certain types of home equity loans (specifically, closed-end home equity loans discussed later in this chapter) are amortizing assets. Any excess payment over the scheduled principal payment is called a **prepayment**. Prepayments can be made to pay off the entire balance or a partial prepayment, called a **curtailment**.

In contrast to amortizing assets, **non-amortizing assets** do not have a schedule for the periodic payments that the individual borrower must make. Instead, a non-amortizing asset is one in which the borrower must make a minimum periodic payment. If that payment is less than the interest on the outstanding loan balance, the shortfall is added to the outstanding loan balance. If the periodic payment is greater than the interest on the outstanding loan balance, then the difference is applied to the reduction of the outstanding loan balance. There is no schedule of principal payments (i.e., no amortization schedule) for a non-amortizing asset. Consequently, the concept of a prepayment does not apply. Credit card receivables and certain types of home equity loans described later in this chapter are examples of non-amortizing assets.

For an amortizing asset, projection of the cash flows requires projecting prepayments. One factor that may affect prepayments is the prevailing level of interest rates relative to the interest rate on the loan. In projecting prepayments it is critical to determine the extent to which borrowers take advantage of a decline in interest rates below the loan rate in order to refinance the loan. As we will see when we discuss valuation modeling for asset-backed securities in Chapter 5, whether or not borrowers will take advantage of refinancing when rates decline will determine the valuation methodology.

As with nonagency mortgage-backed securities, modeling defaults for the collateral is critical in estimating the cash flows of an asset-backed security. Proceeds that are recovered in the event of a default of a loan prior to the scheduled principal repayment date of an amortizing asset represent a prepayment and are referred to as an **involuntary prepayment**. Projecting prepayments for amortizing assets requires an assumption about the default rate and the recovery rate. For a non-amortizing asset, while the concept of a prepayment does not exist, a projection of defaults is still necessary to project how much will be recovered and when.

The analysis of prepayments can be performed on a pool level or a loan level. In **pool-level analysis** it is assumed that all loans comprising the collateral are identical. For an amortizing asset, the amortization schedule is based on the **gross weighted average coupon** (GWAC) and **weighted average maturity** (WAM) for that single loan. We explained in the previous chapter what the WAC and WAM of a pool of mortgage loans is and illustrated how it is computed. In the previous chapter, we did not refer to it as a "gross" WAC. We will do so in this chapter. Pool-level analysis is appropriate where the underlying loans are homogeneous. **Loan-level analysis** involves amortizing each loan (or group of homogeneous loans).

The maturity of an asset-backed security is not a meaningful parameter. Instead, the **average life** of the security is calculated. This measure was introduced in the previous chapter when we discussed agency passthrough securities.

B. Fixed-Rate versus Floating-Rate

There are fixed-rate and floating-rate asset-backed securities. Floating-rate asset-backed securities are typically created where the underlying pool of loans or receivables pay a floating rate.[1] The most common are securities backed by credit card receivables, home equity line of credit receivables, closed-end home equity loans with an adjustable rate, student loans, Small Business Administration loans, and trade receivables. As demonstrated in the previous chapter, fixed-rate loans also can be used to create a structure that has one or more floating-rate tranches. For example, there are closed-end home equity loans with a fixed rate that can be pooled to create a structure with floating-rate tranches.

Based on data provided by Morgan Stanley Dean Witter, of the $269 billion of asset-backed securities issued between January 1, 1998 and July 6, 1999, approximately 55% were fixed-rate securities and 45% were floating-rate securities.

C. Credit Enhancements

All asset-backed securities are credit enhanced. That means that support is provided for one or more of the bondholders in the structure. Credit enhancement levels are determined relative to a specific rating desired by the issuer for a security by each rating agency. Specifically, an investor in a triple A rated security expects to have "minimal," that is to say, virtually no chance of losing any principal due to defaults. For example, a rating agency may require credit enhancement equal to four times expected losses to obtain a triple A rating or three times expected losses to obtain a double A rating. The amount of credit enhancement necessary depends on rating agency requirements.

There are two general types of credit enhancement structures: external and internal. We describe each type below.

---

[1] Issuers of asset-backed securities can also create floating-rate securities using an interest rate swap. We will discuss interest rate swaps in Chapter 7.

1. External Credit Enhancements

External credit enhancements come in the form of third-party guarantees that provide for protection against losses up to a specified level, for example, 10%. This third-party protection is referred to as "first loss protection" since it provides protection against losses before the internal credit enhancements discussed later are drawn upon to provide protection. The most common forms of external credit enhancements are:

1. a corporate guarantee
2. a letter of credit from a bank
3. bond insurance

Typically, external credit enhancement are not used as the primary protection but to supplement other forms of credit enhancement discussed below. For example, suppose that a $300 million asset-backed securities deal is issued and the sponsor (i.e., effectively the seller of the securities) agrees to guarantee $10 million. Then if losses exceed $10 million, the sponsor is not responsible for the excess over $10 million. Bond insurance provides the same function as in municipal bond structures. However, in the case of asset-backed securities, the insurance covers only up to a specified amount of the loss.

An asset-backed security with external credit support is subject to the credit risk of the third-party guarantor. Should the third-party guarantor be downgraded, the issue itself could be subject to downgrade even if the structure is performing as expected. This is based on the "weak link" test followed by rating agencies. According to this test, when evaluating a proposed structure, credit quality of the issue is only as good as the weakest link in credit enhancement regardless of the quality of underlying loans.

2. Internal Credit Enhancements

Internal credit enhancements come in more complicated forms than external credit enhancements. The most common forms of internal credit enhancement are reserve funds, overcollateralization, and senior/subordinated structures.

a. Reserve Funds

Reserve funds come in two forms:

• cash reserve funds
• excess servicing spread accounts

Cash reserve funds are straight deposits of cash generated from issuance proceeds. In this case, part of the underwriting profits from the deal are deposited into a fund which typically invests in money market instruments. Cash reserve funds are typically used in conjunction with external credit enhancements.

Excess servicing spread accounts involve the allocation of excess spread or cash into a separate reserve account after paying out the net coupon, servicing fee, and all other expenses on a monthly basis. For example, suppose that:

1. gross weighted average coupon (gross WAC) is 8.00% — this is the interest rate paid by the borrowers
2. servicing and other fees are 0.25%

3. net weighted average coupon (net WAC) is 7.25% — this is the rate that is paid to all the tranches in the structure

So, for this hypothetical deal, 8.00% is available to make payments to the tranches, to cover servicing fees, and to cover other fees. Of that amount, 0.25% is paid for servicing and other fees and 7.25% is paid to the tranches. This means that only 7.50% must be paid out, leaving 0.50% (8.00% − 7.50%). This 0.50% or 50 basis points is called the **excess servicing spread**. This amount is placed in a reserve account — the excess servicing spread account — and it will gradually increase and can be used to pay for possible future losses.

PRACTICE QUESTION 1

Suppose that the collateral for an asset-backed securities structure has a gross weighted average coupon of 9.50%. The servicing fee is 75 basis points. The tranches issued have a weighted average coupon rate of 7.5%. What is the excess servicing spread?

---

b. Overcollateralization

The total par value of the tranches is the liability of the structure. So, if a structure has two tranches with a par value of $200 million, then that is the amount of the liability. The amount of the collateral backing the structure must be at least equal to the amount of the liability. If the amount of the collateral exceeds the amount of the liability of the structure, the deal is said to be overcollateralized.

The amount of **overcollateralization** represents a form of internal credit enhancement because it can be used to absorb losses. For example, if the liability of the structure is $200 million and the collateral's value is $214 million, then the structure is overcollateralized by $14 million. Thus, the first $14 million of losses will not result in a loss to any of the tranches.

c. Senior/Subordinated Structure

The most popular form of credit enhancement is the **senior-subordinated structure**. In this structure there is a senior tranche and at least one junior or subordinated tranche. For example, suppose a deal has $300 million as collateral (i.e., a pool of loans or receivables). The structure may look as follows:

senior tranche $280 million
subordinated tranche $ 20 million

This means that the first $20 million of losses are absorbed by the subordinated tranche.

There is no reason why there must be only one subordinated tranche. The structure can have more than one subordinated tranche. For example, the structure could be as follows:

senior tranche $280 million
subordinated tranche 1   15 million
subordinated tranche 2   5 million

In this structure, the subordinate tranches 1 and 2 are called the **non-senior tranches**. The senior tranche still has protection up to $20 million as in the previous structure with only one subordinated tranche. In the second structure, the first $5 million of losses is absorbed by the subordinated tranche 2. Hence, this tranche is referred to as the **first loss tranche**. Subordinated tranche 1 has protection of up to $5 million in losses, the protection provided by the first loss tranche.

The basic concern in the senior-subordinate structure is that while the subordinated tranches provide a certain level of credit protection for the senior tranche at the closing of the deal, the level of protection changes over time due to prepayments. The objective after the deal closes is to distribute any prepayments such that the credit protection for the senior tranche does not deteriorate over time.

In real-estate related asset-backed securities, as well as nonagency mortgage-backed securities, there is a well developed mechanism used to address this concern called the **shifting interest mechanism**. Here is how it works. The percentage of the mortgage balance of the subordinate tranche to that of the mortgage balance for the entire deal is called the **level of subordination** or the **subordinate interest**. The higher the percentage, the greater the level of protection for the senior tranches. The subordinate interest changes after the deal is closed due to prepayments. That is, the subordinate interest shifts (hence the term "shifting interest"). The purpose of a shifting interest mechanism is to allocate prepayments so that the subordinate interest is maintained at an acceptable level to protect the senior tranche. In effect, by paying down the senior tranche more quickly, the amount of subordination is maintained at the desired level.

The prospectus will provide the shifting interest percentage schedule for calculating the **senior prepayment percentage** (the percentage of prepayments paid to the senior tranche). For mortgage loans, a commonly used shifting interest percentage schedule is as follows:

Year after issuance	Senior prepayment percentage
1-5	100
6	70
7	60
8	40
9	20
after year 9	0

So, for example, if prepayments in month 20 are $1 million, the amount paid to the senior tranche is $1 million and no prepayments are made to the subordinated tranches. If prepayments in month 90 (in the seventh year after issuance) are $1 million, the senior tranche is paid $600,000 (60% × $1 million).

The shifting interest percentage schedule given in the prospectus is the "base" schedule. The set of shifting interest percentages can change over time depending on the performance of the collateral. If the performance is such that the credit protection for the senior tranche has deteriorated because credit losses have reduced the subordinate tranches, the base shifting interest percentages are overridden and a higher allocation of prepayments is made to the senior tranche.

Performance analysis of the collateral is undertaken by the trustee for determining whether or not to override the base schedule. The performance analysis is in terms of tests and if the collateral fails any of the tests, this will trigger an override of the base schedule.

It is important to understand that the presence of a shifting interest mechanism results in a trade-off between credit risk and contraction risk for the senior tranche. The shifting interest mechanism reduces the credit risk to the senior tranche. However, because the senior tranche receives a larger share of any prepayments, contraction risk increases.

PRACTICE QUESTION 2

Suppose that the structure for an asset-backed security structure is as follows:

senior tranche	$380 million
subordinated tranche 1	$40 million
subordinated tranche 2	$20 million

The value of the collateral for the structure is $440 million and subordinated tranche 2 is the first loss tranche.

a. What is the amount of the loss for each tranche if losses due to defaults over the life of the structure total $15 million?

b. What is the amount of the loss for each tranche if losses due to defaults over the life of the structure total $50 million?

c. What is the amount of the loss for each tranche if losses due to defaults over the life of the structure total $90 million?

D. Passthrough versus Pay Through Structures

In the previous chapter, we saw how a mortgage passthrough security is created. A pool of mortgage loans is used as collateral and certificates (securities) are issued with each certificate entitled to a pro rata share of the cash flow from the pool of mortgage loans. So, if a $100 million mortgage pool is the collateral for a passthrough security and 10,000 certificates are issued, then the holder of one certificate is entitled to 1/10,000 of the cash flow from the collateral.

The same type of structure, a **passthrough structure**, can be used for an asset-backed security deal. That is, each certificate holder is entitled to a pro rata share of the cash flow from the underlying pool of loans or receivables. For example, consider the following asset-backed security structure:

senior tranche	$280 million	10,000 certificates issued
subordinated tranche	$ 20 million	1,000 certificates issued

Each certificate holder of the senior tranche is entitled to receive 1/10,000 of the cash flow to be paid to the senior tranche from the collateral. Each certificate holder of the subordinated tranche is entitled to receive 1/1,000 of the cash flow to be paid to the subordinated tranche from the collateral.

In the previous chapter we saw how a passthrough security can be used to create a collateralized mortgage obligation (CMO). That is, passthrough securities are pooled and used as collateral for a CMO. Another name for a CMO structure is a **pay through structure**. In the case of an asset-backed security, the loans are either pooled and issued as a passthrough security or as a pay through security. That is, unlike in the agency mortgage-backed securities market, a passthrough is not created first and then the passthrough is used to create a pay through security.

In a pay through security the *senior* tranches are carved up to create different tranches. Typically, the subordinated or non-senior tranches are not carved up. So, for example, a pay through structure may be as shown in Exhibit 1. Notice that the par value of the senior tranches is $280 million, as it is in the passthrough structure earlier.

In a pay through structure, the senior tranches can be simple sequential-pays, just as we described for CMOs in the previous chapter. Or, there could be a PAC structure with, say, senior tranche 1 being a short average life PAC, senior tranche 2 being a long average life tranche, and the other two senior tranches being support tranches.

Exhibit 1: Example of Prepayment and Credit Tranching

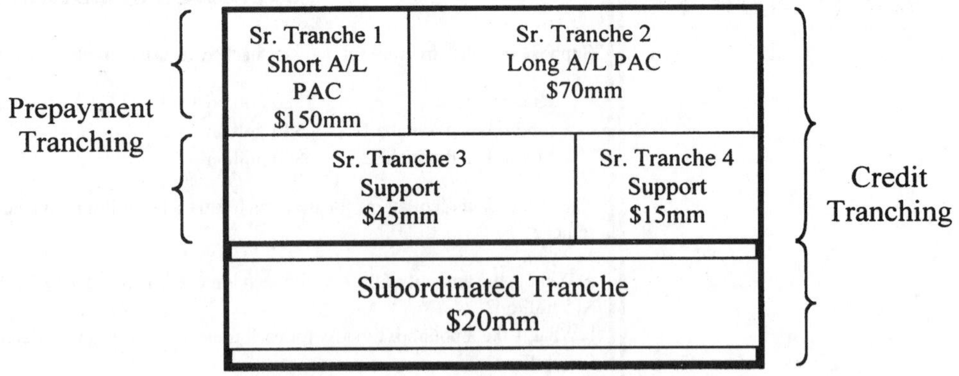

It is important to emphasize that the senior-subordinated structure is a mechanism for redistributing credit risk from the senior tranche to the subordinated tranches and is referred to as **credit tranching**. When the senior tranche is carved up into tranches with different exposures to prepayment risk in a pay through structure, prepayment risk can be transferred among the senior tranches as in a nonagency CMO. This is referred to as **prepayment tranching** or **time tranching**.

E. Optional Clean-Up Call Provisions

For asset-backed securities there is an **optional clean-up call provision** granted to the trustee.[2] There are several types of clean-up call provisions.

In a **percent of collateral call** the outstanding bonds can be called at par value if the outstanding collateral's balance falls below a predetermined percent of the original collateral's balance. This is the most common type of clean-up call provision for amortizing assets and the predetermined level is typically 10%.

A **percent of bonds clean-up call provision** is similar to a percent of collateral call except that the percent that triggers the call is the percent of the amount of the bonds outstanding relative to the original amount of bonds issued. In structures where there is more than one type of collateral, such as in home equity loan-backed securities, a **percent of tranche clean-up call provision** is used.

A **call on or after specified date** operates just like a standard call provision for corporate, agency, and municipal securities. In a **latter of percent or date call** the outstanding bonds can be called if either (1) the collateral outstanding reaches a predetermined level before the specified call date or (2) the call date has been reached even if the collateral outstanding is above the predetermined level. In an **auction call**, common in certain types of home equity loan-backed securities, at a certain date a call will be exercised if an auction results in the outstanding collateral being sold at a price greater than its par value. The premium over par value received from the auctioned collateral is retained by the trustee and eventually paid to the issuer through the residual.

In addition to the above clean-up call provisions which permit the trustee to call the bonds, there may be an **insurer call**. Such a call permits the insurer to call the bonds if the collateral's cumulative loss history reaches a predetermined level.

---

[2] Typically, Freddie Mac CMOs have 1% clean-up calls and Fannie Mae CMOs do not have clean-up calls.

SECTION III HOME EQUITY LOANS

A **home equity loan** (HEL) is a loan backed by residential property. At one time, the loan was typically a second lien on property that was already pledged to secure a first lien. In some cases, the lien was a third lien. In recent years, the character of a home equity loan has changed. Today, a home equity loan is often a first lien on property where the borrower has either an impaired credit history and/or the payment-to-income ratio is too high for the loan to qualify as a conforming loan for securitization by Ginnie Mae, Fannie Mae, or Freddie Mac. Typically, the borrower used a home equity loan to consolidate consumer debt using the current home as collateral rather than to obtain funds to purchase a new home.

A. Securities Backed by Closed-End Home Equity Loans

Home equity loans can be either **closed end** or **open end**. Our focus in this section is on securities backed by closed-end HELs. A closed-end HEL is structured the same way as a fully amortizing residential mortgage loan. That is, it has a fixed maturity and the payments are structured to fully amortize the loan by the maturity date.

There are both fixed-rate and variable-rate closed-end HELs. Typically, variable-rate loans have a reference rate of 6-month LIBOR and have periodic caps and lifetime caps. (A periodic cap limits the change in the mortgage rate from the previous time the mortgage rate was reset; a lifetime cap sets a maximum that the mortgage rate can ever be for the loan.) The cash flow of a pool of closed-end HELs is comprised of interest, regularly scheduled principal repayments, and prepayments, just as with mortgage-backed securities. Thus, it is necessary to have a prepayment model and a default model to forecast cash flows. The prepayment speed is measured in terms of a conditional prepayment rate (CPR).

1. Prepayments

There are differences in the prepayment behavior for home equity loans and traditional residential mortgage loans. Wall Street firms involved in the underwriting and market making of home equity loan-backed securities have developed prepayment models for these loans. Several firms have found that the key difference between the prepayment behavior of HELs and traditional residential mortgages is the important role played by the credit characteristics of the borrower.[3]

Borrower characteristics and the seasoning process must be kept in mind when trying to assess prepayments for a particular deal. In the prospectus of an offering a **base case prepayment assumption** is made — the initial speed and the amount of time until the collateral is expected to be seasoned. Thus, the prepayment benchmark is issuer specific. The benchmark speed in the prospectus is called the **prospectus prepayment curve** or PPC. As with the PSA benchmark described in the previous chapter, slower or faster prepayments speeds are a multiple of the PPC.

However, unlike the PSA prepayment benchmark, the PPC is not generic. By this we mean that the PPC is issuer specific. In contrast, the PSA prepayment benchmark applies to any type of collateral issued by an agency for any type of loan design. This feature of the PPC is important for an investor to keep in mind when comparing the prepayment characteristics and investment characteristics of the collateral between issuers and issues (new and seasoned).

---

[3] Dale Westhoff and Mark Feldman, "Prepayment Modeling and Valuation of Home Equity Loan Securities," Chapter 16 in Frank J. Fabozzi, Chuck Ramsey, Frank Ramirez, and Michael Marz (eds.), *The Handbook of Nonagency Mortgage-Backed Securities* (New Hope, PA: Frank J. Fabozzi Associates, 1997).

Since HEL deals are backed by both fixed-rate and variable-rate loans, a separate PPC is provided for each type of loan. For example, in the prospectus for the Contimortgage Home Equity Loan Trust 1998-2, the base case prepayment assumption for the fixed-rate collateral begins at 4% CPR in month 1 and increases 1.45455% CPR per month until month 12, at which time it is 20% CPR. Therefore, if an investor analyzed the deal based on 200% PPC, this means doubling the CPRs cited and using 12 months for seasoning. For the variable-rate collateral in the ContiMortgage deal, 100% PPC assumes seasoning after 18 months with the CPR in month 1 being 4% and increasing 1.82353% CPR each month. From month 18, the CPR is 35%. Thus, the variable-rate collateral is assumed to season slower than the fixed-rate collateral, but has a faster CPR when the pool is seasoned.

PRACTICE QUESTION 3

The base case prepayment for the Champion Home Equity Loan Trust 1996-1 is provided for the fixed-rate loans (referred to as Group One in the prospectus) and floating-rate loans (referred to as Group Two in the prospectus). The following is taken from the prospectus for the Group One loans:

> The model used with respect to the fixed rate certificates (the "prepayment ramp") assumes that the home equity loans in loan Group One prepay at a rate of 4% CPR in the first month after origination, and an additional 1.5% each month thereafter until the 14th month. Beginning in the 15th month and each month thereafter, the prepayment ramp assumes a prepayment rate of 25% CPR.

What is the CPR assuming 150% PPC for the fixed-rate collateral for the following months

Month	CPR	Month	CPR	Month	CPR
1		11		30	
2		12		125	
3		13		150	
4		14		200	
5		15		250	
6		16		275	
7		17		300	
8		18		325	
9		19		350	
10		20		360	

---

2. Payment Structure

As with nonagency mortgage-backed securities discussed in the previous chapter, there are passthrough and pay through home equity loan-backed structures.

Typically, home equity loan-backed securities are securitized by both closed-end fixed-rate and adjustable-rate (or variable-rate) HELs. The securities backed by the latter are called **HEL floaters**. The reference rate of the underlying loans typically is 6-month LIBOR. The cash flow of these loans is affected by periodic and lifetime caps on the loan rate.

Institutional investors that seek securities that better match their floating-rate funding costs are attracted to securities that offer a floating-rate coupon. To increase the attractiveness of home equity loan-backed securities to such investors, the securities typically have been created in which the reference rate is 1-month LIBOR. Because of (1) the mismatch between the reference rate on the underlying loans and that of the HEL floater and (2) the periodic and life caps of the underlying loans, there is a cap on the coupon rate for the HEL floater. Unlike a typical floater, which has a cap that is fixed throughout the security's life, the effective periodic and life-time cap of a HEL floater is variable. The effective cap, referred to as the **available funds cap**, will depend on the amount of funds generated by the net coupon on the principal, less any fees.

Let's look at one issue, Advanta Mortgage Loan Trust 1995-2 issued in June 1995. At the offering, this issue had approximately $122 million closed-end HELs. There were 1,192 HELs consisting of 727 fixed-rate loans and 465 variable-rate loans. There were five classes (A-1, A-2, A-3, A-4, and A-5) and a residual. The five classes are summarized below:

Class	Par amount ($)	Passthrough coupon rate (%)
A-1	9,229,000	7.30
A-2	30,330,000	6.60
A-3	16,455,000	6.85
A-4	9,081,000	floating rate
A-5	56,917,000	floating rate

The collateral is divided into group I and group II. The 727 fixed-rate loans are included in group I and support Classes A-1, A-2, A-3, and A-4 certificates. The 465 variable-rate loans are in group II and support Class A-5.

Tranches have been structured in home equity loan deals so as to give some senior tranches greater prepayment protection than other senior tranches. The two types of structures that do this are the **non-accelerating senior (NAS) tranche** and the **planned amortization class (PAC) tranche.**

a. Non-Accelerating Senior Tranches

A NAS tranche receives principal payments according to a schedule. The schedule is not a dollar amount. Rather, it is a principal schedule that shows for a given month the share of pro rata principal that must be distributed to the NAS tranche. A typical principal schedule for a NAS tranche is as follows:[4]

Months	Share of pro rata principal
1 through 36	0%
37 through 60	45%
61 through 72	80%
73 through 84	100%
After month 84	300%

The average life for the NAS tranche is stable for a large range of prepayments because for the first three years all prepayments are made to the other senior tranches. This reduces the risk of the NAS tranche contracting (i.e., shortening) due to fast prepayments. After month 84, 300% of its pro rata share is paid to the NAS tranche thereby reducing its extension risk.

---

[4] Charles Schorin, Steven Weinreich, and Oliver Hsiang, "Home Equity Loan Transaction Structures," Chapter 6 in Frank J. Fabozzi, Chuck Ramsey, and Michael Marz, *Handbook of Nonagency Mortgage-Backed Securities: Second Edition* (New Hope, PA: Frank J. Fabozzi Associates, 2000).

Exhibit 2: Average Life for NAS Tranche (Class A9) and Non-NAS Tranche (Class A7) for ContiMortgage Home Equity Loan Trust 1997-2 for a Range of Prepayments

| | % PPC | | | | | | | | | | | | Avg life difference |
	0	50	75	100	120	150	200	250	300	350	400	500	75% to 200% PPC
Plateau CPR	0	10	15	20	24	30	40	50	60	70	80	100	
Avg Life													
NAS Bond	11.71	7.81	7.06	6.58	6.30	6.06	5.97	3.98	2.17	1.73	1.38	0.67	1.09
Non-NAS Bond	21.93	14.54	11.94	8.82	6.73	4.71	2.59	1.96	1.55	1.25	1.03	0.58	9.35

Calculation: Bloomberg Financial Markets
Reported in Charles Schorin, Steven Weinreich, and Oliver Hsiang, "Home Equity Loan Transaction Structures," Chapter 6 in Frank J. Fabozzi, Chuck Ramsey, and Michael Marz, *Handbook of Nonagency Mortgage-Backed Securities: Second Edition* (New Hope, PA: Frank J. Fabozzi Associates, 2000).

The average life stability over a wide range of prepayments is illustrated in Exhibit 2. The deal analyzed is the ContiMortgage Home Equity Loan Trust 1997-2.[5] Class A9 is the NAS tranche. The analysis was performed on Bloomberg shortly after the deal was issued using the issue's PPC. As can be seen, the average life is fairly stable between 75% to 200% PPC. In fact, the difference in the average life between 75% PPC and 200% PPC is slightly greater than 1 year.

In contrast, Exhibit 2 also shows the average life over the same prepayment scenarios for a non-NAS sequential-pay tranche in the same deal — Class A7. Notice the substantial average life variability. While the average life difference between 75% and 200% PPC for the NAS tranche is just over 1 year, it is more than 9 years for the non-NAS tranche. Of course, the non-NAS in the same deal will be less stable than a regular sequential tranche because the non-NAS gets a greater share of principal than it would otherwise.

b. Planned Amortization Class Tranche

In our discussion of collateralized mortgage obligations issued by the agencies in the previous chapter we explained how a planned amortization class tranche can be created. These tranches are also created in HEL structures. Unlike agency CMO PAC tranches that are backed by fixed-rate loans, the collateral for HEL deals is both fixed rate and adjustable rate.

An example of a HEL PAC tranche in a HEL-backed deal is tranche A6 in ContiMortgage 1998-2. We described the PPC for this deal in Section III.A.1 above. There is a separate PAC collar for both the fixed-rate and adjustable-rate collateral. For the fixed-rate collateral the PAC collar is 125%-175% PPC; for the adjustable-rate collateral the PAC collar is 95%-130% PPC. The average life for tranche A6 (a tranche backed by the fixed-rate collateral) is 5.1 years. As explained in Chapter 3, the effective collar for shorter tranches can be greater than the upper collar specified in the prospectus. The effective upper collar for tranche A6 is actually 180% PPC (assuming that the adjustable-rate collateral pays at 100% PPC).[6]

For shorter PACs, the effective upper collar is greater. For example, for tranche A3 in the same deal, the initial PAC collar is 125% to 175% PPC with an average life of 2.02 years. However, the effective upper collar is 190% PPC (assuming the adjustable-rate collateral pays at 100% PPC).

---

[5] This illustration is from Schorin, Weinreich, and Hsiang, "Home Equity Loan Transaction Structures."

[6] For a more detailed analysis of this tranche, see Schorin, Weinreich, and Hsiang, "Home Equity Loan Transaction Structures."

The effective collar for PAC tranches changes over time based on actual prepayments and therefore based on when the support tranches depart from the initial PAC collar. For example, if for the next 36 months after the issuance of the Conti-Mortgage 1998-2 actual prepayments are a constant 150% PPC, then the effective collar would be 135% PPC to 210% PPC.[7] That is, the lower and upper collar will increase. If the actual PPC is 200% PPC for the 10 months after issuance, the support bonds will be fully paid off and there will be no PAC collateral. In this situation the PAC is said to be a **broken PAC**.

B. Securities Backed by Home Equity Lines of Credit

The other type of home equity loan is an open-end home equity loan. Here the homeowner is given a credit line and can write checks or use a credit card for up to the amount of the credit line. The amount of the credit line depends on the amount of the equity the borrower has in the property.

The **revolving period** for a home equity line of credit (HELOC) is the period where the borrower can take down all or part of the line of credit. The revolving period can run from 10 to 15 years. At the end of the revolving period, the HELOC can specify either a balloon payment or an amortization schedule (of up to 10 years). Almost all HELOCs are floating-rate loans, with the interest rate paid by the majority of HELOC borrowers reset monthly to the prime rate (as reported in *The Wall Street Journal*) plus a spread.

The securities created in HELOC deals are floating-rate tranches. While the underlying loans are priced based on a spread over the prime rate, the securities created are based on a spread over 1-month LIBOR.

Because HELOCs are for revolving lines, the deal structures are quite different for HELOCs and closed-end HELs. As with other asset-backed securities involving revolving credit lines such as credit card deals, there is a revolving period, an amortization period, and a rapid amortization period. These periods are discussed later in this chapter when we cover credit card receivable asset-backed securities.

SECTION IV MANUFACTURED HOUSING-BACKED SECURITIES

Manufactured housing-backed securities are backed by loans for manufactured homes. In contrast to site-built homes, manufactured homes are built at a factory and then transported to a manufactured home community or private land.[8] The loan may be either a mortgage loan (for both the land and the home) or a consumer retail installment loan.

Manufactured housing-backed securities are issued by Ginnie Mae and private entities. The former securities are guaranteed by the full faith and credit of the U.S. government. The manufactured home loans that are collateral for the securities issued and guaranteed by Ginnie Mae are loans guaranteed by the Federal Housing Administration (FHA) or Veterans Administration (VA).

Loans not backed by the FHA or VA are called **conventional loans**. Manufactured housing-backed securities that are backed by such loans are called **conventional manufactured housing-backed securities**. These securities are issued by private entities.

---

[7] Schorin, Weinreich, and Hsiang, "Home Equity Loan Transaction Structures."

[8] While these assets are sometimes referred to as "mobile" homes, they are typically costly to move, and should not be confused with recreational vehicles (RVs). RVs have been securitized and are considered automobile loan-backed securities.

A. Cash Flow and Prepayments

The typical loan for a manufactured home is 15 to 20 years. The loan repayment is structured to fully amortize the amount borrowed. Therefore, as with residential mortgage loans and HELs, the cash flow consists of net interest, regularly scheduled principal, and prepayments. However, prepayments are more stable for manufactured housing-backed securities because they are not sensitive to refinancing.

There are several reasons for this. First, the loan balances are typically small so that there is no significant dollar savings from refinancing. Second, the rate of depreciation of mobile homes may be such that in the earlier years depreciation is greater than the amount of the loan paid off. This makes it difficult to refinance the loan. Finally, typically borrowers are of lower credit quality and therefore find it difficult to obtain funds to refinance.

As with residential mortgage loans and HELs, prepayments on manufactured housing-backed securities are measured in terms of CPR.

B. Payment Structure

The payment structure is the same as with nonagency mortgage-backed securities and home equity loan-backed securities. For example, consider the Green Tree Manufactured Housing Contract Trust 1995-3 issue. There are four classes in this $502.1 million issue: A-1, M-1, B-1, and B-2. Class A-1 is the senior class, Classes M-1, B-1, and B-2 are the subordinated or junior classes. The priority of payments is as follows: first payments are made to Class A-1, then to Class M-1, then to Class B-1, and then finally Class B-2. The losses, however, are realized in reverse order; that is, B-2, B-1, M-1, and finally A-1.

SECTION V AUTO LOAN-BACKED SECURITIES

Auto loan-backed securities are issued by

1. the financial subsidiaries of auto manufacturers (domestic and foreign)
2. commercial banks
3. independent finance companies and small financial institutions specializing in auto loans

Auto loans can range in maturity from three years to six years.

A. Cash Flow and Prepayments

The cash flow for auto loan-backed securities consists of regularly scheduled monthly loan payments (interest and scheduled principal repayments) and any prepayments. For securities backed by auto loans, prepayments result from (1) sales and trade-ins requiring full payoff of the loan, (2) repossession and subsequent resale of the automobile, (3) loss or destruction of the vehicle, (4) payoff of the loan with cash to save on the interest cost, and (5) refinancing of the loan at a lower interest cost.

Prepayments due to repossession and subsequent resale are sensitive to the economic cycle. In recessionary economic periods, prepayments due to this factor increase. While refinancings may be a major reason for prepayments of mortgage loans, they are of minor importance for automobile loans. Moreover, the interest rates for the automobile loans underlying some deals are substantially below market rates since they are offered by manufacturers as part of a sales promotion.

Prepayments for auto loan-backed securities are measured in terms of the **absolute prepayment speed**, denoted by ABS. The ABS is the monthly prepayment expressed as a percentage of the original collateral amount. As explained in the previous chapter, the SMM (monthly CPR) expresses prepayments based on the prior month's balance.

There is a mathematical relationship between the SMM and the ABS measures. Letting M denote the number of months after loan origination, the SMM rate can be calculated from the ABS rate using the following formula:

$$\text{SMM} = \frac{\text{ABS}}{1 - [\text{ABS} \times (M - 1)]}$$

where the ABS and SMM rates are expressed in decimal form.

For example, if the ABS rate is 1.5% (i.e., 0.015) at month 14 after origination, then the SMM rate is 1.86%, as shown below:

$$\text{SMM} = \frac{0.015}{1 - [0.015 \times (14 - 1)]} = 0.0186 = 1.86\%$$

The ABS rate can be calculated from the SMM rate using the following formula:

$$\text{ABS} = \frac{\text{SMM}}{1 + [\text{SMM} \times (M - 1)]}$$

For example, if the SMM rate at month 9 after origination is 1.3%, then the ABS rate is:

$$\text{ABS} = \frac{0.013}{1 + [0.013 \times (9 - 1)]} = 0.0118 = 1.18\%$$

Historically, when measured in terms of SMM rate, auto loans have experienced SMMs that increase as the loans season.

PRACTICE QUESTION 4

a. If the ABS for a security is 2% at month 11, what is the corresponding SMM?

b. If the SMM for a security is 1.7% at month 21, what is the corresponding ABS?

B. Payment Structure

There are auto loan-backed deals that are passthrough structures and paythrough structures. A typical passthrough structure for an auto loan-backed deal is as follows:[9]

Tranche	Amount ($)	Average Life (Years)	Coupon Rate
A	$187,050,000	1.87	Fixed
B	18,499,000	1.87	Fixed
IO	6,000,000	1.46	Fixed

In this typical passthrough structure there is a senior tranche (A) and a subordinate tranche (B). There is also an interest-only class. While more deals are structured as passthroughs, this structure is typically used for smaller deals.

Larger deals usually have a paythrough structure. A typical auto loan-backed paythrough structure is as follows:[10]

---

[9] Thomas Zimmerman and Leo Burrell, "Auto Loan-Backed Securities," Chapter 4 in Anand K. Bhattacharya and Frank J. Fabozzi (eds.) *Asset-Backed Securities* (New Hope, PA: Frank J. Fabozzi Associates), Exhibit 7, p. 92. Zimmerman and Burrel obtained this information from Prudential Securities' IMPACT data base.

[10] Zimmerman and Burrell, "Auto Loan-Backed Securities," p. 92.

Tranche	Amount ($)	Average Life (Years)	Coupon Rate
A1	$250,000,000	0.2	Fixed
A2	545,000,000	0.8	Floating
A3	400,000,000	1.9	Fixed
A4	248,760,000	3.0	Fixed
B	56,240	3.3	Fixed

In this typical paythrough structure, the senior tranches are further tranched to create a range of average lives. The subordinate tranche is not tranched further.

SECTION VI
STUDENT LOAN-BACKED SECURITIES

Student loans are made to cover college cost (undergraduate, graduate, and professional programs such as medical and law school) and tuition for a wide range of vocational and trade schools. Securities backed by student loans, popularly referred to as SLABS (student loan asset-backed securities), have similar structural features as the other asset-backed securities we discussed above.

The student loans that have been most commonly securitized are those that are made under the Federal Family Education Loan Program (FFELP). Under this program, the government makes loans to students via private lenders. The decision by private lenders to extend a loan to a student is not based on the applicant's ability to repay the loan. If a default of a loan occurs and the loan has been properly serviced, then the government will guarantee up to 98% of the principal plus accrued interest.[11]

Loans that are not part of a government guarantee program are called **alternative loans**. These loans are basically consumer loans and the lender's decision to extend an alternative loan will be based on the ability of the applicant to repay the loan. Alternative loans have been securitized.

A. Issuers

Congress created Fannie Mae and Freddie Mac to provide liquidity in the mortgage market by allowing these government sponsored enterprises to buy mortgage loans in the secondary market. Congress created the Student Loan Marketing Association (nicknamed "Sallie Mae") as a government sponsored enterprise to purchase student loans in the secondary market and to securitize pools of student loans. Since its first issuance in 1995, Sallie Mae is now the major issuer of SLABS and its issues are viewed as the benchmark issues. Other entities that issue SLABS are either traditional corporate entities (e.g., the Money Store and PNC Bank) or non-profit organizations (Michigan Higher Education Loan Authority and the California Educational Facilities Authority). The SLABS of the latter typically are issued as tax-exempt securities and therefore trade in the municipal market. In recent years, several not-for-profit entities have changed their charter and applied for "for profit" treatment.

B. Cash Flow

Let's first look at the cash flow for the student loans themselves. There are different types of student loans under the FFELP including subsidized and unsubsidized Stafford loans, Parental Loans for Undergraduate Students (PLUS), and Supplemental Loans to Students (SLS). These loans involve three periods with respect to the borrower's payments — deferment period, grace period, and loan repayment period. Typically, student loans work as follows. While a student is in school, no payments are made by the student on the loan. This is the **deferment period**. Upon leaving school, the student is extended a **grace period** of usually six month when no payments on the loan must be made. After this period, payments are made on the loan by the borrower.

---

[11] Actually, depending on the origination date, the guarantee can be up to 100%.

Prior to July 1, 1998, the reference rate for student loans originated under FFELP was the 3-month Treasury bill rate plus a margin of either 250 basis points (during the deferment and grace periods) or 310 basis points (during the repayment period). Since July 1, 1998, the Higher Education Act changed the reference rate to the 10-year Treasury note. Specifically, the interest rate is the 10-year Treasury note rate plus 100 basis points. The spread over the reference rate varies with the cycle period for the loan.

Typically, non-Sallie Mae issues have been LIBOR-based floaters. For Sallie Mae issues, there is an indirect government guarantee. Sallie Mae has typically issued SLABS indexed to the 3-month Treasury bill rate. However, late in the second quarter of 1999, Sallie Mae issued bonds in which the buyer of the 2-year average life tranche had the choice of receiving either LIBOR plus 8 basis points or the 3-month Treasury bill rate plus 87 basis points. There are available funds caps in SLABS because of the different reference rates for the loans and the securities.

Prepayments typically occur due to defaults or loan consolidation. Even if there is no loss of principal faced by the investor when defaults occur, the investor is still exposed to contraction risk. This is the risk that the investor must reinvest the proceeds at a lower spread and in the case of a bond purchased at a premium, the premium will be lost. Studies have shown student loan prepayments are insensitive to the level of interest rates. Consolidations of a loan occur when the student who has loans over several years combines them into a single loan. The proceeds from the consolidation are distributed to the original lender and, in turn, distributed to the bondholders.

SECTION VII
SBA LOAN-
BACKED
SECURITIES

The Small Business Administration (SBA) is an agency of the U.S. government empowered to guarantee loans made by approved SBA lenders to qualified borrowers. The loans are backed by the full faith and credit of the government. Most SBA loans are variable-rate loans where the reference rate is the prime rate. The rate on the loan is reset monthly on the first of the month or quarterly on the first of January, April, July, and October. SBA regulations specify the maximum coupon allowable in the secondary market. Newly originated loans have maturities between 5 and 25 years.

The Small Business Secondary Market Improvement Act passed in 1984 permitted the pooling of SBA loans. When pooled, the underlying loans must have similar terms and features. The maturities typically used for pooling loans are 7, 10, 15, 20, and 25 years. Loans without caps are not pooled with loans that have caps.

Most variable-rate SBA loans make monthly payments consisting of interest and principal repayment. The amount of the monthly payment for an individual loan is determined as follows. Given the coupon formula of the prime rate plus the loan's quoted margin, the interest rate is determined for each loan. Given the interest rate, a level payment amortization schedule is determined. It is this level payment that is paid for the next month until the coupon rate is reset.

The monthly cash flow that the investor in an SBA-backed security receives consists of

- the coupon interest based on the coupon rate set for the period
- the scheduled principal repayment (i.e., scheduled amortization)
- prepayments

Prepayments for SBA-backed securities are measured in terms of CPR. Voluntary prepayments can be made by the borrower without any penalty. There are several factors contributing to the prepayment speed of a pool of SBA loans. A factor affecting prepayments is the maturity date of the loan. It has been found that the fastest speeds on SBA loans and pools occur for shorter maturities.[12] The purpose of the loan also affects prepayments. There are loans for working capital purposes and loans to finance real estate construction or acquisition. It has been observed that SBA pools with maturities of 10 years or less made for working capital purposes tend to prepay at the fastest speed. In contrast, loans backed by real estate that are long maturities tend to prepay at a slow speed. All other factors constant, pools that have capped loans tend to prepay more slowly than pools of uncapped loans.

SECTION VIII CREDIT CARD RECEIVABLE-BACKED SECURITIES

Credit card receivable-backed securities are backed by credit card receivables. Credit cards are issued by:

1. banks (e.g., Visa and MasterCard)
2. retailers (e.g., JC Penney and Sears)
3. travel and entertainment companies (e.g., American Express)

A. Master Trust Structure

Credit card deals are structured as a **master trust**. With a master trust the issuer can sell several series from the same trust. For example, consider the following two deals: Sears Credit Account Master Trust II, Series 1995-4 and Standard Credit Card Master Trust I Series 1995-A.

Sears offers several open-end revolving credit plans. From these various plans, Sears generates a portfolio of receivables. As of July 1995, the master trust was comprised of $4 billion of principal receivables. These receivables were randomly selected from the entire portfolio of receivables of Sears Roebuck and Co. About 38% of the accounts had credit limits of $1,999 and about 61% were seasoned at least five years. All series issued from this Master Trust II share in the cash flow from the pool of receivables that were randomly selected. Information about the specific accounts in the pool selected for Master Trust II was not disclosed; however, because of the random selection process, an investor might expect that the composition did not differ significantly from the entire portfolio of receivables. Each time a new series of securities is issued, more receivables are randomly selected to be added to the trust. The Sears Credit Account Master Trust II, Series 1995-4 was the sixth of a series issued by Group One of Sears Credit Account Master Trust II. There were two classes of certificates that were offered to the public: Class A Master Trust Certificates and Class B Master Trust Certificates. The principal for the former was $500 million and for the latter $22.5 million.

The Standard Credit Card Master Trust I is a Citibank master trust. The master trust as of May 22, 1995 was comprised of 20,092,662 accounts with principal receivables of approximately $24.3 billion and approximately $290.8 million of finance charge receivables. The average credit limit was $3,282 and the average principal balance of the accounts was $1,210. About 69% of the accounts were seasoned more than two years. The SCCMTI Series 1995A is the twenty-second in a series issued by Group One of Standard Credit Card Master Trust I and is a Euro issue. There was only one certificate offered to the public — $300 million of Floating Rate Class A Credit Card Participation Certificates.

---

[12] Donna Faulk, "SBA Loan-Backed Securities," Chapter 10 in *Asset-Backed Securities*.

The 10 largest Master Trusts as of March 1999 were: (1) MBNA Master Trust II, (2) Citibank, (3) First USA, (4) Discover, (5) Chase, (6) First Chicago, (7) AT&T Universal, (8) Sears Master Trust II, (9) Capital One, and (10) Fleet/Advanta.[13]

B. Cash Flow

For a pool of credit card receivables, the cash flow consists of finance charges collected, fees, and principal. Finance charges collected represent the periodic interest the credit card borrower is charged based on the unpaid balance after the grace period. Fees include late payment fees and any annual membership fees.

Interest to security holders is paid periodically (e.g, monthly, quarterly, or semiannually). The interest rate may be fixed or floating — roughly half of the securities are floaters. The floating rate is uncapped.

A credit card receivable-backed security is a nonamortizing security. For a specified period of time, referred to as the **lockout period** or **revolving period**, the principal payments made by credit card borrowers comprising the pool are retained by the trustee and reinvested in additional receivables to maintain the size of the pool. The lockout period can vary from 18 months to 10 years. So, during the lockout period, the cash flow that is paid out to security holders is based on finance charges collected and fees.

After the lockout period, the principal is no longer reinvested but paid to investors. This period is referred to as the **principal-amortization period** and the various types of structures are described later.

C. Payment Structure

There are three different amortization structures that have been used in credit card receivable-backed security deals: (1) passthrough structure, (2) controlled-amortization structure, and (3) bullet-payment structure. The latter two are the more common. One source reports that 80% of the deals are bullet structures and the balance are controlled amortization structures.[14]

In a **passthrough structure**, the principal cash flows from the credit card accounts are paid to the security holders on a pro rata basis. In a **controlled-amortization structure**, a scheduled principal amount is established, similar to the principal window for a PAC bond. The scheduled principal amount is sufficiently low so that the obligation can be satisfied even under certain stress scenarios, where cash flow is decreased due to defaults or slower repayment by borrowers. The security holder is paid the lesser of the scheduled principal amount and the pro rata amount. In a **bullet-payment structure**, the security holder receives the entire amount in one distribution. Since there is no assurance that the entire amount can be paid in one lump sum, the procedure is for the trustee to place principal monthly into an account that generates sufficient interest to make periodic interest payments and accumulate the principal to be repaid. These deposits are made in the months shortly before the scheduled bullet payment. This type of structure is also often called a **soft bullet** because the maturity is technically not guaranteed, but is almost always satisfied. The time period over which the principal is accumulated is called the **accumulation period**.

D. Performance of the Portfolio of Receivables

There are several concepts that must be understood in order to assess the performance of the portfolio of receivables and the ability of the issuer to meet its interest obligation and repay principal as scheduled.

We begin with the concept of the **gross portfolio yield**. This yield includes finance charges collected and fees. **Charge-offs** represent the accounts charged off as

---

[13] Anthony Thompson, *Credit Card Surveillance Chart Book*, Goldman Sachs, Fixed Income Research (March 11, 1999), p. 1.

[14] Thompson, "MBNA Tests the Waters."

uncollectible. **Net portfolio yield** is equal to gross portfolio yield minus charge-offs. The net portfolio yield is important because it is from this yield that the bondholders will be paid. So, for example, if the average yield (WAC) that must be paid to the various tranches in the structure is 5% and the net portfolio yield for the month is only 4.5%, there is the risk that the bondholder obligations will not be satisfied.

Delinquencies are the percentages of receivables that are past due for a specified number of months, usually 30, 60, and 90 days. They are considered an indicator of potential future charge-offs.

The **monthly payment rate** (MPR) expresses the monthly payment (which includes finance charges, fees, and any principal repayment) of a credit card receivable portfolio as a percentage of credit card debt outstanding in the previous month. For example, suppose a $500 million credit card receivable portfolio in January realized $50 million of payments in February. The MPR would then be 10% ($50 million divided by $500 million).

There are two reasons why the MPR is important. First, if the MPR reaches an extremely low level, there is a chance that there will be extension risk with respect to the principal payments on the bonds. Second, if the MPR is very low, then there is a chance that there will not be sufficient cash flows to pay off principal. This is one of the events that could trigger early amortization of the principal (described below).

At issuance, portfolio yield, charge-offs, delinquency, and MPR information are provided in the prospectus. Information about portfolio performance is then available from Bloomberg, the rating agencies, and dealers.

E. Early Amortization Triggers

There are provisions in credit card receivable-backed securities that require early amortization of the principal if certain events occur. Such provisions, which are referred to as either **early amortization** or **rapid amortization**, are included to safeguard the credit quality of the issue. The only way that the principal cash flows can be altered is by the triggering of the early amortization provision.

Typically, early amortization allows for the rapid return of principal in the event that the 3-month average excess spread earned on the receivables falls to zero or less. When early amortization occurs, the credit card tranches are retired sequentially (i.e., first the AAA bond then the AA rated bond, etc.). This is accomplished by paying the principal payments made by the credit card borrowers to the investors instead of using them to purchase more receivables. The length of time until the return of principal is largely a function of the monthly payment rate. For example, suppose that a AAA tranche is 82% of the overall deal. If the monthly payment rate is 11% then the AAA tranche would return principal over a 7.5-month period (82%/11%). An 18% monthly payment rate would return principal over a 4.5-month period (82%/18%).

SECTION IX COLLATERALIZED BOND OBLIGATIONS

A **collateralized bond obligation** (CBO) is an asset-backed security backed by a diversified pool of one or more of the following types of debt obligations:

1. non-investment grade (i.e., high yield) corporate bonds
2. emerging market bonds
3. bank loans to corporate entities

When an asset-backed security has only bank loans, it is referred to as a **collateralized loan obligation** (CLO).

There is an asset manager responsible for managing the portfolio of debt obligations. There are restrictions imposed by the rating agencies as to what the asset manager may do and certain tests that must be satisfied for the tranches in the CBO to maintain their credit rating at the time of issuance. We'll discuss some of these requirements below.

The typical structure of a CBO is as follows. There is (1) a senior tranche, (2) different layers of subordinate or junior debt tranches, and (3) an equity tranche. The senior tranche is between 70% and 80% of the deal and receives a floating-rate payment in order to attract floating-rate investors. The junior tranches, in contrast, receive a fixed coupon rate. So, the collateral from the diversified pool of debt obligations is going to pay the tranche holders, the majority of whom (i.e., the senior tranche investors) are being paid a floating rate. Do the debt obligations pay a fixed or floating rate? While the bank loans are typically floating rate, the other debt obligations in which the asset manager may invest typically pay a fixed rate. Now that presents a problem — paying the majority of the tranche investors a floating rate when the majority of the debt obligations pay a fixed rate.

To deal with this problem, the asset manager uses derivative instruments to be able to convert fixed-rate payments into floating-rate payments. In particular, interest rate swaps are used. We will discuss interest rate swaps in Chapter 7. Because of the mismatch between the nature of the cash flows of the debt obligations in which the asset manager invests and the floating-rate liability for the senior tranche, the asset manager must use an interest rate swap. A rating agency will require the use of swaps to eliminate this mismatch.

The junior tranches receive a fixed rate. The rate is a spread over a comparable maturity Treasury security. The amount of the spread varies with market conditions and the credit rating of a junior tranche. For example, the fixed rate for a junior tranche might be the Treasury rate plus 185 basis points.

The equity tranche receives any remaining interest that is received from the collateral but not paid to the senior and junior tranches. To understand how the equity tranche generates cash flows, consider again the basic CBO structure in terms of collateral and debt tranches and look at what is being received from the collateral and what is being paid to the senior and junior tranches. Depending on market conditions at the time the CBO is issued, the fixed-rate debt obligations that the asset manager invests in will offer a spread to Treasury securities that is quite large to reflect the low credit quality of the bonds purchased. Let's assume the following:

Assumption 1: The CBO is a $100 million structure. That is, the assets purchased will be $100 million.

Assumption 2: The collateral consists of bonds that all mature in 10 years and the coupon rate for every bond is the 10-Treasury rate plus 400 basis points.

Assumption 3: Suppose that the senior tranche comprises 80% of the structure ($80 million) and pays interest based on the following coupon formula (remember the senior tranche is a floating-rate tranche): LIBOR plus 70 basis points.

Assumption 4: There is only one junior tranche ($10 million) with a coupon rate that is fixed. The coupon rate is the Treasury rate plus 200 basis points.

Assumption 5: The asset manager enters into an agreement with another party in which it agrees to pay a fixed rate each year equal to the 10-year Treasury rate plus 100 basis points and receive LIBOR. The notional amount of the agreement is $80 million.

The last assumption may be difficult at this point to appreciate since we have not discussed interest rate swaps. For now, we'll be able to layout the principle without setting forth what an interest swap is. Keep in mind, the goal is to show how the equity tranche can expect to generate a return.

Note that given that the senior tranche is $80 million and the junior tranche is $10 million, the equity tranche must be $10 million ($100 million minus $90 million).

Let's assume that the 10-year Treasury rate at the time the CBO is issued is 7%. Now we can walk through the cash flows for each year. Look first at the collateral. The collateral will pay interest each year (assuming no defaults) equal to the 10-year Treasury rate of 7% plus 400 basis points (Assumption 2). So the interest will be:

Interest from collateral: $11\% \times \$100,000,000 = \$11,000,000$

Now let's determine the interest that must be paid to the senior and junior tranches. For the senior tranche, the interest payment (Assumption 3) will be:

Interest to senior tranche: $\$80,000,000 \times (\text{LIBOR} + 70 \text{ bp})$

The coupon rate for the junior tranche is 7% plus 200 basis points (Assumption 4). So, the coupon rate is 9% and the interest is:

Interest to junior tranche: $9\% \times \$10,000,000 = \$900,000$

Finally, let's look at the interest rate swap. In this agreement, the asset manager is agreeing to pay some third party (we'll call this party the "swap counterparty") each year 7% (the 10-year Treasury rate) plus 100 basis points, or 8%. But 8% of what? In an interest rate swap, payments are based on a notional amount. In our illustration (Assumption 5), the notional amount is $80 million. The reason the asset manager selected the $80 million was because this is the amount of principal for the senior tranche. So, the asset manager pays to the swap counterparty:

Interest to swap counterparty: $8\% \times \$80,000,000 = \$6,400,000$

The interest payment received from the swap counterparty (Assumption 5) is LIBOR based on a notional amount of $80 million. That is,

Interest from swap counterparty: $\$80,000,000 \times \text{LIBOR}$

Now we can put this all together. Let's look at the interest coming into the CBO:

Interest from collateral	$11,000,000
Interest from swap counterparty	$80,000,000 × LIBOR
Total interest received	$11,000,000 + $80,000,000 × LIBOR

The interest to be paid out to the senior and junior tranches and to the swap counterparty include:

Interest to senior tranche..........	$80,000,000 \times (LIBOR + 70\ bp)$
Interest to junior tranche..........	$900,000
Interest to swap counterparty...	$6,400,000
Total interest paid....................	$7,300,000 + \$80,000,000 \times (LIBOR + 70\ bp)$

Netting the interest payments coming in and going out we have:

Total interest received	$11,000,000 + \$80,000,000 \times LIBOR$
− Total interest paid	$7,300,000 + \$80,000,000 \times (LIBOR + 70\ bp)$
Net interest	$3,700,000 - \$80,000,000 \times (70\ bp)$

Since 70 bp times $80 million is $560,000, the net interest remaining is $3,140,000 (= $3,700,000 − $560,000). From this amount any fees (including the asset management fee) must be paid. The balance is then the amount available to pay the equity tranche.

Obviously, some simplifying assumptions have been made. For example, it is assumed that there are no defaults. It is assumed that all of the issues are noncallable and therefore the coupon rate would not decline because issues are called. Moreover, as explained below, after some period the asset manager must begin repaying principal to the senior and junior tranches. Consequently, the interest swap must be structured to take this into account since the entire amount of the senior tranche is not outstanding for the life of the collateral. Despite the simplifying assumptions, the illustration does demonstrate the basic economics of the CBO, the need for the use of an interest rate swap, and how the equity tranche will realize a return.

A. Phases of a CBO

There are three phases in the life of a CBO. The first phase is a **startup phase** or **ramp phase**. In this phase, which is one or two months, the asset manager assembles the portfolio with the proceeds received from the sale of the CBO tranches. Once the portfolio is assembled, the manager monitors the portfolio and is responsible for reinvesting any principal repayments due to any calls or proceeds received from any defaulted issues. This phase is called the **reinvestment phase**. This phase varies from 3 year to 5 years. Finally, principal payments to the senior and junior tranches must be made over the balance of the CBO's life. This phase is called the **pay down phase**.

B. Activities of the Asset Manager

The CBO structure described above is the type that is predominately issued today. The CBO is structured to generate cash flow for the senior and junior tranches *without* the active trading of bonds. Older CBO deals were typically structured so that the cash flow for the structure was based on the active trading of bonds. The cash flow needed to pay principal and interest to the senior and junior tranches had to be generated from capital gains as well as coupon interest. With the difficulties encountered in the high-yield bond sector in the late 1980s and early 1990s, CBOs structured in this way lost their appeal and are no longer issued. Only those CBOs with the type of structure described above are now issued.

Because the cash flows from the structure are designed to accomplish the objective for each tranche, restrictions are imposed on the asset managers. The asset manager is not free to buy and sell bonds. The conditions for disposing of issues held are specified and are usually driven by credit risk management. Also, in assembling the portfolio during the startup phase, the asset manager must meet certain requirements set forth by the rating agency or agencies that rate the deal. These requirements have to do with constructing a diversified portfolio and minimum ratings for the issues acquired. The asset manager during the reinvestment and pay down phases must monitor the collateral to ensure that certain tests or covenants are being met.

SECTION X
KEY POINTS

❏ *The collateral for an asset-backed security can be either amortizing assets (e.g., auto loans and closed-end home equity loans) or nonamortizing assets (e.g., credit card receivables).*

❏ *For amortizing assets, projection of the cash flow requires projecting prepayments.*

❏ *For nonamortizing assets, prepayments by an individual borrower do not apply since there is no schedule of principal repayments.*

❏ *One factor that may affect prepayments is the prevailing level of interest rates relative to the interest rate on the loan.*

❏ *Since a default is a prepayment (an involuntary prepayment), prepayment modeling for an asset-backed security backed by amortizing assets requires a model for projecting the amount that will be recovered and when it will be recovered.*

❏ *Cash flow analysis can be performed on a pool level or a loan level.*

❏ *Since the maturity of an asset-backed security is not a meaningful parameter, the average life of the security is calculated.*

❏ *Asset-backed securities must be credit enhanced; that is, there must be support from somewhere to absorb a certain amount of defaults.*

❏ *Credit enhancement levels are determined relative to a specific rating desired for a security.*

❏ *There are two general types of credit enhancement structures: external and internal.*

❏ *External credit enhancements come in the form of third-party guarantees that provide for first loss protection against losses up to a specified level.*

❏ *The most common forms of external credit enhancements are (1) a corporate guarantee, (2) a letter of credit, and (3) bond insurance.*

❏ *The most common forms of internal credit enhancements are reserve funds and senior/subordinate structures.*

❏ *The senior/subordinated structure is the most widely used internal credit support structure with a typical structure having a senior tranche and one or more non-senior tranches.*

❏ *For mortgage-related asset-backed securities and nonagency mortgage-backed securities there is a concern that prepayments will erode the protection afforded by the non-senior (i.e., subordinated) tranches after the deal closes.*

❏ *A shifting interest structure is used to protect against a deterioration in the senior tranche's credit protection due to prepayments by redistributing the prepayments disproportionately from the non-senior tranches to the senior tranche according to a specified schedule.*

❏ *The creation of a senior-subordinated structure is a means of credit tranching – that is, reallocating credit risk from one tranche to another.*

❏ *When the senior tranche is carved up to create several senior tranches with different exposures to prepayment risk, the structure is referred to as a pay through security.*

❏ *Typically, the subordinated or non-senior tranches are not carved up to create tranches with different exposure to prepayment risk.*

❏ *With an asset-backed security, one of the following optional clean-up call provisions may be granted to the trustee: (1) percent of collateral call, (2) percent of bonds, (3) percent of tranche, (4) call on or after specified date, (5) latter of percent, or (6) date auction call.*

❏ *There may be a clean-up call provision in an asset-backed security that grants an insurer the right to call the bonds if the collateral's cumulative loss history reaches a predetermined level.*

❏ *The collateral for a home equity loan is typically a first lien on residential property and the loan fails to satisfy the underwriting standards for inclusion in a loan pool of Ginnie Mae, Fannie Mae, or Freddie Mac because of the borrower's impaired credit history or too high a payment-to-income ratio.*

❏ *Typically, a home equity loan is used by a borrower to consolidate consumer debt using the current home as collateral rather than to obtain funds to purchase a new home.*

❏ *Home equity loans can be either closed end (i.e., structured the same way as a fully amortizing residential mortgage loan) or open end (i.e., homeowner given a credit line).*

❏ *The monthly cash flow for a home equity loan-backed security backed by closed-end HELs consists of (1) net interest, (2) regularly scheduled principal payments, and (3) prepayments.*

❏ *Several studies by Wall Street firms have found that the key difference between the prepayment behavior of HELs and traditional residential mortgages is the important role played by the credit characteristics of the borrower.*

❏ *Studies strongly suggests that borrower credit quality is the most important determinant of prepayments, with the sensitivity of refinancing to interest rates being greater the higher the borrower's credit quality.*

❏ *The prospectus of an HEL offering contains a base case prepayment assumption regarding the initial speed and the amount of time until the collateral is expected to season.*

❏ *A prospectus prepayment curve is a multiple of the base case prepayments assumed in the prospectus (i.e., base case is equal to 100% PPC).*

❏ *Typically, home equity loan-backed securities are securitized by both closed-end fixed-rate and adjustable-rate (or variable-rate) HELs.*

❏ *Unlike a typical floater which has a cap that is fixed throughout the security's life, the available funds cap of a HEL floater is variable and depends on the amount of funds generated by the net coupon on the principal, less any fees.*

❏ *To provide stability to the average life of a senior tranche, closed-end home equity loan transactions will include either a non-accelerating senior (NAS) tranche or a planned amortization class (PAC) tranche.*

❏ *A NAS tranche receives principal payments according to a schedule based not on a dollar amount for a given month, but instead on a schedule that specifies for each month the share of pro rata principal that must be distributed to the NAS tranche.*

❏ *For a PAC tranche a schedule of the dollar amount for each month is specified.*

❏ *Almost all home equity lines of credit (HELOC) are floating-rate loans, with the interest rate typically reset monthly to the prime rate plus a spread.*

❏ *The securities created in HELOC deals are floating-rate tranches based on a spread over 1-month LIBOR.*

❑ *For HELOC deals, there is a revolving period, an amortization period, and a rapid amortization period.*

❑ *Auto loan-backed securities are issued by the financial subsidiaries of auto manufacturers, commercial banks, and independent finance companies and small financial institutions specializing in auto loans.*

❑ *The cash flow for auto loan-backed securities consists of regularly scheduled monthly loan payments (interest and scheduled principal repayments), and any prepayments.*

❑ *Prepayments on auto loans are not sensitive to interest rates.*

❑ *Prepayments on auto loan-backed securities are measured in terms of the absolute prepayment speed (denoted ABS) which measures monthly prepayments relative to the original collateral amount.*

❑ *Auto loan-backed deals can have a passthrough structure (used for smaller deals) or a paythrough structure (used for larger deals).*

❑ *Manufactured housing-backed securities are backed by loans on manufactured homes (i.e., homes built at a factory and then transported to a site).*

❑ *Manufactured housing-backed securities are issued by Ginnie Mae and private entities, the former being guaranteed by the full faith and credit of the U.S. government.*

❑ *A manufactured housing loan's cash flow consists of net interest, regularly scheduled principal, and prepayments.*

❑ *Prepayments are more stable for manufactured housing-backed securities because they are not sensitive to refinancing.*

❑ *SLABS are asset-backed securities backed by student loans.*

❑ *The student loans most commonly securitized are those that are made under the Federal Family Education Loan Program (FFELP) whereby the government makes loans to students via private lenders and the government guaranteeing up to 98% of the principal plus accrued interest.*

❑ *Alternative loans are student loans that are not part of a government guarantee program and are basically consumer loans.*

❑ *In contrast to government guaranteed loans, the lender's decision to extend an alternative loan is based on the ability of the applicant to repay the loan.*

❑ *Student loans involve three periods with respect to the borrower's payments — deferment period, grace period, and loan repayment period.*

❑ *Prepayments typically occur due to defaults or a loan consolidation (i.e, a loan to consolidate loans over several years into a single loan).*

❑ *Issuers of SLABs include the Student Loan Marketing Association (Sallie Mae, a government sponsored enterprise), traditional corporate entities, and non-profit organizations.*

❑ *Small Business Administration (SBA) loans are backed by the full faith and credit of the U.S. government.*

❑ *Most SBA loans are variable-rate loans where the reference rate is the prime rate with monthly payments consisting of interest and principal repayment.*

❏ *Prepayments for SBA-backed securities are measured in terms of CPR.*

❏ *Voluntary prepayments can be made by the SBA borrower without any penalty.*

❏ *Factors contributing to the prepayment speed of a pool of SBA loans are (1) the maturity date of the loan (it has been found that the fastest speeds on SBA loans and pools occur for shorter maturities), (2) the purpose of the loan, and (3) whether or not there is a cap on the loan.*

❏ *Credit card receivable-backed securities are backed by credit card receivables for credit cards issued by banks, retailers, and travel and entertainment companies.*

❏ *Credit card deals are structured as a master trust.*

❏ *For a pool of credit card receivables, the cash flow consists of finance charges collected, fees, and principal.*

❏ *The principal repayment of a credit card receivable-backed security is not amortized; instead, during the lockout period, the principal payments made by credit card borrowers are retained by the trustee and reinvested in additional receivables and after the lockout period (the principal-amortization period), the principal received by the trustee is no longer reinvested but paid to investors.*

❏ *There are provisions in credit card receivable-backed securities that require early amortization of the principal if certain events occur.*

❏ *Since for credit card receivable-backed securities the concept of prepayments does not apply, participants look at the monthly payment rate (MPR) which expresses the monthly payment (which includes interest, finance charges, and any principal) of a credit card receivable portfolio as a percentage of debt outstanding in the previous month.*

❏ *The MPR for credit card receivable-backed securities is important because (1) if it reaches an extremely low level, there is a chance that there will be extension risk with respect to the principal payments and (2) if the MPR is very low, there is a chance that there will not be sufficient cash flows to pay off principal (which can trigger early amortization of the principal).*

❏ *To assess the performance of the portfolio of credit card receivables and the ability of the issuer to meet its interest obligation and repay principal as scheduled, an investor must analyze the gross portfolio yield (which includes finance charges collected and fees), charge-offs (which represents the accounts charged off as uncollectible), the net portfolio yield, gross portfolio yield minus charge-offs, and delinquencies (the percentage of receivable that are past due as specified number of months).*

❏ *There are three amortization structures that have been used in credit card receivable-backed security structures: (1) passthrough structure, (2) controlled-amortization structure, and (3) bullet-payment structure.*

❏ *A collateralized bond obligation (CBO) is an asset-backed security backed by a diversified pool of one or more of the following types of debt obligations: non-investment grade corporate bonds, emerging market bonds, and/or bank loans to corporate entities.*

❏ *There is an asset manager in a CBO responsible for assembling and managing the debt obligations in which the asset manager may invest, subject to restrictions to prevent active bond management.*

❏ *The typical structure of a CBO consists of a senior tranche (the majority of the structure) that receives a floating rate, different layers of subordinate or junior debt tranches that receive a fixed coupon rate, and an equity tranche.*

❑ *Because of the mismatch between a CBO's collateral (which primarily pays a fixed rate) and the floating-rate payment made to the senior tranche, the asset manager must employ derivatives such as an interest rate swap to better match the interest payments received and paid out.*

❑ *In CBO structures today, there is reliance on the cash flow from the structure to satisfy the CBO obligations rather than active trading by the asset manager.*

END OF CHAPTER QUESTIONS

1. Suppose that the collateral for an asset-backed securities structure has a gross weighted average coupon of 8.6%. The servicing fee is 50 basis points. The tranches issued have a weighted average coupon rate of 7.1%. What is the excess servicing spread?

2. Suppose that the structure for an asset-backed security transaction is as follows:

   senior tranche $220 million
   subordinated tranche 1 $ 50 million
   subordinated tranche 2 $ 30 million

   and that the value of the collateral for the structure is $320 million. Subordinated tranche 2 is the first loss tranche.

   a. How much is the overcollateralization in this structure?

   b. What is the amount of the loss for each tranche if losses due to defaults over the life of the structure total $15 million?

   c. What is the amount of the loss for each tranche if losses due to defaults over the life of the structure total $35 million?

   d. What is the amount of the loss for each tranche if losses due to defaults over the life of the structure total $85 million?

   e. What is the amount of the loss for each tranche if losses due to defaults over the life of the structure total $110 million?

3. What is the difference between a passthrough structure and a pay-through structure?

4. a. Explain why individual loans that are of a non-amortizing type are not subject to prepayment risk.

   b. Explain why securities backed by collateral consisting of non-amortizing assets may expose an investor to prepayment risk.

5. An asset-backed security has been credit enhanced with a letter of credit from a bank with a single A credit rating. If this is the only form of credit enhancement, explain why this issue is unlikely to receive a triple A credit rating.

6. Why is it critical for insurance companies that offer bond insurance for asset-backed security transactions to maintain a triple A credit rating?

7. What is the difference between a cash reserve fund and an excess servicing spread account?

8. Why is the assumption about how defaults may occur over the life of an asset-backed security transaction important in assessing the effectiveness of excess servicing spread as a form of internal credit enhancement?

9. a. Explain why a senior-subordinated structure is a form of internal credit enhancement.

   b. Explain the need for a shifting interest mechanism in a senior-subordinated structure when the underlying assets are subject to prepayments.

10. a. What is meant by the "senior prepayment percentage" in a shifting interest mechanism of a senior-subordinated structure?

    b. Why does a shifting interest mechanism affect the cash flow of the senior tranche and increase the senior tranche's exposure to contraction risk?

11. What is a "call on or after specified date" clean-up call provision?

12. a. Distinguish between the cash flow of a closed-end home equity loan and an open-end home equity loan?

    b. Indicate whether you agree or disagree with the following statement: "Typically, closed-end home equity loans are loans to borrowers of the highest credit quality."

    c. What is the reference rate that is typically used in setting the periodic mortgage rate for an open-end home equity loan?

13. The Izzobaf Home Equity Loan Trust 2000-1 is backed by fixed-rate closed-end home equity loans. The base case prepayment for this deal is specified in the prospectus as follows:

> The model used with respect to the loans (the "prepayment ramp") assumes that the home equity loans prepay at a rate of 5% CPR in the first month after origination, and an additional 1.8% each month thereafter until the 12th month. Beginning in the 12th month and each month thereafter, the prepayment ramp assumes a prepayment rate of 24.8% CPR.

What is the CPR assuming 200% PPC for the following months

Month	CPR	Month	CPR	Month	CPR
1		11		30	
2		12		125	
3		13		150	
4		14		200	
5		15		250	
6		16		275	
7		17		300	
8		18		325	
9		19		350	
10		20		360	

14. James Tellmen is an assistant portfolio manager for a mortgage-backed securities portfolio. Mr. Tellmen's responsibility is to analyze agency mortgage-backed securities. Recently, the portfolio manager has been given authorization to purchase closed-end home equity loan-backed securities. Mr. Tellmen is analyzing his first structure in this sector of the asset-backed securities market. Upon reading the prospectus he finds that the base case prepayment is specified and believes that this prepayment assumption is the benchmark used in all closed-end home equity loan-backed securities. Explain why you agree or disagree with Mr. Tellmen.

15. Why is there is an available funds cap in a home equity loan-backed security in which the collateral is adjustable-rate home equity loans?

16. Suppose that the base case shifting interest percentage schedule for a closed-end home equity loan-backed security is as follows:

Years after issuance	Senior prepayment percentage
1-4	100%
5	90%
6	80%
7	50%
8	20%
after year 8	0%

a. If there are prepayments in month 36 of $100,000, how much of the prepayments is paid to the senior tranche? How much is paid to the subordinated tranches?

b. If there are prepayments in the 8th year after issuance of $100,000, how much of the prepayments is paid to the senior tranche? How much is paid to the subordinated tranches?

c. If there are prepayments in the 10th year after issuance of $100,000, how much of the prepayments is paid to the senior tranche? How much is paid to the subordinated tranches?

17. Larry Forest is an analyst reviewing for the first time a closed-end home equity loan-backed structure in order to determine whether or not to purchase the deal's senior tranche. He understands how the shifting interest percentage schedule is structured so as to provide the senior tranches with protection after the deal is closed. However, he is concerned that the schedule in the prospectus will not be adequate if the collateral's performance deteriorates (i.e., there is considerably greater losses for the collateral than expected). Explain to Mr. Forest what provision is included in the prospectus for protecting the senior tranches if the performance of the collateral deteriorates.

18. How is a non-accelerating senior tranche provided protection to reduce contraction risk and extension risk?

19. a. What are the components of the cash flow for a manufactured housing-backed security?

    b. What are the reasons why prepayments due to refinancing are not significant for manufactured housing loans?

20. a. What are the components of the cash flow for an auto loan-backed security?

    b. How important are prepayments due to refinancing for auto loans?

21. What is the difference between a single monthly mortgage rate and an absolute prepayment speed?

22. a. If the ABS for a security is 1.5% at month 21, what is the corresponding SMM?

    b. If the SMM for a security is 1.9% at month 11, what is the corresponding ABS?

23. A trustee for a pension fund is working with a consultant to develop investment guidelines for the fund's bond portfolio. The trustee felt that the fund should be able to invest in securities backed by student loans because the loans are fully guaranteed by the U.S. government. How should the consultant respond?

24. For a student loan-backed security, what is the difference between the deferment period and the grace period?

25. a. What are the components of the cash flow for a Small Business Administration-backed security?

    b. What reference rate is used for setting the coupon interest and how often is the coupon rate reset?

26. a. What is the cash flow for a credit card receivable-backed security during the lockout or revolving period?

    b. How is the principal received from credit card borrowers handled during the lockout or revolving period?

    c. Explain why you agree or disagree with the following statement: "After the lockout period, the principal is paid to bondholders in one lump sum amount at the maturity date of the security."

27. A manager of a corporate bond portfolio is considering the purchase of a credit card receivable-backed security. The manager believes that an advantage of such securities is that there is no contraction risk and no extension risk. Explain why you agree or disagree with this view.

28. a. What is meant by the monthly payment rate for a credit card deal?

    b. What is the significance of the monthly payment rate?

    c. How is the net portfolio yield determined for a credit card deal?

29. a. What is the typical collateral for a collateralized bond obligation?

    b. Explain why you agree or disagree with the following statement: "The asset manager for a CBO is free to actively manage the portfolio without any constraints."

    c. What is a typical structure for a CBO?

    d. Explain why you agree or disagree with the following statement: "By using an interest rate swap, the asset manager for a CBO increases the risk associated with meeting the obligations that must be paid to the senior tranche."

    e. What is the equity tranche in a CBO entitled to receive?

30. Consider the following CBO transaction:

    1. The CBO is a $200 million structure. That is, the assets purchased will be $200 million.

    2. The collateral consists of bonds that all mature in 8 years and the coupon rate for every bond is the 8-year Treasury rate plus 600 basis points.

3. The senior tranche comprises 75% of the structure ($150 million) and pays interest based on the following coupon formula: LIBOR plus 90 basis points.

4. There is only one junior tranche ($30 million) with a coupon rate that is fixed. The coupon rate is the 8-year Treasury rate plus 300 basis points.

5. The asset manager enters into an agreement with counterparty in which it agrees to pay the counterparty a fixed rate each year equal to the 8-year Treasury rate plus 120 basis points and receive LIBOR. The notional amount of the agreement is $150 million.

a. How much is the equity tranche in this CBO?

b. Assume that the 8-year Treasury rate at the time the CBO is issued is 6%. Assuming no defaults, what is the cash flow for each year and how is it distributed?

c. Ignoring the asset management fee, what is the amount available each year for the equity tranche?

SOLUTIONS TO END OF CHAPTER QUESTIONS

1. The excess servicing spread is determined as follows:

Gross weighted average coupon	=	8.60%
− Servicing fee	=	0.50%
Spread available to pay tranches	=	8.10%
− Net weighted average coupon	=	7.10%
Excess servicing spread	=	1.00% = 100 basis points

2. a. The amount of overcollateralization is the difference between the value of the collateral, $320 million, and the par value for all the tranches, $300 million. In this structure it is $20 million.

   b. If the losses total $15 million, then the loss is entirely absorbed by the overcollateralization. No tranche will realize a loss.

   c. through d.

	total loss	senior tranche	subordinated tranche 1	subordinated tranche 2
c.	$35 million	zero	zero	$15 million
d.	$85 million	zero	$35 million	$30 million
e.	$110 million	$10 million	$50 million	$30 million

3. In a passthrough structure, there is only one tranche at a given seniority level. That is, there is only credit tranching. In a pay-through structure, there may be more than one tranche at a given seniority level. This represents prepayment (or time) tranching. Typically, it is the senior tranche that is prepayment tranched.

4. a. For a non-amortizing loan, there is no schedule for repayment of principal. Consequently, for individual loans of this type there can be no prepayments.

   b. While there may be no prepayments for individual loans that are non-amortizing, the securities that are backed by these loans may be prepayable. For example, credit card receivable-backed securities can be prepaid under certain conditions. Such conditions are referred to as "early amortization" or "rapid amortization" events or triggers.

5. The rating agencies take the weak-link approach to credit enhancement. Typically a structure cannot receive a rating higher than the rating on any third-party providing an external guarantee. Since the question specifies that the only form of credit enhancement is the letter of credit, then the rating will not exceed the single A rating of the bank providing the letter credit. Thus, a triple A rating is not likely.

6. If an insurance company wants to offer bond insurance for an asset-backed security transaction where a triple A credit rating is sought, the insurance company must have a triple A credit rating.

7. Both a cash reserve fund and an excess servicing spread account are forms of internal credit enhancement. A cash reserve fund is provided by a deposit of cash at issuance. Excess servicing spread account is the cash available to absorb losses from the collateral after payment of interest to all the tranches and to the servicer.

8. The excess servicing spread account builds up over time in order to offset future losses. However, if losses occur early in the life of the collateral, there may not be enough time to accumulate the excess servicing spread to adequately cover future losses.

9. a. A senior-subordinated structure is a form of internal credit enhancement because it does not rely on the guarantee of a third party. Instead, the enhancement comes from within the structure by creating senior and subordinated tranches. The subordinated tranches provide credit protection for the senior tranche.

   b. Once a deal is closed, the percentage of the senior tranche and the percentage of the subordinated tranche change when the underlying assets are subject to prepayments. If the subordinated interest in a structure decreases after the deal is closed, the credit protection for the senior tranche decreases. The shifting interest mechanism seeks to prevent the senior tranche's credit protection provided by the subordinated tranche (or tranches) from declining by establishing a schedule that provides for a higher allocation of the prepayments to the senior tranche in the earlier years.

10. a. The senior prepayment percentage is the percentage of prepayments that are allocated to the senior tranche. The senior prepayment percentage is specified in the prospectus.

    b. Because the shifting interest mechanism results in a greater amount of the prepayments be paid to the senior tranche in the earlier years than in the absence of such a mechanism, the senior tranches are exposed to greater contraction risk.

11. A call on or after specified date clean-up call provision acts just like a standard call provision. The outstanding bonds in a structure can be called if either (1) the collateral outstanding reaches a predetermined level before the specified call date or (2) the call date has been reached even if the collateral outstanding is above the predetermined level.

12. a. The cash flow for a closed-end home equity loan is the same as for a standard mortgage loan: interest, regularly scheduled principal repayments (i.e., regular amortization), and prepayments. For an open-end home equity loan, during the revolving period the only payments are interest. At the end of the revolving period, the repayment of principal can be either a balloon payment or based on an amortization schedule.

    b. The statement is incorrect. Typically, a closed-end home equity loan borrower is a credit impaired borrower.

    c. The reference rate for an open-end home equity loan is the prime rate.

13. For month 1, the CPR for 100% PPC is 5%, so the CPR for 200% PPC is 10% (= 2 × 5%). For month 2, the CPR for 100% PPC is 5% plus 1.8% which is 6.8%. Therefore, the CPR for 200% PPC for month 2 is 13.6% (2 × 6.8%).
    In month 12, the CPR for 100% PPC is

    $$5\% + 1.8\% \times 11 = 24.8\%$$

Therefore, the CPR for 200% PPC is 49.6% (2 × 24.8%). For all months after month 12, the CPR for 200% CPR is 49.6%.

Month	CPR	Month	CPR	Month	CPR
1	10.0%	11	46.0%	30	49.6%
2	13.6%	12	49.6%	125	49.6%
3	17.2%	13	49.6%	150	49.6%
4	20.8%	14	49.6%	200	49.6%
5	24.4%	15	49.6%	250	49.6%
6	28.0%	16	49.6%	275	49.6%
7	31.6%	17	49.6%	300	49.6%
8	35.2%	18	49.6%	325	49.6%
9	38.8%	19	49.6%	350	49.6%
10	42.4%	20	49.6%	360	49.6%

14. The base case prepayment specified in the prospectus is called the prospectus prepayment curve (PPC). It is unique to each issuer and should be used instead of the generic PSA prepayment benchmark. However, it is not a generic prepayment benchmark for all closed-end home equity loan-securities as Mr. Tellmen assumes.

15. For adjustable-rate HELs, the reference rate is typically 6-month LIBOR. However, the floating-rate securities that these loans back typically are referenced to 1-month LIBOR in order to make them attractive to investors who fund themselves based on 1-month LIBOR. As a result, there will be a mismatch between the reference rate on the floating-rate HELs used as collateral and the securities backed by that collateral that will prevent the cap from being fixed over the life of the securities. In addition, there are periodic caps and a lifetime cap.

16. a. Since month 36 is in the first five years after issuance, the schedule specifies that all prepayments are allocated to the senior tranche and none to the subordinated tranches. Thus, the prepayments of $100,000 are allocated only to the senior tranche.

    b. According to the schedule, if prepayments occur 8 years after issuance, 20% is allocated to the senior tranche and the balance is paid to the subordinated tranches. Since the prepayments are assumed to be $100,000, the senior tranche receives $20,000 and the subordinated tranches $80,000.

    c. All prepayments that occur 10 years after issuance are paid to the subordinated tranches. Thus, the $100,000 of prepayments some time in year 10 are paid to the subordinated tranches.

17. The schedule in the prospectus is the base schedule. The schedule can change so as to allocate less to the subordinated tranches if the collateral's performance deteriorates after the deal is closed. Determination of whether or not the base schedule should be overridden is made by the trustee based on tests that are specified in the prospectus.

18. The protection is provided by establishing a schedule for the allocation of principal payments (both regularly scheduled principal payments and prepayments) between the NAS tranche and the non-NAS tranches such that contraction risk and extension risk are reduced. For example, a schedule would specify a lockout period for the principal payments to the NAS tranche. This means that the NAS tranche would not receive any payments until the lockout period ends and there-

fore contraction risk is mitigated. Extension risk is provided by allocating a large percentage to the NAS tranche in later years.

19. a. The cash flow is the same as for mortgage-backed securities backed by standard mortgage loans: (1) interest, (2) regularly scheduled principal repayments (amortization), and (3) prepayments.

    b. The reasons why the securities backed by manufactured housing loans tend not to be sensitive to refinancing are:

        1. the loan balances are typically small so that there is no significant dollar savings from refinancing.

        2. the rate of depreciation of manufactured homes may be such that in the earlier years depreciation is greater than the amount of the loan paid off, making it difficult to refinance the loan.

        3. typically borrowers are of lower credit quality and therefore find it difficult to obtain funds to refinance.

20. a. The cash flow for auto-loan backed securities consists of: (1) interest, (2) regularly scheduled principal repayments (amortization), and (3) prepayments.

    b. Prepayments due to refinancing on auto loans tend to be of minor importance.

21. A conditional prepayment rate measures prepayments relative to the amount outstanding in the previous year that could prepay. For a monthly CPR, called the single monthly mortality rate, SMM, prepayments are measured relative to the amount available in the previous month that was available to prepay.

    The absolute prepayment speed, denoted ABS, is the monthly prepayment expressed as a percentage of the *original* collateral amount.

22. a. $\text{SMM} = \dfrac{0.015}{1 - [0.015 \times (21 - 1)]} = 0.0214 = 2.14\%$

    b. $\text{ABS} = \dfrac{0.019}{1 + [0.019 \times (11 - 1)]} = 0.016 = 1.60\%$

23. The trustee is wrong. For certain student loans the government will guarantee up to 98% of the principal plus accrued interest (assuming the loans have been properly serviced). Moreover, there are student loans backed by alternative student loans that carry no government guarantee.

24. While a student is in school, no payments are made by the student on the loan. This period is the deferment period. Upon leaving school, the student is extended a period of time (typically six month) when no payments on the loan must be made. This is called the grace period.

25. a. The cash flow for an SBA-backed security consists of (1) interest for the period, (2) the scheduled principal repayment, and (3) prepayments.

b. The interest is based on a coupon formula where the prime rate is the reference rate. The rate on the loan is reset monthly on the first of the month or quarterly on the first of January, April, July, and October.

26. a. During the lockout period, only finance charges and fees collected are distributed to the bondholders.

b. During the lockout period, principal paid by borrowers is reinvested in new receivables and not distributed to the bondholders.

c. The statement is incorrect because principal repayment can be made by either (1) a bullet payment structure (as stated in the question), (2) a controlled amortization structure, or (3) a passthrough structure.

27. While there is no schedule of principal repayments for credit card borrowers, there is the potential risk of contraction for the securities. This is because there is a provision for early or rapid amortization if certain triggers are reached.

There is also the potential for extension risk because principal repayment from the credit card borrowers and defaults and delinquencies may be such that the schedule specified for principal repayment of the security during the amortization period may not be adequate to completely pay off bondholders by the stated maturity.

While these are nontrivial risks, neither of these occurs frequently.

28. a. The monthly payment rate (MPR) expresses the monthly payment of a credit card receivable portfolio as a percentage of debt outstanding in the previous month. The monthly payment includes finance charges, fees, and any principal repayment collected.

b. There are two reasons why the MPR is important. First, if the MPR reaches an extremely low level, there is a chance that there will be extension risk with respect to the repayment of principal. The length of time until the return of principal is largely a function of the monthly payment rate. Second, if the MPR is very low, then there is a chance that there will not be sufficient cash flow to pay off principal. This is one of the events that could trigger early amortization of the principal

c. The net portfolio yield for a credit card receivable portfolio is equal to the gross portfolio yield minus charge-offs. The gross portfolio yield includes finance charges collected and fees. From the gross portfolio yield charge offs are deducted. Charge-offs represent the accounts charged off as uncollectible

29. a. Typically a CBO is backed by a diversified pool of one or more of the following types of debt obligations: non-investment grade (i.e., high yield) corporate bonds; emerging market bonds; and bank loans to corporate entities.

b. The statement is incorrect. The asset manager responsible for purchasing the debt obligations for the portfolio will have restrictions that are imposed by the rating agencies that rate the securities in the deal. There will be certain tests that must be satisfied for the tranches in the CBO to maintain its credit rating at the time of issuance.

   c. The typical structure of a CBO is as follows. There is (1) a senior tranche (between 70% and 80% of the deal) with a floating rate, (2) different layers of subordinated or junior debt tranches with a fixed rate, and (3) an equity tranche.

   d. The statement is not correct. In fact, it is because of interest rate swaps that the risk is reduced for the senior tranche. This is because the collateral is typically fixed-rate bonds and the senior tranche must be paid a floating rate. An interest rate swap is used to convert the fixed-rate payments from the collateral into floating-rate payments that can be made to the senior tranche.

   e. The equity tranche receives any remaining interest that is received from the collateral but not paid to the debt tranches (i.e., the senior and junior tranches).

30. a. Given that the senior tranche is $150 million and the junior tranche is $30 million, the equity tranche is $20 million ($200 million minus $180 million).

   b. The collateral will pay interest each year (assuming no defaults) equal to the 8-year Treasury rate of 6% plus 600 basis points. So the interest will be:

Interest from collateral: $12\% \times \$200,000,000 = \$24,000,000$

The interest that must be paid to the senior tranche is:

Interest to senior tranche: $\$150,000,000 \times (\text{LIBOR} + 90 \text{ bp})$

The coupon rate for the junior tranche is 6% plus 300 basis points. So, the coupon rate is 9% and the interest is:

Interest to junior tranche: $9\% \times \$30,000,000 = \$2,700,000$

For the interest rate swap, the asset manager is agreeing to pay the swap counterparty each year 6% (the 8-year Treasury rate) plus 120 basis points, or 7.2%. Since the swap payments are based on a notional amount of $150 million, the asset manager pays to the swap counterparty:

Interest to swap counterparty: $7.2\% \times \$150,000,000 = \$10,800,000$

The interest payment received from the swap counterparty is LIBOR based on a notional amount of $150 million. That is,

Interest from swap counterparty: $\$150,000,000 \times \text{LIBOR}$

The interest for the CBO is:

Interest from collateral	$24,000,000
Interest from swap counterparty	$150,000,000 × LIBOR
Total interest received	$24,000,000 + $150,000,000 × LIBOR

The interest to be paid out to the senior and junior tranches and to the swap counterparty include:

Interest to senior tranche..........	$150,000,000 \times (LIBOR + 90 bp)$
Interest to junior tranche..........	$2,700,000
Interest to swap counterparty...	$10,800,000
Total interest paid	$13,500,000 + \$150,000,000 \times (LIBOR + 90 bp)$

Netting the interest payments paid and received:

Total interest received	$24,000,000 + \$150,000,000 \times LIBOR$
− Total interest paid	$13,500,000 + \$150,000,000 \times (LIBOR + 90 bp)$
Net interest	$10,500,000 − \$150,000,000 \times (90 bp)$

Since 90 bp times $150 million is $1,350,000, the net interest remaining is $9,150,000. This is the cash flow ignoring the asset management fee.

c. The amount available for the equity tranche is $9,150,000. This is the cash flow computed in part (b).

SOLUTIONS TO PRACTICE QUESTIONS

1. The excess servicing spread is determined as follows:

$$
\begin{array}{llll}
& \text{Gross weighted average coupon} & = & 9.50\% \\
- & \text{Servicing fee} & = & 0.75\% \\
\hline
& \text{Spread available to pay tranches} & = & 8.75\% \\
- & \text{Net weighted average coupon} & = & 7.50\% \\
\hline
& \text{Excess servicing spread} & = & 1.25\% \quad = 125 \text{ basis points}
\end{array}
$$

2. Losses by tranche

	total loss	senior tranche	subordinate tranche 1	subordinate tranche 2
a.	$15 million	zero	zero	$15 million
b.	$50 million	zero	$30 million	$20 million
c.	$90 million	$30 million	$40 million	$20 million

3. For month 1 the CPR is 4% as per the prospectus. Since we are interested in 150% PPC, the CPR in month 1 is 6% (1.5 × 4%). For month 2, 1.5% is added to 4%, so 100% PPC is 5.5%. Then 150% PPC is a CPR of 8.3% (= 1.5 × 5.5%). In month 15, the CPR is 25% for 100% PPC and for 150% PPC, the CPR is 37.5% (1.5 × 25%). For all months after month 15, the CPR is 37.5%.

Month	CPR	Month	CPR	Month	CPR
1	6.0%	11	28.5%	30	37.5%
2	8.3%	12	30.8%	125	37.5%
3	10.5%	13	33.0%	150	37.5%
4	12.8%	14	35.3%	200	37.5%
5	15.0%	15	37.5%	250	37.5%
6	17.3%	16	37.5%	275	37.5%
7	19.5%	17	37.5%	300	37.5%
8	21.8%	18	37.5%	325	37.5%
9	24.0%	19	37.5%	350	37.5%
10	26.3%	20	37.5%	360	37.5%

4. a. $\text{SMM} = \dfrac{0.02}{1 - [0.02 \times (11 - 1)]} = 0.025 = 2.5\%$

   b. $\text{ABS} = \dfrac{0.017}{1 + [0.017 \times (21 - 1)]} = 0.0127 = 1.27\%$

Chapter 5

VALUING MORTGAGE-BACKED AND ASSET-BACKED SECURITIES

LEARNING OUTCOME STATEMENTS

After reading this chapter you should be able to:

- describe the computation of the cash flow yield for a mortgage-backed security and an asset-backed security.
- identify the limitations of the cash flow yield measure.
- explain the limitations of the nominal spread and the zero-volatility spread for a mortgage-backed security.
- describe the Monte Carlo simulation model for valuing a mortgage-backed security.
- explain why the binomial model or any other model that uses the backward induction method cannot be used to value a mortgage-backed security.
- explain the critical assumptions in the Monte Carlo simulation model.
- explain why adjustments need to be made to the interest rate paths of the Monte Carlo simulation model.
- explain how the option-adjusted spread is computed using the Monte Carlo simulation model and the interpretation of this measure.
- apply the option-adjusted spread analysis to the valuation of mortgage-backed securities to identify rich and cheap securities.
- explain how the effective duration is computed using the Monte Carlo simulation model.
- identify some major assumptions that result in differences in effective durations reported by dealers and vendors.
- identify other measures of duration used by practitioners in the mortgage-backed market (including cash flow duration, coupon curve duration, and empirical duration) and the limitations of these duration measures.
- compute the cash flow duration for a mortgage-backed security and compare this measure to (1) modified duration and (2) effective duration using the Monte Carlo simulation model.
- identify when an asset-backed security should be valued using the zero-volatility spread approach or the option-adjusted spread approach (using Monte Carlo simulation).
- explain how to determine whether the nominal spread, zero-volatility spread, or option-adjusted spread should be used for assessing the value of a specific fixed income security.

SECTION I
INTRODUCTION

In the two previous chapters, we looked at mortgage-backed and asset-backed securities. Our focus was on understanding the risks associated with investing in these securities, how they are created (i.e., how they are structured), and why the products are created. Specifically, in the case of agency mortgage-backed securities we saw how prepayment risk can be redistributed among different tranches to create securities with a prepayment risk profile that is different from the underlying pool of mortgages. For asset-backed securities and nonagency mortgage-backed security, we saw how to create tranches with different degrees of credit risk.

What we did not discuss in describing these securities is how to value them and how to quantify their exposure to interest rate risk. That is, we know, for example, that a support tranche in a CMO structure has greater prepayment risk than a planned amortization class (PAC) tranche. However, how do we determine whether or not the price at which a support tranche is offered in the market adequately compensates for the greater prepayment risk? In this chapter, we will describe and then apply a methodology for valuing mortgage-backed securities and some types of asset-backed securities — Monte Carlo simulation. As we stressed in Chapter 2, a byproduct of a valuation model is the option-adjusted spread. We will see how the option-adjusted spread for a mortgage-backed or an asset-backed security is computed and applied. From a valuation model the effective duration and convexity of any security can be computed. We will explain how to compute effective duration and convexity using the Monte Carlo simulation model. However, in the case of mortgage-backed securities, there have been several alternative measures of duration used by practitioners. These measures will be identified along with their advantages and disadvantages.

Admittedly, the majority of this chapter is devoted to the valuation of mortgage-backed securities and by extension to all real estate-related asset-backed securities. This is because, analytically, they are the more difficult products to value and to quantify the interest rate exposure for. At the end of this chapter, we provide a framework for determining which analytical measures discussed in this chapter are appropriate for valuing any asset-backed security. In fact, the principles apply to all fixed income products.

SECTION II
CASH FLOW
YIELD
ANALYSIS

Let's begin with the traditional analysis of mortgage-backed and asset-backed securities — **cash flow yield analysis**. As explained at Level I (Chapter 6), the yield on any financial instrument is the interest rate that makes the present value of the expected cash flow equal to its market price plus accrued interest. When applied to mortgage-backed and asset-backed securities, this yield is called a **cash flow yield**. The problem in calculating the cash flow yield of a mortgage-backed and asset-backed securities is that the cash flow is unknown because of prepayments. Consequently, to determine a cash flow yield, some assumption about the prepayment rate must be made. And, in the case of all but agency mortgage-backed securities, an assumption about default rates and recovery rates must be made.

The cash flow for mortgage-backed and asset-backed securities is typically monthly. The convention is to compare the yield on mortgage-backed and asset-backed securities to that of a Treasury coupon security by calculating the security's *bond-equivalent yield*. As explained at Level I (Chapter 6), the bond-equivalent yield for a Treasury coupon security is found by doubling the semiannual yield. However, it is incorrect to do this for a mortgage-backed or an asset-backed security because the investor has the opportunity to generate greater reinvestment income by reinvesting the more frequent (i.e., monthly) cash flows. The **market convention** is to calculate a yield so as to make it comparable to the yield to maturity on a bond-equivalent basis. The formula for annualizing the monthly cash flow yield for a monthly-pay product is therefore:

$$\text{bond-equivalent yield} = 2[(1 + i_M)^6 - 1]$$

where i_M is the monthly interest rate that will equate the present value of the projected monthly cash flow equal to the market price (plus accrued interest) of the security.

To illustrate the calculation of the bond-equivalent yield, suppose that the monthly yield is 0.6%. That is, i_M is 0.006. Then

$$\text{bond-equivalent yield} = 2[(1.006)^6 - 1] = 0.0731 = 7.31\%$$

A. Limitations of Cash Flow Yield Measure

All yield measures suffer from problems that limit their use in assessing a security's potential return. The yield to maturity has two major shortcomings as a measure of a bond's potential return. To realize the stated yield to maturity, the investor must:

1. reinvest the coupon payments at a rate equal to the yield to maturity, and
2. hold the bond to the maturity date

As explained at Level I (Chapter 6), the reinvestment of the coupon payments is critical and for long-term bonds can be as much as 80% of the bond's return. Reinvestment risk is the risk of having to reinvest the interest payments at less than the computed yield. Interest rate risk is the risk associated with having to sell the security before its maturity date at a price less than the purchase price.

These shortcomings are equally applicable to the cash flow yield measure:

1. the projected cash flows are assumed to be reinvested at the cash flow yield, and
2. the mortgage-backed or asset-backed security is assumed to be held until the final payout based on some prepayment assumption.

The importance of reinvestment risk, the risk that the cash flow will have to be reinvested at a rate less than the cash flow yield, is particularly important for many mortgage-backed and asset-backed securities because payments are monthly and both interest and principal must be reinvested. Moreover, an additional assumption is that the projected cash flow is actually realized. If the prepayment, default, and recovery experience is different from that assumed, the cash flow yield will not be realized.

B. Nominal Spread

Given the computed cash flow yield and the average life for a mortgage-backed or asset-backed security based on some prepayment, default, and recovery assumption, the next step is to compare the yield to the yield for a comparable Treasury security. "Comparable" is typically defined as a Treasury security with the same maturity as the security's average life. The difference between the cash flow yield and the yield on a comparable Treasury security is called the **nominal spread**.

Unfortunately, it is the nominal spread that some managers will use as a measure of relative value. However, this spread masks the fact that a portion of the nominal spread is compensation for accepting prepayment risk. For example, CMO support tranches have been offered at large nominal spreads. However, the nominal spread embodies the substantial prepayment risk associated with support tranches. The manager who buys solely on the basis of nominal spread fails to determine whether or not that nominal spread offered adequate compensation given the substantial prepayment risk faced by the holder of a support tranche.

Instead of nominal spread, managers need a measure that indicates the potential compensation after adjusting for prepayment risk. This measure is called the **option-adjusted spread**. We discussed this measure in Chapter 2 where we covered the valuation of corporate and agency bonds with embedded options. Before discussing this measure for structured products, we describe another spread measure commonly quoted for structured products called the **zero-volatility spread**, a measure we first described at Level I (Chapter 6).

SECTION III ZERO-VOLATILITY SPREAD

As explained at Level I, the proper procedure to compare any security to a U.S. Treasury security is to compare it to a portfolio of Treasury securities that have the same cash flow. The value of the security is then equal to the present value of all of the cash flows. The security's value, assuming the cash flows are default-free, will equal the present value of the replicating portfolio of Treasury securities. In turn, these cash flows are valued at the Treasury spot rates.

The **zero-volatility spread** is a measure of the spread that the investor would realize over the entire Treasury spot rate curve if the mortgage-backed or asset-backed security is held to maturity. It is not a spread off one point on the Treasury yield curve, as is the nominal spread. The zero-volatility spread (also called the **Z-spread** and the **static spread**) is the spread that will make the present value of the cash flows from the mortgage-backed or asset-backed security when discounted at the Treasury spot rate plus the spread equal to the price of the security. A trial-and-error procedure (or search algorithm) is required to determine the zero-volatility spread. We illustrated this at Level I (Chapter 6).[1]

Also as explained at Level I, in general, the shorter the maturity or average life of a structured product, the less the zero-volatility spread will differ from the nominal spread. The magnitude of the difference between the nominal spread and the zero-volatility spread also depends on the shape of the yield curve. The steeper the yield curve, the greater the difference.

In Section VII we will see when it is appropriate to use the Z-spread instead of the OAS.

SECTION IV MONTE CARLO SIMULATION MODEL AND OAS

In Chapter 2, we discussed one model that is used to value callable agency debentures and corporate bonds, the binomial model. This valuation model accommodates securities in which the decision to exercise a call option is not dependent on how interest rates evolved over time. That is, the decision of an issuer to call a bond will depend on the level of the rate at which the issue can be refunded relative to the issue's coupon rate, and not the path interest rates took to get to that rate. In contrast, there are fixed income securities and derivative instruments for which the periodic cash flows are "interest rate path-dependent." This means that the cash flow received in one period is determined not only by the current interest rate level, but also by the path that interest rates took to get to the current level.

For example, in the case of passthrough securities, prepayments are interest rate path-dependent because this month's prepayment rate depends on whether there

---

[1] Most common spreadsheet programs offer this type of algorithm.

have been prior opportunities to refinance since the underlying mortgages were originated. This phenomenon is referred to as "prepayment burnout." Pools of passthroughs are used as collateral for the creation of CMOs. Consequently, there are typically two sources of path dependency in a CMO tranche's cash flows. First, the collateral prepayments are path-dependent as discussed above. Second, the cash flows to be received in the current month by a CMO tranche depend on the outstanding balances of the other tranches in the deal. Thus, we need the history of prepayments to calculate these balances.

Conceptually, the valuation of agency passthroughs using the Monte Carlo model is simple. In practice, however, it is very complex. The simulation involves generating a set of cash flows based on simulated future mortgage refinancing rates, which in turn imply simulated prepayment rates.

Valuation modeling for agency CMOs is similar to valuation modeling for passthroughs, although the difficulties are amplified because the issuer has distributed both the prepayment risk and the interest rate risk into different tranches. The sensitivity of the passthroughs comprising the collateral to these two risks is not transmitted equally to every tranche. Some of the tranches wind up more sensitive to prepayment risk and interest rate risk than the collateral, while some of them are much less sensitive.

The objective is to figure out how the value of the collateral gets transmitted to the tranches in a deal. More specifically, the objective is to find out where the value goes and where the risk goes so that one can identify the tranches with low risk and high value: the tranches a manager wants to consider for purchase. The good news is that this combination usually exists in every deal. The bad news is that in every deal there are usually tranches with low value and high risk that managers want to avoid purchasing.

A. Simulating Interest Rate Paths and Cash Flows

To generate these random interest rate paths, the typical model used by Wall Street firms and commercial vendors takes as input today's term structure of interest rates and a volatility assumption. (We discussed these topics in Chapter 2.) The term structure of interest rates is the theoretical spot rate (or zero coupon) curve implied by today's Treasury securities. The simulations should be calibrated so that the average simulated price of a zero-coupon Treasury bond equals today's actual price.

On-the-run Treasury issues are often used in the calibration process. Some dealers and vendors of analytical systems use the LIBOR curve instead of the Treasury curve — or give the user a choice to use either the Treasury curve or the LIBOR curve. The reason is that some investors are interested in spreads that they can earn relative to their funding costs and LIBOR for many investors is a better proxy for that cost than Treasury rates. (We will discuss the different types of investors at Level III.)

As explained in Chapter 2, every dealer and vendor of analytical systems employs an interest rate model. This is a model that assumes how interest rates will change over time. The interest rate models employed by most dealers and vendors of analytical systems are similar. However, one input to all interest rate models is the interest rate volatility assumption. It is that assumption that varies by dealer and vendor. As will be illustrated later in this chapter, it is a critical input.

The volatility assumption determines the dispersion of future interest rates in the simulation. Today, many dealers and vendors do not use one volatility number for the yield of all maturities of the yield curve. Instead, they use either a short/long yield volatility or a term structure of yield volatility. A short/long yield volatility means that volatility is specified for maturities up to a certain number of years (short yield volatility) and a different yield volatility for longer maturities (long yield volatility). The short yield volatility is assumed to be greater than the long yield volatility. A term structure of yield volatilities means that a yield volatility is assumed for each maturity.

Based on the interest rate model and the assumed volatility, a series of interest rate paths will be generated. We will see shortly how a security is valued on each interest rate path. However, there is nothing that we have explained thus far that assures us that the values produced by the model will be arbitrage free. Recall from Chapter 2 that the binomial interest rate tree by design is constructed to be arbitrage free. That is, if any of the on-the-run issues that were used to construct the binomial interest rate tree are valued using the tree, the model would produce a value for that on-the-run issue equal to its market value. There is nothing we described so far about the Monte Carlo simulation to assure this.

More specifically, in the case of Monte Carlo simulation for valuing mortgage-backed and asset-backed securities, the on-the-run Treasury issues are typically used. What assurance is there that if an on-the-run Treasury issue is valued using the Monte Carlo simulation model it will be arbitrage free? That is, what assurance is there that the value produced by the model will equal the market price? Nothing. That's right, nothing. What the model builder must do is "adjust" the interest rate paths so that the model produces the correct values for the on-the-run Treasury issues. A discussion of this adjustment process is not important to us. In fact, there are very few published sources that describe how this is done. The key point here is that no such adjustment is necessary in a binomial model for valuing corporate and agency bonds with embedded options because the tree is built to be arbitrage free. In the case of the Monte Carlo simulation model, the builder must make an arbitrary adjustment to the interest rate paths to get the model to be arbitrage free.

The simulation works by generating many scenarios of future interest rate paths. As just explained, the "raw" interest rate paths that are simulated must be "adjusted" so as to make the model generate arbitrage-free values for whatever benchmark interest rates are used — typically, the on-the-run Treasury issues. *So, in the remainder of this chapter, when we refer to interest rate paths it is understood that it is the "adjusted" interest rate paths where "adjusted" means that each interest rate path is adjusted so that the model will produce arbitrage-free values.*

In each month of the scenario (i.e., path), a monthly interest rate and a mortgage refinancing rate are generated. The monthly interest rates are used to discount the projected cash flows in the scenario. The mortgage refinancing rate is needed to determine the cash flows because it represents the opportunity cost the borrower (i.e., mortgagor) is facing at that time.

If the refinancing rates are high relative to the borrower's original coupon rate (i.e., the rate on the borrower's loan), the borrower will have less incentive to refinance, or even a positive disincentive (i.e., the homeowner will avoid moving in order to avoid refinancing). If the refinancing rate is low relative to the borrower's original coupon rate, the borrower has an incentive to refinance.

Prepayments are projected by feeding the refinancing rate and loan characteristics into a prepayment model. Given the projected prepayments, the cash flows along an interest rate path can be determined.

To make this more concrete, consider a newly issued mortgage passthrough security with a maturity of 360 months. Exhibit 1 shows N "adjusted" simulated interest rate path scenarios — adjusted to be arbitrage free. Each scenario consists of a path of 360 simulated 1-month future interest rates. (The number of paths generated is based on a well known principle in simulation which will not be discussed here.) So, our first assumption that we make to get Exhibit 1 is the volatility of interest rates.

Exhibit 1: "Adjusted" Simulated Paths of Arbitrage-Free 1-Month Future Interest Rates*

Month	Interest Rate Path Number						
	1	2	3	...	n	...	N
1	$f_1(1)$	$f_1(2)$	$f_1(3)$	...	$f_1(n)$	...	$f_1(N)$
2	$f_2(1)$	$f_2(2)$	$f_2(3)$	...	$f_2(n)$	...	$f_2(N)$
3	$f_3(1)$	$f_3(2)$	$f_3(3)$	...	$f_3(n)$	...	$f_3(N)$
...	...	...	...	...	...	...	...
t	$f_t(1)$	$f_t(2)$	$f_t(3)$	...	$f_t(n)$	...	$f_t(N)$
...	...	...	...	...	...	...	...
358	$f_{358}(1)$	$f_{358}(2)$	$f_{358}(3)$	...	$f_{358}(n)$	...	$f_{358}(N)$
359	$f_{359}(1)$	$f_{359}(2)$	$f_{359}(3)$	...	$f_{359}(n)$	...	$f_{359}(N)$
360	$f_{360}(1)$	$f_{360}(2)$	$f_{360}(3)$	...	$f_{360}(n)$	...	$f_{360}(N)$

Notation:

$f_t(n)$ = 1-month future interest rate for month t on path n
N = total number of interest rate paths

* As explained in the text, the "raw" interest rate paths that are simulated must be "adjusted" so as to make the model generate arbitrage-free values for whatever benchmark interest rates are used – typically, the on-the-run Treasury issues. The interest rates shown in the exhibit are the "adjusted" arbitrage-free interest rates.

Exhibit 2: Simulated Paths of Mortgage Refinancing Rates

Month	Interest Rate Path Number						
	1	2	3	...	n	...	N
1	$r_1(1)$	$r_1(2)$	$r_1(3)$	...	$r_1(n)$	...	$r_1(N)$
2	$r_2(1)$	$r_2(2)$	$r_2(3)$	...	$r_2(n)$	...	$r_2(N)$
3	$r_3(1)$	$r_3(2)$	$r_3(3)$	...	$r_3(n)$	...	$r_3(N)$
...	...	...	...	...	...	...	...
t	$r_t(1)$	$r_t(2)$	$r_t(3)$	...	$r_t(n)$	...	$r_t(N)$
...	...	...	...	...	...	...	...
358	$r_{358}(1)$	$r_{358}(2)$	$r_{358}(3)$	...	$r_{358}(n)$	...	$r_{358}(N)$
359	$r_{359}(1)$	$r_{359}(2)$	$r_{359}(3)$	...	$r_{359}(n)$	...	$r_{359}(N)$
360	$r_{360}(1)$	$r_{360}(2)$	$r_{360}(3)$	...	$r_{360}(n)$	...	$r_{360}(N)$

Notation:

$r_t(n)$ = mortgage refinancing rate for month t on path n
N = total number of interest rate paths

Exhibit 2 shows the paths of simulated mortgage refinancing rates corresponding to the scenarios shown in Exhibit 1. In going from Exhibit 1 to Exhibit 2, an assumption must be made about the relationship between the Treasury rates and refinancing rates. The assumption is that there is a constant spread relationship between the rate that the borrower will use to determine whether or not to refinance (i.e., the refinancing rate) and the 1-month interest rates shown in Exhibit 1. For example, for 30-year mortgage loans, model builders use the 10-year Treasury rate as a proxy for the refinancing rate.

Given the mortgage refinancing rates, the cash flows on each interest rate path can be generated. For agency mortgage-backed securities, this requires a prepayment model. For asset-backed securities and nonagency mortgage-backed securities, this requires both a prepayment model and a model of defaults and recoveries. So, our next assumption is that the output of these models (prepayments, defaults, and recoveries) are correct. The resulting cash flows are depicted in Exhibit 3.

Exhibit 3: Simulated Cash Flows on Each of the Interest Rate Paths

Month	Interest Rate Path Number						
	1	2	3	...	n	...	N
1	$C_1(1)$	$C_1(2)$	$C_1(3)$	...	$C_1(n)$	...	$C_1(N)$
2	$C_2(1)$	$C_2(2)$	$C_2(3)$	...	$C_2(n)$	...	$C_2(N)$
3	$C_3(1)$	$C_3(2)$	$C_3(3)$	...	$C_3(n)$	...	$C_3(N)$
...	...	...	...	...	...	...	...
t	$C_t(1)$	$C_t(2)$	$C_t(3)$	...	$C_t(n)$	...	$C_t(N)$
...	...	...	...	...	...	...	...
358	$C_{358}(1)$	$C_{358}(2)$	$C_{358}(3)$	...	$C_{358}(n)$	...	$C_{358}(N)$
359	$C_{359}(1)$	$C_{359}(2)$	$C_{359}(3)$	...	$C_{359}(n)$	...	$C_{359}(N)$
360	$C_{360}(1)$	$C_{360}(2)$	$C_{360}(3)$	...	$C_{360}(n)$	...	$C_{360}(N)$

Notation:

$C_t(n)$ = cash flow for month t on path n

N = total number of interest rate paths

Exhibit 4: "Adjusted" Simulated Paths of Monthly Arbitrage-Free Spot Rates

Month	Interest Rate Path Number						
	1	2	3	...	n	...	N
1	$z_1(1)$	$z_1(2)$	$z_1(3)$	...	$z_1(n)$	...	$z_1(N)$
2	$z_2(1)$	$z_2(2)$	$z_2(3)$	...	$z_2(n)$	...	$z_2(N)$
3	$z_3(1)$	$z_3(2)$	$z_3(3)$	...	$z_3(n)$	...	$z_3(N)$
...	...	...	...	...	...	...	...
t	$z_t(1)$	$z_t(2)$	$z_t(3)$	...	$z_t(n)$	...	$z_t(N)$
...	...	...	...	...	...	...	...
358	$z_{358}(1)$	$z_{358}(2)$	$z_{358}(3)$	...	$z_{358}(n)$	...	$z_{358}(N)$
359	$z_{359}(1)$	$z_{359}(2)$	$z_{359}(3)$	...	$z_{359}(n)$	...	$z_{359}(N)$
360	$z_{360}(1)$	$z_{360}(2)$	$z_{360}(3)$	...	$z_{360}(n)$	...	$z_{360}(N)$

Notation:

$z_t(n)$ = spot rate for month t on path n

N = total number of interest rate paths

B. Calculating the Present Value for an Interest Rate Path

Given the cash flows on an interest rate path, the path's present value can be calculated. The discount rate for determining the present value is the simulated spot rate for each month on the interest rate path plus an appropriate spread. The spot rate on a path can be determined from the simulated future monthly rates. The relationship that holds between the simulated spot rate for month T on path n and the simulated future 1-month rates is:

$$z_T(n) = \{[1 + f_1(n)][1 + f_2(n)] \cdots [1 + f_T(n)]\}^{1/T} - 1$$

where

$z_T(n)$ = simulated spot rate for month T on path n

$f_t(n)$ = simulated future 1-month rate for month t on path n

At Level I (Chapter 6) we explained the relationship between spot rates and forward rates. Consequently, the interest rate path for the simulated future 1-month rates can be converted to the interest rate path for the simulated monthly spot rates as shown in Exhibit 4. Therefore, the present value of the cash flows for month T on interest rate path n discounted at the simulated spot rate for month T plus some spread is:

$$PV[C_T(n)] = \frac{C_T(n)}{[1 + z_T(n) + K]^T}$$

where

$PV[C_T(n)]$	=	present value of cash flows for month T on path n
$C_T(n)$	=	cash flow for month T on path n
$z_T(n)$	=	spot rate for month T on path n
K	=	spread

The spread, K, reflects the risks that the investor feels are associated with realizing the cash flows.

The present value for path n is the sum of the present value of the cash flows for each month on path n. That is,

$$PV[\text{Path}(n)] = PV[C_1(n)] + PV[C_2(n)] + ... + PV[C_{360}(n)]$$

where $PV[\text{Path}(n)]$ is the present value of interest rate path n.

C. Determining the Theoretical Value

The present value of a given interest rate path can be thought of as the theoretical value of a passthrough if that path was actually realized. The theoretical value of the passthrough can be determined by calculating the average of the theoretical values of all the interest rate paths. That is, the theoretical value is equal to

$$\text{theoretical value} = \frac{PV[\text{Path}(1)] + PV[\text{Path}(2)] + ... + PV[\text{Path}(N)]}{N}$$

where N is the number of interest rate paths. The theoretical value derived from the above equation is based on some spread, K. It follows the usual practice of discounting cash flows at spot rates plus a spread — in this case the spread is K.

This procedure for valuing a passthrough is also followed for a CMO tranche. The cash flow for each month on each interest rate path is found according to the principal repayment and interest distribution rules of the deal.

D. Option-Adjusted Spread

In the Monte Carlo model, the **option-adjusted spread** (OAS) is the spread that when added to all the spot rates on all interest rate paths will make the average present value of the paths equal to the observed market price (plus accrued interest). Mathematically, OAS is the value for K (the spread) that will satisfy the following condition:

$$\frac{PV[\text{Path}(1)] + PV[\text{Path}(2)] + ... + PV[\text{Path}(N)]}{N} = \text{market price}$$

where N is the number of interest rate paths. The left-hand side of the above equation looks identical to that of the equation for the theoretical value. The difference is that the objective is to determine what spread, K, will make the model produce a theoretical value equal to the market price.

The procedure for determining the OAS is straightforward and involves the same search algorithm explained for the zero-volatility spread. The next question, then, is how to interpret the OAS. Basically, the OAS is used to reconcile value with market price. On the left-hand side of the previous equation is the market's statement: the price of a structured product. The average present value over all the paths on the right-hand side of the equation is the model's output, which we refer to as the theoretical value.

What an investor or a portfolio manager seeks to do is to buy a mortgage-backed security where value is greater than price. By using a valuation model such as the Monte Carlo model, a portfolio manager could estimate the value of a security, which at this point would be sufficient in determining whether to buy a security. That is, the portfolio manager can say that this security is 1 point cheap or 2 points cheap, and so on. The model does not stop here. Instead, it converts the divergence between price and value into some type of spread measure since most market participants find it more convenient to think about spreads than price differences.

The OAS was developed as a measure of the spread that can be used to convert dollar differences between value and price. As we explained in Chapter 2, in the binomial model a spread is measured relative to the benchmark interest rates used to generate the interest rate tree and which is therefore used to make the tree arbitrage free. The same is true in the case of the Monte Carlo simulation model. The spread is measured relative to the benchmark interest rates that were used to generate the interest rate paths and to adjust the interest rate paths to make them arbitrage free. Typically, for a mortgage-backed security the benchmark interest rates are the on-the-run Treasury rates. The OAS is then measuring the average spread over the Treasury spot rate curve, not the Treasury yield as explained in Chapter 2. It is an average spread since the OAS is found by averaging over the interest rate paths for the possible Treasury spot rate curves. Of course, if the LIBOR curve is used, the OAS is the spread over that curve.

This spread measure is superior to the nominal spread which gives no recognition to the prepayment risk. As explained in Chapter 2, the OAS is "option adjusted" because the cash flows on the interest rate paths are adjusted for the option of the borrowers to prepay.

E. Option Cost

The implied cost of the option embedded for a mortgage-backed or asset-backed security can be obtained by calculating the difference between the option-adjusted spread at the assumed volatility of interest rates and the zero-volatility spread. That is,

$$\text{option cost} = \text{zero-volatility spread} - \text{option-adjusted spread}$$

The option cost measures the prepayment (or option) risk embedded in the security. Note that the cost of the option is a byproduct of the option-adjusted spread analysis, not valued explicitly with some option pricing model.

F. Selecting the Number of Interest Rate Paths

Let's now address the question of the number of scenario paths, N, needed to value a security. The number of interest rate paths determines how "good" the estimate is, not relative to the truth but relative to the model used. The more paths, the more the average value produced tends to converge. It is simply a statistical sampling problem.

Most models employ some form of variance reduction to cut down on the number of sample paths necessary to get a good statistical sample.[2] Several vendor firms have developed computational procedures that reduce the number of paths required but still provide the accuracy of a full Monte Carlo analysis. The procedure is to use statistical techniques to reduce the number of interest rate paths to sets of similar paths. These paths are called **representative paths**. For example, suppose that 2,000 sample paths are generated. Using a certain statistical technique, these 2,000 sample paths can be collapsed to, say, 16 representative paths. The security is then valued on each of these 16 representative paths. The theoretical value of the security is then the *weighted* average of the 16 representative paths. The weight for a path is the percentage of that representative path relative to the total sample paths. Vendors

---

[2] The variance reduction technique is described in books on management science and Monte Carlo simulation.

often give the investor or portfolio manager the choice of whether to use the "full Monte Carlo simulation" or to specify a number of representative paths.

G. Illustrations We will use two deals to show how CMOs can be analyzed using the Monte Carlo model/OAS procedure discussed above — a simple structure and a PAC/support structure.[3]

1. Simple Structure

The simple structure analyzed is Freddie Mac (FHLMC) 1915. It is a simple sequential-pay CMO bond structure. The structure includes eight tranches, A, B, C, D, E, F, G, and S. The focus of our analysis is on tranches A, B, and C. All three tranches were priced at a premium.

The top panel of Exhibit 5 shows the OAS, the option cost, and effective duration[4] for the collateral and the three tranches in the CMO structure. However, tranche A had the smallest effective duration and tranche C had the largest effective duration. The OAS for the collateral is 51 basis points. Since the option cost is 67 basis points, the zero-volatility spread is 118 basis points (51 basis points plus 67 basis points).

Exhibit 5: OAS Analysis of FHLMC 1915 Classes A, B, and C
(As of 3/10/98)

All three tranches were trading at a premium as of the date of the analysis.

Base Case (Assumes 13% Interest Rate Volatility)

	OAS (in basis points)	Option Cost (in basis points)	Z-Spread (in basis points)	Effective Duration (in years)
Collateral	51	67	118	1.2
Tranche				
A	32	51	83	0.9
B	33	82	115	2.9
C	46	70	116	6.7

Prepayments at 80% and 120% of Prepayment Model
(Assumes 13% Interest Rate Volatility)

	New OAS (in basis points)		Change in Price per $100 par (holding OAS constant)	
	80%	120%	80%	120%
Collateral	63	40	$0.45	−$0.32
Tranche				
A	40	23	0.17	−0.13
B	43	22	0.54	−0.43
C	58	36	0.97	−0.63

Interest Rate Volatility of 9% and 17%

	New OAS (in basis points)		Change in Price per $100 par (holding OAS constant)	
	9%	17%	9%	17%
Collateral	79	21	$1.03	−$0.94
Tranche				
A	52	10	0.37	−0.37
B	66	−3	1.63	−1.50
C	77	15	2.44	−2.08

[3] These illustrations are from Frank J. Fabozzi, Scott F. Richard, and David S. Horowitz, "Valuation of CMOs," Chapter 6 in Frank J. Fabozzi (ed.), *Advances in the Valuation and Management of Mortgage-Backed Securities* (New Hope, PA: Frank J. Fabozzi Associates, 1998).
[4] We will explain how to compute the effective duration using the Monte Carlo methodology in Section V.A.

At the time this analysis was performed, March 10, 1998, the Treasury yield curve was not steep. At Level I (Chapter 6), we explained that when the yield curve is relatively flat the zero-volatility spread will not differ significantly from the nominal spread. Thus, for the three tranches shown in Exhibit 5, the zero-volatility spread is 83 basis points for A, 115 basis points for B, and 116 basis points for C.

Notice that the tranches did not share the OAS equally. The same is true for the option cost. Both the Z-spread and the option cost increase as the effective duration increases. Whether or not any of these tranches were attractive investments requires a comparison to other tranches in the market with the same effective duration. While not presented here, all three tranches offered an OAS similar to other sequential-pay tranches with the same effective duration available in the market. On a relative basis (i.e., relative to the other tranches analyzed in the deal), the only tranche where there appears to be a bit of a bargain is tranche C. A portfolio manager contemplating the purchase of this last cash flow tranche can see that C offers a higher OAS than B and appears to bear less of the risk (i.e., has lower option cost), as measured by the option cost. The problem portfolio managers may face is that they might not be able to go out as long on the yield curve as tranche C because of effective duration, maturity, and average life constraints relative to their liabilities, for example.

Now let's look at modeling risk. Examination of the sensitivity of the tranches to changes in prepayments and interest rate volatility will help us to understand the interaction of the tranches in the structure and who is bearing the risk. How the deal behaves under various scenarios should reinforce and be consistent with the valuation (i.e., a tranche may look "cheap" for a reason).

We begin with prepayments. Specifically, we keep the same interest rate paths as those used to get the OAS in the base case (the top panel of Exhibit 5), but reduce the prepayment rate on each interest rate path to 80% of the projected rate. As can be seen in the second panel of Exhibit 5, slowing down prepayments increases the OAS and price for the collateral. The exhibit reports two results of the sensitivity analysis. First, it indicates the change in the OAS. Second, it indicates the change in the price, holding the OAS constant at the base case.

To see how a portfolio manager can use the information in the second panel, consider tranche A. At 80% of the prepayment speed, the OAS for this tranche increases from 32 basis points to 40 basis points. If the OAS is held constant, the panel indicates that the buyer of tranche A would gain $0.17 per $100 par value.

Notice that for all of the tranches reported in Exhibit 5 there is a gain from a slowdown in prepayments. This is because all of the sequential tranches in this deal are priced over par. (An investor in a tranche priced at a premium benefits from a slowdown in prepayments because the investor receives the higher coupon for a longer period and postpones the capital loss from a prepayment.) Also notice that while the changes in OAS are about the same for the different tranches, the changes in price are quite different. This arises because the shorter tranches have less duration. Therefore, their prices do not move as much from a change in OAS as a longer average life tranche. A portfolio manager who is willing to go to the long end of the yield curve, such as tranche C, would realize the most benefit from the slowdown in prepayments.

Also shown in the second panel of the exhibit is the second part of our experiment to test the sensitivity of prepayments: the prepayment rate is assumed to be 120% of the base case. The collateral loses money in this scenario because it is trading above par. This is reflected in the OAS of the collateral which declines from 51 basis points to 40 basis points. Now look at the three tranches. They all lost money because the tranches were all at a premium and the speeding of prepayments adversely affects the tranche.

Before looking at the last panel that shows the effect of a change in interest rate volatility on the OAS, let's review the relationship between expected interest rate volatility and the value of a mortgage-backed security. Recall that the investor in a mortgage-backed security has sold an option to homeowners (borrowers). Thus, the investor is short an option. As will be explained in Chapter 8, the value of an option depends on expected interest rate volatility. When expected interest rate volatility decreases, the value of the option embedded in a mortgage-backed security decreases and therefore the value of a mortgage-backed security increases. The opposite is true when expected interest rate volatility increases — the value of the embedded option increases and the value of a mortgage-backed security decreases.

Now let's look at the sensitivity to the interest rate volatility assumption, 13% in the base case. Two experiments are performed: reducing the volatility assumption to 9% and increasing it to 17%. These results are reported in the third panel of Exhibit 5.

Reducing the volatility to 9% increases the dollar price of the collateral by $1.03 and increases the OAS from 51 in the base case to 79 basis points. However, this $1.03 increase in the price of the collateral is not equally distributed among the three tranches. Most of the increase in value is realized by the longer tranches. The OAS gain for each of the tranches follows more or less the effective durations of those tranches. This makes sense, because the longer the duration, the greater the risk, and when volatility declines, the reward is greater for the accepted risk. At the higher level of assumed interest rate volatility of 17%, the collateral is severely affected. The longer the duration, the greater the loss. These results for a decrease and an increase in interest rate volatility are consistent with what we explained earlier.

Using the Monte Carlo simulation/OAS analysis, a fair conclusion that can be made about this simple structure is: what you see is what you get. The only surprise in this structure is the lower option cost in tranche C. In general, however, a portfolio manager willing to extend duration gets paid for that risk in this structure.

2. PAC/Support Tranche Structure

Now let's look at how to apply the methodology to a more complicated CMO structure, FHLMC Series 1706. The collateral (i.e., pool of passthroughs) for this structure is Freddie Mac 7s (7% coupon rate). A partial summary of the deal is provided in Exhibit 6. That is, only the tranches we will be discussing in this section are shown in the exhibit.[5]

While this deal looks complicated, it is relatively simple compared to many deals that have been issued. Nonetheless, it brings out all the key points about application of OAS analysis, specifically, the fact that most deals include cheap bonds, expensive bonds, and fairly priced bonds. The OAS analysis helps identify how a tranche should be classified. A more proper analysis would compare the OAS for each tranche to a similar duration tranche available in the market.

All of the tranches in Exhibit 6 were discussed in Chapter 3. At issuance, there were 10 PAC tranches, three scheduled tranches, a floating-rate support tranche, and an inverse floating-rate support. Recall that the "scheduled tranches" are support tranches with a schedule, referred to in Chapter 3 as "PAC II tranches."

The first two PAC tranches in the deal, tranche A and tranche B, were paid off at the time of the analysis. The other PAC tranches were still available at the time of the analysis. The prepayment protection for the PAC tranches is provided by the support tranches. The support tranches in this deal that are shown in Exhibit 6 are

_____

[5] This deal was described in Chapter 3.

tranches LA, LB, and M. There were other support tranches not shown in Exhibit 6. LA is the shortest average life support tranche (a scheduled (SCH) bond).

The collateral for this deal was trading at a premium. That is, the homeowners (borrowers) were paying a higher mortgage rate than available in the market at the time of the analysis. This meant that the value of the collateral would increase if prepayments slow down but would decrease if prepayments increase. What is important to note, however, is that a tranche could be trading at a discount, par, or premium even though the collateral is priced at a premium. For example, PAC C had a low coupon rate at the time of the analysis and therefore was trading at a discount. Thus, while the collateral (which was selling at a premium) loses value from an increase in prepayments, a discount tranche such as tranche C would increase in value if prepayments increase. (Recall that in the simple structure analyzed earlier, the collateral and all the tranches were trading at a premium.)

The top panel of Exhibit 7 shows the base case OAS, the option cost, and the effective duration for the collateral and tranches in Exhibit 6. The collateral OAS is 60 basis points, and the option cost is 44 basis points. The Z-spread of the collateral to the Treasury spot curve is 104 basis points.

The 60 basis points of OAS did not get equally distributed among the tranches — as was the case with the simple structure analyzed earlier. Tranche LB, the scheduled support, did not realize a good OAS allocation, only 29 basis points, and had an extremely high option cost. Given the prepayment uncertainty associated with this tranche, its OAS would be expected to be higher. The reason for the low OAS is that this tranche was priced so that its cash flow yield is high. Using the Z-spread as a proxy for the nominal spread (i.e., spread over the Treasury yield curve), the 103 basis point spread for tranche LB is high given that this appears to be a short average life tranche. Consequently, "yield buyers" (i.e., investors with a preference for high nominal yield, who may not be attentive to compensation for prepayment risk) probably bid aggressively for this tranche and thereby drove down its OAS, trading off "yield" for OAS. From a total return perspective, however, tranche LB should be avoided. It is a rich, or expensive, tranche. The other support tranche analyzed, tranche M, had an OAS of 72 basis points and at the time of this analysis was similar to that offered on comparable duration tranches available in the market.

Exhibit 6: Summary of Federal Home Loan Mortgage Corporation — Multiclass Mortgage Participation Certificates (Guaranteed), Series 1706

Total Issue: $300,000,000   Issue Date: 2/18/94

Tranche	Original Balance ($)	Coupon (%)	Stated Maturity	Original Issue Pricing (225% PSA Assumed)	
				Average Life (yrs)	Expected Maturity
PAC Tranches					
C (PAC Bond)	25,500,000	5.25	4/15/14	3.5	6/15/98
D (PAC Bond)	9,150,000	5.65	8/15/15	4.5	1/15/99
E (PAC Bond)	31,650,000	6.00	1/15/19	5.8	1/15/01
G (PAC Bond)	30,750,000	6.25	8/15/21	7.9	5/15/03
H (PAC Bond)	27,450,000	6.50	6/15/23	10.9	10/15/07
J (PAC Bond)	5,220,000	6.50	10/15/23	14.4	9/15/09
K (PAC Bond)	7,612,000	7.00	3/15/24	18.8	5/15/19
Support Tranches					
LA (SCH Bond)	26,673,000	7.00	11/15/21	3.5	3/15/02
LB (SCH Bond)	36,087,000	7.00	6/15/23	3.5	9/15/02
M (SCH Bond)	18,738,000	7.00	3/15/24	11.2	10/15/08

Exhibit 7: OAS Analysis of FHLMC 1706 (As of 3/10/98)
Base Case (Assumes 13% Interest Rate Volatility)

	OAS (in basis points)	Option Cost (in basis points)	Z-Spread (in basis points)	Effective Duration (in years)
Collateral	60	44	104	2.6
PAC Tranches				
C (PAC)	15	0	15	0.2
D (PAC)	16	4	20	0.6
E (PAC)	26	4	30	1.7
G (PAC)	42	8	50	3.3
H (PAC)	50	12	62	4.9
J (PAC)	56	14	70	6.8
K (PAC)	57	11	68	8.6
Support Tranches				
LA (SCH)	39	12	51	1.4
LB (SCH)	29	74	103	1.2
M (SCH)	72	53	125	4.9

Prepayments at 80% and 120% of Prepayment Model
(Assumes 13% Interest Rate Volatility)

	Base Case OAS	New OAS (in basis points)		Change in Price per $100 par (holding OAS constant)	
		80%	120%	80%	120%
Collateral	60	63	57	$0.17	−$0.11
PAC Tranches					
C (PAC)	15	15	15	0.00	0.00
D (PAC)	16	16	16	0.00	0.00
E (PAC)	26	27	26	0.01	−0.01
G (PAC)	42	44	40	0.08	−0.08
H (PAC)	50	55	44	0.29	−0.27
J (PAC)	56	63	50	0.50	−0.47
K (PAC)	57	65	49	0.77	−0.76
Support Tranches					
LA (SCH)	39	31	39	−0.12	0.00
LB (SCH)	29	39	18	0.38	−0.19
M (SCH)	72	71	76	−0.07	0.18

Interest Rate Volatility of 9% and 17%

	Base Case OAS	New OAS (in basis points)		Change in Price per $100 par (holding OAS constant)	
		9%	17%	9%	17%
Collateral	60	81	35	$0.96	−$0.94
PAC Tranches					
C (PAC)	15	15	15	0.00	0.00
D (PAC)	16	16	16	0.00	0.00
E (PAC)	26	27	24	0.02	−0.04
G (PAC)	42	48	34	0.21	−0.27
H (PAC)	50	58	35	0.48	−0.72
J (PAC)	56	66	41	0.70	−1.05
K (PAC)	57	66	44	0.82	−1.19
Support Tranches					
LA (SCH)	39	47	24	0.09	−0.18
LB (SCH)	29	58	−4	0.80	−0.82
M (SCH)	72	100	41	1.80	−1.72

The analysis reported in the top panel of Exhibit 7 help us identify where the cheap tranches are in the deal. The long average life and effective duration tranches in the deal are the PAC tranches G, H, J, and K. These tranches have high OAS relative to the other tranches and low option cost. They appear to be the cheap tranches in the deal. These PAC tranches had well protected cash flows and exhibited positive convexity (i.e., these tranches lose less in an adverse scenario than they gain in a positive scenario).

The next two panels in Exhibit 7 show the sensitivity of the OAS and the price (holding OAS constant at the base case) to changes in the prepayment speed (80% and 120% of the base case) and to changes in volatility (9% and 17%). This analysis shows that the change in the prepayment speed does not affect the collateral significantly, while the change in the OAS (holding the price constant) and price (holding OAS constant) for each tranche can be significant.

Tranches C and D at the time of the analysis were priced at a discount with short average lives. The OAS and price of these two tranches were not affected by a slowing down or a speeding up of the prepayment model. Tranche H was a premium tranche with a medium-term average life at the time of the analysis. Because tranche H was trading at a premium, it benefits from a slowing in prepayments, as the bondholder will receive the coupon for a longer time. Faster prepayments represent an adverse scenario. The PAC tranches are quite well-protected. The longer average life PACs will actually benefit from a reduced prepayment rate because they will be earning the higher coupon interest longer. So, on an OAS basis, the earlier conclusion that the long PACs were allocated a good part of the deal's value holds up under our first stress test (i.e., changing prepayments).

The sensitivity of the collateral and the tranches to changes in volatility are shown in the third panel of Exhibit 7. A lower volatility increases the value of the collateral, while a higher volatility reduces its value (This is consistent with our option cost equation in Section IV.E.) The long average life PACs continue to be fairly well-protected, whether the volatility is lower or higher. In the two volatility scenarios they continue to get a good OAS on a relative value basis, although not as much as in the base case if volatility is higher (but the OAS still looks like a reasonable value in this scenario). This reinforces the earlier conclusion concerning the investment merit of the long PACs in this deal. Note, however, that PAC tranches H, J, and K are more sensitive to the volatility assumption than tranches C, D, E, and G and therefore the investor is accepting greater volatility risk (i.e., the risk that volatility will change) with tranches H, J, and K relative to tranches C, D, E, and G.

SECTION V MEASURING INTEREST RATE RISK

As explained at Level I and again in Chapter 2, duration and convexity can be used to estimate the interest rate exposure to parallel shifts in the yield curve (i.e., a measure of level risk). In this section we will discuss duration measures for mortgage-backed securities. There are several duration measures that are used in practice. Two researchers who have done extensive work in measuring duration, Lakhbir Hayre and Hubert Chang, conclude that "No single duration measure will consistently work well for mortgage securities."[6] To that conclusion should be added that there are some measures that do not work at all.

---

[6] Lakhbir Hayre and Hubert Chang, "Effective and Empirical Duration of Mortgage Securities," *The Journal of Fixed Income* (March 1997), pp. 17-33.

A. Duration Measures

Duration is a measure of the price sensitivity to changes in interest rates. At Level I we have seen how to compute the duration of a security by shocking rates up and down and determining how the price of the security changes. Duration is then computed as follows:

$$\text{duration} = \frac{V_- - V_+}{2V_0(\Delta y)}$$

where

$$\Delta y = \text{change in rate used to calculate new values (i.e., the interest rate shock)}$$
$$V_+ = \text{estimated value if yield is increased by } \Delta y$$
$$V_- = \text{estimated value if yield is decreased by } \Delta y$$
$$V_0 = \text{initial price (per \$100 of par value)}$$

For bonds with embedded options such as mortgage-backed securities, the appropriate measure is effective duration and to capture the negative convexity of a bond with an embedded option, effective convexity should be computed. We will see how to calculate the effective duration for a mortgage-backed security using the Monte Carlo simulation model. Then we will see how the assumptions of the model impact the duration estimate. Dealers and vendors use other measures of duration that will be described later.

1. Effective Duration

To calculate effective duration, the value of the security must be estimated when rates are shocked up and down a given number of basis points. In terms of the Monte Carlo model, the yield curve used (either the Treasury yield curve or LIBOR curve) is shocked up and down and the new curve is used to generate the values to be used in the effective duration and effective convexity formulas. This is analogous to the process we used to compute effective duration and effective convexity using the binomial model in Chapter 2.

There are two important aspects of this process of generating the values when the rates are shocked that are critical to understand. First, the assumption is that the relationships assumed do not change when rates are shocked up and down. Specifically, the yield volatility is assumed to be unchanged to derive the new interest rate paths for a given shock (i.e., the new Exhibit 1), the spread between the mortgage rate and the 10-year Treasury rate is assumed to be unchanged in constructing the new Exhibit 2 from the newly constructed Exhibit 1, and the OAS is assumed to be constant. The constancy of the OAS comes into play because when discounting the new cash flows (i.e., the cash flows in the new Exhibit 3), the current OAS that was computed is assumed to be the same and is added to the new rates in the new Exhibit 1.

We'll use an illustration by Lakhbir Hayre and Hubert Chang to explain the calculation of effective duration for a mortgage-backed security, a FNMA 7.5% TBA passthrough on May 1, 1996.[7] On that day, the base mortgage rate was 7.64%. The price of the issue at the time was 98.781 (i.e., 98-25). The OAS was 65 basis points. Based on a shock of 25 basis points, the estimated prices holding the OAS constant at 65 basis points were as follows:

$$V_- = 99.949 \text{ for a decrease in the yield curve of 25 basis points}$$
$$V_+ = 97.542 \text{ for an increase in the yield curve of 25 basis points}$$

---

[7] Hayre and Chang, "Effective and Empirical Duration of Mortgage Securities."

The effective duration based on a Δy of 0.0025 is then

$$\frac{99.949 - 97.542}{2 \times 98.781 \times 0.0025} = 4.87$$

There are differences in the effective durations for a given mortgage-backed security reported by dealers and vendors of analytical systems. Several practitioners have explained and illustrated why there are differences in effective duration estimates reported effective durations of dealers and vendors. The differences result from, among others:[8]

1. differences in the amount of the rate shock used
2. differences in prepayment models
3. differences in option-adjusted spread
4. differences in the relationship between short-term interest rates and refinancing rates

At Level I (Chapter 6), we discussed the first reason. As explained, the rate shock is the amount interest rates are increased and decreased to obtain the two values that are inserted into the effective duration formula. If the change is too large, there is the problem with picking up the effect of convexity.

Prepayment models differ across dealers and vendors. Some dealer models consistently forecast slower prepayments relative to other dealer models and others the reverse.

The effective duration is dependent on the OAS computed. Recall that the calculation of the OAS is a byproduct of the Monte Carlo model. Therefore, the computed value for the OAS depends on all of the assumptions in the Monte Carlo model. Specifically, it depends on the yield volatility assumed and the prepayment model employed. Dealers and vendors make different assumptions regarding yield volatility and use proprietary prepayment models. These can result in differences in OAS. Since the OAS is added to the new simulated short-term rates to compute the new values for V_- and V_+, a different OAS will result in different effective durations.

Finally, recall that in explaining the Monte Carlo simulation model that we stated that in moving from Exhibit 1 (the simulated short-term rates) to Exhibit 2 (the refinancing rates), an assumption must be made about the relationship between short-term rates and the 10-year Treasury rate (i.e., the rate used as a proxy for refinancing). Differences in models about how large the spread between these rates will be affects the value of a mortgage-backed security and therefore the values used in the duration equation when rates are shocked.

2. Other Duration Measures

There have been other measures proposed for estimating the duration of a mortgage-backed security. These measures include **cash flow duration**, **coupon curve duration**, and **empirical duration**. The first two duration measures are forms of effective duration in that they do recognize that the values that should be used in the duration formula should take into account how the cash flows may change due to changes in prepayments when interest rates change. In contrast, empirical duration is a duration that is computed statistically using observed market prices.

[8] Sam Choi, "Effective Durations for Mortgage-Backed Securities: Recipes for Improvement," *The Journal of Fixed Income* (March 1996), pp. 24-30; and, Hayre and Chang, "Effective and Empirical Duration of Mortgage Securities."

a. Cash Flow Duration

Recall from the general duration formula that there are two values that must be substituted into the numerator of the formula — the value if rates are decreased (V_-) and the value if rates are increased (V_+). With effective duration, these two values consider how changes in interest rates change the cash flow due to prepayments. This is done through the Monte Carlo simulation by allowing for the cash flows to change on the interest rate paths.

For a **cash flow duration**, there is recognition that the cash flow can change but the analysis to obtain the cash flow is done following a static methodology. Specifically, the cash flow duration is calculated as follows:

Step 1: Calculate the cash flow based on some prepayment assumption.

Step 2: From the cash flow in Step 1 and the market price (V_0), compute the cash flow yield.

Step 3: Increase the cash flow yield by Δy and from a prepayment model determine the new prepayment rate at that higher cash flow yield. Typically, the prepayment rate will be lower than in Step 1 because of the higher yield level.

Step 4: Using the lower prepayment rate in Step 3 determine the cash flow and then value the cash flow using the higher cash flow yield as the discount rate. This gives the value (V_+).

Step 5: Decrease the cash flow yield by Δy and from a prepayment model determine the new prepayment rate at that lower cash flow yield. Typically, the prepayment rate will be higher than in Step 1 because of the lower yield level.

Step 6: Using the higher prepayment rate in Step 5 determine the cash flow and then value the cash flow using the lower cash flow yield as the discount rate. This gives the value (V_-).

From the change in basis points (Δy), the values for V_+ and V_- found in Steps 4 and 6, and the initial value V_0, the duration can be computed.

We can use the hypothetical CMO structure in Chapter 3 to illustrate how to calculate cash flow duration. Specifically, in FJF-2, there were four tranches, A, B, C, and Z. Let's focus on tranche C. Suppose that the price for this tranche is 100.2813. Then the cash flow duration is computed as follows:

Step 1: Suppose that the assumed prepayment rate for this tranche is 165 PSA.

Step 2: Based on the assumed prepayment rate of 165 PSA and the price of 100.2813, it can be demonstrated that the cash flow yield is 7%.

Step 3: Suppose that the cash flow yield is increased (i.e., shocked) by 25 basis points (from 7% to 7.25%) and suppose that some prepayment model projects a prepayment rate of 150 PSA. (Note that this is a slower prepayment rate than at 7%.)

Step 4: Based on 150 PSA, a new cash flow can be generated. The cash flow is then discounted at 7.25% (the new cash flow yield). It can be demonstrated that the value of this tranche based on these assumptions would be 98.3438. This is the value V_+.

Step 5: Suppose that the cash flow yield is decreased (i.e., shocked) by 25 basis points (from 7% to 6.75%) and suppose that some prepayment model projects a prepayment rate of 200 PSA. (Note that this is a faster prepayment rate than at 7%.)

Step 6: Based on 200 PSA, the new cash flow can be generated. The cash flow is then discounted at 6.75% (the new cash flow yield). It can be demonstrated that the value of this tranche based on these assumptions would be 101.9063. This is the value V_-.

Now we have the following information:

$$V_0 = 100.2813$$
$$V_+ = 98.3438$$
$$V_- = 101.9063$$
$$\Delta y = 0.0025$$

Then using the general form of duration, we obtain:

$$\text{duration} = \frac{101.9063 - 98.3438}{2(100.2813)(0.0025)} = 7.11$$

What type of duration measure is the cash flow duration — effective duration or modified duration? Technically, it is a form of effective duration because notice that in Steps 3 and 5 when the rate is changed, the cash flow is allowed to change. However, as has been stressed throughout, the valuation model that is used to get the new values to substitute into the duration formula is critical. The valuation model in the case of the cash flow duration is based on the naive assumption that there is a single prepayment rate over the life of the mortgage-backed security for any given interest rate shock. This is in contrast to the values produced by the Monte Carlo simulation model that does more sophisticated analyses of how the cash flow can change when interest rates change.

Why bother discussing the cash flow duration if it is an inferior form of effective duration? The reason is that it is a commonly cited duration measure and practitioners should be aware of how it is computed — and because we did discuss in detail yield calculations at Level I despite their limitations.

An interesting question is how does this form of duration compare to modified duration. Recall from Level I (Chapter 7) and Chapter 2 that modified duration does not assume that cash flows will change when rates are shocked. That is, in the steps discussed above to obtain cash flow duration, in Steps 3 and 5 it is assumed that the prepayment rate is the same as in Step 1.

To illustrate this, we'll once again use tranche C in FJF-2. In Step 3, the prepayment rate assumed is still 165 PSA despite the fact that rates are assumed to increase. That is, the cash flow is not assumed to change. Based on a cash flow yield of 7.25% and a prepayment rate of 165 PSA, the value of this tranche would decline to 98.4063. When the cash flow yield is assumed to decline to 6.75%, the prepayment rate is still assumed to be 165 PSA and the value of this tranche would be 102.1875. Then to calculate the modified duration we know:

$$
\begin{aligned}
V_0 &= 100.2813 \\
V_+ &= 98.4063 \\
V_- &= 102.1875 \\
\Delta y &= 0.0025
\end{aligned}
$$

The modified duration is then:

$$
\text{duration} = \frac{102.1875 - 98.4063}{2(100.2813)(0.0025)} = 7.54
$$

Thus, the modified duration is greater than the cash flow duration for this tranche.

It is important to reiterate that the modified duration is inferior to the cash flow duration because the former gives absolutely no recognition to how prepayments may change when interest rates change. While cash flow duration is commonly cited in practice, it is a form of effective duration that does give some recognition that prepayments and therefore cash flow may change when interest rates change, but it is based on a naive assumption about how prepayments may change. The effective duration as computed using Monte Carlo simulation is superior to cash flow duration.

b. Coupon Curve Duration

The **coupon curve duration** uses market prices to estimate the duration of a mortgage-backed security. This approach, first suggested by Douglas Breeden,[9] starts with the coupon curve of prices for similar mortgage-backed securities. The coupon curve represents generic (i.e., TBA as explained in Chapter 3) passthrough securities of a particular issuer with different coupon rates. By rolling up and down the coupon curve of prices, the duration can be obtained. Because of the way it is estimated, this approach to duration estimation was referred to by Breeden as the "roll-up, roll-down approach." The prices obtained from rolling up and rolling down the coupon curve of prices are substituted into the duration formula.

To illustrate this approach, suppose that the coupon curve of prices for a passthrough security for some month is as follows:

Coupon	Price
6%	85.19
7%	92.06
8%	98.38
9%	103.34
10%	107.28
11%	111.19

Suppose that the coupon curve duration for the 8% coupon passthrough is sought. If the yield declines by 100 basis points, the assumption is that the price of the 8% coupon passthrough will increase to the price of the current 9% coupon passthrough. Thus, the price will increase from 98.38 to 103.34. Similarly, if the yield increases by 100 basis points, the assumption is that the price of the 8% coupon passthrough will decline to the price of the 7% coupon passthrough (92.06). Using the duration formula, the corresponding values are:

$$
\begin{aligned}
V_0 &= 98.38 \\
V_+ &= 92.06
\end{aligned}
$$

---

[9] Douglas Breeden, "Risk, Return, and Hedging of Fixed-Rate Mortgages," *The Journal of Fixed Income* (September 1991), pp. 85-107.

$$V_- = 103.34$$
$$\Delta y = 0.01$$

The estimated duration based on the coupon curve is then:

$$\text{duration} = \frac{103.34 - 92.06}{2(98.38)(0.01)} = 5.73$$

Breeden tested the coupon curve durations and found them to be relatively accurate.[10] Bennett Golub reports a similar finding.[11]

While the advantages of the coupon curve duration are the simplicity of its calculation and the fact that current prices embody market expectations, there are disadvantages. The approach is limited to generic mortgage-backed securities and difficult to use for mortgage derivatives such as CMOs.

c. Empirical Duration

When computing effective duration and cash flow duration, the values to be substituted into the duration formula are those based on some valuation model. For coupon curve duration, the observed market prices are used in the duration formula. In contrast, **empirical duration** is estimated statistically using historical market prices and market yields.[12] Regression analysis is used to estimate the relationship. Some firms such as PaineWebber use empirical duration, also called **implied duration**, as their primary measure of the duration of an MBS.

There are three advantages to the empirical duration approach.[13] First, the duration estimate does not rely on any theoretical formulas or analytical assumptions. Second, the estimation of the required parameters is easy to compute using regression analysis. Finally, the only inputs that are needed are a reliable price series and Treasury yield series.

There are disadvantages.[14] First, a reliable price series for the mortgage security may not be available. For example, there may be no price series available for a thinly traded mortgage derivative security or the prices may be matrix priced (i.e., priced by a pricing service based on issues with similar characteristics) or model priced rather than actual transaction prices. Second, an empirical relationship does not impose a structure for the options embedded in a mortgage-backed security and this can distort the empirical duration. This may occur after a sharp and sustained shock to interest rates have been realized. Finally, the volatility of the spread to Treasury yields can distort how the price of a mortgage-backed security reacts to yield changes.

---

[10] Breeden, "Risk, Return, and Hedging of Fixed-Rate Mortgages."

[11] See Bennett W. Golub, "Towards a New Approach to Measuring Mortgage Duration," Chapter 32 in Frank J. Fabozzi (ed.), *The Handbook of Mortgage-Backed Securities* (Chicago: Probus Publishing, 1995), p. 673.

[12] This approach was first suggested in 1986 in Scott M. Pinkus and Marie A. Chandoha, "The Relative Price Volatility of Mortgage Securities," *Journal of Portfolio Management* (Summer 1986), pp. 9-22 and then in 1990 by Paul DeRossa, Laurie Goodman, and Mike Zazzarino, "Duration Estimates on Mortgage-Backed Securities," *Journal of Portfolio Management* (Winter 1993), pp. 32-37, and more recently in Laurie S. Goodman and Jeffrey Ho, "Mortgage Hedge Ratios: Which One Works Best?" *The Journal of Fixed Income* (December 1997), pp. 23-33, and Laurie S. Goodman and Jeffrey Ho, "An Integrated Approach to Hedging and Relative Value Analysis," Chapter 15 in Frank J. Fabozzi (ed.), *Advances in the Valuation and Management of Mortgage-Backed Securities* (New Hope, PA: Frank J. Fabozzi Associates, 1999).

[13] Golub, "Towards a New Approach to Measuring Mortgage Duration," p. 672.

[14] Golub, "Towards a New Approach to Measuring Mortgage Duration."

SECTION VI VALUING ASSET-BACKED SECURITIES

The model that should be used for valuing an asset-backed security (ABS) depends on the characteristic of the loans or receivables backing the deal. An ABS can have one of the following three characteristics:

Characteristic 1: The ABS does not have a prepayment option.

Characteristic 2: The ABS has a prepayment option but borrowers do not exhibit a tendency to prepay when refinancing rates fall below the loan rate.

Characteristic 3: The ABS has a prepayment option and borrowers do exhibit a tendency to prepay when refinancing rates fall below the loan rate.

An example of a Characteristic 1 type ABS is a security backed by credit card receivables. An example of a Characteristic 2 type ABS is a security backed by automobile loans. A security backed by closed-end home equity loans where the borrowers are high quality borrowers (i.e., prime borrowers) is an example of a Characteristic 3 type ABS. There are some real-estate backed ABS we discussed in Chapter 4 where the verdict is still out as to the degree to which borrowers take advantage of refinancing opportunities. Specifically, these include securities backed by manufactured housing loans and securities backed by closed-end home equity loans to borrowers classified as low quality borrowers.

There are two possible approaches to valuing an ABS. They are the

1. zero-volatility spread (Z-spread) approach
2. option-adjusted spread (OAS) approach

For the Z-spread approach the interest rates used to discount the cash flows are the spot rates plus the zero-volatility spread. The value of an ABS is then the present value of the cash flows based on these discount rates. The Z-spread approach does not consider the prepayment option. Consequently, the Z-spread approach should be used to value Characteristic 1 type ABS. (In terms of the relationship between the Z-spread, OAS, and option cost discussed earlier in this chapter, this means that the value of the option is zero and therefore the Z-spread is equal to the OAS.) Since the Z-spread is equal to the OAS, the Z-spread approach to valuation can be used.

The Z-spread approach can also be used to value Characteristic 2 type ABS because while the borrowers do have a prepayment option, the option is not typically exercised. Thus, as with Characteristic 1 type ABS, the Z-spread is equal to the OAS.

The OAS approach — which is considerably more computationally extensive than the Z-spread approach — is used to value securities where there is an embedded option and there is an expectation that the option is expected to be exercised if it makes economic sense for the borrower to do so. Consequently, the OAS approach is used to value Characteristic 3 type ABS. The choice is then whether to use the binomial model (or a comparable model) or the Monte Carlo simulation model. Since typically the cash flow for an ABS with a prepayment option is interest rate path dependent — as with a mortgage-backed security — the Monte Carlo simulation model is used.

**SECTION VII
VALUING ANY
SECURITY**

We conclude this chapter with a summary of the approaches to valuing any fixed income security using the two approaches that we discussed in the previous section — the Z-spread approach and the OAS approach.

Below we match the valuation approach with the type of security.

1. For an *option-free bond* the correct approach is the Z-spread approach.

2. For a *bond with an embedded option where the cash flow is not interest rate path dependent* (such as a callable corporate or agency debenture bond or a putable bond) the correct approach is the OAS approach. Since the backward induction method can be used for such bonds, the binomial model or its equivalent should be used.

3. For a bond with an embedded option where the cash flow is interest rate path dependent (such as a mortgage-backed security or certain real estate-backed ABS) the correct approach is the OAS approach. However, because of the interest rate path dependency of the cash flow, the Monte Carlo simulation model should be used.

**SECTION VIII
KEY POINTS**

❑ *The cash flow yield is the interest rate that makes the present value of the projected cash flow for a mortgage-backed or asset-backed security equal to its market price plus accrued interest.*

❑ *The convention is to compare the yield on mortgage-backed and asset-backed securities to that of a Treasury coupon security by calculating the security's bond-equivalent yield. This measure is found by computing an effective semiannual rate and doubling it.*

❑ *The cash flow yield is based on three assumptions that thereby limit its use as a measure of relative value: (1) a prepayment assumption and default/recovery assumption, (2) an assumption that the cash flows will be reinvested at the computed cash flow yield, and (3) an assumption that the investor will hold the security until the last loan in the pool is paid off.*

❑ *The nominal spread is commonly computed as the difference between the cash flow yield and the yield on a Treasury security with the same maturity as the mortgage-backed or asset-backed security's average life.*

❑ *The nominal spread masks the fact that a portion of the spread is compensation for accepting prepayment risk.*

❑ *An investor or portfolio manager who buys solely on the basis of nominal spread fails to determine whether or not that nominal spread offers an adequate compensation for prepayment risk.*

❑ *An investor or portfolio manager needs a measure that indicates the potential compensation after adjusting for prepayment risk and this measure is the option-adjusted spread.*

❑ *The zero-volatility spread is a measure of the spread that the investor would realize over the entire Treasury spot rate curve if the mortgage-backed or asset-backed security is held to maturity.*

❑ *The zero-volatility spread is not a spread off one point on the Treasury yield curve, as is the nominal spread, but a spread that will make the present value of the cash flows from the mortgage-backed or asset-backed security when discounted at the Treasury spot rate plus the spread equal to the market price of the security.*

❑ *The binomial model and other similar models that use the backward induction method can be used to value securities where the decision to exercise a call option is not dependent on how interest rates evolved over time — that is, the decision of an issuer to call a bond will depend on the level of the rate at which the issue can be refunded relative to the issue's coupon rate, and not the path interest rates took to get to that rate.*

❑ *Mortgage-backed securities and some types of asset-backed securities are products where the periodic cash flows are "interest rate path-dependent" — meaning that the cash flow received in one period is determined not only by the current interest rate level, but also by the path that interest rates took to get to the current level.*

❑ *The Monte Carlo simulation model for valuing mortgage-backed securities involves generating a set of cash flows based on simulated future mortgage refinancing rates, which in turn imply simulated prepayment rates.*

❑ *In the Monte Carlo simulation model there is nothing to assure that the simulated interest rates will generate arbitrage-free values of the benchmark securities used in the valuation process; consequently, the simulated interest rates must be adjusted so as to produce arbitrage-free values.*

❑ *The present value of a given interest rate path can be thought of as the theoretical value of a security if that path was actually realized.*

❑ *The theoretical value of a mortgage-backed security can be determined by calculating the average of the theoretical values of all the interest rate paths.*

❑ *In the Monte Carlo simulation model, the option-adjusted spread is the spread that when added to all the spot rates on all interest rate paths will make the average present value of the paths equal to the observed market price (plus accrued interest).*

❑ *The OAS is measured relative to the benchmark interest rates that were used to generate the interest rate paths and to adjust the interest rate paths to make them arbitrage free.*

❑ *Since typically for a mortgage-backed security the benchmark interest rates are the on-the-run Treasury rates, the OAS measures the average spread over the Treasury spot rate curve, not the Treasury yield curve.*

❑ *The OAS is superior to the nominal spread which gives no recognition to the prepayment risk.*

❑ *The implied cost of the option embedded in a mortgage-backed or an asset-backed security can be obtained by calculating the difference between the option-adjusted spread at the assumed interest rate volatility and the zero-volatility spread.*

❑ *The option cost measures the prepayment (or option) risk embedded in the security and is a byproduct of the option-adjusted spread analysis, not valued explicitly with some option pricing model.*

❑ *In valuation modeling of collateralized mortgage obligations, the objective is to figure out how the value and risks of the collateral get transmitted to the tranches in a deal.*

❑ *There are several duration measures for mortgage-backed securities that are used in practice — effective duration, cash flow duration, coupon curve duration, and empirical duration.*

❑ *For bonds with embedded options such as mortgage-backed securities, the appropriate measure is effective duration and to capture negative convexity, effective convexity should be computed.*

❑ *Effective duration is computed using Monte Carlo simulation by shocking the short-term interest rates for each interest rate path generated up and down and obtaining the new value for the security; the new values determined when rates are shocked up and down are used in the duration formula.*

❏ *There are differences in the effective duration reported for a given mortgage-backed security by dealers and vendors of analytical systems primarily due to differences in: (1) the amount of the rate shock used, (2) the prepayment model used, (3) the option-adjusted spread computed, and (4) the relationship between short-term interest rates and refinancing rates assumed.*

❏ *Cash flow duration and coupon curve duration measures are forms of effective duration in that they do recognize that the values that should be used in the duration formula should take into account how the cash flows may change due to changes in prepayments when interest rates change.*

❏ *Cash flow duration is based on an initial cash flow yield and initial prepayment rate and computes the new values when rates are shocked (i.e., when the cash flow yield is shocked) allowing the cash flow to change based on a new prepayment rate as determined by a prepayment model.*

❏ *Cash flow duration is superior to modified duration (which assumes that cash flows do not change when rates are shocked) but inferior to effective duration as computed using the Monte Carlo simulation model.*

❏ *The coupon curve duration begins with the coupon curve of prices for similar mortgage-backed securities and uses values in the duration formula found by rolling up and down the coupon curve of prices.*

❏ *Empirical duration is a duration measure that is computed statistically using regression analysis based on observed market prices and yields.*

❏ *Empirical duration poses no structure on the embedded option.*

❏ *A limitation of empirical duration and coupon curve duration is that they are difficult to apply to CMOs because of a lack of valid market price data.*

❏ *The zero-volatility spread added to the spot rates can be used to value an asset-backed security if either (1) the security does not have a prepayment option or (2) the borrower has the right to prepay but it has been observed that the borrower does not tend to exercise that option if interest rates decline below the loan rate.*

❏ *The option-adjusted spread approach to valuation using the Monte Carlo simulation model is used for an asset-backed security if the borrower does have the right to prepay and it has been observed that the borrower does tend to refinance when interest rates decline below the loan rate.*

❏ *For any fixed income security, the valuation approaches that can be employed are the zero-volatility spread approach and the option-adjusted spread approach.*

❏ *For option-free bonds, the zero-volatility spread approach should be used.*

❏ *The choice of whether to use the binomial model (or a similar "nomial" model that uses the backward induction method) or the Monte Carlo simulation model for a security with an embedded option depends on the characteristics of the security.*

❏ *For corporate and agency debentures with an embedded option the binomial model or its equivalent should be used for valuation.*

❏ *For securities such as mortgage-backed and asset-backed securities (those where it is observed that borrowers do exercise the prepayment option) the Monte Carlo simulation model should be used since the cash flows are typically interest rate path dependent.*

END OF CHAPTER QUESTIONS

1. Suppose that based on a prepayment assumption of 200 PSA the cash flow yield for a specific agency passthrough security is 7.5% and the stated maturity is 15 years. Suppose further that the average life of this security is 8 years. Assume the following yield curve for Treasuries:

Maturity	Yield
6-year	6.2%
8-year	6.3%
10-year	6.4%
15-year	6.6%

   a. What is the nominal spread for this agency passthrough security?

   b. What must occur over the life of this agency passthrough security for the cash flow yield of 7.5% to be realized?

2. Suppose that the monthly cash flow yield is 0.74%. What is the cash flow yield on a bond-equivalent basis?

3. Jane Howard is a corporate bond analyst. Recently she has been asked to extend her responsibilities to mortgage-backed securities. In researching the methodology for valuing mortgage-backed securities she read that these securities are valued using the Monte Carlo simulation model. She was unfamiliar with this approach to valuation because in valuing callable corporate bonds she used the binomial model. Explain to Ms. Howard why the Monte Carlo simulation method is used to value mortgage-backed securities rather than the binomial method.

4. The following questions have to do with the Monte Carlo simulation model.

   a. What assumption must be made in generating the path of short-term interest rates?

   b. Why must the paths of short-term interest rates be adjusted?

   c. In determining the path of refinancing rates, what assumption must be made?

5. Nat Hawthorne, a portfolio manager, discussed the valuation of a particular mortgage-backed security with his broker, Steven Ruthledge. Mr. Hawthorne is considering the purchase of the security and asked what valuation model the brokerage firm used. Mr. Ruthledge responded that the Monte Carlo simulation model was used. Mr. Hawthorne then asked about what prepayment assumption is used in the Monte Carlo simulation model. Mr. Ruthledge responded that for the particular security Mr. Hawthorne is considering, 175 PSA was assumed. Mr. Hawthorne was confused by the response because he did not believe that a particular PSA assumption was made in the Monte Carlo simulation model. Is Mr. Hawthorne correct? Explain your answer.

6. What interest rates are used to value a mortgage-backed security on each interest rate path when using the Monte Carlo simulation model?

7. Juan Rodriquez is the manager of a portfolio containing mortgage passthrough securities. He is reviewing output of his firm's analytical system for several passthrough securities that are in the portfolio. Below is a portion of the report for three passthrough securities:

Passthrough	Price based on an assumed interest rate volatility of			
	11%	13%	15%	16%
Security 1	100	98	95	93
Security 2	92	90	88	87
Security 3	102	104	106	107

Mr. Rodriquez believes that there is an error in the analytical system. Why does he suspect that there is an error?

8. Suppose that the pool of passthroughs used as collateral for a collateralized mortgage obligation is selling at a premium. Also suppose that one tranche in the deal, Tranche X, is selling at a discount and another tranche, Tranche Y, is selling at a premium.

a. Explain why a slowdown in prepayments will tend to increase the value of the collateral?

b. Explain why a slowdown in prepayments will not affect the value of Tranches X and Y in the same way.

9. Assume for simplicity that only ten interest rate paths are used in the Monte Carlo simulation model to a value Tranche W of a CMO deal. Suppose further that based on a spread of 70 basis points, the present value of the interest rate paths is as follows:

Interest rate path	1	2	3	4	5	6	7	8	9	10
PV for path	80	90	84	88	94	92	86	91	99	87

Based on the Monte Carlo simulation model and assuming a spread required by the market of 70 basis points, what is the theoretical value of Tranche W.

10. Jane Hubert is using an analytical system purchased by her firm to analyze mortgage-backed securities. The analytical system uses the Monte Carlo simulation model for valuation. She is given a choice when using the system to use either the "full Monte Carlo analysis" or "16 representative interest rate paths."

a. What is meant by "16 representative interest path paths"?

b. How is the theoretical value of a mortgage-backed security determined when representative paths are used?

c. What is the trade-off when using representative interest rate paths versus using the full Monte Carlo analysis?

11. A portfolio manager is using an analytical system to value Tranche K of a CMO deal. The Monte Carlo simulation model uses eight representative interest rate paths. The present value of each of the representative interest rate paths and the weight of each path are shown below:

Representative path	1	2	3	4	5	6	7	8
Weight of representative path	20%	18%	16%	12%	12%	12%	6%	4%
PV of representative path	70	82	79	68	74	86	91	93

What is the theoretical value of Tranche K?

12. Suppose that 10 representative paths are used in the Monte Carlo simulation model and that each path has a weight of 10%. The present value for each representative path is based on discounting the cash flows on an interest rate path by the short-term interest rates on that path plus a spread. For the different spreads used, the present value of each representative path is shown below for Tranche L in a CMO deal:

Representative	Present value if the spread used is			
path	70 bps	75 bps	80 bps	85 bps
1	77	72	70	68
2	82	80	77	72
3	86	84	81	78
4	89	86	83	81
5	74	70	68	65
6	88	86	82	80
7	96	92	88	86
8	92	90	86	84
9	74	71	67	65
10	68	64	61	59

   a. Suppose that the market price of Tranche L is 79.5. What is the option-adjusted spread?

   b. Suppose instead of a market price for Tranche L of 79.5 the market price is 73.8. What is the option-adjusted spread?

13. Below are the results of a Monte Carlo simulation analysis using eight representative paths for two tranches of a CMO deal, Tranches M and N:

Representative path	1	2	3	4	5	6	7	8
PV of path for:								
Tranche M	60	55	90	105	110	50	48	70
Tranche N	86	85	89	91	84	92	87	86

One of the tranches is a PAC tranche and the other is a support tranche. Which tranche is probably the PAC tranche and which is probably the support tranche?

14. An analysis of an agency CMO structure using the Monte Carlo simulation model based on 12% volatility found the following:

	OAS (basis points)	Z-spread (basis points)	Effective duration
Collateral	90	130	8.0
Tranche			
PAC I A	50	60	1.5
PAC I B	70	80	3.0
PAC I C	30	120	5.0
PAC I D	30	150	9.0
PAC II A	80	150	4.0
PAC II B	20	280	6.0
Support S1	35	165	11.0
Support S2	50	190	14.0

   a. What is the option cost for PAC IA, PAC II A, and Support S1?

   b. Which of the PAC tranches appears to be expensive in the deal on a relative value basis?

c. PAC II tranches are support tranches with schedules. The four support tranches in the deal are therefore PAC II A, PAC II B, Support S1, and Support S2. Which of the support tranches appears to be expensive on a relative value basis?

d. Despite its low OAS of 20 basis points, why might a yield buyer be induced to purchase PAC II B?

15. How is the effective duration and effective convexity of a mortgage-backed security computed using the Monte Carlo simulation model? Be sure to explain what assumption is made regarding the option-adjusted spread when computing the effective duration and effective convexity.

16. Joel Winters is a junior portfolio manager of a corporate bond portfolio. A decision has been made to include mortgage-backed securities in the portfolio. Mr. Winters is considering the purchase of a CMO tranche called a support bond. Before he buys this tranche, he wants to know its effective duration. Because he does not have the use of an analytical system to compute effective duration, Mr. Winters contacts three dealers and inquires as to the effective duration for this tranche. He is given the following effective duration from the three dealer firms:

Dealer	1	2	3
Effective duration	8.1	4.6	11.6

Mr. Winters is puzzled by the significant variation in the effective durations, especially since all the dealers indicated that the Monte Carlo simulation model was used. In his experience with corporate bonds with embedded options he has never observed such a significant variation in the effective duration from dealer firm to dealer firm.

Explain to Mr. Winters why there is such a significant variation in the effective durations. Be sure to clearly identify the reasons for the variation in the effective durations.

17. Explain why you agree or disagree with the following statement: "If the collateral for a CMO deal has negative convexity, then all the tranches in the deal must have negative convexity. The only difference is the degree of negative convexity from one tranche to another."

18. a. What is the cash flow duration of a mortgage-backed security?

b. What are the limitations of cash flow duration as a measure of the price sensitivity of a mortgage-backed security to changes in interest rates?

19. Suppose that the coupon curve of prices for a passthrough security for some month is as follows:

Coupon	Price
7%	94.00
8%	97.06
9%	99.50
10%	102.60
11%	105.25
12%	106.19

What is the coupon curve duration for the 9% coupon passthrough?

20. Karen Brown is considering alternative measures for estimating the duration of some complex CMO tranches. One measure she is considering is empirical duration. Explain to Ms. Brown the difficulties of using empirical duration for complex CMO tranches.

21. Thomas Larken is a portfolio manager who is considering investing in the asset-backed securities market. In particular, Mr. Larken is considering investing in either credit card receivables, auto loan-backed securities, or home equity loan-backed securities. Examination of the nominal spreads in these three sectors of the market indicates that the largest nominal spread for AAA and AA issues is home equity loan-backed securities. Based on this analysis, Mr. Larken believes that the best sector in which to invest is in home equity loan-backed securities because it offers the greatest relative value as measured by the nominal spread. Explain whether or not you agree with Mr. Larken's assessment of the relative attractiveness of home equity loan-backed securities.

22. An investment banker has created an asset-backed security in which the collateral is the future royalties of a song writer. Which valuation approach do you think should be used to value this security, the zero-volatility spread or the option-adjusted spread?

23. Suppose that empirical evidence on prepayments for manufactured housing loans suggests that borrowers do not take advantage of refinancing when interest rates decline. Explain whether the zero-volatility spread approach or OAS approach is appropriate for valuing securities backed by manufacturing housing loans.

24. Evidence by Wall Street firms on home equity loans strongly suggests that high quality borrowers do take advantage of a decline in interest rates to refinance a loan. In contrast, low quality borrowers tend not to take advantage of a decline in interest rates to refinance.

    a. What is the appropriate valuation approach (option-adjusted spread approach or zero-volatility spread approach) to value home equity loan-backed securities where the underlying pool of loans are those of high quality borrowers? Explain why.

    b. What is the appropriate valuation approach (option-adjusted spread approach or zero-volatility spread approach) to value home equity loan-backed securities where the underlying pool of loans are those of low quality borrowers? Explain why.

SOLUTIONS TO END OF CHAPTER QUESTIONS

1. a. The convention is to determine the nominal spread relative to the spread on a Treasury security with the same maturity as the average life of the mortgage-backed security. Since the average life is 8 years, the benchmark Treasury issue is the 8-year issue. The nominal spread is then 7.5% minus the 6.3% of the 8-year Treasury issue. So, the nominal spread is 120 basis points.

b. For the 7.5% cash flow yield to be realized the following must occur:

- actual prepayments must be 200 PSA over the life of the security
- the monthly cash flow (interest plus principal repayment) must be reinvested at a rate of 7.5%
- the security must be held until the last mortgage pays off

2. The monthly cash flow yield, i_M, is 0.0074. Therefore,

$$\text{bond-equivalent yield} = 2[(1.0074)^6 - 1] = 0.0905 = 9.05\%$$

3. The binomial model used to value a corporate bond with an embedded option can handle securities in which the decision to exercise a call option is not dependent on how interest rates evolved over time. That is, the decision of a corporate issuer to call a bond will depend on the level of the rate at which the issue can be refunded relative to the issue's coupon rate. The decision to call does not depend on the path interest rates took to get to that rate. Ms. Howard must understand that this is not a characteristic of mortgage-backed securities. These securities are "interest rate path-dependent," meaning that the cash flow received in one period is determined not only by the interest rate level at that period, but also by the path that interest rates took to get to that rate.

For example, in the case of passthrough securities, prepayments are interest rate path-dependent because this month's prepayment rate depends on whether there have been prior opportunities to refinance since the underlying mortgages were originated. For CMOs there are typically two sources of path dependency in a CMO tranche's cash flows. First, the collateral prepayments are path-dependent as just described. Second, the cash flows to be received in the current month by a CMO tranche depend on the outstanding balances of the other tranches in the deal. Thus, we need the history of prepayments to calculate these balances.

4. a. To generate the path of short-term interest rates, an assumption about the volatility of short-term interest rates must be made.

b. If the short-term interest rates on each path are used without an adjustment, there is no assurance that the Monte Carlo simulation model will correctly value the on-the-run Treasury issues. An adjustment to the short-term interest rates is required in order to have the model properly price on-the-run Treasury issues so that the model will provide arbitrage-free values.

c. In moving from the short-term interest rates to the refinancing rates, it is necessary to make an assumption about the spread between these rates.

5. In the Monte Carlo simulation model, a prepayment *model* is used. The prepayment model provides a prepayment rate for each month on each interest rate path. Thus,

no specific PSA prepayment assumption is made. Consequently, the statement by Mr. Ruthledge that a 175 PSA was made is inconsistent with the Monte Carlo simulation model. Therefore, Mr. Hawthorne should have been confused by Mr. Ruthledge's response.

6. On an interest rate path, the short-term interest rates are the forward rates. It is the forward rates plus an appropriate spread that is used to value a mortgage-backed security on an interest rate path.

7. The investor in a passthrough security has effectively sold a call option to borrowers (homeowners). The higher the assumed interest rate volatility the greater the value of this embedded call option and therefore the lower the price of a passthrough security. Securities 1 and 2 have the correct relationship between price and assumed interest rate volatility. Security 3 has the opposite relationship. Therefore, the error that Mr. Rodriquez discovered is with the relationship between assumed interest rate volatility and price for Security 3.

8. a. Since the collateral is trading at a premium, a slowdown in prepayments will allow the investor to receive the higher coupon for a longer period of time. This will increase the value of the collateral.

   b. Because Tranche Y is selling at a premium, its value will increase with a slowdown in prepayments. In contrast, because Tranche X is selling at a discount, a slowdown in prepayments will decrease its value. This is because for Tranche X, there will be less principal returned to be reinvested at the new, higher rates. Also, assuming that X was purchased when it was trading at a discount, there will be less of a capital gain realized (since principal is returned at par).

9. The theoretical value based on the ten interest rate paths is the average of the present value of the interest rate paths. The average value is 89.1.

10. a. Rather than sampling a large number of interest rate paths, some vendors of mortgage analytical systems have developed computational procedures that reduce the number of paths required. The procedure involves using statistical techniques to reduce the number of interest rate paths to sets of similar paths. These paths are called representative paths. The security is then valued on each of the representative interest rate paths — 16 in the question.

    b. The theoretical value of a security when the representative interest rate paths are used is the weighted average of the 16 representative paths. The weight for a path is the percentage of that representative path relative to the total paths in a full Monte Carlo analysis.

    c. The trade-off between the full Monte Carlo analysis and the 16 representative paths is one of speed versus accuracy. The full Monte Carlo analysis provides the true value of the security — *true only based on all the assumptions of the model*. Using 16 representative sample is less accurate but requires less computational time.

11. The theoretical value is the weighted average of the present value of the representative interest rate paths. The weighted average of the present value of the representative interest rate paths is 77.94 as shown below:

Weight	PV	Weight × PV
0.20	70	14.00
0.18	82	14.76
0.16	79	12.64
0.12	68	8.16
0.12	74	8.88
0.12	86	10.32
0.06	91	5.46
0.04	93	3.72
Theoretical value		77.94

12. Using the representative interest rate paths, the theoretical value of a mortgage-backed security is the weighted average of the present value of the paths. Since it is assumed in the question that each path has the same weight, the theoretical value is the simple average of the present values of the interest rate paths. For the four spreads, the average PV is given below:

Representative path	Present value if the spread used is			
	70 bps	75 bps	80 bps	85 bps
Average PV	82.6	79.5	76.3	73.8

a. The option-adjusted spread is the spread that will make the theoretical value equal to the market price. Since the question assumes that Tranche L has a market price of 79.5, then a spread of 75 basis points will produce a theoretical value equal to the market price of 79.5. Therefore, the OAS is 75 basis points.

b. If the price is 73.8 instead of 79.5, then the OAS is the spread that will make the theoretical value equal to 73.8. From the table above it can be seen that a spread of 85 basis points will produce a theoretical value equal to 73.8. Therefore, the OAS is 85 basis points.

13. Tranche M has a substantial variation in the present value for the paths. This is a characteristic of a support tranche since a support tranche is exposed to substantial prepayment risk. Tranche N has little variation in the present value for the paths and this is a characteristic of a PAC tranche. Therefore, Tranche M is probably the support tranche and Tranche N is probably the PAC tranche.

14. a. The option cost is the difference between the Z-spread and the OAS. Therefore,

PAC I A: 60 − 50 = 10 basis points
PAC II A: 150 − 80 = 70 basis points
Support S1:   165 − 35 = 130 basis points

b. Typically, the OAS increases with effective duration. The two longer PAC tranches, PAC I C and PAC I D, have lower OAS than the two shorter duration PACs. Therefore, the two longer duration PACs appear to be expensive.

c. On a relative value basis, all but PAC II A appear to be expensive. PAC II B has a lower OAS than PAC II A even though it has a higher effective duration. The other two support tranches without a schedule have a low OAS relative to their effective durations.

   d. Investors who do not appreciate the significance of the option risk associated with a tranche can be induced to buy PAC II B because they look exclusively at the nominal spread. While the nominal spread is not provided as part of the information in the question, it can be estimated from the Z-spread. A Z-spread of 280 basis point is extremely appealing to investors for a security with no credit risk (since the deal is an agency CMO deal). Also, investors who do not realize that a PAC II is a support bond will believe that they have purchased a PAC tranche with a high "spread" to Treasuries.

15. The effective duration and effective convexity require the calculation of V_- and V_+. To calculate V_-, each path of short-term interest rates is decreased by a small number of basis points, say 25 basis points. Then, the cash flows are generated for each interest rate path. When the new cash flows are valued using the short-term interest rates plus a spread, the spread used is the original OAS. That is, it is assumed that the OAS does not change when interest rates are decreased. The same procedure is followed to compute V_+, but each path of short-term rates is increased by the same small number of basis points as was used to compute V_-. Again, it is assumed that the OAS does not change, so the new short-term interest rates plus the original OAS are used to discount the new cash flows on the interest rate paths.

16. First it is important to note that the CMO tranche is a support tranche and therefore has considerable prepayment risk. Despite Mr. Winters having been told that all the dealer firms used the Monte Carlo simulation model to compute the effective duration, there are assumptions in the model that can vary from dealer to dealer. This is the reason for the variation in the effective duration. These different assumptions in computing the value of a mortgage-backed security include:

     1. differences in the amount of the rate shock used
     2. differences in prepayment models
     3. differences in option-adjusted spread (recall that the OAS is held constant when rates are shocked)
     4. differences in the relationship between short-term interest rates and refinancing rates

17. This statement is incorrect. From a collateral with negative convexity, tranches with both positive and negative convexity can be created. For example, a PAC bond that is well protected will have little prepayment risk and therefore positive convexity — effectively the convexity of an option-free bond. However, one or more of the other tranches in the deal would have to have more negative convexity than the collateral itself, since the tranching of the collateral can only reallocate prepayment risk; it cannot eliminate it entirely.

18. a. Cash flow duration is computed assuming that if interest rates are changed the prepayment rate will change when computing the new value.

   b. The problem is that this duration measure is based on one initial prepayment speed and when rates are changed it is assumed the prepayment speed will change to another prepayment speed. It is a static approach because it considers only one prepayment speed if rates change. It does not consider the dynamics that interest rates can change in the future and therefore there is not just one potential cash flow or prepayment rate that must be considered in valuing a mortgage-backed security.

19. To compute the coupon curve duration the assumption is that if the yield declines by 100 basis points, the price of the 9% coupon passthrough will increase to the price of the current 10% coupon passthrough. Thus, the price will increase from 99.50 to 102.60. Similarly, if the yield increases by 100 basis points, the assumption is that the price of the 9% coupon passthrough will decline to the price of the 8% coupon passthrough (97.06). Using the duration formula, the corresponding values are:

$$
\begin{aligned}
V_0 &= 99.50 \\
V_+ &= 97.06 \\
V_- &= 102.60 \\
\Delta y &= 0.01
\end{aligned}
$$

The estimated duration based on the coupon curve is then:

$$\frac{102.60 - 97.06}{2(99.50)(0.01)} = 2.78$$

20. Empirical duration is computed using statistical analysis. It requires good price data for the tranche whose empirical duration is to be computed. A major problem with applying empirical duration to complex CMO tranches is that a reliable series of price data is often not available for a thinly traded mortgage product or the prices may be matrix priced or model priced rather than actual transaction prices. The second problem is that an empirical relationship does not impose a structure for the options embedded in a mortgage-backed security and this can distort the empirical duration. Finally, the volatility of the spread to Treasury yields can distort how the price of a mortgage-backed security reacts to yield changes.

21. The nominal spread of an asset-backed security hides the associated option or prepayment risk. For auto loan-backed securities, refinancing is not an important factor and therefore prepayment risk is not significant. For credit card receivables, there is prepayment risk only at the security level — that is, a credit card borrower cannot prepay because there is no schedule of payments but a security can be prepaid if certain rapid or early amortization triggers are realized. However, prepayment risk is not significant. In contrast, for home equity loan-backed securities prepayment risk is significant and the nominal spread reflects that risk. Consequently, assessing relative value for these three types of asset-backed securities based on the nominal spread is incorrect because the spread is not adjusted for the prepayment risk. Home equity loan-backed securities offer a higher nominal spread because of the prepayment risk.

22. The appropriate valuation approach depends on whether or not the borrower has an option to prepay. Furthermore, even if the borrower has the right to prepay, it depends on whether or not the borrower will take advantage of this option to prepay when interest rates decline. Since the security involves future royalties, there is no prepayment option. Consequently, there is no option value and the appropriate valuation approach is the zero-volatility spread.

23. While there is an option to prepay, if the empirical evidence is correct that borrowers do not prepay when rates decline, then the option value is zero. Consequently, the zero-volatility spread approach is the appropriate approach since the OAS is equal to the zero-volatility spread.

24. a. Since high quality borrowers are observed to take advantage of refinancing opportunities, there is a value to the prepayment option. Consequently, the option-adjusted spread approach is appropriate when the underlying pool of home equity loans of high quality borrowers.

    b. Since low quality borrowers may prepay but have been observed not to take advantage of refinancing opportunities, there is very little value to the prepayment option. Since the option cost has a value of zero, the zero-volatility spread is equal to the option-adjusted spread. Consequently, the zero-volatility spread approach can be used to value securities backed by a pool of home equity loans of low quality borrowers.

       However, there is a caveat here regarding the behavior of low quality borrowers. The answer ignores the adverse selection impact of borrowers who upgrade their credit profile and refinance out, leaving a potentially longer average life, and worse credit, pool.

Chapter 6

A FRAMEWORK FOR ASSESSING TRADING STRATEGIES

LEARNING OUTCOME STATEMENTS

After reading this chapter you should be able to:

- explain what leverage is.
- identify the advantages and disadvantages of leverage.
- explain what a repurchase agreement is.
- compute the dollar interest of a repurchase agreement.
- discuss the credit risks associated with a repurchase agreement.
- distinguish between special (or hot) collateral and general collateral.
- explain the factors that affect the repo rate.
- compute the total return for a bond over some investment horizon.
- describe what scenario analysis is.
- explain how interest rate risk is controlled in a trade.
- explain why total return analysis and scenario analysis should be used to assess the potential performance of a trade before the trade is implemented.

SECTION I
INTRODUCTION

Portfolio managers are inundated with trades suggested by sales people and in periodic publications by dealer firms. Moreover, managers develop trading strategies based on their historical analysis of yields and yield spreads. In this chapter, we will explain the framework for assessing a trade or trading strategy.

A manager may be permitted to use leverage as part of a trade or trading strategy. Leverage means borrowing funds to purchase a part of the securities involved in the strategy. So, we will begin this chapter with a discussion of the advantages and disadvantages of using leverage and then how managers can borrow funds using repurchase agreements. Then we show how to compute the total return for a trade and the use of scenario analysis in evaluating a trade. In the last section, we look at some trades and how to apply the framework developed in this chapter to assess them.

SECTION II
THE PRINCIPLE
OF LEVERAGE

The investment principle of borrowing funds in the hope of earning a return in excess of the cost of funds is called **leveraging**. The attractive feature of leveraging is that it magnifies the return that will be realized from investment in a security for a given change in the price of that security. That's the good news. The bad news is that leveraging also magnifies any loss.

To illustrate this, consider an investor who wants to purchase a 30-year U.S. Treasury bond in anticipation of a decline in interest rates six months from now. Suppose that the investor has $1 million to invest. The $1 million is referred to as the **investor's equity**. Assuming that the coupon rate for the 30-year Treasury bond is 8% with the next coupon payment six months from now and the bond can be purchased at par value, then the investor can purchase $1 million of par value of an 8% coupon 30-year Treasury bond with the equity available.

Exhibit 1 shows the return that will be realized assuming various yields six months from now at which the 8% coupon 30-year Treasury bond will trade. The dollar return consists of the coupon payment six months from now and the change in the value of the 30-year Treasury bond. (There is no reinvestment income.) At the end of six months, the 30-year Treasury bond is a 29.5-year Treasury bond. The percent return is found by dividing the dollar return by the $1 million of investor's equity and then annualizing by simply multiplying by 2 (so the return is computed on a bond-equivalent basis). Notice that the range for the annualized percent return based on the assumed yields six months from now ranges from −29.8% to +63.0%.

Exhibit 1: Annual Return from a $1 Million Investment in a 30-Year 8% Coupon Treasury Bond Held for Six Months

Assumed yield six months from now (%)	Price per $100 par value ($)*	Market value per $1 million par value ($)*	Semiannual coupon payment ($)	Dollar return ($)	Annualized percent return (%)**
10.00	81.12	811,200	40,000	−148,800	−29.8
9.50	85.23	852,300	40,000	−107,700	−21.5
9.00	89.72	897,200	40,000	−62,800	−12.6
8.50	94.62	946,200	40,000	−13,800	−2.8
8.00	100.00	1,000,000	40,000	40,000	8.0
7.50	105.91	1,059,100	40,000	99,100	19.8
7.00	112.41	1,124,100	40,000	164,100	32.8
6.50	119.58	1,195,800	40,000	235,800	47.2
6.00	127.51	1,275,100	40,000	315,100	63.0

* This is the price and market value six months later, rounded to the nearest $100.
** Annualized by doubling the semiannual return.

Exhibit 2: Annual Return from a $2 Million Investment in a 30-Year 8% Coupon Treasury Bond Held for Six Months Using $1 Million of Borrowed Funds

Assumed yield six months from now (%)	Market value per $100 par value ($)*	Market value per $2 million par value ($)*	Semiannual coupon payment ($)	Dollar return to equity ($)**	Annualized percent return (%)***
10.00	81.12	1,622,400	80,000	−342,600	−68.5
9.50	85.23	1,704,600	80,000	−260,400	−52.1
9.00	89.72	1,794,400	80,000	−170,600	−34.1
8.50	94.62	1,892,400	80,000	−72,600	−14.5
8.00	100.00	2,000,000	80,000	35,000	7.0
7.50	105.91	2,118,200	80,000	153,200	30.6
7.00	112.41	2,248,200	80,000	283,200	56.6
6.50	119.58	2,391,600	80,000	426,600	85.3
6.00	127.51	2,550,200	80,000	585,200	117.0

* This is the price and market value six months later, rounded to the nearest $100.
** After deducting interest expense of $45,000 ($1 million × 9%/2).
*** Annualized by doubling the semiannual return.

In our illustration, the investor did not borrow any funds. Hence, the strategy is referred to as an **unleveraged strategy**. Now let's suppose that the investor can borrow $1 million to purchase an additional $1 million of par value of the 30-year 8% coupon Treasury bond. Assume further that the loan agreement specifies that:

1. the maturity of the loan is six months
2. the annual interest rate for the loan is 9%, and
3. $1 million par value of the 30-year 8% coupon Treasury bond is used as collateral for the loan

Therefore, the loan is a collateralized loan. The collateral for this loan is the $2 million par value of the 30-year 8% Treasury bond purchased by the investor. The $2 million invested comes from the investor's equity of $1 million and $1 million of borrowed funds. In this strategy, the investor is using leverage. Since the investor has the use of $2 million in proceeds and has equity of $1 million, this amount of leverage is said to be "2-to-1 leverage." (This means $2 invested for $1 in investor's equity.)

Exhibit 2 shows the annual percent return for this leveraged strategy assuming the same yields at the end of six months as in Exhibit 1. The return is measured relative to the investor's equity of $1 million, not the $2 million. The dollar return on the $1 million of equity invested shown in the exhibit adjusts for the cost of borrowing.

By using borrowed funds, the range for the annualized percent return is wider (−68.5% to +117.0%) than in the case where no funds are borrowed (−29.8% to 63.0%). This example clearly shows how leveraging is a two-edged sword — it can magnify returns both up and down. Notice that if the market yield does not change at the end of six months for the 30-year Treasury bond, then the unleveraged strategy would have generated an 8% annual return. That is, for the $1 million invested the coupon interest is $40,000 for six months. Since there is no change in the market value of the security, this gives a 4% semiannual return and therefore 8% on a simple annual basis (i.e., a bond-equivalent basis). In contrast, consider what happens if $2 million is invested in the 2-for-1 leveraging strategy. Since $2 million is invested, the coupon interest is $80,000 for six months. But the interest cost of the $1 million loan for six month is $45,000 ($1 million × 9%/2). Thus, the dollar return after the financing cost is $35,000 ($80,000 – $45,000). Hence, the return on the $1 million equity of the investor is 3.5% for six months ($35,000/$1 million) and 7% annualized. Thus, without leverage the investor earns 8% if interest rates do not change but only 7% in the same scenario in the 2-for-1 leveraging strategy.

Suppose that instead of borrowing $1 million, the investor can find a lender who is willing to lend for six months $11 million at an annual interest rate of 9%. The investor can now purchase $12 million of 30-year 8% coupon Treasury bonds. That is, there will be $1 million of investor's equity and $11 million of borrowed funds. The lender requires that the $11 million of Treasury bonds be used as collateral for this loan. Since there is $12 million invested and $1 million of investor's equity, this strategy is said to have "12-to-1 leverage."

Exhibit 3 shows the annual return assuming the same yields for the 30-year Treasury six months from now as in Exhibits 1 and 2. Notice the considerably wider range for the annual return for the 12-to-1 leverage strategy compared to the 2-to-1 leverage strategy and the unleveraged strategy. In the case where the yield remains at 8%, the 12-to-1 strategy results in an annual return of –3%. This result occurs because the coupon interest earned on the $12 million invested for six months is $480,000 ($12 million × 8%/2) but the interest expense is $495,000 ($11 million borrowed × 9%/2). The dollar return to the investor for the 6-month period is then –$15,000 or –1.5% (–$15,000/$1 million). Doubling the –1.5% semiannual return gives the –3% annual return.

Exhibit 4 shows the range for different degrees of leverage. The greater the leverage, the wider the range of potential outcomes, and therefore the greater the risk of a leveraging strategy as measured by the greater dispersion of the possible outcomes.

PRACTICE QUESTION 1

Reconstruct Exhibit 2 assuming the investor has $1 million equity and borrows $5 million.

Exhibit 3: Annual Return from a $12 Million Investment in a 30-Year 8% Coupon Treasury Bond Held for Six Months Using $11 Million of Borrowed Funds

Assumed yield six months from now (%)	Price per $100 par value ($)*	Market value per $12 million par value ($)*	Semiannual coupon payment ($)	Dollar return to equity ($)**	Annualized percent return (%)***
10.00	81.12	9,734,900	480,000	-2,280,100	-456.0
9.50	85.23	10,227,900	480,000	-1,787,100	-357.4
9.00	89.72	10,766,000	480,000	-1,249,000	-249.8
8.50	94.62	11,354,700	480,000	-660,300	-132.1
8.00	100.00	12,000,000	480,000	-15,000	-3.0
7.50	105.91	12,708,800	480,000	693,800	138.8
7.00	112.41	13,489,100	480,000	1,474,100	294.8
6.50	119.58	14,349,600	480,000	2,334,600	466.9
6.00	127.51	15,301,200	480,000	3,286,200	657.2

* This is the price and market value six months later, rounded to the nearest 100.
** After deducting interest expense of $495,000 ($11 million × 9%/2).
*** Annualized by doubling the semiannual return.

Exhibit 4: Annual Return For Various Degrees of Leverage

Assumed yield six months from now (%)	Annual return for $1 million of equity and debt of $X million (%)					
	$0	$1	$2	$3	$5	$11
10.00	−29.8	−68.5	−107.3	−146.0	−223.6	−456.1
9.50	−21.5	−52.1	−82.6	−113.2	174.2	−357.5
9.00	−12.6	−34.1	−55.7	−77.2	120.4	−249.7
8.50	−2.8	−14.5	−26.3	−38.0	61.6	−132.1
8.00	8.0	7.0	6.0	5.0	3.0	−3.0
7.50	19.8	30.6	41.5	52.3	73.9	138.8
7.00	32.8	56.6	80.5	104.3	151.9	294.8
6.50	47.2	85.3	123.5	161.6	238.0	466.9
6.00	63.0	117.0	171.1	225.1	333.1	657.2

SECTION III BORROWING FUNDS VIA REPURCHASE AGREEMENTS

A **repurchase agreement** is the sale of a security with a commitment by the seller to buy the same security back from the purchaser at a specified price at a designated future date. The price at which the seller must subsequently repurchase the security is called the **repurchase price** and the date by which the security must be repurchased is called the **repurchase date**. Basically, a repurchase agreement is a **collateralized loan**, where the collateral is the security sold and subsequently repurchased.[1] The agreement is best explained with an illustration.

Suppose a government securities dealer has purchased $10 million of a particular Treasury security. Where does the dealer obtain the funds to finance that position? Of course, the dealer can finance the position with its own funds or by borrowing from a bank. Typically, however, the dealer uses the repurchase agreement or "repo" market to obtain financing. In the repo market the dealer can use the $10 million of the Treasury security as collateral for the loan. The term of the loan and the interest rate that the dealer agrees to pay are specified. The interest rate is called the **repo rate**. When the term of the loan is one day, it is called an **overnight repo** (or RP); a loan for more than one day is called a **term repo** (or RP). The transaction is referred to as a repurchase agreement because it calls for the sale of the security and its repurchase at a future date. Both the sale price and the purchase price are specified in the agreement. The difference between the purchase (repurchase) price and the sale price is the dollar interest cost of the loan.

Back to the dealer firm who needs to finance $10 million of a Treasury security that it just purchased and plans to hold for one day. Suppose that a customer of the dealer firm has funds of $10 million. The dealer firm would agree to deliver ("sell") $10 million of the Treasury security to the customer for $10 million and simultaneously agree to buy back (i.e., "repurchase") the same Treasury security the next day for $10 million plus interest. The amount of the interest is determined by the repo rate.

The dollar amount of the interest is based on the repo rate, the number of days that the funds are borrowed (i.e., the term of the loan), and the amount borrowed. The formula for the dollar interest is:

$$\text{dollar interest} = \text{amount borrowed} \times \text{repo rate} \times \text{repo term}/360$$

Notice that the dollar interest is computed on an actual/360-day basis.

In our example, if the repo rate is 5%, then we know

---

[1] There is a special type of repurchase agreement used in the mortgage-backed securities market. This arrangement is called a "dollar roll." For an explanation of a dollar roll, see Chapter 9 in Frank J. Fabozzi and David Yuen, *Managing MBS Portfolios* (New Hope, PA: Frank J. Fabozzi Associates, 1998).

$$\text{amount borrowed} = \$10,000,000$$
$$\text{repo rate} = 0.05$$
$$\text{repo term} = 1 \text{ day}$$

and therefore the dollar interest is

$$\text{dollar interest} = \$10,000,000 \times 0.05 \times 1/360 = \$1,388.89$$

So, our dealer would sell the Treasury security to the customer for $10 million and agree to repurchase it the next day for $10,001,388.89 ($10,000,000 + $1,388.89).

The advantage to the dealer of using the repo market for borrowing on a short-term basis is that the rate is lower than the cost of bank financing. (The reason for this is explained below.) From the customer's perspective, the repo market offers an attractive yield on a short-term secured transaction that is highly liquid.

While the example illustrates financing a dealer's long position in the repo market, dealers can also use the market to cover a short position. For example, suppose a government dealer sold short $10 million of Treasury securities two weeks ago and must now cover the position — that is, deliver the securities. The dealer can do a **reverse repo** (agree to buy the securities and sell them back). Of course, the dealer eventually would have to buy the Treasury security in the market in order to cover its short position. In this case, the dealer is actually making a collateralized loan to its customer. The customer (or other dealer) is then using the funds obtained from the collateralized loan to create leverage.

PRACTICE QUESTION 2

A dealer needs to finance $5 million of a Treasury security that it plans to hold overnight using a repurchase agreement. Assume that the overnight repo rate is 4% and the dealer can obtain 100% financing.

a. How much dollar interest would the dealer pay?
b. How much would the dealer agree to repurchase the security for the next day?

A. Industry Jargon

There is a good deal of Wall Street jargon describing repo transactions. To understand it, remember that one party is lending money and accepting a security as collateral for the loan; the other party is borrowing money and providing collateral to borrow the money. When someone lends securities (i.e., uses securities as collateral) in order to receive cash (i.e., borrow money), that party is said to be "reversing out" securities. A party that lends money with the security as collateral is said to be "reversing in" securities. The expressions "to repo securities" and "to do repo" are also used. The former means that someone is going to finance securities using the security as collateral; the latter means that the party is going to invest in a repo. Finally, the expressions "selling collateral" and "buying collateral" are used to describe a party financing a security with a repo on the one hand, and lending on the basis of collateral, on the other.[2]

In practice, the term repo transaction and reverse repo transaction are used in a special way in the industry. When a dealer uses a repo agreement to borrow funds,

---

[2] Note that the terms "buying collateral" and "selling collateral" do not mean the same thing in the mortgage-backed securities market as used here. Recall from Chapter 3 that passthroughs are used to create collateralized mortgage obligations. Consequently, passthroughs are referred to as "collateral." In the MBS market, buying collateral means buying passthroughs and selling collateral means selling passthroughs.

the dealer is said to do a **repo transaction**. When a non-dealer entity (such as a portfolio manager) uses a repo agreement to borrow funds, the non-dealer entity is said to do a **reverse repo transaction**. This is important to understand because the expression "repo" and "reverse repo" are used relative to who is borrowing the funds. *The same loan agreement is used whether a dealer or non-dealer is using the loan agreement to finance a position.* That is, it is a repurchase agreement. However, if the dealer needs to borrow funds and uses the repurchase agreement to obtain the funds, the dealer is said to be doing a "repo" or "repo transaction." If, instead, a non-dealer uses a repurchase agreement to obtain financing via a repurchase agreement the non-dealer is said to be doing a "reverse repo" or "reverse repo transaction."

Rather than using industry jargon, investment guidelines should be clear as to what a manager is permitted to do. For example, a client may have no objections to its portfolio manager using a repo as a short-term investment — that is, the portfolio manager may lend funds on a short-term basis. The investment guidelines will set forth how the loan arrangement should be structured to protect against credit risk. We'll discuss this below. However, if a client does not want a money manager to use the repo agreement as a vehicle for borrowing funds (thereby, creating leverage), it should state so.

B. Margin and Marking to Market

Despite the fact that there may be high-quality collateral underlying a repo transaction, both parties to the transaction are exposed to credit risk. Why does credit risk occur in a repo transaction? Consider our initial example where the dealer uses $10 million of government securities as collateral to borrow. If the dealer cannot repurchase the government securities, the customer may keep the collateral; if interest rates on government securities increase subsequent to the repo transaction, however, the market value of the government securities will decline, and the customer will own securities with a market value less than the amount it lent to the dealer. If the market value of the security rises instead, the dealer will be concerned with the return of the collateral, which then has a market value higher than the loan.

Repos should be carefully structured to reduce credit risk exposure. The amount lent should be less than the market value of the security used as collateral, thereby providing the lender with some cushion should the market value of the security decline. The amount by which the market value of the security used as collateral exceeds the value of the loan is called **repo margin** or simply **margin**. Margin is also referred to as the "haircut." Repo margin is generally between 1% and 3%. For borrowers of lower credit worthiness and/or when less liquid or more price sensitive securities are used as collateral, the repo margin can be 10% or more.

For example, consider the dealer who needs to borrow $10 million to finance the purchase of a Treasury security. Suppose that the repo margin is 2%. Then for a Treasury security with a market value of $10 million, only 98% of that amount, $9.8 million, will be lent. That is, the dealer will agree to deliver (sell) $10 million of the Treasury security to the customer for $9.8 million and agree to repurchase the $10 million of the Treasury security the next day for $9.8 million plus the dollar interest. The dollar interest in this transaction for an overnight repo assuming a repo rate of 5% is

$$\text{dollar interest} = \$9,800,000 \times 0.05 \times 1/360 = \$1,361.11$$

Note that the dollar interest is based on $9.8 million (the amount actually lent by the customer), not $10 million as in our earlier example.

Another practice to limit credit risk is to mark the collateral to market on a regular basis. (Marking a position to market means recording the value of a position at its market value.) When the market value changes by a certain percentage, the repo position is adjusted accordingly. The decline in market value below a specified amount will result in a **margin deficit**. In such cases, the borrower of funds typically has the option to take care of the margin deficit by either providing additional cash or by transferring additional acceptable securities to the lender of funds. In cases when the market value rises above the amount required, **excess margin** will result. When this occurs, the lender of funds has the option to give cash to the borrower of funds equal to the amount of the excess margin or to transfer purchased securities to the borrower of funds.

C. Delivery and Credit Risk

One concern in structuring a repo is delivery of the collateral to the lender. The most obvious procedure is for the borrower to deliver the collateral to the lender or to the cash lender's clearing agent. In such instances, the collateral is said to be "delivered out." At the end of the repo term, the lender returns the collateral to the borrower in exchange for the principal and interest payment. This procedure may be too expensive though, particularly for short-term repos, because of costs associated with delivering the collateral. The cost of delivery would be factored into the repo rate. The risk of the lender not taking possession of the collateral is that the borrower may sell the security, or go under and the lender has nothing to liquidate, or use the same security as collateral for a repo with another party.

As an alternative to delivering out the collateral, the lender may agree to allow the borrower to hold the security in a segregated customer account. Of course, the lender still faces the risk that the borrower may use the collateral fraudulently by offering it as collateral for another repo transaction. If the borrower of the cash does not deliver out the collateral, but instead holds it, then the transaction is called a **hold-in-custody repo** (HIC repo). Despite the credit risk associated with a HIC repo, it is used in some transactions when the collateral is difficult to deliver or the transaction amount is small and the lender of funds is comfortable with the reputation of the borrower.

Another method is for the borrower to deliver the collateral to the lender's custodial account at the borrower's clearing bank. The custodian then has possession of the collateral that it holds on behalf of the lender. This practice reduces the cost of delivery because it is merely a transfer within the borrower's clearing bank. If, for example, a dealer enters into an overnight repo with Customer A, the next day the collateral is transferred back to the dealer. The dealer can then enter into a repo with Customer B for, say, five days without having to redeliver the collateral. The clearing bank simply establishes a custodian account for Customer B and holds the collateral in that account. This specialized type of repo arrangement is called a **tri-party repo**. Tri-party repos account for about half of all repo arrangements.

The responsibilities of the third party are as follows. First, it is responsible for marking the collateral to market and reporting these values each day to the two parties. Second, if the borrower of funds wishes to substitute collateral (i.e., change the specific Treasury securities collateralizing the loan), the third-party agent verifies that the collateral satisfies the requirements set forth in the repo agreement.

D. Determinants of the Repo Rate

There is not one repo rate. The rate varies from transaction to transaction depending on a variety of factors:

- quality of collateral
- term of the repo

- delivery requirement
- availability of collateral
- prevailing federal funds rate
- seasonal factors

The higher the credit quality and liquidity of the collateral, the lower the repo rate. With respect to the term of the repo, it is important to understand that there is a repo rate based on the length of time of the repo agreement. This is basically the very short-end of the yield curve. The maturity of the security used as collateral for a repo transaction has nothing to do the repo rate. If delivery of the collateral to the lender is required, the repo rate will be lower. If the collateral can be deposited with the bank of the borrower, a higher repo rate is paid.

The more difficult it is to obtain the collateral, the lower the repo rate. To understand why this is so, remember that the borrower (or equivalently the seller of the collateral) has a security that lenders of cash want, for whatever reason. Such collateral is referred to as **hot collateral** or **special collateral** (or just as "on special"). (Collateral that does not have this characteristic is referred to as **general collateral**.) The party that needs the hot collateral will be willing to lend funds at a lower repo rate in order to obtain the collateral.[3]

While these factors determine the repo rate on a particular transaction, the federal funds rate determines the general level of repo rates in the United States. Banks borrow funds from each other via the federal funds market. The interest rate charged on such borrowing is called the **federal funds rate** (or "fed funds"). The repo rate generally will be a rate lower than the federal funds rate because a repo involves collateralized borrowing, while a federal funds transaction is unsecured borrowing.

SECTION IV
TOTAL RETURN

Now let's look at a framework for assessing trades. A trade is evaluated in terms of its performance. When comparing two possible trades or a trade of a security versus maintaining a current position, the relative performance of the alternatives must be assessed. But what does performance mean? It is the expected **total return** over the investment horizon of the trade. The total return consists of three sources: (1) coupon payments, (2) the change in the value of the bond, and (3) reinvestment income from reinvesting coupon payments and principal repayment (in the case of amortizing securities) from the time of receipt to the end of the investment horizon.

For example, suppose that an investor purchases a security for $90 and expects a dollar return over a 1-year investment horizon from the three sources to be $6. Then the expected total return is 6.7% (= $6/$90).

When a trade involves the borrowing of funds via a repo, the interest cost of the repo must be deducted from the dollar return of these three sources. The dollar return adjusted for the financial cost is then related to the dollar amount invested. For example, suppose the investor purchased the $90 security by borrowing $80 and investing his own funds of $10 (i.e., the investor's equity). Suppose also that the cost of the borrowed funds is 5% or $4. Then the dollar return after adjusting for the financing cost is $2 ($6 − $4). The total return is then 20% ($2 return after adjusting for the borrowing cost divided by the investor's equity of $10 funds invested). This is precisely what was done in Section II when we demonstrated how to compute the total return using various degrees of leverage.

---

[3] Bloomberg provides information on issues on special [Type NI RP<go>].

Below we discuss how to calculate the total return for assessing trades and discuss scenario analysis. At Level III, we discuss total return analysis for a portfolio.

A. Computing the Expected Total Return

The total return considers all three sources of potential dollar return over the investor's investment horizon. It is the return (interest rate) that will make the proceeds (i.e., price plus accrued interest) invested grow to the projected total dollar return at the end of the investment horizon.[4] The total return requires that the investor specify:

- an investment horizon
- a reinvestment rate
- a price for the bond at the end of the investment horizon.

More formally, the steps for computing a total return over some investment horizon are as follows:

Step 1: Compute the total coupon payments plus the reinvestment income based on an assumed reinvestment rate. The reinvestment rate is one-half the annual interest rate that the investor assumes can be earned on the reinvestment of coupon interest payments.[5]

Step 2: Determine the projected sale price at the end of the investment horizon. We refer to this as the **horizon price**. At Level I (Chapter 5) and in Chapters 2 and 5 we explained how the price of a bond is computed based on the term structure of default-free interest rates (i.e., the Treasury spot rate curve) and the term structure of credit spreads. Moreover, for bonds with embedded options, the price will depend on the option-adjusted spread (OAS). So, to determine the horizon price in the total return analysis it is necessary to use at the horizon date an assumed Treasury spot rate curve, term structure of credit spreads, and OAS. Obviously, the assumed values reflect changes in interest rates and spreads from the beginning to the end of the investment horizon. We shall refer to these rates as the **structure of rates at the horizon date**.

However, in the illustrations to follow, to simplify we will assume a single yield to price a security at the horizon date. This yield would reflect the Treasury rate plus a spread and we will refer to it as the **horizon yield**.

Step 3: Add the values computed in Steps 1 and 2. Reduce this value by any borrowing cost to obtain the total future dollars that will be received from the investment given the assumed reinvestment rate and projected structure of rates at the horizon date (or horizon yield in our illustrations to follow).

Step 4: Compute the *semiannual total return* using the following formula:

$$\left(\frac{\text{total future dollars}}{\text{full price of bond}}\right)^{1/h} - 1$$

where the full price is the price plus accrued interest and h is the *number of semiannual periods in the investment horizon*.

---

[4] The total return is also referred to as the **horizon return**.

[5] An investor can choose multiple reinvestment rates for cash flows from the bond over the investment horizon.

Exhibit 5: Graphical Depiction of Total Return Calculation

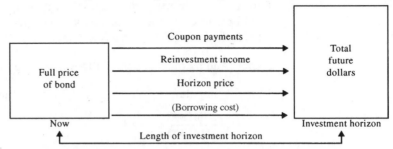

Total return is the interest rate that will make the full price of the bond grow to the total future dollars

---

Step 5: For semiannual-pay bonds, double the interest rate found in Step 4. The resulting interest rate is the total return expressed on a bond-equivalent basis. Instead, the total return can be expressed on an effective rate basis by using the following formula:

$$(1 + \text{semiannual total return})^2 - 1$$

A graphical depiction of the total return calculation is presented in Exhibit 5.

The decision as to whether to calculate the total return on a bond-equivalent basis or an effective rate basis depends on the situation. If the total return is being compared to a benchmark index that is calculated on a bond-equivalent basis, then the total return should be calculated in that way. However, if the bond is being used to satisfy liabilities that are calculated on an effective rate basis, then the total return should be calculated in that way.

To illustrate the computation of the total return, suppose that an investor with a 1-year investment horizon is considering the purchase of a 20-year 6% corporate bond. The issue is selling for $86.4365 for a yield of 7.3%. The issue will be purchased for cash (i.e., no funds will be borrowed). Assume that the yield curve is flat (i.e., the yield for all maturities is the same) and the yield for the on-the-run 20-year Treasury issue is 6.5%. This means that the yield spread over the on-the-Treasury issue for this corporate bond is 80 basis points. The investor expects that:

1. he can reinvest the coupon payments (there will be two of them over the 1-year investment horizon) at 6%.
2. the Treasury yield curve will shift down by 25 basis points and remains flat at the end of 1 year, so that the yield for the 19-year Treasury issue is 6.25% (6.5% minus 25 basis points)
3. the yield spread to the 19-year Treasury issue is unchanged at 80 basis points so the horizon yield is 7.05% (6.25% plus 80 basis points)

The calculations are as shown below.

Step 1: Compute the total coupon payments plus the reinvestment income assuming an annual reinvestment rate of 6% or 3% every six months. The semiannual coupon payments are $3. The future value of an annuity can be used or because the investment horizon is only one year, it can be computed as follows:

First coupon payment reinvested for six months = $3 (1.03)	=	$3.09
Second coupon payment not reinvested since at horizon date	=	$3.00
Total	=	$6.09

Step 2: The horizon price at the end of the 1-year investment horizon is determined as follows. The horizon yield is 7.05% by assumption. The 6% coupon 20-year corporate bond now has 19 years to maturity. The price of this bond when discounted at a flat 7.05% yield (the yield curve is assumed to be flat) is $89.0992.

Step 3: Adding the amounts in Steps 2 and 3 gives the total future dollars of $95.1892.

Step 4: Compute the following (*h* is 2 in our illustration):

$$\left(\frac{\$95.1892}{\$86.4365}\right)^{1/2} - 1 = 4.94\%$$

Step 5: The total return on a bond-equivalent basis and on an effective rate basis are shown below:

$$2 \times 4.94\% = 9.88\% \qquad \text{(BEY)}$$

$$(1.0494)^2 - 1 = 10.13\% \quad \text{(effective rate basis)}$$

PRACTICE QUESTION 3

Consider again the 6% coupon 20-year corporate bond. Assume again a 1-year investment horizon. However, assume that the investor expects that

1. he can reinvest the coupon payments at 4%.
2. the Treasury yield curve will shift down by 25 basis points and remain flat, so that the yield for the 19-year Treasury issue is 6.25% (6.5% minus 25 basis points)
3. the yield spread to the 19-year Treasury issue increases by 10 basis points

---

1. OAS-Total Return

The option-adjusted spread (OAS) can be incorporated into a total return analysis to determine the horizon price. This requires a valuation model. At the end of the investment horizon, it is necessary to specify how the OAS is expected to change. The horizon price can be "backed out" of a valuation model. This technique can be extended to the total return framework by making assumptions about the required variables at the horizon date.

Assumptions about the OAS value at the investment horizon reflect the expectations of the portfolio manager. It is common to assume that the OAS at the horizon date will be the same as the OAS at the time of purchase. A total return calculated using this assumption is referred to as a **constant-OAS total return**. Alternatively, managers or traders will take positions to reflect their views on how the OAS will change — either widening or tightening. The total return framework can be used to assess how sensitive the performance of a bond with an embedded option is to changes in the OAS.

2. Total Return for a Mortgage-Backed and Asset-Backed Security

In calculating total return of mortgage-backed and asset-backed securities, the total future dollars will depend on (1) the projected principal repayment (scheduled plus projected prepayments) and (2) the interest earned on reinvestment of the projected interest payments and projected principal payments. To obtain the total future dollars, a prepayment rate over the investment horizon must be assumed.

The monthly total return for a mortgage-backed security and an asset-backed security that makes monthly payments is computed using the formula:

$$\text{monthly total return} = \left(\frac{\text{total future dollars}}{\text{full price}}\right)^{\frac{1}{\text{number of months in horizon}}} - 1$$

The monthly total return can be annualized on a bond-equivalent yield basis as follows:

$$\text{bond-equivalent annual return} = 2[(1 + \text{monthly total return})^6 - 1]$$

Recall from our discussion in Chapter 5 that the calculation of a bond-equivalent yield for a monthly pay security such as a mortgage-backed or asset-backed security is to compute the effective 6-month yield and then annualize it by doubling the effective 6-month yield. This is precisely what the bond-equivalent annual return formula above does.

So, for example, if the monthly total return for a monthly pay mortgage-backed security or asset-backed security is 0.7%, the bond-equivalent annual return is

$$2[(1 + 0.007)^6 - 1] = 0.0855 = 8.55\%$$

Or, the effective annual return can be computed as follows:

$$\text{effective annual return} = (1 + \text{monthly total return})^{12} - 1$$

The effective annual return is just the compounding of the monthly return. For the previous example where the monthly total return is 0.7%, the effective annual return is:

$$(1 + 0.007)^{12} - 1 = 0.0873 = 8.73\%$$

As explained earlier, the decision as to whether to use the bond-equivalent annual return or the effective annual return depends on the situation.

3. Scenario Analysis

The computation of a total return is based on one or more assumptions regarding interest rates at the end of the investment horizon, spreads at the end of the investment horizon, and reinvestment rates available over the investment horizon. A manager would not want to rely on just one set of assumptions to make an investment decision. Instead, a manager will determine what happens to the total return under different sets of assumptions. A set of assumptions is referred to as a **scenario**. Evaluating what will happen to a strategy under several scenarios selected by the manager is called **scenario analysis**. Regulators also require certain institutions to perform scenario analysis based on assumptions specified by regulations.[6]

Exhibits 6 and 7 provide illustrations of scenario analysis. The bond used in the illustrations is the 6% 20-year corporate bond selling for $86.4365 for a yield of 7.3%. The assumptions in the scenario analysis in both exhibits is that the yield curve is flat and when it shifts it is a parallel shift in the yield curve. In Exhibit 6 it is assumed that only the Treasury yield curve shifts. In Exhibit 7 it is assumed that the yield spread changes and the change varies with how the Treasury yield curve shifts.

---

[6] Scenario analysis is referred to by some broker/dealers, vendors of analytical systems, and regulators as "simulation." They are not the same techniques. Simulation is a more powerful tool that takes into consideration the dynamics of interactions of the factors.

Exhibit 6: Scenario Analysis Assuming only the Treasury Yield Curve Changes (1-Year Investment Horizon)

	Scenario								
	1	2	3	4	5	6	7	8	9
At trade date									
Treasury rate	6.50%	6.50%	6.50%	6.50%	6.50%	6.50%	6.50%	6.50%	6.50%
Spread (bp)	80	80	80	80	80	80	80	80	80
Initial yield	7.30%	7.30%	7.30%	7.30%	7.30%	7.30%	7.30%	7.30%	7.30%
Coupon rate	6.00%	6.00%	6.00%	6.00%	6.00%	6.00%	6.00%	6.00%	6.00%
Maturity	20.0	20.0	20.0	20.0	20.0	20.0	20.0	20.0	20.0
Initial price	86.4365	86.4365	86.4365	86.4365	86.4365	86.4365	86.4365	86.4365	86.4365
At horizon date									
Treasury rate change (bp)	−150	−100	−50	−25	0	25	50	100	150
Spread change (bp)	0	0	0	0	0	0	0	0	0
Horizon yield	5.80%	6.30%	6.80%	7.05%	7.30%	7.55%	7.80%	8.30%	8.80%
Coupon rate	6.00%	6.00%	6.00%	6.00%	6.00%	6.00%	6.00%	6.00%	6.00%
Remaining maturity	19.0	19.0	19.0	19.0	19.0	19.0	19.0	19.0	19.0
Horizon price	102.2846	96.7035	91.5375	89.0992	86.7520	84.4920	82.3155	78.1993	74.3770
Reinvestment rate	6.0%	6.0%	6.0%	6.0%	6.0%	6.0%	6.0%	6.0%	6.0%
Interest + reinvest inc	6.09	6.09	6.09	6.09	6.09	6.09	6.09	6.09	6.09
Total future dollars	108.3746	102.7935	97.6275	95.1892	92.8420	90.5820	88.4055	84.2893	80.4670
Total return (SA)	11.97%	9.05%	6.28%	4.94%	3.64%	2.37%	1.13%	−1.25%	−3.51%
Total return (BEY)	23.95%	18.10%	12.55%	9.88%	7.28%	4.74%	2.27%	−2.50%	−7.03%
Total return (effective)	25.38%	18.92%	12.95%	10.13%	7.41%	4.80%	2.28%	−2.48%	−6.91%

Exhibit 7: Scenario Analysis Assuming Shift in Treasury Yield Curve and Change in Yield Spread (1-Year Investment Horizon)

	Scenario								
	1	2	3	4	5	6	7	8	9
At trade date									
Treasury rate	6.50%	6.50%	6.50%	6.50%	6.50%	6.50%	6.50%	6.50%	6.50%
Spread (bp)	80	80	80	80	80	80	80	80	80
Required yield	7.30%	7.30%	7.30%	7.30%	7.30%	7.30%	7.30%	7.30%	7.30%
Coupon rate	6.00%	6.00%	6.00%	6.00%	6.00%	6.00%	6.00%	6.00%	6.00%
Maturity	20.0	20.0	20.0	20.0	20.0	20.0	20.0	20.0	20.0
Horizon price	86.4365	86.4365	86.4365	86.4365	86.4365	86.4365	86.4365	86.4365	86.4365
At horizon date									
Treasury rate change (bp)	−150	−100	−50	−25	0	25	50	100	150
Spread change (bp)	40	25	20	10	0	−10	−20	−25	−40
Horizon yield	6.20%	6.55%	7.00%	7.15%	7.30%	7.45%	7.60%	8.05%	8.40%
Coupon rate	6.00%	6.00%	6.00%	6.00%	6.00%	6.00%	6.00%	6.00%	6.00%
Remaining maturity	19.0	19.0	19.0	19.0	19.0	19.0	19.0	19.0	19.0
Horizon price	97.7853	94.0708	89.5795	88.1496	86.7520	85.3858	84.0501	80.2191	77.4121
Reinvestment rate	6.0%	6.0%	6.0%	6.0%	6.0%	6.0%	6.0%	6.0%	6.0%
Interest + reinvest inc	6.09	6.09	6.09	6.09	6.09	6.09	6.09	6.09	6.09
Total future dollars	103.8753	100.1608	95.6695	94.2396	92.8420	91.4758	90.1401	86.3091	83.5021
Total return (SA)	9.62%	7.65%	5.21%	4.42%	3.64%	2.87%	2.12%	−0.07%	−1.71%
Total return (BEY)	19.25%	15.29%	10.41%	8.83%	7.28%	5.75%	4.24%	−0.15%	−3.42%
Total return (effective)	20.18%	15.88%	10.68%	9.03%	7.41%	5.83%	4.28%	−0.15%	−3.39%

SECTION V CONTROLLING FOR INTEREST RATE RISK

Unless the objective of a trade is to alter the duration exposure of a position, it is critical in assessing strategies to compare positions that have the same dollar duration. To understand why, consider two bonds, X and Y. Suppose that the price of bond X is 80 and has a duration of 5 while bond Y has a price of 90 and has a duration of 4. Since duration is the approximate percentage change per 100 basis point change in yield, a 100 basis points change in yield for bond X would change its price by about 5%. Based on a price of 80, its price will change by about $4 per $80 of market value. Thus, its dollar duration for a 100 basis point change in yield is $4 per $80 of market value. Similarly, for bond Y, its dollar duration for a 100 basis point change in yield per $90 of market value can be determined. In this case it is $3.6. So, if bonds X and Y are being considered as alternative investments in some strategy, the amount of each bond in the strategy should be such that they will both have the same *dollar* duration.

To illustrate this, suppose that a portfolio manager owns $10 million of par value of bond X which has a market value of $8 million. The dollar duration of bond X per 100 basis point change in yield for the $8 million market value is $400,000. Suppose further that this portfolio manager is considering exchanging bond X that it owns in its portfolio for bond Y. If the portfolio manager wants to have the same interest rate exposure (i.e., dollar duration) for bond Y that he currently has for bond X, she will buy a market value amount of bond Y with the same dollar duration. If the portfolio manager purchased $10 million of par value of bond Y and therefore $9 million of market value of bond Y, the dollar price change per 100 basis point change in yield would be only $360,000. If, instead, the portfolio manager purchased $10 million of market value of bond Y, the dollar duration per 100 basis point change in yield would be $400,000. Since bond Y is trading at 90, $11.11 million of par value of bond Y must be purchased to keep the dollar duration of the position from bond Y the same as for bond X.

Mathematically, the market value of bond Y necessary to have the same dollar duration (per 100 basis point change in rates) as bond X is:

$$\text{market value of bond Y} = \frac{\text{dollar duration of bond X}}{\text{duration of bond Y}/100}$$

The par value of bond Y that must be purchased to obtain the same dollar duration as bond X is then found by:

$$\text{par value of bond Y} = \frac{\text{market value of bond Y}}{\text{price of bond Y per \$1 of par value}}$$

Using our previous illustration to demonstrate how to use these two formulas, we know that:

$$\text{dollar duration of bond X} = \$400,000$$
$$\text{duration of bond Y} = 4$$

therefore,

$$\text{market value of bond Y} = \frac{\$400,000}{4/100} = \$10,000,000$$

This means that $10 million in *market* value of bond Y is needed in order to have the same dollar duration as the $8 market value position in bond X. The amount of the par value of bond Y that must be purchased given its assumed price of 90, or 0.90 per $1 of par value, is:

$$\text{par value of bond Y} = \frac{\$10,000,000}{0.90} = \$11.11 \text{ million}$$

Exhibit 8: Three Hypothetical Treasury Securities

Information on three Treasury securities:

Treasury issue	Coupon rate (%)	Price	Yield to maturity (%)	Maturity (years)
A	6.5	100	6.5	5
B	8.0	100	8.0	20
C	7.5	100	7.5	10

Calculation of duration and convexity (shock rates by 10 basis points):

Treasury issue	Value if rate changes by		Duration	Convexity
	+10 bp	−10 bp		
A	99.5799	100.4222	4.21122	10.67912
B	99.0177	100.9970	9.89681	73.63737
C	99.3083	100.6979	6.94821	31.09724

Failure to adjust a trade based on some expected change in yield spread so as to hold the dollar duration the same means that the outcome of the trade will be affected by not only the expected change in the yield spread but also a change in the yield level. Thus, a manager would be taking a conscious yield spread view and possibly an undesired view on the level of interest rates.

Also note that equating the dollar durations of two positions only means that they will be equal for small changes in rates because of the convexity of a bond.

SECTION VI
AN
ILLUSTRATION

There is no shortage of trading strategies suggested by bond dealer firms or in the popular press. Also, investment management firms have developed what they believe to be proprietary trading strategies. All of these strategies are based on a set of assumptions regarding what will occur in the bond market over the investment horizon and they all involve risk. A trading strategy may involve borrowing funds in the repo market and/or shorting bonds. Some managers and dealers unfortunately use the term "arbitrage" to refer to trading strategies that they may tout to customers. The fact is that such strategies do incur risk, no matter how small that risk may be perceived to be by the proponent of the strategy.

The bottom line is that the potential performance of any trading strategy can be quantified using total return analysis. More specifically, scenario analysis is used to determine what the total return will be under different assumptions about what might occur over the investment horizon. Of course, this should be done before a trade is entered into. The scenario analysis will identify the range of possible outcomes and therefore provide the manager with a feel for the risk associated in a trade.

In this section, a basic illustration will be used to show how to evaluate a trade. We begin with three Treasury securities — A, B, and C. Information about each of these three securities is provided in Exhibit 8. Security A is the short-term Treasury, security B is the long-term Treasury, and security C is the intermediate-term Treasury. Each Treasury security is selling at par, and it is assumed that the next coupon payment is six months from now. The duration and convexity for each security are calculated in the exhibit. Since all the securities are trading at par value, the durations and convexities are then the dollar duration and dollar convexity per $100 of par value.

Suppose that the following two Treasury portfolios are constructed. The first portfolio consists of only security C, the 10-year issue, and shall be referred to as the **bullet portfolio**. (It is called a bullet portfolio because the principal for this portfolio is returned at one time — the maturity date of the 10-year issue.) The second portfolio consists of 51.86% of security A and 48.14% of security B, and this portfolio shall be referred to as the **barbell portfolio**. (It is referred to as a barbell portfolio because the maturity dates for the principal for this portfolio are both shorter than and longer than that of the bullet portfolio.)

As can be seen in Exhibit 8, the duration of the bullet portfolio is 6.94821. The duration of the barbell portfolio is the market value weighted average of the duration of the two Treasury securities in the portfolio and is computed below:

$$0.5186 \, (4.21122) + 0.4814 \, (9.89681) = 6.94826$$

The duration of the barbell is equal to the duration of the bullet. In fact, the barbell portfolio was designed to produce this result.

Duration is just a first approximation of the change in market value resulting from a change in interest rates. As explained at Level I (Chapter 7), the convexity measure provides an improvement to the duration estimate. The convexity measure of the bullet and barbell portfolios is not equal. We explained the issues associated with computing the convexity measure at Level I so we won't repeat them here. The only thing that is important to understand regarding the convexity measure in Exhibit 8 is the relative size of the convexity measures for the two portfolios. The convexity measure of the bullet portfolio is 31.09724. The convexity measure of the barbell is a market weighted average of the convexity measure of the two Treasury securities in the portfolio. That is,

$$0.5186 \, (10.67912) + 0.4814 \, (73.63737) = 40.98722$$

Thus, the bullet portfolio has a convexity measure that is less than that of the barbell portfolio. Below is a summary of the duration and convexity measures of the two portfolios:

	Treasury Portfolio	
Parameter	Bullet	Barbell
Dollar duration	6.94821	6.94826
Dollar convexity	31.09724	40.98722

Given these values, a manager is considering the following trade: buy one portfolio and sell the other. By selling the other it is meant that the manager **sells short** or **shorts** the security or securities in the portfolio. When a manager shorts a security, the coupon interest paid on the shorted security must be paid by the manager to the owner of the security.

Now both the barbell portfolio and the bullet portfolio have the same duration. Since the dollar value that will be invested in both portfolios will be the same, then the two portfolios will have the same dollar duration, but different convexities. Suppose that the manager believes that there will be significant interest rate volatility over the next six months and therefore anticipates a substantial change in interest rates. It is precisely under such circumstances that the a portfolio with higher convexity will benefit. Based on this expectation, suppose that the manager decides to buy the better convex portfolio, the barbell portfolio, because it has a higher convexity than the bullet portfolio, and short the bullet portfolio. Also assume that the manager is basing the trade on a 6-month investment horizon.

Let's assess this trade for the manager. The first thing to note is that expectations based on a large change in interest rates is vague. What is "large"? Can the manager be more specific about how much rates must change in order to benefit from the better convexity of the barbell portfolio relative to the bullet portfolio? Also, is there an implicit assumption about what happens to the shape of the yield curve at the end of the investment horizon? All of this can be quantified by using total return analysis and scenario analysis.

Based on a 6-month investment horizon, the last column of Exhibit 9 shows the total return for this trading strategy assuming that the yield curve shifts in a "parallel" fashion. By parallel it is meant that the yield for the short-term security (A), the intermediate-term security (C), and the long-term security (B) changes by the same number of basis points, as shown in the first column of the exhibit. Since the barbell portfolio is owned and the bullet portfolio is sold, then the difference between the next-to-the last two columns is the total return for this trading strategy. For example, if the yield curve shifts down by 150 basis points (i.e., the row indicating "–150" in the first column), the barbell portfolio would earn a 6-month total return of 29.26%. The bullet portfolio's total return — if it were owned — would be 28.99% for the same scenario of a 150 basis point decline in yield. However, the bullet portfolio was shorted; therefore, the manager must pay this return. Thus, the barbell portfolio earned 29.26% but the manager had to pay 28.99% to short the bullet portfolio, resulting in a 27 basis point 6-month total return for this trading strategy.

The total return for the trading strategy for the different scenarios is shown in the last column. This column helps the manager quantify how much the yield curve must shift (up or down) to realize a positive return from this trading strategy. Notice that the yield curve must change up or down in a parallel fashion by more than 100 basis points (the precise number of basis points is not shown in Exhibit 9) in order to benefit from the better convexity of the barbell portfolio relative to the bullet portfolio. Thus, the manager now knows more than just that he or she is taking a view on a "large" rate change, but a view that rates will change by more than 100 basis points if interest rates shift in a parallel fashion.

Exhibit 9: Performance of Trading Strategy Over a 6-Month Horizon Assuming a Parallel Yield Curve Shift: Scenario Analysis

Yield change (in b.p.)	Price plus coupon ($)			Total return (%)		
	A	B	C	Barbell	Bullet	Trading Strategy[*]
–300	115.6407	141.0955	126.7343	55.79	53.47	2.32
–250	113.4528	133.6753	122.4736	46.38	44.95	1.43
–200	111.3157	126.8082	118.3960	37.55	36.79	0.76
–150	109.2281	120.4477	114.4928	29.26	28.99	0.27
–100	107.1888	114.5512	110.7559	21.47	21.51	–0.05
–50	105.1965	109.0804	107.1775	14.13	14.35	–0.22
–25	104.2176	106.4935	105.4453	10.63	10.89	–0.26
0	103.2500	104.0000	103.7500	7.22	7.50	–0.28
25	102.2935	101.5961	102.0907	3.92	4.18	–0.27
50	101.3481	99.2780	100.4665	0.70	0.93	–0.23
100	99.4896	94.8852	97.3203	–5.45	–5.36	–0.09
150	97.6735	90.7949	94.3050	–11.28	–11.39	0.11
200	95.8987	86.9830	91.4146	–16.79	–17.17	0.38
250	94.1640	83.4271	88.6433	–22.01	–22.71	0.70
300	92.4686	80.1070	85.9857	–26.96	–28.03	1.06

[*] A negative sign indicates that the bullet portfolio outperformed the barbell portfolio; a positive sign indicates that the barbell portfolio outperformed the bullet portfolio.

Exhibit 10: Performance of Trading Strategy Over a 6-Month Horizon Assuming a Steepening of the Yield Curve: Scenario Analysis

Yield change for C (in bp)	Price plus coupon ($)			Total return (%)		
	A	B	C	Barbell	Bullet	Trading Strategy*
−300	116.9785	136.5743	126.7343	52.82	53.47	−0.65
−250	114.7594	129.4918	122.4736	43.70	44.95	−1.24
−200	112.5919	122.9339	118.3960	35.14	36.79	−1.65
−150	110.4748	116.8567	114.4928	27.09	28.99	−1.89
−100	108.4067	111.2200	110.7559	19.52	21.51	−1.99
−50	106.3863	105.9874	107.1775	12.39	14.35	−1.97
−25	105.3937	103.5122	105.4453	8.98	10.89	−1.91
0	104.4125	101.1257	103.7500	5.66	7.50	−1.84
25	103.4426	98.8243	102.0907	2.44	4.18	−1.74
50	102.4839	96.6046	100.4665	−0.69	0.93	−1.63
100	100.5995	92.3963	97.3203	−6.70	−5.36	−1.34
150	98.7582	88.4758	94.3050	−12.38	−11.39	−0.99
200	96.9587	84.8200	91.4146	−17.77	−17.17	−0.60
250	95.2000	81.4080	88.6433	−22.88	−22.71	−0.17
300	93.4812	78.2204	85.9857	−27.73	−28.03	0.30

Assumptions:
Change in yield of A = Change in yield of C minus 30 bp.
Change in yield of B = Change in yield of C plus 30 bp.
* A negative sign indicates that the bullet portfolio outperformed the barbell portfolio; a positive sign indicates that the barbell portfolio outperformed the bullet portfolio.

Moreover, there is another assumption made in this trade — that the yield curve will shift in a parallel fashion. Exhibit 10 shows what happens if the yield curve does not shift in a parallel fashion. The assumption made in computing the total return for the trading strategy in Exhibit 10 is that there is a steepening of the yield curve. There are an infinite number of ways that the yield curve may steepen. The scenario analysis in Exhibit 10 assumes that if there is a change in the yield for security C shown in the first column, the yield on A will change by the same amount less 30 basis points, whereas the yield on B will change by the same amount plus 30 basis points. The last column of Exhibit 10 shows that the trade will result in a loss for the scenarios analyzed in the exhibit except if there is a 300 basis point shift in the yield for C.

Thus, we see the power of using total return analysis and scenario analysis in sharpening our skills in assessing a trading strategy.

SECTION VII KEY POINTS

❑ *Treasury securities can be used as collateral to borrow funds via a repurchase agreement.*

❑ *Leveraging is the investment principle of borrowing funds in the hope of earning a return in excess of the cost of the borrowed funds.*

❑ *Leveraging magnifies the potential gain that will be realized from investing in a security for a given change in the price of that security but also magnifies the potential loss.*

❑ *A repurchase agreement is the sale of a security with a commitment by the seller to buy the security back from the purchaser at the repurchase price at the repurchase date.*

❑ *The difference between the repurchase price and the sale price is the dollar interest cost of the loan.*

❑ *An overnight repurchase agreement is one that has a maturity of one day; a term repurchase agreement is one that has a maturity of more than one day.*

❑ *Interest in a repurchase agreement is computed on a 360-day basis.*

❑ *In a repurchase agreement, the lender of funds is borrowing securities and is making a short-term investment.*

❑ *There is a good deal of Wall Street jargon describing repo transactions but basically one party is buying collateral (and making a short-term investment) and the other party is selling collateral (and obtaining financing).*

❑ *Rather than using industry jargon, investment guidelines should be clear as to what a manager is permitted to do with respect to repo transactions.*

❑ *In a repurchase agreement the lender is exposed to the risk that the borrower will default.*

❑ *To reduce credit risk there is over collateralization of the loan (i.e., there is a repo margin) and the collateral is marked to market on a regular basis.*

❑ *When the market value of the collateral declines by a certain percentage, a repo agreement can specify either a margin call or repricing of the repo.*

❑ *One concern in structuring a repo is delivery of the collateral to the lender.*

❑ *When the borrower must deliver the collateral to the lender or to the cash lender's clearing agent, the collateral is said to be "delivered out" and at the repurchase date the lender returns the collateral to the borrower in exchange for the principal and interest payment.*

❑ *If the lender agrees to allow the borrower to hold the security in a segregated customer account, then the transaction is called a hold-in-custody repo and exposes the lender to greater credit risk than delivering out the securities.*

❑ *A tri-party repo is an alternative to delivering out the collateral which requires that the borrower deliver the collateral to the lender's custodial account at the borrower's clearing bank.*

❑ *The repo rate for a particular transaction will depend on the quality of the collateral, term of the repo, delivery requirement, availability of collateral, and the prevailing federal funds rate.*

❑ *Collateral that is highly sought after by dealers is called hot or special collateral and can be used as a cheap source of repo financing.*

❑ *The three sources of potential return from investing in a bond are: (1) the coupon interest payments, (2) any capital gain (or capital loss), and (3) income from reinvestment of the coupon interest payments.*

❑ *Calculation of the total return to the maturity date requires specification of the reinvestment rate.*

❑ *Calculation of the total return to an investment horizon that is less than the maturity date requires specification of the reinvestment rate and the horizon yield.*

❑ *The horizon yield is needed to obtain the horizon price of the bond at the end of the investment horizon.*

❑ *A semiannual return can be annualized on a bond-equivalent basis or on an effective rate basis, the selection depending on the manager's investment objective.*

❑ *For a mortgage-backed security, total return requires an assumption about prepayment rates.*

❑ *Option-adjusted spread analysis can be incorporated into a total return analysis by specifying the OAS at the end of the investment horizon.*

❑ *When the OAS is not assumed to change from its initial value, the total return is said to be calculated on a constant OAS basis.*

❑ *Scenario analysis involves calculating the total return under different assumptions regarding the reinvestment rate and horizon yield.*

❑ *Total return analysis and scenario analysis should be used to assess the potential outcomes of a trading strategy.*

❑ *Total return analysis and scenario analysis allows the manager to quantify vague notions about what must happen for a trading strategy to be successful.*

END OF CHAPTER QUESTIONS

1. Suppose that an investor has $477,300 in funds to invest and is considering the purchase of a 7% coupon 15.5-year Treasury security. The security is selling for 95.46 (or $954.60 per $1,000 of par value). Assume that there is no accrued interest. The yield to maturity is 7.5%.

   a. How much in par value can this investor purchase with $477,300?

   b. If the investor purchases this bond, what is the annual return assuming the following horizon yield for the bond and the corresponding horizon price for a 6-month time horizon:

Horizon yield	Horizon price
9.00%	83.71
8.50%	87.42
8.00%	91.35
7.50%	95.54
7.00%	100.00
6.50%	104.75
6.00%	109.80

   c. Suppose that the investor borrows $477,300 to purchase an additional amount of the 7% coupon 15.5-year bond. Assume that the annual borrowing rate is 10.8%. What is the annual return for the same scenarios as in part b?

   d. Suppose that the investor borrows $1,909,200 to purchase an additional amount of the 7% coupon 15.5-year bond. Assume that the annual borrowing rate is 10.8%. What is the annual return for the same scenarios as in part b?

   e. Compare the annual return for the scenarios in part b for the cases where no funds are borrowed (part b), $477,300 is borrowed (part c), and $1,909,200 is borrowed and comment on the results.

2. What is the difference between a repo transaction and a reverse repo transaction?

3. In the investment guidelines for a pension fund, the following is specified:

   "The manager of the fund is permitted to enter into a repurchase agreement."

   Why is this provision in the investment guidelines confusing?

4. In an article in a popular daily publication, a statement similar to the following was made: "Repurchase agreements are extremely risky vehicles." Explain why this statement is ambiguous.

5. Suppose that an investor purchases $3 million market value of a bond. The investor decides to borrow the funds via a repurchase agreement and the dealer is willing to lend 97% of the market value of the bond. The overnight repo rate is 7% and the 30-day term repo rate is 7.3%.

   a. Assuming that the investor borrows the funds for 1 day, what is the dollar interest cost of this borrowing arrangement?

   b. Assuming that the investor borrows the funds for 30 days, what is the dollar interest cost of this borrowing arrangement?

6. Explain why you agree or disagree with the following statement: "The repo rate depends on the shape of the yield curve and the maturity of the security used as collateral for the loan."

7. An assistant portfolio manager is reviewing a daily printout of Treasury securities published by a government broker/dealer. He notices that the yield for the on-the-run 10-year Treasury note is trading at a yield considerably less than Treasury securities with a similar maturity or a similar duration. He believes that the issue is expensive (i.e., the price is too high). He asks you whether or not this Treasury issue is rich. What is your response?

8. Suppose that an investor owns a security that is on special in the repo market. If this investor wants to use this security to obtain financing, what will the repo rate be compared to generic collateral for the same term? (No calculation required.)

9. If the repo margin for a 30-day term repo agreement is 2% and the value of the collateral is $10 million, how much will the dealer lend?

10. a. Why is the lender of funds in a repo transaction exposed to credit risk?
    b. What is the credit risk of a hold-in-custody repo?
    c. How do lenders of funds in a repo transaction reduce credit risk?

11. Why is the overnight repo rate generally lower than the federal funds rate?

12. An investor is considering the purchase of an option-free corporate bond with a coupon rate of 7.25% and 15 years remaining to maturity. The price of the bond is 106.1301. The yield to maturity of this bond is 6.6%. Assume that the Treasury yield curve is flat at 6% and that the credit spread for this issuer is 60 basis points for all maturities. Compute the (a) 1-year total return on a bond-equivalent basis and (b) 1-year total return on an effective rate basis assuming:

    i. the reinvestment rate is 4%
    ii. the Treasury yield curve is flat at the horizon date at 5.65%
    iii. the credit spread for this issuer is 50 basis points for all maturities at the horizon date

13. An investor is considering the purchase of an option-free high-yield corporate bond with a coupon rate of 10% and 9 years remaining to maturity. The price of the bond is 95.7420. The yield to maturity of this bond is 10.75%. Assume that the Treasury yield curve is flat at 7.5% and that the credit spread for this issuer is 325 basis points for all maturities. Compute the (a) 1-year total return on a bond-equivalent basis and (b) 1-year total return on an effective rate basis assuming:

    i. the reinvestment rate is 5%
    ii. the Treasury yield curve does not change and therefore remains flat at the horizon date at 7.5%
    iii. the credit spread for this issuer declines by 200 basis points for all maturities at the horizon date

14. Explain why it is essential to have a good valuation model in order to perform total return analysis?

15. "The problem with total return analysis is that it assumes the option-adjusted spread does not change and that the yield curve is flat." Explain why you agree or disagree with this statement.

16. Depository institutions are typically required by regulators to test the sensitivity of their portfolios to an instantaneous parallel shift in the yield curve. Usually, regulators require a shift of ±100 basis points, ±200 basis points, and ±300 basis points. Why is this procedure a special case of total return analysis?

17. Typically, in the collateralized mortgage obligation market the option-adjusted spread (OAS) on planned amortization class tranches (PACs) increases with the average life of the tranche. That is, the OAS for short average life PACs trade tighter (i.e., lower spread) to the collateral than intermediate average life PACs, and intermediate average life PACs trade tighter than long average life PACs. By "collateral" it is meant the passthrough securities used to create the CMO.

In December 1998, the shape of the OAS for PACs became U-shaped such that short average life PACs offered a higher OAS than intermediate PACs. To benefit from this anomaly in the OASs, a portfolio manager could create a "barbell PAC" as a substitute for collateral. A barbell PAC involves buying a combination of a short and a long average life PAC. The PaineWebber Mortgage Group assessed this strategy using scenario analysis. Table A shows the analysis. The PAC barbell was created from 71% FHR 2105 PA and 29% from FHR 2105 PE. The comparison is to a 6% coupon FNMA passthrough. The bottom panel of Table A shows the total return for different scenarios.

Table A: Analysis of PAC Barbell versus 6.0% Collateral

	Face	Proceeds	%	Price	Dur	Cnvx	OAS
FHR 2105 PA	23,082	23,446	71	101:03	1.83	−1.46	70
FHR 2105 PE	10,000	9,762	29	97:04+	9.55	0.66	70
Barbell	—	33,208	100	—	4.10	−0.84	70
30 yr FNMA 6.0%	10,000	9,892	100	98:22+	4.53	−1.72	59

Total Rate-of-Return Analysis

	−200	−150	−100	−50	Unch	50	100	150	200	Steep	Flat
FHR 2105 PA	3.74	4.08	5.24	6.67	6.19	5.36	4.40	3.40	2.38	6.62	5.72
FHR 2105 PE	24.31	20.51	15.70	10.95	6.49	1.99	−2.47	−6.87	−11.13	6.21	6.71
Barbell	10.00	9.04	8.37	7.94	6.28	4.37	2.41	0.44	−1.50	6.50	6.01
30 yr FNMA 6.0%	7.34	7.34	7.68	7.75	6.29	4.19	1.77	−0.68	−3.13	6.57	5.99
Difference	2.66	1.70	0.69	0.18	−0.02	0.18	0.64	1.12	1.63	−0.07	0.03

Source: Table 3 in "PAC Barbells: The Way to Go," *PaineWebber Mortgage Strategist* (December 15, 1998), p.11.

a. How does the duration of the PAC barbell and the collateral suggest that they will perform if interest rates change?
b. What do the convexity measures of the collateral and the PAC barbell suggest about the performance of the two positions if interest rates change?
c. Suppose that a portfolio manager owns the collateral in her portfolio. What do the results of the scenario analysis in Table A suggest as a trade to enhance return?
d. What are some important assumptions that should be kept in mind when reviewing the results of the scenario analysis shown in Table A?
e. Explain why the results in Table A would not have been predicted by just considering duration alone.

18. Suppose that in June 1998 a portfolio manager was considering the purchase of either a 3-year average life nonagency mortgage-backed security or a home equity loan (HEL) issue. The nonagency MBS was a RAST 1998-A5 and the HEL issue was an Amresco 1998-2. Summary information about these two issues is given below:

	3-Year Nonagency MBS	3-Year Home Equity
Issue	RAST 1998-A5	Amresco 1998-2
Class	A2	A3
Speed	100 PPC (16% CPR in 12 Months)	24% PPC
Price	100:06+	100:08+
Yield	6.610	6.136
Avg. Life	3.19 yrs	2.96 yrs
Spread/AL	112 bps	65 bps

The table below shows the PPC (i.e., prospectus prepayment curve) and average life comparison for the two issues at the end of a 12-month investment horizon for different interest rate scenarios (assuming a parallel shift in interest rates):

Spread and Average Life Comparison

	Basis Point Shifts						
	+150	+100	+50	0	−50	−100	−150
Nonagency MBS: RAST 1998-A5 A2							
PPC	63	75	87	100	125	187	218
Avg. Life	5.20	4.25	3.65	3.19	2.57	1.72	1.48
Home Equity: AMRESCO 1998-2 A3							
PPC	75	83	92	100	108	121	133
Avg. Life	4.25	3.76	3.34	2.96	2.64	2.35	2.12

The following table provides a total return comparison for different interest rate scenarios based on a 12-month investment horizon assuming that the spread to the average life is unchanged for each scenario:

Total Return Comparison

	Basis Point Shifts							Wt.
	+150	+100	+50	0	−50	−100	−150	Avg.
Prob of Rate Chg. (%)	1.8	7.4	21.9	35.1	26.1	7.2	0.6	Total
Total Return								Return
Nonagency MBS	2.01	4.13	5.55	6.56	7.18	7.00	6.91	6.27
Home Equity	2.34	3.95	5.17	6.09	6.79	7.24	7.51	5.94
Advantage of Nonagency MBS	−0.33	0.18	0.38	0.47	0.39	−0.24	−0.60	0.33

Source: Adapted from Tables 2, 3, and 4 of "Short Alt-As: Alternative vs. Short Home Equities," *PaineWebber Mortgage Strategist* (June 23, 1998), pp. 10 and 11.

a. Based on the latest prepayment information at the time (June 1998) and the prevailing pricing levels, the PaineWebber Mortgage Group stated that it appeared that the 3-year average life nonagency MBS provides relative value compared to the 3-year average life HEL, especially for investors expecting a modest increase in rates ("Short Alt-As: Alternative vs. Short Home Equities," Paine-Webber *Mortgage Strategist* (June 23, 1998), pp. 8-9.) Explain why.

b. PaineWebber assigned probabilities to the different scenarios. These probabilities are shown below the interest rate scenario. Based on the weighted average total return, which is the better issue to purchase? (Note: The expected total return is simply the weighted average of the total return in each scenario. The weight for the total return for a given scenario is the probability of occurrence for that scenario.)

c. What are the critical assumptions in the relative analysis performed?

19. Explain why in attempting to neutralize two positions against a small parallel shift in interest rates it is necessary to match the effective dollar duration of two positions in a trade and not just the effective duration of the two positions.

20. Mr. Lenox is a portfolio manager who own $15 million of par value of bond ABC. The market value of the bond is $13 million and the effective dollar duration for a 100 basis point change in rates is $1.2 million. Mr. Lenox is considering swapping out of bond ABC and into bond XYZ. The market price of bond XYZ is $75 per $100 of par value and the effective duration is 7. How much of par value of bond XYZ would Mr. Lenox have to purchase to maintain the same exposure to a small parallel shift in interest rates as with bond ABC?

SOLUTIONS TO END OF CHAPTER QUESTIONS

1. a. Since the price per $100 of par value is $95.46, this means that $500,000 of par value [= $477,300/(95.46/100)] can be purchased.

b.

Assumed yield six months from now (%)	Price per $100 par value ($)*	Market value ($)	Semiannual coupon payment ($)	Dollar return ($)	Annualized percent return (%)
9.00%	83.71	418,550	17,500	(41,250)	−17.3%
8.50%	87.42	437,100	17,500	(22,700)	−9.5%
8.00%	91.35	456,750	17,500	(3,050)	−1.3%
7.50%	95.54	477,700	17,500	17,900	7.5%
7.00%	100.00	500,000	17,500	40,200	16.8%
6.50%	104.75	523,750	17,500	63,950	26.8%
6.00%	109.80	549,000	17,500	89,200	37.4%

We will illustrate one of the calculations. Consider the 8% horizon yield. The corresponding horizon price is 91.35. So, for $500,000 in par value, the value of the bonds would equal $456,750 [=$500,000 (91.35/100)].

The coupon interest (for all the scenarios) is $17,500 (=$500,000 multiplied by the semiannual coupon rate of 3.5%). The total proceeds are then the value of the bonds of $456,750 plus the coupon interest of $17,500 which is equal to $474,250.

Given the total proceeds, the dollar return is found by subtracting the initial investment of $477,300. The dollar return is then −$3,050. The semiannual rate of return is found by dividing the dollar return of −$3,050 by the initial investment of $477,300 giving −0.00639. Doubling this return gives an annual return of −0.01278 or −1.3% (rounded).

c.

Assumed yield six months from now (%)	Price per $100 par value ($)	Market value per $1 million par value ($)	Semiannual coupon payment ($)	Dollar return ($)	Annualized percent return (%)
9.00%	83.71	837,100	35,000	(108,274)	−45.4%
8.50%	87.42	874,200	35,000	(71,174)	−29.8%
8.00%	91.35	913,500	35,000	(31,874)	−13.4%
7.50%	95.54	955,400	35,000	10,026	4.2%
7.00%	100.00	1,000,000	35,000	54,626	22.9%
6.50%	104.75	1,047,500	35,000	102,126	42.8%
6.00%	109.80	1,098,000	35,000	152,626	64.0%

Once again, let's illustrate the 8% horizon yield scenario. There is now $1 million of par value invested. The value of the position is $913,500. The semiannual dollar coupon interest is $35,000 (= 3.5% semiannual coupon rate times the $1 million of par value). This is the same for each scenario. The total proceeds are equal to the dollar return (the value of the bonds plus the dollar coupon interest) reduced by the cost of borrowing $477,300. Since the borrowing rate is assumed to be 10.8%, the borrowing cost is $477,300 multiplied by 5.4%. The interest cost is therefore $25,774.20. This is the same interest cost for each scenario. The total dollar proceeds after the interest cost is then −$31,874. Dividing by the equity investment of $477,300 and then multiplying by 2 gives an annual return of −13.4%.

d.

Assumed yield six months from now (%)	Price per $100 par value ($)*	Market value per $1 million par value ($)*	Semiannual coupon payment ($)	Dollar return ($)	Annualized percent return (%)**
9.00%	83.71	2,092,750	87,500	(309,347)	−129.6%
8.50%	87.42	2,185,500	87,500	(216,597)	−90.8%
8.00%	91.35	2,283,750	87,500	(118,347)	−49.6%
7.50%	95.54	2,388,500	87,500	(13,597)	−5.7%
7.00%	100.00	2,500,000	87,500	97,903	41.0%
6.50%	104.75	2,618,750	87,500	216,653	90.8%
6.00%	109.80	2,745,000	87,500	342,903	143.7%

e. The annual returns for the three cases are summarized below.

Horizon yield	No borrowed funds	Borrowed 477,300	Borrowed 1,909,200
9.00%	−17.3%	−45.4%	−129.6%
8.50%	−9.5%	−29.8%	−90.8%
8.00%	−1.3%	−13.4%	−49.6%
7.50%	7.5%	4.2%	−5.7%
7.00%	16.8%	22.9%	41.0%
6.50%	26.8%	42.8%	90.8%
6.00%	37.4%	64.0%	143.7%

The results clearly indicate that borrowing is advantageous in that it offers upside return greater than in the unleveraged case. The advantage is greater the more borrowed. In contrast, the loss is much greater the more leverage that is used. This is the tradeoff when using leverage.

2. A repurchase agreement is a contract that allows a party to either borrow or lend funds using the securities purchased as collateral. In practice, the expression "repo transaction" is used when a dealer uses a repo agreement to borrow funds (i.e., finance a position). A "reverse repo" is a term used when a non-dealer is using the securities to borrow funds (i.e., finance a position).

3. A repurchase agreement can be used to lend funds (i.e., a high quality short-term investment or money market instrument) or as a financing vehicle (i.e., a vehicle to borrow funds). The provision is unclear because as stated, it would suggest that the manager of the funds can use a repurchase agreement as either a short-term investment or a vehicle for financing. This may or may not have been the intent of the trustees of the pension fund.

4. When a repurchase agreement is used to create leverage (i.e., when it is used as a financing vehicle), it is a risky vehicle because of the risk associated with leverage. In contrast, when it is used as a vehicle in which to invest funds on a short-term basis, if properly structured, it is a high quality money market instrument.

5. a. The dollar interest cost is

dollar interest = amount borrowed × repo rate × repo term/360

Since only 97% of the market value can be borrowed,

amount borrowed = $3,000,000 × 0.97 = $2,910,000

The appropriate repo rate is 7% and the term is one day. Therefore,

dollar interest = $2,910,000 × 0.07 × 1/360 = $565.83

b. Since the repo is for 30 days, the 30-day term repo rate of 7.3% is used. The dollar interest cost is

dollar interest = $2,910,000 × 0.073 × 30/360 = $17,702.50

6. This statement is incorrect. The repo rate depends on the number of days or term of the borrowing arrangement. It is this term — the number of days of the repo — not the maturity of the security that is important. That is, a 30-day repo in which the collateral is a Treasury bond with 10 years remaining to maturity and one with 20 years remaining to maturity will have the same repo rate (assuming neither is on special).

7. The Treasury security is not likely to be rich. One reason it will offer a lower yield than similar maturity or similar duration Treasury securities is because of the better liquidity since it is an on-the-run issue. However, the major reason it is trading at a yield considerably less than otherwise comparable Treasury issues is that it is probably on special — that is, it is "hot" collateral. As a result, the issue offers attractive financing and market participants are willing to pay more for this issue, thereby driving down its yield.

8. Because the security is on special, dealers are willing to offer cheaper financing in order to obtain the use of the collateral. Thus, for a given term for the repo, the repo rate will be less for this security than for generic collateral.

9. If the repo margin is 2%, then the dealer will lend 98% or $9.8 million.

10. a. The credit risk of the lender of funds is that the value of the collateral declines and the borrower defaults. As a result, the lender owns the collateral with a market value less than the amount lent. Also, if the borrower holds the collateral, there is the risk that the collateral can be fraudulently used in another borrowing and/or the collateral can be sold without the knowledge of the lender.

b. In a hold-in-custody repo, the borrower retains custody of the collateral. So, there is the risk associated with the collateral being fraudulently used in another borrowing and/or the collateral can be sold without the knowledge of the lender.

c. A lender in a repo can protect itself in several ways. First, it can remove the risk of the collateral disappearing by using a tri-party repo. Second, the loan is for less than the market value of the collateral. This is the repo margin or "haircut." Finally, the collateral is marked to market requiring that if the margin declines below a specified amount the borrower must either provide additional cash or transfer acceptable securities to make up any margin deficit.

11. The repo rate represents a collateralized loan. In contrast, the federal funds rate is a rate on a loan that is unsecured. Hence the repo rate will be less.

12. The horizon yield given the assumptions about the Treasury yield curve and the credit spread is 6.15%. This means that the yield for this corporate bond declined over the 1-year investment horizon from 6.6% to 6.15%. The calculations to compute the 1-year total return are shown below.

Step 1: Compute the total coupon payments plus the reinvestment income assuming an annual reinvestment rate of 4% per year or 2% every six months. The semiannual coupon payments are $3.625. The value is

First coupon payment reinvested for six month = $3.625 (1.02)   = $3.6975
Second coupon payment not reinvested since at horizon date   = $3.6250
Total   = $7.3225

Step 2: The horizon price at the end of the 1-year investment horizon is determined as follows. The horizon yield is 6.15% by assumption. The 7.25% coupon 15-year corporate bond now has 14 years to maturity. The price of this bond when discounted at a flat 6.15% (a flat yield curve is assumed) is $110.2263.

Step 3: Adding the amounts in Steps 2 and 3 gives the total future dollars of $117.5488.

Step 4: Compute the following:

$$\left(\frac{\$117.5488}{\$106.1301}\right)^{\frac{1}{2}} - 1 = 5.24\%$$

Step 5: The total return on a bond-equivalent basis and on an effective rate basis are shown below:

$$2 \times 5.24\% = 10.48\% \text{ (BEY)}$$

$$(1.0524)^2 - 1 = 10.76\% \text{ (effective rate basis)}$$

13. The horizon yield given the assumptions about the Treasury yield curve and the decline in the credit spread is 8.75%. The calculations to compute the 1-year total return are shown below.

Step 1: Compute the total coupon payments plus the reinvestment income assuming an annual reinvestment rate of 5% per year or 2.5% every six months. The semiannual coupon payments are $5. The value is

First coupon payment reinvested for six month = $5 (1.025)   = $ 5.1250
Second coupon payment not reinvested since at horizon date   = $ 5.0000
Total   = $10.1250

Step 2: The horizon price at the end of the 1-year investment horizon is determined as follows. The horizon yield is 8.75% by assumption. The 10% coupon 9-year corporate bond now has 8 years to maturity. The price of this bond when discounted at a flat 8.75% (a flat yield curve is assumed) is $107.0853.

Step 3: Adding the amounts in Steps 2 and 3 gives the total future dollars of $117.2103.

Step 4: Compute the following:

$$\left(\frac{\$117.2103}{\$95.7420}\right)^{\frac{1}{2}} - 1 = 10.64\%$$

Step 5: The total return on a bond-equivalent basis and on an effective rate basis are shown below:

$2 \times 10.64\% = 21.29\%$ (BEY)

$(1.1064)^2 - 1 = 22.42\%$ (effective rate basis)

14. In calculating total return it is necessary to determine the value of a security at the end of the investment horizon. It is in this step of the total return calculation that a valuation model is used. If the valuation model is poor, the horizon price will not be an accurate estimate and the total return computed will be misleading.

15. The statement is incorrect. A total return analysis does allow the analyst to change the OAS at the horizon date. However, a valuation model to compute the horizon price based on the new OAS is required. Moreover, any type of yield curve shift can be accommodated. The yield curve at the horizon date would be a required input into the valuation model to obtain the horizon price.

16. This is a special case of total return analysis assuming that the investment horizon is the next moment in time. Consequently, there is no coupon income nor any reinvestment income. The only concern is with changes in the price of the securities in the portfolio.

17. a. The top panel of Table A shows that the duration of the PAC barbell is less than the duration of the 30-year FNMA 6% (4.10 versus 4.53). Thus, if interest rates increase, the PAC barbell should outperform (based solely on duration) the collateral. The reverse is true if interest rates decrease.

    b. Recall from Level I (Chapter 7) that different dealers and vendors of analytical services scale their convexity measures in different ways. The convexities in Table A — which were referred to as convexity measures at Level I — are based on the scaling used by PaineWebber. There is greater negative convexity for the collateral than the PAC barbell (−1.72 versus −0.84). This means that for large changes in interest rates, the collateral will underperform the PAC barbell.

    c. The results in Table A suggest that it is only in the scenario where rates are unchanged, or the yield curve steepened, that the collateral outperformed the PAC barbell and the underperformance is slight (only 2 and 7 basis points, respectively). Thus, if a manager owns the collateral, there is the potential to enhance return by selling the collateral and purchasing the PAC barbell.

    d. There are three important assumptions. First, it is assumed that the valuation model used to determine the horizon price of the three securities (the collateral and the two PACs) does a good job of estimating what the prices will be for each interest rate scenario. Second, it assumed that the OAS does not change. Third, it is assumed in the ±200 bp scenarios that the yield curve shifts in a parallel fashion.

e. The duration of the collateral is greater than the duration of the PAC barbell. Consequently, in declining interest rate scenarios, using just duration alone one would expect that the collateral would outperform the PAC barbell. This is not the case in Table A. The reason is due to the greater negative convexity of the collateral relative to the PAC barbell.

18. a. The total return comparison based on a 12-month investment horizon assuming a constant spread at the horizon date (i.e., a constant spread to the average life shown for the given scenario) indicates that if the rate change is between −50 basis points and +50 basis points, the 3-year nonagency MBS will outperform the 3-year HEL issue based on the underlying assumptions. Even if rates rise by 100 basis points, the nonagency MBS will outperform by 18 basis points. For a +150 basis point increase, the nonagency MBS underperforms. It also underperforms for a decline in rates of more than 100 basis points. (This is because while not shown in the information supplied for the question there is greater negative convexity for the nonagency MBS than the HEL issue.)

b. Based on the probabilities, there is a higher expected total return for the nonagency MBS than the home equity loan issue (6.27% versus 5.94%) and therefore the nonagency MBS would be the preferred investment if the investor agreed with these probabilities.

c. The critical assumptions are:

1. The yield curve shifts in a parallel fashion.
2. The spread to the average life is unchanged over the 12-month investment horizon.
3. The prepayment speeds for each interest rate scenario for each security are as expected.
4. The valuation model used to derive the horizon prices for each interest rate scenario is a good model.

When using the probability analysis, the assumption is that the probabilities are correct.

19. Matching the effective durations of two positions means only that they will have the same percentage price change for a change in rates. More specifically a small change in rates. However, if two positions have a different dollar value, the dollar price change will not be the same. What is sought in a trade that does not attempt to benefit from changes in interest rates is the neutralization of a trade against interest rate risk. Matching effective dollar durations will do this for a small change in rates.

20. The market value for bond XYZ that must be purchased is found as follows (where duration in the formula refers to effective duration):

$$\text{market value of bond XYZ} = \frac{\text{dollar duration of bond ABC}}{\text{duration of bond XYZ}/100}$$

Since

dollar duration of bond ABC = $1.2 million
duration of bond XYZ   = 7

then

$$\text{market value of bond XYZ} = \frac{\$1,200,000}{7/100} = \$17,142,857.14$$

The par value that must be purchased of bond XYZ is equal to

$$\text{par value of bond XYZ} = \frac{\text{market value of bond XYZ}}{\text{price of XYZ per \$1 of par value}}$$

Since the price of XYZ is \$75 per \$100 of par value, the price per \$1 of par value is 0.75 and therefore

$$\text{par value of bond XYZ} = \frac{\$17,142,857.14}{0.75} = \$22,857,142.86$$

SOLUTIONS TO PRACTICE QUESTIONS

1.

Assumed yield six months from now (%)	Market value per $100 par value ($)*	Market value per $2 million par value ($)*	Semiannual coupon payment ($)	Dollar return to equity ($)**	Annualized percent return (%)***
10.00%	81.12	4,867,200	240,000	(1,117,800)	−223.6%
9.50%	85.23	5,113,800	240,000	(871,200)	−174.2%
9.00%	89.72	5,383,200	240,000	(601,800)	−120.4%
8.50%	94.62	5,677,200	240,000	(307,800)	−61.6%
8.00%	100.00	6,000,000	240,000	15,000	3.0%
7.50%	105.91	6,354,600	240,000	369,600	73.9%
7.00%	112.41	6,744,600	240,000	759,600	151.9%
6.50%	119.58	7,174,800	240,000	1,189,800	238.0%
6.00%	127.51	7,650,600	240,000	1,665,600	333.1%

* This is the price and market value six months later, rounded to the nearest $100.
** After deducting interest expense of $225,000 ($5 million × 9%/2).
*** Annualized by doubling the semiannual return.

2. a. The dollar interest is

$$\$5,000,000 \times 0.04 \times 1/360 = \$555.56$$

b. The repurchase price is $5,000,555.56 (the amount borrowed of $5 million plus the dollar interest of $555.56).

3. The horizon yield is 7.15% (a decrease in the Treasury yield by 25 basis points to 6.25% and an increase in the yield spread by 10 basis points to 90 basis points).
The calculations are as shown below.

Step 1: Compute the total coupon payments plus the reinvestment income assuming an annual reinvestment rate of 4% or 2% every six month. The semiannual coupon payments are $3. The value is

First coupon payment reinvested for six months = $3 (1.02)	=	$3.06
Second coupon payment not reinvested since at horizon date	=	$3.00
Total	=	$6.06

Step 2: The horizon price at the end of the 1-year investment horizon is determined as follows. The horizon yield is 7.15% by assumption. The 6% coupon 20-year corporate bond now has 19 years to maturity. The price of this bond when discounted at a flat 7.15% yield (the yield curve is assumed to be flat) is $88.1496.

Step 3: Adding the amounts in Steps 2 and 3 gives the total future dollars of $94.2096.

Step 4: Compute the following (h is 2 in our illustration):

$$\left(\frac{\$94.2096}{\$86.4365}\right)^{\!\frac{1}{2}} - 1 = 4.40\%$$

Step 5 The total return on a bond-equivalent basis and on an effective rate basis are shown below:

$$2 \times 4.40\% = 8.80\% \qquad \text{(BEY)}$$

$$(1.0494)^2 - 1 = 8.99\% \qquad \text{(effective rate basis)}$$

Chapter 7

INTEREST RATE
DERIVATIVE INSTRUMENTS

LEARNING OUTCOME STATEMENTS

After reading this chapter you should be able to:

- describe the basic features of an interest rate futures contract.
- explain the differences between a futures contract and forward contract.
- explain the margin requirements for a futures contract (i.e., initial margin, maintenance margin, and variation margin).
- explain the role of the clearinghouse associated with a futures exchange.
- explain what a conversion factor is for a Treasury futures contract and the purpose of the conversion factor.
- compute the converted price for an issue that may be delivered to satisfy a Treasury futures contract.
- compute the invoice price for a Treasury futures contract.
- describe the delivery options embedded in the Treasury futures contract.
- compute the implied repo rate for an issue that is acceptable for delivery to satisfy a Treasury futures contract.
- explain what the cheapest-to-deliver issue is for a Treasury futures contract.
- describe what counterparty risk is.
- describe the basic features of an interest rate option.
- explain the differences between a futures contract and an option.
- explain the differences between an exchange-traded option and an over-the-counter option.
- describe what futures options are, their trading mechanics, and the reasons for their popularity.
- explain why over-the-counter interest rate options are used by institutional investors.
- explain what is meant by a notional principal (or notional amount).
- explain the basic features of an interest rate swap.
- compute the periodic payments that the counterparties to an interest rate swap must make.
- explain the relationship between an interest rate swap and forward contracts.
- demonstrate why an interest rate swap can be viewed as a package of cash market instruments.
- explain what an interest rate cap and floor are.
- explain the relationship between a cap and floor and an interest rate option.
- compute the payoff for a cap and a floor.
- explain how a collar is created.

SECTION I
INTRODUCTION

In this chapter we turn our attention to financial contracts that are popularly referred to as **interest rate derivative instruments** because they derive their value from some cash market instrument or reference interest rate. These instruments include futures, forwards, options, swaps, caps, and floors. In this chapter we will discuss the basic features of these instruments and in the next we will see how they are valued. As we will see in Level III, these instruments play an important role in managing the interest rate risk of a portfolio or institution.

SECTION II
INTEREST RATE
FUTURES

A **futures contract** is an agreement that requires a party to the agreement either to buy or sell something at a designated future date at a predetermined price. Futures contracts are products created by exchanges. Futures contracts based on a financial instrument or a financial index are known as **financial futures**. Financial futures can be classified as (1) stock index futures, (2) interest rate futures, and (3) currency futures. Our focus in this chapter is on interest rate futures.

A. Mechanics of Futures Trading

A futures contract is an agreement between a buyer (seller) and an established exchange or its clearinghouse in which the buyer (seller) agrees to take (make) delivery of something at a specified price at the end of a designated period of time. The price at which the parties agree to transact in the future is called the **futures price**. The designated date at which the parties must transact is called the **settlement date** or **delivery date**.

1. Liquidating a Position

Most financial futures contracts have settlement dates in the months of March, June, September, or December. This means that at a predetermined time in the contract settlement month the contract stops trading, and a price is determined by the exchange for settlement of the contract. The contract with the closest settlement date is called the **nearby futures contract**. The next futures contract is the one that settles just after the nearby futures contract. The contract farthest away in time from settlement is called the **most distant futures contract**.

A party to a futures contract has two choices on liquidation of the position. First, the position can be liquidated prior to the settlement date. For this purpose, the party must take an offsetting position in the same contract. For the buyer of a futures contract, this means selling the same number of the identical futures contracts; for the seller of a futures contract, this means buying the same number of identical futures contracts.

The alternative is to wait until the settlement date. At that time the party purchasing a futures contract accepts delivery of the underlying at the agreed-upon price; the party that sells a futures contract liquidates the position by delivering the underlying at the agreed-upon price. For some interest rate futures contracts that we shall describe later, settlement is made in cash only. Such contracts are referred to as **cash settlement contracts**.

2. The Role of the Clearinghouse

Associated with every futures exchange is a clearinghouse, which performs several functions. One of these functions is to guarantee that the two parties to the transaction will perform.

When an investor takes a position in the futures market, the clearinghouse takes the opposite position and agrees to satisfy the terms set forth in the contract. Because of the clearinghouse, the investor need not worry about the financial strength and integrity of the party taking the opposite side of the contract. After initial execution of an order, the relationship between the two parties ends. The clearinghouse interposes itself as the buyer for every sale and the seller for every purchase. Thus investors are free to liquidate their positions without involving the other party in the original contract, and without worry that the other party may default. This is the reason why we define a futures contract as an agreement between a party and a clearinghouse associated with an exchange. Besides its guarantee function, the clearinghouse makes it simple for parties to a futures contract to unwind their positions prior to the settlement date.

3. Margin Requirements

When a position is first taken in a futures contract, the investor must deposit a minimum dollar amount per contract as specified by the exchange. This amount is called **initial margin** and is required as deposit for the contract. The initial margin may be in the form of an interest-bearing security such as a Treasury bill. As the price of the futures contract fluctuates, the value of the investor's equity in the position changes. At the end of each trading day, the exchange determines the settlement price for the futures contract. This price is used to mark to market the investor's position, so that any gain or loss from the position is reflected by the equity in the investor's account.

Maintenance margin is the minimum level (specified by the exchange) by which an investor's equity position may fall to as a result of an unfavorable price movement before the investor is required to deposit additional margin. The additional margin deposited is called **variation margin**, and it is an amount necessary to bring the equity in the account back to its initial margin level. This amount is determined from the process of marking the position to market. Unlike initial margin, variation margin must be in cash, not interest-bearing instruments. Any excess margin in the account may be withdrawn by the investor. If a party to a futures contract who is required to deposit variation margin fails to do so within 24 hours, the futures position is closed out.

Although there are initial and maintenance margin requirements for buying securities on margin, the concept of margin differs for securities and futures. When securities are acquired on margin, the difference between the price of the security and the initial margin is borrowed from the broker. The security purchased serves as collateral for the loan, and the investor pays interest. For futures contracts, the initial margin, in effect, serves as "good faith" money, an indication that the investor will satisfy the obligation of the contract.

B. Forward Contracts   A **forward contract**, just like a futures contract, is an agreement for the future delivery of something at a specified price at the end of a designated period of time. Futures contracts are standardized agreements as to the delivery date (or month) and quality of the deliverable, and are traded on organized exchanges. A forward contract differs in that it is usually non-standardized (that is, the terms of each contract are negotiated individually between buyer and seller), there is no clearinghouse, and secondary markets are often non-existent or extremely thin. Unlike a futures contract, which is an exchange-traded product, a forward contract is an over-the-counter instrument.

Futures contracts are marked to market at the end of each trading day. Consequently, futures contracts are subject to interim cash flows as additional margin may be required in the case of adverse price movements, or as cash is withdrawn in the case of favorable price movements. A forward contract *may* or *may not be marked to market*, depending on the wishes of the two parties. For a forward contract that is *not* marked to market, there are no interim cash flow effects because no additional margin is required.

Finally, the parties in a forward contract are exposed to credit risk because either party may default on its obligation. This risk is called **counterparty risk**. This risk is minimal in the case of futures contracts because the clearinghouse associated with the exchange guarantees the other side of the transaction. In the case of a forward contract, both parties face counterparty risk. Thus, there exists **bilateral counterparty risk**.

Other than these differences, most of what we say about futures contracts applies equally to forward contracts.

C. Risk and Return Characteristics of Futures Contracts

When an investor takes a position in the market by buying a futures contract, the investor is said to be in a **long position** or to be **long futures**. The buyer of the futures contract is also referred to as the "long." If, instead, the investor's opening position is the sale of a futures contract, the investor is said to be in a **short position** or to be **short futures**. The seller of the futures contract is also referred to as the "short." The buyer of a futures contract will realize a profit if the futures price increases; the seller of a futures contract will realize a profit if the futures price decreases.

When a position is taken in a futures contract, the party need not put up the entire amount of the investment. Instead, only initial margin must be put up. Consequently, an investor can effectively create a leveraged position by using futures. At first, the leverage available in the futures market may suggest that the market benefits only those who want to speculate on price movements. This is not true. As we shall see in Level III, futures markets can be used to control interest rate risk. Without the effective leverage possible in futures transactions, the cost of reducing price risk using futures would be too high for many market participants.

D. Exchange-Traded Interest Rate Futures Contracts

Interest rate futures contracts can be classified by the maturity of their underlying security. Short-term interest rate futures contracts have an underlying security that matures in less than one year. Examples of these are futures contracts in which the underlying is a 3-month Treasury bill and a 3-month Eurodollar certificate of deposit. The maturity of the underlying security of long-term futures contracts exceeds one year. Examples of these are futures contracts in which the underlying is a Treasury coupon security, a 10-year agency note, and a municipal bond index. Our focus will be on futures contracts in which the underlying is a Treasury coupon security (a Treasury bond or a Treasury note). These contracts are the most widely used by managers of bond portfolios and we begin with the specifications of the Treasury bond futures contract.

There are futures contracts on non-U.S. government securities traded throughout the world. Many of them are modeled after the U.S. Treasury futures contracts and consequently, the concepts discussed below apply directly to those futures contracts.

1. Treasury Bond Futures

The Treasury bond futures contract is traded on the Chicago Board of Trade (CBT). The underlying instrument for a Treasury bond futures contract is $100,000 par value of a hypothetical 20-year coupon bond. The coupon rate on the hypothetical bond is called the **notional coupon**. Since the inception of the contract, the notional coupon had been 8%. However, beginning with the March 2000 contract, the notional coupon was changed to 6%.

Exhibit 1: Treasury Bond Issues Acceptable for Delivery to Satisfy the September 2000 Futures Contract

Issue	Conversion Factor	Price	Implied Repo Rate(%)	Issue	Conversion Factor	Price	Implied Repo Rate (%)
9⅛ 05/15/18	1.3357	130-26	5.43	7½ 11/15/24	1.1895	116-21	4.40
9 11/15/18	1.3275	130-00	5.43	9¼ 02/15/16	1.3216	129-28	4.39
7⅞ 02/15/21	1.2180	119-06	5.42	9⅞ 11/15/15	1.3798	135-21	4.35
8¾ 08/15/20	1.3156	128-25+	5.40	7¼ 05/15/16	1.1250	110-13	4.32
8⅛ 08/15/19	1.2371	121-03	5.38	6⅞ 08/15/25	1.1119	109-03	4.16
8⅛ 05/15/21	1.2488	122-07	5.35	6 02/15/26	0.9999	98-02+	4.08
8⅞ 02/15/19	1.3161	128-29	5.33	7⅝ 02/15/25	1.2061	118-13	4.08
8¾ 05/15/20	1.3136	128-20	5.33	6¾ 08/15/26	1.0976	107-25	3.84
8½ 02/15/20	1.2830	125-21	5.26	6½ 11/15/26	1.0654	104-21	3.65
8⅛ 08/15/21	1.2502	122-12+	5.26	6⅝ 02/15/27	1.0820	106-10	3.60
7⅝ 11/15/22	1.1971	117-05	5.24	6⅜ 08/15/27	1.0495	103-05+	3.36
8 11/15/21	1.2370	121-05	5.06	6⅛ 11/15/27	1.0166	99-31+	3.10
7⅛ 02/15/23	1.1370	111-10	5.06	5½ 08/15/28	0.9327	91-29	2.34
8⅞ 08/15/17	1.3010	127-18+	4.99	5¼ 11/15/28	0.8989	88-23+	1.63
7¼ 08/15/22	1.1506	112-22+	4.89	5¼ 02/15/29	0.8984	88-30	0.65
8¾ 05/15/17	1.2855	126-02+	4.87	6⅛ 08/15/29	1.0169	101-09	−1.34
6¼ 08/15/23	1.0307	100-29+	4.77	6¼ 05/15/30	1.0344	105-05+	−8.54
7½ 11/15/16	1.1529	113-01	4.72				

Source of information: Bloomberg Financial Markets

The futures price is quoted in terms of par being 100. Quotes are in 32nds of 1%. Thus a quote for a Treasury bond futures contract of 97-16 means 97 and 16/32 or 97.50. So, if a buyer and seller agree on a futures price of 97-16, this means that the buyer agrees to accept delivery of the hypothetical underlying Treasury bond and pay 97.50% of par value and the seller agrees to accept 97.50% of par value. Since the par value is $100,000, the futures price that the buyer and seller agree to for this hypothetical Treasury bond is $97,500.

The minimum price fluctuation for the Treasury bond futures contract is 1/32 of 1%, which is referred to as "a 32nd." The dollar value of a 32nd for $100,000 par value (the par value for the underlying Treasury bond) is $31.25. Thus, the minimum price fluctuation is $31.25 for this contract.

We have been referring to the underlying as a hypothetical Treasury bond. The seller of a Treasury bond futures contract who decides to make delivery rather than liquidate his position by buying back the contract prior to the settlement date must deliver some Treasury bond. But what Treasury bond? The CBT allows the seller to deliver one of several Treasury bonds that the CBT specifies are acceptable for delivery. Exhibit 1 shows the 35 Treasury bond issues that the seller could have selected from to deliver to the buyer of the September 2000 futures contract. The CBT makes its determination of the Treasury issues that are acceptable for delivery from all outstanding Treasury issues that meet the following criteria: an issue must have at least 15 years to maturity from the first day of the delivery month if not callable; in the case of callable bonds, the issue must not be callable for at least 15 years from the first day of the delivery month.

It is important to remember that while the underlying Treasury bond for this contract is a hypothetical issue and therefore cannot itself be delivered into the futures contract, the contract is not a cash settlement contract. The only way to close out a Treasury bond futures contract is to either initiate an offsetting futures position, or to deliver a Treasury issue satisfying the above-mentioned criteria into the futures contract.

a. Conversion Factors

The delivery process for the Treasury bond futures contract makes the contract interesting. At the settlement date, the seller of a futures contract (the short) is now required to deliver to the buyer (the long) $100,000 par value of a 6% 20-year Treasury bond. Since no such bond exists, the seller must choose from one of the acceptable deliverable Treasury bonds that the CBT has specified. Suppose the seller is entitled to deliver $100,000 of a 5% 20-year Treasury bond to settle the futures contract. The value of this bond is less than the value of a 6% 20-year bond. If the seller delivers the 5% 20-year bond, this would be unfair to the buyer of the futures contract who contracted to receive $100,000 of a 6% 20-year Treasury bond. Alternatively, suppose the seller delivers $100,000 of a 7% 20-year Treasury bond. The value of a 7% 20-year Treasury bond is greater than that of a 6% 20-year bond, so this would be a disadvantage to the seller.

How can this problem be resolved? To make delivery equitable to both parties, the CBT has introduced conversion factors for adjusting the price of each Treasury issue that can be delivered to satisfy the Treasury bond futures contract. The conversion factor is determined by the CBT before a contract with a specific settlement date begins trading.[1] The adjusted price is found by multiplying the conversion factor by the futures price. The adjusted price is called the **converted price**.

Exhibit 1 shows for each of the acceptable Treasury issues for the September 2000 futures contract the corresponding conversion factor. The conversion factor is constant throughout the life of the futures contract.

The price that the buyer must pay the seller when a Treasury bond is delivered is called the **invoice price**. The invoice price is the futures settlement price plus accrued interest. However, as just noted, the seller can deliver one of several acceptable Treasury issues and to make delivery fair to both parties, the invoice price must be adjusted based on the actual Treasury issue delivered. It is the conversion factors that are used to adjust the invoice price. The invoice price is:

$$\text{invoice price} = \text{contract size} \times \text{futures settlement price} \\ \times \text{conversion factor} + \text{accrued interest}$$

Suppose the Treasury September 2000 futures contract settles at 118-16 and that the issue delivered is the 8% of 11/15/21. The futures contract settlement price of 118-16 means 118.5% of par value or 1.185 times par value. As indicated in Exhibit 1, the conversion factor for this issue is 1.2370. Since the contract size is $100,000, the invoice price the buyer pays the seller is:

$$\$100,000 \times 1.185 \times 1.2370 + \text{accrued interest} \\ = \$146,584.50 + \text{accrued interest}$$

PRACTICE QUESTION 1

Suppose that the June 200X Treasury bond futures contract settles at 97-24 and the issue delivered has a conversion factor of 1.17. Assume that the accrued interest for the issue delivered is $3,800 per $100,000 par value. What is the invoice price the buyer pays the seller?

---

[1] The conversion factor is based on the price that a deliverable bond would sell for at the beginning of the delivery month if it were to yield 6%.

b. Cheapest-to-Deliver Issue

In selecting the issue to be delivered, the short will select from all the deliverable issues the one that will give the largest rate of return from a cash and carry trade. A cash and carry trade is one in which a cash bond that is acceptable for delivery is purchased with borrowed funds and simultaneously the Treasury bond futures contract is sold. (We will discuss this trade in more detail in the next chapter.) The bond purchased can be delivered to satisfy the short futures position. Thus, by buying the Treasury issue that is acceptable for delivery and selling the futures, an investor has effectively sold the bond at the delivery price (i.e., the converted price).

A rate of return can be calculated for this trade. This rate of return is referred to as the **implied repo rate** and is determined by:

1. the price plus accrued interest at which the Treasury issue could be purchased

2. the converted price plus the accrued interest that will be received upon delivery of that Treasury bond issue to satisfy the short futures position

3. the coupon payments that will be received between today and the date the issue is delivered to satisfy the futures contract.

4. the reinvestment income that will be realized on the coupon payments between the time the interim coupon payment is received and the date that the issue is delivered to satisfy the Treasury bond futures contract.

The first three elements are known. The last element will depend on the reinvestment rate that can be earned. While the reinvestment rate is unknown, typically this is a small part of the rate of return and not much is lost by assuming that the implied repo rate can be predicted with certainty.

The general formula for the implied repo rate is as follows:

$$\text{implied repo rate} = \frac{\text{dollar return}}{\text{cost of the investment}} \times \frac{360}{\text{days}_1}$$

where days_1 is equal to the number of days until settlement of the futures contract. Below we will explain the other components in the formula for the implied repo rate.

Let's begin with the dollar return. The **dollar return** for an issue is the difference between the **proceeds received** and the **cost of the investment**. The proceeds received are equal to the proceeds received at the settlement date of the futures contract and any interim coupon payment plus interest from reinvesting the interim coupon payment. The proceeds received at the settlement date include the converted price (i.e., futures settlement price multiplied by the conversion factor for the issue) and the accrued interest received from delivery of the issue. That is,

proceeds received = converted price + accrued interest received
+ interim coupon payment
+ interest from reinvesting the interim coupon payment

As noted earlier, all of the elements are known except the interest from reinvesting the interim coupon payment. This amount is estimated by assuming that the coupon payment can be reinvested at the term repo rate. We described the repo market in Chapter 6 and the term repo rate. The repo rate is not only a borrowing rate for an investor who wants to borrow in the repo market but also the rate at which an investor can invest proceeds on a short-term basis. For how long is the reinvestment of the interim coupon payment? It is the number of days from when the interim coupon payment is received and the actual delivery date to satisfy the futures contract. The reinvestment income is then computed as follows:

interest from reinvesting the interim coupon payment =
interim coupon × term repo rate × (days$_2$ /360)

where

days$_2$ = number of days between when the interim coupon payment is received
and the actual delivery date of the futures contract

The reason for dividing days$_2$ by 360 is that the ratio represents the number of days the interim coupon is reinvested as a percentage of the number of days in a year as measured in the money market.

The cost of the investment is the amount paid to purchase the issue. This cost is equal to the purchase price plus accrued interest paid. That is,

cost of the investment = purchase price + accrued interest paid

Thus, the dollar return for the numerator of the formula for the implied repo rate is equal to

dollar return = proceeds received − cost of the investment

The dollar return is then divided by the cost of the investment.[2]

So, now we know how to compute the numerator and the denominator in the formula for the implied repo rate. The second ratio in the formula for the implied repo rate simply involves annualizing the return using a convention in the money market for the number of days. (Recall that in the money market the convention is to use a 360 day year.) Since the investment resulting from the cash and carry trade is a synthetic money market instrument, 360 days are used.

Let's compute the implied repo rate for a hypothetical issue that may be delivered to satisfy a hypothetical Treasury bond futures contract. Assume the following for the deliverable issue and the futures contract:

Futures contract
futures price = 96
days to futures delivery date (days$_1$) = 82 days

Deliverable issue
price of issue = 107
accrued interest paid = 3.8904
coupon rate = 10%
days remaining before interim coupon paid = 40 days
interim coupon = $5
number of days between when the interim coupon payment is received and
the actual delivery date of the futures contract (days$_2$) = 42
conversion factor = 1.1111
accrued interest received at futures settlement date = 1.1507

---

[2] Actually, the cost of the investment should be adjusted because the amount that the investor ties up in the investment is reduced if there is an interim coupon payment. We will ignore this adjustment here.

Other information:
    82-day term repo rate = 3.8%

Let's begin with the proceeds received. We need to compute the converted price and the interest from reinvesting the interim coupon payment. The converted price is:

$$\text{converted price} = \text{futures price} \times \text{conversion factor}$$
$$= 96 \times 1.1111 = 106.6656$$

The interest from reinvesting the interim coupon payment depends on the term repo rate. The term repo rate is assumed to be 3.8%. Therefore,

$$\text{interest from reinvesting the interim coupon payment} = \$5 \times 0.038 \times \left(\frac{42}{360}\right)$$

$$= 0.0222$$

To summarize:

converted price	=	106.6656
accrued interest received	=	1.1507
interim coupon payment	=	5.0000
interest from reinvesting the interim coupon payment	=	0.0222
proceeds received	=	112.8385

The cost of the investment is the purchase price for the issue plus the accrued interest paid, as shown below:

$$\text{cost of the investment} = 107 + 3.8904 = 110.8904$$

The implied repo rate is then:

$$\text{implied repo rate} = \frac{112.8385 - 110.8904}{110.8904} \times \frac{360}{82} = 0.0771 = 7.71\%$$

Once the implied repo rate is calculated for each deliverable issue, the issue selected will be the one that has the highest implied repo rate (i.e., the issue that gives the maximum return in a cash and carry trade). The issue with the highest return is referred to as the **cheapest-to-deliver issue**. As explained in the next chapter, this issue plays a key role in the pricing of a Treasury futures contract. Exhibit 1 shows the implied repo rate for the acceptable deliverable issues as reported by Bloomberg Financial Markets. The highest implied repo rate is 5.43% for both the 9⅛% of 05/15/18 and the 9% of 11/15/18 issues. So these two issues are the cheapest-to-deliver.

While an issue may be the cheapest to deliver today, changes in factors may cause some other issue to be the cheapest to deliver at a future date. A sensitivity analysis can be performed to determine how a change in yield affects the cheapest to deliver. For the September 2000 futures contract, the 9⅛% of 05/15/18 and 9% of 11/15/18 issues were the cheapest-to-deliver issues. For the yield changes (i.e., a parallel shift) shown below, the cheapest-to-deliver issue (as reported by Bloomberg) would be as follows:

Yield change	Cheapest-to-deliver issue	
+100 basis points	5.50%	8/15/28
+50 basis points	6.00%	2/15/26
−50 basis points	9.875%	11/15/15
−100 basis points	9.875%	11/15/15

PRACTICE QUESTION 2

Calculate the implied repo rate for a hypothetical issue that is deliverable for a Treasury bond futures contract assuming the following for the deliverable issue and the futures contract:

Futures contract
   Futures price = 97
   days to futures delivery date (days_1) = 62 days

Deliverable issue
   price of issue = 95
   accrued interest paid = 3.0110
   coupon rate = 7%
   days remaining before interim coupon made = 25 day
   interim coupon = $3.50
       number of days between when the interim coupon payment is received and the actual delivery date of the futures contract (day_2) = 37 days
   conversion factor = 0.9710
   accrued interest received at futures settlement date =0.7096

Other information:
   62-day repo rate = 4.7%

Exhibit 2: Delivery Options Granted to the Short (Seller) of a CBT Treasury Bond Futures Contract

Delivery option	Description
Quality or swap option	Choice of which acceptable Treasury issue to deliver
Timing option	Choice of when in delivery month to deliver
Wild card option	Choice to deliver after the closing price of the futures contract is determined

c. Other Delivery Options

In addition to the choice of which acceptable Treasury issue to deliver — sometimes referred to as the **quality option** or **swap option** — the short has at least two more options granted under CBT delivery guidelines. The short is permitted to decide when in the delivery month delivery actually will take place. This is called the **timing option**. The other option is the right of the short to give notice of intent to deliver up to 8:00 p.m. Chicago time after the closing of the exchange (3:15 p.m. Chicago time) on the date when the futures settlement price has been fixed. This option is referred to as the **wild card option**. The quality option, the timing option, and the wild card option (in sum referred to as the **delivery options**), mean that the long position can never be sure which Treasury bond will be delivered or when it will be delivered. These three delivery options are summarized in Exhibit 2.

d. Delivery Procedure

For a short who wants to deliver, the delivery procedure involves three days. The first day is the **position day**. On this day, the short notifies the CBT that it intends to deliver. The short has until 8:00 p.m. central standard time to do so. The second day is the **notice day**. On this day, the short specifies which particular issue will be delivered. The short has until 2:00 p.m. central standard time to make this declaration. (On the last possible notice day in the delivery month, the short has until 3:00 p.m.) The CBT then selects the long to whom delivery will be made. This is the long position that has been outstanding for the greatest period of time. The long is then notified by 4:00 p.m. that delivery will be made. The third day is the **delivery day**. By 10:00 a.m. on this day the short must have in its account the Treasury issue that it specified on the notice day and by 1:00 p.m. must deliver that bond to the long that was assigned by the CBT to accept delivery. The long pays the short the invoice price upon receipt of the bond.

2. Treasury Note Futures

There are three Treasury note futures contracts: 10-year, 5-year, and 2-year. All three contracts are modeled after the Treasury bond futures contract and are traded on the CBT. The underlying instrument for the 10-year Treasury note futures contract is $100,000 par value of a hypothetical 10-year 6% Treasury note. There are several acceptable Treasury issues that may be delivered by the short. An issue is acceptable if the maturity is not less than 6.5 years and not greater than 10 years from the first day of the delivery month. The delivery options granted to the short position and the minimum price fluctuation are the same as for the Treasury bond futures contract.

For the 5-year Treasury note futures contract, the underlying is $100,000 par value of a 6% notional coupon U.S. Treasury note that satisfies the following conditions: (1) an original maturity of not more than five years and three months, (2) a remaining maturity no greater then five years and three months, and (3) a remaining maturity not less than four years and two months. The minimum price fluctuation for this contract is $\frac{1}{64}$ of 1%. The dollar value of a 64th for a $100,000 par value is $15.625 and is therefore the minimum price fluctuation.

The underlying for the 2-year Treasury note futures contract is $200,000 par value of a 6% notional coupon U.S. Treasury note with a remaining maturity of not more than two years and not less than one year and nine months. Moreover, the original maturity of the note delivered to satisfy the 2-year futures cannot be more than five years and three months. The minimum price fluctuation for this contract is $\frac{1}{128}$ of 1%. The dollar value of a 128th for a $200,000 par value is $15.625 and is therefore the minimum price fluctuation.

The 2-year and 5-year note futures are less liquid than the 10-year note futures.

SECTION III INTEREST RATE OPTIONS

An **option** is a contract in which the writer of the option grants the buyer of the option the right, but not the obligation, to purchase from or sell to the writer something at a specified price within a specified period of time (or at a specified date). The **writer**, also referred to as the **seller**, grants this right to the buyer in exchange for a certain sum of money, called the **option price** or **option premium**. The price at which the underlying for the contract may be bought or sold is called the **exercise price** or **strike price**. The date after which an option is void is called the **expiration date**. Our focus is on options where the "something" underlying the option is an interest rate instrument or an interest rate.

When an option grants the buyer the right to purchase the designated instrument from the writer (seller), it is referred to as a **call option**, or **call**. When the option buyer has the right to sell the designated instrument to the writer, the option is called a **put option**, or **put**.

An option is also categorized according to when the option buyer may exercise the option. There are options that may be exercised at any time up to and including the expiration date. Such an option is referred to as an **American option**. There are options that may be exercised only at the expiration date. An option with this feature is called a **European option**. An option that can be exercised prior to maturity but only on designated dates is called a **modified American**, **Bermuda**, or **Atlantic option**.

A. Risk and Return Characteristics of Options

The maximum amount that an option buyer can lose is the option price. The maximum profit that the option writer can realize is the option price. The option buyer has substantial upside return potential, while the option writer has substantial downside risk.

It is assumed in this chapter that the reader has an understanding of the basic positions that can be created with options. These positions include:

1. long call position (buying a call option)
2. short call position (selling a call option)
3. long put position (buying a put option)
4. short put position (selling a put option)

Exhibit 3 shows the payoff profile for these four option positions *assuming that each option position is held to the expiration date and not exercised early.*

B. Differences Between Options and Futures Contracts

Unlike a futures contract, one party to an option contract is not obligated to transact. Specifically, the option buyer has the right, but not the obligation, to transact. The option writer does have the obligation to perform. In the case of a futures contract, both buyer and seller are obligated to perform. Of course, a futures buyer does not pay the seller to accept the obligation, while an option buyer pays the option seller an option price.

Consequently, the risk/reward characteristics of the two contracts are also different. In the case of a futures contract, the buyer of the contract realizes a dollar-for-dollar gain when the price of the futures contract increases and suffers a dollar-for-dollar loss when the price of the futures contract drops. The opposite occurs for the seller of a futures contract. Options do not provide this symmetric risk/reward relationship. The most that the buyer of an option can lose is the option price. While the buyer of an option retains all the potential benefits, the gain is always reduced by the amount of the option price. The maximum profit that the writer may realize is the option price; this is offset against substantial downside risk.

Both parties to a futures contract are required to post margin. There are no margin requirements for the buyer of an option once the option price has been paid in full. Because the option price is the maximum amount that the investor can lose, no matter how adverse the price movement of the underlying, there is no need for margin. Because the writer of an option has agreed to accept all of the risk (and none of the reward) of the position in the underlying, the writer is generally required to put up the option price received as margin. In addition, as price changes occur that adversely affect the writer's position, the writer is required to deposit additional margin (with some exceptions) as the position is marked to market.

C. Exchange-Traded Versus OTC Options

Options, like other financial instruments, may be traded either on an organized exchange or in the over-the-counter (OTC) market. An exchange that wants to create an options contract must obtain approval from regulators. Exchange-traded options have three advantages. First, the strike price and expiration date of the contract are standardized.[3] Second, as in the case of futures contracts, the direct link between buyer and seller is severed after the order is executed because of the interchangeability of exchange-traded options. The clearinghouse associated with the exchange where the option trades performs the same guarantor function in the options market that it does in the futures market. Finally, transaction costs are lower for exchange-traded options than for OTC options.

---

[3] Because of this disadvantage, exchanges have developed put and call options issued by their clearinghouse that have some customization with respect to expiration date, exercise style, and strike price. These options are called *flexible exchange options* and are nicknamed "Flex" options.

Exhibit 3: Payoff of Basic Option Positions If Held to Expiration Date

(a) Long Call Position

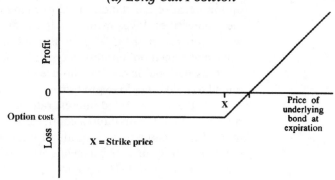

(b) Short Call Position

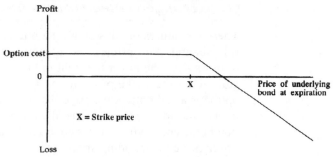

(c) Long Put Position

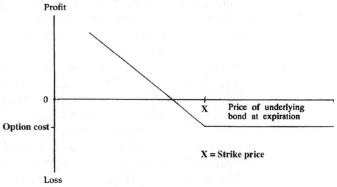

(d) Short Put Position

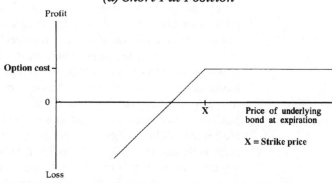

The higher cost of an OTC option reflects the cost of customizing the option for the many situations where an institutional investor needs to have a tailor-made option because the standardized exchange-traded option does not satisfy its investment objectives. Investment banking firms and commercial banks act as principals as well as brokers in the OTC options market. While an OTC option is less liquid than an exchange-traded option, this is typically not of concern to an institutional investor — most institutional investors who use OTC options as part of an asset/liability strategy intend to hold them to expiration.

Exchange-traded interest rate options can be written on a fixed income security or an interest rate futures contract. The former options are called *options on physicals*. For reasons to be explained later, options on interest rate futures are more popular than options on physicals. However, portfolio managers have made increasingly greater use of OTC options.

1. Exchange-Traded Futures Options

There are futures options on all the interest rate futures contracts mentioned earlier in this chapter. An option on a futures contract, commonly referred to as a **futures option**, gives the buyer the right to buy from or sell to the writer a designated futures contract at the strike price at any time during the life of the option. If the futures option is a call option, the buyer has the right to purchase one designated futures contract at the strike price. That is, the buyer has the right to acquire a long futures position in the underlying futures contract. If the buyer exercises the call option, the writer acquires a corresponding short position in the same futures contract.

A put option on a futures contract grants the buyer the right to sell one designated futures contract to the writer at the strike price. That is, the option buyer has the right to acquire a short position in the designated futures contract. If the put option is exercised, the writer acquires a corresponding long position in the designated futures contract.

As the parties to the futures option will realize a position in a futures contract when the option is exercised, the question is: what will the futures price be? That is, at what futures price will the long be required to pay for the instrument underlying the futures contract, and at what futures price will the short be required to sell the instrument underlying the futures contract?

Upon exercise, the futures price for the futures contract will be set equal to the strike price. The position of the two parties is then immediately marked-to-market in terms of the then-current futures price. Thus, the futures position of the two parties will be at the prevailing futures price. At the same time, the option buyer will receive from the option seller the economic benefit from exercising. In the case of a call futures option, the option writer must pay the difference between the current futures price and the strike price to the buyer of the option. In the case of a put futures option, the option writer must pay the option buyer the difference between the strike price and the current futures price.

For example, suppose an investor buys a call option on some futures contract in which the strike price is 85. Assume also that the futures price is 95 and that the buyer exercises the call option. Upon exercise, the call buyer is given a long position in the futures contract at 85 and the call writer is assigned the corresponding short position in the futures contract at 85. The futures positions of the buyer and the writer are immediately marked-to-market by the exchange. Because the prevailing futures price is 95 and the strike price is 85, the long futures position (the position of the call buyer) realizes a gain of 10, while the short futures position (the position of the call writer) realizes a loss of 10. The call writer pays the exchange 10 and the call buyer receives from the exchange 10. The call buyer, who now has a long futures position at 95, can either liquidate the futures position at 95 or maintain a long futures position. If the former course of action is taken, the call buyer sells his futures contract at the prevailing futures price of 95. There is no gain or loss from liquidating the position. Overall, the call buyer realizes a gain of 10. The call buyer who elects to hold the long futures position will face the same risk and reward of holding such a position, but still realizes a gain of 10 from the exercise of the call option.

Suppose instead that the futures option with a strike price of 85 is a put rather than a call, and the current futures price is 60 rather than 95. Then if the buyer of this put option exercises it, the buyer would have a short position in the futures contract at 85; the option writer would have a long position in the futures contract at 85. The exchange then marks the position to market at the then-current futures price of 60, resulting in a gain to the put buyer of 25 and a loss to the put writer of the same amount. The put buyer who now has a short futures position at 60 can either liquidate the short futures position by buying a futures contract at the prevailing futures price of 60 or maintain the short futures position. In either case the put buyer realizes a gain of 25 from exercising the put option.

There are no margin requirements for the buyer of a futures option once the option price has been paid in full. Because the option price is the maximum amount that the buyer can lose regardless of how adverse the price movement of the underlying instrument, there is no need for margin. Because the writer (seller) of a futures option has agreed to accept all of the risk (and none of the reward) of the position in the underlying instrument, the writer (seller) is required to deposit not only the margin required on the interest rate futures contract position but also (with certain exceptions) the option price that is received from writing the option.

The price of a futures option is quoted in 64ths of 1% of par value. For example, a price of 24 means $24/64$ of 1% of par value. Since the par value of a Treasury bond futures contract is \$100,000, an option price of 24 means: $[(24/64)/100] \times \$100,000 = \$375$. In general, the price of a futures option quoted at Q is equal to:

$$\text{Option price} = \left[\frac{Q/64}{100} \right] \times \$100,000$$

There are three reasons why futures options on fixed income securities have largely supplanted options on physicals as the options vehicle of choice for institutional investors who want to use exchange-traded options. First, unlike options on fixed income securities, options on Treasury coupon futures do not require payments for accrued interest to be made. Consequently, when a futures option is exercised, the call buyer and the put writer need not compensate the other party for accrued interest. Second, futures options are believed to be "cleaner" instruments because of the reduced likelihood of delivery squeezes. Market participants who must deliver an instrument are concerned that at the time of delivery the instrument to be delivered will be in short supply, resulting in a higher price to acquire the instrument. As the deliverable supply of futures contracts is more than adequate for futures options currently traded, there is no concern about a delivery squeeze. Finally, in order to price any option, it is imperative to know at all times the price of the underlying instrument. In the bond market, current prices are not as easily available as price information on the futures contract. The reason is that as bonds trade in the OTC market there is no single reporting system with recent price information. Thus, an investor who wanted to purchase an option on a Treasury bond would have to call several dealer firms to obtain a price. In contrast, futures contracts are traded on an exchange and, as a result, price information is reported.

PRACTICE QUESTION 3

a. Suppose an investor purchases a call option on a Treasury bond futures contract with a strike price of 98. Also assume that at the expiration date the price of the Treasury bond futures contract is 103. Will the investor exercise the call option and, if so, what will the investor and the writer of the call option receive?

b Suppose an investor purchases a put option on a Treasury bond futures contract with a strike price of 105. Also assume that at the expiration date the price of the Treasury bond futures contract is 96. Will the investor exercise the put option and, if so, what will the investor and the writer of the put option receive?

---

2. Over-the-Counter Options

Institutional investors who want to purchase an option on a specific Treasury security or a Ginnie Mae passthrough security can do so on an over-the-counter basis. There are government and mortgage-backed securities dealers who make a market in options on specific securities. OTC options, also called **dealer options**, usually are purchased by institutional investors who want to hedge the risk associated with a specific security. For example, a thrift may be interested in hedging its position in a specific mortgage passthrough security. Typically, the maturity of the option coincides with the time period over which the buyer of the option wants to hedge, so the buyer is not concerned with the option's liquidity.

As explained earlier with forward contracts, in the absence of a clearinghouse the parties to any over-the-counter contract are exposed to counterparty risk. In the case of forward contracts where both parties are obligated to perform, both parties face counterparty risk. In contrast, in the case of an option, once the option buyer pays the option price, it has satisfied its obligation. It is only the seller that must perform if the option is exercised. Thus, the option buyer is exposed to counterparty risk — the risk that the option seller will fail to perform.

OTC options can be customized in any manner sought by an institutional investor. Basically, if a dealer can reasonably hedge the risk associated with the opposite side of the option sought, it will create the option desired by a customer. OTC options are not limited to European or American type. Dealers also create modified American (Bermuda or Atlantic) type options.

SECTION IV INTEREST RATE SWAPS

In an interest rate swap, two parties agree to exchange periodic interest payments. The dollar amount of the interest payments exchanged is based on some predetermined dollar principal, which is called the **notional principal** or **notional amount**. The dollar amount each counterparty pays to the other is the agreed-upon periodic interest rate times the notional principal. The only dollars that are exchanged between the parties are the interest payments, not the notional principal. In the most common type of swap, one party agrees to pay the other party fixed interest payments at designated dates for the life of the contract. This party is referred to as the **fixed-rate payer**. The fixed rate that the fixed-rate payer must make is called the **swap rate**. The other party, who agrees to make interest rate payments that float with some reference rate, is referred to as the **fixed-rate receiver**.

The reference rates that have been used for the floating rate in an interest rate swap are those on various money market instruments: Treasury bills, the London interbank offered rate, commercial paper, bankers acceptances, certificates of deposit, the federal funds rate, and the prime rate. The most common is the London interbank offered rate (LIBOR). LIBOR is the rate at which prime banks offer to pay on Eurodollar deposits available to other prime banks for a given maturity. Basically, it is viewed as the global cost of bank borrowing. There is not just one rate but a rate for different maturities. For example, there is a 1-month LIBOR, 3-month LIBOR, 6-month LIBOR, etc.

To illustrate an interest rate swap, suppose that for the next five years party X agrees to pay party Y 6% per year (the swap rate), while party Y agrees to pay party X 6-month LIBOR (the reference rate). Party X is the fixed-rate payer, while party Y is the fixed-rate receiver. Assume that the notional principal is $50 million, and that payments are exchanged every six months for the next five years. This means that every six months, party X (the fixed-rate payer) will pay party Y $1.5 million (6% times $50 million divided by 2).[4] The amount that party Y (the fixed-rate receiver) will pay party X will be 6-month LIBOR times $50 million divided by 2. If 6-month LIBOR is 5%, party Y will pay party X $1.25 million (5% times $50 million divided by 2).[5] Note that we divide by two because one-half year's interest is being paid. This is illustrated in panel a of Exhibit 4.

Exhibit 4: Summary of How the Value of a Swap to Each Counterparty Changes when Interest Rates Change

a. Initial position

Swap rate	=	6%	Settlement	=	semiannual
Reference rate	=	6-month LIBOR	Term of swap	=	5 years
Notional amount	=	$50 million	Payment by fixed-rate payer	=	$1.5 million

Every six months

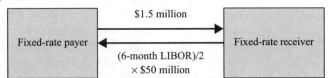

b. Interest rates increase such that swap spread is 7%

Fixed-rate payer pays initial swap rate of 6% to obtain 6-month LIBOR
    Advantage to fixed-rate payer: pays only 6% not 7% to obtain 6-month LIBOR

Fixed-rate receiver pays 6-month LIBOR
    Disadvantage to fixed-rate receiver: receives only 6% in exchange for 6-month LIBOR, not 7%

Results of a rise in interest rates:

Party	Value of swap
Fixed-rate payer	Increases
Fixed-rate receiver	Decreases

c. Interest rates decrease such that swap spread is 5%

Fixed-rate payer pays initial swap rate of 6% to obtain 6-month LIBOR
    Disadvantage to fixed-rate payer: must pay 6% not 5% to obtain 6-month LIBOR

Fixed-rate receiver pays 6-month LIBOR
    Advantage to fixed-rate receiver: receives 6% in exchange for 6-month LIBOR, not 5%

Results of a rise in interest rates:

Party	Value of swap
Fixed-rate payer	Decreases
Fixed-rate receiver	Increases

---

[4] In the next chapter we will fine tune our calculation to take into consideration day count conventions when computing swap payments.

[5] As explained in the next chapter, the floating-rate is determined at the beginning of a period and paid in arrears – that is, it is paid at the end of the period.

The convention that has evolved for quoting a swap rate is that a dealer sets the floating rate equal to the reference rate and then quotes the fixed rate that will apply. The fixed rate is some "spread" above the Treasury yield curve with the same term to maturity as the swap. This spread is called the **swap spread**.

PRACTICE QUESTION 4

Suppose that party G and party H enter into a 4-year interest rate swap. The notional amount for the swap is $100 million and the reference rate is 3-month LIBOR. Suppose that the payments are made quarterly by both the fixed-rate payer and the fixed-rate receiver. Also assume that the swap rate is 4.4%.

a. What are the payments that must be made by the fixed-rate payer every quarter?

b. Suppose for the first floating-rate payment 3-month LIBOR is 7.2%. What is the amount of the first floating-rate payment that must be made by the fixed-rate receiver?

A. Entering Into a Swap and Counterparty Risk

Interest rate swaps are OTC instruments. This means that they are not traded on an exchange. An institutional investor wishing to enter into a swap transaction can do so through either a securities firm or a commercial bank that transacts in swaps.[6] These entities can do one of the following. First, they can arrange or broker a swap between two parties that want to enter into an interest rate swap. In this case, the securities firm or commercial bank is acting in a brokerage capacity. The broker is not a party to the swap.

The second way in which a securities firm or commercial bank can get an institutional investor into a swap position is by taking the other side of the swap. This means that the securities firm or the commercial bank is a dealer rather than a broker in the transaction. Acting as a dealer, the securities firm or the commercial bank must hedge its swap position in the same way that it hedges its position in other securities that it holds. Also it means that the dealer (which we refer to as a **swap dealer**) is the counterparty to the transaction. If an institutional investor entered into a swap with a swap dealer, the institutional investor will look to the swap dealer to satisfy the obligations of the swap; similarly, that same swap dealer looks to the institutional investor to fulfill its obligations as set forth in the swap.

The risk that the two parties take on when they enter into a swap is that the other party will fail to fulfill its obligations as set forth in the swap agreement. That is, each party faces default risk and therefore there is bilateral counterparty risk.

B. Risk/Return Characteristics of an Interest Rate Swap

The value of an interest rate swap will fluctuate with market interest rates. To see how, let's consider our hypothetical swap. Suppose that interest rates change immediately after parties X and Y enter into the swap. Panel a in Exhibit 4 shows the transaction. First, consider what would happen if the market demanded that in any 5-year swap the fixed-rate payer must pay 7% in order to receive 6-month LIBOR. If party X (the fixed-rate payer) wants to sell its position to party A, then party A will benefit by having to pay only 6% (the original swap rate agreed upon) rather than 7% (the current swap rate) to receive 6-month LIBOR. Party X will want compensation for this benefit. Consequently, the value of party X's position has increased. Thus, if interest rates increase, the fixed-rate payer will realize a profit and the fixed-rate receiver will realize a loss. Panel b in Exhibit 4 summarizes the results of a rise in interest rates.

---

[6] Don't get confused here about the role of commercial banks. A bank can use a swap in its asset/liability management. Or, a bank can transact (buy and sell) swaps to clients to generate fee income. It is in the latter sense that we are discussing the role of a commercial bank in the swap market here.

Next, consider what would happen if interest rates decline to, say, 5%. Now a 5-year swap would require a new fixed-rate payer to pay 5% rather than 6% to receive 6-month LIBOR. If party X wants to sell its position to party B, the latter would demand compensation to take over the position. In other words, if interest rates decline, the fixed-rate payer will realize a loss, while the fixed-rate receiver will realize a profit. Panel c in Exhibit 4 summarizes the results of a decline in interest rates

While we know in what direction the change in the value of a swap will be for the counterparties when interest rates change, the question is how much will the value of the swap change. We show how to compute the change in the value of a swap in the next chapter.

C. Interpreting a Swap Position

There are two ways that a swap position can be interpreted: (1) a package of forward (futures) contracts and (2) a package of cash flows from buying and selling cash market instruments.

1. Package of Forward (Futures) Contracts

Contrast the position of the counterparties in an interest rate swap summarized above to the position of the long and short interest rate futures (forward) contract discussed earlier in the chapter. The long futures position gains if interest rates decline and loses if interest rates rise — this is similar to the risk/return profile for a floating-rate payer. The risk/return profile for a fixed-rate payer is similar to that of the short futures position: a gain if interest rates increase and a loss if interest rates decrease. By taking a closer look at the interest rate swap we can understand why the risk/return relationships are similar.

Consider party X's position in our previous swap illustration. Party X has agreed to pay 6% and receive 6-month LIBOR. More specifically, assuming a $50 million notional principal, X has agreed to buy a commodity called "6-month LIBOR" for $1.5 million. This is effectively a 6-month forward contract where X agrees to pay $1.5 million in exchange for delivery of 6-month LIBOR. If interest rates increase to 7%, the price of that commodity (6-month LIBOR) is higher, resulting in a gain for the fixed-rate payer, who is effectively long a 6-month forward contract on 6-month LIBOR. The floating-rate payer is effectively short a 6-month forward contract on 6-month LIBOR. There is therefore an implicit forward contract corresponding to each exchange date.

Now we can see why there is a similarity between the risk/return relationship for an interest rate swap and a forward contract. If interest rates increase to, say, 7%, the price of that commodity (6-month LIBOR) increases to $1.75 million (7% times $50 million divided by 2). The long forward position (the fixed-rate payer) gains, and the short forward position (the floating-rate payer) loses. If interest rates decline to, say, 5%, the price of our commodity decreases to $1.25 million (5% times $50 million divided by 2). The short forward position (the floating-rate payer) gains, and the long forward position (the fixed-rate payer) loses.

Consequently, interest rate swaps can be viewed as a package of more basic interest rate derivatives, such as forwards.[7] The pricing of an interest rate swap will then depend on the price of a package of forward contracts with the same settlement dates in which the underlying for the forward contract is the same reference rate. We will make use of this principle in the next chapter when we explain how to value swaps.

---

[7] More specifically, an interest rate swap is equivalent to a package of **forward rate agreements**. A forward rate agreement (FRA) is the over-the-counter equivalent of the exchange-traded futures contracts on short-term rates. Typically, the short-term rate is LIBOR. The elements of an FRA are the contract rate, reference rate, settlement rate, notional amount, and settlement date.

Exhibit 5: Cash Flow for the Purchase of a 5-Year Floating-Rate Bond Financed by Borrowing on a Fixed-Rate Basis

Transaction:
- Purchase for $50 million a 5-year floating-rate bond:
  floating rate = LIBOR, semiannual pay
- Borrow $50 million for five years:
  fixed rate = 6%, semiannual payments

Six Month Period	Cash Flow (In Millions of Dollars) From:		
	Floating-Rate Bond*	Borrowing Cost	Net = Same as swap
0	−$50	+$50.0	$0
1	+(LIBOR$_1$/2) × 50	−1.5	+(LIBOR$_1$/2) × 50 − 1.5
2	+(LIBOR$_2$/2) × 50	−1.5	+(LIBOR$_2$/2) × 50 − 1.5
3	+(LIBOR$_3$/2) × 50	−1.5	+(LIBOR$_3$/2) × 50 − 1.5
4	+(LIBOR$_4$/2) × 50	−1.5	+(LIBOR$_4$/2) × 50 − 1.5
5	+(LIBOR$_5$/2) × 50	−1.5	+(LIBOR$_5$/2) × 50 − 1.5
6	+(LIBOR$_6$/2) × 50	−1.5	+(LIBOR$_6$/2) × 50 − 1.5
7	+(LIBOR$_7$/2) × 50	−1.5	+(LIBOR$_7$/2) × 50 − 1.5
8	+(LIBOR$_8$/2) × 50	−1.5	+(LIBOR$_8$/2) × 50 − 1.5
9	+(LIBOR$_9$/2) × 50	−1.5	+(LIBOR$_9$/2) × 50 − 1.5
10	+(LIBOR$_{10}$/2) × 50 + 50	−51.5	+(LIBOR$_{10}$/2) × 50 − 1.5

* The subscript for LIBOR indicates the 6-month LIBOR as per the terms of the floating-rate bond at time t.

While an interest rate swap may be nothing more than a package of forward contracts, it is not a redundant contract for several reasons. First, maturities for forward or futures contracts do not extend out as far as those of an interest rate swap; an interest rate swap with a term of 15 years or longer can be obtained. Second, an interest rate swap is a more transactionally efficient instrument. By this we mean that in one transaction an entity can effectively establish a payoff equivalent to a package of forward contracts. The forward contracts would each have to be negotiated separately. Third, the interest rate swap market has grown in liquidity since its introduction in 1981; interest rate swaps now provide more liquidity than forward contracts, particularly long-dated (i.e., long-term) forward contracts.

2. Package of Cash Market Instruments

To understand why a swap can also be interpreted as a package of cash market instruments, consider an investor who enters into the transaction below:

- buy $50 million par of a 5-year floating-rate bond that pays 6-month LIBOR every six months
- finance the purchase by borrowing $50 million for five years on terms requiring a 6% annual interest rate paid every six months

As a result of this transaction, the investor

- receives a floating rate every six months for the next five years
- pays a fixed rate every six months for the next five years

The cash flows for this transaction are set forth in Exhibit 5. The second column of the exhibit shows the cash flow from purchasing the 5-year floating-rate bond. There is a $50 million cash outlay and then ten cash inflows. The amount of the cash inflows is uncertain because they depend on future LIBOR. The next column shows the cash flow from borrowing $50 million on a fixed-rate basis. The last column shows the net cash flow from the entire transaction. As the last column indicates, there is no initial cash flow (no cash inflow or cash outlay). In all ten 6-month periods, the net position results in a cash inflow of LIBOR and a cash outlay of $1.5 million. This net position, however, is identical to the position of a fixed-rate payer/floating-rate receiver.

It can be seen from the net cash flow in Exhibit 5 that a fixed-rate payer has a cash market position that is equivalent to a long position in a floating-rate bond and a short position in a fixed-rate bond — the short position being the equivalent of borrowing by issuing a fixed-rate bond.

What about the position of a floating-rate payer? It can be easily demonstrated that the position of a floating-rate payer is equivalent to purchasing a fixed-rate bond and financing that purchase at a floating rate, where the floating rate is the reference rate for the swap. That is, the position of a floating-rate payer is equivalent to a long position in a fixed-rate bond and a short position in a floating-rate bond.

D. Describing the Counterparties to a Swap Agreement

The terminology used to describe the position of a party in the swap markets combines cash market jargon and futures market jargon, given that a swap position can be interpreted as a position in a package of cash market instruments or a package of futures/forward positions. As we have said, the counterparty to an interest rate swap is either a fixed-rate payer or floating-rate payer.

Exhibit 6 lists how the counterparties to an interest rate swap agreement are described.[8] To understand why the fixed-rate payer is viewed as "short the bond market," and the floating-rate payer is viewed as "long the bond market," consider what happens when interest rates change. Those who borrow on a fixed-rate basis will benefit if interest rates rise because they have locked in a lower interest rate. But those who have a short bond position will also benefit if interest rates rise. Thus, a fixed-rate payer can be said to be short the bond market. A floating-rate payer benefits if interest rates fall. A long position in a bond also benefits if interest rates fall, so terminology describing a floating-rate payer as long the bond market is not surprising. From our discussion of the interpretation of a swap as a package of cash market instruments, describing a swap in terms of the sensitivities of long and short cash positions follows naturally.

Exhibit 6: Describing the Parties to a Swap Agreement

Fixed-rate payer	Fixed-rate receiver
• pays fixed rate in the swap	• pays floating rate in the swap
• receives floating in the swap	• receives fixed in the swap
• is short the bond market	• is long the bond market
• has bought a swap	• has sold a swap
• is long a swap	• is short a swap
• has established the price sensitivities of a longer-term liability and a floating-rate asset	• has established the price sensitivities of a longer-term asset and a floating-rate liability

[8] Robert F. Kopprasch, John Macfarlane, Daniel R. Ross, and Janet Showers, "The Interest Rate Swap Market: Yield Mathematics, Terminology, and Conventions," Chapter 58 in Frank J. Fabozzi and Irving M. Pollack (eds.), *The Handbook of Fixed Income Securities* (Homewood, IL: Dow Jones-Irwin, 1987).

SECTION V
INTEREST RATE
CAPS AND
FLOORS

There are agreements between two parties whereby one party for an upfront premium agrees to compensate the other at specific time periods if the reference rate is different from a predetermined level. When one party agrees to pay the other when the reference rate exceeds a predetermined level, the agreement is referred to as an **interest rate cap** or **ceiling**. The agreement is referred to as an **interest rate floor** when one party agrees to pay the other when the reference rate falls below a predetermined level. The predetermined level is called the **strike rate**. The strike rate for a cap is called the **cap rate**; the strike rate for a floor is called the **floor rate**.

The terms of a cap and floor agreement include:

1. the reference rate
2. the strike rate (cap rate or floor rate) that sets the ceiling or floor
3. the length of the agreement
4. the frequency of settlement
5. the notional principal

For example, suppose that C buys an interest rate cap from D with the following terms:

1. the reference rate is 3-month LIBOR.
2. the strike rate is 6%.
3. the agreement is for four years.
4. settlement is every three months.
5. the notional principal is $20 million.

Under this agreement, every three months for the next four years, D will pay C whenever 3-month LIBOR exceeds 6% at a settlement date. (Actually the payment is made in arrears.). The payment will equal the dollar value of the difference between 3-month LIBOR and 6% times the notional principal divided by 4. For example, if three months from now 3-month LIBOR on a settlement date is 8%, then D will pay C 2% (8% minus 6%) times $20 million divided by 4, or $100,000. If 3-month LIBOR is 6% or less, D does not have to pay anything to C.

In the case of an interest rate floor, assume the same terms as the interest rate cap we just illustrated. In this case, if 3-month LIBOR is 8%, C receives nothing from D, but if 3-month LIBOR is less than 6%, D compensates C for the difference. For example, if 3-month LIBOR is 5%, D will pay C $50,000 (6% minus 5% times $20 million divided by 4).[9]

PRACTICE QUESTION 5

Suppose that a 4-year cap has a cap rate of 7% and a notional amount of $100 million. The frequency of settlement is quarterly and the reference rate is 3-month LIBOR. Assume that 3-month LIBOR for the next four quarters is as shown below. What is the payoff for each quarter?

Period	3-month LIBOR
1	6.7%
2	7.0%
3	7.4%
4	7.6%

---

[9] Interest rate caps and floors can be combined to create an **interest rate collar**. This is done by buying an interest rate cap and selling an interest rate floor. The purchase of the cap sets a maximum rate; the sale of the floor sets a minimum rate. The range between the maximum and minimum rate is called the collar.

A. Risk/Return Characteristic

In an interest rate agreement, the buyer pays an upfront fee which represents the maximum amount that the buyer can lose and the maximum amount that the seller (writer) can gain. The only party that is required to perform is the seller of the interest rate agreement. The buyer of an interest rate cap benefits if the reference rate rises above the strike rate because the seller must compensate the buyer. The buyer of an interest rate floor benefits if the reference rate falls below the strike rate, because the seller must compensate the buyer.

B. Interpretation of a Cap and Floor Position

In an interest rate cap and floor, the buyer pays an upfront fee, which represents the maximum amount that the buyer can lose and the maximum amount that the seller of the agreement can gain. The only party that is required to perform is the seller of the interest rate agreement. The buyer of an interest rate cap benefits if the reference rate rises above the strike rate because the seller must compensate the buyer. The buyer of an interest rate floor benefits if the reference rate falls below the strike rate because the seller must compensate the buyer.

How can we better understand interest rate caps and interest rate floors? In essence these contracts are equivalent to a *package of interest rate options*. As with a swap, a complex contract can be seen to be a package of basic contracts — options in the case of caps and floors. Each of the interest rate options comprising a cap are called **caplets**; similarly, each of the interest rate options comprising a floor are called **floorlets**.

The question is what type of package of options is a cap and a floor. It depends on whether the underlying is a rate or a fixed-income instrument. If the underlying is considered a fixed-income instrument, its value changes inversely with interest rates. Therefore:

• for a call option on a fixed-income instrument:

(1) interest rates increase → fixed-income instrument's price decreases
    → call option value decreases
and
(2) interest rates decrease → fixed-income instrument's price increases
    → call option value increases

• for a put option on a fixed-income instrument

(1) interest rates increase → fixed-income instrument's price decreases
    → put option value increases
and
(2) interest rates decrease → fixed-income instrument's price increases
    → put option value decreases

To summarize:

	When interest rates	
Value of:	increase	decrease
long call	decrease	increase
short call	increase	decrease
long put	increase	decrease
short put	decrease	increase

For a cap and floor, the situation is as follows

Value of:	When interest rates	
	increase	decrease
short cap	decrease	increase
long cap	increase	decrease
short floor	increase	decrease
long floor	decrease	increase

Therefore, buying a cap (long cap) is equivalent to buying a package of puts on a fixed-income instrument and buying a floor (long floor) is equivalent to buying a package of calls on a fixed-income instrument.

In contrast there are options on interest rates. That is, in the over-the-counter market one can purchase an option on an interest rate. These options work as follows in terms of their payoff. There is a strike rate. For a call option on an interest rate, there is a payoff if the reference rate is greater than the strike rate. This means that when interest rates increase, the call option's value increases and when interest rates decrease, the call option's value decreases. As can be seen from the payoff for a cap and a floor summarized above, this is the payoff of a long cap. Consequently, a cap is equivalent to a package of call options on an interest rate. For a put option on an interest rate, there is a payoff when the reference rate is less than the strike rate. When interest rates increase, the value of the put option on an interest rate decreases, as does the value of a long floor position (see the summary above); when interest rates decrease, the value of the put on an interest rate increases, as does the value of a long floor position (again, see the summary above). Thus, a floor is equivalent to a package of put options on an interest rate.

The major reason for providing this explanation is that market participants commonly talk about the equivalency of caps and floors in terms of put and call options. Without specifying what the underlying for the option is, there will be confusion.

C. Counterparty Risk

The seller of an interest rate cap or floor does not face counterparty risk once the buyer pays the fee. In contrast, the buyer faces counterparty risk. Thus, as with options, there is unilateral counterparty risk.

SECTION VI
KEY POINTS

❑ A futures contract is an agreement between a buyer (seller) and an established exchange or its clearinghouse in which the buyer (seller) agrees to take (make) delivery of something at a specified price at the end of a designated period of time.

❑ A forward contract is an agreement for the future delivery of something at a specified price at a designated period of time, but differs from a futures contract in that it is usually non-standardized and traded in the over-the-counter market.

❑ An investor who takes a long futures position realizes a gain when the futures price increases; an investor who takes a short futures position realizes a loss when the futures price decreases.

❑ The parties to a futures contract are required to satisfy margin requirements.

❑ Parties to over-the-counter interest rate contracts are exposed to counterparty risk which is the risk that the counterparty will not satisfy its contractual obligations.

❑ For the Treasury bond futures contract the underlying instrument is $100,000 par value of a hypothetical 20-year 6% coupon Treasury bond.

❏ *Conversion factors are used to adjust the invoice price of a Treasury bond futures contract to make delivery equitable to both parties.*

❏ *The short in a Treasury bond futures contract has several delivery options: quality option (or swap option), timing option, and wildcard option.*

❏ *For all the issues that may be delivered to satisfy a Treasury futures contract, a rate of return can be computed in a cash and carry trade; the rate of return is called the implied repo rate.*

❏ *For all the issues that may be delivered to satisfy a Treasury futures contract, the cheapest-to-deliver issue is the one with the highest implied repo rate.*

❏ *By varying the yield on Treasury bonds, it can be determined which issue will become the new cheapest-to-deliver issue.*

❏ *An option is a contract in which the writer of the option grants the buyer of the option the right, but not the obligation, to purchase from or sell to the writer something at a specified price within a specified period of time (or at a specified date).*

❏ *The option buyer pays the option writer (seller) a fee, called the option price.*

❏ *A call option allows the option buyer to purchase the underlying from the option writer at the strike price; a put option allows the option buyer to sell the underlying to the option writer at the strike price.*

❏ *Interest rate options include options on fixed income securities and options on interest rate futures contracts; the latter, called futures options, are the preferred exchange-traded vehicle for implementing investment strategies.*

❏ *Because of the difficulties of hedging particular fixed income securities, some institutional investors have found over-the-counter options more useful.*

❏ *An interest rate swap is an agreement specifying that the parties exchange interest payments at designated times, with a generic swap calling for one party to make fixed-rate payments and the other to make floating-rate payments based on a notional principal.*

❏ *The swap rate is the interest rate paid by the fixed-rate payer.*

❏ *The swap spread is the spread paid by the fixed-rate payer over the on-the-run Treasury rate with the same maturity as the swap agreement.*

❏ *The convention in quoting swaps is to quote the payments made by the floating-rate payer flat (that is, without a spread) and the fixed-rate payer payments as a spread to the on-the-run Treasury with the same maturity as the swap (the swap spread)*

❏ *A swap position can be interpreted as either a package of forward/futures contracts or a package of cash flows from buying and selling cash market instruments.*

❏ *An interest rate cap specifies that one party receive a payment if the reference rate is above the cap rate; an interest rate floor specifies that one party receive a payment if a reference rate is below the floor rate.*

❏ *The terms of a cap and floor set forth the reference rate, the strike rate, the length of the agreement, the frequency of reset, and the notional amount.*

❏ *In an interest rate cap and floor, the buyer pays an upfront fee, which represents the maximum amount that the buyer can lose and the maximum amount that the seller of the agreement can gain.*

❏ *Buying a cap is equivalent to buying a package of puts on a fixed income security and buying a floor is equivalent to buying a package of calls on a fixed income security.*

❏ *If an option is viewed as one in which the underlying is an interest rate, then buying a cap is equivalent to buying a package of calls on interest rates and buying a floor is equivalent to buying a package of puts on interest rates.*

❏ *Forward contracts and swaps expose the parties to bilateral counterparty risk while buyers of OTC options, caps, and floors face unilateral counterparty risk.*

END OF CHAPTER QUESTIONS

1. What is the counterparty risk associated with a derivative instrument?

2. Explain why you agree or disagree with the following statement: "One difference between futures and forward contracts is that futures contracts are marked to market while forward contracts are not."

3. Explain why you agree or disagree with the following statement: "Futures and forward contracts expose the parties to the same degree of counterparty risk."

4. Eileen Morris is the manager of a bond portfolio and has recently received authorization to use Treasury futures contracts. The chief investment officer of her firm, Rita Gomez, advised Ms. Morris to be sure to keep sufficient cash available to satisfy any contingency payments that must be made as a result of the futures positions. Ms. Morris was not clear as to why any contingency payments must be made. She has asked you to explain why. What is your response?

5. George Salvich is an equity portfolio manager who uses stock index futures. He is considering managing a balanced fund (i.e., a fund that includes both equities and bonds). He would like to use Treasury bond futures in managing the bond component of the fund. He was told by a broker that the underlying for a Treasury bond futures contract is $100,000 par value of a 20-year 6% coupon Treasury bond. The broker noted that no such Treasury bond exists. Mr. Salvich responded that the contract was probably a cash settlement contract because there is no deliverable. How should the broker respond?

6. a. Why is it necessary to have conversion factors for a Treasury futures contract?

   b. How is the converted price of an issue that is acceptable for delivery for a Treasury futures contract computed?

7. Suppose that the June 200X futures contract settles at 105-08 and the issue delivered has a conversion factor of 1.21. Assume that the accrued interest for the issue delivered is $5,300 per $100,000 par value. What is the invoice price the buyer must pay the seller?

8. Calculate the implied repo rate for a hypothetical issue that is deliverable for a Treasury bond futures contract assuming the following for the deliverable issue and the futures contract:

   Futures contract
   Futures price = 102
   days to futures delivery date ($days_1$) = 114 days

   Deliverable issue
   price of issue = 96
   accrued interest paid = 3.2219
   coupon rate = 8%
   days remaining before interim coupon made = 79 days
   interim coupon = $4.00
   number of days between when the interim coupon payment is received and the actual delivery date of the futures contract (day_2) = 35 days

conversion factor = 0.9305
accrued interest received at futures settlement date = 1.7315

Other information:
114-day term repo rate = 5%

9. a. What is the implied repo rate for a deliverable Treasury issue?

b. What is meant by the cheapest-to-deliver issue?

10. Suppose that a government bond futures contract of some country has the same delivery requirements as the U.S. Treasury bond futures contract. Suppose further that there are five possible issues that are acceptable for delivery and the short has the choice of which to deliver. These issues and information about them are shown in the table below. Each of the issues that may be delivered has no accrued interest and the next coupon payment is six months from now. The futures price for the government bond contract that settles in six months (just when each of the five issues matures) is 99.50. (Note: the futures price and the prices of each issue in this question are in decimal form, not $\frac{1}{32}$.)

Issue	Market price	Coupon rate	Conversion factor
1	79.48	4.0%	0.8215
2	86.54	5.7%	0.8942
3	104.77	9.0%	1.0544
4	109.22	9.6%	1.1123

Determine the cheapest-to-deliver issue?

11. What are the following delivery options granted to the seller of the Treasury bond futures contract?

a. quality or swap option
b. timing option
c. wild card option

12. What is the maximum amount the buyer of an option can lose?

13. Suppose an investor purchases a call option on a Treasury bond futures contract with a strike price of 91.

a. If at the expiration date the price of the Treasury bond futures contract is 96, will the investor exercise the call option and, if so, what will the investor and the writer of the call option receive?

b. If at the expiration date the price of the Treasury bond futures contract is 89, will the investor exercise the call option and, if so, what will the investor and the writer of the call option receive?

14. Suppose an investor purchases a put option on a Treasury bond futures contract with a strike price of 97.

a. If at the expiration date the price of the Treasury bond futures contract is 99, will the investor exercise the put option and, if so, what will the investor and the writer of the put option receive?

b. If at the expiration date the price of the Treasury bond futures contract is 91, will the investor exercise the put option and, if so, what will the investor and the writer of the put option receive?

15. a. What is the motivation for the purchase of an over-the-counter option by an institutional investor?

b. Does it make sense for an investor who wants to speculate on interest rate movements to purchase an over-the-counter option?

16. In an interest rate swap what is meant by the swap rate and the swap spread?

17. Suppose that Ted Munson, a portfolio manager, enters into a 3-year interest rate swap with a commercial bank that is a swap dealer. The notional amount for the swap is $40 million and the reference rate is 3-month LIBOR. Suppose that the payments are made quarterly. The swap rate that Mr. Munson agrees to pay is 5.6%.

a. Who is the fixed-rate payer and who is the fixed-rate receiver in this swap?

b. What are the payments that must be made by the fixed-rate payer every quarter?

c. Suppose for the first floating-rate payment 3-month LIBOR is 3.6%. What is the amount of the first floating-rate payment that must be made by the fixed-rate receiver?

18. Give two interpretations of an interest rate swap and explain why an interest rate swap can be interpreted in each way.

19. Suppose that interest rates decrease subsequent to the inception of an interest rate swap.

a. What is the effect on the value of the swap from the perspective of the fixed-rate payer?

a. What is the effect on the value of the swap from the perspective of the fixed-rate receiver?

20. Why is the fixed-rate payer in an interest rate swap said to be "short the bond market"?

21. Suppose that a 1-year cap has a cap rate of 8% and a notional amount of $10 million. The frequency of settlement is quarterly and the reference rate is 3-month LIBOR. Assume that 3-month LIBOR for the next four quarters is as shown below. What is the payoff for each quarter?

Period	3-month LIBOR
1	8.7%
2	8.0%
3	7.8%
4	8.2%

22. Suppose that a 1-year floor has a floor rate of 4% and a notional amount of $20 million. The frequency of settlement is quarterly and the reference rate is 3-month LIBOR. Assume that 3-month LIBOR for the next four quarters is as shown below. What is the payoff for each quarter?

Period	3-month LIBOR
1	4.7%
2	4.4%
3	3.8%
4	3.4%

23. What counterparty risk is the seller of an interest rate floor exposed to?

24. a. What is an interest rate cap or floor equivalent to?

b. What is a caplet and a floorlet?

SOLUTIONS TO END OF CHAPTER QUESTIONS

1. A derivative instrument involves two parties. Counterparty risk is the risk that a counterparty to a derivative instrument will fail to meet its obligation.

2. This statement is not correct. A forward contract is a privately negotiated contract between two parties. One or both parties may require that the positions be marked to market.

3. This statement is not correct. The counterparty in a futures contract is a futures exchange or the clearinghouse associated with a futures exchange. The counterparty risk is viewed as minimal. In contrast, the counterparty risk in a forward contract depends on the credit risk of the counterparty.

4. When a position is taken in a futures contract, initial margin is required. However, the margin obligation does not stop at that point. At the close of each trading day a position is marked to market. If the position falls below the maintenance margin, additional margin in the form of cash must be provided. Failure to provide the cash will result in a liquidation of the position. Any additional margin payments, called variation margin, are the contingency payments that Ms. Gomez is advising Ms. Morris to have sufficient cash available to satisfy.

5. The broker should respond that while there may not be a deliverable, delivery of some Treasury bond issue is required. That is, the contract is not a cash settlement contract. There is a list of issues that are acceptable for delivery and the futures price is adjusted based on which issue is delivered.

6. a. A conversion factor for each deliverable issue is necessary because the value of each issue differs due to the different maturity and coupon rate of each issue. In the case of a Treasury bond futures contract, the buyer expects delivery of the equivalent of $100,000 par value of a 6% coupon 20-year issue. The conversion factor makes delivery equitable to both the long and the short by adjusting the invoice price so that the equivalent of $100,000 par value of a 6% coupon 20-year issue is delivered.

   b. The converted price for a deliverable issue is found by multiplying the futures price by the conversion factor for that issue.

7. The invoice price is equal to

   contract size × futures settlement price × conversion factor + accrued interest

   The futures settlement price is 105-08 or 105.25 (= 105 + 8/32). The futures settlement price per $1 of par value is therefore 1.0225. The invoice price is then:

   $$\$100,000 \times 1.0525 \times 1.21 + \$5,300 = \$132,652.50$$

8. The proceeds received are:

   $$\text{converted price} = \text{futures price} \times \text{conversion factor}$$
   $$= 102 \times 0.9305 = 94.9110$$

The interest from reinvesting the interim coupon based on a term repo rate of 5% is:

$$\text{interest from reinvesting the interim coupon payment} = \$4 \times 0.05 \times \frac{35}{360}$$

$$= 0.0439$$

Summary:

converted price	=	94.9110
accrued interest received	=	1.7315
interim coupon payment	=	4.0000
interest from reinvesting the interim coupon payment	=	0.0194
proceeds received	=	100.6619

The cost of the investment is the purchase price for the issue plus the accrued interest paid, as shown below:

$$\text{cost of the investment} = 96 + 3.2219 = 99.2219$$

The implied repo rate is then:

$$\text{implied repo rate} = \frac{100.6619 - 99.2219}{99.2219} \times \frac{360}{114} = 0.0458 = 4.58\%$$

9. a. The implied repo rate for a deliverable Treasury issue is the rate of return that can be earned by buying the issue in the market, simultaneously selling a Treasury futures contract, and delivering the purchased issue to satisfy delivery at the futures settlement date.

   b. The cheapest-to-deliver issue is the one deliverable Treasury issue that offers the highest implied repo rate.

10. Determination of the cheapest-to-deliver requires computing the implied repo rate (i.e., the rate of return on a cash and carry trade over the next six months). Note that there is no accrued interest paid, nor is there any interim coupon payment that can be reinvested. This is because it is assumed that the next coupon payment is six months from now when the futures contract settles.

   To show how the implied repo rate is computed, let's use the first of the five issues. The cost of the investment for this issue is 79.48. (Remember there is no accrued interest paid to purchase this issue.)

   The proceeds received in six months when the contract settles is the converted price plus accrued interest from delivering the issue. The converted price per $100 of par value is:

$$= 99.50 \times 0.8215 = 81.7393$$

   Since the assumption is that there is no accrued interest and the next coupon payment is six months from now, the accrued interest at the settlement date when the bond is delivered for our five issues is the semiannual dollar coupon. For issue 1, it is $2 per $100 of par value since the coupon rate is 4%. Thus, the proceeds at the settlement date of the contract will be equal to 83.7393 (81.7393 + 2). The semiannual return is then:

$$\frac{83.7393 - 79.48}{79.48} = 0.0536 = 5.36\%$$

The returns can be annualized but the relative return will not change. Ignoring annualizing, the semiannual rate of return can be computed for the other four issues as shown in the table below:

Issue	Market price	Coupon rate	Conversion factor	Dollar coupon	Proceeds at settlement	Dollar return	Semiannual rate of return
1	79.48	4.0%	0.8215	2.00	81.7393	83.7393	5.36%
2	86.54	5.7%	0.8942	2.85	88.9729	91.8229	6.10%
3	104.77	9.0%	1.0544	4.50	104.9128	109.4128	4.43%
4	109.22	9.6%	1.1123	4.80	110.6739	115.4739	5.73%

The cheapest-to-deliver issue is the one that offers the highest rate of return. For the five issues it is Issue 2.

11. a. There are several acceptable Treasury bonds that may be delivered to satisfy a Treasury bond futures contract. The quality or swap option allows the seller to select the issue to deliver.

b. Unlike a typical futures contract, there is not a settlement date for a Treasury bond futures contract but a delivery month. The timing option allows the seller to select when in the delivery month to deliver.

c. The wild card option allows the seller to deliver after the futures price has been determined by the CBT at the end of the trading day up to 8 pm.

12. The maximum that can be lost by the buyer of an option is the option price.

13. a. The investor will exercise the call option because the price of the futures contract exceeds the strike price. By exercising the investor receives a long position in the Treasury bond futures contract and the call option writer receives the corresponding short position. The futures price for both parties is the strike price of 91 The positions are then marked-to-market using the futures price of 96 and the option writer must pay the option buyer 5 (the difference between the futures price of 96 and the strike price of 91).

   After this, the positions look as follows:

   • the investor (the buyer of the call option) has a long position in the Treasury bond futures contract at 96 and cash of 5

   • the writer of the call option has a short position in the Treasury bond futures contract at 96 and has paid cash of 5

b. If the futures price at the option expiration date is 89, the investor will not exercise the call option because it is less than the strike price. Thus, the option will expire worthless.

14. a. If the futures price at the option expiration date is 99, the put option will not be exercised because this price exceeds the strike price.

b. The investor will exercise the put option because the price of the futures contract is less than the strike price. By exercising the investor receives a short position in the Treasury bond futures contract and the put option writer receives the corresponding long position. The futures price for both parties is the strike price of 97. The positions are then marked-to-market using the futures price of 91 and the option writer must pay the option buyer 6 (the difference between the strike price of 97 and the futures price of 91).

After this, the positions look as follows:

- the investor (the buyer of the put option) has a short position in the Treasury bond futures contract at 91 and cash of 6

- the writer of the put option has a long position in the Treasury bond futures contract at 91 and has paid cash of 6

15. a. Institutional investors will purchase an OTC option to obtain a customized option. For example, the option can be customized with respect to the underlying instrument — it could be a particular corporate bond rather than a Treasury bond. It could be customized for the settlement date and/or the strike price. The customization permits an institutional investor to create an option that better satisfies its investment objective.

b. An investor who wants to speculate on interest rate movements using options is better off by using exchange-traded options. OTC options are less liquid and there is no need for customization. Moreover, the counterparty risk may be greater for an OTC option compared to an exchange-traded option.

16. The swap rate is the fixed rate that the fixed-rate payer agrees to pay over the life of the swap. The swap spread is the spread that is added to a benchmark Treasury security (from the Treasury yield curve) to obtain the swap rate.

17. a. The fixed-rate payer agrees to pay the swap rate (i.e., the fixed rate). Since Mr. Munson has agreed to pay the swap rate, he is the fixed-rate payer.

b. Since the swap rate is 5.6%, the fixed-rate payment each quarter will be:

$$\$40,000,000 \times (0.056/4) = \$560,000$$

(In the next chapter, this number will be fine tuned to allow for the fact that not every quarter has the same number of days.)

c. Since 3-month LIBOR is 3.6%, the first quarterly payment will be:

$$\$40,000,000 \times (0.036/4) = \$360,000$$

18. A swap can be interpreted in the following two ways: (i) as a package of forward contracts and (ii) as a package of cash market instruments. It is a package of forward contracts because basically the fixed-rate payer is agreeing to pay a fixed amount for "something." That something is the reference rate and therefore the value of what the fixed-rate receiver is receiving in exchange for the fixed-rate payment at an exchange date will vary. This is equivalent to a forward contract where the underlying is the reference rate. There is not just one forward contract but one for each date at which an exchange of payments will be made over the life of the swap. Thus, it is a package of forward contracts.

The second interpretation is that an interest rate swap is a package of cash market instruments. Specifically, from the perspective of the fixed-rate payer – the party paying fixed and receiving floating – it is equivalent to buying a floating-rate note (with the reference rate for the note being the reference rate for the swap) and funding (i.e., obtaining the funds to buy the floating-rate note) by issuing a fixed-rate bond (with the coupon rate for the bond being the swap rate). The par value of the floating-rate note and the fixed-rate bond is the notional amount of the swap. For the fixed-rate receiver, a swap is equivalent to purchasing a fixed-rate bond and funding it by issuing a floating-rate note.

19. a. If interest rates decrease, the fixed-rate payer will realize a decline in the value of the swap. This is because the swap rate (i.e., a fixed rate) is being paid but that rate is above the prevailing market rate necessary to receive the reference rate.

   b. If interest rates increase, the fixed-rate receiver will realize a decline in the value of the swap. This is because the fixed-rate receiver is being paid a lower rate (i.e., the swap rate) than prevailing in the market in exchange for the reference rate.

20. A investor who is short the bond market benefits if interest rates increase. The party to an interest rate swap that benefits if interest rates increase is the fixed-rate payer. Thus, a fixed-rate payer is said to be short the bond market.

21. There is no payoff to the cap if the cap rate exceeds 3-month LIBOR. For Periods 2 and 3, there is no payoff because 3-month LIBOR is below the cap rate. For Periods 1 and 4, there is a payoff and the payoff is determined by:

   $10 million × (3-month LIBOR – cap rate)/4

   The payoffs are summarized below:

Period	3-month LIBOR	Payoff
1	8.7%	17,500
2	8.0%	0
3	7.8%	0
4	8.2%	5,000

22. There is a payoff to the floor if 3-month LIBOR is less than the floor rate. For Periods 1 and 2, there is no payoff because 3-month LIBOR is greater than the floor rate. For Periods 3 and 4, there is a payoff and the payoff is determined by:

   $20 million × (floor rate – 3-month LIBOR)/4

   The payoffs are summarized below:

Period	3-month LIBOR	Payoff
1	4.7%	0
2	4.4%	0
3	3.8%	10,000
4	3.4%	30,000

23. Once the fee for the interest rate floor is paid, the seller of an interest rate floor is not exposed to counterparty risk. Only the seller, not the buyer, must perform.

24. a. An interest rate cap or floor is equivalent to a package of interest rate options. So, for example, if an interest rate cap is for three years and payments are made quarterly, this is equivalent to 12 interest rate options.

   b. Since a cap is equivalent to a package of interest rate options, each option in the package is called a caplet. So, if an interest rate cap, for example, is for three years and makes quarterly payments, then there are 12 interest rate options and there are then 12 caplets. Similarly, since a floor is equivalent to a package of interest rate options, each interest rate option in the package is called a floorlet.

SOLUTIONS TO PRACTICE QUESTIONS

1. The invoice price is equal to

contract size × futures settlement price × conversion factor + accrued interest

The futures settlement price is 97-24 or 97.75 (= 97 + 24/32). The futures settlement price per $1 of par value is therefore 0.9775. The invoice price is then:

$$\$100,000 \times 0.9775 \times 1.17 + \$3,800 = \$118,167.50$$

2. The proceeds received are:

$$\text{converted price} = \text{futures price} \times \text{conversion factor}$$
$$= 97 \times 0.9710 = 94.1870$$

The term repo rate is 4.7%, so the interest from reinvesting the interim coupon payment is

interest from reinvesting the interim coupon payment

$$= \$3.5 \times 0.047 \times \left(\frac{37}{360}\right) = 0.0169$$

Summary:

converted price	=	94.1870
accrued interest received	=	0.7096
interim coupon payment	=	3.5000
interest from reinvesting the interim coupon payment	=	0.0169
proceeds received	=	98.4135

The cost of the investment is the purchase price for the issue plus the accrued interest paid, as shown below:

$$\text{cost of the investment} = 95 + 3.0110 = 98.0110$$

The implied repo rate is then:

$$\text{implied repo rate} = \frac{98.4135 - 98.0110}{98.0110} \times \frac{360}{62} = 0.0238 = 2.38\%$$

3. a. The investor will exercise the call option because the price of the futures contract exceeds the strike price. By exercising the investor receives a long position in the Treasury bond futures contract and the call option writer receives the corresponding short position. The futures price for both parties is the strike price of 98. The positions are then marked-to-market using the futures price of 103 and the option writer must pay the option buyer 5 (the difference between the futures price of 103 and the strike price of 98).
After this, the positions look as follows:

- the investor (the buyer of the call option) has a long position in the Treasury bond futures contract at 103 and cash of 5

- the writer of the call option has a short position in the Treasury bond futures contract at 103 and has paid cash of 5

b. The investor will exercise the put option because the price of the futures contract is less than the strike price. By exercising the investor receives a short position in the Treasury bond futures contract and the put option writer receives the corresponding long position. The futures price for both parties is the strike price of 105. The positions are then marked-to-market using the futures price of 105 and the option writer must pay the option buyer 9 (the difference between the strike price of 105 and the futures price of 96).

After this, the positions look as follows:

- the investor (the buyer of the put option) has a short position in the Treasury bond futures contract at 105 and cash of 9

- the writer of the call option has a long position in the Treasury bond futures contract at 105 and has paid cash of 9

4. Although the payments are quarterly rather than semiannual as illustrated in the text illustration, the concept is the same.

a. Since the swap rate is 4.4%, the fixed-rate payment each quarter will be:

$100 million $\times$ (0.044/4) = $1.1 million

(In the next chapter, this number will be fine tuned to allow for the fact that not every quarter has the same number of days.)

b. Since 3-month LIBOR is 7.2%, the first quarterly payment will be:

$100 million $\times$ (0.072/4) = $1.8 million

5. There is a payoff to the cap if the cap rate exceeds 3-month LIBOR. For Periods 1 and 2, there is no payoff because the 3-month LIBOR is below the cap rate. For Periods 3 and 4, there is a payoff and the payoff is determined by:

$100 million $\times$ (3-month LIBOR − cap rate)/4

The payoffs are summarized below:

Period	3-month LIBOR	Payoff
1	6.7%	0
2	7.0%	0
3	7.4%	100,000
4	7.6%	150,000

Chapter 8

VALUATION OF INTEREST RATE DERIVATIVE INSTRUMENTS

LEARNING OUTCOME STATEMENTS

After reading this chapter you should be able to:

- compute the profit or loss that will be generated in a cash and carry trade and in a reverse cash and carry trade using futures.
- explain how the theoretical price of a futures contract is determined.
- compute the theoretical price of a Treasury futures contract.
- explain how the theoretical price of a Treasury bond futures contract is affected by the delivery options.
- explain the complications in extending the standard arbitrage pricing model to the valuation of Treasury bond and note futures contracts.
- compute the floating-rate payments in an interest rate swap given the futures price of a Eurodollar CD futures contract.
- explain the appropriate interest rate to use in calculating the present value of the payments in an interest rate swap.
- calculate the forward discount factor used to discount the swap payments given the forward rates.
- explain how the swap rate and swap spread are determined.
- describe how the value of a swap is determined.
- calculate the swap rate, swap spread, and value of a swap.
- compute the new floating-rate payments for a swap if interest rates change.
- explain the two components of the option price and the factors that affect the value of an option.
- identify the limitations of applying the Black-Scholes stock-option pricing model to value interest rate options.
- illustrate how the arbitrage-free binomial model can be used to price options on bonds.
- discuss the Black model for valuing options on futures.
- explain how to measure the sensitivity of an option to the changes in the factors that affect its value.
- explain the similar role that delta and duration play in approximating price changes.
- compute the value of each caplet and the value of a cap given a binomial interest rate tree.

SECTION I
INTRODUCTION

In the previous chapter, we described interest rate derivative instruments — futures, forwards, options, swaps, caps, and floors. In this chapter, we focus on the valuation of these instruments. At Level III we will see how they can be used by portfolio managers to control interest rate risk.

SECTION II
INTEREST RATE
FUTURES
CONTRACTS

In this section we will show how a futures contract is valued using an illustration. Suppose that a 20-year, $100 par value bond with a coupon rate of 8% is selling at par and assume that the next coupon payment is six months from now. Also suppose that this bond is the deliverable for a futures contract that settles in three months. If the current 3-month interest rate at which funds can be loaned or borrowed is 4% per year, what should be the price of this futures contract?

Suppose the price of the futures contract is 105. Consider the following strategy:

Sell the futures contract that settles in three months at $105.
Borrow $100 for three months at 4% per year.
With the funds borrowed, purchase the underlying bond for the futures contract.

This strategy is shown in Exhibit 1.

Notice that ignoring initial margin and other transaction costs, there is no cash outlay for this strategy because the borrowed funds are used to purchase the bond. Three months from now, the following must be done:

Deliver the bond purchased to settle the futures contract.
Repay the loan.

When the bond is delivered to settle the futures contract three months from now, the amount received is the futures price of $105 plus the accrued interest. Since the coupon rate is 8% for the bond delivered and the bond is held for three months, the accrued interest is $2 (8% × $100/4). Thus, the amount received is $107 ($105 + $2). The amount that must be paid to repay the loan is the principal borrowed of $100 plus the interest. Since the interest rate for the loan is 4% and the loan is for three months, the interest cost is $1. Thus, the amount paid is $101 ($100 + $1).[1] To summarize, at the end of three months the following will be the cash flow:

Cash inflow from delivery of the bond	=	$107
Cash outflow from repayment of the loan	=	−$101
Profit	=	$6

Exhibit 1: Cash and Carry Trade

Today
• Sell the futures contract at $105
• Borrow $100 for three months at 4% per year
• Purchase underlying bond for $100 with funds borrowed

3 months later
• Deliver underlying bond for $107
  ($105 plus accrued interest of $2)
• Repay loan plus interest at $101
  ($100 principal + $1 interest)

Arbitrage profit = $107 − $101 = $6

---

[1] Note that there are no interim coupon payments for this bond that must be taken into consideration for potential reinvestment income because it is assumed that the next coupon payment is six months from the time the strategy is implemented.

Exhibit 2: Reverse Cash and Carry Trade

Today
- Buy the futures contract at $96
- Sell the underlying bond for $100
- Lend the $100 from the short bond sale for three months

3 months later
- Buy the underlying bond for $98
  ($96 plus accrued interest of $2)
- Receive loan repayment of $101
  ($100 principal + $1 interest)

Arbitrage profit = $101 − $98= $3

This strategy will guarantee a profit of $6. Moreover, the profit is generated with no initial outlay because the funds used to purchase the bond are borrowed. The profit will be realized *regardless of the futures price at the settlement date*. Obviously, in a well-functioning market, arbitrageurs would buy the bond and sell the futures, forcing the futures price down and bidding up the bond price so as to eliminate this profit.

This strategy where a bond is purchased with borrowed funds and a futures contract is sold is called a **cash and carry trade**.

In contrast, suppose that the futures price is $96 instead of $105. Consider the strategy below and which is depicted in Exhibit 2:

> Buy the futures contract that settles in three months at $96.
> Sell (short) the bond underlying the futures contract for $100.
> Invest (lend) the proceeds from the short sale of $100 for three months at 4% per year.

Once again, there is no cash outlay if we ignore the initial margin for the futures contract and other transaction costs. Three months from now when the futures contract must be settled, the following must be done:

> Purchase the underlying bond to settle the futures contract.
> Receive proceeds from repayment of the funds lent.

When the bond is delivered to settle the futures contract three months from now, the amount that must be paid is the futures price of $96 plus the accrued interest of $2. Thus, the amount paid is $98 ($96 + $2). The amount that will be received from the proceeds invested (lent) for three months is $101 which is equal to $100 plus interest of $1.[2] To summarize, at the end of three months the following will be the cash flow:

Cash inflow from the amount invested (lent)	=	$101
Cash outflow to purchase the bond	=	−$98
Profit	=	$3

A profit of $3 will be realized. It is an arbitrage profit because it requires no initial cash outlay and will be realized regardless of the futures price at the settlement date.

Because this strategy involves initially selling the underlying bond, it is called a **reverse cash and carry trade**.

---

[2] Note that the short seller must pay the party from whom the bond was borrowed any coupon payments that were paid. In our illustration, we assumed that the next coupon payment would be in six months so there are no coupon payments. However, the short seller must pay any accrued interest. In our illustration, since the investor purchases the underlying bond for $96 plus accrued interest, the investor has paid the accrued interest. When the bond is delivered to the party to cover the short position, the bond includes the accrued interest. So, no adjustment to the arbitrage profit is needed in our illustration to take into account accrued interest.

There is a futures price that will eliminate any arbitrage profit. There will be no arbitrage profit if the futures price is $99. Let's look at what would happen if the two previous strategies are followed and the futures price is $99. First, consider the cash and carry trade:

> Sell the futures contract that settles in three months at $99.
> Borrow $100 for three months at 4% per year.
> With the funds borrowed purchase the underlying bond for the futures contract.

When the bond is delivered to settle the futures contract three months from now, the amount received is the futures price of $99 plus the accrued interest of $2. Thus, the amount received is $101 ($99 + $2). The amount that must be paid to repay the loan is the principal borrowed of $100 plus the interest of $1. Thus, the amount paid is $101 ($100 + $1). To summarize, at the end of three months the following will be the cash flow:

Cash inflow from delivery of the bond	=	$101
Cash outflow from repayment of the loan	=	−$101
Profit	=	$0

Thus, there is no arbitrage profit if the futures price is $99.

Next, consider the reverse cash and carry trade. In this trade the following is done today:

> Buy the futures contract that settles in three months at $99.
> Sell the bond underlying the futures contract for $100.
> Invest (lend) the proceeds from the short sale of $100 for three months at 4% per year.

Three months from now when the futures contract must be settled, the amount that must be paid is the futures price of $99 plus the accrued interest of $2. Thus, the amount paid is $101 ($99 + $2). The amount that will be received from the proceeds lent for three months is $101, $100 plus interest of $1. At the end of three months the following will be the cash flow:

Cash inflow from the amount invested (lent)	=	$101
Cash outflow to purchase the bond	=	−$101
Profit	=	$0

Thus neither strategy results in a profit or loss. Hence the futures price of $99 is the equilibrium or theoretical price, because any higher or lower futures price will permit arbitrage profits.

PRACTICE QUESTION 1

a. Suppose that the futures price of a 3-month bond futures contract is $93 and the price of the underlying bond is $90. The underlying bond has a coupon rate of 10% and its par value is $100 and the next coupon payment will be made six months from now. The borrowing rate is 8% per annum. If an investor implemented a cash and carry trade, what would the arbitrage profit be?

b. Suppose that instead of a futures price of $93, the futures price is $87. If an investor implemented a reverse cash and carry trade, what would the arbitrage profit be?

c. Show using both a cash and carry trade and a reverse cash and carry trade that the theoretical futures price is $89.30.

A. Theoretical Futures Price Based on Arbitrage Model

Considering the arbitrage arguments (based on the cash and carry trade) just presented, the theoretical futures price can be determined on the basis of the following information:

1. The price of the bond in the cash market.
2. The coupon rate on the bond. (In our example, the coupon rate is 8% per year.)
3. The interest rate for borrowing and lending until the settlement date. The borrowing and lending rate is referred to as the **financing rate**. (In our example, the financing rate is 4% per year.)

We will let

r = financing rate (in decimal)
c = current yield, or annual dollar coupon divided by the cash market price (in decimal)
P = cash market price
F = futures price
t = time, in years, to the futures delivery date

It can be shown that the equation below is the theoretical futures price that will produce a zero profit (i.e., no arbitrage profit) using either the cash and carry trade or the reverse cash and carry trade:

$$F = P + Pt(r - c) \tag{1}$$

Let's apply equation (1) to our previous example in which

$$r = 0.04 \quad c = 0.08 \quad P = 100 \quad t = 0.25$$

Then the theoretical futures price is

$$F = 100 + 100 \times 0.25 \times (0.04 - 0.08) = 100 - 1 = 99$$

This agrees with the theoretical futures price we derived earlier.

It is important to note that c is the current yield that is found by dividing the coupon rate by the cash market price. In our illustration above, since the cash market price of the bond is 100, the coupon rate is the cash yield. If the cash market price is not the par value, the coupon rate is not the current yield.

The theoretical futures price may be at a premium to the cash market price (higher than the cash market price) or at a discount from the cash market price (lower than the cash market price), depending on $(r - c)$. The term $r - c$ is called the **net financing cost** because it adjusts the financing rate for the coupon interest earned. The net financing cost is more commonly called the **cost of carry**, or simply **carry**. **Positive carry** means that the current yield earned is greater than the financing cost; **negative carry** means that the financing cost exceeds the current yield. The relationships can be expressed as follows:

Carry	Futures Price
Positive ($c > r$)	Will sell at a discount to cash price ($F < P$)
Negative ($c < r$)	Will sell at a premium to cash price ($F > P$)
Zero ($c = r$)	Will be equal to cash price ($F = P$)

In the case of interest rate futures, carry (the relationship between the short-term financing rate and the current yield on the bond) depends on the shape of the yield curve. When the yield curve is upward sloping, the short-term financing rate will generally be less than the current yield on the bond, resulting in positive carry. The futures price will then sell at a discount to the cash price for the bond. The opposite will be true when the yield curve is inverted.

Earlier we explained how the cash and carry trade or the reverse cash and carry trade can be used to exploit any mispricing of the futures contract. Let's review when each trade is implemented based on the actual futures price relative to the theoretical futures price. In our illustration when the theoretical futures price was 99 but the actual futures price was 105, the arbitrage profit due to the futures contract being overpriced was captured using the cash and carry trade. Instead, when the cash market price was assumed to be 96, the arbitrage profit resulting from the cheapness of the futures contract was captured by the reverse cash and carry trade. To summarize:

Relationship between theoretical futures price and cash market price	Implement the following trade to capture the arbitrage profit
theoretical futures price > cash market price	cash and carry trade
theoretical futures price < cash market price	reverse cash and carry trade

---

PRACTICE QUESTION 2

Suppose that the price of a bond that is the underlying for a 3-month futures contract is trading at $90. Assume that the bond has a coupon rate of 10% and its par value is $100. Assume further that the borrowing rate is 8% per annum. What is the theoretical futures price?

B. A Closer Look at the Theoretical Futures Price

To derive the theoretical futures price using the arbitrage argument, we made several assumptions. Below we look at the implications of these assumptions.

1. Interim Cash Flows

No interim cash flows due to variation margin or coupon interest payments were assumed in the model. However, we know that interim cash flows can occur for both of these reasons. Because we assumed no initial margin and variation margin, the price derived is technically the theoretical price for a forward contract that is not marked-to-market. Incorporating interim coupon payments into the pricing model is not difficult. However, the value of the coupon payments at the settlement date will depend on the interest rate at which they can be reinvested. The shorter the maturity of the futures contract and the lower the coupon rate, the less important the reinvestment income is in determining the futures price.

2. The Short-Term Interest Rate (Financing Rate)

In deriving the theoretical futures price it is assumed that the borrowing and lending rates are equal. Typically, however, the borrowing rate is higher than the lending rate. If we will let

r_B = borrowing rate and r_L = lending rate

then the futures price that would produce no cash and carry arbitrage profit is

$$F = P + Pt(r_B - c) \tag{2}$$

and the futures price that would produce no reverse cash and carry arbitrage profit is

$$F = P + Pt(r_L - c) \tag{3}$$

Equations (2) and (3) together provide boundaries for the theoretical futures price. Equation (2) provides the upper boundary and equation (3) the lower boundary. For example, assume that the borrowing rate is 4% per year, while the lending rate is 3.2% per year. Then using equation (2) and the previous example, the upper boundary is

$$F \text{ (upper boundary)} = 100 + 100 \times 0.25 \times (0.04 - 0.08) = 99$$

The lower boundary using equation (3) is

$$F \text{ (lower boundary)} = 100 + 100 \times 0.25 \times (0.032 - 0.08) = 98.8$$

In calculating these boundaries, we assume no transaction costs are involved in taking the position. In actuality, the transaction costs of entering into and closing the cash position as well as the round-trip transaction costs for the futures contract must be considered and do affect the boundaries for the futures contract.

3. Deliverable Bond Is Not Known

The arbitrage arguments used to derive equation (1) assumed that only one instrument is deliverable. But as explained in the previous chapter, the futures contracts on Treasury bonds and Treasury notes are designed to allow the short the choice of delivering one of a number of deliverable issues (the quality or swap option). Because there may be more than one deliverable, market participants track the price of each deliverable bond and determine which bond is the cheapest to deliver. The futures price will then trade in relation to the cheapest-to-deliver issue.

There is the risk that while an issue may be the cheapest to deliver at the time a position in the futures contract is taken, it may not be the cheapest to deliver after that time. A change in the cheapest-to-deliver can dramatically alter the futures price. What are the implications of the quality (swap) option on the futures price? Because the swap option is an option granted by the long to the short, the long will want to pay *less* for the futures contract than indicated by equation (1). Therefore, as a result of the quality option, the theoretical futures price as given by equation (1) must be adjusted as follows:

$$F = P + Pt(r - c) - \text{value of quality option} \tag{4}$$

Market participants have employed theoretical models in attempting to estimate the fair value of the quality option. A discussion of these models is beyond the scope of this chapter.

4. Delivery Date Is Not Known

In the pricing model based on arbitrage arguments, a known delivery date is assumed. For Treasury bond and note futures contracts, the short has a timing and wild card option, so the long does not know when the security will be delivered. The effect of the timing and wild card options on the theoretical futures price is the same as with the quality option. These delivery options result in a theoretical futures price that is lower than the one suggested by equation (1), as shown below:

$$F = P + P(r - c) - \text{value of quality option}$$
$$- \text{value of timing option} - \text{value of wildcard option} \qquad (5)$$

or alternatively,

$$F = P + P(r - c) - \text{delivery options} \qquad (6)$$

Market participants attempt to value the delivery options in order to apply equation (6). A discussion of these models is beyond the scope of this chapter.

5. Putting It Altogether

To summarize, there is not one theoretical futures price that would eliminate any arbitrage profit, but a range for the theoretical future prices based on borrowing and lending rates. Consequently, the futures price can fluctuate within this range and there will be no arbitrage profit. Once recognition is given to the delivery options granted to the short in the futures contract, the theoretical futures price is lower. Specifically, it is reduced by the value of the delivery options. This means that the lower boundary for the theoretical futures price shifts down by an amount equal to the value of the delivery options and the upper boundary for the theoretical futures price shifts down by the same amount.

SECTION III
INTEREST RATE
SWAPS

In an interest rate swap, the counterparties agree to exchange periodic interest payments. The dollar amount of the interest payments exchanged is based on the notional principal. In the most common type of swap, there is a fixed-rate payer and a fixed-rate receiver. The convention for quoting swap rates is that a swap dealer sets the floating rate equal to the reference rate and then quotes the fixed rate that will apply.

A. Computing the Payments for a Swap

While in the previous chapter we described in general terms the payments by the fixed-rate payer and fixed-rate receiver, we did not give any details. That is, we explained that if the swap rate is 6% and the notional amount is $100 million, then the fixed-rate payment will be $6 million for the year and the payment is then adjusted based on the frequency of settlement. So, if settlement is semiannual, the payment is $3 million. If it is quarterly, it is $1.5 million. Similarly, the floating-rate payment would be found by multiplying the reference rate by the notional amount and then scaling based on the frequency of settlement.

It was useful to show the basic features of an interest rate swap using quick calculations for the payments such as described above and then explaining how the parties to a swap either benefit or get hurt when interest rates change. However, we are going to show how to value a swap in this section. To value a swap it is necessary to determine the present value of the fixed-rate payments and the present value of the floating-rate payments. The difference between these two present values is the value of a swap. As will be explained below, whether the value is positive (i.e., an asset) or negative (i.e., a liability) will depend on whether the party is the fixed-rate payer or the fixed-rate receiver.

At the inception of the swap, the terms of the swap will be such that the present value of the floating-rate payments is equal to the present value of the fixed-rate payments. That is, the value of the swap is equal to zero at the inception of the swap. This is the fundamental principle in determining the swap rate (i.e., the fixed rate that the fixed-rate payer will make).

Here is a roadmap of the presentation. First we will look at how to compute the floating-rate payments. We will see how the future values of the reference rate are determined to obtain the floating rate for the period. From the future values of the reference rate we will then see how to compute the floating-rate payments taking into account the number of days in the payment period. Next we will see how to calculate the fixed-rate payments given the swap rate. Before we look at how to calculate the value of a swap, we will see how to calculate the swap rate. This will require an explanation of how the present value of any cash flow in an interest rate swap is computed. Given the floating-rate payments and the present value of the floating-rate payments, the swap rate can be determined by using the principle that the swap rate is the fixed rate that will make the present value of the fixed-rate payments equal to the present value of the floating-rate payments. Finally, we will see how the value of a swap is determined after the inception of a swap.

1. Calculating the Floating-Rate Payments

For the first floating-rate payment, the amount is known. For all subsequent payments, the floating-rate payment depends on the value of the reference rate when the floating rate is determined. To illustrate the issues associated with calculating the floating-rate payment, we will assume that

- a swap starts today, January 1 of year 1(swap settlement date)
- the floating-rate payments are made quarterly based on "actual/360"
- the reference rate is 3-month LIBOR
- the notional amount of the swap is $100 million
- the term of the swap is three years

The quarterly floating-rate payments are based on an "actual/360" day count convention. This convention means that 360 days are assumed in a year and that in computing the interest for the quarter the actual number of days in the quarter are used. The floating-rate payment is set at the beginning of the quarter but paid at the end of the quarter — that is, the floating-rate payments are made in arrears.

Suppose that today 3-month LIBOR is 4.05%. Let's look at what the fixed-rate payer will receive on March 31 of year 1 — the date when the first quarterly swap payment is made. There is no uncertainty about what the floating-rate payment will be. In general, the floating-rate payment is determined as follows:

$$\text{notional amount} \times (\text{3-month LIBOR}) \times \frac{\text{no. of days in period}}{360}$$

In our illustration, assuming a non-Leap year, the number of days from January 1 of year 1 to March 31 of year 1 (the first quarter) is 90. If 3-month LIBOR is 4.05%, then the fixed-rate payer will receive a floating-rate payment on March 31 of year 1 equal to:

$$\$100,000,000 \times 0.0405 \times \frac{90}{360} = \$1,012,500$$

Now the difficulty is in determining the floating-rate payment after the first quarterly payment. That is, for the 3-year swap there will be 12 quarterly floating-rate payments. So, while the first quarterly payment is known, the next 11 are not. However, there is a way to hedge the next 11 floating-rate payments by using a futures contract. Specifically, the futures contract used to hedge the future floating-rate payments in a swap whose reference rate is 3-month LIBOR is the Eurodollar CD futures contract. We will digress to discuss this contract.

a. The Eurodollar CD Futures Contract

As explained in the previous chapter, a swap position can be interpreted as a package of forward/futures contracts or a package of cash flows from buying and selling cash market instruments. It is the former interpretation that will be used as the basis for valuing a swap. In the case of a LIBOR-based swap, the appropriate futures contract is the Eurodollar CD futures contract. For this reason, we will describe this important contract.

Eurodollar certificates of deposit (CDs) are denominated in dollars but represent the liabilities of banks outside the United States. The contracts are traded on both the International Monetary Market of the Chicago Mercantile Exchange and the London International Financial Futures Exchange. The rate paid on Eurodollar CDs is the London interbank offered rate (LIBOR).

The 3-month Eurodollar CD is the underlying instrument for the Eurodollar CD futures contract. The contract is for $1 million of face value and is traded on an index price basis. The index price basis in which the contract is quoted is equal to 100 minus the product of the annualized LIBOR futures rate in decimal and 100. For example, a Eurodollar CD futures price of 94.00 means a 3-month LIBOR futures rate of 6% (100 minus 0.06×100).

The Eurodollar CD futures contract is a cash settlement contract. That is, the parties settle in cash for the value of a Eurodollar CD based on LIBOR at the settlement date.

The Eurodollar CD futures contract allows the buyer of the contract to lock in the rate on 3-month LIBOR today for a future 3-month period. For example, suppose that on February 1, 2000 an investor purchases a Eurodollar CD futures contract that settles in March 2000. Assume that the LIBOR futures rate for this contract is 5%. This means that the investor has agreed to invest in a 3-month Eurodollar CD that pays a rate of 5%. Specifically, the investor has locked in a rate for a 3-month investment of 5% beginning March 2000. If the investor on February 1, 2000 purchased a contract that settles in September 2001 and the LIBOR futures rate is 5.4%, the investor has locked in the rate on a 3-month investment beginning September 2001.

From the perspective of the seller of a Eurodollar CD futures contract, the seller is agreeing to lend funds for three months at some future date at the LIBOR futures rate. For example, suppose on February 1, 2000 a bank sells a Eurodollar CD futures contract that settles in March 2000 and the LIBOR futures rate is 5%. The bank locks in a borrowing rate of 5% for three months beginning in March 2000. If the settlement date is September 2001 and the LIBOR futures rate is 5.4%, the bank is locking in a borrowing rate of 5.4% for the 3-month period beginning September 2001.

The key point here is that the Eurodollar CD futures contract allows a participant in the financial market to lock in a 3-month rate on an investment or a 3-month borrowing rate. The 3-month period begins in the month that the contract settles.

b. Determining Future Floating-Rate Payments

Now let's return to our objective of determining the future floating-rate payments. These payments can be locked in over the life of the swap using the Eurodollar CD futures contract. We will show how these floating-rate payments are computed using this contract.

Exhibit 3: Floating-Rate Payments Based on Initial LIBOR and Eurodollar CD Futures

(1)	(2)	(3)	(4)	(5)	(6)	(7)	(8)
Quarter starts	Quarter ends	Number of days in quarter	Current 3-month LIBOR	Eurodollar CD futures price	Forward rate	Period = End of quarter	Floating-rate payment at end of quarter
Jan 1 year 1	Mar 31 year 1	90	4.05%		—	1	1,012,500
Apr 1 year 1	June 30 year 1	91		95.85	4.15%	2	1,049,028
July 1 year 1	Sept 30 year 1	92		95.45	4.55%	3	1,162,778
Oct 1 year 1	Dec 31 year 1	92		95.28	4.72%	4	1,206,222
Jan 1 year 2	Mar 31 year 2	90		95.10	4.90%	5	1,225,000
Apr 1 year 2	June 30 year 2	91		94.97	5.03%	6	1,271,472
July 1 year 2	Sept 30 year 2	92		94.85	5.15%	7	1,316,111
Oct 1 year 2	Dec 31 year 2	92		94.75	5.25%	8	1,341,667
Jan 1 year 3	Mar 31 year 3	90		94.60	5.40%	9	1,350,000
Apr 1 year 3	June 30 year 3	91		94.50	5.50%	10	1,390,278
July 1 year 3	Sept 30 year 3	92		94.35	5.65%	11	1,443,889
Oct 1 year 3	Dec 31 year 3	92		94.24	5.76%	12	1,472,000

We will begin with the next quarterly payment — from April 1 of year 1 to June 30 of year 1. This quarter has 91 days. The floating-rate payment will be determined by 3-month LIBOR on April 1 of year 1 and paid on June 30 of year 1. There is a 3-month Eurodollar CD futures contract for settlement on June 30 of year 1. That futures contract provides the rate that can be locked in for 3-month LIBOR on April 1 of year 1. For example, if the futures price for the 3-month Eurodollar CD futures contract that settles on June 30 of year 1 is 95.85, then as explained above, the 3-month Eurodollar futures rate is 4.15%. We will refer to that rate for 3-month LIBOR as the "forward rate." Therefore, if the fixed-rate payer bought 100 of these 3-month Eurodollar CD futures contracts on January 1 of year 1 (the inception of the swap) that settle on June 30 of year 1, then the payment that will be locked in for the quarter (April 1 to June 30 of year 1) is

$$\$100,000,000 \times 0.0415 \times \frac{91}{360} = \$1,049,028$$

(Note that each futures contract is for $1 million and hence 100 contracts have a notional amount of $100 million.) Similarly, the Eurodollar CD futures contract can be used to lock in a floating-rate payment for each of the next 10 quarters. Once again, it is important to emphasize that the reference rate at the beginning of period t determines the floating-rate that will be paid for the period. However, the floating-rate payment is not made until the end of period t.

Exhibit 3 shows this for the 3-year swap. Shown in Column (1) is when the quarter begins and in Column (2) when the quarter ends. The payment will be received at the end of the first quarter (March 31 of year 1) and is $1,012,500. That is the known floating-rate payment as explained earlier. It is the only payment that is known. The information used to compute the first payment is in Column (4) which shows the current 3-month LIBOR (4.05%). The payment is shown in the last column, Column (8).

Notice that Column (7) numbers the quarters from 1 through 12. Look at the heading for Column (7). It identifies each quarter in terms of the end of the quarter. This is important because we will eventually be discounting the payments (cash flows). We must take care to understand when each payment is to be exchanged in order to properly discount. So, for the first payment of $1,012,500 it is going to be received at the end of quarter 1. When we refer to the time period for any payment, the reference is to the end of quarter. So, the fifth payment of $1,225,000 would be identified as the payment for period 5, where period 5 means that it will be exchanged at the end of the fifth quarter.

PRACTICE QUESTION 3

Assume a 3-year swap beginning on January 1 of year 1. The reference rate for the swap is 3-month LIBOR and the notional amount is $100 million. The floating-rate and fixed-rate payments are based on the "actual/360" day count convention. Below is the current 3-month LIBOR and the Eurodollar CD futures price for each quarter. Determine the futures rate for each quarter and the floating-rate payment at the end of each quarter.

Quarter starts	Quarter ends	Number of days in quarter	Current 3-month LIBOR	Eurodollar CD futures price	Forward rate	Period = End of quarter	Floating-rate payment at end of quarter
Jan 1 year 1	Mar 31 year 1	90	7.30%		—	1	
Apr 1 year 1	June 30 year 1	91		92.60		2	
July 1 year 1	Sept 30 year 1	92		92.10		3	
Oct 1 year 1	Dec 31 year 1	92		92.05		4	
Jan 1 year 2	Mar 31 year 2	90		92.00		5	
Apr 1 year 2	June 30 year 2	91		91.85		6	
July 1 year 2	Sept 30 year 2	92		91.75		7	
Oct 1 year 2	Dec 31 year 2	92		91.70		8	
Jan 1 year 3	Mar 31 year 3	90		91.55		9	
Apr 1 year 3	June 30 year 3	91		91.40		10	
July 1 year 3	Sept 30 year 3	92		91.25		11	
Oct 1 year 3	Dec 31 year 3	92		91.10		12	

---

2. Calculating the Fixed-Rate Payments

The swap will specify the frequency of settlement for the fixed-rate payments. The frequency need not be the same as the floating-rate payments. For example, in the 3-year swap we have been using to illustrate the calculation of the floating-rate payments, the frequency is quarterly. The frequency of the fixed-rate payments could be semiannual rather than quarterly.

In our illustration we will assume that the frequency of settlement is quarterly for the fixed-rate payments, the same as with the floating-rate payments. The day count convention is the same as for the floating-rate payment, "actual/360". The equation for determining the dollar amount of the fixed-rate payment for the period is:

$$\text{notional amount} \times (\text{swap rate}) \times \frac{\text{no. of days in period}}{360}$$

It is the same equation as for determining the floating-rate payment except that the swap rate is used instead of the reference rate (3-month LIBOR in our illustration).

For example, suppose that the swap rate is 4.98% and the quarter has 90 days. Then the fixed-rate payment for the quarter is:

$$\$100,000,000 \times 0.0498 \times \frac{90}{360} = \$1,245,000$$

Exhibit 4: Fixed-Rate Payments Assuming a Swap Rate of 4.9875%

(1)	(2)	(3)	(4)	(5)
Quarter starts	Quarter ends	Number of days in quarter	Period = End of quarter	Fixed-rate payment if swap rate is assumed to be 4.9875%
Jan 1 year 1	Mar 31 year 1	90	1	1,246,875
Apr 1 year 1	June 30 year 1	91	2	1,260,729
July 1 year 1	Sept 30 year 1	92	3	1,274,583
Oct 1 year 1	Dec 31 year 1	92	4	1,274,583
Jan 1 year 2	Mar 31 year 2	90	5	1,246,875
Apr 1 year 2	June 30 year 2	91	6	1,260,729
July 1 year 2	Sept 30 year 2	92	7	1,274,583
Oct 1 year 2	Dec 31 year 2	92	8	1,274,583
Jan 1 year 3	Mar 31 year 3	90	9	1,246,875
Apr 1 year 3	June 30 year 3	91	10	1,260,729
July 1 year 3	Sept 30 year 3	92	11	1,274,583
Oct 1 year 3	Dec 31 year 3	92	12	1,274,583

If there are 92 days in a quarter, the fixed-rate payment for the quarter is:

$$\$100,000,000 \times 0.0498 \times \frac{92}{360} = \$1,272,667$$

Note that the rate is fixed for each quarter but the dollar amount of the payment depends on the number of days in the period.

Exhibit 4 shows the fixed-rate payments based on an *assumed* swap rate of 4.9875%. (Later we will see how the swap rate is determined.) The first three columns of the exhibit show the same information as in Exhibit 3 — the beginning and end of the quarter and the number of days in the quarter. Column (4) simply uses the notation for the period. That is, period 1 means the end of the first quarter, period 2 means the end of the second quarter, and so on. Column (5) shows the fixed value payments for each period based on a swap rate of 4.9875%.

PRACTICE QUESTION 4

Complete the following table for the fixed-rate payments for the 3-year swap in Practice Question 3 assuming a swap rate of 8.1313%:

Quarter starts	Quarter ends	Number of days in quarter	Period = End of quarter	Fixed-rate payment if swap rate is 8.1313%
Jan 1 year 1	Mar 31 year 1	90	1	
Apr 1 year 1	June 30 year 1	91	2	
July 1 year 1	Sept 30 year 1	92	3	
Oct 1 year 1	Dec 31 year 1	92	4	
Jan 1 year 2	Mar 31 year 2	90	5	
Apr 1 year 2	June 30 year 2	91	6	
July 1 year 2	Sept 30 year 2	92	7	
Oct 1 year 2	Dec 31 year 2	92	8	
Jan 1 year 3	Mar 31 year 3	90	9	
Apr 1 year 3	June 30 year 3	91	10	
July 1 year 3	Sept 30 year 3	92	11	
Oct 1 year 3	Dec 31 year 3	92	12	

B. Calculation of the Swap Rate

Now that we know how to calculate the payments for the fixed-rate and floating-rate sides of a swap where the reference rate is 3-month LIBOR given (1) the current value for 3-month LIBOR, (2) a series for 3-month LIBOR in the future from the Eurodollar CD futures contract, and (3) the assumed swap rate, we can demonstrate how to compute the swap rate.

At the initiation of an interest rate swap, the counterparties are agreeing to exchange future payments and no upfront payments by either party are made. This means that the swap terms must be such that the present value of the payments to be made by the counterparties must be at least equal to the present value of the payments that will be received. In fact, to eliminate arbitrage opportunities, the present value of the payments made by a party will be equal to the present value of the payments received by that same party. *The equivalence (or no arbitrage) of the present value of the payments is the key principle in calculating the swap rate.*

Since we will have to calculate the present value of the payments, let's show how this is done.

1. Calculating the Present Value of the Floating-Rate Payments

As explained earlier, we must be careful about how we compute the present value of payments. In particular, we must carefully specify (1) the timing of the payment and (2) the interest rates that should be used to discount the payments. We already addressed the first issue. In constructing the exhibit for the payments, we indicated that the payments are at the end of the quarter. So, we denoted the timing of the payments with respect to the end of the quarter.

Now let's turn to the interest rates that should be used for discounting. At Level I we emphasized two things. First, every cash flow should be discounted at its own discount rate using a spot rate. So, if we discounted a cash flow of \$1 using the spot rate for period t, the present value would be:

$$\text{present value of \$1 to be received in period } t = \frac{\$1}{(1 + \text{spot rate for period } t)^t}$$

The second thing we emphasized is that forward rates are derived from spot rates so that if we discounted a cash flow using forward rates rather than a spot rate, we would come up with the same value. That is, the present value of \$1 to be received in period t can be rewritten as:

$$\text{present value of \$1 to be received in period } t = \frac{\$1}{(1 + \text{forward rate for period } 1)(1 + \text{forward rate for period } 2)\cdots(1 + \text{forward rate for period } t)}$$

We will refer to the present value of \$1 to be received in period t as the **forward discount factor**. In our calculations involving swaps, we will compute the forward discount factor for a period using the forward rates. These are the same forward rates that are used to compute the floating-rate payments — those obtained from the Eurodollar CD futures contract. We must make just one more adjustment. We must adjust the forward rates used in the formula for the number of days in the period (i.e., the quarter in our illustrations) in the same way that we made this adjustment to obtain the payments. Specifically, the forward rate for a period, which we will refer to as the **period forward rate**, is computed using the following equation:

$$\text{period forward rate } = \text{annual forward rate} \times \left(\frac{\text{days in period}}{360}\right)$$

Exhibit 5: Calculating the Forward Discount Factor

(1)	(2)	(3)	(4)	(5)	(6)	(7)
Quarter starts	Quarter ends	Number of days in quarter	Period = End of quarter	Forward rate	Period forward rate	Forward discount factor
Jan 1 year 1	Mar 31 year 1	90	1	4.05%	1.0125%	0.98997649
Apr 1 year 1	June 30 year 1	91	2	4.15%	1.0490%	0.97969917
July 1 year 1	Sept 30 year 1	92	3	4.55%	1.1628%	0.96843839
Oct 1 year 1	Dec 31 year 1	92	4	4.72%	1.2062%	0.95689609
Jan 1 year 2	Mar 31 year 2	90	5	4.90%	1.2250%	0.94531597
Apr 1 year 2	June 30 year 2	91	6	5.03%	1.2715%	0.93344745
July 1 year 2	Sept 30 year 2	92	7	5.15%	1.3161%	0.92132183
Oct 1 year 2	Dec 31 year 2	92	8	5.25%	1.3417%	0.90912441
Jan 1 year 3	Mar 31 year 3	90	9	5.40%	1.3500%	0.89701471
Apr 1 year 3	June 30 year 3	91	10	5.50%	1.3903%	0.88471472
July 1 year 3	Sept 30 year 3	92	11	5.65%	1.4439%	0.87212224
Oct 1 year 3	Dec 31 year 3	92	12	5.76%	1.4720%	0.85947083

For example, look at Exhibit 3. The annual forward rate for period 4 is 4.72%. The period forward rate for period 4 is:

$$\text{period forward rate} = 4.72\% \times \left(\frac{92}{360}\right) = 1.2062\%$$

Column (5) in Exhibit 5 shows the annual forward rate for all 12 periods (reproduced from Exhibit 3) and Column (6) shows the period forward rate for all 12 periods. Note that the period forward rate for period 1 is $^{90}\!/_{360}$ of 4.05%, which is $^{90}\!/_{360}$ of the known rate for 3-month LIBOR.

Also shown in Exhibit 5 is the forward discount factor for all 12 periods. These values are shown in the last column. Let's show how the forward discount factor is computed for periods 1, 2, and 3. For period 1, the forward discount factor is:

$$\text{forward discount factor} = \frac{\$1}{1 + \text{period forward rate}_1}$$

$$= \frac{\$1}{1.010125} = 0.98997649$$

For period 2,

$$\text{forward discount factor} = \frac{\$1}{(1.010125)(1.010490)} = 0.97969917$$

For period 3.

$$\text{forward discount factor} = \frac{\$1}{(1.010125)(1.010490)(1.011628)} = 0.96843839$$

Given the floating-rate payment for a period and the forward discount factor for the period, the present value of the payment can be computed. For example, from Exhibit 3 we see that the floating-rate payment for period 4 is $1,206,222. From Exhibit 5, the forward discount factor for period 4 is 0.95689609. Therefore, the present value of the payment is:

$$\text{present value of period 4 payment} = \$1,206,222 \times 0.95689609 = \$1,154,229$$

Exhibit 6: Present Value of the Floating-Rate Payments

(1) Quarter starts	(2) Quarter ends	(3) Period = End of quarter	(4) Forward discount factor	(5) Floating-rate payment at end of quarter	(6) PV of floating-rate payment
Jan 1 year 1	Mar 31 year 1	1	0.98997649	1,012,500	1,002,351
Apr 1 year 1	June 30 year 1	2	0.97969917	1,049,028	1,027,732
July 1 year 1	Sept 30 year 1	3	0.96843839	1,162,778	1,126,079
Oct 1 year 1	Dec 31 year 1	4	0.95689609	1,206,222	1,154,229
Jan 1 year 2	Mar 31 year 2	5	0.94531597	1,225,000	1,158,012
Apr 1 year 2	June 30 year 2	6	0.93344745	1,271,472	1,186,852
July 1 year 2	Sept 30 year 2	7	0.92132183	1,316,111	1,212,562
Oct 1 year 2	Dec 31 year 2	8	0.90912441	1,341,667	1,219,742
Jan 1 year 3	Mar 31 year 3	9	0.89701471	1,350,000	1,210,970
Apr 1 year 3	June 30 year 3	10	0.88471472	1,390,278	1,229,999
July 1 year 3	Sept 30 year 3	11	0.87212224	1,443,889	1,259,248
Oct 1 year 3	Dec 31 year 3	12	0.85947083	1,472,000	1,265,141
				Total	14,052,917

Exhibit 6 shows the present value for each payment. The total present value of the 12 floating-rate payments is $14,052,917. Thus, the present value of the payments that the fixed-rate payer will receive is $14,052,917 and the present value of the payments that the fixed-rate receiver will make is $14,052,917.

PRACTICE QUESTION 5

a. For the 3-year swap in Practice Question 3, compute the forward discount factor for each period.

b. Compute the present value of the floating-rate payments given the forward discount factors found in (a) and the floating-rate payments found in Practice Question 3.

C. Determination of the Swap Rate

The fixed-rate payer will require that the present value of the fixed-rate payments that must be made based on the swap rate not exceed the $14,052,917 to be received from the floating-rate payments. The fixed-rate receiver will require that the present value of the fixed-rate payments to received be at least as great as the $14,052,917 that must be paid. This means that both parties will require a present value for the fixed-rate payments to be $14,052,917. If that is the case, the present value of the fixed-rate payments is equal to the present value of the floating-rate payments and therefore the value of the swap is zero for both parties at the inception of the swap. The interest rates that should be used to compute the present value of the fixed-rate payments are the same interest rates as those used to discount the floating-rate payments.

Beginning with the basic relationship for no arbitrage to exist:

PV of floating-rate payments = PV of fixed-rate payments

it can be shown that the formula for the swap rate is:[3]

$$SR = \frac{PV \text{ of floating-rate payments}}{\sum_{t=1}^{N} \text{notional amount} \times \frac{\text{Days}_t}{360} \times \text{FDF}_t}$$

Exhibit 7: Calculating the Denominator for the Swap Rate Formula

(1)	(2)	(3)	(4)	(5)	(6)	(7)
		Number of	Period =	Forward		Forward discount factor
Quarter	Quarter	days in	End of	discount		× Days/360
starts	ends	quarter	quarter	factor	Days/360	× notional
Jan 1 year 1	Mar 31 year 1	90	1	0.98997649	0.25000000	24,749,412
Apr 1 year 1	June 30 year 1	91	2	0.97969917	0.25277778	24,764,618
July 1 year 1	Sept 30 year 1	92	3	0.96843839	0.25555556	24,748,981
Oct 1 year 1	Dec 31 year 1	92	4	0.95689609	0.25555556	24,454,011
Jan 1 year 2	Mar 31 year 2	90	5	0.94531597	0.25000000	23,632,899
Apr 1 year 2	June 30 year 2	91	6	0.93344745	0.25277778	23,595,477
July 1 year 2	Sept 30 year 2	92	7	0.92132183	0.25555556	23,544,891
Oct 1 year 2	Dec 31 year 2	92	8	0.90912441	0.25555556	23,233,179
Jan 1 year 3	Mar 31 year 3	90	9	0.89701471	0.25000000	22,425,368
Apr 1 year 3	June 30 year 3	91	10	0.88471472	0.25277778	22,363,622
July 1 year 3	Sept 30 year 3	92	11	0.87212224	0.25555556	22,287,568
Oct 1 year 3	Dec 31 year 3	92	12	0.85947083	0.25555556	21,964,255
					Total	281,764,282

where

$$SR \quad = \quad \text{swap rate}$$
$$\text{Days}_t \quad = \quad \text{number of days in period } t$$
$$\text{FDF}_t \quad = \quad \text{forward discount rate for period } t$$

Note that all the values to compute the swap rate are known.

Let's apply the formula to determine the swap rate for our 3-year swap. Exhibit 7 shows the calculation of the denominator of the formula. The forward discount factor for each period shown in Column (5) is obtained from Column (4) of Exhibit 6. The sum of the last column in Exhibit 7 shows that the denominator of the swap rate formula is $281,764,282. We know from Exhibit 6 that the present value of the floating-rate payments is $14,052,917. Therefore, the swap rate is

---

[3] The formula is derived as follows. The fixed-rate payment for period t is equal to:

$$\text{notional amount} \times SR \times \frac{\text{Days}_t}{360}$$

The present value of the fixed-rate payment for period t is found by multiplying the previous expression by the forward discount factor for period t (FDF_t). That is, the present value of the fixed-rate payment for period t is equal to:

$$\text{notional amount} \times SR \times \frac{\text{Days}_t}{360} \times \text{FDF}_t$$

Summing up the present value of the fixed-rate payment for each period gives the present value of the fixed-rate payments. Letting N be the number of periods in the swap, then the present value of the fixed-rate payments can be expressed as:

$$SR \sum_{t=1}^{N} \text{notional amount} \times \frac{\text{Days}_t}{360} \times \text{FDF}_t$$

The condition for no arbitrage is that the present value of the fixed-rate payments as given by the expression above is equal to the present value of the floating-rate payments. That is,

$$SR \sum_{t=1}^{N} \text{notional amount} \times \frac{\text{Days}_t}{360} \times \text{FDF}_t = PV \text{ of floating-rate payments}$$

Solving for the swap rate gives the formula in the text.

$$SR = \frac{\$14,052,917}{\$281,764,282} = 0.049875 = 4.9875\%$$

Given the swap rate, the **swap spread** can be determined. For example, since this is a 3-year swap, the convention is to use the 3-year on-the-run Treasury rate as the benchmark. If the yield on that issue is 4.5875%, the swap spread is 40 basis points (4.9875% − 4.5875%).

The calculation of the swap rate for all swaps follows the same principle: equating the present value of the fixed-rate payments to that of the floating-rate payments.

PRACTICE QUESTION 6

What is the swap rate for the swap in Practice Question 3?

D. Valuing a Swap

Once the swap transaction is completed, changes in market interest rates will change the payments of the floating-rate side of the swap. The value of an interest rate swap is the difference between the present value of the payments of the two sides of the swap. The 3-month LIBOR forward rates from the current Eurodollar CD futures contracts are used to (1) calculate the floating-rate payments and (2) determine the discount factors at which to calculate the present value of the payments.

To illustrate this, consider the 3-year swap used to demonstrate how to calculate the swap rate. Suppose that one year later, interest rates change as shown in Columns (4) and (6) in Exhibit 8. Column (4) shows the current 3-month LIBOR. In Column (5) are the Eurodollar CD futures prices for each period. These rates are used to compute the forward rates in Column (6). Note that the interest rates have increased one year later since the rates in Exhibit 8 are greater than those in Exhibit 3. As in Exhibit 3, the current 3-month LIBOR and the forward rates are used to compute the floating-rate payments. These payments are shown in Column (8) of Exhibit 8.

In Exhibit 9, the forward discount factor is computed for each period. The calculation is the same as in Exhibit 5 to obtain the forward discount factor for each period. The forward discount factor for each period is shown in the last column of Exhibit 9.

Exhibit 8: Rates and Floating-Rate Payments One Year Later if Rates Increase

(1)	(2)	(3)	(4)	(5)	(6)	(7)	(8)
Quarter starts	Quarter ends	Number of days in quarter	Current 3-month LIBOR	Eurodollar futures price	Forward rate	Period = End of quarter	Floating-rate payments at end of quarter
Jan 1 year 2	Mar 31 year 2	90	5.25%			1	1,312,500
Apr 1 year 2	June 30 year 2	91		94.27	5.73%	2	1,448,417
July 1 year 2	Sept 30 year 2	92		94.22	5.78%	3	1,477,111
Oct 1 year 2	Dec 31 year 2	92		94.00	6.00%	4	1,533,333
Jan 1 year 3	Mar 31 year 3	90		93.85	6.15%	5	1,537,500
Apr 1 year 3	June 30 year 3	91		93.75	6.25%	6	1,579,861
July 1 year 3	Sept 30 year 3	92		93.54	6.46%	7	1,650,889
Oct 1 year 3	Dec 31 year 3	92		93.25	6.75%	8	1,725,000

Exhibit 9: Period Forward Rates and Forward Discount Factors One Year Later if Rates Increase

(1)	(2)	(3)	(4)	(5)	(6)	(7)
Quarter starts	Quarter ends	Number of days in quarter	Period = End of quarter	Forward rate	Period forward rate	Forward discount factor
Jan 1 year 2	Mar 31 year 2	90	1	5.25%	1.3125%	0.98704503
Apr 1 year 2	June 30 year 2	91	2	5.73%	1.4484%	0.97295263
July 1 year 2	Sept 30 year 2	92	3	5.78%	1.4771%	0.95879023
Oct 1 year 2	Dec 31 year 2	92	4	6.00%	1.5333%	0.94431080
Jan 1 year 3	Mar 31 year 3	90	5	6.15%	1.5375%	0.93001186
Apr 1 year 3	June 30 year 3	91	6	6.25%	1.5799%	0.91554749
July 1 year 3	Sept 30 year 3	92	7	6.46%	1.6509%	0.90067829
Oct 1 year 3	Dec 31 year 3	92	8	6.75%	1.7250%	0.88540505

Exhibit 10: Valuing the Swap One Year Later if Rates Increase

(1)	(2)	(3)	(4)	(5)	(6)	(7)
Quarter starts	Quarter ends	Forward discount factor	Floating cash flow at end of quarter	PV of floating cash flow	Fixed cash flow at end of quarter	PV of fixed cash flow
Jan 1 year 2	Mar 31 year 2	0.98704503	1,312,500	1,295,497	1,246,875	1,230,722
Apr 1 year 2	June 30 year 2	0.97295263	1,448,417	1,409,241	1,260,729	1,226,630
July 1 year 2	Sept 30 year 2	0.95879023	1,477,111	1,416,240	1,274,583	1,222,058
Oct 1 year 2	Dec 31 year 2	0.94431080	1,533,333	1,447,943	1,274,583	1,203,603
Jan 1 year 3	Mar 31 year 3	0.93001186	1,537,500	1,429,893	1,246,875	1,159,609
Apr 1 year 3	June 30 year 3	0.91554749	1,579,861	1,446,438	1,260,729	1,154,257
July 1 year 3	Sept 30 year 3	0.90067829	1,650,889	1,486,920	1,274,583	1,147,990
Oct 1 year 3	Dec 31 year 3	0.88540505	1,725,000	1,527,324	1,274,583	1,128,523
			Total	11,459,495		9,473,390

Summary	Fixed-rate payer	Fixed-rate receiver
PV of payments received	11,459,495	9,473,390
PV of payments made	9,473,390	11,459,495
Value of swap	1,986,105	−1,986,105

In Exhibit 10 the forward discount factor (from Exhibit 9) and the floating-rate payments (from Exhibit 8) are shown. The fixed-rate payments need not be recomputed. They are the payments shown in Column (8) of Exhibit 4. These are the fixed-rate payments for the swap rate of 4.9875% and they are reproduced in Exhibit 10. Now the two payment streams must be discounted using the new forward discount factors. As shown at the bottom of Exhibit 10, the two present values are as follows:

Present value of floating-rate payments $11,459,495
Present value of fixed-rate payments $9,473,390

The two present values are not equal and therefore for one party the value of the swap increased and for the other party the value of the swap decreased. Let's look at which party gained and which party lost.

The fixed-rate payer will receive the floating-rate payments. And these payments have a present value of $11,459,495. The present value of the payments that must be made by the fixed-rate payer is $9,473,390. Thus, the swap has a positive value for the fixed-rate payer equal to the difference in the two present values of $1,986,105. This is the value of the swap to the fixed-rate payer. Notice, consistent with what we said in the previous chapter, when interest rates increase (as they did in the illustration analyzed), the fixed-rate payer benefits because the value of the swap increases.

In contrast, the fixed-rate receiver must make payments with a present value of $11,459,495 but will only receive fixed-rate payments with a present value equal to $9,473,390. Thus, the value of the swap for the fixed-rate receiver is −$1,986,105. Again, as explained in the previous chapter, the fixed-rate receiver is adversely affected by a rise in interest rates because it results in a decline in the value of a swap.

PRACTICE QUESTION 7

The following questions are based on the original 3-year swap that has been used in the illustration. Suppose that one year after the inception of the 3-year swap interest rates have changed as shown in the table below:

(1) Quarter starts	(2) Quarter ends	(3) Number of days in quarter	(4) Current 3-month LIBOR	(5) Eurodollar CD futures price
Jan 1 year 2	Mar 31 year 2	90	3.50%	
Apr 1 year 2	June 30 year 2	91		96.40
July 1 year 2	Sept 30 year 2	92		96.20
Oct 1 year 2	Dec 31 year 2	92		96.00
Jan 1 year 3	Mar 31 year 3	90		95.96
Apr 1 year 3	June 30 year 3	91		95.87
July 1 year 3	Sept 30 year 3	92		95.81
Oct 1 year 3	Dec 31 year 3	92		95.65

a. Compute the floating-rate payments for each period.
b. Compute the forward discount factor for each period.
c. Compute the fixed-rate payments for each period.
d. Compute the present value of the floating-rate payments and the present value of the fixed-rate payments.
e. What is the value of the swap for the fixed-rate payer?
f. What is the value of the swap for the fixed-rate receiver?

The same valuation principle applies to more complicated swaps. For example, there are swaps whose notional amount changes in a predetermined way over the life of the swap. These include amortizing swaps, accreting swaps, and roller coaster swaps. Once the payments are specified, the present value is calculated as described above by simply adjusting the payment amounts by the changing notional amounts — the methodology does *not* change.

SECTION IV
OPTIONS

An option grants the buyer of the option the right, but not the obligation, to purchase from or sell to the contract writer something (the underlying) at a specified price (the strike price) within a specified period of time (or at a specified date). The compensation that the option buyer pays to acquire the option from the writer is the **option price**. (The option price is also referred to as the **option premium**.) A call option grants the buyer the right to purchase the underlying from the writer (seller); a put option gives the buyer the right to sell the underlying to the writer. An American option allows the buyer to exercise the option at any time up to and including the expiration date. A European option only allows the buyer to exercise the option at the expiration date.

The maximum amount that an option buyer can lose is the option price. The maximum profit that the option writer can realize is the option price. The option buyer has substantial upside return potential, while the option writer has substantial downside risk.

A. Components of the Option Price

The option price can be decomposed into two parts. The intrinsic value and the time value. We describe each below.

1. Intrinsic Value

The option value is a reflection of the option's intrinsic value and any additional amount over its intrinsic value. The **intrinsic value** of an option is its economic value if it is exercised immediately. If no positive economic value would result from exercising the option immediately, then the intrinsic value is zero.

For a call option, the intrinsic value is positive if the current price of the underlying security is greater than the strike price. The intrinsic value is then the difference between the current price of the underlying security and the strike price. If the strike price of a call option is greater than or equal to the current price of the security, the intrinsic value is zero. For example, if the strike price for a call option is 100 and the current price for the security is 105, the intrinsic value is 5. That is, an option buyer exercising the option and simultaneously selling the underlying security would realize 105 from the sale of the security, which would be covered by acquiring the security from the option writer for $100, thereby netting a $5 gain.

When an option has intrinsic value, it is said to be **in the money**. When the strike price of a call option exceeds the current price of the security, the call option is said to be **out of the money**; it has no intrinsic value. An option for which the strike price is equal to the current price of the security is said to be **at the money**. Both at-the-money and out-of-the-money options have an intrinsic value of zero because they are not profitable to exercise.

For a put option, the intrinsic value is equal to the amount by which the current price of the security is below the strike price. For example, if the strike price of a put option is 100 and the current price of the security is 92, the intrinsic value is 8. The buyer of the put option who exercises and simultaneously buys the underlying security will net 8 by exercising this option since the security will be sold to the writer for 100 and purchased in the market for 92. The intrinsic value is zero if the strike price is less than or equal to the current market price.

For our put option with a strike price of 100, the option would be: (1) in the money when the security's price is less than 100, (2) out of the money when the security's price exceeds 100, and (3) at the money when the security's price is equal to $100.

The relationships above are summarized in Exhibit 11.

2. Time Value

The **time value** of an option is the amount by which the option price exceeds its intrinsic value. The option buyer hopes that at some time up to the expiration date, changes in the market price of the underlying security will increase the value of the rights conveyed by the option. For this prospect, the option buyer is willing to pay a premium above the intrinsic value.

Exhibit 11: Relationship Between Security Price, Strike Price, and Intrinsic Value

If Security price > Strike price	Call Option	Put Option
Intrinsic value	Security price − Strike price	Zero
Jargon	In-the-money	Out-of-the-money
If Security price < Strike price	Call Option	Put Option
Intrinsic value	Zero	Strike price − Security price
Jargon	Out-of-the-money	In-the-money
If Security price = Strike price	Call Option	Put Option
Intrinsic value	Zero	Zero
Jargon	At-the-money	At-the-money

Exhibit 12: Summary of Factors that Affect the Price of an American Option on a Fixed Income Instrument

Factor	General effect of an increase of factor on:	
	Call price	Put price
Price of underlying security	increase	decrease
Strike price	decrease	increase
Time to expiration	increase	increase
Expected interest rate volatility	increase	increase
Short-term risk-free rate	increase	decrease
Coupon payments	decrease	increase

For example, if the price of a call option with a strike price of 100 is 9 when the current price of the security is 105, the time value of this option is 4 (9 minus its intrinsic value of 5). Had the current price of the security been 90 instead of 105, then the time value of this option would be 9 because the option has no intrinsic value.

B. Factors that Influence the Value of an Option on a Fixed Income Instrument

There are six factors that influence the value of an option when the underlying security is a fixed income instrument:

1. price of the underlying security
2. strike price of the option
3. time to expiration of the option
4. expected interest rate volatility over the life of the option
5. short-term risk-free interest rate over the life of the option
6. coupon interest payment over the life of the option

The impact of each of these factors may depend on whether (1) the option is a call or a put, and (2) the option is an American option or a European option. A summary of the effect of each factor on American put and call option prices is presented in Exhibit 12.

1. Price of the Underlying Security

The option price will change as the price of the underlying security changes. For a call option, as the price of the underlying security increases (holding all other factors constant), the option price increases. This is because the intrinsic value of a call option increases when the price of the underlying security increases. The opposite holds for a put option: as the price of the underlying security increases, the price of a put option decreases. This is because the intrinsic value of a put option decreases when the price of the underlying security increases.

2. Strike Price

All other factors equal, the lower the strike price, the higher the price of a call option. For put options, the higher the strike price, the higher the option price.

3. Time to Expiration of the Option

An option is a "wasting asset." That is, after the expiration date passes the option has no value. Holding all other factors equal, the longer the time to expiration of the option, the greater the option price. This is because, as the time to expiration decreases, less time remains for the underlying security's price to rise (for a call buyer) or to fall (for a put buyer) — that is, to compensate the option buyer for any time value paid — and, therefore, the probability of a favorable price movement decreases. Consequently, for American options, as the time remaining until expiration decreases, the option price approaches its intrinsic value.

4. Expected Interest Rate Volatility Over the Life of the Option

All other factors equal, the greater the expected interest rate volatility (as measured by the standard deviation or variance as explained at Level II (Chapter 1), the more an investor would be willing to pay for the option, and the more an option writer would demand for it. This is because the greater the volatility, the greater the probability that the price of the underlying security will move in favor of the option buyer at some time before expiration due to the asymmetry of the payoff to the owner of the option.

5. Short-Term Risk-Free Rate Over the Life of the Option

Buying the underlying security ties up one's money. Buying an option on the same quantity of the underlying security makes the difference between the security price and the option price available for investment at the risk-free rate. All other factors constant, the higher the short-term risk-free rate, the greater the cost of buying the underlying security and carrying it to the expiration date of the call option. Hence, the higher the short-term risk-free rate, the more attractive the call option will be relative to the direct purchase of the underlying security. As a result, the higher the short-term risk-free rate, the greater the price of a call option. In the case of a put option, the alternative to buying a put is shorting the security. When the security is shorted, the proceeds received can be invested at the short-term risk-free rate. When the short-term risk-free rate increases, this makes it more attractive to short the security relative to buying a put option. Consequently, the value of a put option declines when the short-term risk-free rate increases.

6. Coupon Payments Over the Life of the Option

Coupon interest payments on the underlying security tend to decrease the price of a call option because they make it more attractive to hold the underlying security than to hold the option. That is, the owner of the security receives the coupon payments but the buyer of the call option does not. The higher the coupon payment that the owner of the security receives, the more attractive it is to own the security and the less attractive to own the call option. So, the value of a call option declines the higher the coupon payment.

The opposite is true for the put option. For put options, coupon interest payments on the underlying security tend to increase their price. The buyer of a put option compares the position to a short position in the security. When shorting the security, the coupon payment must be paid. So, the higher the coupon payment the less attractive it is to short the security and the more attractive to buy the put option. As a result, the value of a put option increases the higher the coupon payment.

C. Factors that Influence the Value of a Futures Option

There are five factors that influence the value of an option in which the underlying is a futures contract:

1. current futures price
2. strike price of the option
3. time to expiration of the option
4. expected interest rate volatility over the life of the option
5. short-term risk-free rate over the life of the option

These are the same factors that affect the value of an option on a fixed income instrument. Notice that the coupon payment is not a factor since the underlying is a futures contract.

D. Option Pricing Models

At any time, the intrinsic value of an option can be determined. The question is, what is an approximate time value for an option? To answer this question, option pricing models have been developed. Two models used to value options on a fixed income instrument are the Black-Scholes model and the arbitrage-free binomial model. For options on futures, the most popular model is the Black model, a version of the Black-Scholes model.

1. The Black-Scholes Model

The most popular model for the pricing of equity options is the Black-Scholes option pricing model. By imposing certain assumptions and using arbitrage arguments, the Black-Scholes option pricing model computes the fair (or theoretical) price of a European call option on a non-dividend-paying stock.[4] The factors that we explained earlier that determine the value of an option are included in the formula. However, the

---

[4] The Black-Scholes option pricing formula is:

$$C = SN(d_1) - Xe^{-rt}N(d_2)$$

where

$$d_1 = \frac{\ln(S/X) + (r + 0.5s^2)t}{s\sqrt{t}}$$

$$d_2 = d_1 - s\sqrt{t}$$

ln = natural logarithm
C = call option price
S = current stock price
X = strike price
r = short-term risk-free interest rate
e = 2.718 (natural antilog of 1)
t = time remaining to the expiration date (measured as a fraction of a year)
s = standard deviation of the stock price
$N(.)$ = the cumulative probability density. The value for N(.) is obtained from a normal distribution function.

sixth factor, cash payments (coupon interest in the case of a bond), is not included because the model is for a non-dividend-paying stock. The standard deviation of the stock price must be estimated.

The option price derived from the Black-Scholes option pricing model is "fair" in the sense that if any other price existed, it would be possible to earn riskless arbitrage profits by taking an offsetting position in the underlying stock. That is, if the price of the call option in the market is higher than that derived from the Black-Scholes option pricing model, an investor could sell the call option and buy a certain number of shares in the underlying stock. If the reverse is true, that is, the market price of the call option is less than the "fair" price derived from the model, the investor could buy the call option and sell short a certain number of shares in the underlying stock. This process of hedging by taking a position in the underlying stock allows the investor to lock in the riskless arbitrage profit. The number of shares necessary to hedge the position changes as the factors that affect the option price change, so the hedged position must be changed constantly.

Because the basic Black-Scholes formula is for a non-cash paying security, let's apply it to a zero-coupon bond with three years to maturity. Assume the following values:

> Strike price = $88.00
> Time remaining to expiration = 2 years
> Current bond price = $83.96 (assuming for simplicity annual compounding)
> Expected price volatility = standard deviation = 10%
> Risk-free rate = 6%

The Black-Scholes formula would give a value of $8.116.[5] There is no reason to suspect that this estimated value is unreasonable. However, let's change the problem slightly. Instead of a strike price of $88, let's make the strike price $100.25.[6] The Black-Scholes option pricing model would give a fair value of $2.79. Is there any reason to believe this is unreasonable? Well, consider that this is a call option on a zero-coupon bond that will never have a value greater than its maturity value of $100. Consequently, a call option with a strike price of $100.25 must have a value of zero. Yet, the Black-

---

[5] The value is derived as follows. The current price of $83.96 is the present value of the maturity value of $100 discounted at 6% (assuming a flat yield curve). We know

$$S = 83.96 \quad X = 88.00 \quad t = 2 \quad s = 0.10 \quad r = 0.06$$

Substituting these values into the formula in the previous footnote:

$$d_1 = \frac{\ln(83.96/88) + (0.06 + 0.5(0.10)^2)2}{0.10\sqrt{2}} = 0.5869$$

$$d_2 = 0.5869 - 0.10\sqrt{2} = 0.4455$$

From a normal distribution table it can be determined that $N(0.5869) = 0.7214$ and $N(0.4455) = 0.6720$. Then

$$C = 83.96(0.7214) - 88[e^{-(0.06)(2)}(0.6720)] = \$8.116.$$

[6] Substituting the new strike price, we get

$$d_1 = \frac{\ln(83.96/100.25) + (0.06 + 0.5(0.10)^2)2}{0.10\sqrt{2}} = -0.3346$$

$$d_2 = -0.3346 - 0.10\sqrt{2} = -0.4761$$

From a normal distribution table $N(-0.3346) = 0.3689$ and $N(-0.4761) = 0.3170$. Then

$$C = 83.96(0.3689) - 100.25[e^{-(0.06)(2)}(0.3170)] = \$2.79.$$

Scholes option pricing model tells us that the value is $2.79! In fact, with a higher volatility assumption, the model would give an even greater value for the call option.

Why is the Black-Scholes model off by so much in our illustration? The answer lies in its underlying assumptions. There are three assumptions underlying the Black-Scholes model that limit its use in pricing options on fixed income instruments.

The first assumption is that the probability distribution for the prices assumed by the Black-Scholes model permits some probability — no matter how small — that the price can take on any positive value. But in the case of a zero-coupon bond, the price cannot take on a value above $100. In the case of a coupon bond, we know that the price cannot exceed the sum of the coupon payments plus the maturity value. For example, for a 5-year 10% coupon bond with a maturity value of $100, the price cannot be greater than $150 (five coupon payments of $10 plus the maturity value of $100). Thus, unlike stock prices, bond prices have a maximum value. The only way that a bond's price can exceed the maximum value is if negative interest rates are permitted. This is not likely to occur, so any probability distribution for prices assumed by an option pricing model that permits bond prices to be higher than the maximum bond value could generate nonsensical option prices. The Black-Scholes model does allow bond prices to exceed the maximum bond value (or, equivalently, allows negative interest rates).

The second assumption of the Black-Scholes model is that the short-term interest rate is constant over the life of the option. Yet the price of an interest rate option will change as interest rates change. A change in the short-term interest rate changes the rates along the yield curve. Therefore, to assume that the short-term rate will be constant is inappropriate for interest rate options. The third assumption is that the variance of prices is constant over the life of the option. As a bond moves closer to maturity its price volatility declines. (We discussed this at Level I (Chapter 5) where we demonstrated the "pull to par" characteristic of a bond.) Therefore, the assumption that price variance is constant over the life of the option is inappropriate.[7]

The limitations of the Black-Scholes model to the pricing of options on bonds are summarized below:

Assumptions	Bond Characteristics
1. The price of the underlying has some possibility of rising to any price.	There is a maximum price for a bond and any higher price assumes a negative interest rate is possible.
2. Short-term rates remain constant.	Changes in short-term rates occur which cause bond price to change.
3. Volatility (variance) of price is constant over the life of the option.	Bond price volatility decreases as the bond approaches maturity.

2. Arbitrage-Free Binomial Model

The proper way to value options on bonds is to use an arbitrage-free model that takes into account the yield curve. This model can incorporate different volatility assumptions along the yield curve. The most popular model employed by dealer firms is the Black-Derman-Toy model.[8]

[7] While we have illustrated the problem of using the Black-Scholes model to price interest rate options, it can also be shown that the binomial option pricing model based on the price distribution of the underlying bond suffers from the same problems.

[8] Fischer Black, Emanuel Derman, and William Toy, "A One-Factor Model of Interest Rates and Its Application to Treasury Bond Options," *Financial Analysts Journal* (January-February 1990), pp. 24-32.

Exhibit 13: Valuing a Treasury Bond with Four Years to Maturity and a Coupon Rate of 6.5% (10% Volatility Assumed)

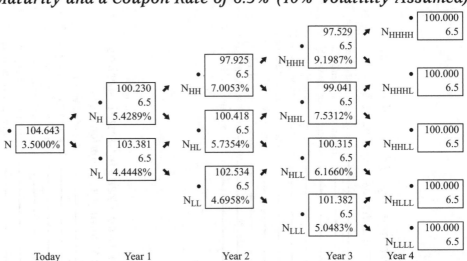

| | Today | Year 1 | Year 2 | Year 3 | Year 4 |

We have already developed the basic principles for employing this model. In Chapter 2, we explained how to construct a binomial interest rate tree such that the tree would be arbitrage free. We used the interest rate tree to value bonds (both option-free and bonds with embedded options). The same tree can be used to value a stand-alone option on a bond.

To illustrate how this is done, let's consider a 2-year American call option on a 6.5% 4-year Treasury bond with a strike price of 100.25. We will assume that the on-the-run Treasury yields are those used in Chapter 2 and that the volatility assumption is 10% per year. Exhibit 6 in Chapter 2, repeated here as Exhibit 13, shows the binomial interest rate tree along with the value of the Treasury bond at each node. It is a portion of Exhibit 13 that we use to value the call option. Specifically, Exhibit 14 shows the value of our hypothetical Treasury bond (excluding coupon interest) at each node at the end of Year 2.

The decision rule at a node for determining the value of an option on a bond is much simpler than for valuing a bond with an embedded option. This is because a complicated rule for the exercise of the option at a node is not required. The rule for determining whether or not an option will be exercised at a node simply depends on whether or not the call or put option being valued is in the money. (Moreover, the exercise decision is only applied at the maturity date.) That is, a call option will be exercised at one of the nodes at the option's maturity date if the bond's price at a node is greater than the strike price (i.e., if the call option is in the money). In the case of a put option, the option will be exercised at one of the nodes at the option's maturity date if the strike price at a node is greater than the bond's price (i.e., if the put option is in the money).

There are three values shown in Exhibit 14: 97.925, 100.418, and 102.534. Given these three values, the value of a call option with a strike price of 100.25 can be determined at each node. For example, if in Year 2 the price of this Treasury bond is 97.925, then since the strike price is 100.25, the value of the call option would be zero. In the other two cases, since the price in Year 2 is greater than the strike price, the value of the call option is the difference between the price of the bond at the node and 100.25.

Exhibit 14: Valuing a European Call Option Using the Arbitrage-Free Binomial Method
Expiration: 2 years; Strike price: 100.25; Current price: 104.643; Volatility assumption: 10%

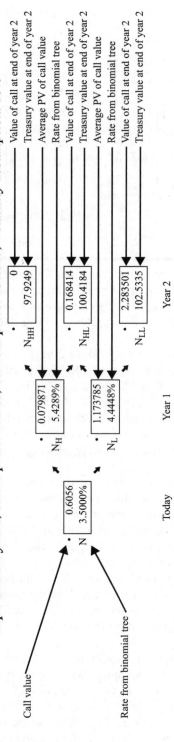

Exhibit 15: Valuing a European Put Option Using the Arbitrage-Free Binomial Method
Expiration: 2 years; Strike price: 100.25; Current price: 104.643; Volatility assumption: 10%

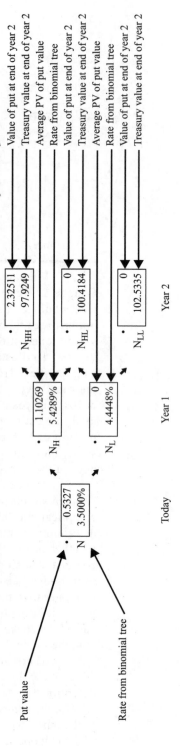

Exhibit 14 shows the value of the call option two years from now (the option expiration date) for each of the three nodes. Given these values, the binomial interest rate tree is used to find the present value of the call option using the backward induction procedure. The discount rates are those from the binomial interest rate tree and are the second number shown at each node. The first number at each node for Year 1 is the average present value found by discounting the call option value of the two nodes to the right using the discount rate at the node. Now let's move back one year to "Today." The value of the option is the first number shown at the root (i.e., today) of the tree, $0.6056.

The same procedure is used to value a put option. This is illustrated in Exhibit 15 assuming that the put option has two years to expiration and that the strike price is 100.25. The value of the put option two years from now is shown at each of the three nodes in Year 2.

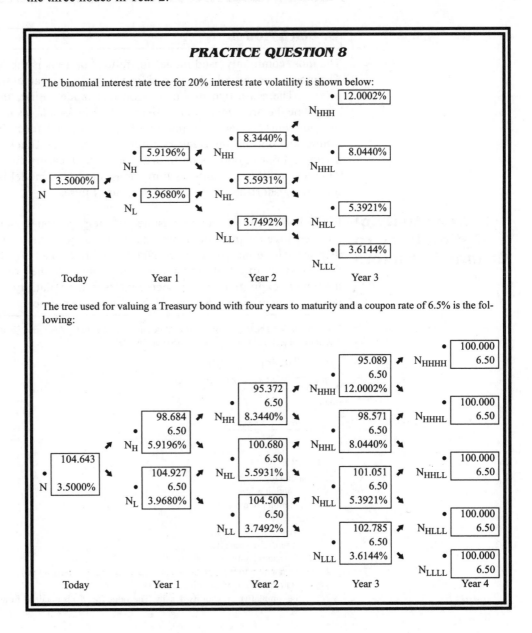

PRACTICE QUESTION 8

The binomial interest rate tree for 20% interest rate volatility is shown below:

The tree used for valuing a Treasury bond with four years to maturity and a coupon rate of 6.5% is the following:

PRACTICE QUESTION 8 (Continued)

a. What is the value of a call option on a 6.5% 4-year Treasury bond with a strike price of 100.25 assuming interest rate volatility of 20%?

b. Compare the value of the call option computed in part a with the value of $0.6056 for an assumed interest rate volatility of 10%. Explain why the value of the call option changed the way it did.

c. What is the value of a put option on a 6.5% 4-year Treasury bond with a strike price of 100.25 assuming interest rate volatility of 20%?

d. Compare the value of the put option computed in part c with the value of $0.5327 for an assumed interest rate volatility of 10%. Explain why the value of the put option changed the way it did.

---

3. Black Model

The most commonly used model for futures options is the one developed by Black.[9] The model was initially developed for valuing European options on forward contracts.

There are two problems with this model. First, the Black model does not overcome the problems cited earlier for the Black-Scholes model. Failing to recognize the yield curve means that there will not be a consistency between pricing Treasury futures and options on Treasury futures. Second, the Black model was developed for pricing European options on futures contracts. Treasury futures options, however, are American options. Despite its limitations, the Black model is the most popular model for pricing short-dated options on Treasury futures.

E. Sensitivity of Option Price to Change in Factors

In employing options in an investment strategy, a money manager would like to know how sensitive the price of an option is to a change in any one of the factors that affects its price. These measures are commonly referred to as the "Greeks." Here we look at the sensitivity of a call option's price to changes in the price of the underlying bond, the time to expiration, and expected interest rate volatility. The same measures apply when the underlying is a Treasury bond futures contract.

---

[9] Fischer Black, "The Pricing of Commodity Contracts," *Journal of Financial Economics* (March 1976), pp. 161-179. The value of a call and put based on the Black model is:

$$C = e^{-rt} [FN(d_1) - XN(d_2)]$$

$$P = e^{-rt} [XN(-d_2) - FN(-d_1)]$$

where

$$d_1 = \frac{\ln(F/X) + 0.5s^2 t}{s\sqrt{t}}$$

$$d_2 = d_1 - s\sqrt{t}$$

ln = natural logarithm
C = call option price
P = put option price
F = futures price
X = strike price
r = short-term risk-free rate
e = 2.718 (natural antilog of 1)
t = time remaining to the expiration date (measured as a fraction of a year)
s = standard deviation of the price
$N(.)$ = the cumulative probability density. The value for $N(.)$ is obtained from a normal distribution function

1. The Call Option Price and the Price of the Underlying Bond

The sensitivity of an option to a change in the price of the underlying bond is called the **delta** of an option. Specifically,

$$\text{delta} = \frac{\text{change in option price}}{\text{change in price of underlying bond}}$$

For a call option, the delta is positive since as we noted earlier, the higher the price of the underlying bond, the higher the option price. For a put option, delta is negative because the higher the price of the underlying bond, the lower the option price.

Let's interpret the delta. Suppose that the delta of a call option is 0.4. This means that if the price of the underlying bond increases by $1, the price of the call option will increase by approximately $0.40. Suppose that the delta of a put option is −0.2. This means that if the price of the underlying bond increases by $1 the price of the put option will decrease by approximately $0.20. The delta of an option changes as the price of the underlying moves closer to or away from the strike price.

For an option that is deep out of the money, the delta is close to 0. For example, consider a call option that expires in one year and has a strike price of $100. Suppose that the current price of the underlying bond is $45. Then an increase in the price of the underlying bond by $1 (from $45 to $46) would not be expected to change the value of the call option.

For an option that is deep in the money, the delta of a call option is close to 1 and the delta of a put option is close to −1. This is because the change in the option's price will closely mirror the change in the price of the underlying bond.

Delta plays the same role in approximating the sensitivity of the option's price to changes in the price of the underlying bond as duration does for measuring the sensitivity of the bond's price to changes in interest rates. In both cases, the changes are approximations. For bonds, the approximation can be improved by using the convexity measure. For an option, the approximation can be improved by calculating the **gamma** of an option. The gamma for an option is:

$$\text{gamma} = \frac{\text{change in delta}}{\text{change in price of underlying bond}}$$

2. The Call Option Price and Time to Expiration

All other factors constant, the longer the time to expiration, the greater the option price. Since each day the option moves closer to the expiration date, the time to expiration decreases. The *theta* of an option measures the change in the option price as the time to expiration decreases, or equivalently, it is a measure of time decay. Theta is measured as follows:

$$\text{theta} = \frac{\text{change in price of option}}{\text{decrease in time to expiration}}$$

Assuming that the price of the underlying bond does not change (which means that the intrinsic value of the option does not change), theta measures how quickly the time value of the option changes as the option moves towards expiration.

Buyers of options prefer a low theta so that the option price does not decline quickly as it moves toward the expiration date. An option writer benefits from an option that has a high theta. This is because a high theta means that as the option moves closer to the expiration date, the option price falls faster than an option with a low theta. The option writer wants the option price to fall quickly as the option moves toward the expiration date because the option then can be bought back at a lower price.

3. The Call Option Price and Expected Interest Rate Volatility

All other factors constant, a change in the expected interest rate volatility will change the option price. The **kappa** of an option measures the change in the price of the option for a 1% change in expected interest rate volatility. (An option's kappa is also referred to as its **vega**.) That is,

$$kappa = \frac{change\ in\ option\ price}{1\%\ change\ in\ expected\ interest\ rate\ volatility}$$

The kappa of an option is positive because, as explained earlier, the option price increases when expected interest rate volatility increases.

SECTION V CAPS AND FLOORS

The arbitrage-free binomial model can also be used to value a cap and a floor. We saw how the backward induction methodology can be used to value a bond with an embedded option in Chapter 2. We also saw that the backward induction methodology can be used to value an option on a bond. However, the methodology is easier to use to value an option on a bond because the decision to exercise at a node is simple, requiring only that the option at each of the nodes at the maturity date be in the money. As will be seen, the same is true in applying the backward induction methodology to valuing caps and floors. The decision to exercise at a node will depend on whether or not the cap or the floor is in the money.

Remember that a cap and a floor are nothing more than a package or strip of options. More specifically, they are a strip of European options on interest rates. Thus, to value a cap, the value of each period's cap, called a **caplet**, is found and all the caplets are then summed. The same can be done for a floor.

To illustrate how this is done, we will once again use the binomial tree given in Exhibit 6 of Chapter 2. Consider first a 5.2% 3-year cap with a notional amount of $10 million. The reference rate is the 1-year rates in the binomial tree. The payoff for the cap is annual.

Exhibits 16a, 16b, and 16c show how this cap is valued by valuing the three caplets. The value for the caplet for any year, say Year X, is found as follows. First, calculate the payoff in Year X at each node as either:[10]

1. zero if the 1-year rate at the node is less than or equal to 5.2%, or

2. the notional principal amount of $10 million times the difference between the 1-year rate at the node and 5.2% if the 1-year rate at the node is greater than 5.2%.

Then, the backward induction method is used to determine the value of the Year X caplet.

For example, consider the Year 3 caplet. At the top node in Year 3 of Exhibit 16c, the 1-year rate is 9.1987%. Since the 1-year rate at this node exceeds 5.2%, the payoff in Year 3 is:

$$\$10,000,000 \times (0.091987 - 0.052) = \$399,870$$

---

[10] Mathematically, the decision at a node is expressed as follows:

$10,000,000 \times$ Maximum [(Rate at node $-$ 5.2%), 0]

Exhibit 16: Valuation of a 3-Year 5.2% Cap
(10% Volatility Assumed)

Assumptions
Cap rate: 5.2%
Notional amount: $10,000,000
Payment frequency: Annual

Panel A: The Value of the Year 1 Caplet

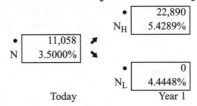

Value of Year 1 caplet = $11,058

Panel B: The Value of the Year 2 Caplet

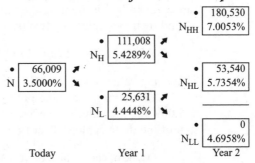

Value of Year 2 caplet = $66,009

Panel C: The Value of the Year 3 Caplet

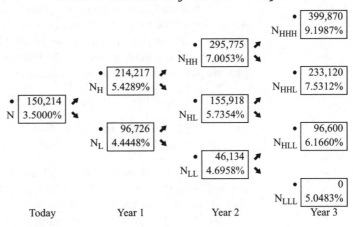

Value of Year 3 caplet = $150,214

Summary: Value of 3-Year Cap = $11,058 + $66,009 + $150,214 = $227,281
Note on calculations: Payoff in last box of each exhibit is

$$\$10,000,000 \times \text{Maximum}[(\text{Rate at node} - 5.2\%, 0)]$$

Let's show how the values shown at the nodes N_{HH}, N_H, and the root of the tree, N, are determined. For node N_{HH} we look at the value for the cap at the two nodes to its right, N_{HHH} and N_{HHL}. The backward induction method involves discounting the values at these nodes, \$399,870 and \$233,120, by the interest rate from the binomial tree at node N_{HH}, 7.0053%, and computing the average present value. That is,

Value at N_{HH} = [\$399,870/(1.070053) + \$233,120/(1.070053)]/2 = \$295,775

This is the value reported at N_{HH}.

Now let's see how the value at node N_H is determined. Using the backward induction method, the values at nodes N_{HH} and N_{HL} are discounted at the interest rate from the binomial tree at node N_H, 5.4289%, and then the present value is averaged. That is,

Value at N_H =   [\$295,775/(1.054289) + \$155,918/(1.054289)]/2 = \$214,217

This is the value reported at N_H.

Finally, we get the value at the root, node N, which is the value of the Year 3 caplet found by discounting the value at N_H and N_L by 3.5% (the interest rate at node N) and then averaging the two present values. Doing so gives:

Value at N =   [\$214,217/(1.035) + \$96,726/(1.035)]/2 = \$150,214

This is the value reported at N.

Following the same procedure, the value of the Year 2 caplet is found to be \$66,009 and the value of the Year 1 caplet is \$11,058. The value of the cap is then the sum of the three caplets. That is,

value of cap = value of Year 1 caplet + value of Year 2 caplet + value of Year 3 caplet

Thus, the value of the cap is \$227,281, found by adding \$11,058, \$66,009, and \$150,214.

Similarly, an interest rate floor can be valued. Exhibit 17 shows how for a 4.8% 3-year floor with a notional amount of \$10 million. Again, the reference rate is the 1-year rate in the binomial tree and the payoff for the floor is annual. The value for the floor for any year, called a **floorlet**, say Year X, is found as follows. First, calculate the payoff in Year X at each node as either[11]

1. zero if the 1-year rate at the node is greater than or equal to 4.8%, or

2. the notional amount of \$10 million times the difference between 4.8% and the 1-year rate at the node if the 1-year rate at the node is less than 4.8%.

Let's see how the Year 2 floorlet is determined using the backward induction method. Specifically, we will see how to get the values at nodes N_{LL}, N_L, and N (the root of the tree and the value of the Year 2 floorlet). Look first at N_{LL}. Since the rate of 4.6958% is less than the floor rate of 4.8%, there is a payoff equal to

\$10,000,000 × (0.048 − 0.046958) = \$10,420

---

[11] Mathematically, the decision to exercise at a node is expressed as follows:

\$10,000,000 × Maximum [(4.8% − Rate at node), 0]

Exhibit 17: Valuation of a 3-Year 4.8% Floor
(10% Volatility Assumed)

Assumptions
Floor rate: 4.8%
Notional amount: $10,000,000
Payment frequency: Annual

Panel A: The Value of the Year 1 Floorlet

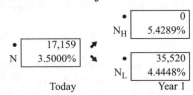

Value of Year 1 floorlet = $17,159

Panel B: The Value of the Year 2 Floorlet

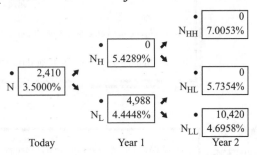

Value of Year 2 floorlet = $2,410

Panel C: The Value of the Year 3 Floorlet

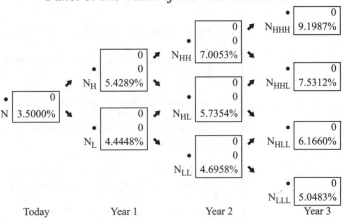

Value of Year 3 floorlet = $0

Summary: Value of 3-Year Floor = $17,159 + $2,410 + $0 = $19,569
Note on calculations: Payoff in last box of each exhibit is

$10,000,000 × Maximum[(4.8% – Rate at node), 0]

This is the value shown at node N_{LL}. Now we use the backward induction method to get the value at N_L. We use the values at N_{LL} and N_{HL} to get the value at N_L. The two values are discounted at 4.4448% (the interest rate at node N_L) and then averaged. That is,

$$\text{Value at } N_L = [0/(1.044448) + \$10,420/(1.044448)]/2 = \$4,988$$

This is the value reported at N_L.

Finally, we get the value for the Year 2 floorlet by discounting the value at N_H and N_L at 3.5% and then averaging, as shown below:

$$\text{Value at } N = [0/(1.035) + \$4,988/(1.035)]/2 = \$2,410$$

This is the value shown at the root of the tree and is the value of the Year 2 floorlet.

Adding the Year 1 floorlet, Year 2 floorlet, and Year 3 floorlet shown in Exhibit 17 gives the value of the 3-year floor: $17,159 + \$2,410 + \$0 = \$19,569$.

PRACTICE QUESTION 9

a. Recompute the value of the cap if the strike rate is 5.6%.

b. Recompute the value of the floor if the strike rate is 5%.

SECTION VI
KEY POINTS

❑ *A cash and carry trade and a reverse cash and carry trade can be used to determine the arbitrage profit available in a futures strategy.*

❑ *A cash and carry trade and a reverse cash and carry trade can be used to determine the theoretical price of a futures contract.*

❑ *The theoretical price of a futures contract is equal to the cash or spot price plus the cost of carry.*

❑ *The cost of carry is equal to the cost of financing the position less the cash yield on the underlying security.*

❑ *The shape of the yield curve affects the cost of carry.*

❑ *The "cash and carry" arbitrage model must be modified to take into consideration the nuances of particular futures contracts.*

❑ *For a Treasury bond futures contract, the delivery options granted to the seller reduce the theoretical futures price below the theoretical futures price suggested by the "cash and carry" arbitrage model.*

❑ *To compute the payments for both parties to an interest rate swap, the number of days in the payment period must be determined.*

❑ *The first floating-rate swap payment is determined by the current value of the reference rate.*

❑ *In a swap where the reference rate is 3-month LIBOR, the Eurodollar CD futures contract provides the forward rate for locking in future floating-rate payments, as well as the forward rates that should be used for discounting all swap payments.*

❏ *In determining the present value of swap payments care must be exercised in determining exactly when the payments will occur.*

❏ *The forward rates obtained from Eurodollar CD futures contracts are used to compute the forward discount factor.*

❏ *The forward discount factor for a period multiplied by the swap payment for a period determines the present value of the swap payment.*

❏ *At the inception of a swap, the present value of the floating-rate payments must equal the present value of the fixed-rate payments to prevent arbitrage.*

❏ *The swap rate is the rate that will produce fixed-rate payments such that the present value of these payments is equal to the present value of the floating-rate payments.*

❏ *The swap spread is the difference between the swap rate and the rate on some benchmark rate selected.*

❏ *When interest rates change in the market, the future floating-rate payments will change, but the fixed-rate payments do not change.*

❏ *When interest rates change in the market, the forward rates change and therefore the present value of the swap payments change.*

❏ *The value of a swap is the difference in the present value of the swap payments for a party to a swap — that is, the difference between the present value of the payments to be received and the present value of the payments to be paid.*

❏ *The value of an option is composed of its intrinsic value and its time value.*

❏ *The six factors that affect the value of an option are the price of the underlying security, the strike price, the time to expiration of the option, the expected interest rate volatility over the life of the option, the short-term risk-free interest rate over the life of the option, and the coupon interest payment over the life of the option.*

❏ *Several assumptions underlying the Black-Scholes model limit its use in pricing options on bonds.*

❏ *The arbitrage-free binomial model is the proper model to value options on bonds since it takes into account the yield curve.*

❏ *The most popular option pricing model for bonds is the Black-Derman-Toy model.*

❏ *The Black model is the most popular model for valuing options on bond futures.*

❏ *Money managers need to know how sensitive an option's value is to changes in the factors that affect the value of an option.*

❏ *The delta of an option measures how sensitive the option price is to changes in the price of the underlying bond and varies from zero (for call options deep out of the money) to one (for call options deep in the money).*

❏ *The gamma of an option measures the rate of change of delta as the price of the underlying bond changes.*

❏ *The theta of an option measures the change in the option price as the time to expiration decreases.*

❑ *The kappa of an option measures the change in the price of the option for a 1% change in expected interest rate volatility.*

❑ *The arbitrage binomial method can be used to value a cap or a floor.*

❑ *The valuation of a cap (floor) involves first determining the value of each caplet (floorlet).*

❑ *The value of a cap (or floor) is the sum of the value of all the caplets (floorlets).*

END OF CHAPTER QUESTIONS

1. a. Suppose that the price of a bond futures contract that settles in four months is $101 and the price of the underlying bond is $98. The underlying bond has a coupon rate of 9% and its par value is $100 with the next coupon payment to be paid in six months. The borrowing rate is 7.2% per annum. If an investor implemented a cash and carry trade, what would the arbitrage profit be?

   b. Suppose that instead of a futures price of $101, the futures price is $96. If an investor implemented a reverse cash and carry trade, what would the arbitrage profit be?

   c. What is the theoretical futures price?

   d. Demonstrate using a cash and carry trade that the theoretical futures price computed in part c will produce no arbitrage profit.

2. a. Suppose that the underlying bond for a futures contract has a coupon rate of 6% and its par value is $100 with the next coupon payment to be paid in six months. Suppose further that the cash market price for this bond is 94. What is the theoretical futures price for a contract that settles in five months if the borrowing rate is 4.6% per annum?

   b. Suppose that the futures price is 93.25. Given your answer to a, is there an arbitrage opportunity and, if so, what strategy will generate that arbitrage profit?

   c. Suppose that instead of a single financing rate of 4.6%, there is a borrowing rate of 4.7% and a lending rate of 4.3%. If the future price is 93.25, is there an arbitrage opportunity available?

3. Explain what the effect of delivery options for the Treasury bond futures contract are on its theoretical futures price and why.

4. Mr. Robert Thompson is an investment manager. Recently, he attended a conference on opportunities in futures markets. Based on the information presented at the conference, he believes that he can enhance returns by exploiting mispriced Treasury bond futures contracts. He saw how a mispriced futures contracts can be exploited to lock in an arbitrage profit by either a cash and carry trade or a reverse cash and carry trade.

   According to the material distributed at the conference, the theoretical price of a futures contract is determined by the cash market price and the cost of carry. Material distributed at the conference provided a general formula for the theoretical price of any futures contract (e.g., stock index futures contracts, foreign exchange futures contracts, commodity futures contracts). When Mr. Thompson applied the general formula for the theoretical futures price to the Treasury bond futures contract he found that the price of the futures contract in the market was always above that of the theoretical futures price given by the general formula. Based on this observation, Mr. Thompson told his clients that there was ample mispricing in the Treasury bond futures market and requested that they give him authorization to trade Treasury bond futures contracts to enhance portfolio returns.

   Do you believe that Mr. Thompson can exploit arbitrage opportunities based on his observation of the mispricing of the Treasury bond futures contract?

5. Consider the following interest rate swap:

- a swap starts today, January 1 of year 1(swap settlement date)
- the floating-rate payments are made quarterly based on "actual/360"
- the reference rate is 3-month LIBOR
- the notional amount of the swap is $40 million
- the term of the swap is three years

a. Suppose that today 3-month LIBOR is 5.7%. What will the fixed-rate payer for this interest rate swap receive on March 31 of year 1 (assuming that year 1 is not a leap year)?

b. Assume the Eurodollar CD futures price for the next seven quarters is as shown below:

Quarter starts	Quarter ends	No. of days in quarter	Eurodollar CD futures price
April 1 year 1	June 30 year 1	91	94.10
July 1 year 1	Sept 30 year 1	92	94.00
Oct 1 year 1	Dec 31 year 1	92	93.70
Jan 1 year 2	Mar 31 year 1	90	93.60
April 1 year 2	June 30 year 2	91	93.50
July 1 year 2	Sept 30 year 2	92	93.20
Oct 1 year 2	Dec 31 year 2	92	93.00

Compute the forward rate for each quarter and the floating-rate payment at the end of each quarter.

c. What is the floating-rate payment at the end of each quarter for this interest rate swap?

6. a. Assume that the swap rate for an interest rate swap is 7% and that the fixed-rate swap payments are made quarterly on an "actual/360 basis." If the notional amount of a 2-year swap is $20 million, what is the fixed-rate payment at the end of each quarter assuming the following number of days in each quarter:

Period quarter	Days in quarter
1	92
2	92
3	90
4	91
5	92
6	92
7	90
8	91

b. Assume that the swap in part a requires payments semiannually rather than quarterly. What is the semiannual fixed-rate payment every six months?

c. Suppose that the notional amount for the 2-year swap is not the same in both years. Suppose instead that in year 1 the notional amount is $20 million, but in year 2 the notional amount is $12 million. What is the fixed-rate payment every six months?

7. Given the current 3-month LIBOR and the five CD Eurodollar CD futures prices shown in the table below, compute the forward rate and the forward discount factor are each period.

Period	Days in quarter	Current 3-month LIBOR	Eurodollar CD futures price
1	90	5.90%	
2	91		93.90
3	92		93.70
4	92		93.45
5	90		93.20
6	91		93.15

8. a. Suppose at the inception of a 5-year interest rate swap in which the reference rate is 3-month LIBOR the present value of the floating-rate payments is $16,555,000. The fixed-rate payments are assumed to be semiannual. Assume also that the following is computed for the fixed-rate payments (using the notation in the chapter):

$$\sum_{t=1}^{10} \text{notional amount} \times SR \times \frac{\text{Days}_t}{360} \times \text{FDF}_t = \$236,500,000$$

What is the swap rate for this swap?

b. Suppose that the 5-year yield from the on-the-run Treasury yield curve is 6.4%. What is the swap spread?

9. An interest rate swap had an original maturity of five years. Today, the swap has two years to maturity. The present value of the fixed-rate payments for the remainder of the term of the swap is $910,000. The present value of the floating-rate payments for the remainder of the swap is $710,000.

a. What is the value of this swap from the perspective of the fixed-rate payer?
b. What is the value of this swap from the perspective of the fixed-rate receiver?

10. Suppose that an interest rate swap has one year remaining. The notional amount of the swap is $50 million and all payments (fixed rate and floating rate) are quarterly based on an "actual/360" day count basis. The reference rate is 3-month LIBOR.

a. Complete the following table for the forward rate, period forward rate, and forward discount factor given the information below:

Period	Days in quarter	Current 3-month LIBOR	Eurodollar CD futures price	Forward rate	Period forward rate	Forward discount factor
1	90	5.90%				
2	91		93.90			
3	92		93.70			
4	92		93.45			

b. Complete the following table for the floating-rate payment given the period forward rate in part a:

Period	Days in quarter	Period forward rate	Floating-rate payment
1	90		
2	91		
3	92		
4	92		

c. If the swap rate is 8%, compute the following:

Period	Days in quarter	Fixed-rate payment based on swap rate
1	90	
2	91	
3	92	
4	92	

d. What is the value of this 1-year swap given the values computed in parts a, b, and c from the perspective of the fixed-rate payer?

e. What is the value of this 1-year swap given the values computed in parts a, b, and c from the perspective of the fixed-rate receiver?

11. Complete the table below for the six options specified in the first column. Assume that the bond's price in the third column means the price of the underlying bond and that each option expires in one year:

Type of option	Strike price	Bond's price	Option price	In, at, or out of the money	Intrinsic value	Time value
call	94	90	7			
call	102	104	6			
call	88	88	3			
put	106	110	5			
put	92	92	9			
put	95	89	11			

12. After a period of extreme interest rate volatility that saw interest rates increase, an investor observed that the price of both put and call options increased even though bond prices decreased. The investor was confused because he thought that a rise in rates resulting in a decline in the price of a bond would adversely affect the price of call options, not increase their price. Explain to this investor why the call options increased in price.

13. Herman Mills is a bond portfolio manager who is just learning about options on bonds. In college, he did learn about options on common stock where he was introduced to the Black-Scholes option pricing model. Mr. Mills has asked you whether or not it is appropriate to apply the Black-Scholes option pricing model to valuing options on bonds. What is your response to him?

14. Use the following arbitrage-free binomial interest rate tree to answer the questions that follow:

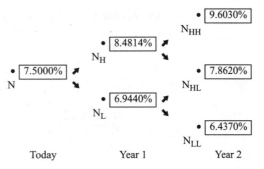

a. What is the value of a 3-year Treasury bond with a 9% coupon rate?

b. What is the value of a 2-year call option on a 3-year Treasury bond with a coupon rate of 9% if the strike price is 98? Assume in this calculation that the current price of the 3-year Treasury bond is the value found in part a.

c. What is the value of a 2-year put option on a 3-year Treasury bond with a coupon rate of 9% if the strike price is 105? Assume in this calculation that the current price of the 3-year Treasury bond is the value found in part a.

15. a. What is the most popular model for valuing options on Treasury bond futures contracts?

b. What are the limitations of this model?

16. Assume the following:

Price of a call option	=	$1.70
Price of underlying bond	=	70
Strike price for call option	=	115
Time to expiration	=	2 years

Without doing any calculations, explain what you believe the value of the delta of this call option is?

17. The duration and convexity measure of a bond are used to approximate the change in the price of a bond if interest rates change. What two measures play a similar role in trying to estimate the price of an option if the price of the underlying bond changes?

18. a. Would the buyer of an option prefer a high or low theta?

b. If an investor anticipates a rise in expected interest rate volatility that is currently not priced into an option, would this investor prefer an option on a bond with a high or low kappa?

19. Answer the following questions based on the following binomial interest rate tree:

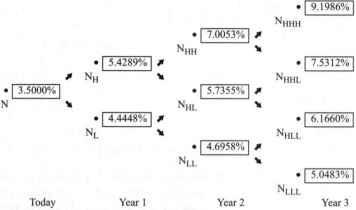

Consider a 3-year cap with a cap rate of 4% and the payoff for the cap is annual. Suppose that the notional amount of the cap is $25 million.

    a. What is the value of the Year 1 caplet?
    b. What is the value of the Year 2 caplet?
    c. What is the value of the Year 3 caplet?
    d. What is the value of the 3-year cap?

20. Using the same binomial interest rate tree in the previous question, answer the following questions for a 3-year floor with a floor rate of 5.5% where the payoff is annual. Assume that the notional amount of the floor is $50 million.

    a. What is the value of the Year 1 floorlet?
    b. What is the value of the Year 2 flooret?
    c. What is the value of the Year 3 floorlet?
    d. What is the value of the 3-year floor?

SOLUTIONS TO END OF CHAPTER QUESTIONS

1. a. The cash and carry trade would involve the following:

> Sell the futures contract that settles in four months at $101.
> Borrow $98 for four months at 7.2% per year.
> With the funds borrowed purchase the underlying bond for the futures contract.

Ignoring initial margin and other transaction costs, the borrowed funds are used to purchase the bond, resulting in no cash outlay for this strategy. Four months from now, the following must be done:

> Deliver the bond purchased to settle the futures contract.
> Repay the loan.

When the bond is delivered to settle the futures contract four months from now, the amount received is the futures price of $101 plus the accrued interest. Since the coupon rate is 9% for the bond delivered and the bond is held for four months, the accrued interest is $3 (9% × $100/3). Thus, the amount received is $104 ($101 + $3). The amount that must be paid to repay the loan is the principal borrowed of $98 plus interest cost. Since the interest rate for the loan is 7.2% and the loan is for four months, the interest cost is $2.35. Thus, the amount paid is $100.35 ($98 + $2.35). Therefore,

> Cash inflow from delivery of the bond   = $104.00
> Cash outflow from repayment of the loan =   −$100.35
> Profit   = $ 3.65

Therefore, the arbitrage profit is $3.65.

b. The reverse cash and carry trade would involve the following:

> Buy the futures contract that settles in four months at $96
> Sell (short) the bond underlying the futures contract for $98.
> Invest (lend) the proceeds from the short sale of $98 for four months at 7.2% per year.

Once again, there is no cash outlay if we ignore the initial margin for the futures contract and other transaction costs. Four months from now when the futures contract must be settled, the following must be done:

> Purchase the underlying bond to settle the futures contract.
> Receive proceeds from repayment of the funds lent.

When the bond is delivered to settle the futures contract four months from now, the amount that must be paid is $99 (the futures price of $96 plus the accrued interest of $3.00). The amount that will be received from the proceeds lent for four months is $100.35. Therefore, at the end of four months the following will be the cash flow:

> Cash inflow from the amount invested (lent) = $100.35
> Cash outflow to purchase the bond   =   −$ 99.00
> Profit   = $ 1.35

An arbitrage profit of $1.35 will be realized.

c. The inputs for computing the theoretical futures price using the notation in the chapter are:

$$r = 0.072 \qquad P = 98 \qquad t = 4/12 = 1/3$$

The current yield is found by dividing the annual dollar coupon of 9 by the cash market price of the bond (98). Thus,

$$c = 9/98 = 9.18\% = 0.0918$$

$$F = 98 + 98 \times (1/3) \times (0.072 - 0.0918) = 97.35$$

The theoretical futures price is 97.35

d. To demonstrate that 97.35 using the cash and carry trade does not allow an arbitrage profit, the following strategy is employed:

Sell the futures contract that settles in four months at 97.35.
Borrow $98 for four months at 7.2% per year.
With the funds borrowed purchase the underlying bond for the futures contract.

When the bond is delivered to settle the futures contract four months from now, the amount received is the futures price of $97.35 plus accrued interest of $3. Therefore the proceeds received will be $100.35. The amount to repay the loan is $100.35. Therefore, at the end of four months the following will be the cash flow:

Cash inflow from delivery of the bond	=	$100.35
Cash outflow from repayment of the loan	=	−$100.35
Profit	=	0

This demonstrates that if the futures price is 97.35, there is no arbitrage profit.

2. a. The inputs for computing the theoretical futures price using the notation in the chapter are:

$$r = 0.046 \qquad P = 94 \qquad t = 5/12 = 0.41667$$

The current yield is found by dividing the annual dollar coupon of 6 by the cash market price of the bond (94). Thus,

$$c = 6/94 = 6.383\% = 0.06383$$

$$F = 94 + 94 \times (0.41667) \times (0.046 - 0.06383) = 93.30$$

The theoretical futures price is 93.30

b. If the future price is 93.25 and the theoretical futures price is 93.30, then there is an opportunity to generate an arbitrage profit. The futures price is cheap. This means that to capture the arbitrage profit, the futures contract is purchased and the bond is sold. That is, a reverse cash and carry trade should be implemented.

c. If the borrowing rate is 4.7%, then the upper boundary for the theoretical futures price would be:

$$r = 0.047 \qquad c = 0.06383 \qquad P = 94 \qquad t = 0.41667$$

$$F = 94 + 94 \times (0.41667) \times (0.047 - 0.06383) = 93.34$$

The lower boundary for the theoretical futures price would be found using 4.3% for r:

$$F = 94 + 94 \times (0.41667) \times (0.043 - 0.06383) = 93.18$$

The range for the theoretical futures price that would not permit an arbitrage profit are then:

93.18 and 93.34

Since the futures price is 93.25, no arbitrage opportunity is available.

3. The delivery options are granted to the short. These options have a value to a short and are a disadvantage to the long. Consequently, the theoretical futures price is reduced by the estimated value of the delivery options.

4. The general formula for the theoretical price of a futures contract that considers only the cash market price and the cost of carry fails to take into consideration the nuances of a Treasury bond futures contract. This includes the delivery options granted to the short which reduce the theoretical futures price below that given by a general formula for any futures contract that considers only the cost of carry. If the general formula is used for Treasury bond futures contracts, the theoretical price derived will be greater than the theoretical futures price after correctly adjusting for the delivery options. Consequently, Mr. Thompson's observation that there is mispricing is incorrect and it is questionable whether he will be able to identify and exploit any opportunities to enhance portfolio return.

5. a. The fixed-rate payer will receive:

$$\text{notional amount} \times (\text{3-month LIBOR}) \times \frac{\text{no. of days in period}}{360}$$

The number of days from January 1 of year 1 to March 31 of year 1 is 90. If 3-month LIBOR is 5.7%, then the fixed-rate payer will receive a floating-rate payment on March 31 of year 1 equal to:

$$\$40,000,000 \times 0.057 \times \frac{90}{360} = \$570,000$$

b. The forward rate for each quarter and the floating-rate payment are shown below:

Quarter starts	Quarter ends	No. of days in quarter	Eurodollar CD futures price	Forward rate (%)	Floating-rate payment at end of quarter
April 1, 1999	June 30, 1999	91	94.10	5.90	596,556
July 1, 1999	Sept 30, 1999	92	94.00	6.00	613,333
Oct 1, 1999	Dec 31, 1999	92	93.70	6.30	644,000
Jan 1, 2000	Mar 31, 2000	90	93.60	6.40	640,000
April 1, 2000	June 30, 2000	91	93.50	6.50	657,222
July 1, 2000	Sept 30, 2000	92	93.20	6.80	695,111
Oct 1, 2000	Dec 31, 2000	92	93.00	7.00	715,556

c. The floating-rate swap payment at the end of each quarter is as follows:

Period	Floating-rate payment at end of quarter
1	570,000
2	596,556
3	613,333
4	644,000
5	640,000
6	657,222
7	695,111
8	715,556

6. a. The fixed-rate payment for each quarter is computed as follows:

$$\text{notional amount} \times (\text{swap rate}) \times \frac{\text{no. of days in period}}{360}$$

Since the swap rate is 7% and the notional amount is $20 million

$$\$20,000,000 \times (0.07) \times \frac{\text{no. of days in period}}{360}$$

For each of the eight quarters the fixed-rate payment is:

Period quarter	Days in quarter	Notional amount	Fixed-rate payment
1	92	20,000,000	357,778
2	92	20,000,000	357,778
3	90	20,000,000	350,000
4	91	20,000,000	353,889
5	92	20,000,000	357,778
6	92	20,000,000	357,778
7	90	20,000,000	350,000
8	91	20,000,000	353,889

b. When payments are made semiannually rather than quarterly, the number of days in the two quarters comprising the 6-month period is determined and the same formula is applied to determine the fixed-rate payment. The semiannual fixed-rate payments for the four 6-month periods are shown below:

Period quarter	Days in period	Notional amount	Fixed-rate payment
1			
2	184	20,000,000	715,556
3			
4	181	20,000,000	703,889
5			
6	184	20,000,000	715,556
7			
8	181	20,000,000	703,889

c. The semiannual fixed-rate payment every six months is:

Period quarter	Days in period	Notional amount	Fixed-rate payment
1			
2	184	20,000,000	715,556
3			
4	181	20,000,000	703,889
5			
6	184	12,000,000	429,333
7			
8	181	12,000,000	422,333

7. The period forward rate is computed as follows:

$$\text{period forward rate} = \text{annual forward rate} \times \left(\frac{\text{days in period}}{360}\right)$$

The forward discount factor for period t is computed as follows:

$$\frac{\$1}{(1 + \text{forward rate for period 1})(1 + \text{forward rate for period 2})\cdots(1 + \text{forward rate for period } t)}$$

Applying the above formulas to current 3-month LIBOR and the forward rates obtained from the Eurodollar CD futures contract, we would find:

Period	Days in quarter	Current 3-month LIBOR (%)	Eurodollar CD futures price	Forward rate (%)	Period forward rate (%)	Forward discount factor
1	90	5.90		5.90	1.4750	0.98546440
2	91		93.90	6.10	1.5419	0.97049983
3	92		93.70	6.30	1.6100	0.95512236
4	92		93.45	6.55	1.6739	0.93939789
5	90		93.20	6.80	1.7000	0.92369507
6	91		93.15	6.85	1.7315	0.90797326

8. a. The swap rate is determined as follows:

$$SR = \frac{\text{PV of floating-rate payments}}{\displaystyle\sum_{t=1}^{20} \text{notional amount} \times \frac{\text{Days}_t}{360} \times \text{FDF}_t}$$

Since the present value of the floating-rate payments is equal to $16,555,000 and the denominator of the swap rate formula is $236,500,000, the swap rate is:

$$SR = \frac{\$16,555,000}{\$236,500,000} = 0.07 = 7\%$$

b. The swap spread is the difference between the swap rate of 7% and yield for the maturity from the on-the-run Treasury yield curve with the same maturity as the swap, 6.4% (the 5-year yield). The swap spread is therefore 60 basis points.

9. a. The present value of what the fixed-rate payer must make over the remaining life of the swap is $910,000; however, the floating-rate payments that will be received only has a present value of $710,000. Thus, the fixed-rate payer has a

liability of $200,000. This means that the value of the swap from the perspective of the fixed-rate payer is −$200,000.

b. The present value of what the fixed-rate receiver will receive over the remaining life of the swap is $910,000; the present value of the floating-rate payments that will be paid is $710,000. Therefore, the fixed-rate receiver has an asset with a value of $200,000.

10. a. The answer is the same as for Question 7 for the first four periods.

Period	Days in quarter	Current 3-month LIBOR (%)	Eurodollar CD futures price	Forward rate (%)	Period forward rate (%)	Forward discount factor
1	90	5.90		5.90	1.4750	0.98546440
2	91		93.90	6.10	1.5419	0.97049983
3	92		93.70	6.30	1.6100	0.95512236
4	92		93.45	6.55	1.6739	0.93939789

b.

Period	Days in quarter	Period forward rate (%)	Floating-rate payment
1	90	1.4750	737,500
2	91	1.5419	770,972
3	92	1.6100	805,000
4	92	1.6739	836,944

c.

Period	Days in quarter	Fixed-rate payment based on swap rate
1	90	1,000,000
2	91	1,011,111
3	92	1,022,222
4	92	1,022,222

d. From part a the forward discount factor is determined. From parts b and c the floating-rate and fixed-rate payments, respectively, are determined. Therefore,

Period	Forward discount factor	Floating-rate payment	PV of floating-rate payment	Fixed-rate payment	PV of fixed-rate payment
1	0.98546440	737,500	726,780	1,000,000	985,464
2	0.97049983	770,972	748,228	1,011,111	981,283
3	0.95512236	805,000	768,874	1,022,222	976,347
4	0.93939789	836,944	786,224	1,022,222	960,273
		Total	3,030,106		3,903,368

For fixed rate payer	−873,263
For fixed rate receiver	873,263

For the fixed-rate payer the present value of the payments is $3,903,368. The amount of the payments to be received by the fixed-rate payer (i.e., the present value of the floating-rate payments) is $3,030,106. Therefore, for the fixed-rate payer, the value of the swap is −$873,263.

e. Given the values for the fixed-rate and floating-rate payments in part d, the value of the swap from the perspective of the fixed-rate receiver is $873,263 because the fixed-rate payments to be received have a present value of $3,903,368 and the floating-rate payments to be paid have a present value of $3,030,106.

11.

Type of option	Strike price	Bond's price	Option price	In, at, or out of the money	Intrinsic value	Time value
call	94	90	7	out of the money	0	7
call	102	104	6	in the money	2	4
call	88	88	3	at the money	0	3
put	106	110	5	out of the money	0	5
put	92	92	9	at the money	0	9
put	95	89	11	in the money	6	5

12. While it is true that a rise in interest rates will decrease the price of a call option because the price of the underlying bond decreases, there are other factors that affect the value of a call option. One such factor is expected interest rate volatility — an increase in interest rate volatility increases the value of a call option. In the question it is specified that the increase in interest rates was a result of extreme interest rate volatility. Consequently, the increase in expected interest rate volatility can increase the price of a call option more than a rise in interest rates decreases it.

13. While the Black-Scholes option pricing model is appropriate for valuing options on common stock, the assumptions underlying the model make it less suitable for valuing bonds on options and in some cases may give an option value that makes no economic sense. The three assumptions that do not reflect the realities of bonds are:

   i. There is no restriction on the possible price of a bond when in fact the maximum price is the sum of the undiscounted cash flows.

   ii. Short-term rates are constant when in fact changes in the short-term rate cause bond prices to change and therefore the value of the option to change.

   iii. Price volatility is assumed to be constant when in fact price volatility declines as a bond moves toward maturity.

14. a. The value of the 3-year Treasury bond is 103.373, as shown below:

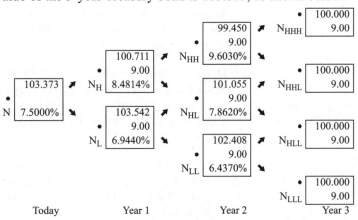

| Today | Year 1 | Year 2 | Year 3 |

b. The current price of the bond is 103.373 as found in part a and the price assumed in the question. The value of the 2-year call option is $2.5886, as shown below:

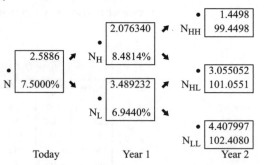

c. Again, it is assumed that the current price is the value found in part a. The value of the put option is $3.4570.

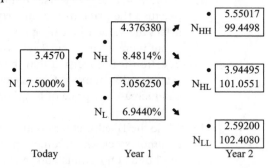

15. a. The most popular model is the Black model that was developed for valuing European options on forward contracts.

b. The Black model does not overcome the problems associated with the Black-Scholes option pricing model. Because it fails to incorporate the yield curve into the model, there will not be a consistency between the pricing of Treasury bond futures and options on Treasury bond futures. The second problem is that the model is for valuing European options, not American options.

16. This call option is deep out of the money — the price of the underlying bond is substantially below the strike price. If the price of the underlying bond increases by $1 to 71, the price of the call option would *not* be expected to change at all. Consequently, the delta is close to zero.

17. Delta measures the sensitivity of an option's price to a change in the price of the underlying bond. This parameter plays the same role as duration. Gamma is used to improve the estimate of the change in the option's price using delta. It plays the same role as the convexity measure for improving the price change estimated using duration.

18. a. Theta measures how quickly the time value of the option changes as the option moves towards expiration. Buyers prefer that the value not decline quickly. Thus, the buyer of an option prefers an option with a low theta rather than a high theta.

b. The kappa of an option on a bond measures the price sensitivity to changes in expected interest rate volatility. An investor who anticipates an increase in interest rate volatility that is not already priced into the option will prefer an option with a high kappa rather than a low kappa.

19. a. The value of the Year 1 caplet is $226,291 as shown below:

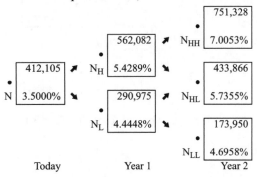

b. The value of the Year 2 caplet is $412,105 as shown below:

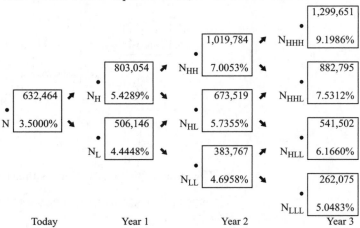

c. The value of the Year 3 caplet is $632,464 as shown below:

d. The value of the 3-year cap is equal to the value of the three caplets:

$226,291 + $412,105 + $632,464 = $1,270,860

20. a. The value of the Year 1 floorlet is $272,055 as shown below:

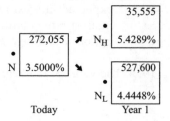

b. The value of the Year 2 floorlet is $92,992 as shown below:

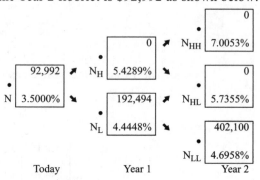

c. The value of the Year 3 floorlet is $24,944 as shown below:

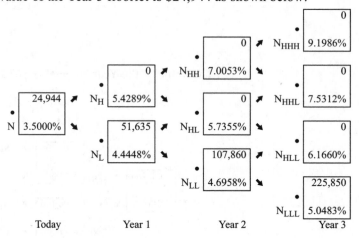

d. The value of the 3-year floor is the sum of the three floorlets:

$272,055 + $92,992 + $24,944 = $389,992

SOLUTIONS TO PRACTICE QUESTIONS

1. a. The cash and carry trade would involve the following:

Sell the futures contract that settles in three months at $93.
Borrow $90 for three months at 8% per year.
With the funds borrowed purchase the underlying bond for the futures contract.

Ignoring initial margin and other transaction costs, the borrowed funds are used to purchase the bond, resulting in no cash outlay for this strategy. Three months from now, the following must be done:

Deliver the bond purchased to settle the futures contract.
Repay the loan.

When the bond is delivered to settle the futures contract three months from now, the amount received is the futures price of $93 plus the accrued interest. Since the coupon rate is 10% for the bond delivered and the bond is held for three months, the accrued interest is $2.50 (10% × $100/4). Thus, the amount received is $95.50 ($93 + $2.50). The amount that must be paid to repay the loan is the principal borrowed of $90 plus the interest. Since the interest rate for the loan is 8% and the loan is for three months, the interest cost is $1.80. Thus, the amount paid is $91.80 ($90 + $1.80). (Notice that interim coupon payments do not occur since it is assumed that the next coupon payment is three months from the time the strategy was implemented.)

To summarize, at the end of three months the following will be the cash flow:

Cash inflow from delivery of the bond   = $95.50
Cash outflow from repayment of the loan   =   −$91.80
Profit   = $ 3.70

Therefore, the arbitrage profit is $3.70.

b. The reverse cash and carry trade would involve the following:

Buy the futures contract that settles in three months at $87.
Sell (short) the bond underlying the futures contract for $90.
Invest (lend) the proceeds from the short sale of $90 for three months at 8% per year.

Once again, there is no cash outlay if we ignore the initial margin for the futures contract and other transaction costs. Three months from now when the futures contract must be settled, the following must be done:

Purchase the underlying bond to settle the futures contract.
Receive proceeds from repayment of the funds lent.

When the bond is delivered to settle the futures contract three months from now, the amount that must be paid is the futures price of $87 plus the accrued interest of $2.50. Thus, the amount paid is $89.50 ($87 + $2.50). The amount that will be received from the proceeds lent for three months is $91.80 which is equal to $90 plus interest of $1.80. To summarize, at the end of three months the following will be the cash flow:

Cash inflow from the amount invested (lent) = $91.80
Cash outflow to purchase the bond   =   −$89.50
Profit   = $ 2.30

An arbitrage profit of $2.30 will be realized.

c. If the futures price is $89.30, the cash and carry trade would involve the following:

>Sell the futures contract that settles in three months at $89.30.
>Borrow $90 for three months at 8% per year.
>With the funds borrowed purchase the underlying bond for the futures contract.

When the bond is delivered to settle the futures contract three months from now, the amount received is the futures price of $89.30 plus the accrued interest. The amount received is $91.80 ($89.30 + $2.50). The amount to repay the loan is $91.80. Therefore, at the end of three months the following will be the cash flow:

Cash inflow from delivery of the bond   = $91.80
Cash outflow from repayment of the loan   =   −$91.80
Profit   =   0

Therefore, there is no arbitrage profit and $89.30 is the theoretical futures price.

Using a reverse cash and carry trade the same is true as shown below. This trade involves the following:

>Buy the futures contract that settles in three months at $89.30.
>Sell (short) the bond underlying the futures contract for $90.
>Invest (lend) the proceeds from the short sale of $90 for three months at 8% per year.

When the bond is delivered to settle the futures contract three months from now, the amount that must be paid is $91.80 (the futures price of $89.30 plus the accrued interest of $2.50.) The amount that will be received from the proceeds lent for three months is $91.80. Thus,

Cash inflow from the amount invested (lent)   = $91.80
Cash outflow to purchase the bond   =   −$91.80
Profit   = $ 0

2. The inputs for computing the theoretical futures price use the notation in the chapter are:

$$r = 0.08 \quad P = 90 \quad t = 3/12 = 0.25$$

The current yield is found by dividing the annual dollar coupon of 10 by the cash market price of the bond (90). Thus,

$$c = 10/90 = 11.11\% = 0.1111$$

$$F = 90 + 90 \times (0.25) \times (0.08 - 0.1111) = 89.3$$

The theoretical futures price is 89.3.

3.

Quarter starts	Quarter ends	Number of days in quarter	Current 3-month LIBOR	Eurodollar CD futures price	Forward rate	Period = End of quarter	Floating-rate payment at end of quarter
Jan 1 year 1	Mar 31 year 1	90	7.30%		—	1	1,825,000
Apr 1 year 1	June 30 year 1	91		92.60	7.40%	2	1,870,556
July 1 year 1	Sept 30 year 1	92		92.10	7.90%	3	2,018,889
Oct 1 year 1	Dec 31 year 1	92		92.05	7.95%	4	2,031,667
Jan 1 year 2	Mar 31 year 2	90		92.00	8.00%	5	2,000,000
Apr 1 year 2	June 30 year 2	91		91.85	8.15%	6	2,060,139
July 1 year 2	Sept 30 year 2	92		91.75	8.25%	7	2,108,333
Oct 1 year 2	Dec 31 year 2	92		91.70	8.30%	8	2,121,111
Jan 1 year 3	Mar 31 year 3	90		91.55	8.45%	9	2,112,500
Apr 1 year 3	June 30 year 3	91		91.40	8.60%	10	2,173,889
July 1 year 3	Sept 30 year 3	92		91.25	8.75%	11	2,236,111
Oct 1 year 3	Dec 31 year 3	92		91.10	8.90%	12	2,274,444

4.

Quarter starts	Quarter ends	Number of days in quarter	Period = End of quarter	Fixed-rate payment if swap rate is 8.1313%
Jan 1 year 1	Mar 31 year 1	90	1	2,032,825
Apr 1 year 1	June 30 year 1	91	2	2,055,412
July 1 year 1	Sept 30 year 1	92	3	2,077,999
Oct 1 year 1	Dec 31 year 1	92	4	2,077,999
Jan 1 year 2	Mar 31 year 2	90	5	2,032,825
Apr 1 year 2	June 30 year 2	91	6	2,055,412
July 1 year 2	Sept 30 year 2	92	7	2,077,999
Oct 1 year 2	Dec 31 year 2	92	8	2,077,999
Jan 1 year 3	Mar 31 year 3	90	9	2,032,825
Apr 1 year 3	June 30 year 3	91	10	2,055,412
July 1 year 3	Sept 30 year 3	92	11	2,077,999
Oct 1 year 3	Dec 31 year 3	92	12	2,077,999

5. a. The forward discount factors are shown below.

Quarter starts	Quarter ends	Number of days in quarter	Period = End of quarter	Forward rate	Period forward rate	Forward discount factor
Jan 1 year 1	Mar 31 year 1	90	1	7.30%	1.8250%	0.98207709
Apr 1 year 1	June 30 year 1	91	2	7.40%	1.8706%	0.96404411
July 1 year 1	Sept 30 year 1	92	3	7.90%	2.0189%	0.94496629
Oct 1 year 1	Dec 31 year 1	92	4	7.95%	2.0317%	0.92615001
Jan 1 year 2	Mar 31 year 2	90	5	8.00%	2.0000%	0.90799021
Apr 1 year 2	June 30 year 2	91	6	8.15%	2.0601%	0.88966194
July 1 year 2	Sept 30 year 2	92	7	8.25%	2.1083%	0.87129219
Oct 1 year 2	Dec 31 year 2	92	8	8.30%	2.1211%	0.85319498
Jan 1 year 3	Mar 31 year 3	90	9	8.45%	2.1125%	0.83554411
Apr 1 year 3	June 30 year 3	91	10	8.60%	2.1739%	0.81776677
July 1 year 3	Sept 30 year 3	92	11	8.75%	2.2361%	0.79988055
Oct 1 year 3	Dec 31 year 3	92	12	8.90%	2.2744%	0.7820923

We will use the forward discount factor for period 5 to illustrate the computation. The period forward rates are shown in the sixth column of the table above. The forward discount factor is

$$= \frac{\$1}{(1.018250)(1.018706)(1.020189)(1.020317)(1.02)} = 0.90799$$

b. The present value of the floating-rate payments is $21,790,770 as shown below:

Quarter starts	Quarter ends	Period = End of quarter	Forward discount factor	Floating-rate payment at end of quarter	PV of floating-rate payment
Jan 1 year 1	Mar 31 year 1	1	0.98207709	1,825,000	1,792,291
Apr 1 year 1	June 30 year 1	2	0.96404411	1,870,556	1,803,298
July 1 year 1	Sept 30 year 1	3	0.94496629	2,018,889	1,907,782
Oct 1 year 1	Dec 31 year 1	4	0.92615001	2,031,667	1,881,628
Jan 1 year 2	Mar 31 year 2	5	0.90799021	2,000,000	1,815,980
Apr 1 year 2	June 30 year 2	6	0.88966194	2,060,139	1,832,827
July 1 year 2	Sept 30 year 2	7	0.87129219	2,108,333	1,836,974
Oct 1 year 2	Dec 31 year 2	8	0.85319498	2,121,111	1,809,721
Jan 1 year 3	Mar 31 year 3	9	0.83554411	2,112,500	1,765,087
Apr 1 year 3	June 30 year 3	10	0.81776677	2,173,889	1,777,734
July 1 year 3	Sept 30 year 3	11	0.79988055	2,236,111	1,788,622
Oct 1 year 3	Dec 31 year 3	12	0.7820923	2,274,444	1,778,825
				Total	21,790,770

6. The denominator for the swap rate formula is computed in the following table:

(1) Quarter starts	(2) Quarter ends	(3) Number of days in quarter	(4) Period = End of quarter	(5) Forward discount rate	(6) Days/360	(7) Fwd. disc. factor × Days/360 × notional
Jan 1 year 1	Mar 31 year 1	90	1	0.98207709	0.25000000	24,551,927
Apr 1 year 1	June 30 year 1	91	2	0.96404411	0.25277778	24,368,893
July 1 year 1	Sept 30 year 1	92	3	0.94496629	0.25555556	24,149,139
Oct 1 year 1	Dec 31 year 1	92	4	0.92615001	0.25555556	23,668,278
Jan 1 year 2	Mar 31 year 2	90	5	0.90799021	0.25000000	22,699,755
Apr 1 year 2	June 30 year 2	91	6	0.88966194	0.25277778	22,488,677
July 1 year 2	Sept 30 year 2	92	7	0.87129219	0.25555556	22,266,356
Oct 1 year 2	Dec 31 year 2	92	8	0.85319498	0.25555556	21,803,872
Jan 1 year 3	Mar 31 year 3	90	9	0.83554411	0.25000000	20,888,603
Apr 1 year 3	June 30 year 3	91	10	0.81776677	0.25277778	20,671,327
July 1 year 3	Sept 30 year 3	92	11	0.79988055	0.25555556	20,441,392
Oct 1 year 3	Dec 31 year 3	92	12	0.78209230	0.25555556	19,986,803
					Total	267,985,021

The present value of the floating-rate payments is $21,790,770. Therefore, the swap rate is

$$\text{swap rate} = \frac{21,790,770}{267,985,021} = 0.081313 = 8.1313\%$$

7. a. The floating-rate payments are shown below:

(1)	(2)	(3)	(4)	(5)	(6)	(7)	(8)
Quarter starts	Quarter ends	Number of days in quarter	Current 3-month LIBOR	Eurodollar CD futures price	Forward rate	Period = End of quarter	Floating-rate payment at end of quarter
Jan 1 year 2	Mar 31 year 2	90	3.50%			1	875,000
Apr 1 year 2	June 30 year 2	91		96.40	3.60%	2	910,000
July 1 year 2	Sept 30 year 2	92		96.20	3.80%	3	971,111
Oct 1 year 2	Dec 31 year 2	92		96.00	4.00%	4	1,022,222
Jan 1 year 3	Mar 31 year 3	90		95.96	4.04%	5	1,010,000
Apr 1 year 3	June 30 year 3	91		95.87	4.13%	6	1,043,972
July 1 year 3	Sept 30 year 3	92		95.81	4.19%	7	1,070,778
Oct 1 year 3	Dec 31 year 3	92		95.65	4.35%	8	1,111,667

b. The forward discount factor for each period is shown below:

(1)	(2)	(3)	(4)	(5)	(6)	(7)
Quarter starts	Quarter ends	Number of days in quarter	Period = End of quarter	Forward rate	Period forward rate	Forward discount factor
Jan 1 year 2	Mar 31 year 2	90	1	3.50%	0.8750%	0.99132590
Apr 1 year 2	June 30 year 2	91	2	3.60%	0.9100%	0.98238618
July 1 year 2	Sept 30 year 2	92	3	3.80%	0.9711%	0.97293788
Oct 1 year 2	Dec 31 year 2	92	4	4.00%	1.0222%	0.96309293
Jan 1 year 3	Mar 31 year 3	90	5	4.04%	1.0100%	0.95346295
Apr 1 year 3	June 30 year 3	91	6	4.13%	1.0440%	0.94361190
July 1 year 3	Sept 30 year 3	92	7	4.19%	1.0708%	0.93361496
Oct 1 year 3	Dec 31 year 3	92	8	4.35%	1.1117%	0.92335038

c. The fixed-rate payments need not be computed they are the same as in Exhibit 4.

d. The present value of the floating-rate payments is $7,664,962 and the present value of the fixed-rate payments is $9,687,560 as shown below:

(1)	(2)	(3)	(4)	(5)	(6)	(7)
Quarter starts	Quarter ends	Forward discount factor	Floating cash flow at end of quarter	PV of floating cash flow	Fixed cash flow at end of quarter	PV of fixed cash flow
Jan 1 year 2	Mar 31 year 2	0.99132590	875,000	867,410	1,246,875	1,236,059
Apr 1 year 2	June 30 year 2	0.98238618	910,000	893,971	1,260,729	1,238,523
July 1 year 2	Sept 30 year 2	0.97293788	971,111	944,831	1,274,583	1,240,090
Oct 1 year 2	Dec 31 year 2	0.96309293	1,022,222	984,495	1,274,583	1,227,542
Jan 1 year 3	Mar 31 year 3	0.95346295	1,010,000	962,998	1,246,875	1,188,849
Apr 1 year 3	June 30 year 3	0.94361190	1,043,972	985,105	1,260,729	1,189,639
July 1 year 3	Sept 30 year 3	0.93361496	1,070,778	999,694	1,274,583	1,189,970
Oct 1 year 3	Dec 31 year 3	0.92335038	1,111,667	1,026,458	1,274,583	1,176,887
			Total	7,664,962		9,687,560

Summary	Fixed-rate payer	Fixed-rate receiver
PV of payments received	7,664,962	9,687,560
PV of payments made	9,687,560	7,664,962
Value of swap	−2,022,599	2,022,599

e. The fixed-rate payer will receive the floating-rate payments that have a present value of $7,664,962. The present value of the payments that must be made by the fixed-rate payer is $9,687,560. Thus, the swap has a negative value for the fixed-rate payer equal to the difference in the two present values of −$2,022,599. This is the value of the swap to the fixed-rate payer. Consistent with what was stated in the previous chapter, when interest rates decrease (as they did in this practice question), the fixed-rate payer is adversely affected because the value of the swap decreases.

f. The fixed-rate receiver must make payments with a present value of $7,664,962 but will receive floating-rate payments with a present value equal to $9,687,560. Thus, the value of the swap for the fixed-rate receiver is $2,022,599. Again, as explained in the previous chapter, the fixed-rate receiver is favorable impacted by a decline in interest rates because it results in an increase in the value of a swap.

8. a. The value of the call option is $1.1854 as shown below:

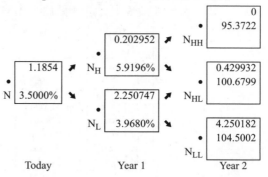

b. When interest rate volatility increases, the value of an option will increase. Consequently, the value of the 2-year call option increases from $0.6056 at 10% volatility to $1.1854 at 20% volatility.

c. The value of the put option is $1.1124 as shown below:

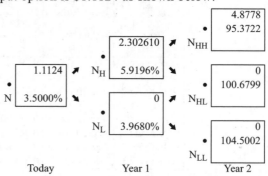

d. Because volatility is higher, the value of the put option increases. For the 2-year put option, the value of the option increases from $0.5327 at 10% volatility to $1.1124 at 20% volatility.

9. a. The value of each caplet is shown below. The assumptions for each are as follows:

Cap rate: 5.60%
Notional amount: $10,000,000
Payment frequency: Annual
Volatility: 10%

The value of the Year 1 caplet is determined as follows:

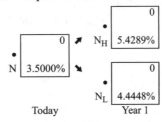

Value of Year 1 caplet = $0

The value of the Year 2 caplet is determined as follows:

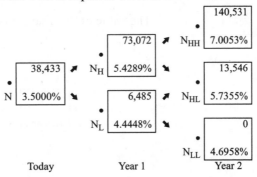

Value of Year 2 caplet = $38,433

The value of Year 3 caplet is determined as follows:

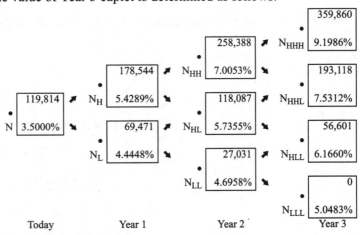

Value of Year 3 caplet = $119,814

The value of the 3-year cap with a cap rate of 5.6% is:

0 + $38,433 + $119,814 = $158,247

b. The value of each floorlet is shown below. The assumptions for each are as follows:

Floor rate: 5%
Notional amount: $10,000,000
Payment frequency: Annual
Volatility: 10%

The value of the Year 1 floorlet is determined as follows:

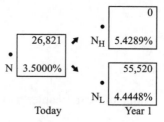

The value of the Year 1 floorlet is $26,821.

The value of the Year 2 floorlet is determined as follows:

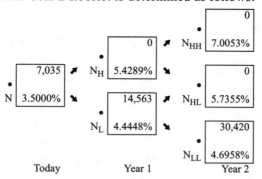

The value of the Year 2 floorlet is $7,035.

The value of the Year 3 floorlet is determined as follows:

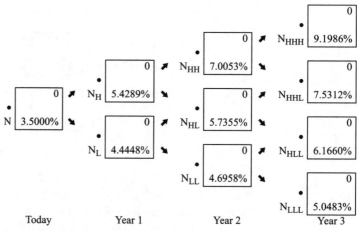

The value of the Year 3 floorlet is 0.
The value of the 3-year floor is:

$$\$26,821 + \$7,035 + 0 = \$33,856$$

Chapter 9

GENERAL PRINCIPLES OF CREDIT ANALYSIS

LEARNING OUTCOME STATEMENTS

After reading this chapter you should be able to:

- explain the different types of credit risk: default risk, credit spread risk, and downgrade risk.
- describe a general framework for credit analysis that involves examination of the borrower's character, the borrower's capacity to repay, the underlying collateral, and the issue's covenants.
- discuss the key elements in the analysis of the debt obligation of a corporate issuer.
- discuss the factors that affect the earnings of a company and the traditional ratios that are used.
- explain the ratios that are used by credit analysts to assess the ability of a firm to satisfy its debt obligations: (1) short-term solvency ratios, (2) capitalization (or financial leverage) ratios, and (3) coverage ratios.
- explain the limitations of traditional ratios and the need to analyze the cash flow from operations to assess the ability of an issuer to service its debt obligations and to identify the financial flexibility of a company.
- identify the various covenants that are important in assessing credit risk.
- explain the unique factors in evaluating the credit worthiness of high-yield corporate issues.
- explain why some investors advocate an equity perspective approach to analyzing the credit worthiness of high-yield corporate issues.
- identify the factors considered by rating agencies in assigning a credit rating to asset-backed securities.
- explain how the credit analysis of asset-backed securities differs from that of corporate bonds.
- explain how the credit worthiness of municipal bonds is assessed and the differences in analyzing tax-backed debt and revenue obligations.
- identify the factors used in assigning local currency debt ratings and foreign currency debt ratings to sovereign bonds.

SECTION I
INTRODUCTION

Credit analysis of any entity — a corporation, a municipality, or a sovereign government — involves the analysis of a multitude of quantitative and qualitative factors over the past, present, and future. The past and present are introductions to what the future may hold. In this chapter, we focus on the credit analysis of a corporation. The analysis is not done in isolation but in conjunction with a review of the issuer's place within the industry and an overall analysis of where the industry fits within the national economy and, with increasing frequency, the global economy. There are some unique factors that should be considered in the analysis of noninvestment grade or high-yield corporate issues. At the end of the chapter we look at the factors considered in the credit analysis of asset-backed securities, municipalities, and sovereign governments and how they are evaluated from a credit perspective in comparison to corporate bonds. The appendix to this chapter provides a case study of one high-yield corporate issuer, Bergen Brunswig Corporation.

SECTION II
CREDIT RISK
AND THE NEED
FOR CREDIT
ANALYSIS

An investor who lends funds to a corporation by purchasing its debt obligation is exposed to credit risk. But what is credit risk? At Level I, we explained that traditionally credit risk is defined as the risk that the borrower will fail to satisfy the terms of the obligation with respect to the timely payment of interest and repayment of the amount borrowed. This form of credit risk is called **default risk**.

In addition to default risk, there are other risks associated with the investment in debt securities that are also components of credit risk. Even in the absence of default, the investor is concerned that the market value of a debt instrument will decline in value and/or the relative price performance of that instrument will be worse than that of other debt obligations which the investor is compared against. As explained at Level I, the yield on a corporate debt instrument is made up of two components: (1) the yield on a similar maturity Treasury issue and (2) a premium to compensate for the risks associated with the debt instrument that do not exist in a Treasury issue — referred to as a **spread**. The part of the risk premium or spread attributable to default risk is called the **credit spread**.

The price performance of a non-Treasury debt obligation and its return over some investment horizon will depend on how the credit spread changes. If the credit spread increases — investors say that the spread has "widened" — the market price of the debt obligation will decline. The risk that an issuer's debt obligation will decline due to an increase in the credit spread is called **credit spread risk**.

Market participants gauge the default risk of an issue by looking at the credit ratings assigned to issues by the three rating companies — Standard & Poor's Corporation, Moody's Investors Service, Inc., and Fitch. Ratings can differ from issue to issue for the same issuer because each issue may give the bondholder a different priority of claim in a bankruptcy. Once a credit rating is assigned to a corporate debt obligation, a rating agency monitors the credit quality of the issuer and can reassign a different credit rating. An improvement in the credit quality of an issue or issuer is rewarded with a better credit rating, referred to as an **upgrade**; a deterioration in the credit quality of an issue or issuer is penalized by the assignment of an inferior credit rating, referred to as a **downgrade**. An unanticipated downgrading of an issue or issuer increases the credit spread sought by the market, resulting in a decline in the price of the issue or the issuer's debt obligation. This risk is referred to as **downgrade risk**.

A credit rating is not a measure of the other aspects of credit risk (that is, credit ratings do not measure credit spread risk and downgrade risk). Yet, an analyst must be aware of how rating agencies gauge default risk for purposes of assigning ratings in order to understand downgrade risk. When an analyst assesses the credit quality of an issuer, he or she often evaluates quantitative measures such as financial ratios as well as the priority of claim in a bankruptcy in terms of what the rating agencies require to achieve a certain rating. When an analyst expresses a view that the credit quality has deteriorated, typically the analyst means that the analysis suggests that the issue may be downgraded because the quantitative measures identified are inferior to the benchmarks for the issue to maintain its current credit rating.

SECTION III
ELEMENTS OF CORPORATE CREDIT ANALYSIS

In conducting this credit examination, the analyst considers the four C's of credit:

- character
- capacity
- collateral
- covenants

Character of management is the foundation of sound credit. This includes the ethical reputation as well as the business qualifications and operating record of the board of directors, management, and executives responsible for the use of the borrowed funds and repayment of those funds. **Capacity** is the ability of an issuer to repay its obligations. **Collateral** is looked at not only in the traditional sense of assets pledged to secure the debt, but also to the quality and value of those unpledged assets controlled by the issuer. In both senses the collateral is capable of supplying additional aid, comfort, and support to the debt and the debtholder. Assets form the basis for the generation of cash flow which services the debt in good times as well as bad. **Covenants** are the terms and conditions of the lending agreement. They lay down restrictions on how management operates the company and conducts its financial affairs. Covenants can restrict management's discretion. A default or violation of any covenant may provide a meaningful early warning alarm enabling investors to take positive and corrective action before the situation deteriorates further. Covenants have value as they play an important part in minimizing risk to creditors. They help prevent the transfer of wealth from debt holders to equity holders.

SECTION IV
ANALYSIS OF AN ISSUER'S CHARACTER

Character analysis involves the analysis of the quality of management. In discussing the factors it considers in assigning a credit rating, Moody's Investors Service notes the following regarding the quality of management:[1]

> Although difficult to quantify, management quality is one of the most important factors supporting an issuer's credit strength. When the unexpected occurs, it is a management's ability to react appropriately that will sustain the company's performance.

In assessing management quality, the analysts at Moody's, for example, try to understand the business strategies and policies formulated by management. Following are factors that are considered:[2]

---

[1] "Industrial Company Rating Methodology," *Moody's Investors Services: Global Credit Research* (July 1998), p. 6.
[2] "Industrial Company Rating Methodology," p. 7.

1. strategic direction
2. financial philosophy
3. conservatism
4. track record
5. succession planning
6. control systems

SECTION V ANALYSIS OF THE CAPACITY TO PAY

A corporation will generate the funds to service its debt from its cash flow. The cash flow is generated from revenues and reduced by the costs of operations. Therefore, in assessing the ability of an issuer to pay, an analysis of the financial statements as discussed later in this chapter is undertaken. In addition to management quality, the factors examined by analysts at Moody's are:[3]

1. industry trends
2. the regulatory environment
3. basic operating and competitive position
4. financial position and sources of liquidity
5. company structure (including structural subordination and priority of claim)
6. parent company support agreements
7. special event risk

In considering industry trends, analysts look at the vulnerability of the company to economic cycles, the barriers to entry, and the exposure of the company to technological changes. For firms in regulated industries, proposed changes in regulations must be analyzed to assess their impact on future cash flows. At the company level, diversification of the product line and the cost structure are examined in assessing the basic operating position of the firm.

In addition to the measures described later in this chapter for assessing a company's financial position over the past three to five years, an analyst must look at the capacity of a firm to obtain additional financing and back-up credit facilities. There are various forms of back-up credit facilities. The strongest forms of back-up credit facilities are those that are contractually binding and do not include provisions that permit the lender to refuse to provide funds. An example of such a provision is one that allows the bank to refuse funding if the bank feels that the borrower's financial condition or operating position has deteriorated significantly. (Such a provision is called a **material adverse change clause**.) Non-contractual facilities such as lines of credit that make it easy for a bank to refuse funding should be of concern to the analyst. The analyst must also examine the quality of the bank providing the back-up facility.

Analysts should also assess whether the company can use securitization as a funding source for generating liquidity. Asset securitization involves using a pool of loans or receivables as collateral for a security. The decision of whether to securitize assets to borrow or use traditional borrowing sources is done on the basis of cost. However, if traditional sources dry up when a company faces a liquidity crisis, securitization may provide the needed liquidity. An analyst should investigate the extent to which management has considered securitization as a funding source.

Other sources of liquidity for a company may be third-party guarantees, the most common being a contractual agreement with its parent company. When such a financial guarantee exists, the analyst must undertake a credit analysis of the parent company.

---

[3] "Industrial Company Rating Methodology," p. 3.

In the analysis of an issuer's ability to pay, the analyst will analyze the issuer's financial statements (income statement, balance sheet, and statement of cash flows), project future financial statements based on certain assumptions, and compute various measures. These measures include traditional ratio measures and cash flow measures. Below we review these measures and explain how an analysis of cash flows provides a better early warning alarm of potential financial difficulties than traditional ratios.

A. Traditional Ratios

Traditional ratios to evaluate the ability of an issuer to meet its obligations include:

- profitability ratios
- debt and coverage ratios

1. Profitability Ratios

Equity analysts focus on the earnings of a firm, particularly the earnings per share. While a holder of the debt obligation of a firm does not have the opportunity to share in the economic growth of the firm, this does not mean that a credit analyst should ignore a firm's profitability. It is from revenues that a firm will continue to grow in order to generate cash flow to meet obligations.

Profitability ratios are utilized to explore the underlying causes of a change in the company's earnings. They show the combined effects of liquidity and asset and debt management on the profitability of the firm. These ratios break earnings per share into its basic determinants for purposes of assessing the factors underlying the profitability of the firm. They help to assess the adequacy of historical profits, and to project future profitability through better understanding of its underlying causes.

Standards for a given ratio will vary according to operating characteristics of the company being analyzed and general business conditions; such standards cannot be stated as fixed and immutable. It is assumed that the analyst has made all adjustments deemed necessary to reflect comparable and true earning power of the corporation before calculating the ratios discussed below. It is important to stress that ratios are utilized to raise significant questions requiring further analysis, not to provide answers. Ratios must be viewed in the context of other ratios and other facts, derived from sources other than the financial statements, such as the statement of cash flows.

Equity analysts use the DuPont formula (explained in textbooks on equity analysis) to assess the determinants of a company's earnings per share. The profitability ratios analyzed to assess earnings per share are:

- return on stockholders' equity
- return on total assets
- profit margin
- asset turnover

Each of these measures and their limitations are explained in textbooks on financial statement analysis and equity analysis so they will not be repeated here.

2. Debt and Coverage Analysis

There are three sets of ratios that are used by credit analysts as indicators to assess the ability of a firm to satisfy its debt obligations:

- short-term solvency ratios
- capitalization (or financial leverage) ratios
- coverage ratios

In addition to these ratios, an analyst should look at the maturity structure of the issuer's debt.

a. Short-Term Solvency Ratios

Short-term solvency ratios are used to judge the adequacy of liquid assets for meeting short-term obligations as they come due. Firms go bankrupt, or get into financial difficulty, because they cannot pay obligations as they come due, not necessarily because they are not profitable.

A complete analysis of the adequacy of working capital for meeting current liabilities as they come due and assessing management's efficiency in using working capital would require a thorough analysis of cash flows and forecasts of fund flows in future periods that will be discussed in the next section. However, ratios provide a crude but useful assessment of working capital. The following two ratios are calculated to assess the adequacy of working capital for a firm:

- the current ratio
- the acid-test ratio

The current ratio is calculated by dividing current assets by current liabilities:

$$\text{current ratio} = \frac{\text{current assets}}{\text{current liabilities}}$$

The current ratio indicates the company's coverage of current liabilities by current assets. For example, if the ratio were 2:1, the firm could realize only half of the values stated in the balance sheet in liquidating current assets and still have adequate funds to pay all current liabilities.

A general standard for this ratio (such as 2:1) is *not* useful. Such a standard fails to recognize that an appropriate current ratio is a function of the nature of a company's business and would vary with differing operating cycles of different businesses.

A **current asset** is one that is expected to be converted into cash in the ordinary operating cycle of a business. Inventory, therefore, is a current asset. In a tobacco or liquor manufacturing company, inventory may be as much as 80% to 90% of current assets. However, for a liquor company that inventory may have to age four years or more before it can be converted into a salable asset. Such a company typically would require a much higher current ratio than average to have adequate liquidity to meet current liabilities maturing in one year. For a public utility company where there is no inventory or receivables collection problem, a current ratio of 1.1 or 1.2 to 1 has proved satisfactory. Industry averages, such as those produced by organizations like Dun & Bradstreet or Robert Morris Associates, should be looked at rather than considering an overall standard. Industry averages have their faults, but they are preferable to general standards that do not recognize operating differences among classes of companies.

The current ratio has a major weakness as an analytical tool. It ignores the composition of current assets, which may be as important as their relationship with current liabilities. Therefore, current ratio analysis must be supplemented by other working capital ratios.

Since the problem in meeting current liabilities may rest on slowness or even inability to convert inventories into cash to meet current obligations, the acid-test ratio (also called the quick ratio) is recommended. This is the ratio of current assets minus inventories, accruals, and prepaid items to current liabilities; that is:

$$\text{acid-test ratio} = \frac{\text{current assets} - \text{inventories} - \text{accruals} - \text{prepaid items}}{\text{current liabilities}}$$

This ratio does assume that receivables are of good quality and will be converted into cash over the next year.

b. Capitalization Ratios

Credit analysts also calculate **capitalization ratios** to determine the extent to which the corporation is trading on its equity, and the resulting financial leverage. These ratios, also called **financial leverage ratios**, can be interpreted only in the context of the stability of industry and company earnings and cash flow. The assumption is that the greater the stability of industry and company earnings and cash flow, the more the company is able to accept the risk associated with financial leverage, and the higher the allowable ratio of debt to total capitalization (the total dollar amount of all long-term sources of funds in the balance sheet).

There are many variations to be found within the industry to calculate capitalization ratios. Two such ratios are shown below:

long-term debt to capitalization

$$= \frac{\text{long-term debt}}{\text{long-term debt} + \text{shareholders' equity including minority interest}}$$

total debt to capitalization

$$= \frac{\text{current liabilities} + \text{long-term debt}}{\text{long-term debt} + \text{shareholders' equity including minority interest}}$$

where shareholders' equity includes preferred stock.

For both ratios, the higher the ratio, the greater the financial leverage. The value used to measure debt in both ratios is book value. It is useful to calculate stockholders' equity at market as well as at book value for the purpose of determining these ratios. A market calculation for common equity may indicate considerably more or less financial leverage than a book calculation.

Commercial rating companies and most Wall Street analysts rely heavily upon the long-term debt to capitalization ratio, and this is often provided in research reports sent out to clients. While this ratio can be useful, it should be noted that in recent years, given the uncertain interest rate environment, many corporations have taken to financing a good deal of their business with short-term debt. Indeed, an imaginative treasurer with a keen insight into money market activities can earn as much for a company as a plant manager, simply by switching debt from long term to short term and vice versa, at the right time.

Other considerations in using the long-term debt to capitalization ratio involves leased assets. Many corporations rent buildings and equipment under long-term lease contracts. Required rental payments are contractual obligations similar to bond coupon and repayment obligations. However, assets acquired through leasing (i.e., those leases classified as operating leases) may not be capitalized and shown in the balance sheet. Two companies, therefore, might work with the same amount of fixed assets and produce the same profits before interest or rental payments, but the one leasing a high proportion of its productive equipment could show significantly lower financial leverage.

c. Coverage Tests

Coverage ratios are used to test the adequacy of cash flows generated through earnings for purposes of meeting debt and lease obligations. The four most commonly used coverage ratios are:

- EBIT interest coverage ratio
- EBITDA interest coverage ratio
- funds from operations/total debt ratio
- free operating cash flow/total debt ratio

EBIT stands for "earnings before interest and taxes." The **EBIT interest coverage ratio** is simply EBIT divided by the annual interest expense. (Interest expense includes "capitalized interest." This is effectively interest expense imputed for capitalized assets, the most important of which is leased assets.) Interest expense is tax deductible and, therefore, all earnings before taxes are available for paying such charges. Also, the interest should be added back to determine the amount available to meet annual interest expenses.

EBITDA stands for "earnings before interest, taxes, depreciation, and amortization." The **EBITDA interest coverage ratio** is simply the ratio of EBITDA divided by the annual interest expense.

The last two ratios listed above indicate the amount of funds from operations relative to the amount of total debt. The funds from operations includes net income plus the following: depreciation, amortization, deferred income taxes, and other non-cash items. The definition of free operating cash flows varies by rating agency. In the next section we describe one variant of free operating cash flow.

Suggested standards for coverage ratios are based on experience and empirical studies relating the incidence of defaults over a number of years to such ratios. Different standards are needed for a highly cyclical company than for a stable company. In the case study presented in the appendix to this chapter, benchmark ratios (as measured in terms of median ratios) by credit rating are presented for the coverage ratios described above, as well as for the capitalization ratios.

B. Cash Flow Analysis

Will the ratios just described be sufficient to help an analyst identify companies that may encounter financial difficulties? Consider the study by Largay and Stickney who analyzed the financial statements of W.T. Grant during the 1966-1974 period preceding its bankruptcy in 1975 and ultimate liquidation.[4] They noted that financial indicators such as profitability ratios, turnover ratios, and liquidity ratios showed some down trends, but provided no definite clues to the company's impending bankruptcy. A study of cash flows from operations, however, revealed that company operations were causing an increasing drain on cash, rather than providing cash.[5] This necessitated an increased use of external financing, the required interest payments on which exacerbated the cash flow drain. Cash flow analysis clearly was a valuable tool in this case since W.T. Grant had been running a negative cash flow from operations for years. Yet none of the traditional ratios discussed above take into account the cash flow from operations.

[4] J.A. Largay III and C.P. Stickney, "Cash Flows, Ratio Analysis and the W.T. Grant Company Bankruptcy," *Financial Analysts Journal* (July-August 1980), pp. 51-54.

[5] For the period investigated, a statement of changes of financial position (on a working capital basis) was required prior to 1988.

Dugan and Samson examined the use of operating cash flow as an early warning signal of a company's potential financial problems.[6] The subject of the study was Allied Products Corporation because for a decade this company exhibited a significant divergence between cash flow from operations and net income. For parts of the period, net income was positive while cash flow from operations was a large negative value. In contrast to W.T. Grant that went into bankruptcy, the auditor's report in the 1991 annual report of Allied Products Corporation did issue a going concern warning. Moreover, the stock traded in the range of $2 to $3 per share. There was then a turnaround of the company by 1995. In its 1995 annual report, net income increased dramatically from prior periods (to $34 million) and there was a positive cash flow from operations ($29 million). The stock traded in the $25 range by the Spring of 1996.[7] As with the W.T. Grant study, Dugan and Samson found that the realities of a firm are better reflected in its cash flow from operations.

Martin Fridson has documented how the typical cash flow generation and uses of companies in different stages of their business life cycle (startup, emerging growth, established growth, mature industry, and declining industry) relate to their statement of cash flows.[8] In addition, he explains how the statement of cash flows allows the analyst to assess a firm's "financial flexibility." An analysis of this statement provides an analyst with the information needed to answer such questions as:

- How 'safe' is the company's dividend?
- Could the company fund its needs internally if external sources of capital suddenly become scarce or prohibitively expensive?
- Would the company be able to continue meeting its obligations if its business turned down sharply?

These questions can be answered by computing a measure called **discretionary cash flow**. Fridson defines this measure as follows:[9]

Cash flow that remains available to a company after it has funded its basic operating requirements. There is no universally accepted, precise definition of discretionary cash flow, but conceptually it includes funds from operations less required new investment in working capital and nondiscretionary capital expenditures. The latter figure is difficult to quantify with precision, but it exceeds the required 'maintenance' level required to keep existing plant and equipment in good working order. Ordinarily, some additional expenditures, which may be designated 'semi-discretionary' are necessary to keep a company competitive with respect to capacity, costs, and technology.

The computation of discretionary cash flow begins with the basic cash flow which includes net earnings, depreciation, and deferred income taxes, less items in net income that do not provide cash. From the basic cash flow, nondiscretionary items are deducted. Subtracting from the basic cash flow increases in working capital (excluding cash and payables) gives **operating cash flow**. Deducting from operating cash

---

[6] Michael T. Dugan and William D. Samson, "Operating Cash Flow: Early Indicators of Financial Difficulty and Recovery," *The Journal of Financial Statement Analysis* (Summer 1996), pp. 41-50.

[7] As noted for the W.T. Grant study by Largay and Stickney, cash flow from operations had to be constructed from the statement of changes in financial positions that companies were required to report prior to 1988.

[8] Chapter 4 in Martin S. Fridson, *Financial Statement Analysis: a Practitioner's Guide* (New York: John Wiley & Sons, 1995).

[9] Fridson, *Financial Statement Analysis*, p. 273.

flow the capital expenditures gives the company's discretionary cash flow. As noted in the above quote, capital expenditures that are nondiscretionary must be estimated. It is common for an analyst to use the capital expenditures reported in the financial statement. This is summarized in Exhibit 1.

For example, consider a company with a basic cash flow of $800 million and operating cash flow of $500 million. Suppose that this company pays dividends of $130 million and that its capital expenditure is $300 million. Then the discretionary cash flow for this company is $200 million found by subtracting the capital expenditure ($300 million) from the operating cash flow ($500 million). This means that even after maintaining a dividend payment of $130 million, its cash flow would be positive. Notice that asset sales and other investing activity are not needed to generate cash to meet the dividend payments because in Exhibit 1 these items are subtracted after accounting for the dividend payments. In fact, if this company planned to increase its capital expenditures, an analyst can use the format in Exhibit 1 to assess how much that expansion can be before impacting dividends and/or increasing financing needs.

A useful ratio to help further assess a company's cash flow is the **cash flow from operations to capital expenditures ratio**. This ratio gives the analyst information about the financial flexibility of the company and is particularly useful for capital-intensive firms and utilities.[10] The larger the ratio, the greater the financial flexibility. The analyst, however, must carefully examine the reasons why this ratio may be changing over time and why it might be out of line with comparable firms in the industry. For example, a declining ratio can be interpreted in two ways. First, the firm may eventually have difficulty adding to capacity via capital expenditures without the need to borrow funds. The second interpretation is that the firm may have gone through a period of major capital expansion and therefore it will take time for revenues to be generated that will increase the cash flow from operations to bring the ratio to some normal long-run level.

SECTION VI ANALYSIS OF COLLATERAL

A corporate debt obligation can be secured or unsecured. In our discussion of creditor rights in a bankruptcy, we explained that in the case of a liquidation, proceeds from a bankruptcy are distributed to creditors based on the absolute priority rule. However, in the case of a reorganization, the absolute priority rule rarely holds. That is, an unsecured creditor may receive distributions for the entire amount of his or her claim and common stockholders may receive something, while a secured creditor may receive only a portion of its claim. The reason is that a reorganization requires approval of all the parties. Consequently, secured creditors are willing to negotiate with both unsecured creditors and stockholders in order to obtain approval of the plan of reorganization.

Exhibit 1: Computing a Company's Discretionary Cash Flow *

	Basic cash flow[1]
Less:	Increase in adjusted working capital[2,3]
	Operating cash flow
Less:	Capital expenditures[3]
	Discretionary cash flow

[1] The basic cash flow includes net earnings, depreciation, and deferred income taxes, less items in net income not providing cash.
[2] The increase in adjusted working capital excludes cash and payables.
[3] Nondiscretionary needs.
* This format was suggested by Martin S. Fridson, *Financial Statement Analysis: A Practitioner's Guide* (New York: John Wiley & Sons, 1995).

---

[10] Fridson, *Financial Statement Analysis*, p. 273.

The question is then, what does a secured position mean in the case of a reorganization if the absolute priority rule is not followed in a reorganization? The claim position of a secured creditor is important in terms of the negotiation process. However, because absolute priority is not followed and the final distribution in a reorganization depends on the bargaining ability of the parties, some analysts place less emphasis on collateral compared to the other factors discussed earlier and covenants discussed later.

At Level I we discussed the various types of collateral used for a corporate debt issue and features that analysts should be cognizant of in looking at an investor's secured position. Other important features are covered in our discussion of covenants below.

SECTION VII
ANALYSIS OF
COVENANTS

Covenants deal with limitations and restrictions on the borrower's activities. Some covenants are common to all indentures, such as

- to pay interest, principal, and premium, if any, on a timely basis
- to pay all taxes and other claims when due unless contested in good faith
- to maintain all properties used and useful in the borrower's business in good condition and working order
- to submit periodic certificates to the trustee stating whether the debtor is in compliance with the loan agreement

These covenants are called **affirmative covenants** since they call upon the debtor to make promises to do certain things.

Negative covenants are those which require the borrower not to take certain actions. There are an infinite variety of restrictions that can be placed on borrowers, depending on the type of debt issue, the economics of the industry and the nature of the business, and the lenders' desires. Some of the more common restrictive covenants include various limitations on the company's ability to incur debt, since unrestricted borrowing can lead a company and its debtholders to ruin. Thus, debt restrictions may include limits on the absolute dollar amount of debt that may be outstanding or may require a ratio test — for example, debt may be limited to no more than 60% of total capitalization or that it cannot exceed a certain percentage of net tangible assets.

There may be an interest or fixed charge coverage test. The two common tests are:

- **maintenance test**: This test requires the borrower's ratio of earnings available for interest or fixed charges to be at least a certain minimum figure on each required reporting date (such as quarterly or annually) for a certain preceding period.
- **debt incurrence test**: only comes into play when the company wishes to do additional borrowing. In order to take on additional debt, the required interest or fixed charge coverage figure adjusted for the new debt must be at a certain minimum level for the required period prior to the financing. Debt incurrence tests are generally considered less stringent than maintenance provisions.

There could also be **cash flow tests** (or **cash flow requirements**) and **working capital maintenance provisions**. The prospectus for Federated Department Stores, Inc.'s debentures dated November 4, 1988, has a large section devoted to debt limitations. One of the provisions allows net new debt issuance if the consolidated coverage ratio of earnings before interest, taxes, and depreciation to interest expense (all as defined) is at least 1.35 to 1 through November 1, 1989, 1.45 to 1 through November 1, 1990, 1.50 to 1 through November 1, 1991, and at least 1.60 to 1 thereafter.

Some indentures may prohibit subsidiaries from borrowing from all other companies except the parent. Indentures often classify subsidiaries as restricted or unrestricted. **Restricted subsidiaries** are those considered to be consolidated for financial test purposes; **unrestricted subsidiaries** (often foreign and certain special-purpose companies) are those excluded from the covenants governing the parent. Often, subsidiaries are classified as unrestricted in order to allow them to finance themselves through outside sources of funds.

Limitations on dividend payments and stock repurchases may be included in indentures. Often, cash dividend payments will be limited to a certain percentage of net income earned after a specific date (often the issuance date of the debt, called the "peg date") plus a fixed amount. Sometimes the dividend formula might allow the inclusion of the net proceeds from the sale of common stock sold after the peg date. In other cases, the dividend restriction might be so worded as to prohibit the declaration and payment of cash dividends if tangible net worth (or other measures, such as consolidated quick assets) declines below a certain amount. However, there are usually no restrictions on the payment of stock dividends. In addition to dividend restrictions, there are often restrictions on a company's repurchase of its common stock if such purchase might cause a violation or deficiency in the dividend determination formulas. Some holding company indentures might limit the right of the company to pay dividends in the common stock of its subsidiaries.

SECTION VIII SPECIAL CONSIDERATIONS FOR HIGH-YIELD CORPORATE BONDS

The discussion thus far has focused on credit analysis for any issuer regardless of credit rating. There are some unique factors that should be considered in the analysis of high-yield bonds. We will discuss the following:

- analysis of debt structure
- analysis of corporate structure
- analysis of covenants

In addition, we will discuss the reasons why an equity analysis approach to high-yield bond issuers is being used.

A. Analysis of Debt Structure

In January 1990, the Association for Investment Management and Research held a conference on high-yield bonds. One of the presenters at the conference was William Cornish, then President of Duff & Phelps Credit Rating Company. In his presentation he identified a unique factor in the credit analysis of high-yield issuers — the characteristics of the types of debt obligations comprising a high-yield issuers debt structure.[11]

Cornish explained why it was necessary for an analyst to examine a high-yield issuer's debt structure. At the time of his presentation, new types of bonds were being introduced into the high-yield market such as deferred coupon bonds (described at Level I (Chapter 1)). He noted that the typical debt structure of a high-yield issuer includes:

- bank debt
- brokers loans or "bridge loans"

---

[11] William A. Cornish, "Unique Factors in the Credit Analysis of High-Yield Bonds," in Frank K. Reilly (ed.), *High-Yield Bonds: Analysis and Risk Assessment* (Charlottesville, VA: Association for Invesment Management and Research, 1990).

- reset notes
- senior debt
- senior subordinated debt
- subordinated debt (payment in kind bonds)

Cornish then goes on to explain the importance of understanding the characteristics of the diverse debt obligations that are included in a typical high-yield debt structure.

Consider first bank loans. While investment-grade issuers also have bank debt in their capital structure, high-yield issuers rely to a greater extent on this form of debt because of a lack of alternative financing sources. Banks loans have three key characteristics. First, holders of bank debt have a priority over other debt holders on the firm's assets. Second, bank debt is typically short-term (usually it is not greater than two years). Finally, the rate on bank debt floats with the level of interest rates.

There are three implications of these characteristics of bank debt for the analysis of the credit worthiness of high-yield issuers. First, because the cost of this source of debt financing is affected by changes in short-term interest rates, the analyst must incorporate changing interest rate scenarios into cash flow projections. A rise in short-term interest rates can impose severe cash flow problems for an issuer heavily financed by bank debt.

Second, because the debt is short term, bank debt must be repaid in the near future. The challenge that the analyst faces is determining where the funds will be obtained to pay off maturing bank debt. There are three sources available:

1. repayment from operating cash flow
2. refinancing
3. sale of assets

Typically, it is a combination of the above three sources that a high-yield issuer will use. The implication is that the analyst must carefully examine the timing and amount of maturing bank debt and consider the sources for repayment.

If the repayment is to come from operations, the projections of cash flow from operations become even more critical than for a high-grade issuer which can rely on a wider range of funding sources such as commercial paper. When refinancing is the source of funds for loan repayment, there is the issue discussed earlier that future conditions in the financial market must be incorporated into the analyst's projections in order to assess future funding costs.

If the source of the loan repayment is the sale of assets, the analyst must consider which assets will be sold and how the sale of such assets will impact future cash flow from operations. If key assets must be sold to pay off maturing bank debt, management is adversely impacting the ability to repay other debt in the future from operating cash flow. In leveraged buyouts, the new management will have a specific plan for the disposal of certain assets in order to pay off bank debt and other debt or related payments. One credit analyst, Jane Tripp Howe, suggests that the analyst ask the following questions regarding asset sales:[12]

"Can the company meet its cash obligations if the sale of assets is delayed?
How liquid are the assets that are scheduled for sale?
Are the appraised value for these assets accurate?"

[12] Jane Tripp Howe, "Credit Considerations in Evaluating High-Yield Bonds," Chapter 21 in Frank J. Fabozzi (ed.), *Handbook of Fixed Income Securities* (Burr Ridge, IL: Irwin Professional Publishing, 1997), p. 408.

Banks will not provide short-term funds where there are insufficient assets to cover a loan in the case of liquidation. If short-term to intermediate-term funds are needed, a high-yield issuer will turn to broker loans (or bridge loans) and/or reset notes. At Level I (Chaper 1) we covered reset notes. A reset note is a security where the coupon rate is reset periodically such that the security price will trade at some specified premium above par value. The presence of reset notes in the debt structure is of particular concern to the analyst for two reasons. First, there is the need to analyze the impact of future interest rates and spreads to assess the impact of higher borrowing costs. Second, to avoid a higher reset rate when interest rates rise due to rising interest rates in general and/or because of a higher spread demanded by the market for the particular issuer, the issuer may seek to dispose of assets. Again the assets sold may have an adverse impact on future operating cash flow.

While there are typically longer term bonds referred to as "senior bonds" in a high-yield issuer's debt structure, the term "senior bonds" is misleading in the presence of bank loans. Moreover, there are deferred coupon bonds. One such bond structure is a zero-coupon bond. Deferred coupon bonds permit the issuer to postpone interest payment to some future year. As a result, the interest burden is placed on future cash flow to meet the interest obligations. Because of this burden, the presence of deferred coupon bonds may impair the ability of the issuer to improve its credit quality in future periods. Moreover, if senior bonds have deferred coupon payments, the subordinated bonds will be adversely affected over time as the amount of senior bonds grows over time relative to the amount of subordinated bonds. For example, one type of deferred coupon bond that was commonly issued at one time was the payment-in-kind (PIK) bond. With this bond structure, a high-yield issuer has the option to either pay interest in cash or pay the equivalent of interest with another bond with the same coupon rate. If the issuer does not have the ability to pay the interest in cash, payment with another bond will increase future interest expense and thereby adversely impact the issuer's future cash flow. If the PIK bonds are senior bonds, subordinated bonds are adversely affected over time as more senior bonds are added to the capital structure and future interest expense is increased further.

B. Analysis of Corporate Structure

High-yield issuers usually have a holding company structure. The assets to pay creditors of the holding company will come from the operating subsidiaries. Cornish explains why it is critical to analyze the corporate structure for a high-yield issuer. Specifically, the analyst must understand the corporate structure in order to assess how cash will be passed between subsidiaries and the parent company and among the subsidiaries. The corporate structure may be so complex that the payment structure can be confusing.

Cornish provides an illustration of this. At the time of his presentation (January 1990), Farley Inc. had the following debt structure: senior subordinated debt, subordinated notes, and junior subordinated debt. The question raised by Cornish was where Farley Inc. was going to obtain cash flow to make payments to its creditors. One possibility was to obtain funds from its operating subsidiaries. At the time, Farley Inc. had three operating subsidiaries: Fruit of the Loom, Acme Boot, and West Point Pepperell. An examination of the debt structure of Fruit of the Loom (20% owned by Farley Inc.) indicated that there was bank debt and no intercompany loans were permitted. While there were restrictions on dividend payments, none were being paid at the time. An examination of the Acme Boot (100% owned by Farley Inc.) showed that there was bank debt and while there were restrictions but no prohibitions on intercompany loans,

Farley Inc. had in fact put cash into this operating subsidiary. Finally, West Point Pepperell (95% owned by Farley Inc.) had bridge loans that restricted asset sales and dividend payments. Moreover, any payments that could be made to Farley Inc. from West Point Pepperell had to be such that they would not violate West Point Pepperell's financial ratio requirements imposed by its bridge loan. The key point of the illustration is that an analyst evaluating the ability of Farley Inc. to meet its obligations to creditors would have to look very closely at the three operating subsidiaries. Just looking at financial ratios for the entire holding company structure would not be adequate. At the time, it was not likely that the three operating subsidiaries would be able to make any contribution to assist the parent company in paying off its creditors.

C. Analysis of Covenants

While an analyst should of course consider covenants when evaluating any bond issue (investment grade or high yield), it is particularly important for the analysis of high-yield issuers. The importance of understanding covenants was summarized by one high-yield portfolio manager, Robert Levine, as follows:[13]

> Covenants provide insight into a company's strategy. As part of the credit process, one must read covenants within the context of the corporate strategy. It is not sufficient to hire a lawyer to review the covenants because a lawyer might miss the critical factors necessary to make the appropriate decision. Also, loopholes in covenants often provide clues about the intentions of management teams.

D. Equity Analysis Approach

Historically, the return on high-yield bonds has been greater than that of high-grade corporate bonds but less than that of common stocks. The risk (as measured in terms of the standard deviation of returns) has been greater than the risk of high-grade bonds but less than that of common stock. Moreover, high-yield bond returns have been found to be more highly correlated to equity returns than to investment grade bond returns. This is why, for example, managers hedging high-yield bond portfolios have found that a combination of stock index futures contracts and Treasury futures contracts has offered a better hedging alternative than just hedging with Treasury bond futures.[14]

Consequently, some portfolio managers strongly believe that high-yield bond analysis should be viewed from an equity analyst's perspective. As Stephen Esser notes:[15]

> Using an equity approach, or at least considering the hybrid nature of high-yield debt, can either validate or contradict the results of traditional credit analysis, causing the analyst to dig further.

He further states:[16]

> For those who work with investing in high-yield bonds, whether issued by public or private companies, dynamic, equity-oriented analysis is invaluable. If analysts think about whether they would

[13] Robert Levine, "Unique Factors in Managing High-Yield Bond Portfolios," in *High-Yield Bonds*, p. 35.
[14] Kenneth S. Choie, "How to Hedge a High-Yield Bond Portfolio," Chapter 13 in Frank J. Fabozzi (ed.), *The New High-Yield Debt Market* (New York, NY: HarperBusiness, 1990).
[15] Stephen F. Esser, "High-Yield Bond Analysis: The Equity Perspective," in Ashwinpaul C. Sondhi (ed.), *Credit Analysis of Nontraditinal Debt Securities* (Charlottesville, VA: Association for Investment Management and Research, 1995), p. 47.
[16] Esser, "High-Yield Bond Analysis: The Equity Perspective," p. 54.

want to buy a particular high-yield company's stock and what will happen to the future equity value of that company, they have a useful approach because, as equity values go up, so does the equity cushion beneath the company's debt. All else being equal, the bonds then become better credits and should go up in value relative to competing bond investments.

We will not review the equity analysis framework here. But, there has been strong sentiment growing in the investment community that an equity analysis approach will provide a better framework for high-yield bond analysis than a traditional credit approach.

SECTION IX CREDIT ANALYSIS OF NON-CORPORATE BONDS

In this section we will look at the key factors analyzed in assessing the credit of the following non-corporate bonds:

- asset-backed securities and non-agency mortgage-backed securities
- municipal bonds
- sovereign bonds

A. Asset-Backed Securities and Non-Agency Mortgage-Backed Securities

Asset-backed securities and non-agency mortgage-backed securities expose investors to credit risk. The three nationally recognized statistical rating organizations rate asset-backed securities. We begin with the factors considered by rating agencies in assigning ratings to asset-backed securities. Then we will discuss how the agencies differ with respect to rating asset-backed securities versus corporate bonds.

1. Factors Considered by Rating Agencies

In analyzing credit risk, the rating companies focus on similar areas of analysis: (1) credit quality of the collateral, (2) the quality of the seller/servicer, (3) cash flow stress and payment structure, and (4) legal structure.[17] We discuss each below.

a. Credit Quality of the Collateral

Analysis of the credit quality of the collateral depends on the asset type. The rating companies will look at the underlying borrower's ability to pay and the borrower's equity in the asset. The latter will be a key determinant as to whether the underlying borrower will default or sell the asset and pay off a loan. The rating companies will look at the experience of the originators of the underlying loans and will assess whether the loans underlying a specific transaction have the same characteristics as the experience reported by the issuer.

The concentration of loans is examined. The underlying principle of asset securitization is that the large number of borrowers in a pool will reduce the credit risk via diversification. If there are a few borrowers in the pool that are significant in size relative to the entire pool balance, this diversification benefit can be lost, resulting in a higher level of default risk. This risk is called **concentration risk**. In such instances, rating companies will set concentration limits on the amount or percentage of receiv-

---

[17] Suzanne Michaud, "A Rating Agency Perspective on Asset-Backed Securities," Chapter 16 in Anand K. Bhattacharya and Frank J. Fabozzi (eds.), *Asset-Backed Securities* (New Hope, PA: Frank J. Fabozzi Associates, 1997).

ables from any one borrower. If the concentration limit at issuance is exceeded, the issue will receive a lower credit rating than if the concentration limit was not exceeded. If after issuance the concentration limit is exceeded, the issue may be downgraded.

Based on its analysis of the collateral and other factors described below, a rating company will determine the amount of credit enhancement necessary for an issue to receive a particular rating. Credit enhancement levels are determined relative to a specific rating desired for a security and can be either internal or external. External credit enhancement can be either insurance, corporate guarantees, letters of credit, or cash collateral reserves. Internal credit enhancements include reserve funds and senior/subordinated structures.

b. Quality of the Seller/Servicer

All loans must be serviced. Servicing involves collecting payments from borrowers, notifying borrowers who may be delinquent, and, when necessary, recovering and disposing of the collateral if the borrower does not make loan repayments by a specified time. These responsibilities are fulfilled by a third-party to an asset-backed securities transaction called a **servicer**. Moreover, while still viewed as a "third-party" in many asset-backed securities transactions, the servicer is effectively the originator of the loans used as the collateral.

In addition to the administration of the loan portfolio as just described, the servicer is responsible for distributing the proceeds collected from the borrowers to the different bondholders in an asset-backed security transaction according to the payment priorities. Where there are floating-rate securities in the transaction, the servicer will determine the interest rate for the period. The servicer may also be responsible for advancing payments when there are delinquencies in payments (that are likely to be collected in the future) resulting in a temporary shortfall in the payments that must be made to the bondholders.

The role of the servicer is critical in an asset-backed security transaction. Therefore, rating agencies look at the ability of a servicer to perform all the activities that a servicer will be responsible for before they assign a rating agency to the bonds in a transaction. For example, the following factors are reviewed when evaluating servicers:[18]

- servicing history
- experience
- underwriting standard for loan originations
- servicing capabilities
- human resources
- financial condition
- growth/competition/business environment.

Based on its analysis, a rating company determines whether the servicer is acceptable or unacceptable. The latter are not rated. The rating companies may require a backup servicer if there is a concern about the ability of a servicer to perform.

Remember that the issuer is not a corporation with employees. It simply has loans and receivables. The servicer therefore plays an important role in assuring that the payments are made to the bondholders. Shortly we will see how the characteristics of the servicer affect the way in which an issue is evaluated in terms of credit quality in comparison to the rating of a corporate bond issue.

[18] Duff & Phelps Credit Rating Co., *Servicer Review Policy*, undated.

c. Cash Flow Stress and Payment Structure

As explained in Chapter 4, the payment structure of an asset-backed security transaction can be either a passthrough or pay through structure. The former simply has one senior tranche and the cash flow is distributed on a pro rata basis to the bondholders. In a pay through structure, the senior tranche is divided into more than one tranche and there are payment rules as to how the cash flows from the collateral are to be distributed amongst the senior tranches.

The decision as to whether a passthrough or pay through structure is used is made by the issuer. Once selected, the rating agencies examine the extent to which the cash flow from the collateral can satisfy all of the obligations of the asset-backed securities transaction. The cash flow of the underlying collateral is interest and principal repayment. The cash flow payments that must be made are interest and principal to investors, servicing fees, and any other expenses for which the issuer is liable. The rating companies analyze the structure to test whether the collateral's cash flows match the payments that must be made to satisfy the issuer's obligations. This requires that the rating company make assumptions about losses and delinquencies and consider various interest rate scenarios.

d. Legal Structure

As explained at Level I, a corporation using structured financing seeks a rating on the securities it issues that is higher than its own corporate rating. This is done by using the underlying loans as collateral for a debt instrument rather the general credit of the issuer. Typically, however, the corporate entity (i.e., seller of the collateral) retains some interest in the collateral. For example, the corporate entity can retain a subordinated class. Because the corporate entity retains an interest, rating companies want to be assured that a bankruptcy of that corporate entity will not allow the issuer's creditors access to the collateral. That is, there is concern that a bankruptcy court could redirect the collateral's cash flows or the collateral itself from the security holders in an asset-backed security transaction to the creditors of the corporate entity if it became bankrupt.

To solve this problem, a bankruptcy-remote special purpose vehicle (SPV) is formed. The issuer of the asset-backed security is then the SPV. Legal opinion is needed stating that in the event of bankruptcy of the seller of the collateral, counsel does not believe that a bankruptcy court will consolidate the collateral sold with the assets of the seller.

The SPV is set up as a wholly-owned subsidiary of the seller of the collateral. Despite the fact that it is a wholly-owned subsidiary, it is established in such a way that it is treated as a third-party entity relative to the seller of the collateral. The collateral is sold to the SPV, which in turn, resells the collateral to the trust. The trust holds the collateral on behalf of the investors. It is the SPV that holds the interest retained by the seller of the collateral.

2. Corporate Bond versus Asset-Backed Securities Credit Analysis

Let's look at how the rating of an asset-backed security transaction differs from that of a corporate bond issue. To understand the difference, it important to appreciate how the cash flow that must be generated differs for an asset-backed security transaction and a corporate bond issue.

In a corporate bond issue, management through its operations must undertake the necessary activities that will produce revenues and collect revenues. Management will incur costs in creating products and services. These costs include management compensation, employees salaries, the costs of raw materials, and financial costs. Consequently, in evaluating the credit risk of a corporate bond issue, an analyst will examine the factors discussed in Section IV regarding the corporation's character and in Section V regarding the corporation's capability to pay.

In contrast, in an asset-backed security transaction, there are assets (loans or receivables) that are to be collected and distributed to bondholders. There are no operating or business risks such as the competitive environment or existence of control systems that are needed to assess the cash flow. What is important is the quality of the collateral in generating the cash flow needed to make interest and principal payments. As mentioned earlier, it is assessing the assurance of cash flow based on different scenarios regarding defaults and delinquencies that the rating agencies will review. It is the greater predictability of the cash flow in an asset-backed security transaction due to the absence of operational risks that distinguishes it from a corporate bond issue.

In a "true" asset-backed security transaction, the role of the servicer is to simply collect the cash flow. There is no active management with respect to the collateral as is the case of the management necessary to operate a corporation to generate cash flow to pay bondholders. Standard & Poor's defines a "true" asset asset-backed security transaction (which this rating agency refers to as a "true securitization") as follows:

> In a true securitization, repayment is not dependent on the ability of the servicer to replenish the pool with new collateral or to perform more than routine administrative functions.[19]

There are asset-backed security transactions where the role of the servicer is more than administrative. Where the role of the servicer is more than administrative, Standard & Poor's, for example, refers to such transactions as **hybrid transactions**. This is because such transactions have elements of an asset-backed security transaction and a corporation performing a service. According to Standard & Poor's:

> In a hybrid transaction, the role of the servicer is akin to that of a business manager. The hybrid servicer performs not only administrative duties, as in a true securitization, but also ... [other] services that are needed to generate cash flow for debt service.[20]

Moreover, Standard & Poor's notes that:

> Unlike a true securitization, where the servicer is a fungible entity replaceable with few, if any, consequences to the transaction, bondholders depend on the expertise of the hybrid servicer for repayment. ... Not coincidentally, these are the same attributes that form the basis of a corporate rating of the hybrid servicer. They also explain the rating linkage between the securitization and its hybrid servicer.[21]

Standard & Poor's provides an illustration of the distinction between a true asset-backed securitization transaction and one requiring a more active role for the

---

[19] Standard & Poor's, "Rating Hybrid Securitizations," *Structured Finance* (October 1999), p. 2.

[20] "Rating Hybrid Securitizations," p. 3.

[21] "Rating Hybrid Securitizations," p. 3.

servicer.[22] Consider a railcar company that has several hundred leases and the leases are with a pool of diversified highly rated companies. Suppose that each lease is for 10 years and it is the responsibility of the customers — not the railcar company — to perform the necessary maintenance on the leased railcars. If there is an asset-backed security transaction backed by these leases and the term of the transaction is 10 years, then the role of the servicer is minimal. Since the leases are for 10 years and the securities issued are for 10 years, the servicer is just collecting the lease payments and distributing them to the holders of the securities. In such a transaction, it possible for this issue to obtain a high investment-grade rating as a true asset-backed security transaction.

Suppose we change the assumptions as follows. The securities issued are for 25 years, not 10 years. Also assume that the railcar company, not the customers, are responsible for the servicing. Now the role of the servicer changes. The servicer will be responsible for finding new companies to release the railcars to when the original leases terminate in 10 years. This is necessary because the securities issued have a maturity of 25 years but the original leases only cover payments to securityholders for the first 10 years. It is the releasing of the railcars that is required for the last 15 years. The servicer under this new set of assumptions is also responsible for the maintenance of the railcars leased. Thus, the servicer must be capable of maintaining the railcars or have on-going arrangements with one or more companies that have the ability to perform such maintenance.

How do rating agency evaluate hybrid transactions? These transactions will be rated both in terms of a standard methodology for rating an asset-backed security transaction and using a "quasi-corporate approach" (in the words of Standard & Poor's) which involves an analysis of the servicer. The relative weight of the evaluations in assigning a rating to an asset-backed security transaction will depend on the involvement of the servicer. The more important the role of the servicer, the more weight will be assigned to the quasi-corporate approach analysis.

B. Municipal Bonds

At Level I we discussed municipal bonds available in the United States — tax-backed debt and revenue bonds. However, municipal governments in other countries are making greater use of bonds with similar structures to raise funds. Below we discuss the factors that should be considered in assessing the credit risk of an issue.

1. Tax-Backed Debt

In assessing the credit risk of tax-backed debt, there are four basic categories that should be considered. The first category includes information on the issuer's debt structure to determine the overall debt burden. The debt burden usually is composed of the respective direct and overlapping debts per capita as well as the respective direct and overlapping debts as percentages of real estate valuations and personal incomes.

The second category relates to the issuer's ability and political discipline to maintain sound budgetary policy. The focus of attention here usually is on the issuer's general operating funds and whether it has maintained at least balanced budgets over three to five years.

The third category involves determining the specific local taxes and intergovernmental revenues available to the issuer, as well as obtaining historical information both on tax collection rates, which are important when looking at property tax levies, and on the dependence of local budgets on specific revenue sources.

---

[22] "Rating Hybrid Securitizations," p. 3.

The final category of information necessary to the credit analysis is an assessment of the issuer's overall socioeconomic environment. The determinations that have to be made here include trends of local employment distribution and composition, population growth, real estate property valuation, and personal income, among other economic factors.

2. Revenue Bonds

Revenue bonds are issued for either project or enterprise financings where the bond issuers pledge to the bondholders the revenues generated by the operating projects financed, or for general public-purpose financings in which the issuers pledge to the bondholders the tax and revenue resources that were previously part of the general fund.

While there are numerous security structures for revenue bonds, the underlying principle in assessing an issuer's credit worthiness is whether the project being financed will generate sufficient cash flows to satisfy the obligations due bondholders. Consequently, the analysis of revenue bonds is similar to the analysis of corporate bonds.

In assessing the credit risk of revenue bonds, the trust indenture and legal opinion should provide legal comfort in the following bond-security areas: (1) the limits of the basic security, (2) the flow-of-funds structure, (3) the rate, or user-charge, covenant, (4) the priority-of-revenue claims, (5) the additional-bonds tests, and (6) other relevant covenants.

a. Limits of the Basic Security

The trust indenture and legal opinion should explain what are the revenues for the bonds and how they realistically may be limited by federal, state, and local laws and procedures. The importance of this is that although most revenue bonds are structured and appear to be supported by identifiable revenue streams, those revenues sometimes can be negatively affected directly by other levels of government.

b. Flow of Funds Structure for Revenue Bonds

For a revenue bond, the revenue of the enterprise is pledged to service the debt of the issue. The details of how revenue received by the enterprise will be disbursed are set forth in the trust indenture. Typically, the flow of funds for a revenue bond is as follows. First, all revenues from the enterprise are put into a **revenue fund**. It is from the revenue fund that disbursements for expenses are made to the following funds: **operation and maintenance fund, sinking fund, debt service reserve fund, renewal and replacement fund, reserve maintenance fund,** and **surplus fund**.

There are structures in which it is legally permissible for others to tap the revenues of the enterprise prior to the disbursement set forth in the flow of funds structure just described. For example, it is possible that the revenue bond could be structured such that the revenue is first applied to the general obligation of the municipality that has issued the bond.

Operations of the enterprise have priority over the servicing of the issue's debt, and cash needed to operate the enterprise is deposited from the revenue fund into the operation and maintenance fund. The pledge of revenue to the bondholders is a net revenue pledge, "net" meaning after operation expenses, so cash required to service the debt is deposited next into the sinking fund. Disbursements are then made to bondholders as specified in the trust indenture. Any remaining cash is then distributed to the reserve funds.

The purpose of the debt service reserve fund is to accumulate cash to cover any shortfall of future revenue to service the issue's debt. The specific amount that must be deposited is stated in the trust indenture. The function of the renewal and replacement fund is to accumulate cash for regularly scheduled major repairs and equipment replacement. The function of the reserve maintenance fund is to accumulate cash for extraordinary maintenance or replacement costs that might arise. Finally, if any cash remains after disbursement for operations, debt servicing, and reserves, it is deposited in the surplus fund. The issuer can use the cash in this fund in any way it deems appropriate.

c. Rate, or User-Charge, Covenants

There are various restrictive covenants included in the trust indenture for a revenue bond to protect the bondholders. A **rate covenant** (or **user charge covenant**) dictates how charges will be set on the product or service sold by the enterprise. The covenant could specify that the minimum charges be set so as to satisfy both expenses and debt servicing, or to yield a higher rate to provide for a certain amount of reserves.

d. Priority-of-Revenue Claims

The legal opinion as summarized in the official statement should clearly indicate whether or not others can legally tap the revenue of the issuer even before they start passing through the issuer's flow-of-funds structure.

e. Additional-Bonds Test

An **additional-bonds test covenant** indicates whether additional bonds with the same lien may be issued. If additional bonds with the same lien may be issued, the conditions that must first be satisfied are specified. Other covenants specify that the facility may not be sold, the amount of insurance to be maintained, requirements for record-keeping and for the auditing of the enterprise's financial statements by an independent accounting firm, and requirements for maintaining the facilities in good order.

f. Other Relevant Covenants

There are other relevant covenants for the bondholder's protection that the trust indenture and legal opinion should cover. These usually include pledges by the issuer of the bonds to have insurance on the project, to have accounting records of the issuer annually audited by an outside certified public accountant, to have outside engineers annually review the condition of the facility, and to keep the facility operating for the life of the bonds.

3. Corporate Versus Municipal Bond Credit Analysis

The credit analysis of municipal bonds involves the same factors and quantitative measures as in corporate credit analysis. For tax-backed debt, the analysis of the character of the public officials is the same as that of the analysis of the character of management for a corporate bond. The analysis of the ability to pay in the case of tax-backed debt involves looking at the ability of the issuing entity to generate taxes and fees. As a corporate analyst would look at the composition of the revenues and profits by product line for a corporation, the municipal analyst will look at employment, industry, and real estate valuation trends needed to generate taxes and fees.

The credit analysis of municipal revenue bonds is identical to that of a corporate bond analysis. Effectively, the enterprise issuing a municipal revenue bond must generate cash flow from operations to satisfy the bond payments. For example, here are the types of questions that a municipal analyst evaluating a toll road, bridge, or tunnel revenue bond would ask. As you read these questions you will see that they are the same types of questions that a corporate analyst would ask in evaluating a corporate issuer if it could issue a bond for a toll road, bridge, or tunnel.[23]

1. What is the traffic history and how sensitive is the demand to the toll charged? Equivalently, does the toll road, bridge, or tunnel provide a vital transportation link or does it face competition from interstate highways, toll-free bridges, or mass transportation?

2. How well is the facility maintained? Has the issuer established a maintenance reserve fund at a reasonable level to use for such repair work as road resurfacing and bridge painting?

3. What is the history of labor-management relations, and can public employee strikes substantially reduce toll collections?

The covenants that are unique to a municipal revenue bond and impact the credit analysis are the rate covenants and the priority-of-revenue covenants. The former dictates how the user charges will be set to meet the bond obligations. Also, just as in the case of a bond issue of a regulated corporate entity, restrictions on pricing must be recognized. In a municipal revenue bond the analyst must determine whether or not changes in the user charge requires approval of other governmental entities such as the governor or state legislature. Priority-of-revenue covenants specify if other parties can legally tap the revenue of the enterprise before the revenue can be passed through to bondholders.

C. Sovereign Bonds

While U.S. government debt is not rated by any nationally recognized statistical rating organization, the debt of other national governments is rated. These ratings are referred to as **sovereign ratings**. Standard & Poor's and Moody's rate sovereign debt. We will first look at the factors considered by rating agencies in assigning sovereign ratings and then look at a structured approach that an analyst familiar with corporate credit analysis can use in assessing sovereign credits.

1. Factors Considered By Rating Agencies

The categories used by S&P in deriving their ratings are listed in Exhibit 2. The two general categories are economic risk and political risk. The former category is an assessment of the ability of a government to satisfy its obligations. Both quantitative and qualitative analyses are used in assessing economic risk. Political risk is an assessment of the willingness of a government to satisfy its obligations. A government may have the ability to pay, but may be unwilling to pay. Political risk is assessed based on qualitative analysis of the economic and political factors that influence a government's economic policies.

There are two ratings assigned to each national government. One is a **local currency debt rating** and the other is a **foreign currency debt rating**. The reason for distinguishing between the two types of debt is that historically, the default frequency differs by the currency denomination of the debt. Specifically, defaults have been greater on foreign currency denominated debt.[24]

---

[23] Sylvan G. Feldstein and Frank J. Fabozzi, *The Dow Jones-Irwin Guide to Municipal Bonds* (Homewood, IL: Dow Jones-Irwin, 1987), p. 72.

[24] David T. Beers and Marie Cavanaugh, "Sovereign Ratings: A Primer," Chapter 6 in Frank J. Fabozzi and Alberto Franco (eds.), *Handbook of Emerging Fixed Income & Currency Markets* (New Hope, PA: Frank J. Fabozzi Associates, 1997).

Exhibit 2: Sovereign Ratings Methodology Profile

Political Risk
- Form of government and adaptability of political institutions
- Extent of popular participation
- Orderliness of leadership succession
- Degree of consensus on economic policy objectives
- Integration in global trade and financial system
- Internal and external security risks

Income and Economic Structure
- Living standards, income, and wealth distribution
- Market, non-market economy
- Resource endowments, degree of diversification

Economic Growth Prospects
- Size, composition of savings, and investment
- Rate, pattern of economic growth

Fiscal Flexibility
- General government operating and total budget balances
- Tax competitiveness and tax-raising flexibility
- Spending pressures

Public Debt Burden
- General government financial assets
- Public debt and interest burden
- Currency composition, structure of public debt
- Pension liabilities
- Contingent liabilities

Price Stability
- Trends in price inflation
- Rates of money and credit growth
- Exchange rate policy
- Degree of central bank autonomy

Balance of Payments Flexibility
- Impact on external accounts of fiscal and monetary policies
- Structure of the current account
- Composition of capital flows

External Debt and Liquidity
- Size and currency composition of public external debt
- Importance of banks and other public and private entities as contingent liabilities of the sovereign
- Maturity structure and debt service burden
- Debt service track record
- Level, composition of reserves and other public external assets

The reason for the difference in default rates for local currency debt and foreign currency debt is that if a government is willing to raise taxes and control its domestic financial system, it can generate sufficient local currency to meet its local currency debt obligation. This is not the case with foreign currency denominated debt. A national government must purchase foreign currency to meet a debt obligation in that foreign currency and therefore has less control with respect to its exchange rate. Thus, a significant depreciation of the local currency relative to a foreign currency in which a debt obligation is denominated will impair a national government's ability to satisfy such obligation.

The implication of this is that the factors S&P analyzes in assessing the credit worthiness of a national government's local currency debt and foreign currency debt will differ to some extent. In assessing the credit quality of local currency debt, for example, S&P emphasizes domestic government policies that foster or impede timely debt service. The key factors looked at by S&P are:

"• the stability of political institutions and degree of popular participation in the political process,
- income and economic structure,
- fiscal policy and budgetary flexibility,
- monetary policy and inflation pressures, and
- public debt burden and debt service track record."[25]

---

[25] Beers and Cavanaugh, "Sovereign Credit Ratings: A Primer," p. 68.

Exhibit 3: Criteria for Lending to Sovereign Borrowers

I. *Character*
   A. Ability to resolve internal conflicts
   B. Potential for social unrest
   C. Orderly succession
   D. External factors
   E. Relations with other nations and membership in regional alliances
   F. Relations with the United States

II. *Capacity*
   A. External liquidity
   B. Domestic policy
   C. Structural variables

III. *Capital*
   A. Internal Reserves ÷ Imports
   B. Debt Service ÷ Exports
   C. Government Surplus ÷ Government Revenues
   D. Bank Net Claims on Government ÷ (Net Foreign Assets + Total Domestic Credit)
   E. Exports ÷ Gross Domestic Product
   F. Domestic Per Capita GDP ÷ US Per Capita GDP

Source: Exhibit 22-2 in Martin S. Fridson, "Sovereign Risk From a Corporate Bond Analyst Perspective," Chapter 22 in Frank J. Fabozzi (ed.), *The Handbook of Fixed Income Securities: Fourth Edition* (Burr Ridge, Il: Irwin Professional Publishing, 1995), p. 474.

For foreign currency debt, credit analysis by S&P focuses on the interaction of domestic and foreign government policies. S&P analyzes a country's balance of payments and the structure of its external balance sheet. The area of analysis with respect to its external balance sheet are the net public debt, total net external debt, and net external liabilities.

2. Corporate Versus Sovereign Bond Credit Analysis

Martin Fridson, a specialist in high yield corporate bonds, has argued that a valid reason for a manager to avoid investing in a sector of the bond market is lack of familiarity with the sector.[26] There are managers who have shunned sovereign bonds because they are uncomfortable with analyzing the credit. However, Fridson believes that this can be remedied. He argues that:

> By several criteria, sovereign debt is inherently no more difficult to analyze than corporate debt. Put another way, there is no greater probability of success in foreseeing credit problems in the private sector than in the public sector. Investors who insist on following a systematic method should perceive no insuperable barriers to a judicious use of sovereign debt.[27]

Fridson suggests a structured framework that an analyst familiar with corporate credit analysis can use to make sense of sovereign risk. Exhibit 3 identifies the

---

[26] Martin S. Fridson, "Sovereign Risk From a Corporate Bond Analyst Perspective," Chapter 22 in Frank J. Fabozzi (ed.), *The Handbook of Fixed Income Securities: Fourth Edition* (Burr Ridge, Il: Irwin Professional Publishing, 1995).

[27] Fridson, "Sovereign Risk From a Corporate Bond Analyst Perspective," p. 480.

information Fridson suggests are needed to assess sovereign risk. The structure in the exhibit was based on ideas of commercial bankers using three Cs — character, capacity, and capital.

In assessing the credit risk of a sovereign entity, an analyst may be uncomfortable with the non-quantitative factors or intangibles such as those listed under "character" in Exhibit 3. However, as noted earlier in this chapter in discussing the analysis of corporate bonds, non-quantitative factors such as the character of the issuer are important in corporate bond analysis. As Fridson notes:

> The necessity of dealing with certain intangibles is inherent to corporate and sovereign risk assessment. Analysts of corporate credits have long recognized the importance of nonfinancial considerations, particularly the quality of management....
>
> Despite their lack of concreteness, such factors significantly influence credit risk. In this respect, corporate and sovereign analysis are not as dissimilar as they might seem at first glance.[28]

While non-quantitative factors are important, a corporate analyst may have more concerns with the quality of the quantitative data provided by a sovereign than a corporation. Fridson addresses this by stating:

> Should we not automatically put more faith in a corporate financial analysis than in an assessment of a sovereign government? Private companies' financial reports, after all, are ordinarily presented in accordance with generally accepted accounting principles (GAAP). Additional confidence should derive from the independent audit that usually accompanies the statements. In contrast, the sovereigns are by definition a law unto themselves. They are invariably confronted with intense political pressures, including the need to sway public opinion regarding economic performance. Surely, the temptation must be great to withhold or manipulate the true economic figures.[29]

However, he concludes that:

> Once again, whatever differences exist between corporates and sovereigns are matters of degree, not of kind. Companies do not invariably publish dependable financial statements, nor are all government-furnished economic reports incomplete or suspect.[30]

He argues that if one uses corporate financial reporting as the benchmark, then based on interviews he conducted with sovereign risk specialists, investors should be comfortable with official government statistics, although it is acknowledged that the quality varies from country to country.

---

[28] Fridson, "Sovereign Risk From a Corporate Bond Analyst Perspective," pp. 475-476.
[29] Fridson, "Sovereign Risk From a Corporate Bond Analyst Perspective," p. 476.
[30] Fridson, "Sovereign Risk From a Corporate Bond Analyst Perspective," p. 476.

SECTION X
KEY POINTS

❑ *There are three types of credit risk: default risk, credit spread risk, and downgrade risk.*

❑ *Default risk is the risk that the issuer will fail to meet its obligation to make timely payment of interest and principal.*

❑ *Credit spread risk is the risk that the spread that the market demands for an issue will increase or widen, resulting in inferior performance of an issue relative to other issues.*

❑ *Downgrade risk is the risk that the issue will be downgraded, resulting in an increase in the credit spread demanded by the market.*

❑ *A credit analyst must consider the four C's of credit — character, capacity, collateral, and covenants.*

❑ *Character relates to the ethical reputation as well as the business qualifications and operating record of the board of directors, management, and executives responsible for the use of the borrowed funds and its repayment.*

❑ *Capacity deals with the ability of an issuer to repay its obligations.*

❑ *Collateral involves not only the traditional pledging of assets to secure the debt, but also the quality and value of those unpledged assets controlled by the issuer.*

❑ *Covenants are important because they impose restrictions on how management operates the company and conducts its financial affairs.*

❑ *The statement of cash flows is used in the analysis of an entity's ability to repay its financial obligations and to gain insight into an entity's financing methods, capital investment strategies, and dividend policy.*

❑ *To assess the ability of a company to meet its financial obligations, an analyst looks at profitability ratios that help explain the underlying causes of a change in the company's earnings.*

❑ *One of the best ways an analyst can predict future downward earnings is through a careful analysis of accounts receivable and inventories; two signs that can indicate problems are a larger than average accounts receivable balance situation and/or a bloated inventory.*

❑ *There are three sets of ratios that are used by credit analysts as indicators to assess the ability of a firm to satisfy its debt obligations: (1) short-term solvency ratios which assess the ability of the firm to meet debts maturing over the coming year, (2) capitalization (or financial leverage) ratios which assess the extent to which the firm relies on debt financing, and (3) coverage ratios which assess the ability of the firm to meet the fixed obligations brought about by debt financing.*

❑ *An analyst should look at the maturity structure of the issuer's debt.*

❑ *Traditional ratios by themselves are not adequate as an early warning signal to an analyst of the financial difficulties that a firm might encounter; analysts have found that an analysis of cash flows from operations provides a better warning signal regarding future potential financial problems than traditional ratio analysis.*

❑ *The statement of cash flows can be recast to provide information about the financial flexibility of a company; from the basic cash flow, the nondiscretionary cash needs are subtracted to determine discretionary cash flow.*

❑ *The cash flow to capital expenditures ratio gives an analyst information about the financial flexibility of the company, particularly for capital-intensive firms and utilities.*

❑ *Negative covenants are covenants which require the borrower not to take certain actions; some of the more common restrictive covenants include various limitations on the company's ability to incur debt.*

❑ *There are two types of interest or fixed charge coverage tests: (1) a maintenance test which requires the borrower's ratio of earnings available for interest or fixed charges to be at least a certain minimum figure and (2) a debt incurrence test when the company wishes to do additional borrowing.*

❑ *In addition, there could be cash flow tests or requirements and working capital maintenance provisions.*

❑ *In analyzing the credit worthiness of high-yield corporate bond issuers, the analyst will want to pay close attention to the characteristics of the debt obligations in the capital structure.*

❑ *The corporate structure is particularly important to investigate when assessing the credit worthiness of high-yield corporate bond issuers where there is a holding company structure because of potential limitations or restrictions on cash flow from operating subsidiaries to the parent company and among operating subsidiaries.*

❑ *Covenants in high-yield corporate bond issues should be reviewed in conjunction with the issuer's overall strategy.*

❑ *Some analysts believe that in assessing the credit quality of a high-yield corporate bond issuer an equity analysis approach is more informative than simply a traditional credit analysis approach.*

❑ *In analyzing the credit risk of an asset-backed security, rating companies basically look at four factors: (1) the credit quality of the collateral; (2) the quality of the seller/servicer, (3) cash flow stress test and payment (financial) structures, and (4) legal structure.*

❑ *A key factor in assessing the quality of the collateral is the amount of equity the borrowers have in the asset.*

❑ *To reduce concentration risk in an asset-backed security, rating companies impose concentration limits.*

❑ *Based on their analysis of the four factors in assigning ratings, rating companies will determine the amount of credit enhancement needed for an issue to receive a particular rating.*

❑ *Fundamentally, because of the absence of operational risk an asset-backed security transaction generally has greater certainty about the cash flow than a corporate bond issue.*

❑ *A true asset-backed security transaction involves minimal involvement by the servicer beyond administrative functions.*

❑ *In a hybrid asset-backed security transaction, the service has more than an administrative function; the greater the importance of the servicer, the more the transaction should be evaluated as a quasi-corporate entity.*

❑ *In assessing the credit risk of tax-backed debt, four basic informational categories should be considered: (1) information on the issuer's debt structure to determine the overall debt burden; (2) information on the issuer's ability and political discipline to maintain sound budgetary policy; (3) information on the specific local taxes and intergovernmental revenues available to the issuer; and, (4) information on the issuer's overall socioeconomic environment.*

❑ *While there are numerous security structures for revenue bonds, the underlying principle in rating is whether the project being financed will generate sufficient cash flows to satisfy the obligations due bondholders.*

❑ *The principles involved in analyzing the credit risk of a revenue bond are the same as for a corporate bond.*

❑ *In assessing the credit risk for revenue bonds, the trust indenture and legal opinion should provide legal comfort in the following bond-security areas: (1) the limits of the basic security, (2) the flow-of-funds structure, (3) the rate, or user-charge, covenant, (4) the priority-of-revenue claims, (5) the additional-bonds tests, and (6) other relevant covenants.*

❑ *Sovereign credits are rated by Standard & Poor's and Moody's.*

❑ *In deriving ratings, the two general categories analyzed are economic risk (the ability to pay) and political risk (the willingness to pay).*

❑ *There are two ratings assigned to each central government: a local currency debt rating and a foreign currency debt rating.*

❑ *Historically, defaults have been greater on foreign currency denominated debt.*

❑ *In assessing the credit quality of local currency debt, rating agencies emphasize domestic government policies that foster or impede timely debt service.*

❑ *For foreign currency debt, rating agencies analyze a country's balance of payments and the structure of its external balance sheet.*

❑ *Analysts familiar with corporate credit analysis can build a structure for the analysis of quantitative and qualitative information of a sovereign issuer.*

❑ *Analysts must assess qualitative factors in assessing the credit risk of both a sovereign and corporate entity.*

❑ *A structure developed for corporate credit analysis can be developed for assessing the credit risk of a sovereign.*

Appendix

CASE STUDY: BERGEN BRUNSWIG CORPORATION

The purpose of this case is to illustrate the how the analysis of financial statements based on traditional ratios discussed in this chapter can be used to identify a corporate issuer that might be downgraded. The corporation used in the illustration is Bergen Brunswig Corporation.

SECTION I BACKGROUND INFORMATION

Bergen Brunswig Corporation is a supply channel management company that provides pharmaceuticals, medical-surgical supplies, and specialty products. The company also provides information management solutions and outsourcing services, as well as develops disease-specific treatment protocols and pharmaco-economic initiatives to assist in the reduction of healthcare costs.

The original corporate bond rating was BBB+. On December 17, 1999, S&P lowered the company's rating to BBB– citing "disappointing results at the company's two recently acquired businesses, PharMerica and Statlander." PharMerica, an institutional pharmacy, suffered from changes in Medicare reimbursement policies which reduced hospital patient occupancy and the use of high-margin drugs.

On February 2, 2000, S&P decided to downgrade the company's corporate rating again to BB. S&P's rationale was "deteriorating conditions in the company's core drug distribution business as well as continued losses at Statlander, a specialty drug distributor acquired in 1999."

SECTION II ANALYSIS

Exhibit A1 shows the financial data for the 1996-1999 fiscal years and various financial ratios. (The financial ratios are shaded in the exhibit.) The company's fiscal year ends on September 30th. Since each rating agency uses slightly different inputs for the ratios it computes, we have included the ratio definitions used by S&P in Exhibit A2.

Exhibit A3 provides a summary of all the ratios that show a deteriorating trend of Bergen Brunswig's financial condition. The eight ratios shown in the exhibit strongly suggest that Bergen Brunswig was losing its financial strength and could possibly be a candidate for downgrade. To show the degree of deterioration, Exhibit A3 also displays for the eight ratios the median ratios for BBB and BB ratings.

Exhibit A4 highlights the trending of two key ratios — EBIT interest coverage and funds from operations/total debt — relative to the BBB benchmark. For 1999, the EBIT fell below 4 times, the median for BBB rated firms. For 1999, the ratio of funds from operations to total debt fell below the median for BB rated firms.

Exhibit A1: Financial Data and Selected Ratios for Bergen Brunswig: Fiscal Years 1996-1999 Based on 10K Data

			1999	1998	1997	1996
1	Revenue	1	$17,244,905	$13,720,017	$11,659,127	
	COGS	1	$(16,145,378)	$(12,969,752)	$(11,004,696)	
	SG & A		$(837,700)	$(534,119)	$(479,399)	
	EBIT		*$261,827*	*$216,146*	*$175,032*	
	Interest Expense	2	*$74,143*	*$39,996*	*$30,793*	
	EBIT interest coverage		3.53	5.40	5.68	
2	EBIT		$261,827	$216,146	$175,032	
	Depreciation & Amortization		$66,031	$37,465	$40,756	
	EBITDA		*$327,858*	*$253,611*	*$215,788*	
	Interest Expense		*$74,143*	*$39,996*	*$30,793*	
	EBITDA interest coverage		4.42	6.34	7.01	
3	Net Income		$70,573	$3,102	$81,679	
	Depreciation & Amortization		$66,031	$37,465	$40,756	
	Current Deferred Income Taxes		$10,840	$41,955	$10,577	
	Other Noncash Items					
	Deferred Compensation		$2,552	$2,809	$2,266	
	Doubtful Receivables		$85,881	$11,934	$11,899	
	Writedown of goodwill			$87,271		
	Abandonment of capitalized			$5,307		
	Funds from operations		*$235,877*	*$189,843*	*$147,177*	
	Long Term Debt		$1,041,983	$464,778	$437,956	$419,275
	Lease Debt Equivalent (see attached)		$82	$53	$59	$43
	Long Term Debt*		$1,042,065	$464,831	$438,015	$419,318
	Current Maturity of LTD		$545,923	$6,029	$1,021	1,125
	Total Debt		*$1,587,988*	*$470,860*	*$439,036*	*$420,443*
	Funds from operations/total debt		14.85%	40.32%	33.52%	
4	Funds from operations		$235,877	$189,843	$147,177	
	Capital Expenditure		($305,535)	($52,361)	($23,806)	
	Working Capital		$1,199,527	$518,443	$474,910	$643,607
	Change in WC		$(681,084)	$(43,533)	$168,697	
	Free operating cash flow	3	*$(750,742)*	*$93,949*	*$292,068*	
	Total Debt		*$1,587,988*	*$470,860*	*$439,036*	
	Free operating cash flow/total debt		−47.28%	19.95%	66.52%	
5	*EBIT*		*$261,827*	*$216,146*	*$175,032*	
	Total debt		$1,587,988	$470,860	$439,036	$420,443
	Equity		$1,495,490	$629,064	$644,861	$666,877
	Non-current deferred taxes				$1,791	
	Total Capital		$3,083,478	$1,099,924	$1,085,688	$1,087,320
	Average Capital		*2,091,701.10*	*1,092,806.15*	*1,086,503.89*	
	Pretax return on capital		12.52%	19.78%	16.11%	
6	Operating Income		$261,827	$216,146	$175,032	
	Sales		$17,244,905	$13,720,017	$11,659,127	
	Operating Income/Sales		1.52%	1.58%	1.50%	

Exhibit A1 (Continued)

	1999	1998	1997	1996
7 *Long Term Debt**	*$1,042,065*	*$464,831*	*$438,015*	
Long-term debt	$1,041,983	$464,778	$437,956	
Shareholders' equity	$1,495,490	$629,064	$644,861	
Capitalization	*$2,537,473*	*$1,093,842*	*$1,082,817*	
Long-term debt/Capitalization	41.07%	42.50%	40.45%	
8 *Total Debt*	*$1,587,988*	*$470,860*	*$439,036*	
Shareholders' equity	$1,495,490	$629,064	$644,861	
Capitalization	*$3,083,478*	*$1,099,924*	*$1,083,897*	
Total debt/Capitalization	51.50%	42.81%	40.51%	

* Bergen Brunswig fiscal year ends September 30th.

1. Revenues and Cost of Goods Sold excludes bulk shipment to customers' warehouse sites. The Company only serves as a intermediary and there is no material impact on the Company's operating earnings.

2. (a) Does not include pre-tax distributions on the Company's Preferred Securities.
   (b) Although the S&P formulas call for "Gross Interest Expense" net interest is used because Gross Interest Expense was unavailable in the filings and could not be inferred.

3. Free operating cash flow = Funds from operations + Capital expenditure + Change in WC.

Note for the above formula for free operating cash flow:
   (a) Capital expenditure is shown as a negative in the exhibit. That is why it is added to obtain free operating cash flow. (This is consistent with S&P's formula for free operating cash flow as given in formula (4) in Exhibit A2.)
   (b) Increase in working capital for 1998 and 1999 is shown as a negative, so is added to free operating cash flow as per the S&P formula (4) in Exhibit A2.

Exhibit A2: S&P's Formulas for Key Ratios

1. EBIT interest coverage $= \dfrac{\text{Earnings from continuing operations** before interest and taxes}}{\text{Gross interest incurred before subtracting (1) capitalized interest and (2) interest income}}$

2. EBITDA interest coverage $= \dfrac{\text{Earnings from continuing operations** before interest and taxes, depreciation, and amortization}}{\text{Gross interest incurred before subtracting (1) capitalized interest and (2) interest income}}$

3. Funds from operations/total debt $= \dfrac{\text{Net income from continuing operations plus depreciation, amortization, deferred income taxes, and other noncash items}}{\text{Long-term debt* plus current maturities, commercial paper, and other short-term borrowings}}$

4. Free operating cash flow/total debt $= \dfrac{\text{Funds from operations minus capital expenditures, minus (plus) the increase (decrease) in working capital (excluding changes in cash)}}{\text{Long-term debt* plus current maturities, commercial paper, and other short-term borrowings}}$

5. Pretax return on capital $= \dfrac{\text{EBIT}}{\text{Average of beginning of year and end of year capital, including short-term debt, current maturities, long-term debt*, non-current deferred taxes, and equity}}$

6. Operating income/sales $= \dfrac{\text{Sales minus cost of goods manufactured (before depreciation and amortization), selling, general and administrative, and research and development costs}}{\text{Sales}}$

7. Long-term debt/capitalization $= \dfrac{\text{Long-term debt*}}{\text{Long-term debt + shareholders' equity (including preferred stock) plus minority interest}}$

8. Total debt/capitalization $= \dfrac{\text{Long-term debt* plus current maturities, commercial paper, and other short-term borrowings}}{\text{Long-term debt* plus current maturities, commercial paper, and other short-term borrowings + shareholders' equity (including preferred stock) plus minority interest}}$

* Including amount for operating lease debt equivalent
** Including interest income and equity earnings; excluding nonrecurring items.

Exhibit A3: Summary of Ratios Showing Deteriorating Trend and Median Ratio for S&P BBB and BB Ratings

	1999	1998	1997	BBB Median	BB Median
EBIT interest coverage	3.53	5.40	5.68	4.10	2.5
EBITDA interest coverage	4.42	6.34	7.01	6.30	3.9
Funds from operations/total debt	14.85%	40.32%	33.52%	32.30%	20.10%
Free operating cash flow/total debt	−47.28%	19.95%	66.52%	6.30%	1.00%
Pretax return on capital	12.52%	19.78%	16.11%	15.40%	12.60%
Operating income/Sales	1.52%	1.58%	1.50%	15.80%	14.40%
Long-term debt/Capitalization	41.07%	42.50%	40.45%	40.80%	55.30%
Total debt/Capitalization	51.50%	42.81%	40.51%	46.40%	58.50%

Exhibit A4: Trending of EBIT Interest Leverage and Funds from Operating/Total Debt Ratios Relative to BBB and BB Benchmark

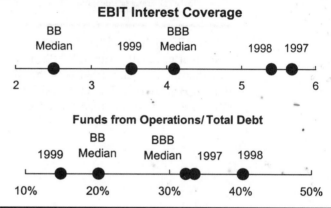

SECTION III CONCLUSION

An analysis of the key ratios would have clearly signaled by December 1999 that Bergen Brunswig was a candidate for downgrading. As noted earlier, S&P lowered the company's corporate credit rating from BBB+ to BBB− on December 17, 1999 and then lowered it again on February 2, 2000 to BB. Among the reasons for the downgrade, S&P indicated that it expected EBITDA/interest to drop below 4 times in fiscal year 2000.

While we have demonstrated that traditional analysis could have identified a potential downgrade, what we did not address was the timing of information for preparing the analysis and reaching our conclusion. Specifically, S&P downgraded Bergen Brunswig the first time on December 17, 1999, but the company did not file its 10K (annual filing with the SEC) until December 29, 1999. Although we use the 10K numbers (since they are more accurate) for this project, an analyst would most probably estimate the ratios by looking at the 10Qs (the quarterly filings with the SEC).

Exhibit A5 shows how this would be done for the first two ratios (EBIT interest coverage and EBITDA interest coverage). An analyst would add the results from the first 9 months of 1999 (fiscal year) to the last quarter of 1998 in order to estimate the annual ratio and show the trend.

As we can see from Exhibit A5, the annualized EBITDA interest coverage ratio (5.65) is much lower than the 1998 ratio. If we take a closer look, the ratio for the first nine months of 1999 is even lower. This strongly suggests a deteriorating trend. Bergen Brunswig filed its 1999 third quarter 10Q on August 17, 1999, so the information was available to the analyst before December 1999.

Exhibit A5: Using Quarterly Financial Data from Bergen Brunswig to Compute EBIT and EBITDA Interest Coverage Ratios

	1999 9 months	1998 4Q	Annualized Estimate
Revenue	$12,716,939	$3,666,166	$16,383,105
COGS	$(11,938,185)	$(3,466,355)	$(15,404,540)
SG & A	$(559,142)	$(144,725)	$(703,867)
EBIT	$219,612	$55,086	$274,698
Interest Expense	47,906.00	$9,657	57,563.00
EBIT interest coverage	4.58	5.70	4.77
EBIT	$219,612	$55,086	$274,698
Depreciation & Amortization	$40,497	$9,847	$50,344
EBITDA	$260,109	$64,933	$325,042
Interest Expense	$47,906	$9,657	$57,563
EBITDA interest coverage	5.43	6.72	5.65

We believe S&P further lowered Bergen Brunswig's rating because of the first quarter result. Again, S&P's action date (February 2) is slightly earlier than the date that the company filed with the SEC (February 17). However, the weakening of Bergen Brunswig's financial position is apparent by the fact that the full-year 1999 ratios are even weaker than those for the first nine months of 1999.

END OF CHAPTER QUESTIONS

1. Explain whether you agree or disagree with the following statement: "The credit risk of a bond is the risk that the issuer will fail to meet its obligation to make timely payment of interest and principal."

2. What are some of the major factors considered by rating agencies in assessing the quality of management?

3. a. There are various forms of back-up credit facilities available to a corporation. What factors should an analyst consider in assessing the back-up credit facilities available to an issuer?

   b. What is a "material adverse change clause provision" in a back-up credit facility and what is its significance in terms of the strength of a back-up credit facility?

4. In 1998 there were several developments in Europe leading to the liberalization of the European telecommunication industry. In October 1998, Moody's Investors Service published a report ("Rating Methodology: European Telecoms") addressing the issues in the rating of European telecommunication companies. Below are quotes from the report followed by questions that should be answered.

   a. "We look carefully at a company's general funding strategy – the debt and equity markets the company accesses, and the sources of bank financing it arranges. ... This becomes more important the lower down the rating scale, particularly in the case of high yield issuers ..." (p. 10) Why is the funding strategy of high-yield issuers of particular concern to Moody's analysts?

   b. "As a very general rule of thumb, the larger the company's cushion of cash and assets above fixed payments due, the more able it will be to meet maturing debt obligations in potentially adverse conditions, and the higher the rating. In many cases, the size of this cushion may be less important than its predictability or sustainability. Moody's views the telecom industry as having generally very predictable revenue streams, which accounts for the relatively high level of ratings of the telecom industry compared to other industries." (p. 10) Explain why "predictability and sustainability" may be more important than size of a coverage ratio.

   c. In discussing the financial measures it uses, the report explains the importance of "cash flow to debt figures." The report stated (p. 11), "We also look at adjusted retained cash flow which includes any items which we view as nondiscretionary to gauge the financial flexibility of a company, ..." What is meant by "financial flexibility of a company"?

   d. The quote in the previous part ends with "as well as adjusted debt figures which include unfunded pension liabilities and guarantees." Why would Moody's adjust debt figures for these items?

   e. In the report, Moody's looks at various measures considered in ratings such as coverage ratios and capitalization ratios, and shows these ratios for a sample of European telecom companies. In each case when discussing ratios, Moody's notes the "loose correlation" between ratings and ratios; that is, it is not necessarily the case that companies with the best ratios will always receive a better rating. Moody's noted that "inconsistencies underscore the limitations of ratio analysis." (p. 11). Explain why one might expect a loose correlation between ratios and ratings.

5. How does a statement of cash flows after adjusting for nondiscretionary cash needs allow the analyst to assess a firm's "financial flexibility"?

6. Karl Hieber is a credit analyst who has been assigned Hot Head Products Inc. The company manufactures hair products for the retail market. For the current year, the firm's operating cash flow is $50 million. The company pays dividends of $25 million. Based on discussions with management, Mr. Hieber believes that the company's capital expenditure for the year will be $30 million.

   a. What is Mr. Hieber's estimate of the discretionary cash flow for Hot Head Products Inc.?
   b. What is the implication of the discretionary cash flow computed in part a for Hot Head Products Inc.?

7. a. Why is the analysis of covenants important in credit analysis?
   b. What is a negative covenant?
   c. Why is covenant analysis particularly important for assessing the credit worthiness of high-yield corporate issuers?

8. a. Why is the cash flow from operations to capital expenditures ratio a useful measure for an analyst?
   b. How can a declining cash flow from operations to capital expenditures ratio be interpreted?

9. Explain the following two statements made by Robert Levine in "Unique Factors in Managing High-Yield Bond Portfolios," in Frank K. Reilly (ed.), *High- Yield Bonds: Analysis and Risk Assessment* (Charlottesville, VA: Association for Invesment Management and Research, 1990), p. 36.

   a. "One must understand the structure because not all debt that is listed as senior is actually senior debt."
   b. "Intellectually zero-coupon bonds are troublesome when they are not at the bottom of the capital structure... From a credit standpoint, it is not desirable to have more senior debt growing faster than the subordinated cash-pay securities, thus offering less protection to the subordinated holders in bankruptcy. We prefer to see less debt that is less senior growing faster than the debt that is more senior — e.g., less above us in the event of bankruptcy."

10. Explain why an understanding of the corporate structure of a high-yield issuer that has a holding company structure is important.

11. The following statement was made by Stephen Esser in "High-Yield Bond Analysis: The Equity Perspective," in Ashwinpaul C. Sondhi (ed.), *Credit Analysis of Nontraditinal Debt Securities* (Charlottesville, VA: Association for Investment

Management and Research, 1995), p. 54: "An equity perspective on high-yield bond analysis can be an important edge for an active manager." Explain why.

12. In the analysis of an asset-backed security, the analysis of the collateral allows the analyst to project the cash flow from the underlying collateral under different scenarios. However, this is not sufficient to assess the credit worthiness of an asset-backed security transaction. Explain why?

13. Why is it necessary for an analyst to assess the financial condition of a servicer in an asset-backed security transaction?

14. a. Some asset-backed security transactions may be characterized as "true securitizations," while others may be more properly classified as "hybrid transactions." What is the distinguishing feature of a "true securitization" and a "hybrid transaction"?
    b. How is the credit quality of a "hybrid transaction" evaluated?

15. What are the four basic categories that are considered in assessing the credit quality of tax-backed municipal debt?

16. a. What is the underlying principle in assessing the credit worthiness of municipal revenue bonds?
    b. In a municipal revenue bond, what is a "rate covenant" and why is such a covenant included?

17. You are reviewing a publication of Moody's Investors Service entitled "Moody's Approach to Rating Regional and Local Governments in Latin America," published in August 1997. On page 3 of the publication, the following was written:

    "A Moody's credit rating is an independent opinion of the relative ability and willingness of an issuer of fixed-income securities to make full and timely payments of amounts due on the security over its life."

    Why in the case of a sovereign entity is the "willingness" of an issuer to pay important?

18. a. Why do rating agencies assign both a local currency debt rating and a foreign currency debt rating to the bonds of a sovereign government?
    b. How do the factors considered in deriving a local currency debt rating differ from those for a foreign currency debt rating?

19. Comment on the following statement: "The difficulty with analyzing bonds issued by foreign governments is the intangible and non-quantitative elements involved in the credit analysis. I would not encounter such complexities when analyzing the credit worthiness of domestic corporate bonds or domestic municipal bonds."

20. Krane Products Inc. is a manufacturer of ski equipment. The company has been in operation since 1997. Ms. Andrews is a credit analyst for an investment management compnay. She has been asked to analyze Krane Products as a possible pur-

chase for the bond portfolio of one her firm's accounts. At the time of the analysis, Krane Products Inc. was rated BB by S&P. The bonds of the company trade in the market with the same spread as other comparable BB bonds.

Ms. Andrews collected financial data for Krane Products Inc. for the years 2000 and 1999 and computed several financial ratios. Information for selected ratios is given below:

Ratios	2000	1999
EBIT interest coverage	3.8	2.7
EBITDA interest coverage	5.9	4.1
Funds from operations/total debt	28.3%	24.5%
Free operating cash flow/total debt	19.2%	1.2%
Pretax return on capital	24.4%	17.1%
Operating income/sales	25.5%	19.5%
Long-term debt/capitalization	55.0%	57.4%
Total debt/capitalization	57.1%	59.5%

Based on the first three quarters of fiscal year 2001, Ms. Andrews projected the following ratios for 2001:

Ratios	2001
EBIT interest coverage	4.5
EBITDA interest coverage	6.9
Funds from operations/total debt	41.5%
Free operating cash flow/total debt	22.5%
Pretax return on capital	24.2%
Operating income/sales	25.12%
Long-term debt/capitalization	40.5%
Total debt/capitalization	45.2%

Ms. Andrews obtained from S&P information about median ratios by credit rating. These ratios are reproduced below:

	AAA	AA	A	BBB	BB	B
EBIT interest coverage	12.9	9.2	7.2	4.1	2.5	1.2
EBITDA interest coverage	18.7	14.0	10.0	6.3	3.9	2.3
Funds from operations/ total debt	89.7	67.0	49.5	32.3	20.1	10.5
Free operating cash flow/total debt	40.5	21.6	17.4	6.3	1.0	(4.0)
Pretax return on capital	30.6	25.1	19.6	15.4	12.6	9.2
Operating income/sales	30.9	25.2	17.9	15.8	14.4	11.2
Long-term debt/capitalization	21.4	29.3	33.3	40.8	55.3	68.8
Total debt/capitalization	31.8	37.0	39.2	46.4	58.5	71.4

What do you think Ms. Andrews' recommendation will be with respect to the purchase of the bonds of Krane Products Inc? Explain why.

SOLUTIONS TO END OF CHAPTER QUESTIONS

1. Credit risk is more general than the statement in the quote. Credit risk encompasses three types of risk: default risk, credit spread risk, and downgrade risk. The quote in the question refers to default risk only. (Credit spread risk is the risk that the credit spread will increase. Downgrade risk is the risk that the issue will be downgraded.) Thus, one should disagree with the statement in the question.

2. The factors considered include strategic direction of management, financial philosophy, management's track record, succession planning, and control systems.

3. a. While there are various forms of back-up credit facilities, some forms are stronger than others. A back-up credit facility where the lender is contractually bound and contains no provisions that permit the lender to refuse to provide funds is the strongest form. There are non-contractual facilities such as lines of credit. For such facilities, the analyst should be concerned because the lender has the right to refuse to lend funds.

   b. A "material adverse change clause" in a back-up credit facility allows a bank to refuse funding if the bank feels that the borrower's financial condition or operating position has deteriorated significantly. Consequently, as explained in part a, this is a weaker form of back-up credit facility.

4. a. With high-yield issuers there tends to be more bank loans in the debt structure and the loans tend to be short term. Also, the loans tend to be floating rate rather than fixed. As a result, the analyst must look at the ability of the issuer to access short-term funding sources for liquidity to meet not only possible higher interest payments (when interest rates rise), but to pay off a maturing loan. High-yield issuers, however, have fewer alternatives for short-term funding sources than high-grade issuers.

   b. At any given point in time, the cushion (as measured by coverage ratios) may be high. However, the concern is with future cash flows to satisfy obligations. If the coverage ratio is adequate and is predicted to change little in the future and the degree of confidence in the prediction is high, that situation would give greater comfort to a bondholder than one where the coverage ratio is extremely high but can fluctuate substantially in the future. Because of this variability it is difficult to assign a high degree of confidence to coverage ratios that are projected and there must be recognition that the coverage ratio may fall well below acceptable levels.

   c. Financial flexibility means the ability to sustain operations should there be a down turn in business and to sustain current dividends without reliance on external funding.

   d. Unfunded pension liabilities may not be listed as debt but they are effectively a form of borrowing by the firm. Hence, S&P is considering them as part of the debt obligation. Guarantees represent potential liabilities if the corporate entity whose debt is guaranteed does not meet its obligations. If S&P views the obligation as one that the company may have to satisfy, the obligation of the corporate entity whose debt is guaranteed is a form of borrowing and should be included in total debt.

e. Ratios represent a snapshot of a particular aspect of a firm's financial position at a given point in time. Ratings reflect an assessment of the future financial position and the assessment of future cash flows. This involves looking at a myriad of factors that impact future cash flows such as competition, potential earnings growth, and future capital requirements. This is a major limitation of ratio analysis as a sole indicator of an entity's financial strength — it is not forward looking in that it does not look at how factors in the future can alter cash flows.

5. It allows an analyst to assess how "safe" is the company's dividend, whether or not the company could fund its needs internally should external sources of capital either become scarce or too expensive, and whether or not a company would be capable of satisfying its obligations if its there was decline in business operations.

6. a. The discretionary cash flow is found by subtracting from the $50 million operating cash flow the estimated capital expenditures of $30 million; thus, the discretionary cash flow is $20 million.
   b. The implication is that if the company wants to maintain a dividend payment of $25 million, it will need to acquire funds in some form because the discretionary cash flow is only $20 million.

7. a. Since covenants deal with limitations and restrictions on the borrower's activities, certain covenants provide protection for a bondholder and this protection must be factored into the credit analysis.
   b. A negative covenant is one that requires the borrower not to take certain actions. An example of a negative covenant is a restriction on the company's ability to incur additional debt.
   c. A review of the covenants in a high-yield corporate issue may help the analyst understand management strategy regarding future funding and operational strategies to determine if they are consistent what management is stating to investors. Loopholes in covenants may provide further clues as to management's future plans.

8. a. A cash flow to capital expenditures ratio is a measure that helps an analyst in assessing a company's cash flow by providing information about the company's financial flexibility — the higher the ratio the greater the financial flexibility. The measure is particularly useful for capital-intensive firms and utilities.
   b. A declining ratio can be interpreted in two ways. The first possible interpretation is that the firm may eventually have difficulty adding to capacity via capital expenditures without the need to borrow funds. The second possible interpretation is that the firm may have undertaken major capital expansion in recent years and therefore it will take time for revenues to be generated that will increase the cash flow from operations to bring the ratio to some normal long-run level.

9. a. The typical structure for a high-yield corporate issuer includes bank debt. This debt is senior to all other debt claims. As a result, bonds that are labeled "senior bonds" are subordinated to bank debt despite their title.
   b. The interest for a zero-coupon bond increases over time due to the accrual of the unpaid interest. As a result, assuming no other changes in the firm's debt struc-

ture, the percentage of a zero-coupon bond in the firm's debt structure increases over time. If these bonds are senior bonds (senior relative to the subordinated bonds, not to bank debt as discussed in part a), then the zero-coupon bond's percentage increases relative to the subordinated bonds. This may increase the credit risk of the subordinated bonds over time and adversely impact subordinated bondholders in the event of bankruptcy. Hence, in the quote Mr. Bernstein is stating that it is preferred to have zero-coupon bonds (or any deferred coupon bonds) as subordinated bonds rather than senior bonds.

10. In a holding company structure, the parent company issues debt as well as the operating subsidiaries. Consequently, the analyst in projecting the cash flows available to pay the creditors of the holding company must understand any restrictions on payments that can be made to the parent company (dividends or loans) by the operating subsidiaries.

11. In the risk-return spectrum, high-yield bonds are between high-grade corporate bonds and common stocks. High-yield corporate bonds have an equity component as evidenced by the higher correlation between stock returns and high-yield bond returns compared to high-grade bond returns and high-yield bond returns. Consequently, some portfolio managers such as Mr. Esser firmly believe that high-yield bond analysis should be viewed from an equity analyst's perspective. It is believed that the equity approach can provide more insight than traditional credit analysis. A manager using an equity approach, it is believed by Mr. Esser, will give that manager an edge in identifying attractive issues for purchase or avoiding or disposing of unattractive issues relative to other managers who rely solely on traditional credit analysis.

12. Given the projected cash flow for the collateral under various scenarios, the next step is to determine how the cash flow would be distributed among the different tranches in the structure. So, by itself projection of the cash flow is insufficient because it will not indicate if any, or all, of the tranches (i.e., bonds) will realize a loss. The allocation of the cash flow in a given scenario will permit the determination of which tranches may realize losses and the extent of those losses.

13. A servicer may be required to make advances to cover interest payments to bondholders when there are delinquencies. Consequently, the servicer must have the financial capacity to fulfill this obligation. This requires an assessment of the financial condition of the servicer.

14. a. In a "true securitization" the role of the servicer is basically routine. There are basic daily administrative tasks performed and the cash flow is not depend to any significant extent on the servicer to perform. Where the role of the servicer is more than administrative in order to generate the cash flow, the transaction is referred to as a "hybrid transaction."
   b. The analysis of a "hybrid transaction" uses both the standard methodology for evaluating an asset-backed security transaction and the analysis of a corporate entity — basically as a service business. The latter approach is referred to by S&P as a "quasi-corporate" approach. The final assessment of a rating agency is a subjective weighting of the credit quality using the two approaches. The

more the transaction's cash flow is dependent on the performance of the servicer, the greater the weight given to the quasi-corporate approach.

15. The four basic categories are: (1) the issuer's debt structure; (2) the issuer's ability and political discipline to maintain sound budgetary policy; (3) the specific local taxes and intergovernmental revenues available to the issuer, as well as obtaining historical information both on tax collection rates, and; (4) the issuer's overall socioeconomic environment.

16. a. The payment of the obligations of a revenue bond must come from the cash flow generated from the enterprise for which the bonds were issued. Thus, just as in the case of a corporate bond, the underlying principle in assessing an issuer's credit worthiness is whether or not sufficient cash flow will be generated to satisfy the obligations due bondholders.

   b. A rate covenant specifies how charges will be set on the product or service sold by the enterprise. A rate covenant is included so the enterprise will set charges so as to satisfy both expenses and debt servicing, or to create a certain amount of reserves.

17. Because the issuer is a sovereign entity, if the issuer refuses to pay there is little legal remedy for the debt holder. Thus, it becomes necessary to understand the factors other than legal recourse that will increase the likelihood that the issuer will repay.

18. a. The reason for assigning two ratings is that the currency denomination of the payments may be either the local currency or a foreign currency. (Historically, the default frequency had differed by the currency denomination of the debt. It has been observed by rating agencies that defaults have been greater on foreign currency denominated debt.)

   b. To generate sufficient local currency to satisfy its debt obligations denominated in its local currency, a government must be willing to raise taxes and control its domestic financial system. In contrast, a national government must purchase foreign currency to meet a debt obligation in that foreign currency. Consequently, a government has less control with respect to its exchange rate and faces exchange rate risk (i.e., depreciation of its currency) when it issues a foreign currency denominated bond.

   The implication of this is that the factors a rating agency will emphasize in assessing the credit worthiness of a national government's local currency debt and foreign currency debt will differ to some extent. S&P, for example, focuses on domestic government policies that affect the likelihood of the government's ability to repay local currency denominated debt. For foreign currency debt, the same rating agency focuses on the interaction of domestic and foreign government policies. Specifically, the areas of analysis that S&P assesses is a country's balance of payments and the structure of its external balance sheet (i.e., the net public debt, total net external debt, and net external liabilities).

19. When analyzing domestic corporate bonds an analyst does factor in intangible and non-quantitative elements, the most important of which is the quality of management. Moreover, a factor that is considered in assessing the credit quality of a tax-

backed municipal bond issue is the willingness of the issuing entity to generate funds to repay the obligation by raising taxes. So, the statement that intangible and non-quantitative elements are not considered in analyzing domestic corporate and domestic municipal bonds but only with sovereign bonds is incorrect.

20. All the financial ratios — actual and projected for 2001 — clearly indicate that the credit worthiness of Krane Products is improving. Using as benchmarks the S&P median ratios, the coverage ratios were already by fiscal year 2000 approaching that of the median BBB rated issuer. The capitalization ratios, while improving, were still well below that of the median BBB rated issuer. Consequently, by fiscal year 2000 an analyst would have been well advised to monitor this issuer's credit for a possible upgrade and to examine how it was trading in the market. That is, was it trading like a BB or BBB credit?

    If Ms. Andrews' projections are correct for fiscal year 2001, the ratios shown in the table are at least as good as the median BBB rated company. Consequently, based on her projections she would recommend the purchase of Krane Products Inc. bonds if that issuer's bonds continue to trade like a BB credit since, based on her analysis, the bonds are likely to be upgraded to BBB.

Index